Republic of Dreams

GREENWICH VILLAGE: THE AMERICAN BOHEMIA, 1910–1960

Ross Wetzsteon

SIMON & SCHUSTER

NEW YORK   LONDON   TORONTO   SYDNEY   SINGAPORE

SIMON AND SCHUSTER
Rockefeller Center
1230 Avenue of the Americas
New York, NY 10020

For information about special discounts for bulk purchases,
please contact Simon & Schuster Special Sales:
1-800-456-6798 or business@simonandschuster.com
Designed by Edith Fowler
Manufactured in the United States of America

10 9 8 7 6 5 4 3 2 1

Library of Congress Cataloging-in-Publication Data

Wetzsteon, Ross.

   Republic of dreams : Greenwich Village: the American
Bohemia, 1910–1960 / Ross Wetzsteon.
     p. cm.
   Includes bibliographical references (p.) and index.
   1. Greenwich Village (New York, N.Y.)—History—
20th century.   2. New York (N.Y.)—History—
1910–1960.   3. Greenwich Village (New York, N.Y.)—
Intellectual life—20th century.   4. New York (N.Y.)—
Intellectual life—20th century.   5. Greenwich Village
(New York, N.Y.)—Biography.   6. New York (N.Y.)—
Biography.   7. Intellectuals—New York (State)—
New York—Biography.   8. Artists—New York (State)
New York—Biography.   9. Bohemianism—New York
(State)—New York—History—20th century.   I. Title.
F128.68.G8 W48   2001
974.7'1042—dc21   2001034229
ISBN 0-684-86995-0

Photo research by Alexandra Truitt,
photoresearching.com

To RACHEL—D.D.
And to LAURA—*forever and a day*.

Contents

PREFACE   *ix*

INTRODUCTION
The Village Becomes "The Village"   1

I   Mabel Dodge's Salon
"Oh, How We Were All Intertwined!"   15

II   Max Eastman and *The Masses*
"Just-Before-Dawn of a New Day"   48

III   Jig Cook, Eugene O'Neill, and the Provincetown Players
"The Beloved Community of Life-Givers"   92

IV   The Feminists of the Village
Meetings with Remarkable Women   162

V   Edna St. Vincent Millay
"A Lovely Light"   240

VI   Eminent Villagers   293

VII   William Carlos Williams, the Little Magazines, and the
          Poetry Wars   347

VIII   Hart Crane
          The Roaring Boy of the Village   360

IX   Maxwell Bodenheim
          "Poems Twenty-Five Cents Each"   380

X   Thomas Wolfe and Aline Bernstein
          "The Knife of Love"   395

XI   Joe Gould
          The Last of the Last Bohemians   418

XII   Djuna Barnes
          *"One's Life Is Peculiarly One's Own When One Has
          Invented It"*   431

XIII   E. E. Cummings and Dylan Thomas
          The Village as Sanctuary, the Village as Stage   449

XIV   Delmore Schwartz
          Alien in Residence   487

XV   Dawn Powell
          The Village as an Idea of Itself   509

XVI   Jackson Pollock and the Abstract Expressionists
          in the Village
          Rearranging the Stars   520

       AFTERWORD   571

       SELECTED BIBLIOGRAPHY   573
       ACKNOWLEDGMENTS   587
       INDEX   589

Preface

"Greenwich Village isn't what it used to be." When I started this book ten years ago, I knew that would be its first sentence. And when I soon discovered that the phrase had been used as early as 1916, I knew the history of the Village would be in large part the ever recurring birth and death and rebirth of bohemia. Youth, romance, adventure—joy, poetry, rebellion—what so quickly recedes into our past?—what more often begins again?

The Village has been called "the most significant square mile in American cultural history," "the home of half the talent and half the eccentricity in the country," "the place where everything happens first." As a young journalist named John Reed said in the teens, "Within a block of my house was all the adventure in the world; within a mile every foreign country." The young scholar named Lionel Trilling declared in the twenties, "There seemed no other place where a right-thinking person might live." And a young actress named Lucille Ball put it in the forties, "The Village is the greatest place in the world."

Many major movements in American intellectual history began or were nurtured in the Village—socialism, feminism, pacifism, gay liberation, Marxism, Freudianism, avant-garde fiction and poetry and theater, cubism, abstract expressionism, the anti-war movement and the counter-culture of the sixties. And nearly every major American writer and artist lived in the Village at one time or another. What other community could claim a spectrum ranging from Henry James to Marlon Brando, from Marcel Duchamp to Bob Dylan, from Gertrude Vanderbilt Whitney to Abbie Hoffman?

But though the Village has had a richer, more exuberant, and more fascinating history than any community in America—its story told in dozens of guidebooks and tangentially in the hundreds of biographies of its major figures—only two histories of the Village have been published, Allen Churchill's engaging *The Improper Bohemians* forty years ago and Terry Miller's charming but perfunctory *Greenwich Village and How It Got That Way* in 1990.

The Village has held such a mythic place in the American imagination that it has often served as kind of iconographic shorthand. A novelist only needed to write "then she moved to the Village" to evoke an entire set of assumptions—she's a bit rebellious, artistically inclined, sexually emancipated, and eager to be on her own. The mythology of the place has been created in large part by those who moved there from elsewhere, of course, but also by the multitude of novels, plays, and movies set there, and by the perceptions of the media, which over the decades have alternated between titillated accounts of fun-loving, sexually uninhibited, and bizarrely attired bohemians and fulminating attacks on the blasphemous, un-American, and unhygienic enclave of nonconformists south of 14th Street. It has, in fact, had two parallel mythologies. It is the community where irresponsibility, naïveté, and self-indulgence are transformed into virtues. It is the magnet that attracts young men and women from all across America to assert their independence. It is the refuge for social misfits. It is the home of poseurs, eccentrics, and drifters, and a romantic alternative to mainstream society. It is a metaphor for iniquity.

The Village has had such a multiplicity of meanings that it has served as a testing ground for many of the major issues of American history, among them the relationship between individual and community, the link between cultural and political revolution, the adversarial stance of writers toward their society, the value of marginality as a spur to creativity, the necessity for a safety valve for social disaffection, the definitions of success and failure, and the role of iconography in cultural history.

·   ·   ·

In the course of my research, I discovered dozens of facts about the Village
that reveal the range of its history beyond bohemianism. One Villager
even went so far as to say that "everything started in the Village except Prohibition."

The Metropolitan Museum of Art and the Whitney Museum
started in the Village, ASCAP and the ASPCA were founded there—and a
claim can be made for the YMCA and the YWCA as well. Unlikely as it
sounds, it was where yet another American institution was born—the National League. Even more unlikely—a fact both parties would be happy
to deny—*The Reader's Digest* began beneath a speakeasy at 113 Macdougal Street in 1922. (The lead article in its first issue was entitled, with
unconscious obeisance to its birthplace, "How to Keep Young Mentally,"
and the article about the theater was headlined "Is the State Too Vulgar?,"
a typographical error perhaps attributable to a free-spirited Village proof-
reader.)

Displaying the same kind of small-town chamber of commerce
chauvinism they came to the Village to escape, Villagers are no less proud
of "firsts" than any other community—not all of them dubious. The first
night court in America was held in the Village, and the first theater devoted
exclusively to films (the 8th Street Playhouse). The first pizza served in
America was served in the Village, also the first spaghetti dinner and the
first ice cream soda. More in keeping with its mythology, the first labor
demonstration in America took place there in the 1830s, when local stone-
cutters protested the use of Sing Sing convicts to cut stone for the construction of New York University (the nation's largest private university). And
where else could the Unitary Household have been founded in 1859 (the
first free-love community in the country), or, for that matter, the American
Civil Liberties Union? The first musical comedy, the first theatrical
cliffhanger, the first cabaret, the first American production of a play by
Oscar Wilde. John L. Sullivan had his first fight there and George M.
Cohan made his stage debut. The first theatrical agency (William Morris),
the first salon, and, naturally, the first professional women's organization.

That quintessential American, the inventor, also had his place in
Village history. For a time Thomas Edison had his office there (his son
Charles was a Village poet, a fact he didn't dwell on, years later, when he
was elected governor of New Jersey). Samuel Colt invented the Colt .45
there, and Samuel F. B. Morse invented the telegraph. Bell Laboratories in
the West Village (now an artists' housing complex called Westbeth) was the
site of the first commercial radio broadcast and the first TV broadcast. The

PA system was developed there as well as the sound-on-disc projector, which made talkies possible.

And speaking of movies, two young Village furriers, Adolph Zukor and Maurice Loew, started their dynasties at the corner of 14th Street and Sixth Avenue with Biograph Films, where Mary Pickford and the Gish sisters made their first pictures. Hundreds of movies were set in the Village in the following years, including *Scarlet Street*, *Daisy Kenyon*, *On the Town*, *My Sister Eileen*, *Barefoot in the Park*, *Funny Face*, *Next Stop*, *Greenwich Village*, *The Group*, and *Desperately Seeking Susan*. In *Wait Until Dark*, Audrey Hepburn awaited assault at 4 St. Luke's Place, and Jimmy Stewart and Grace Kelly solved the murder in *Rear Window* from an apartment overlooking 125 West 9th Street.

The trial of Harry Thaw for murdering Stanford White (who designed the Washington Square Arch) took place in the Jefferson Market Courthouse, and Clement Moore is said to have written "The Night Before Christmas" while a minister of a Village church. *Howdy Doody* was developed in the Village and the USS *Monitor* was built on a pier over by the Hudson River. The buffalo nickel was designed in the Village, as were the giant balloons for the first Macy's Thanksgiving Day parade. The narrowest house in New York City, only nine and a half feet wide, its occupants including Edna St. Vincent Millay and John Barrymore, is on Bedford Street, and the smallest parcel of private property in the country, a twenty-five-inch triangle, sits on the corner of Christopher Street and Seventh Avenue. In the only Shakespeare riot in American history, the adherents of the English actor Charles Macready and the followers of the American tragedian Edwin Forrest came to blows in the Village. And Lindbergh's legendary flight? One of the reasons Lindy took off was to claim the $25,000 offered by the French-born owner of the Brevoort Hotel on lower Fifth Avenue.

The founder of the *New York Times* came from the Village, and Tammany Hall—another institution with an aversion to everything its residents stood for—had its headquarters there. One local organization, in Little Italy in the South Village, has even less connection to the spirit of openness to diverse points of view—the Mafia. One claim Villagers *can* be proud of is that 8th Street has been called "the most integrated street in America."

John Wilkes Booth and his co-conspirators held several of their meetings in the Village, which was also the home of the minister who presided over Lincoln's funeral service. And Eleanor Roosevelt maintained an apartment at 20 East 11th Street during the White House years and lived at 29 Washington Square West after FDR's death.

Several popular phrases in the Village entered the language. The Old Grapevine, a roadhouse located at the corner of 11th Street and Sixth Avenue and so named for the gnarled vine that covered its facade, was a thriving hangout in the nineteenth century, leading to the expression "I heard it through the grapevine." And in the 1880s, Fleischmann's Model Viennese Bakery on the corner of 11th Street and Broadway donated its unsold products to the poor at the end of every day, originating the phrase "bread line."

But the residents of the Village are responsible for its role in the American imagination — its writers and artists and intellectuals, its radicals and bohemians, eccentrics and prophets.

The list of novelists who called it home at some point in their lives is a complete pantheon of American literature. James Fenimore Cooper, Louisa May Alcott, Herman Melville, Mark Twain, William Dean Howells, Stephen Crane, Jack London, Frank Norris, Edith Wharton, and Henry James. Upton Sinclair and Sinclair Lewis. Ford Madox Ford and Sherwood Anderson. John Dos Passos and William Faulkner. Henry Miller and Anaïs Nin. Henry Roth and Katherine Anne Porter, Mary McCarthy, Nathanael West, James T. Farrell, Richard Wright, James Agee, James Baldwin. John Cheever, Saul Bellow, E. L. Doctorow, and James Jones. Jack Kerouac and William Burroughs. Louis Auchincloss and Joan Didion and Gore Vidal. J. D. Salinger and William Gaddis. William Styron and Donald Barthelme. Hubert Selby and Thomas Pynchon. Norman Mailer, of course — who wrote "The Time of Her Time" about a sexual marathon in the Village. And the five novelists who have sections in this book — Willa Cather, Theodore Dreiser, Thomas Wolfe, Djuna Barnes, and Dawn Powell.

From The New Yorker, James Thurber, E. B. White, S. J. Perelman, Dorothy Parker, and Joseph Mitchell. Among the dozens of playwrights who followed Eugene O'Neill were Tennessee Williams (who hung out at the Cedar Bar), Edward Albee (who saw a graffito asking "Who's Afraid of the Virginia Woolf" in the men's room at the Ninth Circle), Sam Shepard (who worked as a busboy at the Village Gate). Kahlil Gibran, the moony Lebanese mystic whose perennial best-seller The Prophet evokes the mysterious Middle East, actually wrote the book at 51 West 10th Street, where he lived from 1911 until his death in 1931.

Among the poets, the Village was once home to Edgar Allan Poe, Walt Whitman, William Cullen Bryant, Edwin Arlington Robinson, John

Masefield, and Louis Untermeyer. Conrad Aiken, Carl Sandburg, and Vachel Lindsay. Stephen Vincent Benét and William Rose Benét. Allen Tate and Wallace Stevens—Mina Loy and Louise Bogan and Elinor Wylie. John Berryman and W. H. Auden. Even Ezra Pound and T. S. Eliot lived in the Village for brief periods, and for a longer time Galway Kinnell, John Ashbery, LeRoi Jones (Amiri Baraka), and Allen Ginsberg. A list of poets who didn't live in the Village would be shorter. Amy Lowell and Robert Lowell visited the Village so often they could be called honorary residents, and Sara Teasdale, sadly, committed suicide in a Village hotel.

The roster of Village intellectuals would include Walter Lippmann, Carl Van Vechten, Randolph Bourne, Van Wyck Brooks, Waldo Frank, Malcolm Cowley, Frances Perkins, Paul Rosefeld, and Kenneth Burke. Add Carl and Mark Van Doren (who told his roommate Joseph Wood Krutch what a liberating act it was, in his first days in the Village, to paint his floors black), Margaret Mead and Meyer Schapiro, Roger Baldwin and Will Durant. Paul Goodman, Dwight Macdonald, Michael Harrington, Alfred Kazin. Jane Jacobs and Susan Sontag.

The list of artists is equally long. In the nineteenth century, Albert Bierstadt, Frederick Church, John La Farge, Albert Pinkham Ryder, Winslow Homer, and Augustus Saint-Gaudens. Stirling Calder and his son Alexander. Diego Rivera and Isamu Noguchi. And of course most of the abstract expressionists, and most of the pop artists who followed, from Andy Warhol to Robert Rauschenberg.

Make a list of the major American photographers and compare it to the list of photographers who have lived in the Village: Mathew Brady, Alfred Stieglitz, Edward Steichen, Jessie Tarbox Beals, Man Ray, Berenice Abbott, Walker Evans, Weegee, Margaret Bourke-White, Robert Frank, and Diane Arbus.

Hundreds of legendary figures in the performing arts either lived here or began their careers here. Norma Shearer worked as a hat-check girl in a Village nightclub, Jessica Lange as a waitress at the Lion's Head. Bette Davis was a leading Village actress, and Lauren Bacall, who lived at 75 Bank Street, was named "Miss Greenwich Village of 1942." Not just Brando, but also James Dean, Montgomery Clift, Al Pacino, Dustin Hoffman, and Martin Sheen were once Villagers, as were John Houseman and Martha Graham, Leontyne Price and Joan Sutherland. Thelonius Monk, Charlie Parker, Charles Mingus, Aaron Copland and Leonard Bernstein, Lenny Bruce, Erwin Piscator and Joe Papp, John Lennon and Yoko Ono.

George Gershwin was born a few blocks from the Village and spent many a Saturday night pounding the piano at Village parties, including the party after the premiere of *Rhapsody in Blue*—and his brother Ira married one of "the Strunsky girls," the three daughters of the legendary Village landlord Papa Strunsky.

I can't ignore the most unlikely Villager of all, Leon Trotsky. Temporarily exiled from Russia, Trotsky briefly settled in New York in the late teens, for a time in the Bronx, then on St. Mark's Place. Village legend claims he worked as a tailor, as a dishwasher, as a movie extra—but like every Villager, he had larger things on his mind.

Prefaces often walk a thin line between explaining the book's contents and apologizing for its deficiencies. (My favorite in the latter category was the author who thanked his parents and added, "Of course any flaws in this book are entirely their fault.") Still, the history of Greenwich Village is such a vast and complex subject, with so many plausible approaches, that I feel compelled to explain—apologize for?—several significant choices.

Iconography is the essence of the Village's history—what it stands for has always transcended what it is. To say that the myths should be disentangled from the "reality"—the usual obligation of the historian—is to ignore the fact that their entanglement *is* its history. If iconography is born at the intersection of reality and myth, and if belief in the myth is itself part of the reality, then it's less important to expose the disparity between them than to explore their connections. The story of the Village is, in large part, the stories old Villagers have told new Villagers about former Villagers.

This version of the Village will no doubt disappoint some readers—old-time Villagers in particular—who expect lengthy descriptions of famous hangouts, or legendary Village publications, or fabled "characters" (I myself miss Maurice, the intrepid, white-haired "Prince of Bohemia"—onetime photographer, poet, lover, now only philosopher with a tinkling bell, who picked up stacks of *The Village Voice* from the circulation department to sell on the subway). And there's no anthropological arcana here either, no architectural details, no walking tours—dozens of guidebooks provide everything anyone would want to know. If some readers complain about the omissions, where were they when my wife and my editor said the manuscript was already too long?

What I hope I've achieved is something best described by the word "synthesis"—in other words, to examine the lives of the leading figures of the Village and the legendary anecdotes of Village mythology in a new context. As for the absence of what is called "scholarly apparatus," I will claim a good deal of what is called "original research," and have included an extensive bibliography.

A word about what may seem an overemphasis on the sex lives of the major figures. The Villagers' commitment to self-fulfillment and the personal as the political were inextricably linked to their attitudes about sex. From the first, sexual emancipation was central to the Villagers' vision of an emancipated society—and indeed, it could even be argued that the degree to which the Village is no longer the locus of bohemia is the degree to which the Village has contributed to winning that battle, from the early days of insistence on the right to premarital sex and access to birth control information to the more recent days of feminism and gay liberation. One of the central convictions of the Villagers' insurrection was the belief that cultural and social change would follow only after personal and sexual liberation. It is easy to forget that throughout most of American history sexual freedom was a taboo rather than a right.

A brief explanation of my use of first names throughout the book. Not an insignificant aspect of what the Villagers called "a revolution of consciousness"—and parallel to their commitment to self-fulfillment— was an emphasis on informality and intimacy. So a usage that might be overly familiar in other contexts seems perfectly appropriate in the case of the Village.

Finally, a word on why the book begins in 1910 and more or less ends in 1960. In 1912 the Village became "The Village," a self-conscious bohemian and radical community, and since the sixties—with the nationalization of bohemia, the replacement of geographic community by electronic community, the blurring of cultural boundaries, and the disappearing hegemony of "the normal"—the Village, in that familiar phrase, actually hasn't been "what it used to be."

I began this book believing the Village spirit has been characterized by youth and romance and adventure, joy and poetry and rebellion—and while that's certainly true, by the time I finished, I also realized the Village has been the scene of many disappointed dreams and miserable deaths. How could it not be, with such exalted expectations? Still, it has cast its spell over hundreds of thousands of young men and women throughout the century and across the country, including the Montana-born author of this book. I first visited in my teens, already entranced by what Jig Cook called "the beloved community of life-givers," and have lived there for nearly forty years. Like everyone else who comes here, I still feel, as I felt that first time, that I'm crossing the border into another country of dreams.

—Ross Wetzsteon
January 1998

Republic
of Dreams

The Village Becomes "The Village"

A shapeless figure crouched in the midnight shadows at the top of Washington Square Park. When the lone policeman had rounded the corner, the figure looked out cautiously, silently opened the door at the base of the arch, and motioned to her fellow revolutionaries gathered on lower Fifth Avenue. Five people emerged from the darkness and stealthily slipped through the doorway. And so, on a frigid, lightly snowing night in January 1917, Marcel Duchamp, John Sloan, and four other Villagers climbed to the top of Washington Square Arch and declared Greenwich Village "a free and independent republic."

The story has been jubilantly told in many memoirs of the period and inaccurately portrayed in nearly every guidebook since. The details vary with each retelling, but all accounts agree that this mock secession symbolized the Golden Age of the Village rebellion against middle-class, puritan, capitalist America. Yet as with so many symbolic moments, the escapade of the Arch-Conspirators—as Sloan titled his famous sketch of the event—signaled not so much the beginning but the end of the era it celebrated.

The leading conspirator wasn't Duchamp or Sloan but a golden-haired, vivacious young woman, Gertrude Drick. She came from a small

1

town in the provinces (Texas) and, realizing that the only thing greater than her ambition to become a violinist was her ineptitude, she became a painting student of Sloan's instead. And though she was fond of pranks, she also fell into fits of dejection, for, as with many apparently lighthearted people, a deep melancholy underlay her effervescence. Gertrude's remedy for her mood swings was to print up hundreds of black-bordered calling cards embossed with the single word "Woe," which she handed out gaily declaring, "Woe is me."

Gertrude had heard of another secession movement the preceding summer. Ellis Jones, an editor at the humor magazine *Life*, had called upon his fellow Villagers to join him in a second American Revolution declaring their community independent of the United States. Believing Washington Square Park would be too small for the expected throngs, Ellis led his cohorts into the heart of enemy territory, Central Park. And fearing an anarchist riot, the New York City police department dispatched dozens of machine-gun-bearing officers and several ambulances. But when the appointed day arrived under a heavy downpour, only a dozen umbrella-carrying insurgents showed up.

One evening several months after Ellis's premature revolution, Gertrude happened to notice that the door at the bottom of the arch's western plinth wasn't locked and that the policeman on duty often wandered away for an hour or two at a time. (The police presence was deemed necessary when several months earlier a vagrant had made his home in a chamber inside the arch, and his crime discovered when, with a soaring sense of security, he hung out his laundry to dry on the parapet.) Gertrude immediately informed John Sloan of her plan, and the two of them rounded up several of their friends to join in the insurrection—the intellectually dapper Marcel Duchamp (whose *Nude Descending a Staircase* had been the scandalous centerpiece of the Armory Show four years earlier), the actors Forrest Mann and Betty Turner, and the Provincetown Players' leading man, Charles Ellis.

On the night of January 23, the six revolutionaries, toting sandwiches, wine, thermoses, hot water bottles, Chinese lanterns, cap pistols, and red, white, and blue balloons, slipped through the unlocked door, mounted the 110 steps of the spiral iron staircase, lifted the trap door, and emerged at the top of the arch. They built a small bonfire in a beanpot and spread out steamer rugs for a midnight picnic. Passing the bottles of wine back and forth, they began their insurrection by reciting verses. Gertrude was also a poet of sorts; her most memorable lyric—the text of which, alas, has not survived—was entitled "The Should That Took Off Its Stockings and Threw Its Shoes Away."

Soon soused, the six Arch-Conspirators decided the moment had arrived. They tied their balloons to the parapet, and, in John's words, "did sign and affix our names to a parchment, having the same duly sealed with the Great Seal of the Village." As the other five fired their cap pistols, Gertrude read their declaration, which consisted of nothing but the word "whereas" repeated over and over—surely Marcel's inspiration—until the final words proclaiming that henceforth Greenwich Village would be a free and independent republic.

The band of revolutionaries then made their inebriated way into the night, "to ply our various callings"—John once more—"till such time as the demands of the state again might become imperative."

When they awoke the next morning, Villagers were pleasantly surprised to see balloons festooned to the ramparts of their arch, but the aristocratic residents of the elegant town houses on the north side of Washington Square were dismayed by yet another example of bohemian tomfoolery. Within twenty-four hours nearly everyone south of 14th Street knew of their new status as a liberated community, and for a week the balloons fluttered in the midwinter breeze as a symbol of a symbol. What could the authorities do? The only result of the Revolution of Washington Square was that the door at the base of the arch was permanently locked.

For a few years, Greenwich Village had already been something close to a free and independent republic—at least in mind and spirit. A few blocks north of the arch, at 23 Fifth Avenue, Mabel Dodge hosted her celebrated salon, introducing the Villagers to the Wobblies and Freud, cubism and free love, anarchism and birth control. A few blocks west of the arch, at 91 Greenwich Avenue, Max Eastman and Floyd Dell presided over the unruly meetings of the staff of *The Masses*, the rebellious monthly that arguably became the most influential magazine in the history of American journalism. A few blocks south of the arch, at 139 Macdougal Street, the lunatic genius Jig Cook and the blackly brooding Eugene O'Neill were transforming the American theater with the Provincetown Players. At the center of this intellectual hullabaloo was Jack Reed, the Golden Boy of the Village—Mabel's lover, Max's leading correspondent, one of Jig's favorite playwrights, and the author of "A Day in Bohemia":

> Yet we are free who live in Washington Square,
> We dare to think as uptown wouldn't dare,
> Blazing our nights with arguments uproarious,
> What care we for a dull old world censorious,
> When each is sure he'll fashion something glorious?

But by 1916, a year before the Arch-Conspirators, Floyd Dell had declared that the Village wasn't what it used to be. The spirit of joyful rebellion had disappeared, he lamented after having been accosted by an up-towner at a local tearoom and asked, "Are you a merry Villager?"—the rents were rising, the poseurs and the tourists were moving in.

From its earliest years the Village was associated with revolution. It was informally called "Green Village" in the eighteenth century for its stretch of game-filled woodlands and marshy pastures several miles north of the thriving settlement on the southern tip of Manhattan. Tobacco plantations occupied the area the Sapokanickan tribe had used for hunting and fishing a century earlier. A young rebel named Thomas Paine lived in a ramshackle building on what is now Grove Street, and among the fine homes of the well-to-do-families who settled in the countryside was a mansion called Richmond Hill, where George Washington established his temporary headquarters during the American Revolution and where John Adams and Aaron Burr later lived.

A series of smallpox and yellow fever epidemics, culminating in the great plague of 1822, forced thousands of lower Manhattanites to flee north, and they settled in hastily constructed shacks in a crazy quilt pattern of streets that followed the contours of Indian trails, cow paths, and meandering brooks.

In 1811, New York City decided to rationalize its rapid expansion northward by imposing a grid system with numbered east–west streets and north–south avenues. But the inhabitants of Green Village—its name changed to "Greenwich" by an early privateer who used part of his plunder to build a country estate—refused to be uprooted, and rose up in protest. So the city planners decided that geometric rigor could bypass the Village, where some streets changed names and numbering system in mid-block, and others bizarrely changed direction at nearly every crossing (including the anomaly of West 4th Street crossing West 10th, West 11th, and West 12th that still leaves bewildered tourists double-checking the street signs). The Village remained a bucolic neighborhood within a bustling metropolis, a quaint sanctuary just a few blocks from the skyscrapers of the world's first vertical city. But Greenwich Village's map had metaphoric resonance as well: rejecting orderliness, refusing conformity, repelling the grid.

Though the population of the Village quadrupled between 1825 and 1840, the northward expansion of the city proceeded even faster—by the end of the Civil War, half of New York's population lived above 14th Street. Developers ignored the area—its labyrinthine layout and the sandy soil made construction too difficult—and, as an early resident said, the Village became "an island of no pressure, a place to pull out for a while."

But before bohemia came Washington Square Park. Used for decades as a potter's field, with an estimated 22,000 graves, and as a hanging ground for the city's more notorious criminals (the last hanging from the great elm in the northwest corner took place in 1822), the park was transformed into a military parade ground in 1828, a purpose it served until the heavy artillery began to sink into the graves below.

By mid-century, a pattern had been established—the rich, taking advantage of the Village's detachment, established New York's first fashionable residential area in a row of elegant town houses on the north side of Washington Square, while the poor settled in the dilapidated tenements on the south side, with saloons, beer gardens, brothels, and sweatshops in the surrounding blocks. For a time, a quarter of the city's black population lived in the South Village—"Little Africa"—with the nation's first black theater and first black newspaper. By the end of the century, the area below the square was scorned for its "fetid fertility," while the square itself had become "the old New York" of Henry James and Edith Wharton, and the neighborhood that later became the nation's Left Bank was called "the American Ward" for its "humanity of the better sort," for its "cleanliness, good citizenship, and self-respect."

Henry James—who was born not on the square, but on an adjoining street—called Stanford White's marble arch, dedicated in 1895, "our lamentable little Arch of Triumph," but remained devoted to the area for its "rural picturesqueness." "It has a kind of established repose," he wrote, "which is not the frequent occurrence in other quarters of the long, shrill city. . . . To come and go where East 11th Street [and] West 10th Street opened their kind short arms was at least to keep clear of the awful hug of the serpent."

In the early years of the twentieth century, as real estate values in the area plummeted and many of the richer residents fled farther north, the Village consisted of three overlapping communities—the increasingly hemmed-in upper class, the Irish and Italian immigrant families in the tenements to the south and west, and a small group of intellectuals, writers, and artists drawn by the bars, clubs, societies, galleries, and libraries. Combining the remnants of aristocracy, the exoticism of Europe, and potential rebels—and, just as important, providing affordable lodging, human scale, places to congregate, and a kind of enforced diversity and tolerance, the polyglot Village was ready for the emergence of bohemia.

In fact, it already had a history of incipient bohemianism. Renowned writers lived in the area throughout the nineteenth century. Herman Melville worked from the mid-1860s to the mid-1880s in the customs office on Gansevoort Pier in the West Village—"a most inglorious vocation," he lamented. And at the turn of the century, the already famous O. Henry was a familiar figure, as was the as yet unknown Stephen Crane. Frank Norris came to the Village with high hopes and left with dashed dreams. "Of the ambitions of the Great Unpublished," he wrote, "the one that is strongest, the most abiding, is the ambition to get to New York. For these, New York is the *point de départ*, the niche, the indispensable vantage ground." But the artists and writers he met around Washington Square, he said, were dilettantes and decadents who drank their beer from teacups.

The most prominent of the pre-"Village" Villagers was Mark Twain, who lived briefly at 14 West 10th Street before settling in splendor at 21 Fifth Avenue from 1904 to 1908. "Efflorescence in white serge," a contemporary called Twain in those years, but guests who came to lionize the legendary writer usually found him under a cathedral vault in his huge canopied bed.

None of these writers could be considered more than semi-bohemians, but the Village could put in a partial claim to America's first true bohemian, Edgar Allan Poe. In the late 1830s and early 1840s, Poe lived at 85 West 3rd Street, 113½ Carmine Street, 137 Waverly Place, and 130 Greenwich Street—at all of which he was said to have written "The Raven" and at none of which did he live abstemiously. The Village is the only community in America where Edgar Allan Poe could score drugs in the 1840s and Henry James could stroll past grazing cows in the 1890s.

Poe was sui generis, a bohemian before Americans even had a word to describe him, but the true birthplace of American bohemianism was at Charlie Pfaff's rathskeller at 653 Broadway, near Bleecker Street, a decade later. Freethinkers and freeloaders, poets and panhandlers, denizens of the demimonde and philosophical drifters—as well as visiting foreigners like Lola Montez—gathered around trestle tables in Charlie's smoky establishment to eat sausages, drink ale, and talk uninhibitedly late into the night.

Henry Clapp, editor of *The New York Saturday Press*, became the center of a high-spirited, low-living coterie. The man who declared his undying opposition to "smug, ponderous, empty, obstructive respectability," and published Twain's first story, "The Celebrated Jumping Frog of

Calaveras County," and who deserves immortality for remarking that Horace Greeley was a self-made man who worshipped his creator, Henry soon won the title "King of Bohemia" from Charlie's clientele. Bohemia's Queen?—Ada Clare, an actress whose ineptitude as Ophelia was forgiven for her grace as a writer, but whose proto-feminist prose ("Only a Woman's Heart") was overshadowed by her scandalous affair with the internationally acclaimed pianist Louis Gottschalk. When she bore a child out of wedlock, Ada refused to be ruined and declared herself a Love-Philosopher. Adah Isaacs Menken, another patron at Pfaff's, could have laid claim to the title "Queen of Bohemia" as well. Adah drank brandy and smoked cigars, didn't take second place to Ada when it came to sexual emancipation, and considerably surpassed her as an actress. Her performance in a potboiler called *Mazeppa* in flesh-colored tights while strapped on the back of a horse won her the title "the Naked Lady."

Walt Whitman—derided elsewhere for "bombast, egotism, vulgarity, and nonsense," for "his exulting audacity of Priapus-worshipping obscenity"—became the rathskeller's resident poet, at least in part, some said, because of the young men loitering around the corner on Bleecker Street. When Ralph Waldo Emerson came to New York and asked to meet Whitman—decorous ecstasy meeting ecstatic indecorum—he was directed to Pfaff's, where he was impressed by the poet but unimpressed by the "noisy and rowdy" acolytes who surrounded him. William Dean Howells also made the pilgrimage to Pfaff's. "A sickly colony," he bristled, "transplanted from the mother asphalt of Paris." Henry Clapp could hardly have been more pleased.

Pfaff's fraternity soon attracted the attention of the uptown press—and several patterns of bohemian iconography were established.

From the beginning, the middle class regarded bohemia with a mixture of revulsion and fascination. "It would be better to cultivate a familiarity with any kind of coarse and honest art, or any sort of regular employment, than to become refined and artistic only to fall into the company of the Bohemians," the *New York Times* editorialized as early as 1858. "The Bohemian cannot be called a useful member of society, and it is not an encouraging sign . . . that the tribe has become so numerous among us as to form a distinct and recognizable class."

Middle-class dismissal of bohemianism took many forms. The most common reproach, of course, repeated decade after decade, was that bohemia was populated by poseurs—as if the middle class would happily accept the real article. This perennial bourgeois response to bohemia served several purposes—it minimized a threat to its own values, it denied the validity of alternative ways of living, and it allowed the peculiarly contradictory fluctuation between outraged denunciation and condescension.

Almost as common was the accusation that bohemians adopted conventions of their own that were just as rigid as those they rejected. The official costume, for instance (from the flannel shirts and batik blouses of the teens to the black stockings and Capezio flats of the sixties), or the bohemian decor (from coal grates and trestle tables to mattresses on the floor and exposed brick walls), or the day that began by rolling out of bed at noon—weren't these codes of behavior just as inflexible as the codes they'd fled? What the middle class never understood is that calling the manners of those of whom one disapproves "conventions" is considerably easier than comprehending the disaffection those manners reflect.

Such middle-class assaults on bohemia followed so closely upon its birth that criticism of its values became almost as central to its definition as articulation of its vision. Bohemia welcomed artistically inspired, politically disaffected renegades living in carefree disarray—and encouraged pseudo-artistic, politically irresponsible outcasts living in unthinkable debauchery. Bohemia rejected hypocritical morality—and had no moral standards. Bohemia repudiated conventional working hours and domestic arrangements—and flaunted its slovenly habits and unstable relationships. Bohemia condemned a money-driven society—and parasitically depended on others to support it. Bohemia educated itself to self-expression—and sank into self-indulgence.

From the first, bohemia existed in an almost symbiotic relationship with the middle class, not so much espousing a new way of life as mirroring an old way—one of the reasons it has so often been called an adolescent rebellion against the adults. But to examine a movement's genesis is not to diminish its goals—"adult" can be just as pejorative as "adolescent"—and in any case, as Charlie Pfaff and Henry Clapp knew, the middle class gets the bohemia it deserves.

Bohemian iconography began with the serialization of Henri Murger's *Scènes de la Vie de Bohème* in Paris in the 1840s. Refusing to become "productive members of society," and castigating bourgeois culture for failing to recognize their genius, Murger's garret-bound poets and painters spoke for the rapidly increasing number of young people who felt creatively gifted and politically disenchanted, just as the middle class was gaining ascendancy.

What did the bohemians care if history was to call them just one of the many by-products of the Industrial Revolution? They were the heirs of romanticism as well, for in its emphasis on idealism, on individualism, on revolt against convention, on artistic self-expression, on political liberation, on sexual emancipation, on the genius as outcast—on everything, in fact, but worship of nature and flirtation with mysticism, bohemianism was romanticism by other means.

"Today, as in the past," wrote Murger—though he sometimes didn't seem sure whether bohemianism should be idealized for its pathos or pitied for its squalor—"any man who enters the path of art, with his art as his sole means of support, is bound to pass by way of Bohemia." And according to Balzac, "Bohemia is made up of young people, all of whom are between twenty and thirty years of age, all men of genius in their own line, as yet almost unknown but with the ability to become known one day, when they will achieve real distinction. Already you can pick them out at carnival-time, giving rein to their superfluous high spirits. . . . Bohemia possesses nothing, yet contrives to exist on that nothing." And as George Du Maurier wrote of bohemia in *Trilby*—a novel that had an even larger cult following in the nineties than Murger's articles and ensuing play had had half a century earlier—"happy times of careless impecuniosity, and youth and hope and health and strength and freedom!" Art Young, the *Masses* cartoonist, was more down to earth. "In this atmosphere a man felt something like his raw self, though he knew well that he had been cooked to a turn by the world's conventions. Here a woman could say 'damn' . . . and still be respected."

But for all the rhapsodizing about "happy days and happy nights," from its very birth, bohemia seemed to exist in the past. "Bohemia is dying," even its most ardent residents lamented; "the great days of bohemia are over." This sense of lost grandeur has been felt in every generation—just as Floyd Dell said in the teens that "the Village isn't what it used to be," Murger's followers were saying in the 1850s that "Paris isn't what it used to be." "Whatever else bohemia may be," a Village magazine editorialized in 1917, "it is almost always yesterday."

One reason for bohemia's ephemerality is the rapidity with which revolt turns into fashion. But bohemians themselves are complicitous, for bohemian days are the days of one's youth—and who will grant the same thrilling sense of *awakening* to succeeding generations? "Bohemia died," said a Villager sardonically, "when we grew old." Even if bohemians understand that when youth fades a new generation replaces them, in their minds the institution originated with them and those who follow can do nothing but repeat their discoveries. Bohemia is a perpetual revolution against an enemy that is never defeated. "What are today's bohemians doing," each generation of bohemians asks of its successors, "but continuing the battle we began?"

What constitutes fulfillment within bohemia? Certainly not what the middle class calls "success": male-dominated careers and female-centered families linked by ever increasing income and status. Bohemia redefines success as personal self-expression, artistic achievement, and political transformation, but soon comes to stress the nobility of failure. If bohemia values unconventionality, irresponsibility, and irregularity because they are anathema to the middle class, then it finds itself in the anomalous position of valuing failure. Too often defining itself by what it is not, bohemia then has to find a way to turn failure into a virtue. Rejection by the middle class has been regarded as the surest validation of vision, acceptance as the surest sign that it has failed to achieve its goals. Clinging to the cliché that great artists are invariably neglected by their culture, bohemia slides imperceptibly into the attitude that works of art neglected by their culture are therefore great. The result is a *cult* of failure. One of the saddest and ultimately most destructive aspects of bohemian life is its tendency to think that to fail on society's terms is necessarily to establish one's integrity and to assure the quality of one's work. The conflict between success and failure confirms the inextricable link between bohemia and the middle class, for bohemia accepts the middle-class definition of the conflict while thinking it can escape the consequences.

"Everything in bohemia changes," Allen Ginsberg said, "—or ought to." But it's merely a rhetorical irony to say that bohemia remains the same precisely *because* it always changes. Nevertheless, bohemia was an old story by the time a new form of it emerged in the Village in the teens.

The years in Greenwich Village between 1912 and 1917 have been called "the lyric years," "the confident years," "the joyous season," "the little renaissance," "the innocent revolution." The years of "the lyrical left" and "the new paganism." But whatever they are called, "something glorious" was happening in New York City in the teens—the Golden Age of the Village.

More or less four square miles, roughly bounded on the north by

14th Street, on the west by the Hudson River, on the south by Houston Street, and on the east by Third Avenue, the Village, as the bespectacled anarchist Hippolyte Havel once said, isn't so much geographical location as a state of mind. In the years before World War I, Villagers talked incessantly about the fusion of revelry and revolt, between artistic creativity and social justice, about the confluence of individual self-fulfillment and political revolution. But they had not so much a philosophy as a temperament. As Walter Lippmann put it, the Village was guided by "a quality of feeling instead of conformity to rules." Yet no matter how imprecise and naive their jubilation—announcing their utopian insurgency not on the barricades but with toy pistols and red balloons—they were galvanized by the feeling that some as yet unfocused energy was about to unleash the spirit of modernity.

But it doesn't diminish the Villagers' revolution of consciousness to say that it was also the result of a confluence of several social and cultural influences. The populist movement and William Jennings Bryan in the nineties, and the progressive movement, Teddy Roosevelt, and the muckrakers in the early years of the century, had created a climate of insurgency. The energy and idealism of the American imagination, focused for half a century on rebuilding the nation after the Civil War, were suddenly released to confront modernity—the New Freedom, the new woman, the new theater, the new art, the new psychology, the new morality. Furthermore, the end of the frontier brought not only a geographic halt but a psychic vacuum. The momentum of "manifest destiny" having suddenly ceased, many of the adventurous and dissatisfied turned inward and became pioneers on the frontier of the self.

For intellectuals, in particular, to move without warning from the world of Henry Wadsworth Longfellow, William Dean Howells, and the New England Brahmins into the twentieth century demanded a vertiginous leap. The works of such native writers as Walt Whitman, William James, Thorstein Veblen, and John Dewey stimulated a search for new values. European writers like Marx, Freud, Darwin, Nietzsche, Dostoyevsky, and Shaw scattered the old complacencies, and radicals and bohemians, writers and artists suddenly found themselves exposed to the full sweep of half a century of European thought.

The rapid urbanization of America and the equally rapid growth of a mass society—both of which contributed to faster communication and stricter conformity—helped create the conditions for a vital enclave of creativity and dissent. And—though the Villagers would have been reluctant to admit it—another condition for a radical bohemian community was the rapidly increasing abundance of the American economy, for poverty is only picturesque to those who can easily escape it.

And in the teens such a community could only have come into existence in New York City. New York was at the intersection between the heartland and Europe. Having only recently replaced Boston as the nation's cultural capital and media center, it was vulgar and vital, the American city that most encouraged diversity, that most lacked cultural consensus. It was seemingly in ceaseless chaos, stimulating creativity and idiosyncrasy. Not coincidentally, it became the focus of provincial hostility.

Superficially inchoate, indiscriminate, with a multitude of personalities and causes, the Village ethos was integrated in its dedication to overthrowing the capitalist, philistine, and puritanical hegemony of the American middle class. As one Villager put it, "We were radicals devoted to anything, so long as it was taboo in the Mid-West!" Whatever their individual obsessions—socialism, anarchism, feminism, pacifism, free verse, cubism, Freudianism, free love, birth control—the Villagers were allied in an assault on social oppression, cultural gentility, and moral repression. For a few brief years—in a configuration not to be repeated until the sixties—justice and poetry seemed complementary goals, for every cause played a role in the revolution that would break the chains of tradition and create a liberated society.

Everyone knew everyone—Wobblies and poets, anarchists and painters, recent Harvard graduates and recently imprisoned strikers, free-lovers and philosophers, pacifists and playwrights—for weren't they all participating in the same joyous crusade? Political revolution would release artistic creativity and more autonomy. Artistic revolution would serve political goals and personal liberation. Lifestyle revolution would engender political justice and artistic inspiration. As Malcolm Cowley wrote, "Villagers might get their heads broken in Union Square by the police before appearing at the Liberal Club to recite Swinburne in bloody bandages." And as Max Eastman put it, "We wanted to *live* our poetry."

One goal in particular unified the apparently contradictory causes of the Villagers—the liberated self. In politics, though most of them espoused a collectivist creed, they sought self-determination. In art, they sought self-expression. And in "the art of living," they sought self-fulfillment.

Dramatic changes in the attitude toward the self between the nineteenth and the twentieth centuries—from an ideal of self-sacrifice to one of self-fulfillment, from the goal of doing good to that of being good—can be traced to a multitude of causes, among them the stability of American social life. But the Villagers made those changes central to their transformation of consciousness. And since displaying the joys of the liberated self would inspire others to join them, the quickest way to win the revolution was to live as if the revolution had already been won. They were self-assured rebels, harbingers of a new social order. "Experiment" was one of their favorite words—radiant with excitement, they were willing to try anything in order to expand the limits, not just of the permissible, but of the possible. And rarely has a revolution relied so heavily on the persuasive power of reason. The Villagers believed it was only necessary to point out the mechanisms of oppression to bring about their dismantling. But more important, they shared three interlinked attributes—joy in the moment, unquenchable optimism, and high moral tone.

The Villagers made a cult of carefree irresponsibility, but in the service of transcendental ideas. Theirs was an attitude, as one historian put it, of "serious unseriousness." Crystal Eastman (Max's sister) summed up their credo: "We wanted to live to help," she said, "and to get fun out of it."

Despite its hostility toward middle-class values and its adulation of such European thinkers as Marx, Freud, and Nietzsche, the Village ethos celebrated nineteenth-century American ideals. The Villagers' creed was closer to Concord and Brook Farm than to Paris or Vienna. What could be more American than the quest for a utopian community of idiosyncratic individuals in which everyone was equal precisely because everyone was unique?

The Villagers may have fled the narrow-minded morality, crude materialism, and barren intellectual life they'd grown up despising—but they retained an image of the pastoral paradise they felt sure small-town America had once been. After all, hadn't they created "the Village"? Their goal was not so much to create as to recapture Eden.

Furthermore, the Villagers' attitude toward America wasn't as unpatriotic as the enraged editorials charged. What were their goals, the rebels asked—the question asked by every American ever accused of lacking in patriotism—but those of the Declaration of Independence and the Founding Fathers? America had wandered from its principles, and they saw it as their task to lead it home. As James Oppenheim addressed his floundering country, "Is it dreamless? I bring it a dream! / Lacks a vision? It shall have mine!"

Nor was the Villagers' attitude toward religion nearly as blasphemous as the outraged preachers of middle America believed. Far from atheistic, they harked back to the ideals of early Christianity that they felt had been distorted and debased by the hypocrisies of institutionalized religion.

They used the Ten Commandments as the moral underpinning of their renegade politics, and even *The Masses* evoked Jesus in its pacifist editorials and cartoons and went so far as to call "the Son of God" "the first socialist." They felt their commitments could be both ecstatic and redemptive.

Young men and women dissatisfied with a small-town or middle-class life but only vaguely attuned to the insurgent sensibility began to hear tales of an almost mythical place called Greenwich Village where radical political creeds were not regarded as un-American, where aspiration to an unordinary life did not result in scorn or unendurable isolation, where people pursued love and beauty and justice without having to respond to parental invocations of responsibility. They packed their bags with either eagerness or trepidation, but at least with the hope of finding a world more challenging, more inspiring, more free than their own. Perhaps the greatest contribution Greenwich Village has made to the American imagination, greater even than the work of its writers and artists, has been to provide a focus for such visions even to those who never made the journey.

Mabel Dodge's Salon

"Oh, How We Were All Intertwined!"

To dynamite New York!"—that's why she'd gathered in her Greenwich Village apartment the writers, artists, journalists, socialists, anarchists, feminists, labor leaders, clergymen, psychiatrists, and poets, all the "movers and shakers," who would "upset America with fatal, irrevocable disaster to the old order!"

Among the more than one hundred guests tonight in Mabel Dodge's legendary salon at 23 Fifth Avenue might be Max Eastman and Walter Lippmann in animated conversation with Big Bill Haywood and Elizabeth Gurley Flynn—or Emma Goldman and Alexander Berkman holding forth for Carl Van Vechten, Alfred Stieglitz, and Marsden Hartley—or Lincoln Steffens, Jo Davidson, and Edwin Arlington Robinson clustered around Margaret Sanger—while a long-haired, walrus-mustached, glitter-eyed anarchist named Hippolyte Havel wandered among them, muttering "goddamn bourgeois pigs." They debated radical politics and free love, psychoanalysis and the single tax, birth control and the Wobblies, cubism and women's suffrage, all the enlightened ideas of the dawning century that they felt certain would cast off the darkness of the past.

Only a few months earlier, in the fall of 1912, Mabel had sat alone in the middle of her huge living room, staring despondently at the walls. Having returned to America after eight years in Europe, shuddering "ugly, ugly, ugly" as her ship sailed into New York harbor, she had taken over the second floor of an elegant brownstone on the corner of Fifth Avenue and 9th Street. On the first floor lived a cranky ninety-two-year-old major general who'd lost a leg at Gettysburg (and who'd been found not guilty by reason of temporary insanity of murdering his wife's lover, the son of Francis Scott Key, on the sidewalk across from the White House). On the top floor brooded an ex-governor of New York who'd been impeached for his dedicated services on behalf of Tammany Hall. But Mabel fought her inclination to sink into their morose seclusion. Determined to experience "the fire of life," and convinced that she had "always known how to make rooms that had power in them," she shook off her malaise and promptly redecorated.

As if to counteract the tenacity of the drab and dismal past, as well as her listless moods, Mabel surrounded herself with white—white wallpaper, white woodwork, white velvet chairs, white silk curtains, a white marble mantelpiece, a white porcelain chandelier, a white bearskin rug. But now that she'd created her tabula rasa, what was she to write upon it? Elation, dejection—the constant counterpoint of her life. "Nothing to do again!" she wailed. But recalling her passion "to know the Heads of things, Heads of Movements, Heads of Newspapers, Heads of all kinds of groups of people," she opened her doors and "let the town pour in!"

A wealthy socialite of thirty-three, with a voracious curiosity and an insatiable need for stimulation—"I wanted to know everybody!"—Mabel quickly befriended the prominent journalists Hutchins Hapgood, Carl Van Vechten, and Lincoln Steffens, and dispatched her lackluster husband, who was "unaware of the possibilities lingering in the soul," and whose "commonness and mediocrity" contrasted so strongly with her own "broad-mindedness," to the Hotel Brevoort across the street. Hapgood, a writer for the *New York Globe* who virtually invented the solemnly effusive style that still plagues American newspaper columnists, knew virtually everyone in New York and obediently brought several of his most interesting friends to Mabel's home, and Van Vechten, the urbane music critic for the *New York Times*, invited a pair of Harlem entertainers. While Mabel was distressed by the way they "leered and rolled their suggestive eyes" as they played the banjo and sang off-color songs, she comforted herself with the thought that "one must let Life express itself in whatever form it will."

Steffens, America's "messiah at large," told her one day as they took tea, "You have . . . a centralizing, magnetic social faculty. You attract, stimulate, and soothe people. . . . If you had lived in Greece long ago, you would have been called a hetaira. Now why don't you see what you can do with this gift of yours. Why not organize all this . . . coming and going of visitors?" "But I thought we don't believe in 'organization,'" protested Mabel, already a devotee of the Village cult of spontaneity. "Oh, I don't mean you should 'organize' the evenings," Steffens replied wryly. "I mean . . . let [people] feel absolutely free to be themselves and see what happens." Gather interesting people around her, then listen to them exhort and denounce and declaim—at last Mabel could satisfy her craving for stimulation. Evenings!

It is Mabel's Dangerous Characters Evening, and her posh salon is under police surveillance. Big Bill Haywood is talking about the IWW tonight, Emma Goldman about anarchism, English Walling about socialism. With half the nearly two hundred guests in evening dress sipping Graves Supérieur, the other half in working clothes and sandals, waiting to put together a free dinner from the lavish buffet of Virginia ham, cold turkey, and Gorgonzola, she quietly signaled her butler to open the door to the dining room at midnight. The future, classless organization of American society was to be debated, perhaps even decided. Insurrectionary ideas were socially respectable to the degree that they were intellectually provocative— and since the stirrings of radicalism were beginning to awaken the middle-class conscience, the restructuring of industrial capitalism and bourgeois politics seemed less a matter of class conflict than of rationally selecting the most persuasive agenda.

Big Bill was feared by upright citizens as a fiery advocate of labor violence—a reputation enhanced by his hulking body and black eyepatch— but naturally that made him a folk hero to the Villagers, the Cyclops of the revolution. But unfortunately the Wobbly spokesman, like so many leaders who become impassioned orators when addressing thousands of angry followers in a driving rain, was inarticulate, almost reticent, when asked to explain rather than exhort. Sprawled on a chaise longue, "this great battered hulk of a man, with one eye gone and an eminent look to him," Big Bill seemed, said Mabel, "like a large, soft, overripe Buddha," with two or three Village maidens—schoolteachers by day, bohemians by night—seated enraptured at his feet. And when the brilliant young Harvard graduate Walter Lippmann, in his somber, precise manner, tried to question him about Wobbly strategy, Big Bill's "lid drooped over his blind eye and his heavy cheeks sagged even lower."

Emma Goldman, editor of the anarchist magazine *Mother Earth* and advocate of Direct Action—she and her constant companion, Alexander "Sasha" Berkman, had served time in prison for attempting to assassinate the steel magnate Henry Clay Frick—scolded Mabel's guests for their dilettantism and "endless quibbles and hair-splitting of issues." But though Emma warned the working men and women not to listen to the "college professors and lawyers who with the philanthropically-minded ladies"—whom could she mean?—"only succeed in sentimentalizing the cause and making compromises which in turn become real evils again," she showed little inclination to satisfy the guests' curiosity about the differences between the competing philosophies.

The socialist English Walling, one of the founders of the NAACP, was the most articulate speaker, everyone agreed, but also the most bland—though with Eugene Debs receiving six percent of the vote for president in the 1912 election, socialism had never before, or since, been such a prominent voice in the American political dialogue.

Some of Mabel's guests expressed shock at the inflammatory ideologies of the speakers, others felt their minds quickened by startling new ideas, while a few felt that the debate merely exposed the innocence of the Villagers, their commitment to conversational radicalism. "They all talk like goddamn bourgeois pigs!" Hippolyte Havel cried out shrilly, and as the Evening came to an end, he embraced Mabel with tears in his eyes. "My little sister! My little goddamn bourgeois capitalist sister!"

Tonight's topic, Mabel announced a few weeks later, is Sex Antagonism. Doctrines of free love periodically surface in American life—the practice, of course, is considerably more consistent—but in the Village in the teens the concept flourished by allying itself with feminism, socialism, Freudianism, anarchism, birth control, and the assault on marriage as a bourgeois institution. And while it's tempting to say that never has so much ideology been called upon in support of instinct—for nothing seems quite as quaint as the erotic rationalizations of previous generations—this was in fact the first generation of Americans to realize the role of sexual repression in social control. As the critic James Hunecker complained, in America "the whole man ends at the collarbone." The sexual revolution of the years preceding World War I alternated between the frivolous and the fearless—and as those who lived through the sixties can confirm, in the midst of a revolution it's sometimes difficult to discern the difference.

In 1914, to take a not untypical example, a buxom Villager named Babs, sympathizing with the plight of those young men unfortunately forced to resort to prostitutes for the happiness that was their birthright as

Americans, persuaded a number of her friends to freely give their bodies to anyone who asked, a movement that proved as short-lived as it was enthusiastically encouraged. Somewhat less self-deluded, prominent Village intellectuals constantly experimented with ways to reconcile erotic independence and emotional commitment. Lincoln Steffens pretended he was married when he wasn't—and later pretended he wasn't when he was— while Max Eastman and his wife, Ida Rauh, who at one point denied they were married in order not to disturb the free-love ideologues, later shocked the pulpit from coast to coast by putting their names separately on their Village mailbox. Still others, like the flamboyant Hippolyte Havel and his mistress, Polly Holladay, proprietor of the Village's most popular restaurant, fell into the familiar pattern of adopting free love for themselves and bitterly denouncing their partners for exercising the same privilege. And then there were men like Hutch Hapgood, Mabel's closest confidant, who, having once been told by William James himself that he was "in thrall to the absolute," felt that he was obligated by this distinction not only to have extramarital affairs but to report their subtle effects on his soul to his resigned wife—and even to write a book about his wanderings for circulation among his Village friends.

It was Hutch who Mabel felt would be most qualified to address her guests on the subject of the relationship between the sexes—though it was Mabel, recently converted by Margaret Sanger to "the joys of the flesh," who came up with the unambivalent title Sex Antagonism. Still, even to discuss the topic openly, and in mixed company, was daring for the time. A little drunk, Hutch stood before Mabel's assembled guests, announced that "my wife is always telling me that love is a misunderstanding between a man and a woman," and concluded by observing that "men are the victims"—apparently because they do not have "the vitality that the working class has, that the women have," and are thus forced to resort to clandestine affairs. "The problem is how to get the heat without the lie," he went on.

Steffens, the chairman for the Evening, remarked wryly, "Quite Steinesque"—referring to Mabel's friend Gertrude. When Hutch elucidated his thesis by remarking that "the sex distinctions are only a thing like time and space, something by which we go through our experiences," and attempted to throw an ecumenical bouquet to the unimpressed anarchist faction by gushing that "Emma Goldman represents an infinitely greater amount of law than the government does," it was apparent that Villagers committed to the principle of free love but hoping for some guidance as to its practice were still on their own.

Undaunted, Mabel turned from sexual to aesthetic liberation. Despite the shift in cultural power from Boston to New York and the fierce assaults on moral and literary respectability in the novels of Frank Norris, Stephen Crane, and Theodore Dreiser (who lived in the Village but kept a sullen distance from Mabel's salon), the complacent conventions of the Genteel Tradition, so named by George Santayana only a year earlier, still ruled the American literary imagination. Within months of her return to the United States, Mabel embarked on "my own little Revolution" in literary and artistic taste by introducing Gertrude Stein to the American reading public and by serving as one of the sponsors of the explosive Armory Show of 1913.

Believing that political, sexual, and artistic rebels were equal partners in the struggle against capitalism, Mabel invited "that sturdy old eagle" Big Bill Haywood back to address her modernist friends, including Marsden Hartley, Andrew Dasburg, Max Weber, and John Marin, at an Evening on Proletarian Art.

Artists think themselves too special, too separate, Big Bill argued with a rather condescending smile. Someday the state will recognize that everyone is an artist. Torn between sympathy with the working-class cause and dedication to their own revolution, the artists were momentarily silent—until sculptress Janet Scudder rose from her seat, and asked, with the same scorn with which she'd address a Terre Haute matron, "Do you realize that it takes twenty years to make an artist?"

On another Arts and Politics Evening, Mabel invited both the artists who drew for *The Masses*, the newly founded leftist magazine (to which she contributed several articles), and the editors of the uptown *Metropolitan Magazine* (the most popular 10-cent periodical of the day, featuring plutocratic politics and pretty-girl covers), who had refused the artists' work because of their radical politics. But the "gatling gun talkers" of the Village, as the *Metropolitan* editor characterized them, left the uptowners launching even more pointed epithets—such as "your prostitute of a magazine."

To the Poets Evening, over which Edwin Arlington Robinson presided as an owlish, grimly mute eminence, Mabel invited not only published poets, but those whose masterpieces were too "advanced" to reach print—or in some cases paper. George Sylvester Viereck's "quite startling verses" were the most memorable, though not as memorable as Amy Lowell's shocked departure in mid-reading, leaving, as Mabel described her, "like a well-freighted frigate."

· · ·

The Dangerous Characters Evening, the Sex Antagonism Evening, the Evenings of Art and Unrest—all ended in ideological disarray. But Mabel's curiosity combined with her diffidence, her need for self-expression with her impulse to self-effacement, to make her the perfect salon hostess. For three years, beginning in January 1913, her salon became the center of the country's radical intelligentsia. Experts on "good government" and women's suffrage appeared, on prison reform and eugenics, on unemployment and "the Mexican question," on "primitive life" and "the corrupting influence of money"—the debaters, even in the last case, smoking imported cigarettes and sipping imported liqueurs provided by Mabel's imported servants.

She was constantly exhorted to open her rooms to discussion of such Village cults as vegetarianism and Esperanto, but in politics she focused on the labor movement, in sex she stressed women's rights, and in art she emphasized modernist painting and prose.

She managed the Evenings so skillfully, as Steffens noted, that "no one felt they were managed. . . . Practiced hostesses in society could not keep even a small table of guests together; Mabel Dodge did this better with a crowd of one hundred or more people of all classes. Her secret, I think, was to start the talk going with a living theme."

Feeling that she was merely "an instrument of the times," that "I'm not doing anything . . . I let them come, that's all. Life decides, not me," Mabel never participated in the "living themes" herself but acted as their conduit. "I had a little formula for getting myself safely through the hours without any injury to my shy and suspicious sensibilities. . . . I never uttered a word during my Evenings beyond the remote 'How do you do?' or the low 'Good-by.' . . . I never talked myself except to one or two people at a time, and preferably to *one.*"

Some Villagers were enthralled by Mabel's regal inscrutability, others felt she was concealing her incomprehension, yet most agreed with Carl Van Vechten, who recalled that "she remained in the room without being present," and that though her face was "a perfect mask," her "electric energy presided." Max Eastman, never one of Mabel's admirers—in his heart he thought her "witchlike"—wrote that "for the most part she sits like a lump and says nothing. She seems never to have learned the art of social intercourse. . . . She has neither wit nor beauty, nor is she vivacious or lively-minded or entertaining. . . . [Yet] there is something going on, or going round, in Mabel's head or bosom, something that creates a magnetic field in which people become polarized and pulled in and made to behave queerly. . . . And they like it—they come back for more." Mabel's fetish was other people's conversations—and her genius at listening catalyzed an entire generation of vociferous radicals.

Carl Van Vechten stressed the way she forced her guests to test their convictions by confronting them with others who held opposing points of view, combining "dissimilar objects to their mutual benefits." As Max Eastman put it, "Many famous salons have been established by women of wit or beauty; Mabel's was the only one established by pure will power." But its very simplicity made it, as Lincoln Steffens said, "the only successful salon I have ever seen in America."

A particularly striking example of the benefit of juxtaposing apparently incongruous ideas, of the Villagers' emphasis on the importance of self-expression in both personal and public life, were Mabel's Evenings devoted to the New Psychology. It was there that many of America's leading radicals and intellectuals first heard of the theories of Freud and Jung that were to play such a crucial role—and in some cases to create such havoc—in their public as well as private lives.

Walter Lippmann, a rather unlikely acolyte of the unconscious, led the first Evening's discussion, and not surprisingly the conversation focused on such issues as the environmental causes of nervous disorders, the "unhealthy" aspects of the Protestant work ethic, and the repressiveness of genteel, middle-class "civilization."

On another New Psychology Evening, Dr. A. A. Brill, Freud's American translator and a founder of the American Psychoanalytic Association (and later to become Mabel's psychiatrist—nothing but the best), alarmed many of the guests, who got up and left in mid-discussion, "incensed at his assertions about unconscious behavior and its give-aways." But Brill's Evening, and the awareness of the new theories that soon swept through the Village, made Freud a fad. As the playwright Susan Glaspell recalled, "You could not go out to buy a bun without hearing of someone's complex." But Freud's theories, though invariably simplified and warped to fit the Villagers' optimistic creeds, didn't just energize the sexual radicals with a new vocabulary, they also inspired modernist artists with a new muse and provoked political radicals to reconsider the premises of middle-class progressivism. As Steffens recalled after the Brill Evening, "It was there and thus that some of us first heard of psychoanalysis and the new psychology of Freud and Jung, which . . . introduced us to the idea that the minds of men were distorted by unconscious suppressions, often quite irresponsible and incapable of reasoning or learning. . . . I remember thinking how absurd had been my muckraker's description of bad men and good men and the assumption that showing people facts and conditions would persuade them to alter them or their conduct."

Margaret Sanger had learned the frustrations of "showing people facts and conditions," and those who characterized as frivolous Mabel's Evenings devoted to free love, feminism, and birth control ignored the hostility, even brutality, with which such ideas were greeted in America in 1913. When Mabel's apartment was opened to meetings of the Sanger Defense Committee, Margaret had not only spent numberless nights in jail for distributing information on birth control, but had lost nine teeth when one inflamed jailer, zealously defending traditional moral values, had kicked her in the mouth. Labor unrest involved more than a cozy debate of ideologies. Mabel might feel a frisson up her spine at entertaining "murderers," but she also exhibited much courage in juxtaposing classes as well as causes. One evening in the late winter of 1914, Mabel welcomed IWW leaders "Wild Joe" O'Carroll, "Chowder Joe" O'Brien, "Omaha Doc" Roth, and "Baldy" McSween for an Unemployment Evening, "a great gathering" of nearly two hundred Village figures. A red banner hung on the wall. Feminists in bobbed hair and sandals accepted cigarettes from bankers in starched linen and tails. Society women mingled with laborers. And everyone listened raptly to the Wobblies, who'd just returned from a protest meeting that had been circled by mounted police.

When one of her guests urgently whispered to Mabel that "There are some newspaper men coming in," she promptly delegated Walter Lippmann, who had made it clear that he felt her Evenings were becoming too raucous, to act as her bouncer. As he tried to eject the intruders from the press, Mabel began to have second thoughts. "Surely we should not put them out. They are just *people*, too. They are part of Life trying to express Itself." So she countermanded her order, and the newspapers were also allowed to express themselves. "I.W.W. THRONG ARE GUESTS OF SOCIETY FOLK ON FIFTH AVENUE," exclaimed the headline in one New York paper. "WOMEN IN EVENING GOWNS ENTERTAIN BILL HAYWOOD, AGITATORS, AND THE UNEMPLOYED IN HOME OF MRS. MABEL DODGE." "About 200 men and women, in evening dress, and nearly all, women included, smoking cigarettes, took part in the meeting," the article reported. "Women in low-necked gowns hid behind escorts and tried to hide their cigarettes." "I.W.W. MEN STARVE AS LEADERS EAT," another paper proclaimed. "LEADERS OF I.W.W. FIFTH AVE. GUESTS MINGLE WITH MEN AND WOMEN IN EVENING CLOTHES AT MRS. DODGE'S HOUSE." "There were present some men with long, black, flowing locks, who say they are anarchists, some of the Haywood type who say they are leaders of industrial organizations, some who belong to social uplift movements in New York . . . [and] some women who didn't appear to have any occupations. . . . A heavy set young man [Lippmann] came out and said that the gathering was for the purpose of discussing social problems and that all present were friends of Mrs. Dodge and that positively nothing should be published about it."

And so, with the emphasis on emblems that was rapidly moving from advertising into journalism, evening clothes transformed muckrakers and editors of *The Masses* into "society folk," cigarettes signaled sexual audacity, and the press responded to the incomprehensible, as it always has and always will, by adopting a tone both ominous and condescending, which would come to characterize American attitudes to the Village itself.

Long accounts of Mabel's salon soon appeared in the press almost weekly, and Mabel herself became one of the country's first celebrities. She was widely regarded by the tabloid public as a "sphinx," an appellation that, given her anathema to mystery, she loathed. Most of the papers mocked the very fame they were heaping upon her, but according to the *Morning Telegraph*, "If you ever get a card from Mona Mabel Dodge with the word 'discussion' in the corner, drop what you had planned to do and get on the ground floor." Recalled the widow of a president of Yale, "Simply *everybody* went."

Patron of geniuses or collector of celebrities? Siren of spirit or dabbler in ideas? Feeling a void at the center of her being, she became adept, as did so many women, at discerning the needs of others and then adopting a persona that would fulfill them. At first in her salon, and especially in her many love affairs, she resigned herself to living through others—as if she could only be real to herself if she saw her reflection. "I wanted to lie back and float on the dominating decisive current of an all-knowing, all-understanding man," she confessed of her lovers, though in practice, and not at all paradoxically, this meant she aspired to be either their muse, their mother, or their master.

Inevitably dissatisfied with floating, Mabel soon became resentful and manipulative and sought in domination the only alternative to submission. "People were always warning other people about me," Mabel said, not without a touch of pride. How could a woman so committed to following the flow be so willful? Her contemporaries did not understand, though nearly all considered themselves feminists, that with no outlet for her talent and ambition other than devoting herself to the men she hosted and the men she loved, these were the only two choices available to her. Most of the epithets directed at Mabel—femme fatale, queen bee, sorceress, Venus flytrap, spiritual vampire, and, of course, bitch goddess—and most of the fictional portraits of her written by fascinated and appalled novelists who considered her a kind of female principle—resulted from her dubious relationships with men.

But it's too easy to dismiss Mabel as a "werewolfess"—as she once characterized herself—for the neurotic qualities that proved so disastrous in her romances made her the ideal hostess. Her psychic emptiness, her dread of purposelessness, led her not only to devour the men who, she vainly hoped, would provide her with authenticity of self, but also to crave experiences, and causes, that through her salon might provide her with a sense of identity. "That woman will drive me crazy," Van Vechten told Hapgood, more in admiration than dismay. Still, he said, "She had more effect on my life than anybody I ever met." In the freewheeling, experimental vortex that was the Village in the years before World War I, who was more perfectly suited to gather together the "movers and shakers" to debate the contours of the future? Her refusal to crystallize her commitments, her ultimate indifference to the causes she sponsored, while leaving her in a state of psychic disarray, also kept the Villagers who attended her salon in a state of ideological flux. Mabel could never cease experimenting—but her emotional indecisiveness quickened the Village's intellectual glory.

Many of Mabel's critics dismissed her as less hetaera than "a species of Head Hunter," as she herself acknowledged—as nothing but a dilettante of radicalism, mixing champagne and dynamite, confusing feelings with thought, regarding insurrection as entertainment, the latest in the long, ignoblesse oblige tradition of aristocratic voyeurs of bohemia, seeking titillation by flirting with revolutionary credos she had no desire to embrace. But more than any other person, Mabel recognized, if only intuitively, that the repressive traditions against which the Village radicals were rebelling—political, economic, sexual, artistic—were inextricably linked, and that the most immediately necessary radical act was not to focus on specific reforms but to break down the barriers between the radicals themselves, to affirm both the range and the unity of the insurgent spirit itself.

One Evening might founder in factionalism, another might degenerate into disputation, another might conclude in incoherence—but the Lyrical Left defined itself more by its energy than by its ideas. Mabel's fabled openness to all those willing to risk "shattering themselves for the sake of their ideas"—which led Steffens to remark that "she believed, for a while, everything," and one historian to claim that she "all but established the pattern of the 'free-lance intellectual' of the early twentieth century"—had a greater impact than any one of those ideas, for they would not have received such vigorous mutual reinforcement had they not been disseminated at her salon. As Mabel exclaimed, "Oh, how we were all intertwined!" Without an original idea in her head, Mabel helped sow every original idea of her decade.

The catalyst of Mabel's fabled openness to divergent points of view was less philosophical curiosity than psychological circumstance—her real need was to create and then ameliorate emotional conflict. Like most prominent Villagers, she was raised in the intellectual hinterland, but more than most, she seemed, as she said, to have a life "destined for sorrow."

Born into a wealthy family in Buffalo in 1879, Mabel was shaped by the proper Victorian gentility her remote parents adopted as a mask. Of their marriage one need know only that whenever Mabel's mother returned home from one of her frequent trips, her father honored the occasion by lowering his monogrammed flag to half-mast. Unloved, miserably lonely, and surrounded by formalized contentiousness, Mabel soon learned that the only way to avoid sinking into a pit of purposelessness was to manipulate others. Yet driven by the panic of nonbeing, and determined to flout her mother's hypocritical "respectability," she obsessively tried on roles, causes, ideas, identities—as a teenager even flirting with a kind of chaste lesbianism, for which there was little peer pressure in late-nineteenth-century Buffalo—then instantly dropping them when they inevitably failed to fulfill her. Neurasthenia, they called it, that feeling of placid desperation, of restless passivity all too familiar to gifted women in all ages.

At twenty-one, Mabel married a young man who, despite awakening her to what she called "fiery fountains falling on black velvet," failed to gratify the longings of her soul. Within a few months, she began an affair with an older man who satisfied her on both counts—her gynecologist—and when her husband was killed in a hunting accident and her illicit relationship became a public scandal, her mother shipped her off to Europe, not least because Mabel had seen her in the gynecologist's arms herself. Before the boat landed in Le Havre, a Boston architect named Edwin Dodge had fallen in love with her and they were married four months later.

Settling into a Florentine villa constructed by the Medicis in the fifteenth century—its courtyard designed by Brunelleschi, and one of its inhabitants, Raphael—Mabel immediately adopted the pose of voluptuous

Renaissance lady. "I will make you mine!" she addressed Florence from a Tuscan hilltop. *"Questo angelo vestito di bianco"* ("this angel dressed in white"), the local merchants called her. Already as unhappy in her second marriage as she'd been in her first, she indulged in a series of not-quite affairs (one with her Italian chauffeur, whom she transformed into "a knight, a page, a courtier"), attempted a series of not-quite suicides (in one instance mixing figs and broken glass), embarked on a fully consummated affair with her son's tutor, and, in a last effort to save her marriage, designed a bedroom with a trapdoor in the ceiling from which descended a silken ladder that could facilitate more episodes of "fiery fountains falling on black velvet"—though Edwin used it only once, to certify that it wasn't a safety hazard. Wealthy, well connected, intelligent, charming—when not indulging in her pose of elegant ennui—Mabel had no difficulty collecting both objets d'art and objets de personnalité, and the Villa Curonia soon became a prominent international salon—a "constant carousel," in the words of Artur Rubinstein. Emotionally immobilized by her lack of any sense of self, she frantically surrounded herself with the vibrant intellects who might provide it. Among her many guests were Bernard Berenson, Roger Fry, Gordon Craig, Eleanora Duse, André Gide, Norman Douglas, Paul and Muriel Draper, and Lord and Lady Acton, and she flattered everyone with a passive yet desperate curiosity that seemed to say she'd discovered the one person who could answer the questions about the nature and purpose of existence she'd been vainly asking all her life.

Mabel, in short, was precisely the kind of person Gertrude Stein was willing to bestow her presence upon, and when Gertrude visited Florence in 1911 they immediately became friends. "She has a laugh like beefsteak," said Mabel. Fascinated by Mabel's enigmatic, volatile moods, Gertrude wrote "Portrait of Mabel Dodge at the Villa Curonia," one of her series of cubist word portraits of prominent figures of the first years of the century. (Among her other subjects were Picasso and Matisse, though it was her portrait of Mabel that Oliver Gogarty liked to read aloud in a Dublin pub, where it may have been heard by James Joyce.)

Mabel wanted to transform her life into a work of art, but when this proved beyond her talents, she began to see herself as a muse who would accomplish her purpose through others—Gertrude's was the first of many portraits of Mabel by entranced if not always admiring writers, including novels by Carl Van Vechten and Max Eastman and several stories by D. H. Lawrence. Focusing on the discontinuity of Mabel's moods, with touches of sexual innuendo (her bedroom was next to Mabel's, the walls were thin), Gertrude found Mabel the ideal subject for her emphasis on the fluidity of personality. "So much breathing has not the same place when there is so much beginning . . ." "There is that desire and there is no pleasure . . ." "There is no action meant . . ."

Mabel wasn't entirely sure what such sentences signified, but she was sure that what she regarded as her unstructured personality could be interpreted as dynamic rather than passive. Gertrude helped Mabel understand that no metaphysic, no aesthetic could substitute for an absent identity, and that perhaps she could find herself in the disorderly present more easily than in the formalized past. So, still dissatisfied with her life, with her husband, and, most of all, with herself, Mabel abandoned the search in Europe and resumed it in America.

Even before beginning her salon, Mabel had three hundred copies of Gertrude's portrait printed and bound in Florentine wallpapers for her friends, and when a copy found its way into the hands of one of the organizers of the 1913 Armory Show, he asked her for permission to distribute it at the show and to write an accompanying article explicating Gertrude's genius. "There will be a riot & and revolution & things will never be quite the same afterward," Mabel wrote Gertrude in Paris.

"Gertrude Stein is doing with words what Picasso is doing with paint," she concluded. "She is impelling language to induce new states of consciousness." Gertrude's introduction into the world of American letters had turned both women into perhaps the earliest examples of what was soon to become a staple of the twentieth-century media, the incomprehensible celebrity.

"*Everyone* is saying, '*Who* is Gertrude Stein?' " Mabel reported to Gertrude. "*Who* is Mabel Dodge at the Villa Curonia?" Despite Mabel's effusions, however, their friendship soon cooled. Mabel attributed Gertrude's withdrawal to Alice Toklas's jealousy over some innocent flirting—she was one of those fortunate people who find flattering explanations even for flagrant rejections—although the more likely explanation was advanced by Gertrude's brother, Leo. "In Gertrude Stein's mind," he said, "there had begun to be some doubt as to who was the bear and who was leading the bear." Mabel was never a self-starter, but once started she was unstoppable. Soon she became the vice president of the Armory Show, one of its financial backers, its most indefatigable publicist; she even contributed her chauffeur. "The most important public event that has ever come off since the signing of the Declaration of Independence," she called the exhibition in a letter to Gertrude. "I think it the most important thing that ever happened in America, of its kind," she added less grandiosely. Indeed, it was one of her rare understatements, for the Armory Show *was* the most important art exhibit of the twentieth century and detonated like a bomb in the national consciousness. The most controversial painting, of course, was Marcel Duchamp's *Nude Descending a Staircase*, which was called, in perhaps the best example of philistine wit in the history of art criticism, "an explosion in a shingle factory."

"It should be borne in mind," editorialized the *New York Times* in a typical media response to the Armory Show, "that this movement is surely a part of the general movement, discernible to all the world, to disrupt, degrade, if not destroy, not only art but literature and society too . . . the Cubists and the Futurists are cousins to anarchists in politics." On one level, this reaction marked the beginning of a common phenomenon of the twentieth century—success measured not by praise but by notoriety. On another, it acknowledged the unity of art and politics and hinted that art no longer served a comfortable cultural function but expressed an alienation from society. And on yet a third level, while superficially just another instance of philistine incomprehension, it actually articulated the goals of modernist art as clearly as any of its supporters. Disrupt, degrade, destroy?—wasn't that precisely what the artists intended?

As for Mabel, she could at least take some of the credit for introducing Picasso, Matisse, Van Gogh, Cézanne, Gauguin, Braque, Brancusi, Seurat, and Kandinsky to the New World. "Many roads are being broken—what a wonderful word—'broken'!" she exulted. "Nearly every thinking person nowadays is in revolt against something, because the craving of the individual is for further consciousness, and because consciousness is expanding and is bursting through the molds that have held it up to now." But while she found a characteristically dizzying and detached gratification in her overnight notoriety—"if Gertrude Stein was born at the Armory Show, so was 'Mabel Dodge' "—she remained self-effacingly committed to "my own little revolution," the credo of her salon.

Not all the guests at Mabel's salon were movers and shakers. Indeed, the It that Mabel idolized occasionally revealed Itself in eccentrics and out-and-out crackpots. Bizarre behavior, whether annoying or amusing, came to symbolize freedom and authenticity, and "unconventional" became just as much an ideal for the Villagers as "conventional" was for the bourgeoisie they despised. Among the pioneers of individuality were those who discovered nothing but their own idiosyncrasies—but whether outrageous, lunatic, or merely pathetic, they joined the ranks of Legendary Village Characters.

Hippolyte Havel! Outrageous, lunatic, and pathetic, first of a noble breed. Raised in Hungary by his Gypsy mother, confined as a teenager in an insane asylum and released at the advice of Krafft-Ebing himself, Hippolyte embraced anarchism in late Victorian London, moved to Chicago to edit an anarchist newspaper, and, after a less than delirious stint as one of Emma Goldman's many lovers, surfaced in New York, in the words of Max Eastman, like a "ragged chrysanthemum."

When not berating Mabel's guests as "goddamn bourgeois pigs," which sometimes seemed the full extent of his radicalism, Hippolyte could usually be found either as a short-tempered cook, waiter, and dishwasher at Polly Holladay's restaurant on the west side of Washington Square or standing on street corners shouting anarchist slogans at bewildered passersby. As for Polly, she found no fault with his cooking, but was severely disappointed in his companionship. He keeps breaking his promises, she complained to a friend, explaining that on more than one occasion he had promised to kill himself for her but as yet had failed to keep his word.

One night, over drinks with two friends at the Brevoort bar, Hippolyte suddenly suggested a Trimordeur evening. Trimordeur? Trimordeurs, he explained impatiently, were knights-errant of the spirit of wine and dance. So they drew up an announcement of a meeting of the Trimordeurs at an Italian restaurant on Mulberry Street and sent postcards to ten or fifteen friends. On the night of the party, friends brought friends and friends of friends—was it the knight-errant grapevine?—and by midnight over seventy Villagers were celebrating the spirit of wine and dance, one of the first occasions when Villagers began to form their own bohemian community. "Goddamn bourgeois pigs," yelled Hippolyte, stroking his goatee, grinning.

On one memorable occasion, Hippolyte relieved himself in the gutter at the corner of Fifth Avenue and 8th Street at 3:00 A.M. and raved at the policeman who arrested him, "You mean I don't even have the rights of an ordinary horse?" Yet Mabel fondly welcomed Hippolyte to all her Evenings, even if his only contribution was "Goddamn bourgeois pigs!"

Mabel became muse to a Village variation of the prototype—the After-Working-Hours Genius. A copy editor at the *New York Times* by day, Donald Evans turned to the Quest for Immortality at night, differing only from most night-dreamers in that he actually published his effusions, an achievement somewhat diminished by the fact that his publishing house, Claire-Marie Press, one of the first of those small, avant-garde enterprises, was owned, managed, and staffed by a single person, Donald Evans himself. Reading his letters to Mabel ("You opened up avenues of joy today for me. . . . The vision of your freedom was intoxicating. . . . You yourself are ineffable; Your name will be blessed above the Virgin's") and the poems she inspired ("She tried to rouge her heart, yet quite in vain. . . . Her hidden smile was full of hidden breasts"), it's not entirely clear whether he was trying to give expression to infinite yearning or just wanted to get laid. As a potential lover, Donald had—how to put it?—a kind of vegetable magnetism, but Mabel concluded that "this fin de siècle attitude of his was rather boring"—an opinion she expressed of several other Village men who fell in love with her. Undiscouraged, Donald informed Mabel of "the golden voyage I have embarked upon, a thousand and one sonnet portraits of you," of a "slender vol." describing in verse a dozen ways of commiting suicide. Of the latter, one way was all Donald needed, however—unsuccessful in his poetic projects, he proved all too successful in taking his life.

For a few years, a Donald Evans cult sprang up. As the poet Arthur Davison Ficke wrote in the foreword to a proposed book called *The Donald Evans Legend*, "Probably no figure so mythical as that of Donald Evans has ever had even an imaginary existence. Faust, Til Eulenspiegel, the Wandering Jew, and Haroun al Raschid are all solid, demonstrable, and documented persons in comparison. Already the Evans-Legend has assumed large proportions; in fact, we must even today make a discrimination between the archaic—or as I shall call it, the Ur-Legend—and the latter and doubtful form, which I shall call the Neo-Legend." The book was never completed, however, and very soon Donald Evans became a nonlegend.

Mabel sometimes showed as little understanding of the significance of her salon as the newspapers that hooted at its "radical chic"—an epithet that surfaced fifty years before the sixties. But her ingenuousness gave her courage, and she never faltered in her quest for emotional or intellectual adventure. Even if Mabel had never hosted a single Evening, she would have entered Village lore, for in one of her more prescient experiments, she threw the Village's first peyote party.

In the spring of 1914, when Raymond Harrington, a visiting cousin of Hutch Hapgood, told them about a strange medicine he had discovered while doing ethnological research among the Oklahoma Indians that enabled the mind to pass beyond ordinary consciousness, Mabel announced that they must all try it.

Harrington and Hutch and his wife, Neith Boyce, were the first to be invited. Max Eastman and Ida Rauh were always eager to try something new. Her old friend Bobby Jones, the famous set designer. Andrew Dasburg, the pioneering modernist painter. Genevieve Onslow, an actress and friend of the Hapgoods—one of those familiar Village figures who, though embarked on a quest for ultimate wisdom, had difficulty expressing the simplest idea. And of course Terry.

Another figure in the gallery of Legendary Village Characters, Terry Carlin, a true anarchist, had vowed as a young man never to earn so much as a dollar under the exploitative capitalist system. A man of his word, he lived on the verge of starvation, but since he was an ingratiating conversationalist, his many friends gave him money for food, and since he was an alcoholic, he spent it all on booze. With his huge thatch of iron-gray hair, sparkling Irish blue eyes, "beautiful skeleton, and splendid head with noble features"—Mabel's phrase—Terry would sit for days in various bars, the Hell Hole on 8th Street and Sixth Avenue in particular, spinning tales until he dropped. One of those helplessly charming dreamers called poets though they've never written a word, he became one of Eugene O'Neill's closest companions.

So one evening—having fasted, as Raymond insisted—they gathered at Mabel's and sat cross-legged on her living room floor. Holding an arrow in one hand and eagle feathers in the other, Raymond stationed himself behind the "fire"—one of Mabel's Chinese silk shawls draped over an electric bulb. He popped a peyote button into his mouth and soon began to howl like a dog. The others took pieces of peyote and gulped them down. "The mere presence of that peyote seemed already to have emphasized the real nature in us all," Mabel recalled. "I was laughing, but Neith looked down at the fire, distantly grave and withdrawn, beautiful and strange. Hutch appeared rather boyish, like a boy in church who lowers his head and peeps over his prayer book at another boy. Bobby's face was simulating a respectful attention, while it hid his thoughts. Ida looked more like a superior lioness than ever, cynical and intolerant; Max grinned amiably, and Terry seemed more remote than the others as he contemplated the end of his cigarette. . . . Genevieve Onslow's frog-like eyes were brilliant and intense. . . . Andrew's brows twitched as he gave and yet did not give himself to the occasion; a half smile played over his sulky lips, but it was an irritated smile. Only I seemed to myself to be just exactly as usual, unaffected by anything and observant of it all."

Raymond motioned everyone to join his howling song, but only Hutch obeyed, then motioned everyone to take a second button. This time everyone obeyed but Mabel, who, finding herself more affected than she'd realized, palmed the button and placed it on the floor behind her. "Everything seemed ridiculous to me," Mabel continued—"utterly ridiculous and immeasurably far away from me. . . . Several little foolish human beings sat staring at a mock fire and made silly little gestures. Above them I leaned, filled with an unlimited contempt for the facile enthrallments of humanity, weak and petty in its activities, bound so easily by a dried herb, bound by its notions of everything—anarchy, poetry, systems, sex, and society."

Hutch, who liked to describe himself as "God drunk," wasn't one to so readily scorn "the facile enthrallments of humanity." "It didn't seem strange to me when Raymond left his seat and ascended through the air to the ceiling," he recalled. Soon afterward, however, he left his seat and knelt before the toilet watching lurid flames dart out of his mouth, then lay down in one of Mabel's bedrooms and turned into an Egyptian mummy, "making a complete review of my whole life, applying to it an intense criticism, which amazed me for its complete unworthiness." As for Raymond, he reported that he had departed on "a long voyage to wander for months in a tropical valley full of huge birds and animals of hitherto unknown colors."

Hours passed; Max and Ida quietly went home. Long after midnight, Mabel discreetly retired to her all-white bedroom. Hutch, Neith, Andrew, and Bobby departed to Mabel's guest rooms, leaving Raymond, Genevieve, and Terry in their oblivious trances.

Mabel lay in a fitful half-sleep, trembling with rage. "To think that that was going on there in my house and I could not stop it." "Oh, Great Force, hear me!" she prayed, and in almost immediate response she heard Andrew stalking furiously into the living room, where he opened the windows, threw out the remaining buttons, and cursed the entranced trio.

Mabel heard a dreadful cry, then silence, then a tap at her door. Genevieve stood before her like an apparition. "Oh Mabel!" she moaned. "It is terrible!" Mabel hurried to the living room. Raymond, horrified at the defiling of a sacred ceremony, was trying to restrain Andrew when suddenly they noticed that Genevieve had disappeared. By this time, the others had been awakened. The sudden startling ring of the telephone. "Genevieve is here," Max said. "We heard her crying under our window. We'll put her to bed and see you in the morning."

The participants were suddenly sobered. "Mabel," Hutch said with his usual solemn exultation, "I have learned tonight something wonderful. I cannot put it into words exactly, but I have found the short cut to the Soul." "What is it?" Mabel asked eagerly. "The death of the flesh." "I saw what Sex is," Andrew contributed. "And it is a square crystal cube, transparent and colorless, and at the same time I saw that I was looking at my Soul."

Max soon showed up with Genevieve, gibbering and rolling her eyes, and Hutch rang up Harry Lorber, a discreet Village doctor. After a

quick examination, Lorber offered his half-amused, half-chiding diagnosis—"Dope, hey?" The word brought Mabel crashing down. She had failed
to achieve the visionary consciousness reported by Hutch and Andrew—or
even Genevieve, who was now mumbling tearfully about God—and felt
compelled to take the public stance that "such gatherings . . . were the antithesis of all I wished to stand for. The level of my life, at least in my own
eyes, was infinitely raised above such sordid sensationalism." Mabel took
some measure of solace, however, in the fact that "every one of the others
who had been at the apartment that night talked about it for years . . . un-
doubtedly that legend has encircled the world."

Terry? Terry finally spoke for the first time since nine o'clock the
previous evening. "I have seen the Universe," he exclaimed with what
Mabel was forced to describe as "the most illumined smile I have ever
seen," and "man!," he concluded, "it is wonderful!"—whereupon he
walked out without another word, and, in all likelihood, repaired to the
Hell Hole for his morning pick-me-up.

Mind cures," spiritualism, astrology, New Thought, Divine Science—
Mabel tried every cult with the same blend of promiscuous enthusiasm
and disenchanted skepticism with which she listened to Wobblies advocate
revolution or watched Villagers pop peyote. In the years 1912 to 1917, such
therapies seemed to hold out as much healing potential as the rather im-
plausible "talking cure" recently introduced from Vienna. What all the various new therapies shared, and what made the radical intellectuals flock to
them with evangelical ardor, was the conviction that mind could triumph
over matter, that the environment could be mastered by the will.

Mabel's motives were less ideological. Sunk in emotional paralysis,
she gave herself over to each of the new cures with the wholeheartedness
and detachment that allowed her both to explore every idea of her generation and commit herself to none.

Dear Hutch wrote of "my sister Mabel," "Her eager, sometimes
graceless searchings . . . her inability to let go of anything even for a moment casually within her domain, all this seems often ugly and reprehensible. But to me it is not so at all; for I know that even the harsher more
unattractive elements of her activity are there because of her eager love of
'It'—the infinite—with which she wants to be naturally, strongly connected." Why not try to connect herself through the as yet unfashionable
science of psychiatry? Even if Mabel felt the new doctrine from Vienna was

"apparently a kind of tattle-taleing," hadn't her New Psychology Evenings been among her most provocative? So Mabel became one of the first Americans to undergo psychoanalysis, and not the last to change analysts. Mabel's first psychiatrist, Smith Ely Jelliffe, America's leading Jungian and the man who coined the word "psychosomatic," quickly arrived at his diagnosis. Mabel obviously suffered from penis envy and responded by trying to castrate men, a conclusion that not only followed inevitably from her confession that she wanted to cut off her hair, but had the added advantage of being applicable to all women. Mabel expressed her willingness to see gender as one of the sources of her emotional disturbances—an intuitive feminist, she recognized all too clearly that she derived her sense of self largely from her identification with the achievements of men—but this organ business seemed dogmatic and about as healing as "the Intense Inane." "I am afraid I did not learn much about myself with Jelliffe," said Mabel, "but I did get a very complete line on *him*."

So Jelliffe didn't work out? Go for the best. Go for Brill. When Brill informed her he was too busy to see her until fall, she told him she simply couldn't survive until then. Brill well understood that one of an analyst's most effective tools, in addition to the nuances of Freudian methodology, was a brisk dose of psychic cold water, and replied that not only could Mabel survive until fall, but that she would. "I have a very bad Oedipus complex—" Mabel began one of their first sessions, but Brill cut her off. "Never mind about that," he said. "You are not here for conversation." "I believe *people* constitute your best medium," he soon told her, and his insistence on sublimation, translated into encouragement that she find some sort of "meaningful work," inspired her to at last take her writing seriously.

Soon after starting her analysis with Brill, she began a syndicated biweekly advice column in the Hearst papers—some historians even credit her with being the first female columnist in American journalism. Typically, she called her contributions *feuilletons*, at once belittling them and giving them a kind of snobbish éclat—but in writing frequently about psychological problems she became one of Freud's first and most widely read popularizers.

For an acolyte of It, Mabel showed a surprising disinclination to search in the one place where a large number of Village men would have been happy to help. Not a beauty, she was described by Gertrude Stein as "a stoutish woman" and by Max Eastman as "a rather dumpy and stumpy little girl," but Gertrude went on to say that she had "very pretty eyes," and certainly it was her "very old-fashioned coquettry" that made her seem so attractive to so many men.

In principle, of course, Mabel championed sexual intercourse as "a scientific, wholly dignified, and prophylactic part of right living," a position she adopted at the urging of Margaret Sanger. Although Mabel aided her in establishing clinics, she was frankly more interested in Margaret's views of the process that led to the *need* for birth control. "She was the first person I ever knew," gushed Mabel, "who was openly an ardent propagandist for the joys of the flesh." In a cozy tête-à-tête, Margaret had taught her "the way to a heightening of pleasure and of prolonging it . . . the spreading out and sexualizing of the whole body until it should become sensitive and alive throughout, and complete"—a lesson she learned with alacrity but that she remained reluctant to apply. (When Emma Goldman's companion, Alexander Berkman, an ardent devotee of free love as a philosophical obligation of anarchism, tried to steal a kiss in a taxi, Mabel was as horrified as any Victorian matron—"this scared me more than murder.")

Mabel finally persuaded herself "that I was very old-fashioned and that what I needed and had never admitted to myself was this very sex-expression other people were so intent upon." But as is well known to everyone who's tried to talk themselves into opening their arms, ideology is a poor seducer. Mabel carefully selected a young man from her Village circle and invited him into her all-white bedroom, but instead of the fountains on black velvet redux felt only a kind of detached observation. Let's try a hotel, the dogged fellow suggested—after all, she was technically still married, maybe that was the problem—and while Mabel complied, she couldn't help feeling that "he had suddenly become a dose of medicine I must take . . . that would lead me into the world of free souls." Her companion, unaware of the pharmacological role he had come to play in her erotic imagination, was proceeding with the movements of ecstatic communion, if in a more or less solitary manner, when a waiter suddenly popped open the door and inquired, "You ring?"; it was at last clear to both of them that insofar as untrammeled, free-souled "sex-expression" went, Mabel was much more adept at talking about it.

This was the woman, however, who was later called America's leading exponent of the cult of orgasm (she even named her dog Climax) and who would soon embark on one of the legendary Village love affairs—for when Mabel's flesh finally declared itself ready, it didn't have to listen to any arguments.

There was candlelight in the cozy apartment of Hutch's schoolteacher heroine, where enraptured Villagers had gathered to hear Big Bill Haywood. Just released from jail, he reported on the Paterson silk workers' strike for an eight-hour day. "There's no way to tell our comrades about [the strike]," he grumbled. "The newspapers have determined to keep it from the workers in New York."

"Why don't you bring the strike to New York and *show* it to the workers?" a shy voice blurted out—and even Mabel was surprised to realize it was hers, "this idea speaking through me . . . another case of It!" "Why don't you hire a great hall," It continued, "and reenact the strike over here? Show the whole thing!" How? Where? "Madison Square Garden! Why not?"

Mabel had been addressing Big Bill, but suddenly a voice cried out "I'll *do* it!" and a young man moved from the back of the room to sit beside her. "That's a *great* idea. I'll go over to Paterson the first thing in the morning. We'll make a pageant of the strike! Where do you live? I'll come and see you when I get back." At first Mabel didn't quite get his name. "My name," he said, "is Reed."

Everyone in the Village had heard of Jack Reed, but Mabel had never met him. Flattered by his eagerness to implement her idea, amused by his breezy enthusiasm, she took even more careful note of his appearance. "His olive green eyes glowed softly, and his high, round forehead was like a baby's with light brown curls rolling away from it and two spots of light shining on his temples, making him loveable."

Who could resist? Poet of adventure, aflame with dreams, Jack Reed—raised in cultivated Oregon, educated in the wilds of Harvard—descended on the Village like a whirlwind. He endowed everything he pursued with the nimbus of romantic rebellion, and pursued everything with what Hutch called his "three-dimensional self-confidence." (Befriended by the much older Lincoln Steffens, Jack took a cheap apartment with three other young men at 42 Washington Square South. When Steff took an adjoining apartment, the building became celebrated as the successor to the fabled House of Genius at number 61, whose residents were said to have included Jack London, O. Henry, Frank Norris, Stephen Crane, Upton Sinclair, Theodore Dreiser, Willa Cather, and Edwin Arlington Robinson.)

Before his mid-twenties, Jack had made his mark as a crusading journalist, widely published in both the commercial press and the radical *Masses*. And his exuberant ode "A Day in Bohemia" had established him as the Byron of the Village.

At five o'clock the morning after he and Mabel met, Jack hurried to

Paterson, and before they met again, three weeks later, he'd interviewed dozens of strikers, gotten himself arrested for refusing to obey a policeman's order—"I returned airy persiflage to his threats," he boasted—spent four well-publicized days in jail with angry Wobblies and nodding cocaine-fiends and "a lineal descendant of the Republican doctrinaires of the French Revolution" (a particularly exhilarating experience for a Harvard man), and written a long, colorful, teeming account of "The War in Paterson" for *The Masses*.

Already on the way in his conversion from Village playboy to international provocateur, he was forging the solidarity between workers and intellectuals in a common revolutionary struggle the Villagers had only prophesied! Mabel led several meetings at Margaret Sanger's apartment, and enlisted the help of her friends, especially Bobby Jones, John Sloan, and Walter Lippmann. Her main task, she thought, was to act as an inspiration for Jack. "I kept having ideas about what to do and he carried them out. . . . I knew I was enabling Reed to do what he was doing . . . pouring all the power in the universe through myself to him."

Writing the scenario, enlisting the painters and designers, preparing Madison Square Garden, rehearsing the striking silk workers, even teaching them to sing their insurrectionary slogans to the tune of "Harvard, Old Harvard" (with Jack, a former cheerleader, on the megaphone)—as they worked themselves into a state of physical exhaustion and spiritual exaltation, Mabel and Jack fell in love. "That we loved each other seemed so necessary a part of working together," recalled Mabel, "we never spoke of it once. . . . There wasn't time, and that it was no time for lovemaking was accepted without words between us. . . . We had taken for granted the inevitability of our love for each other, Reed and I. We got each other through our pores."

And Jack? Who fell in love so often it was considered a joke among his friends? But as Hutch put it, "When I saw that look on her face, I knew it was all over for Mabel . . . and also probably all over for Reed."

But first the pageant. On June 7, 1913, Mabel watched in delight as nearly 1,500 strikers marched through the Village, up Fifth Avenue, and into Madison Square Garden. The letters "IWW" blazed ten feet high in red electric lights on all four sides of the Garden Tower. The city sheriff foamed at the mouth over what he called these "fulminations of paranoiacal ebullitions," but fifteen thousand spectators whooped and sobbed in a continuous roar for four, five, six hours as the strikers jammed the stage reenacting the fierce battles with the police, and, at the climax, the funeral of a slain worker, his coffin carried through the crowd as each striker placed in it a red carnation. "The Marseillaise," followed by "The Internationale," tore off the ceiling.

"These scenes," reported a New York paper, "unrolled with a poignant realism that no man who saw them will ever forget." The pageant proved a financial fiasco—and helped precipitate the break between Big Bill Haywood and Elizabeth Gurley Flynn, who felt that he had succumbed to the romantic allure of the Village. But even though the strike was soon broken, anarchists and socialists had been united with painters and poets, by two Villagers who were falling in love, to create what one historian has called "one of the most unusual cultural events in American history," and the quintessential Village link of politics, art, and sex.

The morning after the pageant, accompanied by Carl Van Vechten and Jack's old Harvard roommate Bobby Jones, Mabel and Jack sailed for Europe to spend the summer at the Villa Curonia. But when Jack tried to enter Mabel's cabin the first night at sea, she rebuffed him. "Inevitability" was one thing, decorum (what the other passengers would think) was another. "You shouldn't care about that," Jack reproached her bitterly. "If you cared for me nothing would matter." The same scene ensued on the second night, and again on the third, whereupon Jack took out his frustration—what choice did she leave him?—in poetry. "Wind smothers the snarling of the great ships," he wrote, "And the serene gulls are stronger than turbines / Higher than high heaven and deeper than sighs. / . . . But the speech of your body to my body will not be denied!" An "occasional" poem if ever there was one.

Jack had his plea delivered to Mabel's cabin at midnight, but her body remained mute. She feared, she said, "descending into the mortality of love." She found herself enamored instead of "the high clear excitement of continence."

Mabel proved right in thinking people were watching but wrong in thinking they disapproved, for even before they consummated their love, their friends began mythologizing their romance. "I feel there's something wonderful and immortal between you and Jack," Bobby shyly offered in mid-Atlantic. And when they arrived in Paris a letter from Hutch confessed that he had slept alone in her parlor, described *their* relationship as "a flower . . . full of an unfolded, a comprehensive, serene *bien être* floating beneficently on invisible and insentient things," and unnecessarily assured her, and himself, in a magnaminously discreet reference to Jack, that "what is between you and me can do no Wrong to anybody."

Of course Mabel was too sophisticated to think it Wrong to sleep with Jack, but while her reluctant rhetoric echoed the virginal Victorianism of her childhood reading, her circumspect behavior presaged, if only intuitively, the feminist awakening in the Village. If at first the Village women demanded sexual equality as part of their liberation, they soon learned that many men all too enthusiastically encouraged them to throw off their clothes along with their shackles. Women like Mabel, struggling to find a sense of identity other than through their relationships with men, began to see that the only power they possessed was erotic — which sometimes meant that only in withholding sex could they achieve sexual equality. Mabel's resistance to Jack, in short, resulted from her incipient self-respect as well as from her manipulative coyness, but when, the first night in Paris, at the Hôtel des Saints Pères, she finally tasted "my own elixir of love," she sank back into the bliss of submission. "In one night I threw it all away," she said — the "it," in this case, being "power."

Off the lovers went to the Villa Curonia, and for the entire summer of 1913, night after passionate night, into the low bed with four gold lions at its corners, Jack descended from the silken ladder.

Happy affairs are all alike — and so are all unhappy ones. Almost from the first, Mabel realized that her fears of "descending into the mortality of love" had been prophetic. "Nothing counted for me but Reed," she said in a tone mingling bliss and remorse, "to lie close to him and to empty myself over and over, flesh against flesh." Part of her wanted to strengthen her independence, another part wanted to devote herself to her lover — the one enhancing the self, the other enslaving it.

Even in Paris, Mabel had been dismayed when Jack leapt out of bed to greet an old friend knocking at the door and insisted they immediately take a walk. Only two days his inamorata and already abandoned! And in Florence, every minute of every day was a jubilant new adventure. "He always went from thrill to thrill," Mabel complained. "He was sturdily loyal to his own wonder." The very aspect of his personality that had attracted her soon became a curse.

When she was forced to submit to "the terror of seeing his eyes dilate with some other magic than my own," Mabel's old depression returned. "Everything seemed to take him away from me and I had no single thing left in my life to rouse me save his touch. But I could not hold him day and night. Only at night." In the morning the joy with which he greeted the day cast her into despondency. Only when Jack fell briefly ill with diphtheria did Mabel feel "a resurgence of delight." "A lover sick in bed, one is safe for the moment!" Mabel was perceptive enough to recognize her dilemma, if not strong enough to extricate herself, and confessed that "a man completely at a disadvantage, disempowered, and delivered up to us, we find to be no man at all."

As for Jack, uninterested in the tangled emotional relationships that were Mabel's métier, the summer was little more than a brief interlude of white peacocks and Etruscan grottoes from the causes to which he had committed his life. "I feel," he wrote a friend, "like the fisherman caught up by the Genie's daughter and carried to her palace on the mountaintop." When Mabel attempted to consecrate their idyll by revealing to him the treasures of Tuscany, he responded, "It's old, Mabel. It's beautiful, but it's so *old*."

The lovers returned to 23 Fifth Avenue in the fall to discover that they had entered the realm of legend—the Queen of Bohemia united with the Poet Laureate of the Village. He was greeted as the heroic radical-poet-lover who would define the style of an entire generation. "From the break of day he was eager to be off and doing," Mabel recounted. "The world had won him away from me again. . . . Each day as soon as he was gone out of the house I felt deserted and miserable. . . . My triumphs served to stimulate him to greater achievements in that world where men do things in order to prove themselves powerful to themselves. So a spirit of competition sprang up between us! If I had power, he, then, must have more power. . . . Desperate, I tried to hold him closer by laments. . . . I grew more and more domestic except for the Evenings, when I sat tragic and let It do what It wanted." Nothing worked—not her laments, not her tears, not her hysterics—not even her attempts to join him on his excursions, for when Jack said he wanted to show her the misery of the Lower East Side, Mabel, to his mortification, insisted on making the tour in her chauffeur-driven limousine.

One night, when Jack told her about an encounter with a Village prostitute, how he "had felt her beauty and her mystery, and through her, the beauty and mystery of the world," she conjured up a not entirely successful faint. A few weeks later, when he stormed out of her apartment she took a carefully insufficient overdose of Veronal. And a few weeks later, when Jack invited another young rebel to 23 Fifth Avenue and talked into the night she tried to convey her loneliness by belittling his friend. To her astonishment, Mabel discovered a note beside her bed the next morning. "Good-by, my darling. I cannot live with you. You smother me. You crush me. You want to kill my spirit. I love you better than life but I do not want to die in my spirit. I am going away to save myself. Forgive me. I love you—I love you. Reed." Jack had vanished, "taking the universe with him."

Mabel sobbed out her misery to Hutch. "If you suffer enough," Hutch reassured her in his dolefully optimistic way, "you will know the Absolute." But for the moment Mabel preferred Jack. After two days of nonstop weeping, she lunched with Carl Van Vechten, dined with Walter Lippmann, distracted by the one's self-amusement, the other's self-effacement—and the next morning, just as "a faint beginning of gladness for aloneness was lifting in me," Jack burst into her apartment, pale and worn, buried his head in her lap, and cried out, "Oh, I couldn't *bear* it. I can't live without you. I missed your love, your selfish, selfish love!"

So the cause of Mabel's misery was removed at the precise moment she was beginning to glimpse its benefits. Jack got an assignment to go to Mexico to write a series of articles on Pancho Villa; Mabel tried to talk him out of it; Jack protested. "I will take you with me in my heart, but we must be free to live our own lives!"

The morning Jack departed Mabel sobbed to her pillow, then suddenly resolved to follow him. By midday, she'd wired him to meet her in Chicago, and boarded a train. But alas, "when we met I was disappointed that he looked merely glad instead of overjoyed." By the time they reached El Paso and she began to realize that tents and troop trains awaited her in Mexico, Mabel returned to the Village, "very much out of sorts." "I think she expect[ed] to find General Villa a sort of male Gertrude Stein," Jack wrote a friend, "or at least a Mexican Stieglitz." But he also sent Mabel long, loving letters—"I will write all our names across the sky in flames!"

Dimly recognizing that her love diminished rather than enhanced her sense of self, Mabel tried to escape the web in which she felt trapped only to create another. Upon her return from El Paso, she discovered on her living room wall a painting by her old friend Andrew Dasburg, one of the peyote celebrators, boldly entitled *The Absence of Mabel Dodge*, and clearly intended as the anguished love letter he was too reticent to write. Although she felt "chemically all avowed" to Jack, Mabel encouraged Andrew's attention and asked another pioneering modernist in her circle, Marsden Hartley—that "gnarled New England spinster man," Mabel's euphemism for homosexual—to write Jack about the painting in order to stir his jealousy.

"It is full of the lightning of disappointment," Marsden wrote Jack. "It is a pictured sensation of spiritual outrage—disappointment carried way beyond mediocre despair." The critic for the *New York World* outperformed even Marsden's strenuous effort. "Mrs. Dodge is not only literary, aspiring, and a charming hostess," he wrote, "but also appears to wave a mesmeric wand over Mr. Dasburg. In her presence he seems to feel like a torso stripped of skin and palpitating in roast beef layers of deep red and shining white; away from her his thrill collapses and the torso is jammed, twisted, and flattened as if a motor car had run over it." Unfortunately, the painting that evoked such prose—they don't write like that anymore—has disappeared.

She began to see Andrew every day, though she conscientiously reminded herself after each visit that "I was all for Reed." While Mabel had hoped to stir Jack's jealousy, the only jealousy stirred, alas, was Mabel's, for when Jack breezed back from Mexico intoxicated by the enthusiastic reception of his articles on Villa, he dedicated the resulting book, to the chagrin of Mabel, to his mother. He departed almost immediately to cover the miners' strike in Ludlow, Colorado. Mabel wanted a hero, but had no one to remind her to be careful what you want because you might get it. She began to pull away from Jack, as dissatisfied lovers so often do, by disguising her criticism of her lover as questioning of herself. Why, she wondered, do I always seem to "choose men too immature to satisfy me"?

And so the curtain slowly descended on their love. They spent a few weeks in Provincetown, on Cape Cod, sleeping in a silken tent on the dunes, before Mabel left for another summer in Florence; then they met for a few days in Naples when Jack rushed to Europe to cover the war. But "how [to] recount the gradual fall from bliss" that followed? "Did the return to earthly love bring it about? Did I forfeit my wholeness when I lay in Reed's arms again, tearing open the entrance to the nether world until I was like a wound that gaped between heaven and hell? . . . Even though his had been the hand that thrust me below once more, he himself remained above in the light. . . . He was not essentially radical or revolutionary; he loved it when things happened and always wanted to be in the center of Events." Operatic lovemaking, protestations of undying love, the charades that signal the end.

In saying goodbye to Jack, Mabel also bid farewell "to the labor movement, to Revolution, and to anarchy. To the hope of subtly undermining the community with Hutch; and to all the illusions of being a power in the environment." The Evenings ceased as well, but not her capitalization, for now Mabel determined to devote herself to Art and Nature.

Mabel's first project, early in 1915, was to aid Isadora Duncan in establishing a school to teach the joys of modern dance to the children of the

New York slums. With Walter Lippmann's aid, she persuaded New York's Irish Catholic mayor to visit Isadora's Ark, a Manhattan loft that the priestess of erotic dance had decorated with billowing blue curtains to evoke an Aegean island. Isadora may have had a superb sense of decor, but she had only a marginal sense of decorum, and tore into the mayor with such agitated passion that her gown slipped from her shoulder, exposing a breast. "If this is Greece and Joy and the Aegean Isles and the Influence of Music," Walter informed Mabel, falling into a fit of capitalization of his own, "I don't want anything to do with it."

Mabel's interest in Isadora wasn't a total loss, however, for a few months later, at a performance at the Duncan school, she met a patriarchal painter named Maurice Sterne and discovered that Men were still among her goals. Maurice's face made her think of the "undisclosed soul of Russia," and she promptly invited him to spend the summer in Provincetown to paint a series of portraits of her. Mabel may have wanted another Andrew, but she got another Jack, for while she hoped to remain on the Threshold, Maurice informed her that he couldn't work without sex. Well, if it'll help complete the portraits . . .

Who should show up, soon after Mabel and Maurice had moved in together that fall, but the crestfallen Jack. He could not live without her. Lincoln Steffens persuaded her, since Jack was almost immediately going back to Europe, to defer the final break, and Jack exultantly told everyone they were going to be married as soon as he returned. But Mabel forgot him the moment he "plung[ed] away into a heavy rainstorm," as Max Eastman said, "none of us knew where."

As for Mabel and Maurice, some lovers meet each other's needs too perfectly. Maurice, who longed to lose himself to a woman who would give shape to his life, certainly picked the right one. Mabel, who was fearful of once more losing her independence in love, was more than willing to comply. Momentary bliss—quick disaster. She became calculating, controlling, domineering, he slavish, then morose, finally enraged. Maurice was less her lover than her job, she complained. Noticing that after orgasm he would study her body with an artist's eye, rapturously explaining his theories of curves, volumes, and masses, she decided that sculpture was his true medium, and bullied him into trading in his oils for clay. Mabel was now muse with a vengeance, but of course the more pliant Maurice became, the less manly he seemed.

Torn between submissiveness and anger, Maurice had no choice—he begged Mabel to marry him. Torn between gratification and contempt, she was equally helpless—and agreed. A few days after the ceremony, a distraught Village feminist berated Mabel for betraying women. Hadn't she been an example of women's right to love without the constraints of marriage? "You have *counted* so much for Women! Your Example has stood for courage and strength! I wonder if you realize that hundreds of women and girls have been heartened and fortified by the position you took." To which the bewildered Mabel could only respond, "Which one?"

Only a few days after their wedding, aware that now she had the rights of marriage without the constraints of love, and aware that theirs was a romance that provided its greatest pleasures when they were separated, Mabel informed Maurice that she thought it advisable that he go on their honeymoon alone. The compliant groom departed for the Southwest without his bride. Mabel's marriage was no more a total loss than her visit to Isadora's Ark, however, for in one of his first letters from Santa Fe, Maurice wrote, half in affection, half in desperation, "Dearest Girl — Do you want an object in life? Save the Indians."

The Indians! "My life broke in two right then," Mabel said, "and I entered the second half . . . curing me of my epoch." In the Village, she had struggled for individuality, for achievement, for self-expression, but in New Mexico she surrendered herself to the acceptance and wholeness she discerned in the Indian way of life. She settled in the Eden of Taos for the rest of her life, replacing It with One.

Unfortunately, she still had Maurice to deal with. On one of their first excursions, however, they entered a pueblo and saw a tall, handsome Indian dressed in a white sheet singing in a low murmur. When he looked up, Mabel recognized the placid yet leonine face that had superimposed itself over Maurice's in a dream she had had shortly before leaving the Village. "I sing you a little song," the Indian said solemnly. "I wish you'd come and see us down in Taos," Mabel responded after he'd finished. "I seen you before already," he replied calmly, a remark that Mabel interpreted as predestination, Maurice as a roving eye.

They were both right. Antonio Luhan, a Tiwa Indian who had once made a tour to Coney Island with a Wild West show, quietly but persistently took over Mabel's life, introducing her to native customs, and, with his emotional dignity, acting as the spiritual guide for whom she still yearned. "Goin' by, goin' by, just like water," Tony once described Mabel, which pleased her more than anything Gertrude Stein had ever said. Most of the time they spent together they remained silent, somewhat a novelty to Mabel — and indeed, whenever her talking annoyed Tony, he simply walked away, an even more unusual experience. "It seems to me," Tony once told her when she complained of his silences, "my heart is talking to you all the time"—and that quieted her, as it would quiet anyone, for several months.

When Maurice finally announced that he was thinking of returning East, she eagerly approved. For it was Tony who promised psychic stability, Tony who inspired her to plant a teepee in her front yard, Tony who said one evening, "I comin' here to this teepee tonight, when darkness come. That be right?" "Yes, Tony," answered Mabel, "that will be right."

Mabel and Tony married in 1923, to the amused astonishment of her Village friends. "Lo, the poor Indian," commented Edwin Dodge.

"Why Bohemia's Queen married an Indian Chief" trumpeted the headlines in the national press, though Tony was in fact a "blanket Indian" whose fellow tribesmen were under the impression that Mabel was merely renting him. Mabel's restless pursuit of peace was over, but she remained a hostess to the end. Famous guests descended on Taos; Tony, wrapped in his blanket, took particular delight in chauffeuring them to the neighboring pueblos in Mabel's Cadillac, and Mabel almost singlehandedly transformed Taos into a kind of Village West. Willa Cather and Thornton Wilder were seduced by "the regent of New Mexico," as she came to be called (Paul Horgan dubbed her "the Morgan le Fay of Taos"), followed by Georgia O'Keeffe, Ansel Adams, Edna Ferber, Robinson Jeffers, Leopold Stokowski, John Marin, Jean Stafford, and Thomas Wolfe, who showed up drunk, with two whores in tow, and was promptly dispatched.

But Mabel's most notable conquest was D. H. Lawrence, whom she summoned "across continents" with the ineffable power of One—and with a bombardment of letters. "Before I went to sleep at night," she recalled, "I drew myself all in to the core of my being where there is a live, plangent force lying passive—waiting for direction. Becoming entirely that, moving with it, speaking with it, I leaped through space, joining myself to the central core of Lawrence, where he was in India, Australia. . . . I became that action that brought him across the sea. . . . Come, Lawrence! Come to Taos! This is not prayer, but command."

Mabel's conviction was that Lawrence would "take *my* experience, *my* material, *my* Taos, and . . . formulate it all into a magnificent creation." After briefly toying with the idea of collaborating with Mabel on a book about her life, Lawrence—or Lorenzo, as she came to call him—decided it would be wiser to write his "American book" by himself. Upon seeing a manuscript of Mabel's, he had advised her to "Take a boat out to the middle of the Atlantic and sink it."

Initially attracted to each other by their imperious wills, Mabel and

Lorenzo soon found themselves in ceaseless combat. "I wanted to seduce his spirit," Mabel confided, but Lorenzo's wife, Frieda—whom Mabel described as having "a mouth rather like a gunman"—smelled sex in the air, and the two women spent much of their time trying to rescue the genius from each other's possession. As for Lorenzo, once his initial fascination had faded, he quickly passed from wry amusement—referring to Taos as "Mabeltown" and warning prospective guests not to fall "under the wing of the padrona"—to outright horror, and eventually came to see Mabel as "the prototype of that greatest living abomination, the dominating American woman." He was determined to break the spirit of that "cooing raven of ill-omen" and Mabel briefly capitulated, even scrubbing the floors of her kitchen, one of the few times in her life she had ever visited that part of the house.

But some things even a muse won't put up with, and when Lorenzo went on berating Mabel for her "terrible will to power" and for trying "to compel life," she decided to return to the behavior she would be accused of. Years later, his anger recollected in tranquillity, Lorenzo called Mabel's memoirs "the most serious 'confessions' that ever came out of America, and perhaps the most heart-destroying revelation of the American life-process that ever has or will be produced. It's worse than Oedipus and Medea, and Hamlet and Lear and Macbeth are spinach and eggs in comparison." When they finally separated, after four tumultuous years, Lorenzo published a story about Mabel in which he not only revealed his desire to murder her but described in ingenious detail precisely how he would accomplish the task.

"Lorenzo thought he finished me up," Mabel mused wryly, but she survived for nearly four decades, even returning briefly to the Village in 1940 in a halfhearted attempt to revive her salon at One Fifth Avenue.

This extravagant, insatiable, courageous, silly, indomitable woman —so easy to mock, so difficult to comprehend—whose openness to experience and curiosity about ideas contributed so much to inventing the Village, died in Taos in 1962 at the age of eighty-three. Tony, who'd remained silent throughout the funeral service and most of the burial ceremony, suddenly began to talk. "Where's Mabel?" he asked as he wandered plaintively among the mourners. "We can't start without Mabel."

II

Max Eastman and *The Masses*

"Just-Before-Dawn of a New Day"

Jack Reed eagerly opened the envelope and out fell a gold ring. He was on assignment in the Balkans, covering the early months of the war on the Eastern Front, and awaiting him in Bucharest was a solemn letter from Hutch. Since Mabel's "old feeling is dead," Hutch reported, she'd asked him to return the ring Jack had given her. "If I know her at all, I know she cannot repeat an experience, feeling, that is gone." Love still lingered in Jack's heart, but with nearly all of Europe preparing for war his thoughts were far from an all-white bedroom in the Village. "Talk about talking and think about thinking," he had lampooned the Villagers in "A Day in Bohemia" even before he'd met Mabel, "and swallow each other without even thinking." Jack threw Mabel's ring into a canal, and returned to his hotel to begin work on his dispatch.

Among the many magazines for which Jack wrote was a newly founded monthly called *The Masses*, which was as rebellious and as exuberant as he. In 1913, not yet a member of the staff, he'd even contributed a draft of a manifesto to run under the masthead.

"We refuse to commit ourselves to any course of action except this: *to do with the Masses exactly as we please. . . .* We don't even intend to conciliate our readers. . . . We have perfect faith that there exists in America a wide public, alert, alive, bored with the smug procession of magazine platitudes, to whom what we please will be as a fresh wind. . . . The broad purpose of *The Masses* is a social one: to everlastingly attack old systems, old morals, old prejudices—the whole weight of outworn thought that dead men have saddled up us; and to set up many new ones in their places. . . . We intend to lunge at specters—with a rapier rather than a broad-axe, with frankness rather than innuendo. We intend to be arrogant, impertinent, in bad taste, but not vulgar. We will not be bound by one creed or theory of social reform, but will express them all, providing they be radical. We shall keep a running destructive and satiric comment upon the month's news. Poems, stories, and drawings rejected by the capitalist press on account of their excellence will find a welcome in this magazine; and we hope some day to even be able to pay for them. Sensitive to all new winds that blow, never rigid in a single view. . . . And if we want to change our minds about it—well, why shouldn't we?"

　　The final version of the manifesto, though using only a few of Jack's words, conveyed the same joyously insurrectionary spirit. "This Magazine is Owned and Published Cooperatively by its Editors. It has no Dividends to Pay, and nobody is trying to make Money out of it. A Revolutionary and not a Reform Magazine; a Magazine with a Sense of Humor and no Respect for the Respectable: Frank; Arrogant; Impertinent: Searching for the True Causes; a Magazine Directed against Rigidity and Dogma wherever it is found, printing what is too Naked or True for a Money-Making Press; a Magazine whose final Policy is to do as it Pleases and Conciliate Nobody, not even its Readers—there is a Field for this Publication in America."

　　When *The Masses* began publishing in January 1911, its goals were less audacious. Founded by Piet Vlag, a Dutch immigrant, and financed by Rufus Weeks, a wealthy life insurance executive whose passion for efficiency translated into an infatuation with socialism, the magazine was "devoted to the interests of the working people" in general and the promotion of consumer cooperatives in particular. Vlag had no difficulty finding writers and artists who would contribute without pay—many members of the "silk stocking" Branch One of the Socialist party welcomed the opportunity to express political views uncongenial to popular periodicals such as *Collier's* and the *Saturday Evening Post,* but despite hawking the magazine himself, crying "Masses, Masses" in Union Square, he had difficulty finding readers. When Weeks withdrew his backing, Vlag, again ahead of his time, retired to Florida. *The Masses* ceased publication in August 1912.

　　Not so fast. In September, cartoonist Art Young, a former Republican now famous for his caricatures of bloated plutocrats, called an emergency meeting of the staff to try to keep *The Masses* afloat. Everyone confessed that Vlag's emphasis on consumer cooperatives and the noble proletariat had led to some pretty boring issues, but where else could writers and artists find a magazine that would also print what *they* wanted to express, a magazine unbeholden to advertisers and stockholders—even, if the truth be told, a magazine unburdened by subscribers? So they decided "to keep on publishing the magazine without funds—something," Young mused, "nobody but artists would think of doing." There'd be changes, though. They'd get rid of all that dreary uplift and replace it with a more sophisticated, irreverent tone. And they'd abolish the position of editor and replace it with group decisions at monthly meetings.

Group decisions seemed splendid, but shouldn't someone be in charge? Not to make policy—everyone bristled at that—but to implement the staff's wishes? An excellent suggestion, but none of the free spirits seemed inclined to volunteer. Fortunately, Art remembered meeting, at a dinner honoring Jack London, a former member of the Columbia philosophy department named Max Eastman who said he was looking for "a paid part-time job in the service of socialism." Most of the staff had heard of Max—he'd published essays on political themes, founded the Men's League for Women's Suffrage, and was a charismatic lecturer on social issues. In lieu of any other candidate, and conveniently ignoring his proviso about pay, they unanimously approved the nomination. The painter John Sloan and the poet Louis Untermeyer were delegated to contact Max, and after hours of deliberation arrived at what they felt was the most persuasive approach. John ripped a piece of drawing paper off a pad and scrawled a note in huge letters—"You are elected editor of *The Masses*. No Pay."

The man who soon became the most famous radical in America was born in upstate New York in 1883, a mix of "Christian moralism and pagan revolt against it." Max's mother was the most prominent woman minister of the time (she was asked to conduct Mark Twain's funeral service), which influenced her son in becoming one of America's first male feminists. And after his birth, "she did not want any more of the experience which produced me," which aroused in him a lifelong desire to find women who would prove her wrong. After attending Williams, where, in his "general thirst of life's experience," he attempted to emulate Nietzsche's Übermensch by pricking his finger on a red-hot scarf pin—he studied for his Ph.D. in philosophy at Columbia, completing every requirement but refusing to pay the $30 commencement fee in a gesture of disaffiliation. His life, he recalled nearly a half-century later with his characteristic self-irony, was "the story of how a pagan and unbelieving and unregenerate, and carnal and seditious and not a little idolatrous, Epicurean revolutionist emerged out of the very thick and dark of religious America's deep, awful, pious, and theological zeal for saving souls from the flesh and the devil." Where else could such a person go but Greenwich Village?

As for the "Epicurean revolutionist," Max was the kind of rebel who simultaneously took pleasure in a reputation for pagan irrationality and took pains to behave with moral logic. So strong was the Puritan strain in the American mind that even an unbeliever dedicated to its destruction "felt compelled to lay out his goals with the sobriety of a minister's son." His life, the young Max decided, would be divided into equal parts creative and scientific writing: earning a living, and aiding humanity. But just as Mabel Dodge, in the throes of exhorting her salon guests to overthrow the old order, insisted that their souls have a little fun along the way, Max proceeded to fulfill his goals with irrepressible cheer—and even confessed that in his ideal world he'd be renowned foremost as a humorist. Never, in fact, has a generation of radicals dedicated itself so fervently to experiencing the happiness in the making of revolution.

Max organized the Men's League for Women's Suffrage in 1909 not only because he considered the movement "the big fight for freedom in my time," but also because, as he wryly admitted, he had a "basic need to suffer a little in the cause of an ideal." For several months, the league consisted of little more than Max and newspaper headlines. But then, a year later after Max had tirelessly licked stamps and raised money and lectured to cheering audiences, several thousand members of the Men's League paraded up Fifth Avenue.

Max had neglected female companionship in his list of life's goals, but this was an oversight he soon attempted to remedy. If Jack was the Byron of the Village, Max was the Adonis. Tall, blond, lithe, he dazzled his friends (and it must be admitted, himself) with his gorgeous good looks, which a contemporary described as "like some kind of messenger from Olympus." As with many male feminists, his devotion to the principle of sexual equality seemed to stem, at least in part, from the delights of sexual variety.

Max's first Village approach was a prominent Village feminist, Inez Milholland, a Vassar graduate whom he joined on picket lines. "There is a species of people whose conversation, while radically democratic, always, as though by some gravitational magic, takes place among the rich, swanky, or distinguished," he said. Though Max and Inez were "twin rising stars on the feminist horizon . . . her female beauty and my masculine oratory providing just the combination that the movement wanted," and though, "there was almost, you might say, a public demand that we fall in love," Max remained unmoved. Even though he saw himself as an incipient hedonist and her as a wooden virgin, he felt he should fall in love, he tried to fall in love, he declared himself falling in love, but the more he saw of Inez, the more he admired her mind—an unpropitious sign. On East 9th Street, Inez informed him that it was her impression he was experiencing more passion than she was, an observation he denied. Inez misunderstood his protests, however, "thinking I was attributing more feeling."

Inez had been too likely a candidate for his Great Village Romance; well then, who most unlikely? A year earlier, Max had met Ida Rauh, an attractive, intelligent woman who, in her rebellion against the bourgeois values of her uptown Jewish family, had adopted a philosophy mingling Marx, Nietzsche, anarchism, free love, a free proletariat, and a kind of semi-pauper truancy. But despite these impeccable credentials, Max found her "remote, indolent, impersonal, and willfully unalive—as alien to me as a beautiful groundhog . . . a decorative negation." But what lonely young man, wandering through Washington Square Park on a balmy spring morning, running into a lovely young lady who asked him to come to her apartment on 4th and Macdougal for tea, would brood on such ungracious memories?

"Ida Rauh has a motto on her wall—'Honesty, Simplicity, Intolerance,' " he wrote his mother. "I didn't like it at first, but I do now. It suggests an untrammeled and dynamic character. I want to be one." How often, alas, the desire to become the other lies behind the avowal of love.

Max and Ida's ensuing marriage immediately showed signs of turning trammeled and listless. On the first day of their honeymoon, Max awoke with "a craving to escape," soon followed by an overwhelming sleepiness and a severe case of hives. He was convinced that "I had lost, in marrying Ida, my irrational joy of life. . . . I had committed—irrevocably, it seemed to me—The Folly of Growing Up." The newlyweds were soon accused of a somewhat different folly when they rented a sixth-floor walk-up on Charles Street for $12 a month, and, in their disdain for bourgeois convention, put the names Ida Rauh and Max Eastman on their mailbox. They were promptly visited by a reporter from the *New York World*. His article was headlined "No 'Mrs.' Badge of Slavery Worn by This Miss Wife." They were promptly reviled in editorials and pulpits from coast to coast for adopting what one columnist called "the Rabbit system" and for betraying what multitudes of ministers regarded as the heart of the republic. "Against the entrance of this serpent of lush falsehood," declaimed one pastor, "let every man's hand be raised, and let every sword of manly and fatherly honor flash death to the intruder who would maim the tree of life."

This assault did little to bring the spark back into Max and Ida's relationship, and lacking romance in his marriage Max sought it in revolution—or at least in books about revolution. Ida, more adept as his teacher than as his lover, had introduced him not only to numerous Village radicals but to the Marxist doctrine of class struggle, a concept the Ph.D. philosophy candidate had not so much as heard of until he moved to the Village. "It seems fine to work for an ideal like that," Max told Ida, "even though you may never achieve it. . . . Only I can't understand the rant about class struggle and class war." "Didn't you ever read anything about Marx or Engels?" Ida responded in amazement and launched into such a perspicacious and persuasive summary that he called the conversation "a turning point in my intellectual life."

Max was too much the Deweyite pragmatist to experience the flash of conversion—"a suggestion that seemed practical had been proposed to my mind, that was all"—and was even reluctant to call his newfound conviction socialism, preferring the idiom "hard headed idealism." "This man Marx seemed to offer a scheme for attaining an ideal!—based on the very facts which make it otherwise unattainable." But he found himself ready, given his commitment to the axioms of Greek reason, Christian sympathy, and Founding Father democracy, to join the socialist cause, and willing to listen to an offer of a "part-time job" in its service. So when, in the late fall of 1912, at almost precisely the moment Mabel Dodge was redecorating her apartment at 23 Fifth Avenue, the staff of *The Masses* made its offer. Max accepted with a kind of amused indecisiveness that seemed the last quality the foundering magazine needed in its new editor.

Max had actually heard of *The Masses*. But though he was scornful of its limp humanitarianism, and though he charged Art Young with having "turned my design for living exactly upside down, making my service to socialism the unpaid factor," he couldn't resist looking up the "whimsical bunch" who'd made such an intriguing offer. He didn't want a job without pay and he didn't want to be an editor, he informed Art, but though these were the precise terms involved, his objections seemed trifling. The job? Merely nominal, we all edit the magazine together. No pay? We'll gladly give you a salary as soon as the magazine is on its feet. "Come on up and meet the bunch," Art went on heartily.

And there they were, the staff of *The Masses*, gathered in Charles

Winters's studio—Winters and his wife, Alice; Young; John Sloan; Maurice Becker; Eugene Wood; Louis Untermeyer; Ellis Jones; Horatio Winslow; Mary Heaton Vorse; Inez Haynes Gillmore. "The whole scene and situation lent itself to my effort and my then very great need to romanticize New York life and romanticize the revolution," Max recalled. "The talk was radical; it was free-thought talk and not just socialism. There was a sense of universal revolt and regeneration, of the just-before-dawn of a new day in American art and literature and living-of-life as well as in politics. I never more warmly enjoyed liking people and being liked by them."

And if universal revolt and regeneration weren't enough to shake Max's resolve, the dummy was. He had never heard of the word "dummy" before, but there it lay, innocently spread out on a table, and when Winters showed him how to paste up an issue—cutting up the galleys of the texts and the proofs of the pictures and gluing them onto a previous issue—he was hooked. "No more fascinating sport has ever been invented," he said, combining "the infantile delight of cutting out paper dolls . . . with the adult satisfaction of fooling yourself into thinking you are molding public opinion."

Within twenty minutes, Max had a vision of how such a magazine might be edited—a vision, moreover, uncontaminated by the "cooperation of the staff." While he understood how misleading Art's word "nominal" had been as a description of the editor's job, pay or no pay, this could be fun. Convinced that it was little more than a lark, the new editor agreed to put out one issue, write an editorial laying out the magazine's new policy, and insert an appeal for money—on the condition that everyone on the staff canvassed their rich friends for funds. He'd join in the cooperative on equal terms and contribute an occasional editorial.

Max's inaugural issue, dated December 1912, which featured a cover by Charles Winters of a clown looking into a crystal ball, established three standards that would guide the magazine for the rest of its existence.

First, Piet Vlag's solemn, cumbersome layout was replaced by John Sloan's lively, graceful design, with bold headlines, wide margins, and large drawings—indeed, *The Masses* would remain one of the most beautifully designed publications in the history of American journalism.

Second, Max's editorial, entitled "Knowledge and Revolution," made it clear that the magazine now pledged itself to revolution rather than reform—though his bravado in publishing it without the approval of the staff was somewhat undercut by the fact that none of them seemed to notice. Politically, Max supported left-wing rather than right-wing socialism—backing the IWW strike in Lawrence, Massachusetts, for example—

and ideologically, he committed the magazine to openness rather than doctrine, even, and especially, socialist doctrine. "By Knowledge," the new editor wrote, "we do not mean a set of intellectual dogmas which can not change and to which every new fact must conform whether it wants to or not. By Knowledge, when it is spelled by a capital, we mean experimental knowledge—a free investigation of the developing facts and a continuous re-testing of the theories which pertain to the end we have in view. The end we have in view is a social and economic revolution. . . . To be accomplished only when and if the spirit of liberty and rebellion is sufficiently awakened in the classes in which are now oppressed."

And third, the tone as well as the subject matter of the magazine challenged the decorum of mainstream journalism, as in Art Young's double-page cartoon depicting the capitalist press as a whorehouse with the editor as madam, advertisers as clients, and reporters as prostitutes.

If the editorial wasn't clear enough, Max sent over a press release— this revolution wasn't going to sneak up on anybody. "We are going to make *The Masses* a *popular* Socialist art and freedom of expression . . . [and with] a literary policy equally . . . radical and definite. . . . [The magazine will have a socialist emphasis but will be] hospitable to free and spirited expression of every kind. . . . We shall have no further part in the factional disputes within the Socialist Party; we are opposed to the dogmatic spirit which creates and sustain these disputes. . . . Our appeal will be to the masses, both Socialist and non-Socialist, with entertainment, education, and the livelier kinds of propaganda."

That December issue brought immediate furor. When Max received letters from old friends containing phrases like "vulgar beyond anything I have ever seen in an American magazine," or "deliberately throw away that refinement which is true power," or "invites to careless living both as to care of body and mind," he knew he was on the right track. But bohemian radicalism was not yet fashionable enough to elicit funds from those it flayed. The results of his appeal totaled $80. Worse still, Max discovered that not only had the staff failed to raise a cent, but none of them had even made an effort, curing him of the illusion that his job was "nominal" and that the magazine was a "cooperative." He felt "as far as the North Pole from the part-time paid job I had set out to get," but he had made "too energetic" a start to back out now.

Furthermore, Max was "afflicted with the ability to organize a job and stick at it until it is finished." He realized that his most immediate task was to raise enough money to pay the printer and hold off the landlord— "social and economic revolution" would have to wait until the magazine found sound capitalist backing. The "creative geniuses" on the staff, this "bunch of utopians," as he characterized them, had not only selected an editor sight unseen, but, as they cheerfully returned to their studios, had appointed him chairman, president, publisher, and financial manager as well.

None of the members of the staff recognized that their selection of Max was uncommonly fortuitous. In the first place their "cooperative" ideology conveniently convinced them that the magazine could run itself, and in the second, Max's personality was so perfectly suited to sustaining this illusion that it was several years before they realized that their socialist enterprise had become, almost immediately, a kind of participatory monarchy. In addition to his office manager efficiency, which made it seem that all the magazine's financial difficulties solved themselves, Max had an even stronger streak of wry, lackadaisical charm, which made it seem that all the ideological disputes resolved themselves before it became necessary for a strong editorial presence to intervene. His unruffled manner in the midst of chaos made everyone feel they were participating in a workers' cooperative, an idea he had abandoned on virtually his first day on the job.

In principle, all the magazine's major decisions were made by the staff at its monthly editorial meetings. Twenty or thirty writers and artists would get together on a Wednesday or Thursday evening at one of the artists' studios—the magazine's cramped offices at 91 Greenwich Avenue being too small for such a large gathering—and while eating crackers and cheese and drinking beer pretend they were determining the contents of next month's issue. Max, one of his legs slung over the arm of a chair, would select manuscripts at random from the piles strewn over the table and read aloud—withholding the authors' names—after which the staff would applaud or hoot, make specific suggestions, or drift off into ruminations on political or aesthetic theory. Louis Untermeyer might interrupt, "Oh my God, Max, do we have to listen to this tripe?" or a voice from the back of the room could be heard—"Chuck it!"

The staff turned from voting on manuscripts to voting on drawings, also unsigned. Debate was briefer but no less acerbic. "There is only one thing left for you to do," John Sloan advised one artist. "Pull off your socks and try with your feet." "Nothing more horrible can be imagined than having one's pieces torn to bits by the artists at a *Masses* meeting," recalled Mary Heaton Vorse. "On the other hand, there was no greater reward than having them stop their groans and catcalls and give close attention; then laughter if the piece was funny; finally applause." Finally Max would call for a vote. In keeping with the magazine's commitment to openness, even frequent visitors such as Bill Haywood, Lincoln Steffens, and Clarence Darrow were given an equal voice in the proceedings. Only after a decision had been reached was the author's name finally revealed—on one occasion, two poems by Carl Sandburg were roundly rejected. These meetings made the "*Masses* crowd" an aristocracy of merit, "a little republic," said John Sloan; "We worked for the approval of our fellows, not for money. . . . It took a lot of time and we had a lot of arguments, but that was one reason why *The Masses* at its best was a fine thing."

Everyone agreed this was the only workable procedure for a radical magazine—everyone but its editor, who knew he'd have to pick up the pieces after the group merrily disbanded at 2:00 or 3:00 A.M.

Once the selections had been made, the group turned to writing captions. "Fitting a gag to a picture," Kenneth Russell Chamberlain sarcastically called the process. Occasionally an artist would submit a drawing with no particular point in mind, only to find it transformed into a cartoon. In the early years the artists enthusiastically endorsed the procedure; like the writers, they regarded satire as a crucial ingredient in the editorial mix. Sometimes the captions were savage ("The Southern Gentleman Demonstrates His Superiority" under a Robert Minor drawing of crucified blacks), sometimes whimsical ("Your Honor," intones a corpulent attorney, "this woman gave birth to a naked child"), sometimes wry ("Nearer, My God to Thee" under an Art Young portrayal of a tiny church flanked by two enormous Wall Street towers).

The most successful example of great decision-making was the caption added to a controversial drawing by Stuart Davis, in later years a renowned modernist. A portrait of two hags from Hoboken, it caused a furor at the April 1913 editorial meeting. Art scorned it as too grotesque to print; John threatened to resign if the staff voted it down; Stuart listened to the uproarious debate with mute detachment. The battle lines remained firmly drawn until suddenly John thought of the perfect caption, turning Stuart's hymn to ugliness into a satiric rebuke to the pretty-girl covers *Masses* artists despised. "Gee, Mag," John's underline read, "Think of Us Bein' on a Magazine Cover!" Two months later, in June 1913, the drawing appeared on the front of the magazine, and it remains one of the most famous covers in the history of American journalism.

The captions being the last order of business, the members of the staff congratulated themselves on putting together another issue, broke out more beer, and left Max to sort out the manuscripts and drawings.

For there wasn't nearly enough material to fill an issue, and accepted pieces often needed massive revision. Max never felt bound by the decisions made at the meetings—which never got him into trouble, as no one remembered what they were—but assiduously proceeded to make the rounds of the writers and artists he admired to cajole, beg, provoke, or shame them into making the contributions *he* wanted. He was so persuasive—and so low-key in his bullying charm—that at the next month's meeting the members of the staff would invariably applaud one another on the material he'd selected, reserving their criticism for the few contributions they'd voted in themselves.

It would be a mistake to dismiss the editorial meetings as a sham, however, for if Max made most of the day-to-day decisions himself, the idealistic and gaily militant tone of the magazine was established at what even he conceded were their "warm, witty, colorful, and brilliantly lively gatherings." "I doubt if socialism was ever advocated in a more life-affirming spirit," he recalled, as fond of the "amazing fertility, force, wit and imaginative caring" of the staff as he was exasperated by their delusions about decision-making. One of the reasons so many gifted writers and artists contributed to *The Masses*, in addition to their socialist ideology and their contempt for the commercial press, was this sense of rollicking camaraderie, and Max, understanding the importance of cohesion, wisely kept his reservations about efficiency to himself.

John Sloan was not alone when he said, "If I got a good idea I gave it to *The Masses*. If a got a second-rate one, I might sell it to *Harper's*." During the five years of Max's tenure, most of the leading writers, poets, artists, and political theorists of the prewar decade, and those who would be among the country's leading intellectuals in the decades that followed, contributed—including Sherwood Anderson, Upton Sinclair, Djuna Barnes, Vachel Lindsay, Amy Lowell, William Carlos Williams, Elizabeth Gurley Flynn, Louis Untermeyer, Randolph Bourne, Babette Deutsch, even Mabel Dodge, and, from abroad, Maksim Gorky, Bertrand Russell, Romain Rolland, and Pablo Picasso. To be published in *The Masses* became a badge of acceptance in the radical community worth more, to these idealistic rebels, than any amount of money. In the matter of money, in fact, "cooperative" was merely a tactful way of saying that no one was paid for contributions, and only when the staff finally managed to come up with a salary of $25 a month for its editor was Max paid anything at all.

That Max's job would be "nominal" was a farce from the first. Simply dealing with the flood of mail provoked by the magazine's militancy and irreverence occupied much of his time, though he enjoyed this part of his work too much to complain. When George Bernard Shaw wrote from England in 1914, for instance, sniffing that "in the last few numbers you were admitting vulgar and ignorant stuff just because it was blasphemous, and coarse and carnal work because it was scandalous," Max rejoined, "When we read the first page of your letter we imagined our correspondent as a very liberal Unitarian prelate who enjoyed shocking with his intelligence the good ladies of a New England congregation, and was a little jealous of our liberty to shock him. . . . We never published anything that was vulgar or coarse *to our tastes,* because we are not any of us vulgar or coarse. I don't say the same thing about your word carnal. . . . You ought to try to be a little more carnal [yourself]."

From George Santayana came this charge: "You are spoiling life for others and for yourself in the very ignorant and factious pursuit of some inopportune ideal."

To all of the objectors Max replied: "*The Masses* exists to publish what commercial magazines will not pay for, and will not publish. . . . [We] offer you the goods whose value is too peculiar, or too new, or too subtle, or too high, or too naked, or too displeasing to the ruling class to make its way financially in competition with slippery girls in tights and tinted cupids, and happy stories of love."

Of course, praise poured in as well. "The current number of *The Masses* [Max's first issue] abounds with vital matter from the virile pens of some of the ablest writers in the movements," wrote the socialist presidential candidate Eugene Debs. "The clear cry of the revolution rings all through its pages, and the illustrations are such as could be produced only by artists animated by the militant spirit of Socialism." From abroad, a letter from Romain Rolland—"Liberty, lucidity, valor, humor, are rare virtues, still more rarely found in combination in these days of aberration. . . . They make the high value of *The Masses.*" And even Shaw wasn't entirely critical. "At least one American paper has produced . . . cartoons superbly drawn as well as striking in comment," he wrote in *The New Statesman.*

Max's two major tasks at *The Masses,* in addition to the grueling chore of putting out the monthly, were raising funds from capitalists for a magazine devoted to undermining capitalism and trying to establish professional relationships with writers and artists enamored of their carefree idiosyncrasies.

Max hated fund-raising, as people often hate their greatest talent, but he loved the irony of capitalists financing their own destruction. The first six issues found their patron in the person of Mrs. O. H. P. Belmont, a pink-painted aristocrat who'd divorced a Vanderbilt, married a Belmont, and become, in the words of one social historian, "the indefatigable duchess of the Gilded Age." Mrs. Belmont was hardly a habitué of Max's circles, but she had the habit of enlisting ardent young suffragists as semi-adopted daughters, including Inez Milholland. When Max poured out his financial troubles to Inez one day, she suggested a solution. But it would be difficult to describe Mrs. Belmont as a socialist, Max demurred. "What of it?" Inez replied. "You're a militant—that's all that matters."

Within three days Max found himself in the palatial presence of Mrs. Belmont, and within three hours—for he had a certain skill at ingratiating himself with people who fancied themselves supporters of militants so long as militants knew their place—had received a pledge of $2,000. Furthermore, it took only an imperious glance from Mrs. Belmont at her other guest, a commercially successful novelist named John Fox, to raise an additional, though more reluctant, $1,000.

Amos Pinchot of the Wall Street Pinchots became another $2,000 contributor, and other members of the Rebel Rich soon followed. "Our getting money from the rich," confided a member of the staff, "was a sort of skeleton in our proletarian revolutionary closet." Funds also came from annual balls, from radical and labor groups across the nation, from meetings, rallies, and what Max candidly called "personal holdups." He toured the country, contributing his lecture fees on such topics as "Revolutionary Progress," "What Is Humor and Why," "Feminism and Happiness," and "Poetry Outside of Books"—though the questions afterward usually dealt with the scandalous lifestyle of the Village.

Dealing with the radicals who shared his commitments proved just as difficult as persuading the bourgeoisie to finance their own downfall, for when Max returned from his fund-raising ventures to put out the next issue, he discovered that the Villagers clearly regarded pulling together an issue as nothing but drudgery—the very middle-class "responsibility" against which their revolutionary ardor and artistic integrity rebelled.

Take Harry Kemp, for instance, the Hobo Poet. Max hired Harry as his editorial assistant at $10 a week, more than his own salary, and gave him a pile of manuscripts to read and edit, only to find them alongside his mail the next morning, accompanied by the note, "Dear Max. I don't want to be an editor any more. I must live and die a poet. Please don't get mad. I leave this note because I hate to come up and tell you. Harry."

Max nearly resigned in frustration, but John Sloan came to his rescue. A painter who'd come to New York in 1904, John was a member of the famous group the Eight (later dubbed the Ashcan School by Art Young for their emphasis on harsh realism), but had yet to sell a single painting, making his living by commercial art and teaching. Like many artists of the period, John was a socialist, even campaigning for public office, but unlike most he had a degree of executive ability and took over two summer issues in 1913. John loved *The Masses* more than any of its contributors—and his wife, Dolly, intermittently served as its office manager between bouts of alcoholism—but his real calling lay elsewhere. Once more Max considered resigning—but his wry skepticism rescued him. What could he actually resign? he asked himself. And to whom could he resign it? The time had come to admit to himself that his ironic fate was that of "a poet and philosophic moralist, with special distaste for economics, politics, and journalism, [who] became known to the public as a journalist campaigning for a political ideal based primarily on economics."

Disenchanted by the intimacies of marriage yet enchanted by the companionship of women, Max soon found himself in bed with a liberated young Villager named Elsa, "an extremely rosy apple" whose straightforward approach—"I hope you don't mind if I strip"—stirred his erotic inclinations even as it disturbed his romantic soul. Prevailing Village doctrine made sexual adventure virtually mandatory, but some residue of bourgeois morality still inhibited the minister's son. And after making "demi-virgin" love the demi-adulterer pondered the only two words Elsa had spoken since she'd taken off her clothes—"Poor Max."

To the followers of free love, openness was just as obligatory as adventure, and if Max couldn't entirely succeed at seduction he certainly could at candor. But Ida's devotion to Nietzsche hadn't prepared her for *this*—among other things, she considered Elsa one of her closest friends—and for a few minutes the agonized couple dutifully enacted their ideologies, Ida insisting on "knowing it all," Max explaining that he had merely been "living life to the fullest." Theory soon gave way to theatrics. "I can't bear it," Ida sobbed, while the mortified Max shrank in withering guilt. "Few women understand," he wryly reflected some years later, "the tribute contained in a man's desire to tell the truth." Nor, for that matter, did Max understand the tribute contained in Ida's anguish, and for weeks, putting himself to sleep with the aid of opium, he brooded about the hand of gloom "which had reached out and snatched me back from any feeling of joy." The more he brooded, the more he came to define joy as uninhibited eroticism, and though he felt self-contempt for the way his fidelity had been "cerebrally motivated," he decided that the only way out of his blighted mood—he remained a rational pagan—was "to use my brains about my problem."

To a man simultaneously enamored of science and sexuality, committed equally to intellect and instinct, the only possible recourse was the newest import from the Continent, psychoanalysis. Freud's revolutionary doctrines promised not only hedonistic self-fulfillment but creative self-expression, and soon became an integral part of the Villagers' assault on the conventions and institutions of American society they felt were inhibiting their development as free individuals. Of course this pan-radical platform remained little more than a parlor game for many, but it was in a utopian spirit that Max joined Mabel Dodge as one of America's first analysands, even choosing the same analyst, Smith Ely Jelliffe, for four sessions a week for several months. His immediate motive may have been "poor Max," but he was equally committed to poor humanity. Weren't all forms of repression evil, didn't Freud reveal the hidden springs of convention just as Marx revealed the hidden springs of exploitation, wasn't heightened consciousness the path to both individual happiness and social justice? Change yourself and change the world—the agenda of the Lyrical Left in the prewar Village may have been naive but it was hardly modest.

Alas, Max's sessions with Jelliffe, a robust and gregarious doctor, resembled a classroom more than a clinic, with the therapist lecturing and the patients returning home with reading assignments. Indeed, Max's intellectual curiosity got in the way of his treatment. "Homosexuality, mother fixation, Oedipus, Electra, and inferiority complexes, narcissism, exhibitionism, autoeroticism," he recalled, "I never heard of an infantile fixation of which I could not find traces in my makeup."

It seemed he was learning more about Freud than about himself. Like Mabel, he then consulted A. A. Brill. The only apparent result of his consultations were two articles in *Everybody's Magazine* in 1915 in which he extolled Freud's simple, effective, and socially salutary technique for triumphing over emotional disorders. Explaining such concepts as the unconscious, repression, and wish fulfillment, and calling therapy a kind of surgery that could remove "mental cancer," leaving the patient "sound and free and energetic" and able to "think out a deliberate course of conduct in the light of the facts," Max's articles were as influential as they were simplistic, and introduced Freud to the American public—including a teenager in Red Bank, New Jersey, named Edmund Wilson.

For all his yearning after an "irresponsible" paganism, Max viewed psychoanalysis as the use of reason in the service of self-improvement. "I was not sick, I was merely bewildered. What I needed was not scientific

picking down on my patter, but a little common sense about handling it."
Willpower could achieve what "the talking cure" could not, even if the
goal of willpower was release from cerebral self-control. Jelliffe and Brill
may not have comprehended Max's unconscious, but they confirmed his
common sense—in Max's view, the last thing a revolutionary consciousness required was a sublimated sexuality.

Reason: Think it but with the precision of a logician, then act with
the dedication of a revolutionary. What did Max want? "The sole object of
perfect and eternal desire in me is life in the universe, a life that has to be
free and be my own. At the same time, I have an inclination to put my arms
around some loving girl. . . . I do not know that there is anything I wish
more than that I might have that girl at my pleasure, an adventure and
heart-whole pleasure, and yet not lose the recourse to my dearer daily companion [Ida]." Well, why not have both? After several months of philosophic brooding, Max approached Ida and suggested that, all things
considered, when you look at things from a rational standpoint, seeking the
most sensible way of saving their marriage, didn't it seem logical that he
should have, well, you know, casual affairs? Nothing serious, nothing
threatening. Weren't they rebelling against the false constraints of bourgeois morality? Didn't they understand that what he needed, having
suffered through a deprived, no, a *repressed* childhood, and having prematurely accepted adult responsibilities, was to play out his youthful, even
adolescent longings? The affairs upon which he would embark would be
nothing but "brief true love." Surveying the debris of their marriage, reflecting on her ideological commitment to free love, yet not neglecting to
warn Max—prophetically, as it turned out—"that he was in danger of turning into a professional Don Juan," Ida reluctantly agreed to the arrangement.

Permission turned out to be what Max wanted—not psychoanalysis
or common sense. Ida may have intuited that allowing freedom would forestall its exercise, but Max had too long lusted to be easily lulled, and before
she could begin to restructure their marriage on the basis of the new
ground rule, he had fulfilled both his philosophy and his fantasies.

Max and Ida's marriage soon ended, of course. Perhaps the most
handsome man in New York, probably the most charming, and certainly
the most romantic, Max was a great love waiting to strike. And his "Divine
Accident" happened at last at *The Masses* ball in December 1916.

The Masses ball? At the suggestion of the business manager—for
even a socialist magazine wasn't above cashing in on its cachet—*The
Masses* sponsored annual fund-raising frolics, "gay and tumultuous affairs,"

Max recalled, "where all bars against 'Greenwich Villageism' were let down. They were a reflection within the frame of American morals, of the 'Quatz' Arts ball in Paris, and many curious visitors came down from the upper bourgeoisie to see them"—as well as reporters anxious to record the degenerate entertainments of the rich and infamous.

The ball immediately became a Village institution. Admission was $1 for those in costume, $2 for those without, resulting, wrote one chronicle, "in a procession of sheiks, cave-women, circus dancers, and the like, frequently showing, for the times, generous amounts of flesh. For reasons of economy as well as titillation, hula skirts, ballet costumes, and ragged beggars' garments were favored."

The revolution against repression had self-indulgent, even elitist elements—it would have been difficult to convince an imprisoned IWW striker that the dancing Villagers served the same cause—but in allying moral and sexual with political and economic rebellion, the Villagers sought not only the gratifications of self-expression but an integrated vision of the quality of life in a post-capitalist, post-puritan world.

No such thoughts intruded on the revels, of course, and among those attending the 1916 ball was John Fox, author of *The Lonesome Pine*, and donor of $1,000 to *The Masses*, escorting a bona fide movie star. Florence Deshon was considered by many the most beautiful woman in America, and had recently starred in *The Beloved Vagabond*. As editor of the publication sponsoring the ball, Max felt entitled to a dance.

Max and Florence circled the floor. "She was twenty-one and in exactly the state of obstreperous revolt against artificial limitations which I had expressed in my junior and senior essays at college," he recalled wryly. "What do I care about a flag?" Florence told him, describing the day she had refused to rise for "The Star-Spangled Banner." "I'm living in the world, not a country!" Little wonder, then, that he "went to sleep believing that I had miraculously found what all young men forever vainly dream of, the girl who is at once ravishingly beautiful and admirable to what lies deepest in their minds and spirits."

In the rapturous affair with Florence that followed, he soon added "open" to the "brief" and "true" he sought in love. "The highest kind of relationship is one of which the lovers both feel free to have other experiences of love," Florence told him after nearly a year together, and while "six months earlier, she had aroused my apprehension by suggesting that I might love someone else and it wouldn't make much difference," now "the same thing gave me, together with my sadness, a feeling of relief."

For a time, Florence enjoyed "the highest kind of relationship" with Charlie Chaplin as well as Max, commuting from coast to coast between her two adoring lovers. But some demon in Max's psyche rebelled against his commitments—to women, to ideologies—some demon neither Jelliffe nor Brill had exorcised, which inevitably announced one day, "It's over." Disenchantment with ideologies took months, years, of reflection, but disenchantment with women—as with Ida, on the first day of their honeymoon—took place in a monstrous moment. Though his affair with Florence continued intermittently for five years, Holy Communion had long ceased when she took her own life in a gas-filled Village apartment in February 1922.

Even in his remorse, Max remained faithful only to his inconstancy. An uncommonly gifted lover—combining Village openness, Victorian courtliness, and feminist tenderness in a way hundreds of women found irresistible—he even acquired a legendary reputation as an American Casanova, which, he noted, "stood somewhat in my way as a real lover." But however dubious his behavior, he was never duplicitous. His candor with the women he wooed matched his candor before the world, his passionate advocacy of feminism and birth control and free love in particular. Max's social principles had as their goal the happiness of the individual. To Max, the "one steady and arrogant and implacable thing in my heart" remained "to live my earthly life to the full"—and in the Village, and at *The Masses*, he found a place where love and poetry and truth and liberty seemed part of a single revolution. While most American socialists rejected these Village doctrines—indeed, the sexual and cultural conservatism of the laboring classes made them almost as suspicious of the intellectuals championing their cause as they were hostile to the capitalists denouncing it—*The Masses* linked free love to proletarian revolution, alternated nude drawings with pro-IWW cartoons, birth control editorials with anti-business harangues, and, in its advertising, sex manuals with Marxist tracts. In rebelling against all constraints Max and his colleagues even transformed hedonism into a social principle. The very titles of Max's two autobiographies attest to this multifaceted commitment—*Enjoyment of Living* and *Love and Revolution*.

Max was by temperament as well as conviction open to multifold points of view and skeptical of creeds; he believed that even revolutionary principles were essentially experimental, so when he selected manuscripts for publication, and especially when he wrote his own editorials, the results were diverse rather than doctrinaire. "It is the catholicity of *The Masses*, its freedom from the one-track mental habit of the rabid devotee of cause, for which I as editor was most responsible," he recalled—its emphasis, in short, was on provoking debate rather than promoting dogma.

To be sure, *The Masses* committed itself to certain general principles under the umbrella of radicalism. According to Floyd Dell, the magazine stood for "fun, truth, beauty, realism, freedom, peace, feminism, revolution," and opposed capitalism, militarism, sexism, racism, and organized religion. But the principle to which it gave its ultimate allegiance was the struggle for liberty, confronting restraints in any and all forms—social, cultural, economic, institutional, moral—with lyrical anger and outraged enthusiasm. None of its specific causes had any validity unless they contributed to a society in which, in Max's words, "every individual should be made free to live and grow in his own chosen way." So even socialism, in the Village, was transformed into a doctrine of self-expression.

This emphasis made it necessary to monitor themselves as well as their enemies. In one issue, an Art Young cartoon depicted a cherub at the seashore staring complacently into a pail of water labeled "dogma," while behind him surged the ocean of "truth." "I publish this little picture," Max wrote in the accompanying editorial, "in answer to numberless correspondents who 'want to know just what this magazine is trying to do.' It is trying *not* to try to empty the ocean, for one thing. And in a propaganda paper that alone is a task." Even as early as Max's second issue, he wrote of the debate between political action and direct action, then the central argument among socialists: "All these questions of method are to be answered differently at different times, at different places, in different circumstances. . . . The one thing continually important is that we keep our judgement free. Tie up to no dogma whatever."

Still, Max realized that even a nondogmatic publication could founder in the solemnity of its high-minded aspirations, and once more the tenor of his character perfectly coincided with the spirit of the age. "I never could see why people with a zeal for improving life should be indifferent to the living of it," he wrote. "Why can not one be young-hearted, gay, laughing, audacious, full of animal spirits, and yet also use his brains?" What this meant, in editorial terms, was selecting not just articles, essays, stories, poems, and drawings that would foment the revolution, but material that would exemplify the kind of joyous, expressive life readers might hope to enjoy after the revolution succeeded.

A typical issue of twelve or fourteen pages might include on-the-scene accounts of labor strife unreported in the mainstream press—Max from Ludlow, for instance, or Elizabeth Gurley Flynn from Minnesota, or

Jack from Paterson. There were articles on the IWW effort to organize the unemployed, or exposés of attempts by manufacturers to influence Congress, or dispatches on revolutions in Mexico, China, the Philippines unavailable elsewhere. Essay subjects ranged from psychoanalysis to the link between capitalism and militarism, from birth control to prison reform, from free love to the Boy Scouts (who were being trained, the magazine charged, to become soldiers). Writers would debate the relative merits of direct versus political action, anarchism versus socialism, free verse versus meter. And in its editorials, *The Masses* didn't leave a subject untouched—Margaret Sanger's defense fund, the general strike in Belgium, the right to suicide, mutiny in the French army, organized charity, suffragists, the stock exchange, religious hymns, industrial sabotage, poets laureate, indicted IWW leaders, the Manufacturers Association, Fabianism, welfare. Even the advertisements captured the ethos of the era—everything from Karl Marx five-cent cigars to birth control pamphlets, from Jung's books to cubist prints.

The Masses' record on racism, though ahead of its time—right-wing elements in the Socialist party, hoping for "respectability," still advocated segregation—was tainted by racial stereotyping, particularly in its cartoons, and by the kind of condescending admiration all too familiar to women. As at Mabel's salon, blacks were regarded as "uncivilized," but this was a virtue to the Villagers, who were determined to find pagan release from the restraints of puritanism. Victims, yes, but all ethnic minorities, except those who happened to live in the Village, also represented unrepressed "experience," and Villagers like Hutch prowled Harlem and the Lower East Side, less to aid the downtrodden than to find the "authenticity" they felt so lacking in their own lives.

Although the fiction, poetry, and drawings in *The Masses* seemed radical when compared to the material in mainstream publications, Max and his colleagues remained actively hostile to the stirring of radical arts on the continent. Gertrude Stein's prose, for instance, seemed to them pretentious and silly, and inspired *Masses* writers no further than parody. And nothing could have been more uncongenial to their sensibilities than the masterpieces of Proust, Joyce, Kafka, and Eliot composed during the very period when they were dynamiting the aesthetic orthodoxies of the past.

And as for painting, despite the magazine's publication of a Picasso drawing in an early issue, more characteristic was John Sloan's response to the Armory Show, a lighthearted but dismissive caricature in the April 1913 issue captioned, "He had a cubic cat which caught a cubic mouse, and they lived together in a little cubic house." Their commitment to artistic "experiment" confined itself largely to "realism," which is to say that their radicalism remained more a matter of class than aesthetics. Ironically, even as their revolution stressed the link between politics and art, its aesthetic stance already seemed reactionary to the revolutionaries abroad. Yet in the case of *The Masses*, this apparent paradox of the political vanguard remaining in the artistic rear guard—or vice versa, neither position unfamiliar in the twentieth century—reflected the extent to which the magazine's radicalism was rooted in the serene idealism of the American past rather than in the ideological turmoil of the European present.

The character of *The Masses* was defined less by its contents than by its tone—"frank, arrogant, and impertinent," as its declaration of principles stated. "What made us so objectionable," Max recalled, "was not primarily our attack on capitalism—that question was still a trifle academic in America. But we voiced our attack in a manner that outraged patriotic, religious, and matrimonial, to say nothing of ethical and aesthetic tastes and conventions." For whether inflammatory or exultant, idealistic or impious, *The Masses* was always infused with a spirit of brash and lively urgency.

Though *The Masses'* circulation hovered between fifteen thousand and forty thousand—despite its notoriety, its contents remained too sophisticated for commercial success, and, because of its notoriety, too iconoclastic for most of the working class at which it was ostensibly aimed—it had an impact far beyond mere numbers. It was the first major American expression of the link between the radical intelligentsia and the revolutionary labor movement that would continue, in often confused configurations, for several decades, and it immediately became a decisive force, along with Mabel Dodge's salon, in bringing to the rebels a sense of political, intellectual, artistic community. "Them Asses" they might be called—often by themselves—but, as Irving Howe has written, "For a brief time . . . *The Masses* became the rallying center—as sometimes also a combination of circus, nursery, and boxing ring—for almost anything that was then alive and irreverent in American culture."

The success of *The Masses* could be measured, in part, by the continuing efforts to suppress it. Every lawsuit, every sanction, not only offered a chance to demonstrate the repressiveness of the social system the staff had vowed to overthrow, but also indicated that their policy of "conciliating nobody" had exposed fissures in that system.

At first the unconciliated confined themselves to indignant letters and canceled subscriptions, but on December 14, 1913, almost a year to the day since Max's first issue, he learned from an evening newspaper that he and Art Young had been indicted for criminal libel on a complaint from the Associated Press. The suit cited Max for an editorial in the July issue charging that the AP reports of a coal miners' strike in West Virginia had deliberately concealed information from the public, and named Art for his accompanying cartoon depicting the news as a reservoir "poisoned at the source" by the head of the AP, who surreptitiously poured "lies" out of a bottle into water already contaminated by "prejudice," "slander," "suppressed facts," and "hatred of labor organizations."

Max suspected that his special Christmas issue had spurred the suit—and quite an issue it was: a frontispiece called "Their Last Supper," by Maurice Becker, showed a crew of clergymen gorging themselves while blithely ignoring Christ hanging on a cross behind them; Kenneth Russell Chamberlain depicted the Rock of Ages as a dollar sign; an illustration by Stuart Davis was captioned, "That's right, girls, on Sunday the cross, on weekdays the double cross."

Depicting the Judean carpenter as "comrade Jesus," "the first socialist," and "militant champion of the oppressed workers" may have inflamed the Associated Press—it enabled the radicals to find a link between their idealism and their impiety—but the court would not be concerned with such theological niceties or disingenuous sophistries. *The Masses* hired Robert La Follette's ex-partner, who cannily suggested that Ida Rauh, a licensed attorney, enter the not guilty plea ("Prisoner Represented in Court by His Own Wife," read one scandalized headline), and Max, "a little to my poetic regret," wasn't jailed but released on bail. Hundreds of radicals, muckrakers, writers, and intellectuals held a fiery meeting at Cooper Union in support of freedom of the press—assaulted, ironically, by one of the pillars of the press. It was not the First Amendment, however, but the subpoena of its record, and the fear of what it might reveal during a trial, that finally brought the AP to its senses, such as they were, and after a few years of maneuvering and mumbling, the charges were withdrawn. Art Young crowed their revenge with a cartoon entitled "Madame, you dropped Something" in which a plump elderly matron labeled "The Associated Press" walked out of an "exclusive park" carrying a bag of money, oblivious to *The Masses'* libel proceeding lying on the ground behind her.

Max's attribution of theological motives to the Associated Press may have been problematic, but many of *The Masses'* difficulties with the authorities did stem from its assaults on organized religion. "Printing what is too naked or true for a money-making press," as the masthead proclaimed, meant one thing when it came to capitalism, quite another when it came to the church. Indeed, organized religion occupied much the same position in American culture before World War I that sex occupied in the fifties, in the sense that the behavior and attitudes of a large portion of the population were excluded from public discussion. Much of the impact of *The Masses*, in fact—like that of nearly all groundbreaking publications— derived from its impoliteness, from what Max called its "athletic honesty." "Even more 'objectionable' than our juvenility," he recalled, "was our determination to say the same things in public that we said in private."

While the watchdogs of *The Masses* found its attacks on the state, the capitalists, and the press objectionable, they found its attacks on religion actionable. The first effort to bar the magazine from the newsstands, in January 1916, resulted not from a call to arms but from a ballad comparing the Virgin Mary to an unwed mother. Ward and Gow, distributors of periodicals to newsstands in the New York subway system, finding the sentiment "blasphemous," ordered its dealers to stop carrying the magazine. Despite ringing testimonials from John Dewey, Helen Keller, Charles Scribner, Walter Lippmann, Herbert Croly, and Franklin P. Adams, the ban stood, severely hampering the magazine's circulation but considerably raising its morale. (The company offered to rescind the ban if the magazine would agree to model itself more along the lines of, say, *The Atlantic Monthly*, which gave the editors a good laugh.)

Max's fund-raising lecture tours also benefited from the brouhaha. As attacks on *The Masses* increased, so did Max's audiences. Barred from the University of Wisconsin campus merely meant a quadrupled turnout off-campus. When a pastor in Detroit began to read the Virgin Mary ballad to his congregation, stopped mid-poem to exclaim, "I cannot go on, it is too horrible," then fulminated to the press, "I protest against a Christian church being polluted by a man like Max Eastman, whose blasphemy . . . is a desecration of the most sacred ideals of the Christian people," the only result was that Max doubled his schedule—and his fees.

Soon after the Virgin Mary episode, and for similarly offensive high crimes against taste, *The Masses* found itself barred from newsstands in Boston and Philadelphia and stopped at the border by Canadian postal officials. The library and bookstore at Columbia, where Max had been a member of the faculty, canceled their orders, and were joined by colleges from Cambridge to San Diego. Even the advertisements elicited rage. A discreet ad in the September 1916 issue for August Forel's book *The Sex Question* led to a raid by John Sumner, Anthony Comstock's successor as head of the New York Society for the Suppression of Vice, the arrest of business manager Merrill Rogers, and the temporary confiscation of the indelicate issue. *The Masses* was a success!

And to signal his delight at the efforts at suppression, Max inserted a brief note in the August 1913 issue requesting that all legal proceedings "be postponed until fall, as our jail editor, John Reed, has gone to Europe."

The tone of *The Masses* inevitably sobered as corpses began to fill the trenches of Europe. The urgency of the situation seemed to call for a modification of the magazine's policy of no policy. In the face of possible American participation in the war, shouldn't *The Masses* speak with a single voice? And what should that voice say? The staff agreed that it was a war to save not democracy, but capitalism, and everyone opposed the mood of militarism rapidly infecting the country, the patriotic hysteria in the guise of "preparedness." But some contributors felt that the United States must enter the war sooner or later, and began to defect when Max declared the magazine unalterably opposed to American intervention. This split, however, was foreshadowed by another internal dispute.

In the early months of the magazine, none of the staff had cared that their "nominal" editor was turning out a one-man periodical in the guise of a cooperative—indeed, given their publishing naïveté, they scarcely noticed. But gradually some of them began to feel uneasy when Max or Floyd would affix captions to their drawings without consulting them first, and once this issue was raised, they began to wonder why all the drawings needed captions. Didn't it demean their work to turn it into mere illustration of political polemic, even one with which they wholeheartedly agreed?

As often happens, a small dissatisfaction masked a larger grievance and the grumbling grew into an insurrection. The magazine had betrayed its premises, the artists argued, not only in allowing one person to assume such a dominant position, but in raising funds from the very class it had vowed to overthrow. Some members of the staff, in fact, would have agreed with the words of one New York newspaper that "its armchair anarchy is parlor entertainment for the uptown aristocrats these days."

In March 1916, five members of the editorial board—John Sloan, Stuart Davis, Glenn Coleman, Robert Carlton Brown, and Henry Glintenkamp—demanded a restructuring or they would heed the magazine's editorials on the inalienable rights of labor and go out on strike. They called for the magazine to return to the nonexistent days when all editorial decisions were made by the staff as a whole, appoint a committee to implement their decisions, and hire a makeup man to dummy the issue. Furthermore, the staff would be divided into writers and artists, with each group making its decisions independent of the other—which would solve the problem that some members felt was behind all the grandiose grumbling about "policy": the affixing of the captions to drawings.

Since the dissidents essentially proposed a structure that Max had been counting on when he reluctantly accepted the editorship three and a half years earlier, and since the major changes in the magazine had come as a result of the staff's inability to follow through on its pledge to put out a publication cooperatively and the phenomenal success of Max's single-handed orchestrations of their talents, he was naturally miffed. Max called for a vote on the insurgents' proposals and agreed to resign if they passed. The initial vote was five to five; they realized they didn't have a quorum, but failed to notice that such a split was a comical comment on a revolt on behalf of increased staff participation. There was nothing to be done but call another meeting, and a few weeks later—a quorum now rounded up— Sloan's proposal was voted down eleven to five.

One of the characteristics of twentieth-century politics, however, is that nothing more quickly succeeds a left-wing revolt than a left-wing purge, and instead of getting back to revolution-as-usual, Floyd promptly moved that the five dissenters be dropped from the magazine. This bombshell was seconded by none other than tolerant, almost lackadaisical Art Young, the most beloved member of the staff. "To me, this magazine exists for socialism," he declaimed with uncharacteristic fervor. "That's why I give my drawings to it, and anybody who doesn't believe in a socialist policy, so far as I go, can get out." Max quickly called for a vote, and when Floyd's motion was defeated by the same eleven-to-five vote, he proposed that instead of casting out the rebels, the staff elect them to office. He meant it in a spirit of reconciliation, but what better way to trounce his opposition than to make them share his responsibilities. The vote carried and everyone parted amiably.

The next day, however, Max received a letter from John Sloan. "If thy right hand offend thee, cut it off," he began. "This afternoon I played the part of one of the five fingers in the above suggested tragedy, and foolishly resisted amputation"—whereupon he resigned as vice president of *The Masses*, a position he had occupied for less then twenty-four hours. "Dear Sloan," Max briskly responded, "I shall regret the loss of your wit and artistic genius as much as I shall enjoy the absence of your cooperation."

Four other fingers followed John, and what Floyd called the "practical dictatorship" resumed.

While the artists' strike seemed to reflect a functional dispute about the magazine's structure, it actually represented a philosophical disagreement about the relationship between art and politics. The artists' demands that the position of editor be eliminated and that the publication return to the ideal of a workers' cooperative were only means to an end—assurance that the art not be made subservient to the magazine's politics. Roughly speaking, two types of artists contributed to *The Masses*, those who felt their work served socialism and those who felt socialism served their work. The first group had no argument with Max, but the second regarded the magazine as a model of the socialist society where their art would be free to speak for itself, independent of its political meaning. As usually happens, parameters of debate soon expanded into parameters of invective, each side caricaturing the other's position, former allies speaking angrily of "mere art's for art's sake" on one hand and "blatant propaganda" on the other.

The Masses frequently published artwork with no political point, but the threat of war brought growing pressure to make an ideological commitment, which meant, as the artists saw it, that their work was valued only as illustration—intolerable word to an artist—of political policy. All of them shared the magazine's sense of urgency—indeed, Maurice Becker, one of the angriest protesters, later became a conscientious objector and served several months in Leavenworth—but while those who regarded themselves as essentially cartoonists couldn't understand what the fuss was about, those who regarded themselves as essentially painters felt their art was being degraded. Wasn't the magazine embarking on the very huckstering it was supposed to be rebelling against?

In all these debates over "art for art's sake" versus "propaganda," however, no one thought to consider the relationship between artistic and political *radicalism*. The linkage of artistic and political revolution, though central to *The Masses'* achievement, was problematic from the first. Unencumbered by ideology—or borrowing it piecemeal from Europe without regard to coherence or even consistency—the contributors' rationale for their twin rebellion focused on vague invocations of the liberating role of art in the transformation of culture that must precede political, etc., etc., whatever. Since the Villagers' rejection of stultifying middle-class convention owed more to temperament than theory, they often went little further than energetic exhortations about something called Life.

Max, the professional philosopher, could wander in the foggiest of effusions. "Oh how foolish it is to try to justify poetry and art on the ground of their service to the revolution. They are but life realizing itself utterly, and only by appeal to the value of life's realization can the revolution be justified." And Jack, the dedicated revolutionary, could lapse into undergraduate Byronism. "I am not a socialist temperamentally any more than I am an Episcopalian. I know now that my business is to interpret and live life, where it may be found—whether in the labor movement or out of it."

Though they indulged in musings about rejecting all forms of repression and celebrating all forms of creativity, and despite the talk about the value of heightened aesthetic consciousness as a political act, when it came time to transform these putative principles into works of art, they had no idea how to proceed. Lacking any inclination or aptitude for the kind of formal innovation that characterized the Continental modernists, they focused their rebelliousness almost solely on content, on what they called "realism." While the magazines' writers produced no radical novels, no enduring poetry, they turned journalism into the kind of art form they advocated—spontaneous, "realistic," "transforming."

So while the radicals of The Masses must be given credit for raising the possibility of the synthesis of art and politics, in practice their commitment virtually ignored the difficult issues that a later generation of Villagers would endlessly debate—the apparent contradiction between the elitist impulses of their art and the democratic assumptions of their politics, or the degree to which art must become socially conscious in order to serve the class struggle, or the discrepancy between the aesthetic conservatism and the political radicalism of the proletariat. It's even tempting to speculate that a number of Village poets and painters, suspecting that their own work was insufficiently radical, supported labor insurrection in precise proportion to their envy of those who manned the picket lines.

Despite this refusal to think through the ramifications of their stance, The Masses' staff nevertheless succeeded in bringing the political implications of art and the aesthetic implications of politics into public discourse after a century in which they were considered entirely separate activities. For some Villagers defining the self, creative self-expression, Enjoying the Revolution, may have been part of a purely personal revolt, but in acknowledging the capacity of art to alter consciousness and in insisting on the personal dimensions of politics, it also revealed the compatibility of individual aspirations and socialist programs. They formed an entirely new character type in the American intellectual gallery, the bo-hemian/artist/radical, equally committed to all three vocations. They may not have been able to answer the question posed in the famous ditty—

> *They draw nude women for* The Masses
> *Thick, fat, ungainly lasses—*
> *How does that help the working classes?*

—but their intellectual inadequacies shouldn't overshadow their humanist aspirations.

When Jack, in the midst of wearily toiling to establish a Bolshevik party in the United States, complained wryly to Max, "This class struggle plays hell with your poetry!," his concern wasn't ideological incoherence but simply the lack of time. They wanted everything. They wanted love and poetry and revolution all at once!

Come on in, America, the Blood's Fine!" read the caption on M. A. Kempf's drawing of a skeleton ankle-deep in blood, embracing three terrified youths. "Glory" was the simple title of Will Hope's portrait of a sol-dier with his arm in a sling and a patch over his blinded eyes. And Robert Minor captioned his cartoon of an army medical examiner gloating at the brutish but headless lout standing before him, "At last a perfect soldier!"

The tenor of *The Masses* irrevocably altered in 1916 and 1917. As Jack wrote in the April 1917 issue, "The press is howling for war. The church is howling for war. . . . I know what war means. I have been with the armies of all the belligerents except one, and I have seen men die, and go mad, and lie in hospitals suffering hell; but there is a worse thing than that. War means an ugly mob-madness crucifying the truth-tellers, choking the artists, side-tracking reforms, revolutions, and the working of social forces."

As events began to make real "the kind of fact implied by our ideas"—Max's ironic phrase—those ideas were at once narrowed and in-tensified. Worldwide revolution against the capitalist system, random at-tacks on all the "old systems," both would have to wait—the magazine must commit itself to a single, immediate goal, keeping the United States out of war. War, far from "an exploit in glory, had become a mere business of slaughter," in which "blind tribal instincts" swept up millions of people in hysterical blood lust, all in the service of the capitalists and the imperialists and the militarists who were making the world safe for profits.

The policy-versus-no-policy conflict initiated by the artists' strike of

1916 flared up with more urgency. In March 1917, Max drew up a manifesto against American intervention and asked the editors to sign it as a statement of the magazine's position. The artist George Bellows, who regarded *The Masses* as "the finest and most necessary magazine in America," spoke for many of them when he replied, "I decidedly will not sign the enclosed paper. . . . *The Masses* has no business with a 'policy.' It is not a political paper and will do better without any platform. Its 'policy' is the expression of its contributors. They have the right to change their minds continually, looking at things from all angles." (Bellows exercised this right almost immediately—he became an active advocate of American intervention and volunteered for the tank corps.) Bellows's response was a concise statement of the principles that had always guided Max, but now, faced with an unambiguous crisis, he shot back: "*The Masses* has certainly as pronounced an editorial policy as any paper in the country and as long as I am this editor and raise money for it, it will have."

If *The Masses* had no official policy in 1916 and 1917, none of its readers could tell—for every issue featured editorials eloquently attacking the war and cartoons bitterly condemning militarism, "as if," said Floyd, *The Masses* "were the last spark of civilization left in America." Month after month the magazine linked capitalism to militarism, protested preparedness, denounced the draft, and castigated the clergy for justifying the fight on religious grounds, for to Max and the other socialists the war was nothing less than "the business of slaughter."

Jack, in particular, wrote with anger and anguish. "The country is rapidly being scared into a heroic mood. The workingman will do well to realize that his enemy is not Germany, nor Japan; his enemy is that 2% of the people of the United States who own 60% of the national wealth, and are now planning to make a soldier out of him to defend their loot. We advocate that the workingman prepare himself against that enemy. This is our Preparedness."

Such sentiments struck the authorities as taking the First Amendment somewhat too seriously, and the government decided to curtail democracy in order to protect it. On June 13, 1917, Congress passed an espionage act making it unlawful to "make or convey false reports or false statements with intent to interfere with the operation or success of the military or naval forces of the United States . . . to promote the success of its enemies . . . to attempt to cause insubordination, disloyalty, or refusal of duty in the military or naval forces . . . or willfully obstruct the recruiting or enlistment services of the United States." Three weeks later, on July 5, *The Masses* received a letter from the postmaster of New York City declaring that under the terms of this act the August issue was "unmailable." Hoping to avoid a confrontation—it seemed more important to continue publishing attacks on the war than to get involved in a lengthy court battle—Max offered to omit the "unmailable" material. But the postmaster refused to cite the offensive sections, and *The Masses* had no choice but to seek an injunction.

Fortunately, the judge turned out to be Learned Hand, and when the "unmailable" material was finally identified, the case turned into a mockery. Four cartoons incurred the wrath of the government—a drawing of the Liberty Bell falling apart, another of a wheel of destruction titled "Conscription," a third called "Making the World Safe for Capitalism," and finally an Art Young portrait of a group of arms dealers dismissing Congress with the caption, "Run along now! We got through with you when you declared war for us!" The passages of text cited were two editorials by Max, one defending Emma Goldman's and Alexander Berkman's right to advocate draft resistance and another deploring their imprisonment, and an unsigned article (by Floyd) upholding the rights of conscientious objectors.

Judge Hand forcefully ruled for *The Masses*. The cited cartoons and editorials "fall within the scope of that right to criticize, either by temperate reasoning or by immoderate and indecent invective, which is normally the privilege of the individual in countries dependent upon the free expression of opinion as the ultimate source of authority."

But those with little understanding of the Constitution often display great understanding of the legal system, and the sly postmaster filed an appeal and brought it before the nearest sympathetic judge—in the metropolis of Windsor, Vermont. Having been sought out, the flattered judge could hardly fail to cooperate, and, in Max's words, "decided to hold up our August issue until its value was lost in order to find out whether it should be held up or not."

When *The Masses* presented its September issue for mailing, the postmaster declared he was revoking the magazine's second-class privileges on the grounds that since it had not mailed its August issue it no longer qualified as a periodical. Back to Vermont, where the judge, after learning that the postmaster had denied mailing privileges on the grounds of an interruption in publication for which the postmaster himself was responsible, allowed that the decision was, all things considered, "a rather poor joke," but that, in effect, poor jokes were not necessarily adjudicative. Finally, in November, the vaudeville turned somber when a three-judge court overruled Judge Hand's decision and *The Masses* was officially declared "unmailable." Since the magazine could not survive solely on newsstand sales, Max had no choice but to announce that the November-December issue would be its last.

Almost on the very day the staff closed up the office—giving away the furniture and selling the empty safe—they learned of the long-awaited Bolshevik victory in Russia. "It was as though we had achieved the revolution," Max said with a mixture of elation and wistfulness, "and could now take a rest."

The government had stopped publication of *The Masses*—what more could it do? But early in 1918, as Max stood in the wings of a lecture hall in Oak Park, Illinois, a young man rushed up and handed him a telegram. YOU DELL REED YOUNG GLINTENKAMP MERRILL ROGERS AND JOSEPHINE BELL INDICTED UNDER THE ESPIONAGE ACT STOP BAIL HAS BEEN POSTED AND A DEFENSE COMMITTEE IS BEING FORMED STOP EVERYTHING WILL BE TAKEN CARE OF STOP DON'T WORRY.

United States v. Eastman et al. charged the seditious seven with conspiracy to obstruct enlistment, and, given the mood of the country, that was tantamount to treason. But as if to show that the government had no monopoly on "poor jokes," the ex-contributors sent out "mailable" postcards to their friends that read, "We expect you for the—shh!—weekly sedition. Object: Overthrow of the Government. Don't tell a soul."

Only five of the defendants showed up at the federal courthouse opposite New York's City Hall on April 15, 1918. Jack in Petrograd learned of his indictment too late to return, and Glintenkamp had skipped the country to join what he called "the Soviet of Slackers" in Mexico. *The Masses* was once more fortunate in its judge. Augustus Hand shared his cousin Learned's flinty devotion to the Constitution. A Liberty Bond rally was taking place in the square below, and the proceedings had hardly begun when a band outside the window struck up "The Star-Spangled Banner." *The Masses'* business manager, Merrill Rogers, stood at rigid attention in a solemn and somewhat disingenuous display of patriotism. Judge Hand, realizing he had no choice, reluctantly rose to his feet, whereupon the entire courtroom, including the seditious defendants, reverently followed suit. Twenty minutes later, as the prosecution was explaining its indictment to the jury, the band once more struck up the national anthem, Rogers once more shot to his feet, and once more Judge Hand and the courtroom followed his lead. When it happened a third time, Judge Hand, while joining Rogers in pious ritual, stared down at the patriot with something close to exasperation. And when it happened a fourth time, and nearly everyone in the courtroom strained to hold back their laughter, Judge Hand announced rather testily, "I think we shall have to dispense with this ceremony from now on."

Max, to whom Merrill's canny charade was erroneously attributed in later years, regarded it as a disaster. By rising to his feet he was submitting to the "religion of patriotism" he had so vehemently denounced, abandoning the very position for which he was on trial. But by refusing to stand he would have offered the jury the spectacle of one stubbornly seated figure in a courtroom of standing patriots—he might as well have thrust out his arms and accepted the handcuffs. "I did get up, of course—reluctantly, and no doubt with a very solemn expression," he recalled, "for my thoughts were concerned with the relative merits of different ways of murdering Merrill Rogers."

Max's political enemies would ridicule him as a phony revolutionary who "went star spangled banner" in order to save his skin, but his immediate problem was the prosecution's possession of a letter in which he ridiculed patriotic ritual that required standing up for the national anthem. "Will you tell us if the sentiments therein expressed, which I have just read to you," asked the prosecutor with a sly smile, "are still your sentiments?" The jury had just seen Max stand; now they'd hear him mock such shams—if he seemed to be trying to bamboozle them, all was lost. But among the philosophers he had studied at Columbia were the Greek Sophists, and his mentor, John Dewey, had never been one to feel that the study of philosophy was without practical application. He stood by the sentiments in the letter, Max replied firmly, but the situation had changed since he'd written them, and when he'd stood up earlier he'd been thinking of "those boys over there . . . dying for liberty"—neglecting to mention as technically immaterial that he was putting "dying for liberty" in savagely ironic quotation marks. The jury seemed to accept the clarification and the prosecutor changed the subject.

The final proceedings were characterized by ringing appeals to principles and tedious documentation of the self-evident—the prosecution even spent several hours proving beyond a reasonable doubt that *The Masses* had, in fact, existed. Max the educator spent most of his nearly three days on the stand expounding on socialism, civil liberties, and the contradictions of American foreign policy. Floyd the romantic fervently defended conscientious objection, his eloquence enhanced by the fact that he had recently been inducted into the army. And Art the genial humorist testified with forthright bemusement. When asked, "What did you intend to do when you drew this picture, Mr. Young?" he replied, "Intend to do? I intended to draw a picture," and when pressed to explain what he'd meant by his impounded cartoon depicting an editor, a capitalist, a politician, and a minister merrily dancing to war under the patronage of the devil, he responded, "What do you mean by meant? You have the picture in front of you."

The crime of defendant Josephine Bell was a poem in defense of Emma Goldman, but as for conspiracy, well, this was going to be a tough nut for the prosecution. When *The Masses'* lawyer, Morris Hillquit, many times Socialist candidate for mayor of New York, submitted Josephine Bell's traitorous verses to Judge Hand, the jurist/critic asked with unconcealed scorn, "You call that a poem?" "Your honor," Hillquit replied, "it is called so in the indictment." "Indictment dismissed," Judge Hand announced with a bang of his gavel, and Josephine Bell's chance for martyrdom came to an abrupt end.

After nine days of testimony and two days of deliberation, the members of the jury reported that they were "hopelessly deadlocked"—eleven for conviction, one for acquittal. It wasn't clear if the lone holdout—one H. C. Fredricks, who was subsequently stricken from the rolls of future jurors—was devoted to the constitutional liberties of the defendants or under the impression that, since the defendants apparently never agreed on anything, it was hardly plausible that they'd engaged in a conspiracy.

Max had founded a new publication called *The Liberator* within a few weeks, taking many of *The Masses'* writers and artists with him and making sure—since he'd had his fill of publishing "cooperatives"—that 51 percent of the stock was owned by him and his sister, Crystal. Jack remained his ace correspondent and when he returned from Russia only a few days after the trial ended, he was dismayed at having missed such a splendid show.

The government that had tried to send Josephine Bell away for twenty years for her innocuous verses saw Bolsheviks everywhere. The war was over, but the Red Scare was growing more hysterical. Upon Jack's arrival he'd been interrogated for eight hours before being allowed to disembark. He was put under constant surveillance by Department of Justice agents, and would soon be arrested for making "seditious statements." At moments, Jack still embodied the spirit of what was already being called "the old Village," but fresh from the bloodshed of the front and the revolutionary turmoil of St. Petersburg, he found the Village frivolous and *The Liberator* conciliatory. He continued to write for the new magazine but resigned from the editorial board to protest the increasingly pro-Wilson tone of Max's editorials.

"Events grand and terrible are brewing in Europe," Jack had written in *The Masses* in July 1917, "such as only the imagination of a revolutionary poet could have conceived," and upon his arrival in Petrograd (as St. Petersburg was renamed) in September he threw himself into the task of chronicling those events. He careened from place to place, interviewing the Bolshevik leaders in his rudimentary Russian, even, on occasion, hurling leaflets from the back of trucks or addressing cheering crowds as a spokesman for American socialism. The "stirring spectacle of proletarian mass organization, action, bravery, and generosity" reawakened his faith in his political principles, and he at last fused socialist, poet, reporter, and adventurer. He had come to Russia as a rebel; he left as a revolutionary.

On his return to the Village in the spring of 1918 Jack began work on his eyewitness account of the ten tumultuous days that had shaken the world. He signed a book contract with Boni & Liveright, the company co-founded by old friends Albert and Charles Boni from the Washington Square Book Shop and one of the occasional actors at the Provincetown Playhouse.

He rented a small top-floor room on Sheridan Square and worked around the clock. Between chapters, he lectured across the country, electrifying his audiences with his vision of Lenin and Trotsky transforming the world, raising his fist at the end of his fevered orations and shouting, in Russian, "Long Live Revolution!"

The government soon announced that the editors of the now defunct *Masses* would be retried. The defendants fully expected to lose this time around, but undaunted, they decided to turn the courtroom into a "classroom for socialism"—for though the press focused more on the comeuppance of middle-class radicals than on the abuse of the Constitution, the Villagers, even at their most playful, always had a touch of the didactic.

Having missed the first trial, Jack was eager to strike an uncompromisingly insurrectionary note, and in his high-pitched, intense voice he testified that he had witnessed warfare on five fronts and had personally been under fire fifty-five times, experiences that had brought an impassioned militancy to his anti-militaristic ideology. Asked about class war, he instantly answered, "Well, to tell you the truth, it's the only war that interests me." But the jurors apparently paid less attention to his words, which might have seemed inflammatory coming from someone else, than to his boyish gusto.

Max, making sure to mention that he was a descendant of Daniel Webster, summed up with an extemporaneous, three-hour speech, later circulated as a pamphlet, in which he presented a history of socialism, defended the principle of free speech, and explained the defendants' objections to the war. "My father and mother were both ministers," he intoned, "and I was brought up with the utmost love for the character and beauty of the teachings of Jesus of Nazareth, and I count Him much nearer in His faith and His influence to the message of any political body of men." Socialists, he explained to the spellbound jurors, were not unpatriotic. They believed in "liberty and democracy exactly in the same way" as did Thomas Jefferson, Patrick Henry, Samuel Adams, and the rest of the true revolutionary fathers. "And so I ask you that whatever your own judgement of the truth or wisdom of our faith may be, you will respect it as one of the heroic ideas and ardent beliefs of humanity's history. Its faith which possesses more adherents all over the surface of the earth who acknowledge its name and subscribe to its principles than any other faith ever has, except those private and mysterious ones that we call religious. It is either the most beautiful and courageous mistake that hundreds of millions of mankind ever made, or else it is really the truth that will lead us out of misery, and anxiety, and poverty, and war, and strife and hatred between classes, into a free and happy world. In either case it deserves your respect."

"The one great factor in our victory," wrote Jack in *The Liberator* of the speech. "Standing there, with the attitude and attributes of intellectual eminence, young, good-looking, he was the typical champion of ideals — ideals which he made to seem the ideals of every real American. . . . After it was all over . . . it [was] rumored that [the marshal] began to preach socialism to his deputies." Eugene Debs, serving a sentence in the Atlanta penitentiary on similar charges, sent the message, "Your speech before the court was a masterpiece, and will stand as a classic in the literature of the revolution." There was even a surprising tribute from one of the prosecuting attorneys, who wrote Max, "As an address of a man accused of a crime, it will probably live as one of the great addresses of modern times."

Hard-pressed to match Max's eloquence, the prosecutor pulled out all *his* oratorical stops, concluding with the tragic tale of a friend who had died to make the world safe for democracy. "Somewhere in France he lies dead, and he died for you and he died for me. He died for Max Eastman, he died for John Reed. He died for Floyd Dell. He died for Merrill Rogers. His voice is but one of the thousand silent voices that demand that these men be punished!"

The jury retired after five days of testimony and soon reported itself unable to reach a verdict—this time with only four votes for conviction, eight for acquittal. The government, having achieved its goal of driving *The Masses* out of business, was disinclined to pursue the case any further. But how could the Villagers celebrate such an ambiguous victory with any enthusiasm? Not only had they lost their beloved magazine; they had avoided prison only because, for all their rebelliousness, they were perceived as articulate, sophisticated, well-educated, but misguided scions of mainstream American stock. Indeed, the trial was virtually the only setback the government suffered in dozens of similar "espionage" cases, many of which were brought against recent immigrants with thick accents.

The impotence of their resistance, their quarrels among themselves, the persecution by the authorities, most of all the tragedy of the Great War—the exuberance had gone out of their cause. They couldn't even tell if the society against which they rebelled considered them threats to the republic or innocuous idealists, for if the government brought indictments against them, they had also met that peculiar combination of frightened outrage and condescending mockery the American middle class reserves for its apostates, until, decades later, they are transformed into icons of individualism in college curricula.

Margaret Sanger urged Max to "go down with your colors flying," but by this time, the most famous radical in America decided that *The Liberator* should sacrifice intransigence for influence, thus abandoning, like so many radicals before and since, the very qualities that had brought him influence. Professional, responsible, eliminating both the rambunctious tone and freewheeling diversity of *The Masses*, the new publication nevertheless kept the radical banner aloft. Jack's report on the Bolshevik revolution in the first issue in March 1918 ended with the words, "Lenin and Trotsky send through me to the revolutionary proletariat of the world the following Message, Comrades! . . . We call you to arms for the international Socialist revolution." Max editorialized that Lenin's establishment of an industrial parliament was "without doubt the most momentous event in the history of people." And Lenin himself appeared in a subsequent issue with a message to American workers smuggled back from Moscow by Carl Sandburg.

But *The Liberator* also supported President Wilson's war effort and the League of Nations, and even invested its surplus cash, itself an anomaly, in U.S. bonds. When Jack, despairing of "a magazine which exists on the sufferance of [the postmaster general]," finally resigned from the editorial board, Max replied, "Personally I envy you the power to cast loose when not only a good deal of the dramatic beauty, but also the glamour of abstract moral principle has gone out of our venture, and it remains for us merely the most effective and therefore the right thing to do."

The circulation of *The Liberator* leapt to sixty thousand—double that of *The Masses*—and the roster of writers and artists, paid for their contributions this time around, foretold the firmament of the coming decades. John Dos Passos, Ernest Hemingway, William Carlos Williams, Edna St. Vincent Millay, E. E. Cummings, Sherwood Anderson, Vachel Lindsay, Elinor Wylie, Heywood Broun, Amy Lowell, Louise Bogan, and Edmund Wilson were among the writers, and its artists included George Grosz and Pablo Picasso. Even H. L. Mencken wrote in to say, "You produce the best magazine in America—not now and then, but steadily every month."

Not that the enterprise lacked its moment of bohemian folly. E. F. Mylius, a free-spirited Village character who unaccountably showed up on the masthead as business manager, dutifully enacted a prophetic-in-more-ways-than-one pamphlet he had written entitled "The Socialization of Money" by absconding with the magazine's cash reserve and losing it all in a stock market frenzy. But the lighthearted spirit of *The Masses* had turned sober, and even though Max regarded *The Liberator* as a superior publication, he soon tired of radical respectability.

In 1922, Max visited Russia to witness firsthand the Bolsheviks he had so ardently applauded, and while his preconceptions led him to extol Lenin and befriend former Villager Leon Trotsky—whose American translator he later became—he was one of the first Americans to perceive the totalitarian tendencies of Stalin's rule. Arranging for the publication of "Lenin's Testament," which warned the Bolsheviks against Stalin, damaged rather than enhanced his reputation as a radical. A series of books in the thirties and forties denouncing Stalin and Marxism made him a pariah on the left, and when he became a "roving editor" of *The Reader's Digest* and a supporter of Senator Joseph McCarthy in the fifties, his *Masses* heirs dismissed him as the kind of crank who saw Russian tanks at the borders of Idaho. "He represents a pitiable spectacle," wrote Dwight Macdonald, "similar to that of persons in an advanced state of alcoholism, in which all emotional cerebral responses have atrophied and there remains only a reflexive reaction to alcohol. Eastman's drink is anti-Stalinism."

But Max's plummeting reputation could be attributed not to failing intellect but to untimely insight. He even lashed out against socialism. It was not a science, he concluded, but a secular religion that helped believers to endure life. "We shall have to renounce this alluring pleasure of drawing up plans for new worlds, which would run like a mechanical toy if we could only get somebody to start them."

While Max's anti-communism in the early fifties undeniably resembled the Red Scare he had deplored in the teens, Edmund Wilson remained virtually alone in realizing that his books of the thirties and forties perceptively challenged the philosophical premises of communism and prophetically warned against the excesses of Stalinism. Max's best books, wrote Wilson, have "a clarity and terseness of form, an intellectual edge, which it would be hard to match elsewhere today in the American literature of ideas."

He retained his youthful vigor until the end—remaining more a Village individualist than an embittered conservative. He wrote eighty-six books (including a novel loosely based on the affair between Mabel Dodge and Jack Reed), had numberless lovers (though he unaccountably failed in his efforts to seduce Edna St. Vincent Millay), and occasionally resurfaced in the media as a whatever-happened-to celebrity, most notably in his well-publicized encounter with Ernest Hemingway in Maxwell Perkins's office (Hemingway belligerently ripping open his shirt in reply to Max's accusation that he had "false literary hair on his chest") and in his notorious march through the streets of Paris during a Beaux Arts ball bronzed like an American Indian and clad in nothing but a jockstrap.

Max may have been an exemplar of the frequent charge that the American left of the twentieth century consists of few striking ideas but many striking personalities—and of the repeated characterization of American rebels as constituting a party of one—yet his legacy to the left remains less his ideology than his life, his ceaseless search.

For a trained philosopher, Max displayed a remarkable disinclination to develop a coherent set of theoretical principles. Indeed, in his hostility to ideology, he found himself frequently accused of fuzzy thinking, contradictory pronouncements, and even a kind of intellectual promiscuity. But it's possible to discern in his editorials and speeches and books three strands of thought that reveal, if more temperamentally than philosophically, clarity, consistency, and commitment. It's not too much to say, in fact, that like many American political theorist-activists, he transformed ideological looseness into an intellectual virtue.

First, he insisted to the point of obsession on the primacy of fact over faith. His favorite word of praise was "scientific," of contempt "theological." By "scientific" he meant practical and objective; by "theological" he meant imposition of dogma on reality, and what he called "the undiscriminating hurrah" of the "sentimental rebels," who at one time or another included most of his colleagues. He adopted Marxism when it seemed to provide a scientific analysis of particular economic relationships, Freudianism when it seemed to provide a scientific explanation of specific human motivations, then rejected both when their adherents turned their concepts into cathedrals. At the slightest sign that reality was being twisted to fit doctrine—a phenomenon he was particularly adept at detecting, sometimes when it didn't exist—he abandoned the doctrine, overlooking the fact that the genius of Marx and Freud lay precisely in their discovery of new realities. For all his flirtation with Continental thought, Max remained faithful to John Dewey—which is to say that he regarded all ideologies as instruments rather than revelations and considered metaphysics a disease that transformed independent judgment into intellectual slavery. A pragmatist before he was a socialist—though it sometimes seemed that he was doctrinaire in his pragmatism—he declared himself more devoted to progress than to party. "To me socialism was never a philosophy of life, much less a religion. [It is] an experiment that ought to be tried." He had made, he said, "a vow of unconsecration."

Second, given the danger of rigidity inherent in any ideology, Max insisted on free, open-minded inquiry. He raised doubt itself into a principle. So when he became disillusioned with a doctrine, he didn't founder in despair or decamp to the opposing party with venomous fervor, as have so many twentieth-century intellectuals, but, with a kind of invigorating equanimity, changed his mind in response to experience. Max's sadly ironic fate is that he remains best known for his single lapse from intellectual openness—his rigid anti-communism at the end of his life—but even then he based his opposition on what he regarded as communist rigidity. "The vice of soft-headedness, now better called wishful thinking, is what has caused liberals and liberalism the world over to fall for the organized deceit and principled lying of the totalitarians. I have done my full share of it, but I still deem it the chief enemy of human progress." At once receptive and skeptical, he was the ideal editor, filling the pages of *The Masses* with an astonishing diversity of opinion without losing sight of its revolutionary goal.

The goal, at least in Max's mind—the third thread in his thought— can be loosely defined as joy. While this might seem simultaneously meaningless and self-evident, Max's life and writing centered on the assumption that capitalism and Puritanism had falsely elevated other values over "the pursuit of happiness" on which the nation was founded. But the principal goal of politics was to create a society that would restore the choice to each and every person. If this meant adopting a collectivist politics for individualist ends, or using one's brains to satisfy one's heart, well, the pragmatic only seemed paradoxical. So he regarded Marxism and Freudianism merely as means to an end, the liberation of the individual from the exploitations of capitalism and the inhibitions of puritanism.

Max's positions—on the class struggle and liberated sexuality in particular—may not have accorded with the morality of the *Mayflower,* but the premises from which they derived accorded with the principles of the Founders. Indeed, the three major strands of his thought—which he summed up in the quintessentially American phrase, "hardheaded idealism"—served not so much to overthrow society as to return it to the values from which it had strayed.

One problem with putting values in the place of philosophy, of course, is that character all too soon replaces values, and it's not long before personality gets put in the place of character—the progression of not a few American intellectuals, radical or otherwise. Max's impact on his contemporaries seemed to derive not from his mind but from his charm, and unfortunately for his reputation among later generations, the legacy of charm is convincing only by hearsay.

Max sensed the disparity between his aspirations and his achievement, and while fervently enjoying his semi-heroic status as the John Barrymore of American radical letters during the teens and early twenties, frequently suffered from feelings of failure. He had wasted his talents. Even at *The Masses* he had merely been playing. Ironically, the qualities of his character that cast him into self-doubt were the very qualities that most enchanted his admirers. What he saw as drifting, they saw as wide-ranging. What he saw as uncentered, they saw as mercurial. What he saw as contradictory, they saw as protean.

One hardly has to fall back on "the enduring mystery of human nature" to account for the contradictory strains in Max's philosophy and character. The child of two ministers, a weak father and an adored mother, he rejected passively rigid dogma while retaining an energetically moral vision. Max came of age as Enlightenment ideals were intersecting with bohemian impulses, as the optimistic scientism of the nineteenth century was confronting the irrational terrors of the twentieth, as the American trinity of Emerson, Whitman, and Twain, all of whom he idolized, suddenly faced the Continental trinity of Nietzsche, Marx, and Freud. His autobiography reveals a man witty, charming, even relentlessly self-aware—except for one facet of his personality about which he is both candid and confused. A moment occurs again and again in his relationships with women when for no reason he suddenly realizes that rapture is lost. He tries to understand—some subtle shift in her personality? some gradual growth in his needs?—but the closest he can come seems to be words like "surrender" or "possess," which fill him with a terror he cannot comprehend, and finally he just shrugs it off as his nature.

A. A. Brill's "mother fixation" diagnosis, rudimentary as it was, would seem to be conclusive, except that the same "demon" acted up in Max's intellectual life as well. Some small but stubborn core of his being must remain impenetrable, inviolate, untouched—by causes as well as by women. Renowned for the variety of his vocations—philosopher, teacher, editor, writer, lecturer, humorist, critic, poet—he secretly sensed that his intellectual contributions remained superficial, inconclusive, incomplete—a judgment, aside from his editorship of *The Masses*, history has seemed happy to confirm. It was as if he sought an ideal, only to find some part of himself holding back at the last moment, undercutting himself. If he made the final leap of commitment—to a lover, to a cause—he'd lose his independence, and with it his sense of self.

Max's words "Cut off from life" echo, oddly enough, those of Mabel Dodge. Though two people could scarcely have been less alike, they shared both a voracity for self-fulfillment and an insatiable emptiness. Two of the most active personalities of their generation—and the most self-conscious and willful—they struggled against an implacable, inexplicable passivity. The kind of independent self they sought—calling the least trace of cultural or social influence repressive or inhibiting—could result only in a disembodied self without contours or direction, and could be attained only at the price of isolation, drift, and unfulfillment. Max and Mabel demonstrated that voracity for experience can be the cause of rather than the cure for free-floating anxiety, and it's not too much to say that they were among the precursors of that particularly twentieth-century malaise—alienation.

Max and Mabel—along with Jack, whose voracity seemed to foretell his early death—defined a community obsessed with individualism, independence, self-expression, and self-fulfillment far more than with the radicalism and bohemianism for which it became famous. The Villagers adopted radicalism and bohemianism not as enduring ideals but as temporary means of rebellion. Still, at the turn of the century, with the increasingly repressive dominance of middle-class capitalism, the individual desperately needed a haven for self-expression, the culture a myth of independence—which accounts for the slight haze of nostalgia that always hovers over the Village. Golden youth, irreverent radicalism, madcap bohemia, that's what the Village promised, and, in a few people, exemplified. It was Max's fate, like Mabel's, to become such an archetype, but for all his disillusionments, few people have enjoyed such a golden youth.

Though the birth of the Village coincided with the birth of *The Masses*, Max took every opportunity to denounce what he called "Greenwich Villageism." Radicalism embodied the best values of the Village, but bohemianism the worst. Bohemians distorted radical ideals—gaiety degenerated into frivolity, self-expression into self-indulgence, the flouting of middle-class morality into grunginess and sloth. "Bohemian dilettantism" remained one of his favorite epithets, "arty pretentiousness" one of his favorite sarcasms. "We were radicals, revolutionaries," he complained in an uncharacteristic whine, "unposing pioneers of what was soon to become a conscious pose called 'Greenwich Village.'"

The artists' strike of 1916, Max said, was a war of the bohemian art rebels "against the socialist who loved art." As he elaborated in a letter to Norman Thomas, who had protested that *The Masses* angered more readers with its sexual bravado than it convinced with its anti-war arguments, "I do think you might feel a little differently about *The Masses* if you got a deeper taste of its mood. I think there is an Elizabethan gusto and candor in the strong taste for life which must be won back over the last relics of Puritanism." When Upton Sinclair made a similar protest, Max replied that what he objected to was not the result of "an indiscriminate habit of rebellion." "If you knew how much continual resistance I have put up to what you call a Greenwich Village atmosphere, from the very start, you would be satisfied upon that point."

Like the Village, *The Masses* was less an institution than an impulse, and like the Village, it was occasionally tainted by elitism, naïveté, and intellectual incoherence. It may have been intended for the masses, but it never aspired to be of them or by them. Unlike other radical magazines of the period, Emma Goldman's *Mother Earth* in particular, it rarely published pieces by workers or organizers, but depended almost exclusively on contributions from disaffected middle-class intellectuals. Even in praising the magazine, Max unconsciously revealed a patronizing attitude. *The Masses*, he wrote, was "a luxurious gift to the working-class movement from the most imaginative millionaires in the Adolescence of the Twentieth Century."

Its subscribers were almost exclusively confined to writers, artists, intellectuals, college students, big-city radicals, small-town iconoclasts, and the Rebel Rich for whom it served less as a guilty pleasure than as a gesture of conscience. George Santayana read *The Masses* and so did H. L. Mencken and Woodrow Wilson, but not the Saccos and Vanzettis of Lowell or Ludlow—indeed, one of the few participants in the Ludlow conflict to read *The Masses'* outraged account of the ensuing massacre was John D. Rockefeller. "You *Masses* boys," the conservative *New York Evening Post* editor, Arthur Brisbane, told Art Young," are talking to yourselves!" The very qualities that made such an impact on its elite readership—its uncompromising impertinence toward conventional morality, religion, and family, its advocacy of feminism, psychoanalysis, and free love—alienated the very working class that gave the magazine its name.

But for all its blasé sophistication, *The Masses* naively misunderstood power, believing that denouncing it was nearly equivalent to weakening and defeating it. Point out injustice, exploitation, and repression, and who would not rally to their cause?—as if injustice, exploitation, and repression were merely unexposed flaws in the social order rather than the mechanisms of its power. When their enemies on the left called them "playboys of revolutions," they accepted the charge with delight. "Play"— the word keeps coming up in justification of their rebellion. And while the word was meant to contrast with the joylessness of puritanism and the grimness of capitalism, it's hard not to contrast it with the decades-long struggle to set up structures of countervailing power that follows, not so much from the rhetoric of persuasion the magazine exemplified, as from the drudgery of activism it underestimated. The intellectuals of *The Masses* provided all the bugles the revolution needed but none of the troops.

Max, in retrospect, recognized the innocence of *The Masses'* rebellion as well as anyone. "It is easy to denounce the whole existing world," he wrote, "when you believe that a millennium lies just over the hill or behind the sky—or on the other side of the planet. And there was a good deal of that too easy denunciation in our magazine. We had no sense of history; we were pretty juvenile." But *The Masses* can be faulted for another form of naïveté—intellectual incoherence. As a contemporary writer put it—and the charge was made by both the far left and the bourgeoisie—"*The Masses* has found no trouble in mixing Socialism, Anarchism, Communism, Sinn Feinism, Cubism, Sexism, direct action, and sabotage into a more or less homogeneous mass. It is peculiarly the product of the restless metropolitan coteries who devote themselves to the cult of Something Else; who are ever seeking the bubble Novelty of the door of Bedlam."

In their enthusiastic eclecticism, the radicals who wrote for *The*

Masses made no sustained effort to reconcile the often contradictory claims of anarchism and socialism, socialism and Freudianism, Freudianism and free love, free love and the rights of labor. They used creeds and causes piecemeal, with no concern for intellectual consistency, to say nothing of systematic analysis. The astonishing range of their concerns reflected their conviction that all issues were intimately interconnected. Their emphasis on free expression opened few prisons but did open many minds. Their vision of a better life created no lasting institutions but drove the search for them. The ardor of their insurgency overcame the tension between their conflicting ideals. So though the radicals of *The Masses* were naive about the means of implementing their goals, they nevertheless succeeded in creating the demand for change and in awakening the vision that must precede any genuine transformation of social policy.

Indeed, what some saw as "a more or less homogenous mass," the writers for *The Masses* saw as a kind of creative eclecticism. To anyone who argued that style thus took precedence over substance, they would have replied, yes, but style can *become* substance—not a bad summary, for that matter, of the history of the Village itself.

For several years after the demise of *The Masses*, the Village spirit lay dormant, its joyous iconoclasm and insurrectionary energy replaced by political disillusionment and bohemian dissipation. "*The Masses*," said *Quill* editor Bobby Edwards, was "a magazine that didn't give a damn—and got caught." But a more suitable epitaph for *The Masses*—and the epitaphs of great enterprises are sometimes prophecies as well—would have been the last words for the last issue, an announcement of an upcoming series of articles printed in large type on the back cover: "John Reed is in Petrograd . . . his story of the first proletarian Revolution will be an event in the world's literature."

Jig Cook, Eugene O'Neill, and the Provincetown Players

"The Beloved Community of Life-Givers"

In 1914, Jack and Mabel had entered the off-again, off-again phase of their affair. Paris, Naples, Berlin, London, Bucharest while Jack reported the horrors of war; he found, as he wrote Lincoln Steffens, nothing but "a clash of traders." In a trench on the German front in occupied France, knee-deep in mud after a night of drenching rain, he borrowed a Mauser from a Wehrmacht soldier and fired two heedless shots in the general direction of the French lines. In another act of boyish bravado, when he had made his way through the Balkans into Russia, he presented his passport to the authorities inscribed with the words, "I am a German and an Austrian spy. I do it for money. Reed." Such insouciance masked his unease, however, for whereas some people seek a cause to fill their yawning emptiness, he sought one into which he could pour his abundant passions.

After Reed explored Russia in the summer of 1915, his despair turned into delirium. "Russian ideals are the most exhilarating, Russian thought the freest, Russian art the most exuberant," he wrote. "Russian food and drink are to me the best, and Russians themselves are, perhaps, the most interesting human beings that exist. . . . There the people live as if they know it was a Great Empire. . . . There are no particular times for get-

92

ting up or going to bed or [for] eating dinner, and there is no conventional way of murdering a man, or of making love." This glowingly apolitical vision—he was speaking, it shouldn't be overlooked, of czarist Russia—revealed that Jack remained as committed to a bohemian as to a bolshevik utopia, and he returned to the Village in the fall of 1915 prepared to ignore the war he increasingly despised.

Not to be in love—either with a cause, with his work, or with a woman—what could be more unendurable? In December, Jack dutifully returned to Oregon to spend the Christmas holidays with his family in Portland. Two weeks later he wrote a friend in the Village, "This is to say, chiefly, that I have fallen in love again, and that I think I've found her at last. Not sure about it, of course. She doesn't want it. She's two years younger than I, wild and brave and straight, and graceful and lovely to look at. A lover of all adventure of spirit and mind, a realist with the most silver scorn of changelessness and fixity. Refuses to be bound, or to bind . . . has done advertising, made a success, worked on a daily newspaper for five years. And in this spiritual vacuum, this unfertilized soil, she has grown (how, I can't imagine) into an artist, a rampant, joyous individualist, a poet and a revolutionary. She is coming to New York to get a job—with me, I hope. I think she is the first person I ever loved without reservation."

Louise Bryant—in his breathless paean Jack had neglected to give the goddess a name (or to mention that she was married)—actually bore some resemblance to her conquest's description. Short, slender, dark-haired, with pale skin and flashing gray-green eyes, Louise had a restless vivacity. If beneath Jack's bravado lay moments of self-doubt, beneath Louise's recklessness lay elements of self-aggrandizement. How could he know that this charm would wreak such calamity? And as far as "she doesn't want it," how little he knew about how much she knew about men, for Louise wanted Jack even before she'd met him.

Louise had been married for six years, but she'd known about Jack for at least four. He was something of a celebrity in Portland, for his scorn for the middle-class background he'd rejected was overshadowed by the fame this scorn had brought him. Louise's husband, Paul Trullinger, was a prominent dentist, but this comic condition was modified, in Louise's eyes, by a quasi-bohemian disposition, for he proudly proclaimed himself a "free thinker." Paul's free thoughts, when he first met Louise, were largely confined to living on a houseboat, but under her tutelage he soon supported women's suffrage and magnanimously ignored her occasional extramarital affairs.

Radicalism by permission, adventure through sufferance—Louise soon became as exasperated by Paul's complaisance as she was bored by provincial propriety. She defiantly wore lipstick, wrote poetry, and avidly read *The Masses*—she had sold so many subscriptions that Max Eastman knew her by name—and after listening to the tales of friends about the joyous rebelliousness of a place called Greenwich Village, its artistic and political insurgency, its contempt for the convention of marriage and advocacy of the independence of women, she determined to join the thousands of young men and women flocking to this Mecca. These romantic reveries were accompanied by a ruthless resolve, and when she heard that the Golden Boy of Bohemia planned a trip to Portland, she regarded him as a combination of shining knight and convenient opportunity—not realizing that this cast her in the rather anomalous role of ambitious damsel.

Louise had persuaded an artist friend to introduce them at a dinner party, but they ran into one another in the rain that afternoon, took shelter in Louise's studio—where she treated Jack's cold with hot milk and honey, selections from her unpublished poetry, conversation about war and women's suffrage, and discreet hints that her marriage was not utterly fulfilling—and when they finally arrived at the dinner at which they were to have been introduced, not only had Jack's cold disappeared, but they had obviously fallen in love. What self-dramatizing bohemian manqué could fail to fall for a six-foot, green-eyed, pugnacious troubadour of rebellion with clumsy gestures and ill-fitting clothes, talking of lands far from Oregon? Louise exulted, "I know there isn't another soul anywhere so free and exquisite and so strong!"

Jack, though playing the role of rescuer, thought himself the one who had been rescued—the foundation of the love that lasted the rest of their lives. Their athletic lovemaking sometimes left marks on Louise's body, which under other circumstances might have tested her husband's magnanimity, but the enraptured lovers didn't even allow him the dignity of being an inconvenience, and by the time Jack returned to the Village a few weeks later, they had agreed she would join him shortly after the New Year.

On January 4, 1916, Jack met Louise's train at Grand Central Station and had rented her an apartment near his own at 43 Washington Square South.

The Village! Jack took as much delight in showing her its magical sights as she took in seeing them—meeting Max Eastman and Floyd Dell at the *Masses* office, lunching at Polly's restaurant, chatting with Albert and Charles Boni at the Washington Square Book Shop, taking tea at the

Brevoort Hotel at Fifth Avenue and 8th Street, attending rowdy anarchist meetings, talking, laughing, loving until dawn.

"The wonder boy of Greenwich Village," Van Wyck Brooks called Jack. He was already legendary not only for his exploits from Paterson to Mexico to the trenches of Europe—which he covered for the highest fees in the profession for the commercial press and for no fee at all for *The Masses*—but as a lover as well. The Villagers thus regarded his new inamorata with curiosity and skepticism. Louise charmed many of his friends with her vivacity, but others, sensing her steely opportunism, dismissed her as an interloper.

Conrad Aiken, an old Harvard friend of Jack's, first met Louise at Three Steps Down, a café on West 8th Street. Lunching with a friend who spotted Louise at a nearby table and whispered "I think she can be made," Conrad was more formally introduced when Jack burst in and proclaimed, "Come over and meet my wife!" (Unlike Max and Ida, who pretended they weren't married when they were, Jack and Louise pretended they were married when they weren't.) According to Roger Baldwin, another friend of Jack's and later one of the founders of American Civil Liberties Union, Louise "was eccentric, of course, but her eccentricities fit right in with the period. She had a lot of courage, was a flame in the protest socialism of the day. She was on her way, although she didn't know where she was going. That, too, was typical. . . . You felt she sensed what was stirring, and was ready to take off in the wind."

Other Villagers remained aloof, either because they were jealously protective of "big Jack, beloved by all," or because they understood the volatility of his devotions and saw Louise as nothing but a legend's passing fancy. Some of Jack's friends found Louise shallow and ambitious—a frequent complaint about the girlfriends of deep and ambitious young men. Emma Goldman, matriarch of the anarchists, could only condescend to one who aspired to be queen of the bohemians. "One had to like [Louise]," she remarked, "even when not taking her social protestations seriously." She had no right to have brains and be so pretty. They were constantly minimizing her.

And Mabel? What could Mabel be expected to feel? One of those people who assume that their ex-lovers lurch through the remainder of their lives if not exactly destroyed, at least devastated, she responded to the news of Jack's new flame with avid curiosity masked as serene indifference. She had a new lover of her own, of course—so what could *his* new lover be but a form of revenge on her and consolation for him? "[Jack] had to stiffen inside himself and feel coldly toward me," she said, "so as not to mind too much."

On reflection, Mabel described Louise as "a very pretty, tall young woman with soft, black hair and very blue eyes"—Louise was short, with gray-green eyes—but less generously, Mabel went on, "The girl was clever with a certain Irish quickness, and very eager to get on. I think Reed was a stepping stone and through him she met a lot of people she never would have known otherwise. It had not seemed to me that she cared very much for him. When he was away on one of the writing commissions he always had, [Louise] had a brief passion with a friend of Reed's and mine."

This accusation, alas, wasn't distorted by jealousy, for while Mabel had the timing wrong she had the temperament to a T. Jack had noted Louise's "fixity," but hadn't realized that it was a fixed resolve to follow her whims, particularly when a man took the approach that she could fulfill his romantic yearnings by satisfying his sexual desires. Very early in their relationship, like many Village couples of the era, Jack and Louise entered into what Max called "a kind of gypsy compact," which in the abstract meant "freedom to live life to the fullest," and, in practice, permission to fool around—though most of the men seemed to assume that as far as their own mates were concerned, the practice would remain entirely theoretical. Not Louise. Love must be free, without merely moralistic obligations, and while she adored Jack, she also adored spontaneous impulse—and her image of herself as a kind of nurturing femme fatale. As for those merely moralistic obligations, well, unlike Villagers whose concept of free love extended no further than earnest candor in discussing their temptations, she felt it more "free" to succumb to the temptation and forgo candor—though how this differed from conventional bourgeois cheating she never bothered to explain.

For his part, Jack "lived life to the fullest" on several occasions during their years together, differing from Louise mainly in that his liaisons were more short-lived, but they caused him more remorse and elicited a kind of vague honesty. "I've had four or five of these things that have worn you down," he wrote her in 1917. "Still my darling *you've* got to make up your mind to trust me to a certain extent or our life together will be a farce." But in early 1916, in the first flush of romance, when Jack took an out-of-town assignment to interview William Jennings Bryan for *Collier's*—their longings were relegated to passionate, lonely letters. "My little lover," he wrote her from a bumpy train, "I become more and more gloomy and mournful to think I'm not going to sleep all over you in our scandalous and sinful voluptuous bed. All my enthusiasm begins to run out of my toes when you get farther and farther away, and I can't go rushing into your room and kiss you four or five hundred times."

Only a few months later, however, with Jack off on yet another adventure leaving Louise with no outlet for *her* restlessness—she knocked on the door of Andrew Dasburg, the painter whose *The Absence of Mabel Dodge* had failed so utterly to make Jack jealous. Whether or not she knew about this, she knew Andrew was a prominent artist who had returned from Paris to champion the new art of the Continent—and soon learned that in his dryly paternal manner, and with his lame leg from a childhood fall, he had exactly the kind of vulnerable manliness to which nurturing femme fatales are particularly susceptible.

Nothing happened on this occasion requiring either candor or discretion, but later that spring, with Jack once more out of town, and under the mistaken impression that Andrew and his wife were "separated," Louise traveled to Woodstock in the Catskill Mountains just north of the city, to spend the weekend with the painter at his studio, the first of several such interludes over the next four years in a long-running but strictly confined love affair. That same spring, Jack's chronic kidney problem flared up, and he was directed by his doctor to take a prolonged rest. For once he didn't resist.

Mary Heaton Vorse, who did labor reporting for *The Masses*, and who had "discovered" Provincetown in 1906, almost single-handedly turning the quaint Cape Cod village into a Villager summer retreat, had invited Jack and Louise to stay with her, but they rented a furnished, white clapboard cottage with its own private stretch of beach instead. They swam in the morning, took long walks and sunbathed nude in the afternoon, and got together with Hutch Hapgood and Neith Boyce or Mary Heaton Vorse and her then husband, Joe O'Brien, in the evening, or with other Village familiars who seemed to arrive almost daily: the painters Charles Demuth and Marsden Hartley, *Masses* business manager Merrill Rogers, set designer Bobby Jones, even Max Eastman and Ida Rauh, who lived across the street.

To Jack, a "prolonged rest" meant a week, maybe even ten days. He turned down most assignments, but couldn't resist a three-week offer from *Metropolitan Magazine* to cover the 1916 national political conventions in Chicago and St. Louis with the added opportunity of dispatching editorial commentary to *The Masses*, and a side jaunt to Detroit to interview Henry Ford with the vain hope of persuading the isolationist millionaire to finance an anti-war daily. Kidneys be damned! Jack vented his anger at what he called "the great American farce" in *The Masses*, excoriating the conventions as boss-manipulated shams and denouncing Teddy Roosevelt as a man who had "sold out" to "the munitions makers and the money trust."

"O how I wish I was in my sweetheart's arms in bed together!" he wrote Louise back on the Cape, but immediately added, "I've had a glorious trip . . . I think a vacation from each other every now and then is wonderful for two lovers."

During his absence, Louise found solace in her own work. She began a play for the local troupe, wrote an essay on the Easter Rebellion in Ireland for *The Masses*, and sent six poems to Floyd Dell, who replied, "Those poems hit me hard. I think they are almost terribly beautiful—like Greek fragments." To Jack, she sent a snapshot of herself in the nude, half-reclining on the sand, and wrote on the back, "Run away from the silly Conventions. . . . I have eaten my dinner in 'solitary confinement' and Hippolyte called me Marie-Antoinette-in-Prison."

Hippolyte? Yes, poor mad Hippolyte Havel. Anarchists need vacations, too, and having spotted Jack and Louise on practically their first day in Provincetown, he peremptorily informed them that they needed a cook. His superb cooking had made Polly Holladay's the most frequented restaurant in the Village, and after some capitalist bargaining between the anarchist and the socialist, a magnificent salary of $80 a month was agreed upon and Havel helped turn the Reed-Bryant household into one of the most popular gathering spots on the Cape, forcing Jack to rent a second cottage in which to escape escape. Hippolyte once shouted at Jack over a dinner, "You're nothing but a parlor socialist," to which Jack rejoined, labeling Hippolyte forever, "And you're nothing but a kitchen anarchist!"

Even the charming anarchist alcoholic Terry Carlin showed up, living in a ramshackle cabin on the dunes. Intertwining them all even further would be two other summer residents, who would transform American theater—an old friend of Floyd Dell's from Davenport, Iowa, named George Cram Cook, but known to his friends simply as Jig, and Terry Carlin's cabin mate and drinking companion, Eugene O'Neill.

A failed novelist, a failed critic, a failed professor, a failed farmer—indeed, a failed son, husband, and father—in his early forties, Jig was turning his unpropitious attention to the theater in hopes of establishing an alternative to the commercial, corrupt Broadway for which he had so much contempt. As a playwright Jig was unimaginative, as a director incoherent, as an actor unmemorable. A crackpot visionary, a soulful charlatan, he had only talent—his genius. In the summer of 1915—"that remarkable and never [to be] repeated summer," in the words of Marsden Hartley—the

Provincetown Players, the third great Village institution of the teens—were
born out of the inebriated energy and windy rhetoric of this one man.

Born in 1873, George Cram Cook, like so many prominent Villagers, came from a family that blended strict middle-class propriety with
vaguely eccentric impulse. Jig's father's father served in the House of Representatives and later lost most of his wealth when he developed an excessive regard for whiskey. Jig's corporate lawyer father—confirming the
theory that vice often skips a generation—was as straitlaced a man as could
be found in all of Iowa. His mother—whose father had captained steam-
boats on the Mississippi River in the age of Samuel Clemens—was a
theosophist, vegetarian, and lover of the arts who converted the family's
summer cabin into what she called "the Vale of Bohemia," a gathering
place for local poets and painters and occasional celebrities, including
Mark Twain himself.

At first Jig tried to take after both parents, leading to the rather
schizoid comment in his school yearbook—"Poet, Philosopher, Pessimist,
Prohibitionist, Proctor, and Professor's Pet." Off to Harvard, where he announced that he hoped to "make life glorious for myself and others before
I die," only to leave after a year when he learned that glory wasn't included
in the curriculum. Then, after a *Wanderjahr* at Heidelberg, during which
he quaffed far too much Nietzsche—"I was the third man in America to
read him with my blood of my soul."

After teaching Greek at the University of Iowa and at Stanford, he
grew weary of the "bourgeois" academic world and decided to emulate Tolstoy, dedicating his life equally to farming and writing, a project that
yielded thousands of muskmelons but not a single publishable manuscript.
By now he was more often intoxicated than not. "Without stimulants," he
argued, "I might miss a certain brilliancy of performance that I might otherwise attain."

If alcohol served as one source of inspiration, women served as another. Since adolescence, Jig had longed for "that not impossible she" who
would become his soul-mate, and felt confident that, as a lover, he would
"rank spiritually among the great ones of the earth." His first wife, an incipient matron, soon sued for divorce on the grounds of mental cruelty, citing,
among other indignities, his refusal to shave daily.

In his travels Jig had met a vivacious young anarchist named Mollie Price, a road company dancer who later worked on Emma Goldman's
Mother Earth, and, now that he had discovered at last an "emancipated"
woman, one familiar with "the haunts of the bohemians," one who some-

times earned her rent by modeling in the nude, his sensuality unfolded in lieu of his soul. "You opened to me [your] more than velvet softness, laid bare the entrance to your sacred womb," he wrote Mollie shortly before she became his second wife. "I felt delight in being able to penetrate—when penetration is an urgent spiritual necessity—oh nature is good to man."

The spiritual exaltation of sacred wombs and tender tunnels all too soon gave way to the spiritual lassitude of quotidian life, however, and in 1910, with Mollie pregnant with their second child, the bored and restless Jig began an affair with a differently emancipated woman from Davenport, a thirty-four-year-old writer named Susan Glaspell.

Sad-eyed and sweet-smiling, "as fragile as old lace," said a friend, "until you talked with her and glimpsed the steel lining beneath the tender surface"—Susan had a stabilizing effect on Jig. Her quiet, whimsical intelligence forgave him his faults. Furthermore, "Little Bear," as Jig called her, was physically frail, which allowed him to play the protective husband, but emotionally imperturbable, which allowed him to play the capricious child—the basis for more than a few enduring relationships. Jig soon fled to Chicago with Susan, leaving behind two failed marriages, two failed novels (A Balm of Life and The Chasm), two failed philosophical texts (Evolution and the Superman and The Third American Sex), a failed run for Congress on the Socialist ticket, and an unquenchable conviction that the two "lovers-writers" would "radiate . . . ideals of art and love."

In Davenport, Jig had befriended a young newspaperman, poet, and socialist named Floyd Dell—with whom he founded the Monist Society, a group of "free-thinkers" who regarded themselves as "master minds" destined to "reject conventional belief" and create a kind of socialist/bohemian utopia in Iowa, only to be stymied, raged Jig, by a 10:00 P.M. tavern curfew that threatened to bring about "a pitiful end of [Davenport's] vaunted literary supremacy." No such tyranny existed in Chicago, however, and though nearly twenty years older than his friend, Jig became Floyd's assistant at the Friday Literary Review, which, along with Harriet Monroe's Poetry magazine, became the hub of the burgeoning bohemia of the Midwest.

Soon sensing himself chosen for even greater tasks, Jig departed for Greenwich Village at the end of 1912, almost at the precise moment when Mabel Dodge began her salon and Max Eastman accepted the editorship of The Masses.

•   •   •

Jig intended to devote himself to "serious writing," but like so many new-comers to the Village, he devoted himself instead to conviviality and dissipation. Supported by Susan, he attempted spasmodically to compose his masterpiece, but spent most of his time pontificating in the Liberal Club, or carousing in the basement of the Brevoort, or fooling around behind Susan's back and drinking half the Village under the table. Painter William Zorach remarked that sober he was "dull and commonplace and plodding," while drunk he became "dynamic and intelligent"—talk about motivation!

Now nearly forty, and prematurely gray, having at last escaped the society of unappreciative hog farmers and discovered a community of sympathetic "free spirits," Jig developed a vaguely Arcadian theory of cultural anarchism, communal creativity, and national awakening based on a mystical mélange of Greek soul, Nietzschean philosophy, socialist doctrine, and bohemian whoopee. Ninety million Americans were poised on the brink of a renaissance, but its animating ideals would be more aesthetic than activist—poverty of spirit remained the only poverty that concerned Jig—and it would be led not by the masses but by an elite one hundred, of whom he only had to find ninety-nine more. As Jig summed up the principles for the middle class: in the Village one could "*live* without the wretched necessity of earning money."

Some dim instinct led Jig to realize that theater might be the most congenial outlet for his otherwise thwarted creativity. Gifted at articulating visions but inept at realizing them, wouldn't he work best in a collaboration? And hadn't his most inspiring oratory resulted from his infatuation with Greek drama? His greatest regret, in fact, was that he had been born in modern Davenport rather than ancient Athens.

In Chicago, Jig had seen the Irish Players and Maurice Browne's Little Theater productions of the Greek classics. "What he saw done for Irish life he wanted for American life," Susan recalled. Tears had come into his eyes when he saw a production of Aristophanes' *Lysistrata*. "Its beauty, its coming from so far away in time, its revelation of man and woman as they were two thousand years ago . . . struck something tremulous in me."

In New York, aside from Jack Reed's exhilarating Paterson Pageant, true feelings and tremulousness were hard to find. The American theater of the time consisted almost exclusively of musical spectacles, meretricious melodramas, and frantic farces—the industry of entertainment. As Susan put it, "We went to the theater, and for the most part we came away wishing we had gone somewhere else. Those were the days when Broadway flourished almost unchallenged. Plays, like magazine stories, were patterned. They didn't ask much of *you*, those plays. . . . Your mind came out where it went in, only tireder. Audience, Jig said, had imagination. What was this 'Broadway,' which could make a thing as interesting as life into a thing as dull as a Broadway play?"

Other Villagers felt the same contempt for commercialism, among them some members of the Liberal Club, who had begun a series of amateur theatricals. Floyd not only wrote and directed and designed his own one-act bills but, a kind of downtown George M. Cohan, starred in them as well. Soon several members of the club formed a drama group, led by Ida Rauh, who, said Max Eastman, "had long talked of founding a theater to be sustained by subscriptions instead of ticket sales, one which could ignore the box office and adhere to pure standards of art."

Disillusioned when an art dealer who had offered free space in his gallery decided to charge rent, harassed by fire and health and building inspectors when they found a temporary home in an empty stable just down Macdougal Street from the club, the dejected group sat in the Boni brothers' bookstore one evening in the winter of 1915. Albert Boni had moved to the Village after graduating from Harvard to found the store with his brother Charles. Located right next door to the Liberal Club, the Washington Square Book Shop soon became one of the Village's most fashionable gathering places, where impecunious Villagers settled in at the open fireplaces as if they were at home.

Sympathetic to the aspiring thespians, Albert Boni asked Robert Edmond Jones—Mabel Dodge's Bobby, who had studied stage design with Max Reinhardt—"Do you have to have a stage to put on a play?" Bobby responded that a theater wasn't necessary for theater, that there was no reason they couldn't mount a play on the spot. Since there weren't any patrons in the store at the time—patrons being about the last people you'd expect to find at the Bonis' store—the Villagers discovered several copies of Lord Dunsany's *The Glittering Gates*. Bobby hastily improvised two columns and two spears from a roll of wrapping paper, spread coats over the heads of kneeling volunteers to simulate boulders, found several candles for footlights, and with the frame of the sliding mahogany doors that separated the two rooms representing the proscenium, the performance proceeded. In later years, this impromptu evening would become legendary as the beginnings of the Washington Square Players.

Such Village luminaries as Lawrence Langner (a patent attorney by day and a playwright by night), Helen Westley (a duskily beautiful actress who carried her bankbooks in her stockings and filled her bathtub with books), and Ida Rauh (of whom Lawrence said, "She suffered considerably as an actress from having once been told that she resembled Sarah Bernhardt") met regularly at Lawrence's apartment on West 11th Street or at the Eastman-Rauh apartment on West 13th Street to plan a season of one-act plays and report on their largely futile efforts at fund-raising. The Washington Square Players issued a manifesto deploring "the present condition of the American drama," vowing to strive for "a high standard" based on "experiment and initiative," and pledging themselves to "the sincere, truthful, and effective"—hardly goals one associated with bohemia, unless one realizes that a strong strain of Village bohemianism, in direct contradiction of its image as sophisticated and degenerate, rejected the debased values of the middle class in favor of a renewed purity and simplicity.

The Washington Square Players' first bill, in February 1915, featured three one-act plays, a propaganda piece in defense of birth control, a naughty jeu d'esprit discussing Shaw's ideas on mating, and Maeterlinck's *Interior*—followed by a divertissement in which the mise-en-scène represented, in Langner's words, "the inside of a man's stomach, into which various foods portrayed by the actors passed through the esophagus," Helen Westley superbly portraying an oyster and another Villager, to use the word in its precise meaning, a nauseating liqueur. Though the Players aspired to "the subtler nuances of drama," the critic for the *New York Evening Post* wrote that "The appeal is distinctly to the 'highbrow' or revolutionary tendencies. That it will ever win an audience outside of the spiritual frontiers of Greenwich Village is not probable." The *Times* critic, revealing highbrow or revolutionary tendencies not hitherto associated with that paper, wrote that the Players gave "every indication of fully realizing their aim, which is to present the unusual pieces in an unpretentious and yet effective way in the hope of adding impetus to the artistic movement in the New York theatre."

When Jig had heard that members of the Liberal Club were mounting amateur theatricals as the Washington Square Players, he and Susan—to whom he was now more or less married—had eagerly set about writing a play for the new group. *Suppressed Desires* spoofed the fad for Freud—new codes of morality being popular subjects for satire among the very Villagers who most ardently practiced them (Susan observed that "Those were the early years of psychoanalysis in the Village [when] you could not go out to buy a bun without hearing of someone's complex").

When the Washington Square Players rejected the play—too esoteric, too experimental—Jig and Susan, almost as an afterthought, packed it in their luggage when they departed for Provincetown.

Alternately ecstatic about his destiny and despondent about his life, Jig felt fated both to transform the American theater and to die unknown. The paradoxical fate of genius, according to Village mythology in the teens and for decades thereafter, was to fail in the realm of commerce in precise proportion to one's success in the realm of culture. But Jig had little notion that the process that would prove both prophecies would begin on a vacation.

The usual Village gang showed up in Provincetown in the summer of 1915. On a chilly evening, several couples gathered around a driftwood fire—Hutch and Neith, Mary and Joe, the Wilbur Daniel Steeles, Jig and Susan. The conversation soon turned to the lack of worthy outlets for writers, and since the newest outlet was the Washington Square Players, Jig became animated. The commercial theater? Everyone knew its intolerable shortcomings. But the new, the "daring," the "artistic" Washington Square Players? Jig railed against their policy of stressing foreign works at the expense of native playwrights, and since he happened to be "a native playwright" the Players had rejected . . . well, the listeners might have been forgiven had they been skeptical, but the enthusiasm behind his vehemence enchanted them instead.

When Jig finally wound down, Wilbur, a prolific magazine writer, announced that he'd been thinking of writing a play himself, and the reserved, even diffident Neith confided that she'd already *written* one. Come on Neith, what is it? Well, she'd written this one-act play based on Jack and Mabel's affair, she'd called it *Constancy*—and everyone laughed. Within minutes, the group decided to put on *Suppressed Desires* and *Constancy* in a couple of weeks.

At 10:00 P.M. on Wednesday, July 21, 1915, the vacationers' romp—and Jig's revolution—began. The cast of *Constancy* was the author herself and Joe O'Brien, and the "set" was the Hapgoods' veranda overlooking the bay at 621 Commercial Street. The audience sat in the adjoining low-ceilinged room with the open double doors serving as a proscenium.

Constancy focused on the disastrous denouement of Jack and Mabel's affair. Rex/Jack returns to Moira/Mabel after having abandoned her for another woman (in a nice touch, Joe made his entrance in a rowboat, which he tied up at the Hapgood dock, disembarking onto the veranda/stage), and when she says she no longer loves him, they argue over the meaning of "constancy." *You're* inconstant because you always cheat, she says. *You're* inconstant because you let little things like that stand in the way of our love, he replies. And that's pretty much it.

Only a few months earlier, Mabel had sent Neith a letter in which she had poured out her despair. "One of us had to give in on this issue [of sexual fidelity]. . . . To [Jack] the sexual gesture has no importance, but infringing on his right to act freely has the first importance. Are we both right & wrong—and how do such things end? Either way it kills love—it seems to me. This is so fundamental—is it what feminism is all about? . . . I know all women go thro this—but *must* they go on going thro it?" No one in the audience knew the extent of Mabel's anguish, but everyone knew the extent of Jack's libido, and everyone also must have realized that Neith was quietly addressing her philandering husband as well.

During the performance, Mabel's house guest, the ever-present Bobby, quietly set the stage for the second play behind the backs of the audience, and at intermission asked them to turn their chairs around. Voilà! Hutch and Neith's cozy alcove had been transformed into a Village apartment for Jig and Susan's *Suppressed Desires*, subtitled "A Freudian Comedy."

Henrietta, played by Susan, prattles on about Freud, "the new Messiah," and applies his doctrines of the "unconscious," "complexes," and "suppressed desires" with such blithe disregard for common sense that her husband, Steve, played by Jig, is nearly driven loony. "I couldn't even take a bath without its meaning something," he complains, and concludes that Freudianism is nothing but "the latest scientific method of separating families." "Think of the living libido in conflict with the petrified moral codes!" a female friend breathlessly tells Henrietta in anticipation of seducing her husband—and Henrietta is instantly cured of her devotion to the new messiah from Vienna. The play may have been too esoteric for the Washington Square Players, but not for a Provincetown critic, who expressed amazement that "they not only write about modern things, but satirize them."

Overnight the performance became the talk of Provincetown, and the next morning Jig, Susan, Hutch, Neith, and a few friends trooped over to Mary Heaton Vorse's house to urge her to donate her ramshackle wharf at 571 Commercial Street. In a model display of philanthropic zeal, Mary agreed.

Each of the thirty or so members of the burgeoning company contributed $5, and Jig proceeded to build a ten-by-twelve-foot stage. Through the sliding door at the back of the fish house the audience could gaze past the performance to the bay beyond, and they could smell the sea through the wide gaps between the floor planks. Jig improvised a row of lanterns with tin reflectors and stationed four members of the company backstage with handheld lamps, and in case of fire he designated four others to bring shovels and sand. Everything was ready for the gala opening but the seats. Since lumber was scarce and their funds were depleted, word passed around Provincetown that members of the audience should bring their own chairs.

Finally, in late August, the Wharf Theater was officially christened with the revival of *Constancy* and *Suppressed Desires*. And on September 9, the Provincetown Players presented two new one-act plays written expressly for the occasion.

Contemporaries, by Wilbur Daniel Steele, was loosely based on an incident in New York City a year earlier—a young IWW organizer named Frank Tannenbaum had received six months in jail for leading a group of homeless men into a church.

Mabel returned in the fourth play, Jig's *Change Your Style,* in the guise of Myrtle Dart, a wealthy, om-chanting "Lover of the Buddhistic." A satire of the dispute between objective and nonobjective art and a wry caricature of the relationship between art and money, the play featured performances by Jig, Max, Ida, and the painter Charles Demuth.

A makeshift stage, a cast characterized more by enthusiasm than by skill, an audience of only a couple dozen friends—all this hardly seemed like "signaling through the flames." None of the plays contained a hint of the psychological or moral depth of Chekhov or Shaw, or a trace of anything resembling the dramaturgical innovations of Brecht or Beckett. Yet they brought to the stage the real lives and passionate concerns of both the participants and the audience—the emancipated woman, the debate over Freud, the political struggle, and the artistic awakening.

Furthermore, those two throwaway double bills were a rebuke to the melodramatic grandiloquence and calculated theatrics that characterized contemporary American theater. Hardly aware of what they were doing—and hardly any of them with any previous interest or experience in theater—the group focused on creativity rather than commercialism, sincerity rather than spectacle, passion rather than self-aggrandizement. But Jig glimpsed Greece. What to the others seemed little more than a summer lark seemed to him the embryo of a revolution.

• • •

Throughout the winter of 1915–1916, Jig cornered his friends, barraged them with letters and telegrams, organized them into committees, cajoled and badgered and charmed in an effort to keep "the Provincetown moment alive." Jig may have advocated a Greek-based American nationalism—and all with a kind of incandescent pomposity—but the inchoate stirrings of his soul would be satisfied with nothing less than what he called "the beloved community of life-givers," an American Athens, a "dream city" with a theater as its temple. In thrall to an ideal of spiritual oneness, and the concept of communal drama with its members celebrants in primitive ritual, he believed not so much that the community would create theater as that the theater would create community.

"One man cannot produce drama," Jig wrote in one of his many missionary manifestos. "True drama is born only of one feeling animating all the members of a clan—a spirit shared by all and expressed by the few for the all. If there is nothing to take the place of the common religious purpose and passion of the primitive group, out of which the Dionysian dance was born, no vital drama can arise in any people." To a Village friend he declaimed, "Why not write our own plays and put them on ourselves, giving writer, actor, designer a chance to work together without the commercial thing imposed from without? A whole community working together, developing unsuspected talents. The city ought to furnish the kind of audience that will cause new plays to be written."

Confronted with the drama-drunk fervency of his appeals, the Villagers must have felt that the *least* they could do was dash off a one-act play—and if Jig made little progress in establishing a spiritual polis in the byways of the Village, he *did* manage to put together an expanded theatrical program for the summer of 1916.

By the middle of June, most of the Villagers were back in Provincetown. Max and Ida returned, Hutch and Neith, Mary and Joe, a dozen others, joined by the unkempt poet Harry Kemp, the sultry actress Kirah Markham (an old flame of Theodore Dreiser's), Floyd Dell, Mabel Dodge, the artists William and Marguerite Zorach, and Jack and Louise. Jig commandeered "volunteers" to install electricity and construct seating for nearly one hundred subscribers—the average cost of a production, he proudly calculated, was a mere $13—then blithely announced a season of four programs of three one-act plays, although only six of the plays had actually been written. Never mind, hadn't they been *imagined*?

On July 13, the Provincetown Players presented the first bill of their second season to a sold-out house—a revival of *Suppressed Desires*, Neith's *Winter's Night* (yet another meditation on constancy in which the woman's virtue remains inviolate—oh Hutch!), and Jack's *Freedom* (a prison parable which also had the distinction of having been turned down by the Washington Square Players). Giddy with success, Jig and the Provincetowners set about putting together the second triple bill. They could lead off with a new comedy called *Not Smart* by the proficient Wilbur Steele, and Louise's parable *The Game* could fill the second slot. Wilbur's play seemed slight, however, and Louise's effort, with characters called "Life," "Death," "Youth," and "The Girl" (with Jack slated to play "Death"), seemed, to put it generously, a bit stilted. A strong third play to carry the second bill was needed.

One day Susan ran into Terry Carlin, and asked, "Haven't you a play to read to us?" No, Terry said, "I don't write, I just think—and sometimes talk." But he had a friend, with whom he was sharing a cabin on the dunes who had "a whole trunk full of plays." "What's your friend's name?" asked Susan. "O'Neill," said Terry. "Gene O'Neill." "Well," she said, "tell O'Neill to come to our house tonight at eight and bring some of his plays."

That casual encounter between a director's wife and an alcoholic anarchist in a small fishing village in the summer of 1916 changed the course of the American theater. If Susan and Terry had known of the playwright's psychic struggles of the last twenty-seven years, they might have wondered if their meeting was chance or destiny.

"Gene talks to me for hours," wrote his wife, Carlotta, in her diary on June 21, 1939, "about a play (in his mind) of his mother, father, his brother, and himself. . . . an ache in our hearts for things we can't escape." Mother, father, brother, himself—the inescapable configuration began with Eugene O'Neill's birth in October 1888 in a theatrical hotel at Broadway and 43rd Street, then called Long Acre Square, soon to be renamed Times Square. During his delivery, his mother received morphine to ease her pain, and developed a lifelong addiction—so his very birth, Gene came to believe, was the source of the guilt that became his lifelong companion. "I should never have borne [you]," says the mother in *Long Day's Journey into Night*. "It would have been better for [your] sake."

Gene's father, James, an extravagantly gifted actor in the dashing/heroic line, seemed destined to succeed Edwin Booth as the greatest performer of his era, but became a mere legend instead. Enormously popular, he was trapped in a swashbuckling adaption of Dumas's *The Count of Monte Cristo*—he performed the role more than six thousand times over a quarter of a century, in nearly every city in the country—and could credit the Count with making him rich, famous, and miserable. The aggrieved, avenging Count became part of Gene's psychic landscape as well, and so did his father's sense of desolation. The Count's story was one of escape and vengeance, James's one of entrapment and victimization, his son's one of rejection and retribution—how Gene hated the hammy grandiloquence of nineteenth-century theater, how he emulated its grandiose passions. No actor has been so ensnared by success as James O'Neill; few sons have been so ambiguously rebellious as Gene. Determined to reject every trace of his father's world, he reshaped it to fit his own needs instead, his life and work at once an act of rebellion and an act of reconciliation.

The gulf between father and son was widened by the gulf between father and mother. James O'Neill reveled in the hotel-theater-train hurly-burly of the itinerant matinee idol, while Ella O'Neill, though she reluctantly accompanied her husband on many of his travels, withdrew into the serene rituals of the Catholic Church, or, more accurately, into mystic reverie. Ella nevertheless became the focus of the family, not only in the way that invalids determine household rituals, but in the sense that an emotional vacuum sucks up attention. Her frailty became as domineering as James's energy. James and Ella endured one of those marriages in which the partners are yoked by their very incompatibilities, James hypnotized by a mysticism he despaired of comprehending, Ella entranced by a glamour for which she felt contempt.

How could a boy survive in this emotionally entangled atmosphere in which love seemed inseparable from daily instability, hate from lifelong commitment? Unfortunately, Gene had as a guide his older brother, Jamie (James Junior), who responded to their parents' miserable marriage with cynical despair and sneering dissipation. A wastrel—the epithet seemed invented for Jamie. And when he came to enact his rituals of rejection, which consisted largely of drowning in cheap alcohol and seeking out "loose" women, he found an entranced witness in his younger brother.

Gene quickly developed an instinct for dramatic gesture and a contempt for theatrical convention. In one of his earliest memories, he wrote, his father appeared "dripping with salt and sawdust, climbing on a stool behind the swinging profile of dashing waves. With arms outstretched he declared that the world was his. This was a signal for the house to burst into deafening applause that drowned out the noise of the mechanical storm being manufactured backstage." Emotions must have seemed either meretricious or menacing, and Gene withdrew into books and moodiness, a wretched childhood, rootless and forlorn.

Father and mother, parent and child, man and woman, self and others—to James and Ella's son, they all seemed at once utterly alienated and inextricably bound, and if the great anguish of Gene's life was his failure to transcend this paradox, his great task was to transform it into tragedy, for tragedy, to his sensibility, was ceaseless yearning for the never attainable.

At twelve, Gene returned home unexpectedly one day and surprised his mother as she was giving herself an injection of morphine. She flew into a rage, his father frantically tried to explain the circumstances, his brother derisively let him in on the family secret—all to a boy who still only dimly understood what he'd seen.

At fifteen, having gradually comprehended the source of his mother's anguish and his father's bitterness, he announced one Sunday morning that he was never going to church again. Since their God had been no help to them, why should they expect him to become a believer? James shouted at his son to stop blaspheming. Gene jeered back. They grappled on a stairway, and James finally had to leave for church alone.

These two events marked Gene's passage from withdrawal to open rebellion, though for several years his defiance of his parents and his rejection of religion were confined to brooding over books. Tolstoy, Dostoyevsky, Wilde, Conrad, London—he simultaneously declared his adherence to atheistic nihilism and sought a surrogate redemption in the literature of repudiation. Like Max Eastman and Jig Cook, he discovered Nietzsche too young, and soon became inebriated less by the specific doctrines than by the heady vapors of Nietzschianism. The great appeal of Nietzsche to the teenage sensibility was that he could so easily be misread. In seeming to validate the claims of the ego, his work allowed young men to turn their whims into philosophy, to justify any need from seducing a virgin to overthrowing a government. To Gene, Nietzsche meant the loss of faith, the outcast superman, the association of emotional volatility with creative inspiration—what better way to transform the angst of adolescence into the stirrings of genius?

A shy rebel, at first Gene could only timidly act out his fierce drama. At Betts Academy, a prank involving chamber pots led the headmaster to proclaim he'd surely die in the electric chair, a prediction that only flattered the bookish boy. At Princeton, he drank absinthe in his dormitory, visited prostitutes in Trenton, and declaimed to a group of trembling classmates, "If there is a God, let Him strike me dead!," all of which secured him a reputation as a kind of undergraduate Übermensch. But his pain was real, and he left Princeton after only nine unhappy months. (The legend that he was kicked out for heaving a beer bottle through Woodrow Wilson's window was the invention of drama critic George Jean Nathan.)

Gene vowed to devote himself to "experience," which he defined (like most young men of such inclinations) as alcohol and women. Jamie, who was his guide, had no illusions about their mother, or about women — which is to say he had the illusion they could be judged by their gender. All women are whores, he believed, and since his experience with women was largely confined to brothels, it was difficult to dissuade him from this conviction. Gene, who tagged along behind his older brother on many of these visits — "Here comes the kindergarten!" the ladies called out — may have thought his own view of women was more generous than Jamie's, but in romanticizing the whores Jamie scorned, in attributing to them the large-bosomed love his mother never showed him, in imagining in them the earthy archetypes who would come to fill his plays, he merely created a mirror image of his brother's cynical caricature.

Still, Gene gave the impression of shielding a hurt that needed soothing. He was brooding, tortured, aggrieved; no wonder that so many women felt so attracted to him, or that he could be both a swooning lover and a heartless rake. Barely twenty, he secretly married a New York woman named Kathleen, sailed off to Honduras in a banana boat a week later, failed to look her up when he returned after half a year, and discovered he'd become a father only when a winking bartender showed him a newspaper announcement. Gene felt guilty — guilt was his permanent affliction, as inescapable as a stutter — but he was too trapped in his psychic struggle with his father, alternately submitting to his authority and fleeing his tyranny, to accept any adult responsibility.

For a few months after returning from Central America, Gene trailed along on tour with his father and took on titles like "assistant company manager," but they were phantom jobs between bouts of brooding and boozing. In mid-1910 Gene suddenly succumbed to the allure of the open sea, and impulsively signed on as a deckhand on a ship sailing to Buenos Aires. The open sea gave him a sense of freedom, and sweat and the fatigue of honest work gave him a feeling of manliness for which he'd always longed. He may have earned only $10 in wages for his sixty-five-day journey, but he'd traveled six thousand miles from his father, from his family, from his past. He was a man at last.

Upon returning to New York, Gene couldn't face his father, so he holed up in a dingy lower Manhattan rooming house called Jimmy-the-Priest's for $3 a month, befriended by the sailors, whores, Wobblies, and drifters who later populated his plays. Running out of money, he finally wrote his father, but when James sent him enough cash to come home, he impulsively signed on as an able-bodied seaman for a voyage to Europe and back before finally getting up enough nerve to rejoin his family. He had proven he could live on his own, he even had a wife and child, but some unresolved need led him to submit to his father's dominion yet once more, and he met up with the touring troupe in New Orleans.

By this time, *The Count* had been reduced to a forty-five-minute vaudeville version on a bill with trained horses and flying acrobats. James, behind his hearty showman's front, felt humiliated, Ella wandered backstage in a morphine trance, Jamie had become so dissipated he was unemployable, and Gene, who had one line in the current version—"Is he . . . ?" to which another actor responded, "Yes, he's dead"—never drew a sober breath until the tour terminated. But when James had to cancel a performance because both of his sons were too drunk to go on, Gene abandoned the company and returned to Jimmy-the-Priest's in nearly unendurable anguish.

In 1912—the year of Mabel Dodge's salon and the founding of *The Masses*, and the year in which *Long Day's Journey into Night* takes place—Gene's life touched bottom. Unable to drown his rage and helplessness in alcohol, he flirted with death by swallowing varnish diluted with water, and, a few weeks later, deliberately ingested an overdose of Veronal. Gene later confessed that the suicide attempts had merely been a dramatic gesture aimed at attracting his father's attention. But it was clear that his misery was more than a difficult "stage," as his father continued to insist, and that for all his gentleness and sentimentality, he would always have a strain of violence and despair.

That year two events pivoted Gene's life in another direction. In the becalmed aftermath of his suicide attempts, he returned to the family home in New London for the summer and took a job his father had secured for him as a reporter for the local newspaper. Though he annoyed his employers with his momentarily radical political views, he managed to stay sober and perform more than perfunctorily, and the interlude provided him with a relatively peaceful period. In late fall, after failing to shake a "bad cold," Gene was diagnosed with tuberculosis, and spent the next half year in a sanatorium. He had one of the mildest cases on record—"never coughed a cough in six months," he said—but a kind of perverse romance was still associated with the disease, and he wasn't averse to seeing himself transformed into a delicate poet in a brutal world, or seeing his father as penuriously denying him the best possible care.

Partly as an escape from the emotional turmoil of his family, perhaps even as a result of the odd euphoria that often overcomes TB patients, Gene began writing plays. He wrote more than a half dozen plays during his treatment and recuperation. His wild swings of mood—from black brooding to tender reveries, from maudlin self-pity to angry lashing out—softened. He even came to feel a tinge of compassion for his parents.

Gene's first completed effort, a bizarre vaudeville sketch with Oedipal overtones (a young man unwittingly steals an elderly friend's wife), must have been written with his father very much in mind. Though bewildered by his son's scripts—groaningly melodramatic by today's standards, they seemed too harshly realistic to an early-twentieth-century sensibility—James nevertheless encouraged Gene, even paying for publication of a volume of one-act plays and arranging for him to attend George Pierce Baker's renowned English 47 playwriting course at Harvard in the fall of 1914.

"I want to be an artist or nothing," Gene wrote Professor Baker in his application letter, his tone typically combining earnestness and arrogance. After admission to Baker's Dozen, as the course was called, he maintained that tone by sitting in disdainful silence throughout the discussions of the other students' plays and walking out of a guest lecture by a leading commercial playwright to go downtown and get drunk. He churned out scripts characterized by a heavy-handed blend of florid symbolism and grandiloquent realism. "Rotten" was his own word for them, yet he was angered when Baker casually suggested that one of his plays—a script called *Bound East for Cardiff*—wasn't really a play at all. Gene decided not to return for a second year.

In the fall of 1915—only a few weeks after Jig, Susan, and the others finished their first season of plays in Provincetown and returned to New York, Gene landed in the Village. He'd visited before, and had met Jack Reed in 1914. Though totally opposite in temperament (Gene taciturn and gloomy, Jack gregarious and buoyant) and prospect (Gene a drunken ne'er-do-well, Jack a blazing legend), they immediately became fast friends. Gene was enchanted by Jack's commitment to "raw experience," so unlike the poseurs and dilettantes of the Village, while Jack was impressed by Gene's spirit of adventure and feelings of kinship with the wretched underclass of day laborers, prostitutes, and social outcasts whose cause he so ardently championed. Indeed, Jack had been one of the first people to encourage Gene to become a writer, but in the fall and winter of 1915, Gene's father's Broadway friends showed no interest in his plays, film studios returned his scenarios, and the Washington Square Players rejected several of his one-act scripts. Gene relapsed into drunken drifting and his path rarely crossed Jack's.

Eking out a living on the dollar-a-day dole from his father, Gene spent most of his time slumped in saloons, occasionally fooling around with accessible women (including Becky Edelson, a union leader and Big Bill Haywood's Village mistress whenever he happened to be in town), and frequently attending the six-day bicycle races at Madison Square Garden (which appealed to him, a friend speculated, because the cyclists pedaled in an endless circle, going nowhere).

In later generations of Villagers there would be a skid row sentimentality, a romance of the riffraff—authenticity of experience measured by degree of degradation—and in a sense Gene found his self-worth precisely in the extent to which his dissipation displeased his father. But he gradually shifted from self-destruction to self-expression and, in finally articulating his pain, transcended it. In Eugene O'Neill the Village had its first tormented genius.

Among Gene's closest friends was Louis Holladay, another struggling young writer he'd met at Princeton, and with whom he'd spent boozy weekends in the Tenderloin, mid-Manhattan's notorious red-light district, gambling center, and opium den. Since Louis was Polly Holladay's younger brother, Gene soon began hanging out at her legendary restaurant, whose clientele, by 1915, included Floyd Dell, Theodore Dreiser, and a young Midwesterner named Sinclair Lewis.

Polly had seduced Louis when they were both barely past childhood, and as an adult she had to struggle to keep her boyfriends out of her mother's arms—O'Neill may have derived many of his themes from the Greeks, but he could draw on his Village acquaintances as well. In the winter of 1915–1916, Louis attempted to emulate his sister's success, but his own bar, called Sixty, at 60 Washington Square South, was closed by the police after only a few months because its owner neglected to secure a liquor license (more likely, he neglected to pay off the precinct).

Another close friend entered Gene's life through the short-lived Sixty. Christine Ell, its cook, was a green-eyed, untidy, and sturdily proportioned woman who had worked in factories as a child, was seduced by her stepfather at fourteen, but became renowned for her earth-mother zest. Christine won some of her fame as a devoted wife who slept around, occasionally bestowing her ample favors on Gene ("What would have been simple promiscuity in someone else," wrote one of his biographers, "seemed in her a generous giving"). Like many delicate-souled but overweight women who consider themselves unattractive to men, Christine disguised her self-doubt in bawdy self-deprecation. To Gene she became "the female Christ," and many years later she served as a model for the heroine of A Moon for the Misbegotten.

Gene's life also intersected with those of the bohemians and radicals at a bar named Columbia Gardens, operated by a jovial Irishman named Luke O'Connor, who blithely cashed checks from Village artists and who served as his own bouncer. Located at the junction of Sixth Avenue, Greenwich Avenue, and 8th Street, conveniently across the street from the courthouse, it was where the English poet laureate John Masefield was said to have once worked as a barboy. The establishment was more popularly known as the Working Girls' Home—a name bestowed by Mary Heaton Vorse in honor of its streetwalker clientele.

In his first year in the Village, Gene was most likely to be found in the seedy saloon located on the southeast corner of Sixth Avenue and 4th Street officially named the Golden Swan, but known to its patrons, a colorfully disreputable collection of hoodlums, thieves, pimps, touts, gamblers, politicians, socialists, anarchists, artists, and writers, as the Hell Hole. With sawdust on the floor, a potbellied stove, a player piano, and photos of boxers, racehorses, and nude women on its walls, the Hell Hole couldn't have appealed more to the Irish alcoholic in Gene, while the free lunch, cheap rooms upstairs, and the dingy light and clanging noise from the Sixth Avenue El satisfied his self-pitying romanticizing of degradation.

According to Mary Heaton Vorse, the Hell Hole was "something at once alive and deadly . . . sinister. It was as if the combined soul of New York flowed underground and this was one of its vents." Women weren't allowed in the front room—the "family entrance," through which many of the Village's prostitutes also passed, was on 4th Street—and in this all-male enclave, presided over by proprietor Tom Wallace and bartender/bouncer

Lefty Louie, Gene and his friends drank—some to euphoria, some to oblivion, and Gene, in the dismal winter of 1915, closer to self-destruction.

Among the attractions of the Hell Hole, in Gene's eyes, were Kid Yorke, Circular Jack, Goo Goo Knox, Rubber Shaw, Honey Stewart, and Ding Dong, members of a Greenwich Village gang called the Hudson Dusters. Occasionally acquainted with an honest dollar as stevedores or truck drivers, the Dusters preferred burglary or hijacking and sometimes even took part in local politics, particularly when Tammany Hall intimated that certain ballot boxes might best serve the commonweal from the bottom of the Hudson River.

The Dusters adopted Gene as a kind of honorary member, calling him "the Kid" and crying out "Get the Kid out of the way!" whenever a beer bottle was about to be broken over someone's head. One freezing day, when Gene showed up at the Hell Hole with his thin jacket lined with newspapers, one of the more nimble-fingered Dusters politely asked him to scrutinize all the men's clothing stores in the neighborhood and select any coat he wanted, it'd be personally delivered to him the next day, no questions asked—an offer Gene declined, but which flattered him so much he told the story until his dying day.

The chief attraction of the Hell Hole—and the greatest influence on Gene—was the penniless drifter and spellbinding dreamer Terry Carlin.

A wreck of his former self when he first met Gene in the winter of 1915, Terry, then in his early sixties, nevertheless remained a striking figure, and not just because he constantly scratched himself in search of ever-elusive lice. As Gene described him in *The Iceman Cometh*—in his portrait of Larry Slade, the ex-anarchist—"[he had] a gaunt Irish face with a big nose, high cheekbones, a lantern jaw with a week's stubble of beard, a mystic's meditative pale-blue eyes with a gleam of sharp sardonic humor in them—His face [had] the quality of a pitying weary old priest's." He seemed impervious to misfortune and unencumbered by commitment. Is it any wonder that Gene instantly adopted him as a spiritual father? An ex-Catholic, ex-socialist, ex-anarchist, Terry propounded a philosophy loosely mingling unionism, Nietzsche, free love, anarcho-syndicalism, and a kind of serene, mentorlike mysticism that was occasionally indistinguishable from passing out. While not wholly taken in by this weird, half-baked, autodidactic amalgam—he called Slade "the old foolosopher" in *The Iceman Cometh*—Gene found in Terry's emotional detachment and intellec-

tual agility an antidote to his own emotional turmoil and intellectual confusion.

Born to impoverished Irish peasants in the 1850s, Terry was
brought across the Atlantic and went to work in a sweatshop when he was
eight years old. He apprenticed as a tanner—a profession he followed with
decreasing enthusiasm until his twenties, when he quit altogether, vowing
never to do another day's labor as long as he lived on the theory that "honest living there is none."

For several years, Terry lived with a onetime streetwalker named
Marie, who gave Gene many ideas for his characterization of Anna
Christie. Terry was one of those saintly souls in whom disillusionment and
idealism reinforced each other—the more wronged by society he felt, the
more he dreamed of a better world; the more desperate he found his circumstances, the more visionary became his convictions. "Oh, that I might
expand my written words into an Epic of the Slums, into an Iliad of Prole-
taire!" he wrote to Hutchins Hapgood. In a later letter he said, "I am very
'crummy,' badly flea bitten, overrun with bed bugs, but, redemption of it
all, I am free and always drunk."

A strain of self-destruction buttressed Terry's almost Franciscan embrace of poverty. Like many people who make a principle of renunciation,
he had an instinct for self-indulgence, and his dedication to dissipation
seemed to stem as much from addiction as from conviction—particularly
when he began to experiment with hashish and chloroform. Gene may
have transfigured Terry into an earth father, but every day he spent with
him was a day Gene drank himself closer to death.

Gene soon began sharing lodgings as well as bars with Terry—the
cagey old hobo and the drifting young writer were now inseparable. A
proud "product of the slums," Terry would ask a marginally less disrep-
utable-looking friend to visit a real estate agent under the pretense of seeking an apartment, and show the friend how to jam the door surreptitiously
upon finishing his inspection of the premises. That night Terry and Gene
would drag in a flea-ridden mattress and a couple of crates to live in the
apartment in hobo splendor until they were discovered.

Terry helped Gene through the rougher spots, dragging him down
to the Fulton Fish Market for oysters or bringing home tin containers of
soup from the Hell Hole's free lunch or panhandling enough for an occasional sandwich. But he wasn't just accustomed to this derelict life, he was
committed to it, and the dark side of his fondness for Gene revealed itself
one day when he staggered into their flat to discover his protégé trembling
in alcoholic withdrawal. Gene announced in a bleary but determined

voice that he'd decided to quit drinking. Disconcerted, perhaps even threatened, Terry came up with a cunning, almost Dickensian plan. He corralled half a dozen winos, whores, and drug addicts, and sent them into the apartment one by one, to walk slowly past Gene's bed and stare at him in silent reproach. Aghast at this nightmarish spectacle, and twitching fiercely, Gene soon pleaded with Terry for a drink—which Terry was all too delighted to provide.

The downward spiral continued. Propped against a bar, no longer even conscious of what he was fleeing, Gene would drape a towel around his neck, clutch a shot glass of whiskey and the end of the towel in his right hand, and pulling down with his left hand with what little strength remained would pull the shot glass to his trembling lips.

"Cheer up," Terry would say at such moments, "the worst is yet to come!" Yet while Terry almost killed Gene, he ultimately saved him, for he was the first person to understand both his despair and his aspirations.

In the spring of 1916, Gene began to emerge from his bleakest winter. Even while sunk in besotted oblivion, he had continued to write, poetry mostly and he'd kept in touch with a few friends, people like Polly and Louis Holladay, Christine Ell, Becky Edelson, and even Jack Reed.

The days were turning balmy when Jack made one of his whirlwind forays into the Village. This time he was accompanied by "the new girl" he'd met in Oregon only a few months earlier. Gene was curious to meet his friend's new lover, and naturally chagrined when he found that he was almost instantly smitten himself. For several months he had remained too self-absorbed for romance, but something slyly brazen suddenly renewed his sense of longing. A passing fancy, certainly—after all, she was Jack's girl.

For her part, Louise, like so many women, immediately responded to Gene's haunted good looks, his sense of poetic dejection—she never could resist a man who seemed unable to resist her. Still, the thought that Louise was in love with Jack restrained Gene, so worldly in so many ways but so naive about women, so unwilling to understand that that made her accessible. One of the surest signs of his restored health was that, against his will, he fell in love with Louise, and one of the surest signs that he was ready to return to writing was that he remained content to adore from afar.

As the weather warmed, Gene yearned to escape the Hell Hole, the Village, the city. Talk of Provincetown filled the salons and saloons; even Jack and Louise planned to spend the summer there. Accompanied by Terry, Gene set out in late June on his fateful journey to the Cape.

• • •

The Players' second Provincetown season was well under way, and Jack and Louise had settled into their boisterous household, when Gene and Terry disembarked at the dock. In the few weeks before Terry ran into Susan, the two Hell Hole refugees had taken possession of a shipwrecked boat on the beach at nearby Truro, an arrangement that had the dual advantage of keeping the shy Gene out of the social scene (and at a safe distance from Louise) and providing the impecunious pair with free rent.

Gene showed up at Jig and Susan's house at nine o'clock on the evening the Players were to select the third play for the second bill, and diffidently handed Jig the script for *Bound East for Cardiff*—after all, no less a critic than Professor Baker had dismissed it as "not a play." Among those seated in the living room as Frederic Burt, a professional actor, read Gene's tragic tale of the Glencairn were Jig and Susan, Jack and Louise, Harry Kemp and his wife, Mary Pyne, and Kirah Markham, while Gene anxiously paced around the dining room. When Burt finished reading the group sat in stunned silence for several moments, then burst into applause. As Harry Kemp later recalled, "We heard the actual speech of men who go to sea; we shared the reality of their lives. This time no one doubted that here was a genuine playwright."

Jig instantly saw in Gene the native playwright who could embody his dream of a transfigured theater, and he set to work with the calm of visionary certitude. He immediately put the play into rehearsal, with Jack and Harry playing seamen, Gene, the mate—with his single line, "Isn't this your watch on deck, Driscoll?"—and Jig performing the role of a dying sailor, Yank. Gene wanted a couple of actors to roll around the floor under a sheet to simulate the sea, but the others quickly rejected such a theatrical contrivance. Two weeks later, on the evening of July 28, 1916, on a triple bill with Wilbur Steele and Louise Bryant, Eugene O'Neill made his debut as a produced playwright.

What playwright's premiere was ever better served by nature? The play took place on board a ship, and the audience could see the bay behind the actors with the fog rolling in and hear the foghorns in the distance and the waves sloshing under the wharf's stage. "It seems to me I have never sat before a more moving performance than our *Bound East for Cardiff*," Susan recalled. "There was a fog, just as the script demanded, and a fog bell in the harbor. The tide was in, and it washed under us and around, spraying through the holes in the floor, giving us the rhythm and the flavor of the sea while the big dying sailor talked to his friend Drisc of the life he had always wanted deep in the land, where you'd never see a ship or smell the sea. It is not merely figurative language to say the old wharf shook with applause."

Encouraged by his success, Gene began to emerge from seclusion. At Jack's insistent invitation, he and Terry moved out of the shipwreck into a sailmaker's shack diagonally across the street from Jack and Louise's cottage and took most of their meals with them. But he still remained aloof from the hubbub of the summer colony. He felt more comfortable with Portuguese fishermen, sailors from the coast guard station, or local businessmen like John Francis, a grocery story owner who made sure that Gene and Terry never went hungry.

Gene hadn't given up drinking altogether, but between binges he'd lean against the door of his shack for hours staring out to sea, or take long swims heading straight out into the ocean until he almost vanished. And he started writing with fitful energy. Louise must have pondered how different Gene was from Jack—cheerful, gregarious Jack, but a Jack whose attention, as Mabel had also learned to her dismay, was distracted by house guests and friends and work, leaving her uncared for and abandoned. She was still in love, but it wasn't hard for her to feel a bit put upon, then a bit restless, then a bit . . . Well, they'd entered into a pact of mutual freedom, hadn't they? They'd agreed that fidelity was a bourgeois convention, hadn't they? And hadn't her pleasant weekend liaisons with Andrew Dasburg proven that her love for Jack couldn't be damaged by an occasional fling? And if he insisted on leaving her alone . . . and if this shy and wounded writer who had suddenly become the focus of everyone's admiration . . . if that young man's intense unease in her presence made her realize that yes, he desired her, too . . .

Louise watched Gene on his long swims, then wandered casually down to the beach as he strode back through the surf. They'd sit in the sand and talk for hours. Gene was falling deeply in love, yet he was the only person in Provincetown who didn't see how obviously Louise was pursuing him. Why did he so stubbornly cling to the idea that his yearning was hopeless? Part of him idealized his beloved too much to believe she could love him in return—which is another way of saying that part of him was enamored of his image of himself as doomed to heartbreak. Years later he would call Louise "something out of the old Irish legends, betrayed by life . . . always the pivotal person, beautiful, passionate, and strange." But now, as he told Terry, "When that girl touches me with the tip of her little finger it's like a flame."

Naturally Louise would have liked to hear such talk firsthand. Those casual conversations on the beach—then a quiet word after rehearsals, covert glances, then gently touching his hand as they parted; finally in frustration, she nearly spelled it out. She'd written several poems that summer, one of them, published in *The Masses*, called "Dark Eyes," and one night, as she was about to depart on a brief trip to the Village, and just as Gene was leaving her house, she slipped him a book of poems with a note between the pages that read, "Dark eyes, what do you mean?" Gene still didn't understand, so upon her return, Louise sent him a note through Terry that she had to see him—she had something to explain. Louise "shyly" told him that Jack was in bad health, that he had a serious kidney problem, that though she and Jack lived together they weren't . . . they didn't . . . Well, Gene mustn't say a word to anybody, but actually she and Jack lived together not as lovers but as, well, brother and sister. It wasn't true, of course, but by this time Gene had very little inclination for skepticism, and that very night he and Louise finally became lovers.

As often happens, at that moment the long-awaited obsession vanished. Gene must have realized almost immediately that Louise had lied to him and his all too familiar feelings of guilt were no less troubling because they were justified. Louise had made her conquest, and had provided herself with a lover during Jack's absences—now she could get back to her own writing. And Jack behaved so nonchalantly that despite his commitment to the principle of free love, everyone in Provincetown assumed he must have been oblivious to what was happening right before his eyes, forgetting that he had the instincts of a superb reporter and the steadfastness of a true believer. The trio settled in for a compatible summer and the rest of the Provincetowners soon professed to lose interest—though there's nothing quite as annoying as pretending to be bored by a scandal and having everyone take you at your word. Mabel? Mabel had achieved some degree of honesty with herself. "When I saw Reed on the street, he steeled himself against me," she recalled. "Though I wanted to be friends, he wouldn't. People said Louise was having an affair with young Gene O'Neill . . . and I thought Reed would be glad to see me if things were like that between him and Louise—but he wasn't."

Renewed most of all by success and guilt, Gene plunged into his work, writing with discipline, vigor, confidence. At Jack's encouragement he finished a short story about the inhabitants of a waterfront flophouse who run out of "tomorrows" (a distant forerunner of *The Iceman Cometh*), a farce about an art heiress who displeases her father by adopting self-consciously bohemian poses (a rough predecessor of *Ah, Wilderness!*), and a Strindbergian monologue by a shrewish wife directed at her sensitive husband, who only appears as a hand reaching out of the wings for a pot of hot water with which to shave and who shortly thereafter, unseen by the audience, responds to his wife's nagging by using his razor to cut his throat (this role was performed by Gene in his "farewell" appearance as an actor when the play was produced in the Village that winter).

Thirst, Gene's second play of the summer, presented on a special bill in early September, came out of his "whole trunkful of plays," though given its parallels to Louise's tactics of seduction it must have seemed uncannily prescient to the two lovers. Louise and Gene took the leads, Louise as the Dancer, and Gene the Mulatto Sailor.

Mary Vorse's son, Heaton, then twelve years old, many years later assessed Louise's performance. She was "too conscious of her good looks to be able to act well. The thing that struck me was her amazing complexion and brightly colored cheeks. She was a perfectly beautiful person."

A Boston journalist, A. J. Philpott, published a long and laudatory account of the troupe in the *Boston Globe* in mid-August. "These players are revolutionists. . . . They are paying more attention to that thoughtful class of people whose numbers seem to be increasing in this country . . . the class that thinks less about profits and more about human aspirations, justice, and equality of opportunity. . . . Idealists! Dreamers! They believe that the tendency of the age is toward such idealism, and that from the crude productions of their little theater on the wharf—or similar theaters—will flow some of the big theatrical success of the future."

"Many people will remember James O'Neill, who played *Monte Cristo*," Philpott also wrote. "He has a son—Eugene O'Neill. . . . He has written some little plays which have made a very deep impression."

As Susan put it, "Life was all of a piece, work not separated from play, and we did together what none of us could have done alone." Yet the sense of communal optimism stemmed from one man's obsession. Jig directed many of the plays, acted major roles, helped design the sets, and almost single-handedly drummed up an audience. A summer that might have been a challenge became a crusade.

The son of James O'Neill knew a bit about rhetorical fervor, of course, and one might have suspected that Jig's resemblance to James would have made Gene flee in dismay. But he needed the stimulation, the approval, the validation of an older man—in the summer of 1916 Jig was forty-two, Gene twenty-seven—and in his eyes Jig's devotion to drama outweighed his bombastic style. At last Gene had found a man with many of the alluring, repelling characteristics of his father, but what he had to contend with in James he was able to use with Jig. James gave him two choices—surrender to me and win my approval, or assert yourself and suffer my rejection. But Jig, though playing the role of authority figure, allowed him to win approval precisely in the act of self-assertion.

But if Gene had found a father figure with whom he could disentangle the psychic knots that had kept him creatively immobilized, that didn't mean that he felt close to Jig. To Gene, emotional intimacy would have carried with it emotional blackmail. He didn't need affection from Jig, or solace; he needed to feel valued. He needed to feel independent without feeling murderous. This desire for a kind of emphatic distance, further than a father, closer than a colleague, coincided with Jig's needs, for he didn't want a son whose soul he could shape, he wanted a playwright whose career he could promote.

Despite his indifference to and occasional hostility toward Jig's full-sailed fantasies of communal creativity and Dionysiac ecstasy, Gene shared his desire to shatter "everything that suggested the worn-out conventions and cheap artificialities of the commercial stage" and a religious, almost cosmic vision of the potential of theater. Their aesthetic visions were similar, the cultural context made them natural allies, the economics of theater encouraged their collaboration, the extraordinary combination of their psychic needs transformed them both.

Summer was coming to a close but Jig remained in a state of visionary intoxication. Why stop now? Why not take the theater back to the Village with them?

Gene fervently supported the plan, of course. Jack would back anything that promised revolution. But Susan expressed her reluctance. Actually, the word she used was "appalled." She knew that Jig got an almost erotic charge out of capturing people, but still "I was afraid people would laugh at him, starting a theater in New York—new playwrights, amateur acting somewhere in an old house or a stable—I feared we couldn't make it go. 'Jack Reed thinks we can make it go,' he said. Those two were the first to believe—adventurers both, men of faith."

On Monday evening, September 4, the troupe gathered to formally organize—twenty-nine members, including Jig and Susan, Jack and Louise, Gene, Hutch and Neith, Max and Ida, Mary, William and Marguerite Zorach. The first order of business was an impassioned declamation, this time delivered not by Hippolyte but by Hutch, that "organization is death!" After rejecting the suggestion that they call themselves the Tryout Theater, they settled on the name they'd been using, the Provincetown Players. Election of the officers followed, with Jig the uncontested choice as president. One of his first duties was to find a way to pay himself the agreed-upon salary of $15 a week. Finally, the members asked Jig, Jack,

Max, and Frederic Burt to draw up a constitution to present for their approval the following night.

Never one to pass up a chance to write a manifesto, Jack contributed most of the wording to the document. "Be it resolved," Louise, the secretary pro tem, noted in the minutes, "that it is the primary object of the Provincetown Players to encourage the writing of American plays of real artistic, literary, and dramatic — as opposed to Broadway — merit. That such plays be considered without reference to their commercial value, since this theatre is not to be run for pecuniary profit. . . . That the president shall cooperate with the author in producing the play under the author's direction. The resources of the theater . . . shall be placed at the disposal of the author. . . . The author shall produce the play without hindrance, according to his own ideas. The author, with the assistance of the president, must select his own cast, see to it that they are rehearsed, and generally direct his production."

These may have been their overt, organizational principles but the implicit, animating principles remained Jig's obsessive, unwritten theories — communal creativity, spontaneous impulse, and amateur spirit. He never bothered to resolve — any more than did the radicals of *The Masses* — the apparent paradox of a group endeavor dedicated to personal self-expression, but his selfless dedication paralleled Max's philosophical open-mindedness, and so both institutions provided a communal context within which individual expression could flourish.

The players authorized Jig to find a theater, his sublime faith authorized him to play a bill of three new plays every two weeks. Three new plays every two weeks? With no money, no theater, not even any scripts? Jig snapped his fingers at such trifling obstacles. "Some day this little theater will be famous," he told a newspaperwoman from Chicago. "Gene's plays aren't the plays of Broadway; he's got to have the sort of stage we're going to find in New York. You don't know Gene yet," he said with the strange blend of egomania and selflessness that characterized his attitude toward his young protégé. "You don't know his plays. But you will. All the world will know Gene's plays some day."

Almost lunatic with optimism, Jig departed for the Village in mid-September. Jack and Louise stayed a few weeks longer. Even on vacation Jack bustled about, finding a house to buy in nearby Truro, planning renovations, writing articles to pay for his extravagance. Poor Louise paid "visits" to Gene, unfettered by the fact that Jack's kidney operation was scheduled for November and that they planned a clandestine wedding before he went into the hospital. Louise saw no reason — including marriage — why the arrangement that had proven so satisfactory couldn't continue during the winter in the Village.

Gene also stayed on a few weeks after Jig's departure. After the desolate winter of 1915–1916, in only a few weeks in Provincetown he'd found a sensual mistress and a supportive producer. The constraints of his affair with Louise may have caused him some melancholy moments, but they healed his spirit. His relationship with Jig turned out to be even more salutary: no longer having to thrash around to escape his father, he could now focus on letting his genius thrive.

In late June Gene had left the Village a drunk—in late September he returned a playwright.

Gene moved into a one-room apartment at 38 Washington Square South, just a few doors down from Jack and Louise. He still kept his distance from the writers-and-artists crowd, but now he also stayed away from Terry and his other drinking companions at the Hell Hole.

Jig found a theater for the troupe on his first day back in the Village—"139 Macdougal Street leased by Provincetown Players!" he wrote Susan on September 19. "Hurray! Paid $50 first month's rent from Oct. 1st, so that much is settled!"

A block south of Washington Square and next door to the Liberal Club, 139 Macdougal was a former stable converted into a brownstone, and owned by Jenny Belardi, who had once thought of herself as an actress but who—anticipating the careers of so many Villagers—had turned to real estate instead. Taking over the three and a half rooms of the parlor floor, the Players knocked down partitions, making a fifteen-by-forty-four-foot auditorium of the first two rooms, constructed a ten-and-a-half-by-fourteen-foot stage in the third, and improvised a backstage in the tiny half room at the rear. The curtain?—a drop cloth. The box office?—a table in the entrance hall. They busily constructed plank seating for 140 spectators—tiered benches, supported on stilts, with wooden backs, "unparalleled," said one participant, "for discomfort." Dark gray paint, brightly decorated proscenium, primitive lighting (but no heating)—within a few weeks the theater was ready. They still needed space for more dressing rooms and offices. Luckily, several members of the group lived nearby and volunteered their apartments for quick changes. Neighbors soon became used to the sight of actors trooping up and down Macdougal in their costumes.

Jig may have started a revolution, but as far as the bureaucrats were concerned, he still had to adhere to the rules. Though established as a "theater club," and thus supposedly exempt from routine fire and building codes, the Players soon found themselves harassed by a round of stone-faced city inspectors, impervious to every reason, every argument, every-thing but a discreet envelope filled with cash. Jig tried charm instead. Remembered Susan Glaspell, "The person from the building department looked a little less impersonal as Jig talked to him of the plays out of Amer-ican life, quite as if this were one of the man's warm interests. The Irish po-liceman remained a friend to the last, more than once telling us what to do when we would have blundered." But the building inspector remained un-moved, and insisted that the proscenium arch be buttressed by a steel girder. This $200 expense, added to the $50 rent, left the players only $70 from the money they'd raised in Provincetown.

Ticket sales should finance the season and Jig tried to entice every-one he met to attend an evening's performance. He sent a circular to a thousand lucky New Yorkers, promising ten evenings of one-act plays for $4.

The response, while encouraging, was hardly overwhelming. But one day a matronly lady stopped by the theater, asked a few polite ques-tions, and left. Who was that? No one knew. It was Hutch's sister-in-law, in her capacity as president of the New York Stage Society, which decided on her recommendation to buy two hundred double subscriptions for $4 a seat, adding a bonanza of $1,600 to the Players' coffers. Jig didn't learn until some time later that she'd secretly been sent by Jack.

Their season now assured, in early October the Players voted on the opening program. Gene's *Bound East for Cardiff*, in which Hippolyte was cast as one of the sailors, headed the bill this time, with Louise's *The Game* and Floyd's *King Arthur's Socks*, a comic treatment of modern man-ners superimposed on medieval myth. Committed, as Jig had put it in his circular, to "the true amateur spirit," the players decided not to invite crit-ics, but after a long and contentious debate, they invited the few they re-spected to attend as paying customers.

On Friday, November 3, 1916, the Provincetown Players debuted with Floyd's farce, Jack as Death in Louise's allegory, and Jig as the dying Yank in Gene's saga of the sea. The audience cheered wildly, word of mouth spread, and the giddy Players were soon performing to packed houses. Ten days later Stephen Rathburn of the *Evening Sun* gave the troupe its first review. "Oyez! Hear Ye! Make way there! New players are come to town." Louise's effort was "so amateurish that the less said about it the better"—but he called Floyd's play "good fun" and found Gene's "sub-tly tense." "The first night," he reported, "they turned away ten limousines

... and on the nights the Stage Society was taken they have to install a carriage caller—in Macdougal Street!"

The limousines and carriages returned on November 17 for the opening of the second bill, one of the few times in his life Jack missed all the fun. On November 12 he had entered Johns Hopkins hospital in Baltimore to have his left kidney removed.

In the fall of 1916, Jack was suffering from a crisis of commitment—was this really the life he wanted to live? Though only in his twenties, he realized that his legend had already become a threat to his sense of self. But even his most ardent admirers, focusing on his robust activism, didn't know of the doubts, disillusionment, and despair that occasionally overwhelmed him. The causes he championed sometimes seemed hopeless, the public man's commitments sometimes threatened the private man's fulfillment. Part of him wanted to remain on the barricades of radicalism, but part wanted to retire to the realm of poetry.

Some verses Jack composed during this period and dedicated to Max spoke to this dilemma:

> There was a man, who, loving quiet beauty best,
> Yet could not rest
> For the harsh moaning of unhappy humankind,
> Fettered and blind—
> Too driven to know beauty and too hungry-tired
> To be inspired. . . .
> A vision of new splendor in the human scheme—
> A god-like dream—
> And a new lilt of happy trumpets in the strange
> Clangor of Change!

And shortly before entering the hospital, Jack wrote a poem about death entitled "Fog":

> Death comes like this I know—
> Snow-soft and gently cold;
> Impalpable battalions of thin mist,
> Light-quenching and sound-smothering and slow.

After the successful surgery, his Harvard friend Robert Benchley wrote, "Allow me to condole you on your recent bereavement. We never realize, I suppose, what a wonderful thing a kidney is until it is gone. How true that is of everything in life, after all, isn't it?" And Jack had a cheering secret too—after playing a particularly jolly Death in *The Game* for five nights on the Players' opening bill, he and Louise had taken the train to Peekskill and gotten married on November 9. Louise insisted on secrecy because her divorce from the dentist had not yet become final, because their Village friends hooted at marriage as an outmoded bourgeois convention, and, perhaps more pertinently, because she intended to continue her affair with Gene. "Hang on to this, lady," the clerk told her as he handed over the certificate, "you may need it some day."

Louise couldn't keep her marriage a secret from Gene for long, of course, but as a Villager also in on the secret put it, "We all had a rationale about sex—we had discovered Freud—and we considered being libidinous a kind of sacred duty." She soon found herself unable to perform her sacred duty, however—not out of commitment to Jack but because she fell ill. Many of their Village friends believed that her "illness" was a pregnancy, but it seems certain she suffered a tubal abscess. In any case, Jack worried more about her condition than his own, and the affection aroused by their twin illnesses made it clearer to the lovesick but guilt-ridden Gene that his great romance couldn't last.

Meanwhile, Jig plunged ahead with his lunatic schedule of three new plays every two weeks over a twenty-one-week season, a pace his playwrights couldn't maintain. Gene's *Before Breakfast* headlined the third bill, but Neith's *The Two Sons* was utterly unmemorable, and Alfred Kreymborg's *Lima Beans* split the audience squarely down the middle, those who hated it on one side, those who didn't understand it on the other.

The enthusiastic emphasis on amateurism, group participation, and new, native playwrights meant that any Villager could walk into the theater and get a hearing (and be rejected only if the work showed disconcerting signs of the slick professionalism of the despised commercial stage). It also meant that rehearsals lacked discipline, sets remained half-finished, and actors often disappeared the afternoon before opening night. Group participation gave everyone an equal voice, but as at Max's *Masses* it also created friction and chaos. The members began to mount works in smaller, more private clusters—even, dread word, in committees—and plays would show up on bills with many members wondering who'd approved that piece of trash.

Worst of all, Jig's conviction that legions of talented Villagers would write dozens of inspired plays proved wildly optimistic. Obsessed by the frantic scramble to produce three plays every two weeks, the Players had no time to wonder if the plays were worth producing. By midway in the first season it was obvious that the group most lacked what it had most depended on—gifted playwrights.

Jack's buoyant spirit was sorely missed, personal animosities flared up, morale plummeted, but Jig didn't give a moment's thought to giving up. Glimmers of encouragement came from the despised critics. N. P. Dawson in the *New York Globe* wrote: "The players are almost uniformly interesting. . . . There is nothing amateur about their literary qualities." The *New York Tribune*'s influential Heywood Broun, yet another member of Jack's Harvard class, reviewing the eighth bill—which included one of the group's most popular plays, *Cocaine*, in which a pair of Village addicts decide to commit suicide by turning on the gas, only to discover that the gas has been shut off because they were too poor to pay the bill—wrote: "An experiment is something which turns cinders into gold dust or explodes with a fearful crash and odor. In this sense the Provincetown Players have established a most efficient experimental theater. . . . There is only a little gold dust, but then there never is much gold dust."

But Jig was probably most heartened by an ear-steaming screed written for the *New York Herald* by none other than David Belasco, the nearly universally acknowledged (especially by himself) Great Man of the American Theater, and thus symbol of all Jig despised. Under the headline in the *New York Herald* "DAVID BELASCO SEES A MENACE TO TRUE ART OF THE STAGE IN TOY PLAYHOUSES AND LITTLE REPERTORY THEATERS," the impresario declared, "Theaters and acting organizations devoted to false ideals are not new, but never until this season have they been so vicious, vulgar, and degrading. . . . I have attended every one of these places devoted to the so-called 'new art,' whose clumsy and amateurish directors have decided to be 'different.' . . . This so-called new art of theater is but a flash in the pan of inexperience. It is the cubism of the theater—the wail of the incompetent and the degenerate. As cubism became the asylum of those pretenders in art who could not draw and had no conception of composition in painting, so 'new art of the theater' is the haven of those who lack experience and knowledge of the drama. . . . My opposition to this cult had made for me many enemies among the younger and inexperienced writers . . . but I must endeavor to protect our drama, the stage, and the legitimate theater of America from those who would make a freak of it. . . . O Art, Art, how many freakish things are committed in thy name!" If that was Belasco's reaction they must be on the right track!

Belasco was no less a despised symbol to Gene, and he, too, must have felt exhilarated by his enemies. Unhappily realizing that Louise's love was slipping away, remaining aloof from the troupe to which he owed so much and which depended upon his plays, even lapsing into binges with Terry and Louis, he nevertheless continued to write—whatever else he was, he was at last a playwright. Even to his father.

James attended *Bound East for Cardiff,* his son's New York debut, expecting nothing more than amateurish enthusiasm, but came away acknowledging Gene's talent. Greeting the Players backstage, he exclaimed with parental pride—"Yes, yes, I think the boy has something in him!" He managed to concede that he was impressed without making it sound condescending.

James went to rehearsals of Gene's second production, *Before Breakfast,* but showing how much he still had to learn, his professional advice largely consisted of adding melodramatic gestures and grandiloquent line readings. He also attended rehearsals of *Fog,* Gene's play on the fifth bill. William Carlos Williams, who acted with the troupe on occasion, noted with fascination that "during the rehearsal the father would often interrupt the course of the play and when he did the son would be closely attentive. God knows he had to be because the father made no bones about it. . . . [Gene] would leave the theater still talking with his father." That Gene didn't explode in rage at his father's interference certainly had less to do with respect for the old man's advice than self-respect for his own talent. As so often happens, the young man had finally won a measure of paternal approval precisely at the moment it no longer mattered.

Revolutions don't pay royalties, of course, and though he was the Players' leading asset, Gene was still living on his father's dole. Polly Holladay and Romany Marie, who ran the Brevoort Hotel's basement café, provided his meals free of charge, but he owed $46 in rent on his Washington Square room and skipped out to bunk with friends, leaving behind a trunkful of clothes and manuscripts that the landlady threw into the garbage. Gene soon felt suffocated by the Village, distracted by its bustle. He needed seclusion, companionship with his genius. Finally, in frustration, Gene fled to Provincetown—bleak in March, but at least he could breathe.

Jack's operation was a success. He moved back with Louise into their Village apartment and he was having trouble working, too—or at least Louise thought so. She wrote to him when he convalesced in Baltimore, "I was so afraid you might not get through it and I kept thinking to myself—the pity, the unpardonable pity you had always *wasted* yourself with Greenwich Villagers. . . . That's why I think it will be so fine to do *work* out here, uninterrupted." "Out here" referred to the house in Croton-on-Hudson they'd recently purchased, the very house only a few years earlier that Mabel had rented as a weekend retreat for herself and Jack.

Reluctantly, they sent Jig their resignations from the Provincetown Players. *Metropolitan Magazine* had commissioned Jack to write a series of articles from China, and Louise planned to travel with him. Other magazines deluged Jack with assignments to cover the war, but after two lengthy visits to the Continent he'd become convinced that the conflict was less a matter of liberty than of greed, spoils, and capitalist exploitation. In his articles in *The Masses*, in his letters, in his conversations, he passionately argued that "it is not our war."

On April 6, 1917, however, President Wilson and the U.S. Congress made it "our war," and Jack immediately devoted all his energy to the anti-war cause. Addressing rallies, taking part in demonstrations, testifying against conscription before congressional committees, he became a hero to the radical movement and a pariah to everyone else. The China trip was canceled, and many of the magazines that had pleaded for his services now hesitated to give him assignments.

Louise understood Jack's passion, she even shared it, but she couldn't help worrying about her own problems. Suddenly an outcast because of their anti-war stand, she also felt isolated in the Village because of her affair with Gene. Never popular with Jack's friends for winning his love, she was now actively disliked for betraying it. The last thing she expected to encounter was the double standard. What happened to that community of idealists she'd so longed to join? She could understand why so many Villagers supported the war effort, and even defended her brother against the taunts of her few friends when he visited her in uniform on his way to the front, but how could they pretend to support women's rights when they disapproved in her the behavior they admired in Jack?

Lonely, discontented, in May Louise told Jack she wanted to go to Provincetown herself for a few weeks. Jack knew that Gene was already there, and certainly guessed that they were resuming their affair, but understood her confusion too much to persuade her not to go. Gene greeted Louise with renewed hope, but a week later, she received a telegram from Jack—"Peach tree blooming and wrens have taken their house." The joyous tenderness of those few words, their unspoken respect for her independence, their poignant plea for her return, contrasted so dramatically with the gloomy, taciturn, and possessive love Gene offered that she hurried home to Croton, finding that Jack had gone out at dawn to pick wood violets and decorated the house for her arrival.

Their idyll didn't last long. Perhaps assuming that his honesty would help her overcome her guilt, perhaps letting her know that he claimed the same freedom for himself that he honored in her, Jack confessed that he had had a brief affair when Louise had been in Provincetown.

She had lied to Jack while Jack had been truthful to her, she'd carried on a nearly year-long affair while he'd merely slept with a woman whose name he could hardly remember, but she flew into a fury. Gene's name was unmentioned, but in a sense Gene was beside the point; even sexual jealousy wasn't the real issue. Maybe Louise unfairly applied a standard to Jack that she refused to apply to herself, but maybe, too, she saw in his behavior a deeper betrayal than in her own. She might well have reacted rationally, forgivingly, if Jack had told her he'd been seeing someone he loved—yes, it would have hurt her deeply, but how much worse that he'd hurt her for an experience he called meaningless. And maybe she sensed that loving a man so much threatened her hard-won, but never wholly stable, sense of independence—and thus resented Jack as much for her need for him as for his betrayal of her.

Shaken by the episode, dismayed to find herself in the position of so many supposedly "liberated" Village women—enraged at clinging to the men in their lives—Louise once more decided to go away for a while. She got credentials as a foreign correspondent to cover the war "from a woman's point of view" for the Bell Syndicate. Jack felt too guilty to stand in her way. He paid her fare, arranged interviews with friends in Europe, and saw her off in early June.

Even before her ship sailed, Louise wrote a hasty note. "Please believe me Jack—I'm going to try like the devil to pull myself together over there and come back and act like a responsible human being. . . . It's a terrible thing to love as much as I do."

"Dearest of honies," Jack answered, "Got here to find your pitiful little note—it isn't you who must learn, my honey, but me. In lots of ways we are very different, and we must both try to realize that—while loving each other. But of course in this last awful business, you were humanly right and I was wrong. I know that one thing I cannot bear any more is consciously to hurt you, honey."

Another letter from Jack, referring to a woman he'd met in Washington, D.C.: "She wanted to make love. I didn't and couldn't. I've been true all right. But I think perhaps there's something terribly wrong with me—that I may be a little crazy, for I had a desire once, just the other day, I can't tell you how awful, how wretched that made me feel. You see, my dearest lover, I was once a free person. . . . Then along came women, and they set out deliberately, as they always instinctively do, to break that armor down, to make the artist a human being and dependent upon human beings. Well, they did it, and so now without a mate I am half a man, and sterile. (Now, honey, there is no use denying this. It is true I'm not regretful for it—I'd rather be human than artist.)

"I feel that I am always on the verge of something monstrous," he continued, "this is not as bad as it seems, dear—it's just that no one I love has ever been able to let me express myself fully, freely, and trust that expression. . . . I realize how disappointed and cruelly disillusioned you have been. You thought you were getting a hero—and you only got a vicious little person who is fast losing any spark he may have had."

Jack's love had shriveled under Mabel's bondage and blossomed under Louise's openness, but in either case he couldn't help feeling that he was being punished for cherishing freedom. The difference was that Mabel, irrationally jealous, even suffocating, punished him herself and thus drove him away, while Louise, equally hurt and with better cause, but understanding and forgiving, forced him to punish himself and thus drew him closer. Since Jack knew almost nothing about women's erotic needs—like most Village male feminists, he fought for women's sexual freedom while still believing that sex was a gift women bestowed upon men—nothing assured him that he'd take all the blame for their sexual fidelity problems quite as much as her insistence that it was all her fault. Despondent over Louise's departure, despairing at the progress of the war, Jack could hardly be expected to understand that at last he'd found a love and a cause that would sustain him for the rest of his life.

Jig had reason to be discouraged, too—Jack had gone, Gene had gone, the Players' morale had gone, many of their principles had gone, and he was only midway through his first season. But like many great leaders, Jig's genius lay largely in his stubbornness.

In midwinter, a young woman who'd graduated from Stanford came to New York to become an actress. Nina Moise wasn't looking for a revolution, she was looking for a job, so she wrote Jig a note, and presented herself as an experienced director.

In spite of his prejudice against professionalism, he was impressed by Nina and knew the time had come to admit that the Players could benefit from theatrical expertise. To her astonishment, such fundamentals as blocking were virtually unknown to the poetic sensibilities of the Players. "They had a very definite idea that anything one did in life could be done on the stage. If people stood in front of each other and bumped each other in a room, why not do it on the stage—which is exactly what they were doing."

Convincing Jig that actors didn't have to step on one another's toes in order to express their integrity, Nina almost immediately took over rehearsals of the sixth bill. She took charge of the seventh bill as well—"the war bill," the players called it, including *The Sniper*, an anti-war play Gene had written in Baker's seminar—and was elected chairman of the producing committee in late February. Her calm competence, perfectly complementing Jig's volatile ebullience, not only lifted the Players' spirits but impressed outsiders as well. "I wasn't paid anything," Nina said, then immediately added a remark repeated by tens of thousands of Villagers in the next half century, "but I rarely went north of 14th Street again."

And so, with Nina's help, the first Village season of the Provincetown Players came to a close. They'd sought out the new, and untried, and it worked. Everyone rotated functions. They'd fallen short of Jig's vision in some ways—neglecting larger social issues and focusing on comedies of bohemia in a kind of narcissism, stressing experimentation so much that it became a kind of orthodoxy in itself—but Susan said, "Even knowing we did it, I am disposed to say what we did that first year couldn't be done."

Yet few of the Players seemed pleased. At the tempestuous meeting a few nights after the final production, the members split into two camps, the purists and the pragmatists. The principles and the memberships of the Players would remain in a constant state of flux for the rest of the troupe's existence, with Jig the only one who understood that nothing mattered if they didn't stay afloat. He could only point out that a certain degree of skill hardly compromised the amateur spirit and that even in a collective certain responsibilities had to be delegated. The stance united them—at least temporarily—and soon the Players closed ranks behind another manifesto before dispersing until the fall.

"We have a theater because we want to do our own thing in our own way," Jig wrote in a widely distributed circular. "We have no ambition to go uptown and become a 'real theater.' We believe that hard work done in the play spirit of the pure joy of doing it is bound to have a freshness not found in the commercial theater."

Jig and Susan returned to Provincetown for the summer of 1917 and found Gene and Terry living rent-free in an apartment over John Francis's store on Commercial Street, still subsisting on handouts from James plus $50 Gene had made on a short story for *Seven Arts* magazine. Gene seemed adrift, writing a bit but mostly drinking, swimming, brooding over the war and Louise. The only thing he ingested, beyond booze, seemed to be oatmeal. His bout with tuberculosis made him ineligible for the draft, but his anti-war sentiments made him eligible for suspicion—while wandering over the dunes he'd even been arrested as a possible German spy. As for Louise, he seemed to his friends to get a certain perverse pleasure out of his role as rejected lover, but when she wrote him upon her return to the Village in late summer that she planned to leave with Jack for Russia almost immediately, no one doubted that his pain was real.

Because of his fierce stand against the war, Jack couldn't get an assignment to cover the impending revolution from any of the commercial magazines. *The Masses* had managed to raise enough money to fund the trip, however, and Gene's hope also departed with Jack and Louise. He sat on a bench one afternoon with a mentally retarded boy he'd befriended. "What's beyond Europe?" the boy asked. "The horizon," Gene answered. "Yes," the boy persisted, "but what's beyond the horizon?" Gene didn't know the answer to the question, but he once more began to transform his loss into art. *Beyond the Horizon*, written several years later, would become his first enduring play.

In the fall of 1917, Jig sent out another circular. "We mean to go on giving artists of the theater—playwrights, actors, roaches [directors], designers of set and costume—a chance to work out their ideas in freedom. . . . We are still not afraid to fail in things worth trying. We will let this theater die before we let it become another voice of mediocrity. If any writers in this country—already of our group or still to be attracted to it—are capable of bringing down fire from heaven to the stage, we are here to receive and help."

Even with a rise in prices from $4 to $5 for a season's subscription, the response was so encouraging—nine hundred members, double the first season—that the Players could afford to renovate the theater. And thanks to the munificence of the banker Otto Kahn, a freelance Maecenas of the American arts, they even added a small restaurant on the third floor, its sixty-cent meals prepared by Gene's old friend Christine Ell.

The second season of the Provincetown Players opened on November 2, 1917—almost the very day Jack and Louise were witnessing the outbreak of the Russian Revolution in Petrograd—featuring Gene's *The Long Voyage Home*. His *In the Zone* had opened the Washington Square

Players season only a week earlier. (In a neat reversal, the Provincetowners had turned it down as not experimental enough.) A headline in the Sunday *Times* asked, "Who Is Eugene O'Neill?" Burns Mantle of the *Mail* declared Gene "a genius."

Jig continued commandeering recruits for the cause, "anyone fired with an unquenchable desire to become a thespian," said Alfred Kreymborg, "and even anyone who had no such ambition." In a letter to Edgar Lee Masters, Jig wrote, "What you did in 'Spoon River'—a direct, first hand, new version of our new life, is what we are seeking to do on our little amateur stage. . . . No one has brought to the stage so much straight truth of life as you brought to the pages of 'Spoon River.' That truth would be immeasurably powerful on the stage. Can you do it? . . . I am sure we could help you if you were with us."

Villagers strolling down Macdougal Street encountered Jig trying to drag them into the theater. Didn't you ever dream of writing? Performing? Making costumes? Just take five minutes to let me show you our theater! Such haphazard conscription led to haphazard production, of course—as the writer Edna Kenton put it, "Some of the very worst acting on any stage has been on the stage of [the Provincetown Playhouse], and some of the best"—but for every new member who learned that his dramatic aspirations were unwarranted, another discovered gifts he never knew he possessed.

One new member arrived more conventionally, through a casting call for an ingenue to play opposite Jimmy in Floyd's *The Angel Intrudes*. "A slender little girl with red-gold hair . . . read Annabelle's lines," Floyd recalled. She left her name, 'Edna Millay'. Soon Vincent, as the Villagers called her, was joined by her sister, Norma, who became one of the troupe's leading actresses.

Shortly after the final curtain on opening nights, half the Village would cram into Christine's restaurant. Jig would ritually dip his cup into the giant punchbowl and down the first drink. "It's for the good of the Provincetown Players," he'd parody his own pontifications while raising his glass. "I am always ready to sacrifice myself for a cause." Though some members questioned Jig's assurances that such communal carousing descended from the religious revels of Periclean Athens, all joined in the convivial spirit.

It wouldn't have been a revolution without a splinter group, of course, and early in 1918 a number of dissidents formed the Other Players. Financed by Alfred Kreymborg, still smarting over the debacle of *Lima Beans*, this poetic fringe complained that the Players were "not sufficiently daring and elastic." Granted the use of the Players' theater, the Others mounted three pieces experimenting with structure, language, and movement. *Manikin and Minikin*, Alfred's "Duologue in Bisque," juxtaposed British and Bostonian accents and featured "an ancient clock whose ticks act as the metronome." Kathleen Cannell's *Static Dances*, presented under the pseudonym Rihani, lived up to its title. "I never moved from one spot," Kathleen said. "All the movement was for the head, torso, arms, and hands." Vincent Millay's *Two Slatterns and a King* picked up things a bit, with the two Millay sisters playing the slatterns. *Jack's House*, a "melo-poem" by Alfred, co-starring Rihani and Vincent, rounded out the evening. The production played to sold-out houses, but when Alfred tried to move the company uptown—foreshadowing the fantasies of hundreds of Village troupes in the next half-century, and the Provincetown Players only three years later—Broadway audiences proved unready for static dances and melo-poems, and the Other Players quickly went broke.

During the winter of 1917–1918—Gene's third in the Village—the joyous rebelliousness of the bohemians and radicals began to fade. Commercialization was well under way, the tourists had discovered the titillations of immorality, the poseurs had learned how to capitalize on unconventionality. More important, the war and the Bolshevik revolution splintered the Village sensibility. Ebullient insurgency turned bitter, despairing, and romantic idealism became fevered, dogmatic, apocalyptic. Many Villagers deserted the anti-war cause, and those who remained found themselves increasingly isolated or hounded by the authorities. While Jig was preparing another season, Jack and Max and Floyd were under indictment in federal court. And Gene brooded over the loss of Louise.

Now virtually living in the back room of the Hell Hole for weeks at a time, Gene drank himself into a stupor. He could write only fitfully, without enthusiasm or focus, and destroyed the three dismal plays he did manage to complete during the winter.

When he wanted to pour out his soul, he turned to women—sometimes Christine Ell, sometimes Nina Moise (to whom he confided in one of their chaste 5:00 A.M. talks that Louise was "the only woman I love or will ever love"), but most often a new arrival, an assistant to Max and Floyd at *The Masses*, a willowy twenty-year-old named Dorothy Day.

Raised as a Republican and Episcopalian, Dorothy turned socialist and suffragist as an undergraduate, dropped out to become a reporter, was jailed for picketing the White House, moved to the Village while still in her teens, and got the job at *The Masses*. Dorothy was independent, idealistic, unconventional, but beneath the fun-loving bohemian rebel lived a somber, mystic spirit, unfulfilled by work, uninterested in revels, yearning for grace. Gene and Dorothy soon discovered that though one was fleeing God, the other seeking Him, there was a place where their souls over-lapped. Introduced by Mike Gold—who, like many men in the Village, wanted to marry her—the two soon became constant companions.

Their closest bond was formed by Francis Thompson's "The Hound of Heaven," the fearfully exhilarating poem about the pursuit of God through flight, which Gene recited to Dorothy from memory.

> *I fled Him, down the nights and down the days;*
> *I fled Him, down the arches of the years;*
> *I fled Him, down the labyrinthine ways*
> *Of my own mind.*

Once, more because he seemed to think it was expected of him than because he desired her, Gene halfheartedly suggested that they sleep together, but Dorothy, knowing he still longed for Louise and wanted companionship more than romance, quietly changed the subject. "He couldn't bear to be alone," she said. "Only an hour after I'd left him to go to work . . . he'd be calling me from the Hell Hole or some other bar to come back." And come back she would.

Blessed in friendship, Gene remained tormented in love. As if he could find carnal fulfillment only when accompanied by emotional turmoil, by the linked passions of love and hate, by the high drama of possessiveness, rejection, and reconciliation, he continued to portray himself as enslaved to Louise. So urgent was his need for a transfiguring love that it carried with it the threat of emotional annihilation, leaving him with no recourse but to repel the very love he sought—or find his sense of self in brooding over betrayal and loss. Into this psychic morass wandered a shy, insecure, and unsuspecting twenty-four-year-old woman named Agnes Boulton.

Raised in Philadelphia, the daughter of a painter, and herself a widowed mother of a two-year-old girl, Agnes came to the Village in October 1917 to find a part-time job while trying to make her name as a writer of short stories for pulp magazines. She already knew Harry Kemp and Mary Pyne and Christine Ell and on their recommendation took a room at the Brevoort Hotel on Fifth Avenue and 8th Street. One evening, having agreed to meet Christine at the Hell Hole at 10:30, she took a table and casually lit a cigarette. Within minutes she sensed that a man was staring at her. How could Agnes know that Gene was thinking how much she looked like Louise?

Gene's brooding scrutiny began to disturb Agnes, and she was just about to leave when Christine breezed in and embraced her two friends. They were soon joined by Jamie O'Neill, who of course was soused. When the foursome finally broke up near dawn, Jamie staggered off with Christine and Gene offered to escort Agnes back to the Brevoort. They stood in awkward silence before the entrance when suddenly Gene burst into a torrent of talk. His family, his plays, his loneliness, it all came pouring out. "I want to spend every night of my life from now on with *you*," he said before disappearing into the streets.

Several days later, at a party at the Provincetown Theater, Agnes glimpsed Gene standing in a corner, but he hardly seemed to recognize her. "Hello, remember me?" she asked. If Gene wanted a woman who'd enter into an affair based on a struggle for dominance, he'd met his match. He excused himself for a moment and took a quick swig in the next room. Making sure he had everyone's attention, he stepped onto a chair, opened the glass face of a large clock on the mantelpiece, and dramatically turned back the hour hands while intoning "Turn back the universe and give me yesterday!" Agnes suddenly sensed the meaning of his ostentatiously forlorn behavior. Gene wanted her to think he couldn't get over Louise, he wanted to make her jealous, he wanted to hurt her—yes, he was falling in love with her!

Dorothy was skeptical from the first. Agnes was "much better-looking than Louise," she said, "but without Louise's brains and sophistication. . . . Gene fell in love with Louise first of all because Jack loved her. Gene needed a hopeless love. . . . So I hoped [Agnes] would not be too hurt." Mary Pyne went so far as to confide to Agnes that "Louise will come back from Russia and want him back. She is much more clever than you, and they were very much in love. . . . [Gene] may want to go back to the pleasure of being tortured."

The pleasure of being tortured was hardly eluding the new couple, especially in their all too public quarrels and Gene's sudden outbursts of abuse. At a small party, Hutch saw Gene jerk Agnes to her feet and push her from the room, apparently in a jealous rage at her conversation with another man. At the Hell Hole, the habitués saw Agnes suddenly bolt from their table and run out the door, Gene in angry pursuit.

Gene had told the Players that once more he planned to leave for Provincetown even though it was still midwinter. Jig and the others encouraged him to leave soon as possible. They depended on his plays and they knew he'd drink away another winter if he stayed. What they didn't know was that Gene had asked Agnes to go with him. The only reason he didn't depart immediately was a long-awaited reunion with his old friend Louis Holladay. Having served his jail sentence for violation of the liquor laws, and having been told by *his* Louise that she wouldn't marry him unless he sobered up and showed he could hold a job, Louis had spent several months in Oregon drying out and running an apple orchard. Now he had returned—cured of his alcoholism and with enough money saved to get married, and he invited his old friends to join him in celebrating his happiness at the Hell Hole.

On January 22, they all gathered at the saloon—Gene, Agnes, Dorothy, Christine, Terry, Charles Demuth. Expecting their old friend to be in ebullient spirits, they found Louis oddly subdued and drinking heavily. He quietly announced that Louise had met another man—a composer named Edgard Varèse—and she'd broken off their engagement.

Before or after the now despondent party moved from the Hell Hole to Romany Marie's, Louis took a small bottle out of his pocket, tapped some white powder onto the back of his hand, and snorted it. "What's that?" someone asked. "Heroin," Louis casually replied. Most members of the group suspected that he had gotten it from Terry, and according to one witness, he and Demuth joined Louis in using it. It would have been just like Terry—a friend in despair, a friend saying he needed to obliterate his pain, even intimating that he wanted to commit suicide—kindly old Terry would shrug his shoulders and produce the drug.

Agnes had already gone home. Gene had left in a fury the moment he realized Louis was sniffing heroin; only Dorothy and a few others remained, too far gone themselves to understand what was happening, or, in Dorothy's case, feeling she might be needed. Louis continued to inhale the heroin, and at around 6:30 in the morning, he began to foam at the mouth. Within minutes he was dead.

Marie called for an ambulance. Even though a policeman had already arrived, Dorothy surreptitiously removed the bottle of heroin from Louis's pocket. Polly and the doctor showed up, and she told him that her brother had chronic heart trouble. On the death certificate, the cause of Louis's death was listed as "chronic endocarditis."

Louis's fatal overdose, whether accidental or suicidal, traumatized the Villagers. Hutch was breakfasting at the Brevoort when Demuth "came in looking like a crazy man, I never saw such a look of complete horror on any human being's face." Christine fell into a hysterical fit. Dorothy moved out of the Village and took a job in a city hospital, now on the road that would eventually lead to the founding of the Catholic Workers. At the Provincetown Theater "the feeling of death" lingered for weeks. Could this be the result of the Village's much-vaunted freedom?

Gene had no illusion about the freedom or innocence of the Village. As far as he was concerned, Terry had virtually killed Louis. But unable to confront the turmoil of his emotions, he tried to drink himself into oblivion. After several days, he realized he had to leave. He managed to pull himself together long enough to pack his bags, pick up Agnes, and take the boat to Provincetown. He had to get back to work—writing was the only thing that could save him. And when the boat slowly pulled away Eugene O'Neill's romance with Greenwich Village came to an end.

Taking stock at a season-ending meeting, the Provincetown Players could point to the acclaim Gene's and Susan's plays had received as a sign of artistic achievement and to the $4,515 box office take as a sign of fiscal stability. "All receipts . . . were consumed in putting on the seven bills of the season," Jig reported—"nothing left on hand to cover summer's rent." But merely surviving counted as a triumph.

The trend away from the principles of amateurism, spontaneity, and collectivism continued. Jig was reelected president and given expanded powers, and a professional secretary was hired to run the operation in a more businesslike manner. The Players' principles were further eroded when they decided after another bristling debate to seek a larger audience for their third season. Critics would be invited, posters would be put up, a publicity machine would be activated. The ostensible purpose was to put the group on sounder financial footing, and the unstated though friction-provoking goal was to receive recognition for their personal contributions.

So Jig began yet another fund-raising drive and sent out another stirring circular to attract more members. Both projects proved successful. Contributions of $5 and $10 had slowly accumulated $1,700—little over half of what they needed—when Albert C. Barnes, a Philadelphia art collector and avid theatergoer, came through with a $1,000 donation. And when Mrs. Belardi offered the Players a four-story building three doors down at 133 Macdougal for $400 a month, and discreetly intimated that she well understood the difficulty artistic temperaments had with prompt payments, Jig jubilantly announced the move for the 1918–1919 season. Yet in modifying their purpose, the Provincetown Players had moved almost imperceptibly from an emphasis on process to an emphasis on product. Even Jig could not have foreseen—though in revolutions based on artistic principles it sometimes seems inevitable—that expansion actually signaled the beginning of the end.

Every organization inspired by a charismatic leader needs a practical, stabilizing influence behind the scenes, and when Nina Moise announced she was leaving the troupe to work for the Red Cross in California, many feared that the creative chaos would soon degenerate into directionless fervor. Fortunately, Mary Eleanor Fitzgerald, Emma Goldman's former secretary, whom they'd hired as an office manager, turned out to be one of those people with bourgeois talents often found at the center of bohemian causes. Fitzi, as everyone called her, a tall, broad-shouldered, auburn-haired woman in her forties, with no artistic ambitions of her own, could handle the day-to-day operations of the Players with a serene indulgence that placated the artistic temperaments of the troupe. "What are the geniuses and near geniuses up to now?" she'd ask, and orders that might have been resented coming from Jig were promptly carried out. With Jig officially installed as director and Fitzi as executive secretary, the third season promised to be even more successful than the first two.

To no one's surprise—and to Jig's pride rather than dismay—Broadway producers had begun to woo Gene, the downtown "genius." Another of Professor Baker's former students had even optioned *Beyond the Horizon* for a possible uptown production with John Barrymore. Gene's first full-length play finished during the winter and spring of 1918, *Horizon* dealt with two brothers in a bitter father-son conflict who loved the same woman, but though the script suffered from Gene's usual contrivance and verbosity, it revealed for the first time his capacity to transform personal agony into tragic art. Though not produced until 1920, when it won him his first Pulitzer Prize, *Horizon* clearly signaled to Jig and the Players that Gene's talent would soon take him beyond their small experimental theater.

Louise was as drawn to drama as Gene, and upon returning from Russia in February 1918, and hearing that he had departed for Provincetown with another woman she immediately wrote him an impassioned letter avowing that she'd made a terrible mistake in leaving him, and concluding—after promising to forgive him for picking up some girl to soothe his loss—that she desperately needed to see him. She loved Jack, she loved Gene, but she loved more the image of herself as a beloved romantic heroine pursued by two gallant leading men. Jack was too trusting, to be drawn into this kind of emotional morass, so her lies to him had to be straightforward—she loved only him, Gene was just a friend. As for Gene, she instinctively realized that the more complicated the web the more completely he'd be caught, so her lies to him were devious and manipulative.

Partly to hurt Agnes, partly to protect himself, Gene showed her the letter. He knew Agnes was jealous of Louise—she'd despaired to friends that Gene was still in love with "that girl"—but he also knew that she had too much common sense to be taken in by Louise's ruses. For one thing, that story that Jack and Louise lived together like brother and sister. How could Gene believe such a ridiculous fabrication? He must have wanted Agnes to persuade him not to return to Louise, but still he argued that he owed it to Louise to go back to New York to talk to her. Shouldn't he explain that he was in love with Agnes? Shouldn't he at least tell Louise in person that their affair was over? But Agnes was adamant.

In another letter, Louise intimated that she'd told Jack she was leaving him for Gene, that Jack understood and gave them his blessing. The struggle between the attraction of torment and the dictates of reason flared up once more in Gene's volatile psyche, but soon he was able to reassure Agnes, with halfhearted conviction, that he wasn't going to leave her, and he stayed up half the night composing a letter to Louise. Oh, how they'd loved one another, he wrote. But he was now in love with Agnes. Furthermore, a trip to the Village wasn't convenient at the moment since he was finishing work on a new play. Why didn't Louise come up to Provincetown instead? Satisfied that he'd hit upon the right tone, Gene showed the letter to Agnes before mailing it.

Louise's reply renewed her protestations of love, but ended with the retort that a trip to Provincetown wasn't particularly convenient for her. But nothing is quite as shameless as hurt pride. Louise told Village friends she'd thrown Gene out of her apartment and had found him next morning lying drunkenly on her doorstep. In fact, Gene went back to work with surprising equanimity, and a few weeks later, on April 12, he and Agnes were quietly married in Provincetown. Louise burned all Gene's letters and they never saw each other again.

But if Jig thought Gene had settled comfortably into marriage, he was mistaken. The jealous outbursts and possessive rages that had characterized his courtship of Agnes continued on the Cape. He would show up unexpectedly as she lunched with friends, berate her for leaving him alone, and literally drag her home, then, after a period of remorseful tenderness, would abuse her with melodramatic tirades like "Go back to the gutter you came from!" Alcohol couldn't be blamed—despite occasional binges, he fell into an ascetic routine in Provincetown. "Altogether too much damn nonsense had been written since the beginning of time about the dissipation of artists," he claimed years later. "The artist drinks, when he drinks at all, for relaxation, forgetfulness, excitement, for any purpose except for his art. . . . I never try to write a line when I'm not strictly on the wagon. . . . This is not morality, it's plain physiology."

No, Gene's drinking resulted from, more than caused, his tempestuous relationships with women. Many of his friends felt he demanded too much—an idealized partner who would devote herself to his genius, part muse, part typist, part housewife, part mistress, part madonna, and total devotee. Agnes was willing to go even that far. What she could never satisfy—because at bottom it expressed a need to be *dissatisfied*—was Gene's unspoken, unconscious desire for the high drama of love-hate, exhilaration-torture, adoration-contempt. His changing but contradictory impulses meant that his partner didn't merely have to submerge her personality to his, she also had to be his companion in ambivalence, a kind of psychic counter-twin who would provide him with the gratifications of opposition. He longed for utter union with a woman, yet pushed her away when she got too close. He dreaded being left alone, yet retreated into unbreachable solitude. He yearned for complete commitment, yet soon complained of claustrophobia. None of this passion found more than momentary outlet in sex. Gene's fascination with prostitutes and his unwavering devotion to earth-mother figures like Christine and Fitzi—two types he tended to merge—meant that he could relate to women only when he consigned them to narrowly defined roles. And when they violated the images he'd imposed upon them, he felt betrayed. He made women believe he desperately needed their love, that they could soothe the agony that clung to him like an aura. But they never understood that he cherished that agony. He seemed incapable of entering into a relationship with a woman without rage, without cruelty, without pain.

Throughout the summer and early fall of 1918, Gene remained largely oblivious to the activities of the Players, but when he left Provincetown in the late fall, choosing to live in New Jersey, he found himself involved in the controversy over his new play. He'd written *Where the Cross Is Made* to lead off the Players' third season. Far from the "strong" O'Neill play Jig was counting on, *Cross* carried the unconventional a bit too far. Without a trace of irony Gene described the play as an "experiment in treating the audience as insane." The production history of *Cross* was "one prolonged argument," but Gene prevailed. One critic wrote that any theatergoer who wanted to "enjoy the sensation of going mad" would "find the want supplied" down in the Village.

The Players' third season ended with yet another deficit and more internal discord. The general outline of the problem was presciently described in an article in *The Nation* in May 1919. "The Little Theater movement is now in its second and perhaps its most difficult stage.... The voluntary character of the Provincetown Players is one of their chief assets. If they reorganize, as is probable, and decide to pay their actors, they must make more money, and the need of money begets a caution in production which limits, if it does not nullify, the purely experimental character of the enterprise.... To justify a paid company they will be tempted to give more ambitious productions, which promise a wider appeal, and will be forced to turn ... from the immaturity of the native playwright to the finished product of Europe."

The rift between the two groups of Players was rapidly widening. Jig assumed a permanent rebellion against the official culture, but many of the younger members, feeling that the official culture could be reformed from within, wanted to find their place in the larger world. The debate initially raged over the issue of amateurism. Those who wanted a career in the theater, and saw their work with the Players as a kind of apprenticeship, found Jig's devotion to amateurism less liberating than inhibiting. Those who wanted to continue an emphasis on experimentation noticed that Jig was now scheduling plays of almost commercial conventionality. Those who believed in group decision-making felt that he was committed to democracy only so long as no one disagreed with him.

Increasingly embittered, Jig began to talk about devoting more of his energies to his own writing. In the late spring of 1919, he announced a Season of Youth for the following winter, with Jimmy and Ida in charge. Making the best of a bad situation, he described the change as a new experiment, grumbling "We never meant to do it forever," and departed for Provincetown.

In Truro, Jig worked on a fresco on the walls of his cottage depicting the history of theater—"Theater born of Primitive Dance. Theater hardening into Church. Pure Dead Church. Church giving birth to Theater. Pure Dead Theater. Theater transforming itself into Living Church." Still obsessed with "the oneness of all men's minds," he studied the Swiss alchemist Paracelsus, experimented with automatic writing, and disappeared for days at a time into the occult.

Jack made a short visit to the Cape, and he, too, was despondent.

His *Ten Days That Shook the World* had been published that spring to great acclaim, but his ceaseless work on behalf of the revolution, particularly his well-publicized hostile testimony before a Senate committee investigating Bolshevik propaganda in the United States, had accelerated his transformation from a famous journalist into a notorious revolutionary. Though the most prominent victim of the Red Scare, unable to obtain assignments from the national magazines, and worried about money for the first time in his life, Jack refused to forsake his principles. "I wish I could stay here," he told Susan and Jig. "Maybe it will surprise you, but what I really want is to write poetry." But when they encouraged him to heed his impulses, he responded wearily, "I've promised too many people"—and after only a few days, the last time Susan and Jig would see him, he returned to the Village to plunge back into his work.

Gene was withdrawing from Jig as well. He hadn't broken with the Players, but it was only a matter of time before the despised uptown theater would woo away the playwright Jig so lovingly nurtured, an inevitability Jig had difficulty regarding as a betrayal since he could no longer pretend he didn't feel envy. Gene was also enjoying a newfound domestic comfort. Agnes was expecting a child in the fall, and when the couple returned to the Cape in the spring of 1919, James, as a surprise gift for his grandchild, had purchased the converted coast guard station from Mabel Dodge. In his relative tranquillity at Peaked Hill, the name he gave his new home, Gene didn't even spend much time with Terry, whom he established for the summer in a nearby shed. Terry and Agnes didn't particularly take to each other, Terry having no use for women who dragged home one's drinking companions and Agnes dismayed by the temptations Terry offered. Well, if he'd lost a friend to pick up his tab, Terry had other resources. He filled jars with blueberries, added yeast, and buried them in the sand to let the concoction ferment. Weeks later, he put his ear to the ground to hear if the fizzing had stopped and raised a jar to his lips. On one occasion, impatient with nature, Terry tried to separate out wood alcohol from shellac through a homemade centrifuge device he'd heard about from Jack London, only to discover, when he greedily imbibed the drink, that his mouth was glued shut and his tongue was stuck to the roof of his mouth.

Agnes regarded it as one of her duties to gradually distance Gene from his drinking cronies, and not the least of their difficulties over the next several years was that Gene implicitly asked her to provide this kind of protection, then chafed when she did so. On more than one occasion, Agnes made the frantic trip to the Village and spent hours trying to track him down, the trail usually leading to the Hell Hole or the Working Girls'

Home, where his buddies tried to hide him from the woman who'd once been indifferent to his work but who now saw herself as its guardian.

Even when Prohibition had closed many of his hangouts, Gene remained in daily danger. Tom Wallace, the proprietor of the Hell Hole, boarded up its windows, made a discreet "contribution" to Tammany Hall, and continued to serve his regulars under the guise of running a drugstore. Luke O'Connor ostentatiously locked the front door of the Working Girls' Home, while a steady stream of patrons entered through the side door. Gene's new favorite was conveniently located around the corner from the Provincetown Playhouse, presided over by a former Hudson Duster, now bootlegger, named Spanish Willie.

Back at the Playhouse, the Season of Youth proceeded with a professionalism rebuking the "personal, slightly haphazard methods of the first years" under Jig. The roster of authors presented in the six bills — including two plays by Gene, three by Djuna Barnes, and one each by Vincent Millay, Edna Ferber, Alfred Kreymborg, Lawrence Langner, Mike Gold, and a young poet named Wallace Stevens — seems impressive, but only Vincent's *Aria da Capo*, a satiric harlequinade, lived up to the standards the group had set for itself. Few of the other plays proved more than mediocre, and the critic Burns Mantle concluded that "these earnest amateurs [are] not living up to their promise of a few seasons ago."

Reacting "smartly to the critics' whip," Jimmy complained bitterly that unless native writers submitted substantially better scripts to the Players, "the hitherto American theater on Macdougal Street will be adulterated" by European work.

Looking for a miracle, the Players were confronted by a catastrophe. The IRS descended with an audit based on 1917 war tax legislation affecting noncharitable and noneducational institutions engaged in public entertainment. Believing themselves a private club, the Players had failed to collect the required ten percent tax on admissions. The legal battle continued for months, but in the end the IRS submitted a bill for $5,000, most of which the stunned Players managed to pay off before the books were finally closed on the case in 1923.

The Broadway production of *Beyond the Horizon* claimed most of Gene's attention, and in June he received a telegram notifying him that he'd won the Pulitzer Prize for drama. In February, his father had suffered a stroke and tests revealed that he had cancer of the intestines. Shortly after the Pulitzer announcement, James returned to New London to die. Gene's award momentarily raised James's spirits—to one visitor he whispered, with the merest semblance of a smile, "Between us, I didn't think he'd amount to anything." But his last words to Gene revealed the bitterness of his final years: "Eugene—I'm going to a better sort of life—this sort of life—here—all froth—no good—rottenness!" Those dying words, Gene said, "are . . . seared on my brain—a warning from the Beyond to remain true to the best that is in me though the heavens fall."

Gene also had been working on a play called *The Emperor Jones* throughout most of the spring and summer, and in August, in Provincetown, he told Jig and Susan he had an unusual new play he wanted to show them.

Virtually a monologue, the play deals with a black Pullman porter wanted for murder who flees to a tropical island, sets up a dictatorship, and tries to escape when his subjects revolt. Trapped in the jungle, Brutus Jones succumbs to superstitious fear, then to primitive terror, and is finally murdered by his victims. Though superficially conforming to the stereotypes of the darkie, the protagonist conveys Gene's conviction that a hunted savage lives just beneath mankind's civilized veneer.

An intermissionless, one-hour play with only one major character, and that character a black man, an experiment violating all the conventions of structure, theme, and even casting—who else could mount this script but the Provincetown Players? Entranced by the play's hypnotic theatricality, Jig exclaimed to Susan the next morning, "This is what I have been waiting for—a play to call forth the utmost each one can do, and fuse all into unity. This marks the success of the Provincetown Players! Gene . . . wrote it to compel us to the untried, to do the 'impossible.' " That very afternoon he caught a train to New York to begin preparations for *The Emperor Jones*.

Jig was back in his element, but he discovered that the rest of the Players were reluctant to relinquish the reins. No one doubted Jig's description of *The Emperor Jones* as a masterpiece, but when he began to talk euphorically of a dome for the play, he soon found himself at odds with the entire company.

"We listened to Jig, truly a madman, telling us over and over and over that we must risk our all in a dome for *The Emperor*," said a member of the troupe. Jig's folly, they called it—it'd never work, it'd be too expensive, at the very least it should be postponed.

The dome, a celebrated device in the European avant-garde, had never been tried in America. Usually constructed of plaster and hanging in an elongated semicircle from the ceiling of the stage, it would provide a reflective surface to represent the horizon, giving the illusion of far greater space than a cyclorama. A dome would be perfect for Gene's script, but since it would cost $500 in materials alone, the executive committee voted it down. Jig, the apostle of collective decision-making, began to work on the dome by himself.

When Edna Kenton, a member of the executive committee, one day found Jig at work in a clutter of steel netting and cement, he turned to her and said abruptly, "There is to be no argument about this. . . . *The Emperor* has *got* to have a dome."

Jig labored around the clock, mixing cement, cutting rebar, installing lathe. The troupe soon became awed by the magnitude of his inspiration—the Michelangelo of MacDougal Street!—and when at last they dared enter the dome after weeks of whispered suspense—behold, hanging from the ceiling of the stage, in all its resplendence, was not Jig's folly but Jig's masterpiece.

The entire company set about preparing Gene's play for production with renewed enthusiasm. Jig would serve as the director, obviously, but who would play the role of the Emperor? Gene had no objection to casting a white actor in blackface, but Jig, Ida, and several others argued that the role should be played by a black actor—a momentous move when no black actor had ever performed a leading role for a white American company. Someone recalled seeing an actor named Charles S. Gilpin playing a slave in a recent Broadway production about Abraham Lincoln, and Jig set out in search of his Emperor.

In his forties, the youngest of fourteen children, Gilpin had worked as a printer, a barbershop porter, and, appropriately enough, a Pullman porter, but he'd also managed to gain considerable theatrical experience in vaudeville, with black stock companies, and in minstrel shows. Intelligent, sensitive, and gifted, Gilpin gave a superb reading and won the part on the spot.

Another experienced actor almost won a role as well. Charlie Chaplin attended one of the early rehearsals and told Jig he'd like to play a small, pantomimed part under the name "Harry Spencer." Jig reluctantly declined his offer, depriving Gene of the opportunity to meet the man who, decades later, and much to his dismay, would become his son-in-law.

Gene stayed away on opening night—his common practice—but the next day learned that the audience had cheered the play, cheered

Gilpin, even cheered the dome. Lines of ticket buyers appeared at the box office and the subscription list quickly rose to 1,500. To Jig, the triumph was the group's—and not the least element of his euphoria was that Gene had at last become "an initiate of our community."

The Players soon realized that they had by far their biggest hit. "Eugene O'Neill's *The Emperor Jones*," wrote Heywood Broun, "seems to us just about the most interesting play which has yet come from the most promising playwright in America. . . . We have no disposition to say, 'If only the play had been done in the commercial theater!' . . . *The Emperor Jones* is so unusual in its technique that it might wait in vain for a production anywhere except in so adventurous a playhouse as the Provincetown Theater." Alexander Woollcott found the play "an extraordinarily striking dramatic study of panic. . . . It reinforces the impression that for strength and originality [O'Neill] has no rival among the American writers for the stage." Gilpin's performance was praised for its "heroic stature."

The Provincetown Players had reached the point from which there was no turning back—and without a moment's hesitation they succumbed. Only one member of the executive committee voted against moving the play to Broadway—not Jig—though they remained divided on details, the few remaining idealists still arguing that the script should merely be signed over for royalties, the more ambitious advocating that the production should reach what is always called in such cases "a wider audience." The group finally accepted an offer to take the play uptown for an unlimited engagement with the original company intact.

The Emperor Jones ran for 204 performances on Broadway, gave Gene his first substantial income as a playwright, made Gilpin a star, and nearly tripled the Players' income. The engagement hardly ran smoothly, however, for Gilpin, disoriented by his sudden fame, began drinking heavily, and, increasingly sensitive about some of Gene's dialogue, started to substitute lines of his own (particularly offended by the word "nigger," he'd substitute "black baby" or "colored man," leading Gene to warn him, "If I ever catch you rewriting my lines again, you black bastard, I'm going to beat you up"). "That role belongs to me," Gilpin told one of Gene's friends years later. "That Irishman, he just wrote the play." When it came time to cast the London production, Gene decided to use another actor, "with a . . . wonderful presence and voice, full of ambition and a damn fine man personally with real brains"—a young fellow named Paul Robeson. Still, near the end of his life, Gene would say, "There was only one actor who carried out every notion of a character I had in mind. That actor was Charles Gilpin."

• • •

Meanwhile, after its enthusiastic start, the Players' fifth season soon turned lackluster. The second bill featured Gene's *Diff'rent*, the story of a sexually repressed New England woman—influenced by the Lizzie Borden case and foreshadowing *Mourning Becomes Electra*—but the production was memorable only for the debut of a young actress named Mary Blair, later Edmund Wilson's first wife, and for the ominous importation, Gene insisting on a more professional production, of a Broadway-trained director. Though the critics found the play too harsh and gloomy, it, too, moved uptown.

By the time Jig's new play, *The Spring*, went into rehearsal for the third bill, most of the group's resources and many of its members were tied up on Broadway—though given the distance between Jig's ambition and Jig's talent, no amount of attention would have transformed his mystic mélange into the hit he hoped for. National recognition and Village mediocrity—the irony was complete.

The group began its sixth season in shambles. The membership degenerated into embittered cliques, the actors competed for parts in the London production of *Emperor*. The careerists schemed to rid the company of the amateurs. The budget, even after the financially successful fifth season, lurched out of control. Worst of all, the new scripts turned out to be audience failures. In desperation, the players had to turn over the theater to a guest company—Maurice Browne's Chicago Repertory—to provide subscribers with a fourth bill.

Once more, the Players counted on Gene to come to the rescue. *Anna Christie* had opened on Broadway the preceding fall, but he'd promised another play, *The Hairy Ape*, for the Players' fifth bill. An attempt to explain the suicide at sea of one of his friends, the story had simmered in his mind for years, and in a frenzied six-week period during the winter of 1921–1922 "it just oozed out of every pore."

Dismayed at what he regarded as the slipshod, haphazard treatment his plays had received on Macdougal Street, and without informing Jig, Gene arranged for a professional director, cast the Broadway actor Louis Wolheim in the leading role, and privately negotiated for an uptown run after three weeks in the Village. "So you see it will not be an amateur affair," Gene wrote the critic George Jean Nathan, "but can be relied upon to achieve results."

The strain between Gene and Jig soon accelerated to open hostility.

First Gene announced that he would co-direct with Jig, then he called in his friend Jimmy Light, and eventually the program stated, in the spot usually reserved for the director's credit, "Produced by the Provincetown Players."

Unlike previous rehearsal periods, which were usually character-ized by leisurely chaos, this one proceeded with professional dispatch. Pushed into the background, humiliated in front of his own company, and feeling that Gene had repaid his devotion by using the Players as a mere try-out theater for Broadway, Jig fell back on alcohol.

While preoccupied with plans for the opening of *The Hairy Ape*, Gene received a telegram from Jamie in California informing him that their mother had suffered a stroke. Less than two weeks later Ella died, and the train bearing her body arrived at Grand Central the very night of the Village premiere. Jamie—who would die within two years—had accompa-nied the casket in a state of alcoholic oblivion, but Gene struggled to stay sober through the ordeal. He had found a measure of release for his thwarted love and overpowering guilt in his writing, and later based *A Moon for the Misbegotten* on the incidents surrounding his mother's death.

The Hairy Ape opened on March 9 to disappointed reviews. Broun called the play propaganda, Woollcott found it a "wildly fantastic play," "monstrously uneven . . . now flamingly eloquent, now choked and thwarted and inarticulate." Gene found consolation in the reaction of a group of Village hoodlums, bootleggers, and barroom riffraff he invited to the Broadway premiere several weeks later, who greeted the play's rough seafaring language with cheers and whistles. The police proved less enthu-siastic, and asked a magistrate to close the play as "indecent, obscene, and impure," containing, as it did, such imprecations as "Yuh lousy stinkin' yel-low mut of a Catholic-moiderin' bastard." But even before the complaint against *The Hairy Ape* was summarily dismissed, Gene received word that *Anna Christie* had won his second Pulitzer. More propitious, though he didn't realize it at the time, was a change in the Broadway cast of *The Hairy Ape*, when Mary Blair was replaced by the exotic beauty Carlotta Monterey.

In the aftermath of the Broadway experience Jig was dispirited and broken. "The Provincetown moment" had come to an end. "It is time," Jig told Susan, "to go to Greece," and on March 1, 1922, they set sail on the SS *Themistocles* for Athens.

The theater on Macdougal Street remained open until the end of the decade, but the Provincetown Players had died, the building no longer animated by Jig Cook's lunatic vision.

Somewhat belatedly, Gene realized that he still needed a place like the Provincetown to produce his more experimental work, and before it became evident that Jig and Susan had no intention of returning to the Village, he began to think about how the Playhouse might serve this function. He thought that Jig would oppose the idea, but was also convinced that "unless something of this kind is done a year from now, I am going to resign instantly, there is no good sitting up with a corpse."

In the summer of 1923, the executive committee cabled Jig in Athens, informed him that they were debating whether to resume operations or discontinue the Players, and asked for his vote. "For termination," Jig tersely cabled back. Gene suggested that the critic Kenneth Macgowan should run the reorganized Players. Kenneth approved, but suggested that he, Gene, and Bobby Jones jointly take charge as a triumvirate. At first Gene demurred. "To hell with democracy!" he wrote Kenneth from Provincetown. "Director with a capital D!" But laying aside his distaste for committees, his less than fond memories of Jig's "collective" decision-making in particular, he reluctantly agreed.

But the time had long since passed to save "the P.P. theater and stimulus," and season after season passed in lackluster solidity. Only Gene's *All God's Chillun Got Wings*, in 1924, caused a stir, and not because of any merit in the script. Described by Gene as "a character study of two human beings," the story dealt with the bitter misunderstandings between a black husband and a white wife. The cast featured Mary Blair and Paul Robeson, and one minor bit of business called for Mary to kiss Paul's hand. When a national newspaper syndicate distributed a photograph of Mary with the caption "White Actress Kisses Negro's Hand," the controversy escalated so rapidly that Kenneth claimed *Chillun* "received more publicity before production than any play in the history of the American theater, possibly the world." The Society for the Suppression of Vice warned that "such a play might easily lead to racial riots," and Gene received a letter from the Grand Kleagle of the Ku Klux Klan concluding, "If your play goes on, don't expect to see [your son] again"—a letter Gene promptly returned to the Grand Kleagle after scrawling across the bottom, "Go fuck yourself!"

Gene had hoped to escape "the old bickering," but the new management had more than its share. By the end of 1926, he no longer actively participated in the affairs of the Playhouse, and in 1929 the organization finally folded—an enterprise established to separate art and commerce unable to continue because its major investors lost most of their money in the stock market crash.

Though he'd reached the land of Sophocles, Euripides, and

Aeschylus, Jig felt that his sojourn in Greece was less a pilgrimage to the fabled past than a flight from the failed present. Distance often lends perspective, but to prophets, distance rigidifies ideals. And to Jig, as to so many Villagers, ideals weren't vague guides to help focus aspirations, they were precise goals to be achieved through unwavering commitment. Ideals, in short, were prophecies.

No wonder the Villager felt an overwhelming sense of failure. But whose failure was it? The more Jig brooded, the more convinced he became that it was Gene's. He'd discovered Gene, he'd nurtured Gene, he'd devoted most of the Players' energies to Gene—and Gene had betrayed him and had joined the hated uptown theater as soon as it beckoned. Even Belasco, who had attacked Jig's theater as "vicious, vulgar, and degrading," whom Gene himself had characterized as running nothing but a "Broadway show-shop," would soon receive a letter from Gene saying, "I now have a play to submit to you." Gene, said Floyd Dell, "broke George Cook's heart."

Gene, of course, remained the Players' greatest success. And success, in a dynamic Villagers have failed to understand for years, threatens to deprive the rebellious, the avant-garde, the experimental, of their function. The artistic breakthrough accomplished, the creative energy vanishes—leaving them with achievement but without purpose. Jig had rejected the socialism of his youth, Floyd said, to become the disciple of "another gospel, of the beauty of failure," a principle according to which "Failure would be Success." "When the Provincetown Players succeeded," said Susan more succinctly, "Jig felt they had failed."

Jig could find no consolation in such thoughts. In regarding ideals as prophecies, the best he could hope for was magnificent failure. In falsely defining their goals, in wrongly reading their relationship to their culture, the prophetic idealists of the Village erroneously regarded the difference between their aspirations and their achievements as the measure of their shortcomings. At first, Jig and the Villagers alternated between despondency and blame—between attributing failure to their own weaknesses and to the betrayal of their colleagues—but unable to endure this overwhelming sense of impotence, they began to see it as inevitable, proof of their superiority to a monolithic, stultifying, and alienating culture. A quintessential American, Jig remained enslaved to his society's false definitions of success and failure—and, a quintessential Villager, even while measuring his worth by these definitions, he rebelled against the very society that embraced them.

Self-exiled, what else could Jig do but pretend he was Greek? Tak-

ing up residence in a small village on the slopes of Parnassus, he grew a patriarchal beard and dressed in native costumes. In the flush of inebriation,
and in fluent Greek, he'd sit from morning to midnight in outdoor cafés exhorting the baffled but entranced peasants to recapture the glories of Periclean Athens.

Jig even planned to rebuild the ancient theater in nearby Delphi,
but these euphoric illusions soon gave way to embittered anguish. "My
Provincetown Players never swerved ½ an inch right or left for money in
that New York hog trough," he wrote a friend in the Village. He even intimated that shooting "certain men" would "purify" America, and, alternat-
ing between maudlin self-inflation and morbid self-pity, contemplated a
glorious suicide. "I have had an automatic pistol revolver for two years—I
have lived with that implement," he wrote Edna Kenton. "Now that youth
is gone, I'm keen for a good cause to die in." Even this last pitiful ideal was
denied Jig, however, for while playing with his dog he contracted glanders,
a painful animal disease rarely communicated to humans, and after a few
weeks of agony died on January 14, 1924.

"When the word went up Parnassus that he was sick," wrote Susan,
"shepherds left their flocks . . . and came down the mountain. And when
in Delphi they were told he would not be with them again, they did not go
back to their flocks, but stayed on in the house of this man they loved—
through the day, the night, another day and until midnight, they were
there. Villagers and shepherds carried him, uncovered, through . . . Delphi, round the bend of the mountain to the graveyard."

At the order of the Greek government, in honor of the devotion Jig
had shown his adopted homeland, a sacred stone was solemnly borne aloft
from the Temple of Apollo, near the navel of the earth, and mounted as a
headstone over his grave. In the words of Sappho, in a poem Jig himself had
translated:

> *Though we know that never a longing mortal*
> *Gains life's best—Oh better it is to pray for*
> *Part in what we cherished and shared of old than*
> *Fail to remember.*

Upon hearing of Jig's death, Gene wrote Susan that he remained "one of
the best friends I had ever had or ever would have . . . ! And then when
I thought of all the things I hadn't done, the letters I hadn't written, . . . I
felt like a swine, Susan. Whenever I think of him it is with the most self-

condemning remorse." And in a public tribute, he called Jig "the big man, the dominating and inspiring genius of the Players . . . he represented the spirit of revolt against the old worn-out traditions, the commercial theater, the tawdry artificialities of the stage."

But controversy continued. Edna Kenton, with the grieving Susan's support, wrote a series of acrimonious letters to the triumvirate charging that since they had abandoned Jig's principles they had no right to Jig's name. Gene finally convinced Susan that the word "Provincetown" should be retained as a tribute to Jig, and they collaborated on the inscription for a bronze plaque to be placed in the lobby of the theater. "To the memory of George Cram ('Jig') Cook, poet of life, priest of the ideal, lovable human being, to whose imagination and unselfish devotion this Playhouse owes its original inspiration and development as a home for free creative expression."

Two wildly disparate geniuses who worked for a time in perfect harmony, Jig Cook and Gene O'Neill transformed the American theater. Before the Players, drama in this country was nothing but an industry, but by the end of the institution's life it was also an art. In its eight years the Provincetown Players produced ninety-seven original American plays by forty-seven authors (seventeen of them women), including fifteen by Eugene O'Neill and eleven by Susan Glaspell. Alexander Wollcott described it as, "that preposterous little theater . . . yet on it the artists have created the illusion of vast spaces and endless perspectives."

And though Jig's vision of the theater as the temple of a reawakened nation remained a quixotic fantasy, he was the first American to gather a group of artists into a creative collective. Always a dilettante, often a dictator—Jig had a genius for ferment, for provocation, for awakening artistic ambition, and presided over the resulting disorder with a maniacal serenity. Jig's life, recalled Floyd, was "hardly within his own control; it was as if he were being driven on by a demon to some unknown goal." Jig Cook failed in his fatuous fantasy of becoming "one of the creators of the world's future," but his life can best be measured by the way he helped his "beloved community of life-givers" create it.

Since Gene had met Jig at the Cook summer cottage only eight years earlier, so nervous and insecure he had to retreat to the next room while his play was being read, the father and mother and brother who'd irrevocably shaped his psyche had all died, he'd married twice and fathered children, and he'd grown from a brooding drunk to an internationally acclaimed playwright. His vision exasperated by Jig's utopian idealism, his temperament alienated by Jig's overbearing selflessness, he nevertheless knew the magnitude of his debt. Gene needed a theater that would give him the freedom to develop the mixture of tragic themes and experimental modes that characterized his plays, he needed an audience that would sustain his will when he stumbled and groped, but most of all he needed the faith in his genius that was Jig's most generous gift.

And though Gene felt contempt for the bohemians, radicals, and intellectuals of the Village, he needed the place's openness, tolerance, and diversity if his long and painful struggle to find his own voice were to succeed.

Despite his contempt, Gene returned to the Village after he became famous. Something in his psyche instinctively drew him to the sources of his pain, and his lingering friendships with his cronies continued to be one of the main causes of his increasingly troubled relationship with Agnes. He wrote to a friend, "Agnes wants the goddamned *Social Register* crowd. I don't learn anything about human beings from them. They're living corpses."

When Gene and Carlotta Monterey met again in the mid-twenties, Carlotta recalled, "I thought him the rudest man I'd ever seen. And he had no use for me." But in the winter of 1927–1928, Gene abandoned Agnes and their two children for Carlotta, the woman with whom he remained until the end of his life.

Ambitious, manipulative, devoted, Carlotta had the qualities necessary to become the mother-mate-manager Gene had unconsciously sought. Her adoration could contain the tempestuous quarrels her fiery spirit guaranteed; her control of his career was so complete he could depend on her to shelter him from the temptations he could not resist. Carlotta almost immediately began to cut Gene off from his Village past. Convinced that the Provincetowners had used Gene for their own ends—reversing Jig's complaint—she wrote a friend, "[Gene] is going thro' a *new development*—new pleasures—new riches—new objects of study—are coming into his life—the old skin is being shed! And with it the old parasites."

Fitzi, Jimmy Light, Mary Vorse, Susan Glaspell, Kenneth Macgowan—one by one his former intimates were dropped, in some cases simply because Carlotta didn't pass on their letters. Carlotta disapproved of Djuna Barnes's *Nightwood*—a friendship ended. Fitzi, seriously ill, asked if Gene could help pay her hospital bills, and, annoyed when Gene seemed sympathetic and began to reminisce about the old days, Carlotta walked out on him for several weeks. Gene knew better than to see Terry more than once every few years, but Carlotta knew better than to resist when Gene insisted on supporting him with monthly checks. In the winter of 1933–1934, hearing that one of Gene's plays was trying out in Boston, the seventy-nine-year-old Terry, living there in rapidly declining health, asked Gene to visit him when he came to town. Gene didn't even call. He couldn't bear seeing his old friend bedridden, and Carlotta probably made sure he was too busy. A few days later, Terry died of pneumonia.

In the early twenties a storm destroyed the wharf on which the Players had produced their first plays, and at the end of the decade Susan cabled Gene that the ocean had finally claimed the converted coast guard station James had bought from Mabel Dodge. Years later, walking through Times Square, Gene discovered that the hotel in which he had been born had been razed. "There is only empty air now," he said, "where I came into this world."

Upton Sinclair had called Jack Reed "the playboy of the social revolution," but even if this label had once been appropriate, in the last years of his life his innocent idealism gave way to exhausting struggle. His fervor for revolution had led him to sacrifice his personal life, his poetry, his income, his reputation, even his health.

Despite the distractions of the Village and the harassment of the government, Louise and Jack finished their books on the Russian revolution in only a few months. The "partisanship" of Louise's *Six Red Months in Russia*, said *The Dial*, "does not mitigate her reporter's gift for accurate observation." But Louise's work was overshadowed by *Ten Days That Shook the World*. Published in March 1919, it was in its fourth printing in July. "This book is a slice of intensified history," wrote Jack in his preface, "—history as I saw it. . . . It does not pretend to be anything but a detailed account of the November Revolution . . . a chronicle of those events which I myself observed and experienced, and those supported by reliable evidence." Lenin himself, in an introduction to the 1922 edition, wrote, "Unreservedly do I recommend it to the workers of the world. Here is a book which I should like to see published in millions of copies and translated into all languages. It gives a truthful and most vivid exposition of the events so significant to the comprehension of what really is the Proletarian Revolution and the Dictatorship of the Proletariat."

Jack's prose, wrote one of his biographers, blended "fact and fiction, life and art, history and poetry—often over the years he had ignored or transcended the kind of distinction by which most men nail reality to a cross." And the painter Boardman Robinson, one of his colleagues on *The*

Masses, frequently told a story illustrating Jack's approach to his writing. Boardman: "But it didn't happen that way!" Jack: "What the hell difference does it make?" Jack grabs a picture of Boardman's. "She didn't have a bundle as big as that," he says. "He didn't have so full a beard." But drawing isn't a matter of accuracy, Boardman answers, it's a matter of overall impression. "Exactly!" exclaims Jack. "That's just what I'm trying to do!"

Jack had no time to rest after the arduous months of writing, for he regarded the revolution in Russia and the revolution that must soon follow in the United States as urgent. Speeches, fund-raising, rallies—no longer a dilettante of revolution, he poured his passion into each, but behind the scenes he devoted even more time to committee meetings, editorial conferences, and organizational squabbles—drudgery that couldn't have been further from the adventure he craved.

Hounded by the authorities, separated from Louise for weeks at a time, dismayed by the bureaucratic squabbling of his comrades, he lost much of his ebullience but none of his commitment. His old brashness occasionally resurfaced. He wrote a satirical play for the Provincetown Players called *The Peace That Passeth Understanding* based on the Versailles peace conference, representing Woodrow Wilson, Georges Clemenceau, David Lloyd George, and the other delegates in grotesque masks, with a clock on the mantelpiece behind them "fifty years slow." He treated state and federal surveillance of his activities with lighthearted scorn—when the writer Don Marquis spotted him about to board a double-decker bus on Fifth Avenue and wondered why he wasn't in hiding, he responded jovially, "The red-hunters never catch anybody." His humor was directed at his allies as well as his enemies. He and a friend secretly published a parody of a socialist periodical and put it on sale at party headquarters. On another occasion, after sitting through a solemn debate about communism, he quoted at length from Marx, leaving his listeners unable to refute his arguments—and unaware that he'd invented the quotation on the spot.

By the fall of 1919, Jack had to make another trip to Russia as the representative of one of the two competing factions of American communism. Since the government now banned such trips, he arranged to be smuggled aboard ship as a stoker named "Jim Gormley," and in late September he bade Louise goodbye and boarded a Swedish freighter for his eleventh and last crossing of the Atlantic.

"Jim Gormley" jumped ship in Norway, stowed away on another freighter to Finland, and was smuggled across the border into Russia, where Jack found the Bolshevik bureaucracy firmly in place, the political situation "frightfully mixed up," and factionalism more devious than anything he'd ever encountered in the States. He soon became disillusioned with the communist commitment to doctrine over compassion, yet he never lost his romantic hope in the revolution. Criticized by Upton Sinclair for his support of a repressive regime, he replied, "I was in a better position to overlook the violence and injustice which cannot help going on in times of Revolution, and see beyond them to the beauty and bigness of the thing as a whole." And when he had a joyful reunion with Emma Goldman in Petrograd, he countered her anarchist skepticism by saying, "You are a little confused by the Revolution in action because you have dealt with it only in theory. You'll get over that."

Month after month, Louise waited for word in their Village apartment, fearful and lonely—and apprehensive for her own safety during the Palmer raids on suspected communists.

But Louise could never be wholly satisfied with love at a distance—Jack himself had confessed to several passing affairs in his travels—and after trying unsuccessfully to contact Gene, and enjoying a brief relationship with "a French sweetheart," she spent several weekends in Woodstock with the always comforting, always available Andrew Dasburg. Word finally reached her that Jack had been arrested traveling back through Finland, again under the name Jim Gormley, carrying over a hundred diamonds to help finance the communist cause. After thirteen weeks in solitary confinement, he was released and returned to Moscow, where Louise joyously joined him in September 1920.

"He ran shouting into my room," Louise wrote Max. "I found him older and sadder and grown strangely gentle and ascetic. . . . The effects of the terrible experience in the Finnish jail were all too apparent." Jack talked wistfully of returning to the Village to work on a second book about the revolution, maybe even a novel. But first he had to regain his health, then join his comrades in America who'd been indicted for anarchy. Louise tried to dissuade him, but "My dear little Honey," he told her firmly, "I would do anything for you, but don't ask me to be a coward."

A few weeks later, Jack began to suffer from headaches and dizziness, and it soon became apparent that he had contracted typhus. He lingered in a feverish delirium and Louise later recalled that when the hallucinations momentarily ceased, his mind was "full of stories and poems and beautiful thoughts." Ten days later he suffered a stroke, and for five more days he was unable to speak. Shortly after midnight on October 17, 1920—five days before his thirty-third birthday and only ten years after he had arrived in the Village as a brash young Harvard graduate—Jack Reed died in a shabby Moscow hospital.

Four years before Jig was to be laid to rest near the Temple of Apollo in Delphi, Jack's body lay in state at the Temple of Labor in Moscow. Rain and sleet fell on the funeral. "The faces of the crowd around betrayed neither sympathy nor interest," reported the *New York Times*. "They looked on unmoved." Jack was buried in the walls of the Kremlin— like Jig, halfway around the world from the Village he loved.

After working for three years as one of the leading correspondents for the Hearst chain, in 1923 Louise married William Bullitt, who later served as U.S. ambassador to France and Russia. Their cosmopolitan life seemed to suit her for a few years, but she began drinking heavily, and Bullitt divorced her in 1930. Virtually penniless, dependent on alcohol and pickup lovers, she returned to the apartment on Patchin Place she'd shared with Jack.

Louise moved to Paris in 1935, lived in a series of seedy Left Bank hotels, turned to drugs when alcohol proved insufficient to obliterate her unhappiness, and was the subject of rumors of lesbianism. Recalled her friend Janet Flanner, "When she came back to Paris she was in the lowest stage of degradation. One of the last times I saw her was on a rainy night . . . along Rue Vavin. . . . Her face was so warped, I didn't recognize her." On January 6, 1936, the year Gene received the Nobel Prize, Louise collapsed with a cerebral hemorrhage on the stairs of her hotel and died in a hospital a few hours later.

By the time of Jack's death, the bohemian insurgency of the Village had lost its glow and the revolutionary movement of the Bolsheviks ushered in years of bloodshed, injustices, and terrors. Jack's principles were drawn more from Tom Paine than from Karl Marx, but the Golden Boy of Greenwich Village became known as one of his country's lonely, misguided outcasts, "the only American buried in the Kremlin."

As for Mabel Dodge, Max Eastman, and Jig Cook—all served less as programmatic leaders than as creative catalysts. The guiding principles of the informal structures they established were freedom, openness, diversity, and experimentation. With a kind of contentless charisma, they brought cohesion to what were essentially anarchist collectives. The secret of the success of Mabel's salon, *The Masses*, and the Provincetown Players, in short, lay in their selfless devotion to the self-expression of others.

IV

The Feminists of the Village

Meetings with Remarkable Women

S o long as any woman is denied the right to her own life and happiness," wrote Floyd Dell in *Confessions of a Feminist Man*, "no man has a right to his; and every man who walks freely in his man's world, walks on an iron floor, whereunder, bound and flung into her dungeon, lies a woman-slave." "It is no longer possible to hedge the life of women in a set ritual," wrote Walter Lippmann, first awakened to feminism at Mabel's salon, "where their education, their work, their opinion, their love, and their motherhood are fixed in the structure of custom. . . . For one fact is . . . the prime element in any discussion. That fact is the absolute necessity for a readjusting of women's position." "When the world began to change," wrote Hutch Hapgood, "the restlessness of women was the main cause of the development called Greenwich Village, which existed not only in New York but all over the country."

In the teens, male radicals and bohemians frequently wrote of the role of feminism in the transformation of society, but the women of the Village didn't wait for an invitation to voice their aspirations. Men like Floyd, Walter, and Hutch may have rhapsodized about the revolution, but between 1912 and 1917 women like Henrietta Rodman, Mary Heaton Vorse,

162

Elizabeth Gurley Flynn, Marie Jenney Howe, Neith Boyce, Crystal East-man, Emma Goldman, and Margaret Sanger made a Golden Age of Feminism, chronicling oppression, defining goals, organizing movements, rallying supporters, disdaining custom, and defying the law.

Nearly every passion of the prewar Village—anarchism, socialism, Freudianism, pacifism, bohemianism—had a feminist dimension, and the Village cults of creativity, spontaneity, instinct, and pleasure aimed at the liberation of women as well as men. Rigid bourgeois codes were cracking under the demand for more flexibility, more alternatives, more freedom. The byword of the teens was "new," epitomized by Woodrow Wilson's New Freedom, but also by the New Society, the New Arts, the New Morality, the New Psychology, and, of course, the New Woman.

Educated, white, and middle-class, the New Woman was privileged by Victorian standards, yet realized not only that her "privileges" were a form of enslavement but that she had abilities society would not allow her to use, aspirations society would not allow her to attain. As a character said in Mary Austin's novel *A Woman of Genius,* "Women everywhere [are] getting courage to live lives of their own. . . . The more women there are like you, the less there will be of [oppression and abuse] for any of them."

Breaking old conventions and claiming new options proved frustrating as well as exhilarating—but a fierce optimism was a component of women's determination. More and more women were entering the workforce, more and more women were entering the professions. Over eight percent of the physicians in the country were women, a figure that actually declined in the next half century, and over fifteen percent of the Ph.D.'s at the end of the decade were granted to women, a figure that also declined. In fact, the percentage of women college students and professors was greater in 1920 than in 1960.

The New Woman emerged in cities and towns across the country, but the center of the movement was the Village. In the teens, Village women could have careers beyond home without inspiring antagonism, they could have sex outside of marriage without eliciting condemnation, they could drink, smoke, wear nonconstricting clothing. "Life was ready to take a new form of some kind," said Mabel Dodge. The liberation of women, they believed, would lead to a new political, social, and cultural order, for the New Woman was part of a larger movement in which *everyone* would be liberated.

The feminists of the Village—and the word "feminism" was first heard in 1910—had several specific causes. Suffrage, obviously, but also economic self-sufficiency, free love, birth control, the ending of child labor, divorce reform, repeal of discriminatory legislation, and as war engulfed Europe, pacifism. But each was part of a larger commitment to the liberation of women from capitalist exploitation and bourgeois morality, to economic, social, political, cultural, and sexual independence. They subsumed their assault on gender discrimination in their assault on the entire system. "Feminism," said the platform of the Feminist Alliance, formed in 1914, is not only "a movement which demands the removal of all social, political, and other discriminations which are based upon sex," but demands "the award of all rights and duties in all fields on the basis of individual capacity alone."

This idealistic vision—for seldom has a dedication to self-fulfillment been so selfless—was so all-encompassing that confusion, conflict, and contradiction inevitably resulted, not just with men but within the feminist movement itself. Even the simple and self-evident goal of suffrage caused disputes. Some women argued that gaining the vote would allow women equal rights to express their opinions. Others countered that it would merely allow women to participate in a corrupt process and that electoral politics would have little impact on the social, economic, and cultural conditions that lay at the root of women's oppression.

As for socialism, while some members of the party asserted that women were among the foremost victims of capitalism and that women's rights were central to a socialist world (what good would economic independence do women in a male, capitalistic society?), others asserted that women's issues were marginal and distracting, and that mere reform of women's place would have to wait for the restructuring of the economic basis of society (how could women stress individual over communal needs, by what rationale could they insist that gender take priority over class?). Such issues as labor reform and peace seemed clear-cut, but should feminists seek special laws protecting women in the workplace or demand the elimination of all distinctions based on sex? Should feminists protest American participation in World War I or support the democratic countries that were their best hope for progress?

But the arena of greatest confusion, conflict, and contradiction, of course, was sex. Since repression of sexuality was seen as central to the repressiveness of bourgeois capitalism, liberated sexuality was a crucial component of the coming revolution. With sexuality one of the major concerns of the social sciences, sex was moving beyond one's private life and into the public realm. And since equality of the sexes in all things was now a moral imperative, women's sexuality should be as taken for granted as men's.

But while liberated sexuality might be central to the coming revolution, many Villagers asked themselves how they could justify elevating erotic yearnings into a political program. While sexual behavior might be part of the new politics of personal life, hadn't they had enough of sexual codes as a form of social control? And while women's lives should be as free as men's, why should they emulate sexual behavior they'd always found oppressive? Weren't the new doctrines of female eroticism defined from a male perspective? Who most benefited from the new codes of free love? Feminist theories of sexual liberation seemed unequivocal, but many of their consequences seemed unacceptable.

Even the self-evident goal of eliminating the double standard raised unsettling questions. Do we seek freedom for sex or freedom from sex: liberation to become sexual beings or liberation from being regarded as little more than sexual beings? Do we want women to become more erotic or men to become more chaste? Do we desire more morality in sexual relationships or less? Aren't our goals of more autonomy and more intimacy fundamentally irreconcilable? Is free love the basis for female sexual emancipation or merely a way to legitimize male promiscuity?

The answers might have come more easily if Village men weren't such ardent champions of the sexual liberation of women, for in advocating the democracy of sexuality—precisely what women wanted—weren't they merely seeking willing companions, weren't they asking women to fulfill the old triad of mother, mistress, and muse in a new guise, weren't they less interested in emancipating women than in making them more available for their own needs? If women had always been the guardians of morality, if their roles had always been the care and preservation of family, of culture, of sexual relationships, how could they at one and the same time reassert those roles and mount an assault on respectability? And if women were adopting a masculine image of independence, wouldn't they become amateur males, wouldn't they succumb to an insidious form of self-enslavement?

The intellectual turmoil and psychic confusion and emotional frustration of the New Women of the Village might easily have immobilized them, but instead gave them an explosive energy. They understood that the rebellion of women was central to the rebellion against economic oppression, cultural convention, and political injustice, and realized that their challenge was to redefine work and love, career and family, institutions and self-fulfillment.

In the teens, a series of remarkable women—some focusing on specific causes, others advocating a total transformation of society—addressed these concerns with passion, determination, and courage. "Restlessness! Restlessness!" wrote the novelist Margaret Deland in *The Atlantic Monthly* in 1910. "A prevailing discontent among women—a restlessness infinitely removed from the content of a generation ago."

Henrietta Rodman

Henrietta Rodman's dinner guests would start to arrive at her top-floor apartment on Bank Street, but she was so busy she hadn't prepared a thing. Hurriedly handing a $5 bill to Harry Kemp or Floyd Dell or Jack Reed she'd say, "Here, buy four or five loaves of bread, about 15 cans of spaghetti, three pounds of butter, and when you come back you can take [a] pail down for beer." She'd ask her guests to set up the table—long planks on wooden saw horses with benches on each side and tell everyone to take their places. "Coming up to my apartment is like the progress of the soul," she'd say cheerfully, stirring the spaghetti with one hand, downing a mug of beer with the other. "A long, tortuous climb, a difficult step after step, but at the top you burst into the sky."

"A professor, a leader of demonstrations and ever-new factions, a blazer of trails," as one friend called her, she was proudest of founding the Feminist Alliance in 1914. She fought for suffrage and socialism, but she also dispensed birth control information to young women, supported workers' rights to strike, argued against prejudicial college admissions policies, entered the fight whenever free speech was threatened, espoused free love with such conviction that her friends were afraid to tell her if they got married, became one of the first women in America to smoke in public, and for several months opened her door stark naked until she reluctantly decided that nudism was a cause whose time had not yet come.

But a fully mechanized apartment house for working mothers, a twelve-story building with a kitchen in the basement and a school on the roof—*that* was long overdue. A writer in the *New York Times* declared that the project was a perfect example of the "monstrous egotism" of Henrietta and her fellow feminists, but argued that "at the present time the care of the baby is the weak point in feminism," and that in order to make a career in any of the professions women had to be first freed from the "four primitive home industries," "care of the children, preparation of food, care of the house, and of clothing." Henrietta understood the connection between economic independence and the feminist ideal long before most leaders of the women's movement, and went so far as to hire an architect and select a site on Washington Square. Only the tightness of the mortgage market fore-stalled her project.

But Henrietta's renown in the Village survived this failure and re-sulted from three resounding successes: school reform, the migration of the Liberal Club to Macdougal Street, and the seemingly innocuous but in-flammatory issue of women's clothing.

Supporting herself as an English teacher at Wadleigh High School, Henrietta was appalled by the Board of Education's policy forbidding mar-ried women from teaching in the New York City school system. Having herself married in her mid-thirties—indeed, since she was an ardent advo-cate of free love and her husband was rarely in evidence, many Villagers suspected that she'd exchanged vows for no other reason than to test the policy—Henrietta didn't keep her status a secret, as did many other teach-ers, but openly confessed her crime. Promptly suspended, she challenged the ruling.

How confessing to being married could be construed as proof of immoral behavior was a question the board proved unable to answer, but immoral they called her, supported by most of the city's outraged editorial-ists. Max brought *The Masses* into the fray, writing with his typical wry rad-icalism, "The impulse of life to reproduce itself will probably not be entirely annihilated by the New York Board of Education, but we are glad to see that institution doing what it can to suppress this craze. Women teachers at least shall not be allowed leave of absence to have children. Maybe it does not come within the province of 'education' to prevent ba-bies from being born, but at least it makes their education unnecessary."

But Henrietta's chief target was a *liberal* institution—called, in-deed, the Liberal Club. Founded in Gramercy Park in 1908 by the muck-raker Lincoln Steffens, the Reverend Percy Stickney Grant, and other progressive-minded gentlemen to press for reform legislation, the club put particular emphasis on liberalizing the divorce laws but had few female members. Henrietta joined its ranks, and instantly began to urge expansion of its agenda. "Why aren't you supporting my case against the Board of Ed-ucation?" she asked. "Why doesn't the club have any black members?" These questions were disconcerting enough, but when her passionate ad-vocacy of free love so inspired one of the more prominent members that he not only took a mistress but asked her to move in with him and his wife, the leadership of the Liberal Club had heard enough about liberalism. Rally-ing her supporters, Henrietta discovered that what had seemed a mere splinter group consisted of the vast majority of the members, and in 1913 they moved en masse to 137 MacDougal Street above Polly's restaurant, where thanks to Henrietta the renowned Liberal Club became another of the seminal Village institutions of the teens.

Henrietta's assault on the pious progressivism of the Liberal Club may have made its elder members sputter, but her assault on the clothing conventions of women made the city gasp. Female finery may have seemed mere fashion, but it made a powerful statement about women's role in society. When Henrietta strolled though the neighborhood wearing a flowing gown, brown socks, and sandals, she scandalized the guardians of propriety more than when she advocated socialism or free love. Even her bobbed coiffure represented an outrageous affront to common decency.

Soon hundreds, soon *thousands* of "free young women" of the Village were emulating Henrietta. One of her followers tore down the draperies of her Washington Square apartment, pinned them around her waist, and set off for an evening at the Brevoort café. Henrietta's credo was that to do anything merely because others did it was "the most immoral act I can conceive," but eventually her revolutionary dress of gown, socks, sandals, and bobbed hair became a kind of bohemian costume, and she found herself watching the public paradoxically transform her passion for individuality into a concern for conformity.

Henrietta may have been, in the words of a friend, "incredibly naive and preposterously reckless, believing wistfully in beauty and goodness." But the militance of her naïveté, the dynamism of her craziness—combined with her contempt for convention and the range of her causes—so charmed and energized her multitude of friends and followers that Floyd Dell said the Village began with Henrietta Rodman.

Mary Heaton Vorse

Mary Heaton Vorse was present at the birth of all the seminal institutions of the Village of the teens. All but Mabel Dodge's salon. "Woman of shallow curiosities about the things in which I was most interested," said Mary of Mabel, "a rich woman amusing herself in meeting celebrities of different kinds." For her part, Mabel found Mary "small and domestic." Mabel regarded her as a threat to her hostess hegemony—and while everyone else was amused at Mabel's foibles, Mary remained annoyed at her frivolity.

Born into an upper-crust family in Amherst in 1874, Mary had an independent spirit that rebelled against New England decorum. "There is an awful gulf," she wrote. "They think I talk of serious things lightly and I think they talk of light things ponderously." Sent to Paris in her late teens to study art, Mary was promptly whisked home when it became apparent she was having a good time, but three years later she escaped to New York to study at the Art Students League. In the Village she exulted, "I am an escaped bird, flying through the clear air of heaven!"

Mary fell in love with Bert Vorse, a semitalented writer and semi-successful bohemian—and after their marriage in 1897 they moved into an eighth-floor walk-up apartment on Sheridan Square, a neighborhood shared by bohemian radical newcomers and Italian Catholic immigrants. With a daring born of middle-class comfort, Mary wore no corset and smoked in public. On one occasion, asked again and again to put out her cigarette, again and again she relit it, going through the ritual "with the air of someone performing a public service."

But when Bert started fooling around with other women shortly after she became pregnant, Mary felt that the "new world" was approaching faster than she'd expected. She began writing partly to supplement their income, partly to achieve economic independence. Their marriage was further strained when it became obvious that Mary was a far more gifted writer than Bert, and by the time he suddenly died in 1910 she had established herself as a highly regarded and well-paid contributor of short stories and essays to women's magazines and genteel journals like *The Atlantic*. In 1911 she became one of the original cooperative owner-writers of Piet Vlag's *Masses*.

"[I was one of] the gay, warmhearted girls who [entered] the nineties in their teens," Mary wrote. "And [who] felt it was up to them to be doing something about saving the world. . . . We had the feeling that we were important civic factors who could put in a thumb almost anywhere and pull out a plum, ranging from votes for women to a fine new building law."

Even as early as 1906, while Mabel Dodge was still in Italy, Max Eastman at Columbia, and Jig Cook in Iowa, Mary helped form a cooperative housing project at 3 Fifth Avenue, the first Village organization to articulate the spirit of insurgency of the new century. Christened A Club when one of the members, frustrated at the effort to find an appropriate name, said in exasperation, "Oh, just call it a club," the group consisted of the usual collection of writers and artists and activists. "Everybody was a liberal, if not a radical," said Mary, who added, one of the first to express the Village's unity of political and cultural rebellion, "and all for Labor and the Arts."

People "who questioned the system under which they lived" were gathering together in search of a "new consciousness," and though she wryly noted that their main activity seemed to be talk, the talk engendered a sense of community. Among those who stopped by for an evening of high-spirited conversation — in a kind of informal precursor of Mabel's salon and the Liberal Club — were John and Dolly Sloan, Frances Perkins, Theodore Dreiser, Mother Jones, and even Mark Twain with his jovial tales, caustic wit, and foul cigars.

After Bert's sudden death, Mary moved with her two children into an apartment near Sheridan Square. She was by now radicalized intellectually, but two events in particular committed her emotionally as well.

Five hundred garment workers toiled at the Triangle Shirtwaist Company in the top three floors of a ten-story building near Washington Square. On a late March afternoon in 1911, Mary and several hundred Villagers watched aghast from the sidewalks as smoke and flames billowed out. The fire company ladders reached only six floors, and the single, eighteen-and-a-half-inch-wide fire escape almost immediately collapsed. Dozens of women leapt to their deaths; the calamity claimed 146 lives.

By the time she visited the Lawrence, Massachusetts, textile workers' strike in 1912 with her second husband, Joe O'Brien, a man devoted equally to alcohol, blarney, and socialism, she knew where she belonged — "on the side of the workers and not with the comfortable people among whom [I had been] born." "Before Lawrence," she later recalled, "I had known a good deal about labor, but I . . . had not got angry. In Lawrence, I got angry." For the rest of her life she was the preeminent labor reporter in the country.

In covering nearly every major strike in the country for over three decades, she not only shrewdly analyzed the economic issues, but eloquently portrayed the misery and courage of the striking workers and their impoverished families. Starving children in Appalachian shacks, immigrant couples in dilapidated tenements, workers in tent cities in the mining towns of the Rockies — raucous street-corner rallies, angry and defiant factory workers picketing in the pouring rain, the fear that crackled through company towns as word spread that hired goons had been spotted on the outskirts with clubs and rifles — all this Mary conveyed to hundreds of thousands of readers in her impassioned prose.

Murray Kempton wrote in 1955, "Whenever you read across forty years about an event in which men stood in that single, desperate moment which brings all past, all present, and all future to one sharp point for them, you could assume that Mary Vorse had been there."

One of her friends called her a "quiet firebrand." An emancipated, sensual woman well acquainted with Victorian sexual codes (her mother informed her that sex twice a week was excessive, leading her to write Bert that she was "horribly scared to think to what frightful excess we had gone, and all my fault") and the male double standard (when she caught Bert emerging from the dunes of Provincetown with a woman in excessive deshabille, "Ah," he simply shrugged, "such is the way of the world"), she skillfully depicted in her fiction women's romantic yearnings and the rigid rituals that so often warped and thwarted them. And as a working mother—and when Joe died in 1915 a twice-widowed mother with three children—she well understood the conflict between self-fulfillment and domesticity. "My failure is that of almost every working woman who has children and a home to keep up," she wrote, "whether she scrubs floors, . . . or is a high-priced professional woman. . . . So most women fail in either or both. Their energy and thoughts are divided."

So by 1912, the year the Village became "the Village," Mary, at thirty-eight, was already a kind of elder stateswoman of insurgency, a role model, and inspiration for the young men and women who were flocking to the country's "center of contagion." Mary appeared in Max's first issue of The Masses—a scathing demolition of the Goddess of Domesticity, "the sisterhood of amalgamated wives," and it was Mary who said, "Nothing more horrible can be imagined than having one's pieces torn to bits by the artists at a Masses meeting."

But if Mary was only one of many figures around whom the Villagers congregated, she single-handedly made Provincetown the place where they vacationed when she bought her summer home in 1907 and invited her closest friends, Neith Boyce and Susan Glaspell, and their husbands, Hutch Hapgood and Jig Cook, to spend several sunny weeks with her.

If all three wives were struggling to find equality in marriage without granting license to their husbands, the war in Europe clouded their political optimism. "Companionate marriage" wasn't as easily attainable as they'd hoped, or a socialist utopia as near as they'd assumed, and in the summer and fall of 1914, particularly after Sarajevo, their revolutionary rhetoric became feverish, and the parties turned into binges foreshadowing despair. Only Mary wasn't stunned by this turn of events—she'd foreseen the coming conservative reaction as early as 1911, when she'd noticed that her house on East 11th Street was under surveillance by the New York City police because of her activities on behalf of the unemployed.

Everyone's spirits revived during the summer of 1915, with the birth of the Provincetown Players. But only two weeks after Gene O'Neill gave them Bound East for Cardiff, Mary received a disturbing letter from

Big Bill Haywood and promptly left Provincetown to cover the Mesabi Range strike in Minnesota.

I love my golden wings," Mary wrote in 1896, "and I want to fly right into the sun until they are all bedraggled and battered." Far she flew. For the last five decades of her life she not only wrote about the significant labor disputes but reported from Hitler's Germany and Stalin's Russia. She became the oldest accredited journalist covering World War II, and for her opposition to the Vietnam War she became the oldest American with an active FBI file. In sixteen books and hundreds of articles—for such mainstream magazines as *The Atlantic, Harper's,* and *Scribner's,* and for such radical journals as *The Masses* and *The New Republic*—Mary illuminated the lives of sharecroppers and the minutiae of Senate hearings, chronicled the struggles of factory workers and the rise of dictatorships, proselytized for unions and for feminism.

Mary numbered many of the major novelists of her time among her friends. Sinclair Lewis always quoted her advice to him as a young writer— "Place your unpaid bills before you, then apply the seat of your pants to the seat of your chair." John Dos Passos used her as the model for Mary French, "The Rebel Girl," in *U.S.A.* Ernest Hemingway invited her to Key West and praised her prose as "clear and cool"—though for her part, she described in her diary the novel of his she read during her stay as "a very juvenile performance." And during a visit to Nazi Germany in 1933, she saw books by all three of her friends tossed onto a blazing pyre.

Mary could be as stubborn as she was open-minded, as exasperating as she was enchanting, and her emotional life was marked by lapses from the idealism of her intellect. She was estranged from her children for long periods of time, and suffered for years from morphine addiction that began when Robert Minor, the former *Masses* artist with whom she'd been living, left her for a younger woman.

But the paradox that most characterized her was her unassuming intransigence. Her dedication to feminism—combining militant anger and romantic yearnings, insistence on career and longing for family—was nourished by her years in the Village, and greatly extended its influence. "She had not been *in* history," wrote Kempton, "but *of* history." And at the age of eighty-eight, venerable but still audacious, she wrote of herself, "You must understand that when I was very young, Life said to me, 'Here are two ways—a world running to mighty cities, full of the spectacle of bloody adventure, and here is home and children. Which will you take . . . ?' 'I will take *both*,' I said."

Elizabeth Gurley Flynn

When Big Bill Haywood—bearish, rough-hewn, gregarious—strode into Mabel Dodge's parlor for her IWW Evening, he brought with him two other organizers of the Paterson silk workers' strike. The crowd immediately recognized Carlo Tresca, tall, slender, strikingly handsome, his beard covering a scar where one of his many enemies had slashed him—"the most pugnaciously hell-raising male rebel I could find in the United States," said Max Eastman. But who could that woman be beside him, obviously his lover? Petite, pretty, and vivacious, Elizabeth Gurley Flynn, "the Joan of Arc of American labor," seemed more like an actress than an IWW militant. Indeed, David Belasco had once asked her to appear in one of his plays. Mabel's guests were as mesmerized by her as by Carlo and Big Bill, and she soon became a legend to the downtown radicals and bohemians not only for struggling for the rights of labor but for proving that a woman could lead the battle.

She later became one of the leaders of the American Communist party and in the fifties served several years in prison for her activities. Few Villagers followed her as far, and most rejected her call for class warfare, but all admired the courage and dedication with which, as a woman, she made "a life of her own."

Elizabeth's earliest "indelible impressions" were the poverty of her family and the example of Susan B. Anthony, and even as a child she was deeply influenced by her grandfather "Paddy the Rebel," who told her of the Molly Maguires, Edward Bellamy's *Looking Backward*, and the writings of Peter Kropotkin. She made her first speech at the age of fifteen at the Harlem Socialist Club in 1906—"What Socialism Will Do for Women"—and though she spoke in a quaking voice, she had enough presence of mind that when silence greeted her conclusion, she declared "Just because I'm young and a girl is no reason you shouldn't ask me questions!"

Only a few months later, she was arrested for the first time. "Speaking without a permit" was the dubious charge, plus "blocking traffic" at 38th Street and Broadway. And when she appeared before a magistrate at the Jefferson Market Courthouse the next day he discharged her with the admonition that girls her age ought to be in school. Unheeding, Elizabeth not only continued her streetcorner speaking but traveled across the country leading demonstrations, organizing strikes, and marching on picket lines—resulting in fifteen more arrests by 1920, several brutalizing nights in jail, but not a single conviction.

"They call her Comrade Elizabeth Flynn," wrote Theodore Dreiser, "and she is only a girl just turned sixteen. . . . But she is also an ardent Socialist orator. . . . Mentally, she is one of the most remarkable girls that the city has ever seen."

Her mother, Elizabeth said, "was strong for girls 'being somebody,' and 'having a life of their own.' . . . I saw no reason why I . . . should give up my work for [my husband's]. I knew . . . I could make more of a contribution to the labor movement than he could. I would not give up."

The Women of the Heterodoxy Club

"Remains of the early Heterodites, a tribe of women living on the Island of Manhattan . . . are still to be found by the ardent traveler. Relics of their former civilization are fairly well preserved . . . found them frank and friendly, ready to share their folk lore. . . . Among some of the tribe was a good deal of reticence about their personal habits and previous experiences, but others had an innate feeling for the value of loquacity to scientific observers."

Actually, the tribe discouraged loquacity—just about its only rule was that members refrain from disclosing what took place at its meetings—and Florence Guy Woolston's 1919 anthropological parody "Marriage Customs and Taboos Among the Early Heterodites" is itself one of the group's few remaining relics. Still, Heterodoxy—a club for unorthodox women, said Mabel Dodge, "women who did things and did them openly," or, in the words of another member, "a little band of willful women, the most unruly and individualistic females you have fell among"—became a part of Village folklore within months of its inception in 1912. Its long, private, and tumultuous luncheons, every other Saturday for nearly thirty years—usually at Polly's or other fashionable bohemian restaurants—served not only as a way for feminists to share ideas and experiences, but as a kind of precursor to the women's consciousness-raising groups of the sixties and seventies.

The only qualifications for membership were an interest in women's issues and any sort of work that could remotely be called "creative." Among those who gathered for the biweekly lectures, and, more important, to talk, to argue, to proselytize, and even *more* important, to break down isolation, provide emotional support—were Democrats, Republicans, radicals, socialists, and anarchists. They might be teachers, journalists, lawyers, or sociologists, settlement house workers or popular novelists, labor organizers or stockbrokers, Freudian or Jungian psychoanalysts, actresses or physicians or interior decorators or cartoonists, married women, single women, free love advocates, and lesbians. Diversity of background was Heterodoxy's striving point, community of aspiration its achievement. The only taboo of Heterodoxy, its members proudly proclaimed, was taboo.

Heterodoxy had over a hundred members, thirty-five to fifty of whom showed up at the meetings—and the only reason the rest didn't attend, someone said, was because they were the kind of women who were always "somewhere else, usually working for various reform causes."

Mabel Dodge was a member—she never saw a membership list she could resist—and Susan Glaspell, Crystal Eastman, Inez Milholland, Ida Rauh, and Henrietta Rodman. Fitzi, Eleanor Fitzgerald, was a member, and Helen Westley, the Washington Square Players actress who kept her bankbook in her stockings. The novelists Fannie Hurst and Edna Kantor and Zona Gale were members, as was the radio personality Mary Margaret McBride. Add Elizabeth Gurley Flynn and Rose Benton Stokes, later leaders of the American Communist party; Stella Ballantine, Emma Goldman's niece and a member of the prominent publishing family; Fola La Follette, actress and daughter of the Wisconsin progressive. Grace Neil Johnson, the group's sole black member, wife of James Weldon Johnson and one of the founders of the NAACP; Charlotte Perkins Gilman, feminist theorist and author of *Herland*, a utopian fantasy about an all-woman society discovered by white male invaders; Mary Heaton Vorse and Elisabeth Irwin, founder of the Village's renowned Little Red School House. Rose Strunsky, one of three oft-wooed daughters of legendary Papa Strunsky, soft-touch landlord to dozens of writers and artists, was legendary for storing dynamite under her bed in her boardinghouse in anticipation of the anarchist insurrection soon to come. Ruth Hale joined as well—wife of Heywood Broun, mother of Heywood Hale Broun, and founder of the Village's Lucy Stone League, which advocated the right of married women to keep their maiden names. And Agnes George de Mille, the daughter of Henry George, and her own daughter, the choreographer Agnes de Mille, who became Heterodoxy's last survivor.

The woman who wielded the Heterodoxy gavel with warmth and wit was a woman who, in the words of one member, "did not choose to be important." "What does she do anyway?" added another. She doesn't write books or plays or poems, "she has only a genius for friendship. She only throws her great motherheart open to us all."

Marie Jenney Howe, Heterodoxy's founder, was ordained as a Unitarian minister in 1898—"only [a secret involvement with] a man could explain such a beautiful girl . . . at the theological seminary," whispered her fellow students . . . and became beloved to her Midwest flock as "the Little Minister" before abruptly giving up her career to marry a liberal lawyer in 1904. Six years later the Howes moved to West 12th Street and "began in earnest our New York Life."

"Brilliant young people, full of vitality, ardent about saving the world, floated in and out of our apartment," recalled Marie's husband, but Marie soon narrowed their focus to saving *half* the world. Shortly after spotting the best-selling novelist Fannie Hurst watching a women's suffrage parade down Fifth Avenue and pulling her out to help hold aloft a feminist banner, she decided to pull other notable women into the cause by forming a biweekly luncheon club. A place where women could share their ideas and explore their feelings, a gathering where women could air their grievances, debate solutions, and clarify their hopes—all without the restraints of feminine "decorum," without fear that their disagreements would damage their common cause, without the constraining presence of men—such was Marie's vision of Heterodoxy.

The first meeting, in the same year Mabel began her salon, brought two dozen prominent women together in Polly's restaurant. For a membership fee of $2 a year, the women of Heterodoxy received "Loud talk and simple feasting: Discussion of philosophy, investigation of subtleties. Tongues loosened and minds at one. Hearts refreshed by discharge of emotion."

Sometimes Marie would ask members to give "a background talk" about their childhood or relationships or work experiences as a way of breaking down emotional restraints, and forming a community dedicated to the larger issues of women's liberation. Sometimes she would invite outside speakers such as Emma Goldman, Margaret Sanger, Louise Bryant, Helen Keller, or Elizabeth Gurley Flynn to stimulate debate about the tactics and goals of the women's movement.

The ensuing discussions were often raucous but always enlightening—with two exceptions. During Margaret Sanger's 1914 appearance at Heterodoxy, she "struck no responsive chord," she reported almost angrily, adding that one found it "unbelievable that the Heterodites could be serious in occupying themselves with what I regarded as trivialities" like keeping their maiden names after marriage—although Margaret's response was probably the result of the Heterodites' reluctance to devote themselves exclusively to the birth control movement.

The Amy Lowell luncheon was even more dismaying. After asking members what poems they'd like her to recite, and hearing them request what she regarded as the most insipid examples of her work, the poet exclaimed, "I'm through. They told me I was to be speaking to a group of intellectual, tough-minded leaders in the woman's world. Instead, I find a group that wants nothing but my most sentimental things." Sticking her cigar firmly into her mouth, Amy snarled "Good afternoon!" and strode out of the restaurant.

On two occasions, both in 1914, Heterodoxy briefly went public with "feminist mass meetings" at Cooper Union, where Marie's husband, in addition to his duties as head of Ellis Island, served as director of the Greenwich Village People's Institute, a kind of popular university which sponsored a series of weekly forums. At the first meeting, a dozen speakers, including Frances Perkins, Crystal Eastman, Max Eastman, and Floyd Dell, addressed the topic "What Feminism Means to Me," and at the second, six women took on "Breaking into the Human Race," with talks entitled "The Right to Work," "The Right of the Mother to Her Profession," "The Right to Her Convictions," "The Right to Her Name," "The Right to Organize," "The Right to Ignore Fashion," and "The Right to Socialize in Home Industries."

Marie, serving as chairman, passionately declaimed, "We're sick of being specialized to sex. We intend simply to be ourselves, not just our little female selves, but our whole, big, human selves." And the Village men in the audience, who outnumbered the women, and who were getting their only glimpse of Heterodoxy in action, cheered the sentiment while reluctantly integrating it into their lives. Hutch Hapgood, for one, despite his disclaimers of sexism, fervent advocacy of free love, and ardent championship of suffrage, couldn't quite understand why the women of Heterodoxy, "women of character and personal charm and beauty," felt that in having "husbands and lovers like other women" they were merely gratifying some of their "commonplace instincts." Maybe it was because "women of character" understood all too well how most Village men practiced feminism— they enjoyed women's sexual freedom, but feared women's sexual power.

Knowing that many of Heterodoxy's members were professional writers and that most were compulsive talkers, and realizing that publicity about Heterodoxy's meetings would inhibit emotional intimacy and restrain freewheeling discussion of differences within the feminist movement, Marie imposed a strict off-the-record rule. Just as Max brought order out of chaos at *Masses* meetings with charm, ideological openness, and efficiency, Marie succeeded with nurturing, ideological commitment, and kindhearted wit.

The club members were unanimously in favor of suffrage, but divided—as was the Village itself—between those who felt that winning the vote was the primary goal and those who felt that a constitutional amendment was only one aspect of a much broader assault on legal discrimination, social customs, and cultural conventions.

For her part, Marie creatively employed irony. One of her standard speeches exposed the assumptions and convictions of the anti-suffrage position by solemnly pretending to embrace them. "Enfranchisement is what makes feminism," she declaimed. "Disenfranchisement is what makes woman woman. . . . If the women were enfranchised they would . . . desert their families, and spend all their time at the polls."

Marie continued her exposure of the illogic and misogyny of the anti-suffrage argument. "For me . . . the effect of the mental strain [of voting] on woman's delicate nervous organization and on her highly wrought sensitive nature . . . [will be that] they will come out of the voting booths and be led away by policemen . . . while they are fainting and weeping. . . . Divorce and death will rage unchecked, crime and contagious disease will stalk unbridled throughout the land."

While all the Heterodites cheered Marie's feminism, some questioned her pacifism. The approach of American intervention in the European war caused considerable controversy within the club—as it did everywhere else. Though most Heterodites supported the anti-war movement led by Fola's father, several members placed their patriotism ahead of their progressivism and resigned from the group. One outraged member supposedly wrote a letter alerting the Secret Service to the large number of pacifists and radicals in the club and suggested surveillance of its meetings. But professional spy-catchers in Washington needed no help from amateur sleuths in Greenwich Village—they were already monitoring Heterodoxy's activities. Several members, in fact, had been arrested for their suffrage protests—Marie among them—and others had been beaten by police in front of the White House, imprisoned, and force-fed when they undertook a hunger strike. But the anti-pacifist hysteria made the anti-suffrage hysteria seem benign.

Beyond direct political action, Heterodoxy provided a place for clarifying and releasing the New Woman's feelings about sexuality, especially the ideal of a free erotic life.

Florence Guy Woolston's spoof of "Marriage Customs and Taboos Among the Early Heterodites" had divided the members' personal lives into three types of sexual relationships, which she labeled "monotonists, varietists, and resistants." The monotonists were women who had "mated young and by pressure of habit and circumstance have remained mated. . . . Some monotonists have practiced variety, secretly. Some varietists would like to become monotonists."

Contrary to the cliché that the "complaining" and "immoral feminist—like the bohemians and radicals—were merely rebelling" against their families and their marriages, most of the monotonists of Heterodoxy came from supportive families and were married to feminist men. Yet even the most articulate ideological sympathy was often undermined by ingrained cultural attitudes, and inertia took its toll on even seemingly ideal marriages.

"Sheer inertia" may have been the problem for some monotonists, but participation in the "new morality" was a problem for others. Heterodite Elsie Clews Parsons, who went so far as to advocate trial marriages in her book *The Family*, found her feminist husband so willing to exercise the principle that he embarked on a series of guilt-free love affairs with liberated women. "Modern" in his attitude, he could accept his wife's ways with equanimity—in all probability, because she didn't embark on affairs of her own—so how could she do less when it came to *his*?

The varietists, Woolston's spoof went on—some of whom "distinguish themselves by short hair"—"have never been ceremonially mated but have preferred a series of matings." Sex before marriage, in fact, remained such a taboo that in the minds of many Villagers it became virtually synonymous with free love—which itself sometimes threatened to become a form of institutionalized liberation. The economic independence of most Heterodites (who were beginning to comprehend the connection between economic and sexual independence), the underground availability of birth control information, the encouragement of the Village's feminist men—all made nonmarital sex appear easier for women. But in reality, the lingering sexism of even the most feminist men and the increasing rigidity of the free love credo itself (which often transformed emancipation into an imperative) made nonmarital sex difficult.

In any case, most of the unmarried Heterodoxy women would probably have agreed with Susan Glaspell when she wrote, "We were supposed to be a sort of special group—radical, wild, Bohemians. . . . Most of us were from families who had other ideas—who wanted to make money, play bridge, voted the Republican ticket, went to church. . . . And so, drawn together by the thing we really were, we were as a new family. . . . Each could be himself, that was perhaps the real thing we did for one another."

Florence's third group, the resistants, "have not mated at all. . . . True resistants are rare. As virginity is an asset outside of monotony, many varietists assume an outward resistancy. I recall one resistant who had cleverly concealed 16 varieties of mating." But despite Florence's gibe, celibacy was the intimation, lesbianism the fact that even she remained reluctant to acknowledge—for probably two dozen participants in Heterodoxy were gay, or roughly a fifth of the total membership. If the Village was an enclave for women of "loose morals," it was a *haven* for lesbians, for nowhere else in the country could they live even semi-openly. Even there they were treated with tolerance rather than acceptance, and even among the feminists were the subject of whispers and innuendo.

Among the lesbians of Heterodoxy—and Charlotte, Mabel, and Florence all had brief affairs with women—were two couples, Katherine Anthony and Elisabeth Irwin, and Ida Wylie and Sara Josephine Baker (Sara, ironically, acknowledged that in her work as a doctor she found it professionally advisable to look as "unfeminine" as possible). Lou Rogers, the political cartoonist, cryptically remarked that "Love is good wherever it comes from"—an appropriate motto for Heterodoxy, even if not all of its members realized all its implications.

But love has an even shorter life as a social credo than as a marriage vow, and all too soon the members of Heterodoxy began to find it elsewhere. Though many members continued to meet under a revolving leadership until the early forties, the flame that had been lit in the teens flickered only fitfully in the twenties and thirties. The women's movement became an outdated whim. Women had won the vote; what more did they want? The flapper replaced the feminist, the dance hall replaced the luncheon lecture, and the desire for free fashions replaced the commitment to a freer society. Emancipation? With the gin fizz, the Charleston, the short skirt, the diaphragm, Village women who only a decade earlier were "ardent about saving the world" were now ardent about having a good time.

"I have never met a man who at any time wanted to be a woman. I have met few women who have not at some time or another wanted to be men." So wrote one of the Heterodites in *Harper's Bazaar* in 1912. But if this tone of wistful despair was rarely heard after the teens, and even if Heterodoxy's early critics correctly asserted that its members were "less inclined toward activism" than toward a kind of "religious excitement," Marie Jenney Howe and the Heterodites provided what Elizabeth Gurley

Flynn called "a glimpse of the women of the future, big-spirited, intellectually alert, devoid of the old feminism."

Neith Boyce and Hutch Hapgood

When Hutchins Hapgood published *The Story of a Lover* in 1919—a
brooding account of his marriage to Neith Boyce in which he confessed
many affairs and revealed his efforts to persuade her to experiment with infidelity herself—both of them felt compelled to write letters of disavowal to
their mothers. "It's not all true," Hutch wrote. "I misrepresented myself because I took her point of view and misrepresented her because of my un-
balanced feeling." "Don't believe it," Neith wrote. "It isn't all true to *my*
facts or feelings, that is, it represents a very different truth from my truth."

But though *The Story of a Lover* was pathetically self-justifying and
comically self-deluding, it also touched thornier truths than Hutch's and
Neith's mothers, or most of Hutch's readers, were ready to understand.
It's the story of an early-twentieth-century couple struggling to move beyond the constraints of nineteenth-century marriage, but on a deeper level
it's the chronicle of a modern couple struggling to redefine the relationships between men and women—especially the role of sex in the era of
Freud and the role of autonomy in the era of feminism.

Hutch and Neith's marriage, as related not only in Hutch's psycho-
sexual autobiography but in Neith's novel *The Bond* and in a play the two
co-authored, revealed the ways in which the Villagers' restructuring of
their personal affairs had revolutionary social consequences.

Hutch and Neith met in New York in 1898 when both worked as writers
for a liberal newspaper edited by Lincoln Steffens. Hutch, who'd
grown up in Illinois as an "odd stick," was an extroverted conversationalist
and an introverted dreamer, ebullient and sensitive. Neith, a native of Indiana whose family moved to California—where her father became one of
the founders of the *Los Angeles Times*—was quiet and even a bit remote,
qualities that, combined with her sardonic asides and aura of calm self-
sufficiency, made her seem "unfeminine" to her contemporaries despite
her red hair and sultry green eyes. Ambitious, independent, and iconoclastic, she was told to choose between marriage and a career—and didn't hesitate for a moment. Naturally, the endearingly childlike Hutch and the
mature Neith were destined to fall in love.

"She is a new woman," Hutch wrote his mother, "more or less disliked by all my friends that know her, and she has no idea of getting married, at any rate to me." As for Neith, she found herself drawn to the "warm, life-quality in him."

Hutch and Neith married in 1899, and within the next decade they had four children and wrote four books each. Hutch focused on what he called "the underlife" of New York, "the immigrants, radicals, prostitutes, and ex-convicts," while Neith wrote observant, unmelodramatic novels about middle-class marriage. They traveled extensively, and in 1911 settled in Dobbs Ferry. For most of the teens they were commuters to bohemia, always present at Mabel's salon, close friends of many of the writers for *The Masses*, and instrumental in the founding of the Provincetown Players.

Hutch and Neith's discovery that a common purpose can lead to both cooperation and competition makes their forty-five-year marriage an intriguing test of the new relationships between men and women that began to emerge in the Village in the years before World War I.

In every aspect of their marriage, they found themselves adjusting traditional gender roles, a daily balancing act that resulted in accommodations more or less satisfying to each. Hutch's financial inheritance from his father allowed them to hire household help—including that gifted Village cook Hippolyte Havel, who alternately served them sumptuous meals and raged that he'd never work another day for such bourgeois pigs—but his psychological inheritance from his mother, a warm zest for family life, allowed him to feel comfortable with the homemaking duties Neith disdained. Hutch's emotionally accessible temperament made him eager to share in child-rearing as well, and even complain that Neith was too emotionally aloof with their children. Hutch's easygoing disinclination to undertake a conventional male career also meant that he'd often disappear for months at a time, wandering around America or Europe casually researching his books. And it also meant that he couldn't understand Neith's dedication to *her* work, the single aspect of her life that gave her the feeling of autonomy she craved.

Their central conflict soon emerged. For two decades it threatened to drive them apart, yet eventually sealed their union. Sex.

Hutch believed that a husband should give "his wife some occasion for jealousy" or he was "deficient in the art of life," and added that "a jealous wife" had "great attractiveness." So during the second year of their marriage, and during Neith's first pregnancy, he began a series of what he called "conventional affairs," but, unconventionally, he not only told Neith about them, he encouraged her to have affairs of her own. "To have her know other men intimately," he wrote in *The Story of a Lover* in the familiar rhetoric of free love, "was with me a genuine desire. I saw in this one of the conditions of greater social relations between her and me, of a richer material for conversation and for a common life together." Like that of most Village men who practiced promiscuity and persuaded their partners to join them, Hutch's sincerity might be questioned, but Neith had reason to believe Hutch, for the one thing he enjoyed more than sex was "richer material for conversation."

On and off for the next two decades, Neith tried her best to emulate Hutch's infidelities, sometimes in perfunctory obeisance to his precepts when his philandering left her lonely. She'd flirt with their male friends, form intimate friendships of her own, and contemplate, but probably not consummate, sexual liaisons. The ensuing "conversations" invariably revolved around her failure to understand his principles. No, no, that's not what I meant by free love, he'd rant. Didn't she see that if she developed an emotional attachment to another man she was detracting from her relationship with him, and if she was sleeping with another man she'd develop an emotional attachment? None of his affairs threatened their marriage, he'd sputter, but all of her behavior caused him pain. There was nothing wrong with free love, it was just that Neith never seemed to get the hang of it.

Neith wrote Hutch in 1901, "I assure you that I shall tell you if anything at all occurs beyond friendly and (at times) coolly flirtatious talks."

Four years later she wrote him, "There is no doubt in my mind that the ideal on which marriage is based (theoretically)—mutual fidelity—is the most attractive that has been discovered so far."

While Hutch always found very sound reasons why her innocent behavior was reprehensible, she nearly always found very sound reasons why his reprehensible behavior was pardonable. Like so many Village women of the time she felt vaguely ashamed of her jealousy, silently berating herself for her shortcomings. His principles made sense, so why couldn't she live up to them? Free love was rational, so why was she behaving so irrationally?

When Mabel wrote Neith about her jealousy over Jack Reed's affairs, Neith responded, "Why want anybody to be what they are not? . . . An absolutely faithful man, but what's the use of discussing him. He's a mythical creature. . . . I like them as they are."

So while Hutch reacted angrily to her innocent friendships, Neith tolerated his sexual betrayals, shifting uneasily between blithe acceptance and painful resignation and maintaining an emotional stability that irrationally but lovingly kept their marriage intact.

Emotionally they reversed gender roles—Hutch open, sensitive, even effusive, Neith aloof, withdrawn, remote—but sexually, despite their earnest efforts, they remained almost Victorian. Hutch, who like many Village bohemians had his first sexual experience in France, and who, like so many puritans, had a lifelong fascination with prostitutes, regarded Neith as sexually passive and morally restraining, qualities he probably would have found in Messalina herself, and without which he probably never would have married her in the first place. For her part, Neith, likely a virgin when they married, gradually and gratefully found herself becoming sexually responsive, but took it as a matter of course that men wanted sex more than women, and, despite her occasional exasperation, wouldn't have found Hutch so attractive if he hadn't.

Hutch approached free love less with a wandering eye than with a romantic heart, and regarded sex not so much a physical impulse as a spiritual quest for "higher truths." Neith wasn't nearly as sentimental as her husband about free love and was more down-to-earth about sex. As a result, their attempts at free love forced them to re-examine their own attitudes. Ironically, Hutch discovered how much he cherished intimacy, and Neith learned how much she desired independence—setting up precisely the opposite conflicts from the ones with which they'd begun.

So a curious combination of circumstances—their approach to free love, their complex psychological constitutions, and, most of all, their courageous determination to make their union work—allowed them to move beyond the conventional unconventionality of most Village relationships, to avoid the dreary stalemate of philandering-husband-and-patient-wife marriages, and to become one of the first couples of the post-Victorian, pre-feminist era.

Drawn to Hutch's warmth, so unlike the emotional chill of her family, Neith was opening up to form intimate friendships with other men. Although her male friends were so like her in temperament that she felt no erotic charge, she felt less dependent on Hutch for companionship. Furthermore, Hutch's affairs made him considerably less physically attractive to her, so she became less sexually dependent as well. Neith found herself able to work more creatively. "When I'm not working," she said in a kind of pre-echo of what so many women would be saying decades later, "I hate the world and myself—when I am, I have peace." And since so much of her self-image centered around her writing, her sense of self began to blossom under the conditions that had once shriveled her soul.

As Neith became less dependent on him, Hutch found himself becoming more dependent on her. If this had happened early in their relationship, he probably would have fled in fear—after all, she initially attracted him largely because of her emotional remoteness—but as she moved even further away, he had to move closer to maintain the same distance between them. In a sense, then, their conflicts over free love saved their marriage, allowing Neith to insist on her independence and allowing Hutch to express his dependence, and like dance partners, one moving forward, the other backward, they remained in each other's arms.

"The deeper relation between [us] was founded not on compromise," he wrote in *The Story of a Lover*, "but on attraction and repulsion, on a kind of interesting warfare." And in a remarkable letter to Neith in 1916, he wrote, "Tell me you love me and also tell me about the flirtations you are having. Have you been unfaithful? Have you sinned? Did you like it? . . . Is he younger than I? Warmer? Handsomer?" Hutch, a voyeuristic narcissist.

The man who flew into a rage at the slightest possibility of infidelity became sexually excited at the fantasy of infidelity, since now he was in complete control of his imagination, and since, as he intimated, it led not to intercourse but to masturbation. But even Hutch, for all his sexual sophistication and familiarity with Freud, would have been shocked if anyone had suggested that his fantasy also had homoerotic overtones. What better way to ease into bed with a man than to join Neith and her lover? Emma Goldman, in fact—who knew her Freud far better than did Hutch—always suspected that Hutch and her longtime lover Ben Reitman were sexually attracted to each other. The two men did strike up a brief friendship, but even given Hutch's fascination with outcasts, he found Ben a sleazy buffoon.

For the most part, Neith refused to take Hutch's mystical flights seriously. As Mabel put it, "Neith let him think he was pursuing God, but she held the end of the leash in her enigmatic white hand and smiled a secret smile. . . . She was sweetly half-attentive, half-distrait when he talked, as when one of the children told of his exploits."

Still, Hutch and Neith's marriage might have failed if they both hadn't been so self-conscious about personal relationships, so committed to exploring their every nuance, so obsessed with examining their every permutation. And who better to take the foreground in this revolution of consciousness than a pair of writers?

• • •

Neith wrote several novels about marriage, but the aptly titled *The Bond*, published in 1908, most closely paralleled her own. Teresa and Basil, a sculptress and a painter, talk about their feelings, quarrel, talk some more about their feelings, reconcile, and talk some more about their feelings. They become more or less innocently involved with other people and talk some more. The talk never ceases, except for their occasional silences, which they then talk about.

Yet easy as Neith's pedestrian novel is to mock, it's also a genuine attempt to explore a modern marriage, to establish a balance of power between men and women, to find some psychic equilibrium between love and work, domesticity and creativity, intimacy and autonomy, submission and independence. And if these themes, commonplace as they might seem to later generations, were relatively revolutionary in Neith's day, so was her tone—a woman's point of view about love not swooning and romantic, but matter-of-fact and psychological.

Without claiming too much for what could easily be regarded as a turgid novel, it's fair to say that Neith pioneered the fictional treatment of woman's consciousness. Analyzing the relationships as a continually unresolved exploration of emotional intimacy, she not only helped bring new material into the novel but helped envision a more modern form of union.

Neith's reward was to be misunderstood and mocked. "We are getting a little tired of the neurotic young woman who makes unreasonable demands upon life," wrote the critic for *The Dial*, "and is unhappy because it turns out to be less exciting than she would like to find it. A typical example of this sort of woman, who worries over her own emotions until her whole moral fiber is weakened, is found in the heroine of *The Bond*. This morbid type of character occurs, of course, as a by-product of the life which we moderns lead at such high pressure, and the novelist has a right to describe it; we could wish that the author's delicate talent had been employed upon a worthier theme, or a theme bearing a closer relation to normal existence." And the *New York Times* characterized the novel as a matter of "bicker, quarrel, jar and nag."

Not a single reviewer brought up the issue of the double standard, which was examined so subtly in the novel.

Less interested in sex than in self, Hutch had long had the annoying habit of analyzing his friends at generous length and in exhaustive detail, and in *The Story of a Lover* he turned the full force of this impulse on himself, then distributed copies of the manuscript to his friends years before it was published.

With minimal social or historical context and virtually no narrative, the book soon degenerates into vapid metaphysical musings and tepid Nietzschean aphorisms. "He who has never desired a revaluation of all values," read one typically unmemorable passage, "has never fully loved a woman." Yet for all his floundering self-indulgence and failures of self-understanding, Hutch relentlessly attempted to discover a new ideal of masculinity incorporating "female" impulses and a new basis for more fulfilling sexual relationships.

Hutch set as one of his major themes the contrast between his profound love "for the essence of [Neith's] being" and her mere love "for what I was able to say and feel"—"she did not love me," he complained. Readers might have sympathized with Hutch's frustration at Neith's failure to love him as unconditionally as he loved her, until it became clear, though not to Hutch, that the commitment he sought was less marital than maternal, and that the imperative of his Soul she refused to accept was his impulse to fool around.

Hutch set forth the "varietal" credo of the Village with a kind of ecclesiastical zeal. "To free love from convention and from the economic incubus seemed a profound moral need. . . . I met men and women who, with the energy of poets and idealists, attempted to free themselves from that jealousy which is founded on physical possession. . . . —believing that love is of the soul, and is pure and intense only when freed from the gross superstitions of the past. . . . They traced this feeling to old theology and to the sense of ownership extended until it includes the body of the loved one!"

So free love, Hutch argued, was not so much in service of the libido as of the spirit—and even of feminism!

With his "fragmentary and idealistic hopes of a superior race of men and women . . . capable of maintaining beautiful and intense relations," he introduced Neith to "new and excited feelings." To his surprise, she agreed to give them a try, but his delight was shaded by apprehension. "The ease and calmness with which she could take a mental proposition filled me with uneasiness, I felt that if she loved me she would have more in her instincts to overcome."

And when Neith tells him she's having lunch with another man, they have a violent quarrel, and she, who'd been asked to accept his explicitly sexual adventures, "accused me of hopeless inconsistency. Inconsistent

I was, but not in the way she meant," Hutch acknowledged with an argument a Jesuit would envy. "My inconsistency lay in demanding from her what her nature could not give"—and what *his* nature could all too easily give was the assurance that having sex (but not lunch) with another person in no way threatened their own relationship.

So for all his vaunted efforts to build a relationship upon equality, Hutch not only instinctively reverted to the "It didn't mean anything" defense of his promiscuity, but even blamed Neith for his irrational jealousy of her innocent friendships. "I retorted with what I think was not entire hypocrisy. Despairingly and passionately I insisted that she had as yet shown herself incapable of giving to others without taking away from the relation with me. . . . Never, I repeated, had I been able to forget, even for a moment, even in the arms of another woman, my bond with her: even when I desired to forget it, this spiritual love, stronger than death, was unshaken.

"But with her it was different, I insisted. Had she ever loved in that strange, temperamental way, had she ever had that passionate liking for my real self, independent of my qualities, she would have been incapable of spiritual infidelity. Over and over again I vehemently asserted the difference between the conventions of her sex and of mine: conventions that I hated and wished undone and obliterated from society: but which nevertheless existed and which were a painful element in every human relation."

Like many people who talk incessantly about freedom, Hutch was clearly in the grip of a compulsion. He kept on having affairs, he kept telling Neith about them, he kept encouraging her to become intimate with other men, he kept feeling devastated whenever she did. Nothing could stop him, for he was motivated by an ideology he couldn't forsake.

But was Hutch motivated solely by ideology? Had he known more about the Freud he idolized, had he realized how compulsively he pursued a path that led only to pain for them both, another word might have come to mind—sadomasochism. At moments he glimpsed this element of his psyche—he had, he admitted, "an idealistic instinct for self-torture." And of his treatment of Neith he confessed, "I did all I could to disturb, to wound, to arouse, to make her calm soul discontented and unhappy." He defended this behavior as an attempt to penetrate her reserve, to deepen her allegiance, but he also noted, almost in passing, that "the deeper relation between us was founded not on compromise but on attraction and repulsion, on a kind of interesting warfare."

Well, as Hutch himself observed, "If our relation had remained simple it might not have endured." At the end of his book, he both described himself as "passionately unsatisfied" and wrote that "this inaccessible woman . . . consciously rejecting me as a lover and accepting me warmly as a child . . . is the one perfect experience of my life."

Shortly after the publication of *The Story of a Lover*, the New York police confiscated all copies and brought obscenity charges against its publisher.

Critically, *The Story of a Lover* met the same unfortunate fate as Neith's *The Bond. The Dial* may have called the book "one of the extraordinary pieces of literature of recent years," but far more typical was the review of a Chicago critic: "That any educated person could be so naive is fairly incredible." "It is not the story of a lover; it is the story of a sexual psychasthenic . . . a constitutional neurotic. Far from representing the universal, or even not very uncommon experience of lovers, it belongs in the class of the pathological." The *New York Times*, echoing Hutch himself, and revealing how quickly psychological jargon had entered the language, summed up the book as "the history of the love life of a self-conscious neurasthenic."

Writing *The Story of a Lover* documented Hutch's obsessions but failed to free him from them. One of his most intense affairs, in fact, took place between the year he wrote the book and the year he published it.

In May 1915, he found himself deeply involved with Lucy Collier, the wife of John Collier, a close friend of Mabel's and later commissioner of Indian Affairs under FDR. Lucy, like Hutch, saw no reason not to have a lover as well as a spouse, and, since both Neith and John accepted Hutch and Lucy's affair with relative equanimity, the Villagers seemed at last to have an exemplary model of the free love they so heartily advocated and so haphazardly practiced—until Mabel entered the picture.

Even before he began his affair with Lucy, Hutch and Neith corresponded with Mabel about their mutual misery. "Anything that you can write me about [Neith], that you observe, that will help me to understand," Hutch wrote, "I will receive gratefully." He entreated her to be straightforward.

Mabel opened her mail a few days later and found a letter from Neith. "I knew we were killing one another," she wrote. "It was the culmination of long years of strains and of savage intensity. . . . It got to a point where the only way out seemed to be physical murder."

After a flurry of tense letters, everything seemed to be proceeding more or less smoothly—until Hutch and Neith again corresponded with Mabel, forgetting her compulsion to meddle. She decided to use all her charms to resolve a situation that she could only make worse. But even Mabel understood, at this point, that some hapless people have to be left to their own devices, and the ménage à cinque reverted to a ménage à quatre. There had always been more talk than sex in Hutch's affairs, however, and soon he was sated. In the spring of 1916, the two couples resumed their old friendly relationship, and Hutch and Neith began their inevitable postmortems.

One year after the Lucy fiasco, Hutch once more fell in free love, this time with a young actress with the Provincetown Players named Mary Pyne, twenty-five years his junior and who, even more infelicitously, was married to Harry Kemp. Hutch claimed that it was a "spiritual intimacy" only, but Harry was less accommodating than John, and threatened to thrash Hutch if he continued his advances. Hutch also claimed that Neith approved of his relationship, but Neith's letters revealed that this interpretation was something of a misunderstanding.

Neith's patience with Hutch's promiscuity was partly principle, but partly sheer weariness. In any event, her common sense and shrugging acceptance outlasted his metaphysical musings and wandering eye. What saved their marriage, finally, was a secret Neith never realized she'd discovered—that an important part of love is the forgiveness of foolishness.

Ever eager to play out his private life in the public domain, Hutch prevailed upon Neith to join him in co-authoring a play for the Provincetown Players based on the conflicts in their marriage. Neith had already written *Constancy* for the troupe, its narrative based on the affair between Mabel and Jack but its subtext revealing her own feelings about Hutch's philandering. So in Provincetown in 1916—the year after the production of *Constancy*—Hutch and Neith wrote and acted a dialogue between a man and a woman called, with Hutch's self-conscious irony, *Enemies*.

The play opens with Hutch in a tirade and proceeds with a series of sarcastic put-downs that must have made their friends in the audience experience that peculiar uneasiness we often feel in the presence of truth. Hutch calls Neith "a cold-blooded person that you have to hit with a gridiron to get a rise out of," while Neith tells him "you keep your unsociability for me" and freely expresses her exasperation—"If you're not talking it's [only] because you're sulking."

Soon, they stop inflicting mere flesh wounds and begin to expose raw nerves. Neith argues that she wants sexual fidelity and he argues that he wants sexual freedom. But in a deeper sense, Neith wants emotional autonomy and Hutch wants spiritual union—the true conflict in their relationship.

She: "But what you want is to censor and control me, while you feel perfectly free to amuse yourself in every possible way."

He: "I am never jealous without cause and you are. You object to my friendly and physical intimacies and then expect me not to be jealous of your soul's infidelities."

Enemies revealed, far more than anything either of them ever wrote, the central dynamic of their relationship—that Hutch, in setting the terms of their dispute, seemed the dominant partner; Neith, in resisting his demands for mystic union, slowly asserted her emotional independence. The mystic union of love—the ideal to which women of the nineteenth century were supposed to aspire, was Neith's for the taking. But female autonomy—the ideal which the modern women of the Village were struggling to achieve—was hers only if she resisted.

The new candor about "human relations" was in many ways comic (particularly Hutch's solemn scrutiny of his every motive for promiscuity except his libido, and the Villagers' eager attempts to elevate gossip into a principle of liberation), in some ways destructive, and in one way problematic (the preoccupation with self that led some Villagers toward political indifference). Yet the new candor was also a provocative challenge to conventional morality and social structures, and the first step in the politicization of self-fulfillment and personal relationships. "The new sexuality" remained largely male-defined, for while women's right to sexual fulfillment was acknowledged, men assumed it would follow male patterns and hoped it would enhance male pleasures. Hutch and many other Village men who insisted on women's sexual freedom remained reluctant to deal with gender issues, women's desire to work in particular. He failed to see the role of work in women's emancipation, resenting Neith's writing as a distraction from her commitment to their marriage. Still, he was one of the first men who dimly comprehended the role of women's issues in the revolution of consciousness, writing that "woman's soul . . . is a spiritual abode of deep rebellion against man's conventional moralities and laws." Yet for all Neith and Hutch's "rich conversations," and for all the radical feminist visions of the Villagers, the two remained unable to find equality in love and work.

As for Neith, she was no ideologue; she never joined the handful of leaders who were developing a feminist doctrine; she was just one among thousands of restless Village women whom they spoke for and whose energies they mobilized. She struggled for independence in love, in sex, in work, and almost unconsciously she understood that women's liberation depends not so much on the sexual freedom Hutch advocated as on the emotional autonomy she achieved. If feminism in the Village can be defined as women's demand that personal concerns become public issues, Neith Boyce, in her patient courage, imperturbable common sense, and stubbornness, was one of the women who led the way.

Crystal Eastman

When Crystal Eastman was fifteen, her mother started a series of summer "symposiums" at their home in upstate New York. Once a week, the neighborhood mothers and children—"and any fathers who happened to be around"—gathered on the front porch, listened to a paper, and then discussed it. Crystal's contribution was called "Woman."

"The trouble with women," wrote the teenage girl, "is that they have no impersonal interests. They must have work of their own, first because no one who has to depend on another person for his living is really grown up: and, second, because the only way to be happy is to have an absorbing interest in life which is not bound up with any particular person. Children can die or grow up, husbands can leave you. No woman who allows a husband and children to absorb her whole time and interest is safe against disaster."

Nearly as prominent a figure in the Village in the teens and early twenties as her younger brother, Max—a pioneering feminist and socialist, an influential labor lawyer, a founder of the Women's Peace Party and the American Civil Liberties Union, a co-editor of *The Liberator,* and one of the most beloved women of her generation—Crystal embodied not only the principles of her adolescent essay but the reasons for its necessity. For despite all this "work of [her] own," she is remembered, if at all, only as Max's older sister—and "the trouble with women," at least to the historians of the period who have largely ignored her remarkable achievements, is nothing but their gender.

• • •

The story of my background," recalled Crystal, "is the story of my mother." After her minister husband suffered a nervous breakdown, Annis Eastman was herself ordained as a Congregational minister—at a time when few women entered the profession—and became celebrated as "the most noted minister of her time" for her eloquent, impassioned sermons. But it was her energetic mind, her sparkling humor, her "stormy, troubled soul, capable of black cruelty and then again of the deepest generosities"—her daughter's memory—that had a decisive influence on her children.

Both parents were suffragists, but the young Crystal's feminism was instinctive—and initially domestic. "When I insisted that the boys must make their beds if I had to make mine, [my father] stood by me. When I said that if there was dishwashing to be done they should take their turn, he stood by me. And when I declared that there was no such thing in our family as boys' work and girls' work, and that I must be allowed to do my share of wood-chopping and outdoor chores, he took me seriously and let me try."

While such behavior seemed, to most friends of the family, little more than amusing adolescent obstinacy, Crystal was already learning to draw parallels to adult life. "If boys, *as well as girls*, must be taught . . . the rudiments of home-making," didn't it follow that "girls, *as well as boys*, must be brought up as a matter of principles not through an adult's intellectual analysis but through a child's sense of household fairness." As a result, "I grew up confidently expecting to have a profession and earn my own living, and also as passionately determined to have children as I was to have a career. And my mother was the triumphant answer to all doubts as to the success of this double role."

At Vassar, Crystal wrote in her journal that men were "clever, powerful, selfish, and animal," except for her brother, Max, and that if she ever were to marry, her husband would have to have Max's qualities. "I don't believe there is a feeling in the world too refined and imagined for him to appreciate." Crystal worked at a settlement house while studying for her M.A. in sociology at Columbia and her law degree at New York University. Her apartment with Ida Rauh became one of the social centers of the Village in the years before Mabel Dodge's salon. Her multitude of friends were drawn to her company to discuss suffragism and labor reform—the forms feminism and socialism took before expanding their scope in the teens—and by her vivacious personality.

Crystal was "a natural leader," recalled Max's friend Roger Baldwin, a founder of the ACLU, "outspoken (often tactless), determined, charming, beautiful, courageous." "The moment I saw her and heard her voice," said Claude McKay, poet of the Harlem Renaissance, "I liked Crystal Eastman. I think she was the most beautiful white woman I ever knew. Her beauty was not so much of her features . . . but in her magnificent presence."

A quintessential early Villager in her combination of the practical and the rebellious, she wore short skirts at work and flamboyant dresses in the evening, stressing that such a style was not only "comfortable, hygienic, and becoming," but "a step in the direction of freedom." One of the first women in the country to bob her hair, she saw such seemingly trivial decisions as crucial components of women's initial steps on the road to liberation but justified as well on grounds of comfort and equality. "What the short skirt has done for women's legs, short hair is doing for their heads. And outside of musical comedy, a woman's head is ever more important than her legs."

After graduating second in her class at NYU Law, specializing in labor legislation, Crystal moved to Pittsburgh to undertake America's first comprehensive study of industrial accidents, a project that led to her appointment as the first female member of New York's Employers' Liability Commission, where she drafted the state's first workers' compensation law. Starting to identify herself as a socialist, she wanted to shift the burden of responsibility for industrial safety from the workers to the industry. When laborers are injured or killed, she said angrily, she didn't want to see them dependent on relief funds, she wanted "to start a revolution."

But unlike many of her Village friends, Crystal didn't vaguely envision the new social order, or merely lend eloquent vocal support to the workers, but wrote the statistic-filled reports and undertook the tedious lobbying efforts that might actually result in meaningful change. Though she knew her efforts would lead to reform rather than revolution, and though she grudgingly accepted the necessity for compromise, she never lost sight of her socialist ideals. "The tigress," friends called her—aggressive, fearless, often flushed with anger. "Very realistic but not very docile," said a colleague.

And since, as a radical feminist, she espoused equality as her abiding principle, Crystal firmly opposed as discriminatory and condescending the trend toward industrial safety legislation that regulated working conditions only for women—"protective" legislation, it was called by male lawmakers who saw themselves as responding to the "special" needs of women. "Feminism has entered upon a new phase," wrote Crystal. "No longer content with asking for their rights, women have begun to question their privileges. They have begun to examine, with some shrewdness, the whole body of more or less benevolent legislation which has been gradually built up during the last half century for the 'protection' of women in industry." She advocated, instead, the goals of the British feminist societies — "legislation for the protection of the worker . . . based not upon sex but upon the nature of the work."

"It was fifty-fifty with men," Crystal had said — career and marriage. But she wanted a child more than she wanted a husband, and vowed that if she wasn't married before she reached thirty she'd take a year-long "vacation" in Italy and return with an "adopted" baby. Several men proposed and less than a month before her thirtieth birthday, after a series of casual liaisons and a consultation with the Village's favorite psychoanalyst, A. A. Brill, to help bring her "libido down," she married an insurance salesman named Wallace Benedict.

Max married Ida Rauh within the same week, and brother and sister were not alone in noting that both had waited for wedlock until they were nearly thirty. Among their friends there was little doubt that they loved each other more than they loved their spouses. Max had frequently declared in his childhood that "I would never marry any girl but my sister," and later didn't hesitate to express his conviction that "of all Freud's plain and fancy inventions, the concept of an 'incest barrier' is one of the most easily verifiable in my experience." Perhaps in Crystal's, too, for shortly after her engagement she fell ill and wrote Max, "I've been feeling very scared about getting married all through this sickness. Getting back to New York and living with you was the hope I fed my drooping spirits on, not . . . the married state. Your suggestion that if I can't stand it, you'll know it's not for you, gives me a humorous courage. Perhaps after we've both experimented around a few years, we may end up living together again."

Although her handsome husband, Bennie, supported her work and satisfied her sexually, Max and her friends weren't entirely happy with Crystal's choice, not the least because it meant moving to Milwaukee. Whatever qualms she might have felt about letting the man's career predominate were partially relieved by her own work in Wisconsin's burgeoning suffrage movement, but after two melancholy years she left Bennie and returned to the Village.

. . .

For the next two years, Crystal led the suffrage movement in New York, but like Emma Goldman she had no illusion that gaining the vote would bring meaningful equality. "Today when there is no longer a single, simple aim and a solidarity barrier to break down," she wrote, "there are a hundred difficult questions of civil law, problems of education, of moral and social custom to be solved before women can come wholly into their inheritance of freedom."

Crystal personally addressed dozens of those questions, writing, lecturing, organizing, founding institutions, chairing committees, dealing with subjects ranging from housework to birth control, from living arrangements to the Equal Rights Amendment and prostitution.

In one of her few compromises with principle, she hired domestic servants and when she had children of her own rarely so much as changed a diaper; as a result, she saw that homemaking symbolized women's inequality and proposed what she called a Motherhood Endowment, wages for housework as skilled labor. "It seems that the only way we can keep mothers free," she wrote, "at least in a capitalist society, is by the establishment of a principle that the occupation of raising children is peculiarly and directly a service to society, and that the mother upon whom the necessity and privilege of performing this service naturally falls is entitled to an adequate economic reward from the political government. It is idle to talk of real economic independence for women unless this principle is accepted. But with a generous endowment of motherhood . . . there is no reason why woman should not become almost a human thing. It will be time enough then to consider whether she has a soul."

As part of her effort to reveal to women the small but insidious ways in which they were kept powerless—and often unconsciously conspired in maintaining male supremacy—Crystal was one of the first to emphasize gender roles. Why shouldn't it be considered "manly" to cook, clean, and sew, she argued, and then made sure that the men in her life paid more than rhetorical attention. She even spoke out on the physical equality of the sexes. Almost six feet tall, vigorous and athletic, she scorned the notion that women were delicate creatures. "When women were expected to be agile, they became agile; when they were expected to be brave, they developed courage; when they had to endure, their endurance broke all records."

Women also had the right to be sexually active. "Feminists are not nuns," Crystal wrote. "That should be established." And though she believed most women have "the normal desire to be mothers," she insisted that they have the right to choose when. One of the earliest supporters of birth control, she was also one of the first to stress its connection to economic independence. Women must demand "such freedom to choose one's way of making a living as men now enjoy, and definite economic rewards for one's work when it happens to be 'home-making.' . . . Until women learn to want economic independence . . . it seems to me feminism has no roots. . . . But on this we [feminists] are surely agreed, that Birth Control is an elementary essential in all aspects of feminism. . . . We must all be followers of Margaret Sanger. . . . I would almost say that the whole structure of the feminists' dream of society rests upon the rapid extension of scientific knowledge about birth control."

Crystal also recognized "the fact that women by their passivity have made [women's oppression] possible." "WE WILL NOT WAIT FOR THE SOCIAL REVOLUTION TO BRING US THE FREEDOM WE SHOULD HAVE WON IN THE 19TH CENTURY."

In one of her most popular and provocative articles, published in *Cosmopolitan* in 1923, Crystal made the feminist case in "Marriage Under Two Roofs." After divorcing Bennie in 1913—and refusing alimony—in 1916 she married a dapper and witty pacifist named Walter Fuller, with whom she'd been living, and the couple raised two children while they traveled between the United States and Walter's native England. The arrangement saved their marriage, Crystal told her *Cosmopolitan* readers, her breezy tone only partially disguising how seriously she felt about the erosion of romance by domesticity.

> "You're breaking up our home," my husband said.
> "No I'm not. I'm trying to hold it together."
> We tried it. And it has given us the one serene and happy period of all our married life. . . . For the first time the fact that we love each other and have two splendid children is making us happy instead of miserable. . . .
> My husband may come home with me and he may not, according to our mood. . . . And because neither course is inexorably forced upon us, either one is a bit of a lark. . . .
> Women, more than men, succumb to marriage. They sink so easily into that fatal habit of depending on one person to rescue them from themselves. And this is the death of love.
> The two-roof plan encourages a wife to cultivate initiative in rescuing herself, to develop social courage, to look upon her life as an independent adventure and get interested in it.

. . .

Crystal's greatest contribution to the feminist cause remains her comprehensive vision, which took the women's movement far beyond suffrage by seeing the connections among the emotional basis of women's bondage, the cultural preconceptions and legal manifestation of women's inequality, and the economic sources of women's dependency.

" 'Oh, don't begin with economics,' my friends often protest. 'Woman does not live by bread alone. What she needs first of all is a free soul.' And I can agree that women will never be great until they achieve a certain emotional freedom, a strong healthy egotism, and some unpersonal sources of joy—that in this inner sense we cannot make woman free by changing her economic status. What we can do, however, is to create conditions of outward freedom in which a free woman's soul can be born and grow."

Crystal always believed that women's rights were more likely to be achieved in a socialist than in a capitalist economy, and unlike most Villagers who professed both feminism and socialism, she was a feminist first. When it became clear to her that women's issues remained secondary to most of her socialist colleagues, she declared in her opening statement to the First Feminist Congress, in 1919, "Many feminists are socialists, many are communists. But the true feminist, no matter how far to the left she may be in their revolutionary movement, sees the women's battle as distinct in its objects and different in its methods from the workers' battle for industrial freedom. . . . She counts herself a loyal soldier in the working-class army that is marching to overthrow that system. [But] if we should graduate into communism tomorrow . . . man's attitude to his wife would not be changed."

As early as 1913, she also realized that militarism would not only threaten the women's movement but could bring an instant end to social reforms. In 1914, seeing that the women's movement could become a leading force in the effort to keep the United States out of the war, she founded the Women's Peace Party of New York, which soon became a national organization. Forming committees to support anti-militarism strikes, confronting speakers at preparedness rallies, and frequently subjected to arrest or physical assaults by "patriots" in uniform, Crystal ignored criticism from more polite members of the anti-war movement. She also helped launch the American Union Against Militarism and in 1915 organized the Truth

About Preparedness Campaign, which used her detailed research into the economic profiteering evident in America's war preparation for a series of dramatic mass meetings across the country.

Like Max at *The Masses*, Crystal included the Village spirit of gay mockery in her anti-war tactics, especially "The War Against War" exhibit she and Walter helped organize in New York, featuring satirical cartoons, sardonic posters, and an enormous dragon symbolizing the munitions makers. Though five to ten thousand visitors a day crowded the skillfully publicized display, some members of the anti-war movement added public criticism of Crystal's "extreme and dangerous" sentiments to their private chastisements of her "casual sex life."

In 1917, she further antagonized some of her colleagues, Jane Addams in particular, by initiating a newsletter of the New York branch of the Women's Peace Party called *Four Lights*, modeled on *The Masses*, which declared itself "the voice of the young, uncompromising peace movement in America, whose aims are daring and immediate."

The dispute within the peace movement over Crystal's "radical" methods and goals seemed insignificant compared to the dispute within the feminist movement in the 1916 presidential election. Woodrow Wilson promised peace but not suffrage; his Republican challenger, Charles Evans Hughes, promised suffrage but not peace. Crystal continued to support suffrage, but she endorsed Wilson — and the bitterness felt by many of her feminist colleagues culminated in a speech Inez Milholland gave shortly before her death. "There are people who honestly believe — HONESTLY BELIEVE . . . that there are more important issues before the country than suffrage. . . . Now I do not know what you feel about such a point of view . . . but it makes me mad. . . . We must say, 'Women First.' " But to Crystal, personal friendships transcended political differences — she organized the largest of the many memorial services for Inez, and after Wilson's reelection the tension between the two groups ceased.

When *The Masses* was forced to stop publication in 1917, Crystal and Max immediately made plans for a successor, and in March 1918 the first issue of *The Liberator* appeared. Less gay-spirited than *The Masses*, less open to divergent points of view, the new magazine nevertheless lived up to its motto — "a Journal of Revolutionary Progress." Under Crystal's guidance it was virtually the only source of information about socialist movements around the world, printed the only accounts of the Allied intervention in Russia, published significant literature and poetry, and featured John Reed,

Louise Bryant, Floyd Dell, Norman Thomas, Roger Baldwin, Dorothy Day, Helen Keller, Eugene Debs, Bertrand Russell, and Lenin himself.

She was even more radicalized by the war and the Red Scare than Max and joined him in declaring, in *The Liberator*'s initial editorial, "Never was the moment more auspicious to issue a great magazine of liberty. With the Russian people in the lead, the world is entering upon the experiment of industrial and real democracy. . . . We must unite our hands and voices to make the end of this war the beginning of an age of freedom and happiness for mankind undreamed by those whose minds comprehend only political and military events. . . . We issue *The Liberator* into a world whose possibilities of freedom and life for all are now certainly immeasurable."

Crystal's ardent support of the Bolshevik revolution alienated many of her followers in the peace movement who shared her commitment but not her courage, and the government added her name to its list of "dangerous Reds" and monitored her activities. Most of her work of the last several years was made illegal under the Espionage and Sedition Acts passed in 1917 and 1918. Arguing that "it is the tendency even of the most 'democratic' of governments embarked upon the most 'idealist of wars' to sacrifice everything for complete military efficiency," she along with Roger Baldwin and Norman Thomas founded the American Civil Liberties Union in 1920.

The division in the women's movement in the 1916 election had momentarily disheartened Crystal, but the division in the twenties between supporters and opponents of an equal rights amendment to the Constitution threatened to demoralize her permanently. A Supreme Court decision in 1908 had upheld "protective" legislation for women and minors and implied women's biological inferiority. So when the National Women's Party supported the Equal Rights Amendment in 1923, and many reformers opposed it as a threat to the "protections" they'd already won, Crystal and her colleagues once more found themselves in a battle with other women.

Protection or equality? For the woman who, as a girl, had demanded that she help her brothers chop wood, there couldn't be any doubt. But winning the vote halted the impetus of the women's movement, and the opposition of so many women doomed the amendment. Feminism is "a fight worth making if it takes ten years," Crystal had said in a rare lapse from prescience, and now, those ten years nearly gone, the flapper was about to become the dominant image of woman.

. . .

When the war finally came to an end, Crystal established a kind of commune in the Village—"a delightful half-way family," as Max put it—with Crystal, Walter, and their son sharing two houses and a courtyard with Max, the actress Florence Deshon, and several friends, including Inez Milholland's widower, Eugen Boissevain.

Max cheerfully admitted that Crystal "really ran" *The Liberator*. She was the only person whose advice he regularly sought, and she traveled extensively as a reporter and fund-raiser for the magazine. After the premature birth of her second child in 1922 her doctor gave her the order she dreaded more than death—she had to rest. While Crystal thought modern medical science often fell back on this patronizing prescription for "women's ailments," she had to acknowledge that she was overworked, that her blood pressure had always been dangerously high, and that she suffered from a painfully debilitating kidney condition finally diagnosed as nephritis. Reluctantly, she resigned from *The Liberator*—soon followed by Max— and, in large part because she continued to work for the fusion of the feminist, socialist, and pacifist causes, the woman who'd been educated as a labor lawyer and who'd established herself as the nation's leading expert on industrial safety couldn't find even a part-time job.

Walter had returned to England to seek work, and for five years Crystal and their two children traveled between the Village and London— the "life under two roofs" she'd cheerfully advocated now a grim necessity. Her nephritis grew worse, and though severe headaches roared in her head "like a train puffing uphill," she continued to write bracing, farsighted articles synthesizing the feminist and socialist causes that still seemed so unrelated to so many of her colleagues. "Life is a big battle for the complete feminist," she wrote—and it was a lonely battle in her last years.

"I go from acute sorrow to my usual joy," Crystal wrote after one of her many operations in 1928, "still half doped with morphine and veronal," "and there IS SO MUCH for me to do. . . ." Only a few weeks later "this good for nothing body of mine" finally failed. She died at the age of forty-six.

Crystal was as respected by her enemies as she was adored by her friends—a diverse group including IWW organizers and titled nobility, anarchist leaders and government officials, Charlie Chaplin and Harlem intellectuals like Claude McKay. When a friend called her "impatient of more sober councils," what could this mean but admiration for her commitment?

What exasperated her was condescending praise from people who expressed surprise that a woman could accomplish so much, such as the female journalist who described her as a "modern Portia," and reported that she had "none of that fanaticism usually credited to the feminine enthusiast."

"She poured magnetic streams of generous love around her all the time," wrote Max, who remained bereft for three decades. Freda Kirchwey wrote in her obituary in *The Nation*, "wherever she moved she carried with her the breath of courage and a contagious belief in the coming triumph of freedom and decent human relations. . . . Force poured from her strong body and her rich voice, and people followed where she led. . . . She was to thousands of young women and young men a symbol of what the free woman might be."

Crystal created in her own being the modern woman she so relentlessly prophesied. In the forefront of every major movement for social progress in her time, she exemplified a post-suffragist feminism that could have continued to make "a little headway against tremendous odds." But with the passage of the Nineteenth Amendment—which Crystal saw as the beginning of the struggle, not the end—the first wave of feminism lost its impetus, and a woman who might have served as its forebear and inspiration, disappeared into history.

Emma Goldman

When Emma Goldman dedicated the October 1906 issue of *Mother Earth* to the memory of Leon Czolgosz, the anarchist who had assassinated President McKinley in 1901, she made it clear to everyone—the United States government in particular—that despite unceasing harassment, frequent jailings, and even beatings, she remained the most dangerous woman in America.

Mother Earth, a monthly advocating anarchism, atheism, and free love, began publication in March 1906 at 210 East 13th Street in an apartment Emma shared with several members of the magazine's staff. So many people congregated at 210—visiting anarchists, rebels on the run, lumpen revolutionaries, even Lower East Side gamblers who used her home to hide their equipment—that it became fondly known throughout the Village as "the inn for wounded souls."

What few knew was that Emma, contrary to her harsh, humorless image, was herself a wounded soul. Though overflowing with maternal tenderness toward the victims of injustice she encountered almost daily, in her personal life she remained confused and distraught, tormented by the disparity between her vision of erotic love and the reality of sexual conflict.

Born in 1869 in the Jewish quarter of Kovno, Lithuania—then part of czarist Russia—Emma quickly learned the tribulations of being female. Her parents never hid their disappointment that their first child was a girl: when she had her first period her embittered mother slapped her face, and when she was raped in her early teens, her enraged father acted as if she were to blame. Emma responded to the prospect of an arranged marriage by threatening to kill herself, and finally fled to America. She was sixteen years old.

Settling in Rochester, New York, Emma found work as a seamstress for $2.50 a week, and, not yet eighteen, married a textile worker who, she discovered on their wedding night, was impotent. Within two years she scandalized the Jewish community by getting a divorce and moving to New Haven, Connecticut, where she joined a group of Russian immigrants who gathered after work to debate socialism versus anarchism. Her political passion had been inflamed by the Haymarket Affair in Chicago in 1886 and 1887—the trial and execution of several anarchists and labor organizers for killing a policeman during a general strike. "I had the distinct sensation that something new and wonderful had been born in my soul," she wrote of her epiphany on the night of their deaths, "a great ideal, a burning faith, a determination to dedicate myself to the memory of my martyred comrades, to make their cause my own."

Upon arriving in New York City in August 1889 with nothing but $5 and her sewing machine, Emma gravitated to the Lower East Side. At the Sachs café on Suffolk Street—the meeting place for the city's anarchists—she met a cigar-maker and shirt-packer named Alexander "Sasha" Berkman, whose kindly, energetic temperament and uncompromising radicalism captivated her. Emma's sexuality was as ardent as her politics, and she and Sasha were soon lovers. They vowed "to dedicate themselves to the cause in some supreme deed and to die together if necessary" to prove their revolutionary commitment. Armed with a pistol and a knife, Sasha forced his way into the Pittsburgh office of Henry Clay Frick, chairman of the board of Carnegie Steel, and unsuccessfully attempted to assassinate the notorious strike-breaker. Sasha was sentenced to fourteen years in jail, and the police, correctly assuming that Emma had taken part in the plot, raided her by then empty apartment. After several months in hiding—often sleeping on streetcars or in brothels—Emma spoke at a Union Square demonstration on behalf of the unemployed, was arrested for "inciting a riot and . . . disbelief in God and government," and then sentenced to a year in prison. Upon her release in 1894, she had become a national celebrity.

From the age of twenty-five on, Emma lived most of her life in public and moved from one "exalted moment" to another—crossing the country speaking on radical causes to increasingly larger and more enthusiastic crowds, and adding birth control and other feminist issues to her repertoire of revolution. From the first she faced constant threats of imprisonment and hysterical vilification in the press—"a wrinkled, ugly Russian woman" who "would kill all rulers," said the *New York World*. On trips to Europe she studied nursing and midwifery, which, she said, led her "out of a dark cellar and into broad daylight," and which validated her own conviction that sexual repression lay at the root of women's oppression.

Emma was by nature a sensualist and by conviction an advocate of free love, but the psychic bruises left by her adolescent rape were slow to heal. "Their lure remained strong," she said of men, "but it was always mingled with violent revulsion." Still, the homicidal harridan was a youthful, vibrant, and tenderly passionate woman. Five feet tall and weighing 120 pounds, she was invariably described as "stocky" or "sturdy"—but her firm chin, determined mouth, and penetrating blue eyes made her attractive to men more drawn to unconventional strength than to conventional beauty.

Initially, Emma hoped to enjoy a multitude of lovers, only to find that her own nature tended toward stability, and that the anarchists with whom she became sexually involved, though disdaining monogamy for themselves, expected it of her. Furthermore, though unwavering in their dedication to free love, most of them took it for granted that a sexual relationship involved a surrender of female independence, and even, on occasion, argued that she had to choose between their relationship and her career, the very career that had done so much to promote the cause they cherished. The contradiction between feminist principles and personal behavior that characterized most of the men in the movement struck Emma all the more forcibly when she realized, to her dismay, that in some ways she herself remained just as unliberated.

At a gathering of anarchists in London in 1899, Emma met a short, dark man "with large eyes gleaming in his pale face" who gruffly exclaimed, when she asked why he seemed so vindictive, "because I can't bear sham!" Hippolyte Havel, he introduced himself. To Emma's compassionate heart, however, Hippolyte seemed less comic than forlorn. At first she found him a rather fastidious dandy for an anarchist—when he gallantly asked her to dine with him, he kept his gloves on—but she soon discovered that his hands were covered with blisters from the menial labor he undertook to support himself.

Haltingly, Hippolyte told Emma his story—how he'd been born in Czechoslovakia of mixed Czech and Gypsy blood, discovered anarchism in his teens, and spent several months in jail, on one occasion transferred to a psychopathic ward and only released when Krafft-Ebing himself declared his ravings all too rational. After dinner, when he called a cab to take her home, and she lightheartedly protested that it was rather bourgeois to object to a woman's right to pay for herself, "Just like an American, flaunting your money!" he raged in his staccato voice. "I'm working, and I can afford to pay!"

In the following weeks, Emma and Hippolyte took the anarchist message to the poor quarters of London, and she "began to realize that the pleasure I found in his company was due to more than ordinary comradeship." Hippolyte may have been acrimonious and morose, but he was also exotic and stimulating. As a generation of Villagers was soon to learn, even his irritability had a certain flamboyance. And, said Emma with uncharacteristic coyness, "love was making its claims again, daily more insistent." Finally, one night "we found ourselves, hardly conscious how, in each other's embrace."

Emma may have felt reborn "with new joy," but Hippolyte remained as depressed and irascible as ever. Never mind, Emma loved her "bitter Putzi" for his wounds. When his anger was exacerbated by heavy drinking she quickly forgave him. And when he grew impatient with the implicit free love contract, resenting the attentions he imagined other men paid her, even raging over common courtesies, she just forgave him again. But gradually his instability soured their love, and though he followed her back to New York, they soon drifted into friendship. One more temporary liaison for Emma—one more heartbreak.

Hippolyte continued his anarchist activities and polemical diatribes in his adopted homeland, but to Emma, anarchism was more than an outlet for personal rage, it was an expression of an idealistic vision. She supported herself as a midwife and nurse, for a time as a drama critic, as the proprietor of a massage parlor on Broadway and 17th Street, and as the manager of an experimental theater troupe on East 3rd Street. In the service of the cause, and to prove her superiority to bourgeois convention, she even briefly and unsuccessfully tried to raise money as a streetwalker on 14th Street.

Emma finally found her base at 210 East 13th Street. "There were no facilities for heating at 210," Emma recalled, "except the kitchen stove. . . . My room was the living-room, dining-room, and *Mother Earth* office, all in one. I slept in a little alcove behind my bookcase. There was always someone . . . who had stayed too late and lived too far away or who was too shaky on his feet and needed cold compresses or who had no home to go to. . . . It was flattering, but at the same time wearying, never to have any privacy by day or night. . . . The entire kaleidoscope of human tragedy and comedy had been reflected in colourful variegation within the walls of 210."

Emma devoted most of her considerable energies to her increasingly successful calling as a public speaker. "Her name was enough in those days to produce a shudder," said Margaret Anderson of *The Little Review.* "She was considered a monster, an exponent of free love and bombs." In an editorial the *New York Times* characterized Emma and her colleagues as "the most virulent and dangerous preachers and practitioners of the doctrine of destruction." Naturally, the Villagers flocked to her New York lectures, Jack and Max frequently bailed her out of jail, and across the country, in lecture halls, in mine shafts, in colleges and churches, in vacant lots and barns, she spread her gospel to the workers, the intelligentsia, the unemployed, the immigrants, the radicals, the merely curious.

Mabel persuaded her to take part in the famous Dangerous Characters Evening featuring a debate between advocates of political action and supporters of direct action, the largest gathering ever assembled at 23 Fifth Avenue, though Mabel found her disappointing. Emma "was not at all to the point. She was more than ever like a severe schoolteacher in a scolding mood." The Evening was a pivotal event, however, marking the meeting of intellectuals and radicals, bohemians and workers, artists and activists, immigrant militants and middle-class rebels that was to characterize the revolution in consciousness.

Emma and the Villagers, in fact, discovered one another almost simultaneously. Though most of the Villagers were nominal socialists, they were infatuated by the more incendiary members of the working class—the anarchists and the Wobblies in particular—and regarded them as a kind of avant-garde of insurrection. Emma was quick to take advantage of this romantic admiration, hoping to radicalize the intellectuals, even going so far as to call them "proletarians."

Eugene O'Neill and Floyd Dell were among those captivated by Emma. Only Max Eastman resisted the charms of her anarchism. He argued that her eloquence and fervor were less striking than "her impermeability to humor and logic." Her "whole life wisdom," he concluded, "consisted of comparing reality with an absolute ideal, and breaking her neck, and if need be all necks, in some obviously desperate leap for the ideal."

Unlike many of her anarchist colleagues who disapproved of her fascination with intellectuals, artists, and bohemians, Emma had no fundamental quarrel with the "frivolities" of the Villagers. She believed in their attempts to find common cause between intellectuals and workers, and if they might better have devoted their energies to political activism she understood they were nevertheless trying to lead the liberated lives her own political activism had as its goal.

In 1910, Emma visited thirty-seven cities in twenty-five states and in 120 lectures spoke to forty thousand people. By 1915, she was giving more than three hundred speeches a year on such topics as "Anarchism: The Moving Spirit in the Labor Struggle," "Art and Revolution," "The Failure of Christianity," "Communism: The Most Practical Basis for Society," and "Sex: The Great Element for Creative Work." Everywhere she was greeted with both ovations and catcalls.

On several occasions she collapsed from exhaustion, but she remained indefatigable. Speaking with a nobility that belied her image as hysterical and hate-filled, she defined anarchism as "the philosophy of a new social order based on liberty unrestricted by man-made law; the theory that all forms of government rest on violence, and are therefore wrong and harmful, as well as unnecessary."

Although Eugene Debs attracted nearly a million voters as the Socialist candidate in the presidential election of 1912, and Big Bill Haywood and the Wobblies rallied hundreds of thousands of workers to the labor cause, it was Emma—though her anarchist movement drew far fewer followers—who most vividly symbolized the radical unrest of the early teens.

In private, Emma's personality was as unpredictable as it was powerful. Some of her friends found her an irrepressible fountain of gaiety, others "as serious as the deep Russian soul itself." But everyone agreed that she had a sovereign aura. As Margaret Anderson put it, "Life takes on an intenser quality when she is present. There is something cosmic in the air, a feeling of the world in the making."

Unlike most of her anarchist colleagues who were solemnly scornful of "luxuries," Emma relished food, wine, flowers, music, dancing, parties, and up to forty cigarettes a day. After all, she would say with vigorous laughter, anarchism meant individual fulfillment as well as social liberalism. But rather inappropriately for an anarchist, she could also be as imperious as royalty. She displayed what one friend called "a genius for hurting people." Her ambiguous relationship with Sasha in the years after his release from prison was symptomatic of her double-edged temperament. She treated him with a resentment that probably reflected her admiration for his bold attempt on Frick's life and her guilt over her failure to match his zeal, her compassion for his suffering and her shame over not sharing it.

Emma's public image, early in her speaking career, was just as sharply divided. Many listeners found her rhetorical and zealous, others called her logical and cool. Her opponents, particularly the nation's newspapers, found her "a despicable creature"; a San Francisco paper described her as "a snake," "unfit to live in a civilized country," while another paper called her "synonymous with everything vile and criminal," and yet another proclaimed that she should "be hanged by the neck until dead and considerably longer." Harry Kemp said "she made me think of a battleship going into action."

"The magnetism of her sledgehammer style," as one colleague called her oratorical mode, was only the beginning, for where she truly triumphed was in the question-and-answer sessions that followed her speeches and invariably brought her into direct combat with her enemies. Emma found the verbal confrontations exhilirating. "The more opposition I encountered," she said, "the more I was in my element and the more caustic I became with my opponents."

If to some Emma's oratory seemed a threat to the republic, to others an invocation of utopia, Emma made no secret of relishing both reactions. Indeed one of her greatest creations remains her public persona. Inventing herself as rebel queen, as earth mother, as menace, as martyr, even frequently referring to herself in the third person, she consciously exploited her image as terrorist of the status quo and as harbinger of hope. One of America's first self-mythologizers, she understood that even anarchism needed a rallying center. One of the world's first media manipulators, she knew that even newspaper headlines contributed to her legend.

The anxieties aroused by Emma's message and charisma were hardly confined to the press. The police intimidated auditorium owners, declared meeting halls "unsafe," locked out her audiences, even arresting her before she spoke, claiming "fear for her safety," but in doing so exemplified the very violence they accused her of encouraging. One policeman knocked out one of her front teeth, but Emma invariably retained both her composure and her humor. "Behave yourself," she chided one officer: "Talk like a man, even if you are a policeman." Arriving in Chicago, she called the police chief and announced, "This is Emma Goldman. I just wanted you to know I am back." Naturally her notoriety increased the more the government tried to suppress her, and her crowds grew larger the more the press depicted her as speaking only for a tiny band of lunatics.

Emma's notoriety made her search for love even more difficult—overthrowing the government seemed easier. Since she stressed not only anarchist violence but illicit sex, and since such controversial concepts as birth control remained crucial to her program, she had to maintain a certain propriety in her personal relationships so as not to compromise her political platform. (In America, those who would overthrow the government have some of the same constraints as those who would lead it.) It was one thing for a frumpy woman with rimless glasses to preach free love, another for a cheerful, full-bodied woman with overflowing sensuality to practice it. So she conducted her many love affairs with considerable circumspection—never displaying affection in public, always registering in separate hotel rooms—and behaved with a respectability that sometimes made her feel sordid.

On a trip to Chicago in 1908, the national celebrity and unhappy woman, Emma Goldman, Queen of the Anarchists, met Ben Reitman, King of the Hobos. At once a respectable doctor who pioneered the treatment of venereal disease, and a disreputable iconoclast who consorted with bums, prostitutes, and pimps, Ben described himself as "single by good fortune, a physician and teacher by profession, cosmopolitan by choice, a socialist by inclination, a rascal by nature, a celebrity by accident, a tramp by twenty years' experience, and a Tramp Reformer by inspiration." From the moment they met, she found herself erotically transfixed by this "handsome brute" ten years her junior. "I was caught in the torrent of an elemental passion I had never dreamed any man could rouse in me," she recalled. "I responded shamelessly to its primitive call, its naked beauty, its ecstatic joy."

The object of all this adoration was, in fact, a bit of a buffoon, with more than a touch of the charlatan—brash and swaggering. Emma may have seemed austere to her colleagues, but she was also a woman seething with "the sublime madness of sex." She would sit up long past midnight to write long impassioned letters to "the Great Grand Passion of my life." "You have opened up the prison gates of my womanhood. And all the passion that was unsatisfied in me . . . leaped into a wild reckless storm boundless as the sea. . . . I will give you my soul only let me drink, . . . from the Spring of my master lover. . . . There. You have the confession of a starved tortured being."

Emma's need to self-dramatize coincided with her imperative to rebel. The woman who could say "I love you with a madness that knows no bounds, no patience, no logic" was also an anarchist who could assault the citadels of society with no hesitations, no compromises. Furthermore, her ideology, unlike that of her European mentors, contained a critique of sexual as well as political repression. She had found a man who would "love the woman in me and yet who would also be able to share my work. I had never had anyone who could do both."

Now that she was embracing her dream lover in the flesh, her swooning effusions turned into heated eroticism. Since the law prohibited sending obscenities through the mails, and since her correspondence was routinely scrutinized by the authorities, Emma and Ben developed a private erotic code—hardly indecipherable to any reader but probably unindictable in court. Her "treasure box" longed for his "Willie," she yearned to have his face buried between her "joy mountains"—"Mt. Blanc and Mt. Jura"—she longed to suck the head of his "fountain of life," "to drink every drop of W juice," and after reading his replies, poised between the coy and the raunchy, she frequently had to "take a bath" to relieve herself.

"I press you to my body close with my hot burning legs," Emma wrote the "animal" who had "awakened lust in me." "My t-b___ is hot and burning with the desire to run it up and down up and down W." "My m scream in delight and my brain is on fire." "The day seems unbearable if I do not talk to you"—another letter—but "I would prefer to do something else to you. . . . How I would press my lips to the fountain and drink, drink, every drop."

Ben cut back on his medical practice and devoted most of his time, when not running his W up and down her t-b, to being Emma's personal manager. He made travel arrangements for her tours to raise money for *Mother Earth*, arranged her meetings, advertised her appearances, rented halls for her lectures, sold anarchist literature.

He was arrested along with Emma on several occasions, and later wrote, "I've been in jail with her a dozen times, and have seen the mob howling for her blood, and she never lost her poise or her courage. I only saw her weep once, and that was when she learned that she was not pregnant." Still, Emma sometimes doubted the depth of his dedication. "Intellectually crude," she called him, "socially naive," a man enamored of the turbulence of their life without making any commitment to its message, a man who, "like so many other liberal Americans . . . was a reformer of surface evils, without any idea of the sources from which they spring."

Emma's friends wondered what she could possibly see in this often overbearing, frequently uncouth man, this man whom even Harry Kemp described as "a fat nincompoop." He was even suspected of skimming money from her lecture receipts and sending it to his mother in Chicago. Ben's sexual power remained a mystery to Emma herself. All she knew was that she would have skipped speeches, canceled fund-raisers for an hour of sexual abandon. She found herself so overwhelmed by erotic longing she even questioned her commitment to the cause, and feared she had lost her sense of independence. The woman who regarded female emancipation as a crucial component of the anarchist revolution, the woman who in every other regard subordinated her personal happiness to her political goals, was she herself so unliberated she would give up everything for a man?

Emma might have achieved her dream of uniting political commitment and erotic abandonment if Ben had proven worthy of either. She already knew, of course, that most of the men in the movement behaved as if sexual equality were only an opportunity for sexual conquest, but Ben was no hypocrite, he made clear his unwavering dedication to free love every chance he got. He even encouraged her to "go to it!" with other men. His anarchism seemed to reside in his sex organs and in what she called his "fuck talk." He had a "disease for women," she accused him, a "sex morbidity." He'd seduce women who'd come to hear Emma speak; he'd use their room to practice her doctrine with women she'd converted.

Among Ben's many conquests was the earnest Mary Eleanor Fitzgerald—the same Fitzi who later brought order to the Provincetown Players and became one of Eugene O'Neill's matronly muses and occasional bedmates. A cheerful, hardworking presence at the *Mother Earth* office for many years, Fitzi also had a brief affair with Sasha Berkman—and with several women as well, her friends suspected—and remained so devoted to Emma and Sasha that when they were deported to Russia she tried to have herself deported with them.

Emma's letters were filled with torrents of jealousy. His promiscuity, she wrote him, "tears at my very vitals, fills me with gall and horror and twists my being into something foreign to myself." Confronted with so much pain, even Ben knew better than to remind Emma of her principles, and momentarily ignoring his own, he extravagantly expressed remorse and vowed to reform. All too soon, though, he would succumb to the claims of anarchism and the cycle would begin again.

Ben's struggle wasn't on behalf of, but in opposition to, his conscience. "Little black devils dance before me," he wrote, "there is fire in my blood. I cry for water, for a cooling thought, but only breasts, legs, and eyes float before me. What an awful thing it is to develop a conscience. . . . I did not stop to think 'whose wife is she' or 'is the act of satisfying passion fair or moral,' but now when my primitiveness is gone and civilization's ideas and standards have been forced upon me, I find that I cannot freely and savagely set about to get a woman. What is this strange influence, Civilization, that makes me stop and think when lust and fire are in my blood? Civilization! God, how terrible it is! . . . If civilization means that a man must stop and think when he desires another man's wife, it is time to do away with it!"

Like many Village women of the teens—berating themselves for their "irrational" unhappiness—Emma desperately tried to reconcile her politics and her feelings. Her principles told her free love would liberate her from sexual oppression, her experience told her it only brought pain. Her exalted vision of an anarchist relationship implied monogamy, but her skeptical analysis of monogamy kept her from demanding it. Trapped between the ideal Ben's love promised and the torment his behavior caused, she couldn't call on her politics to rescue her, for they remained part of the trap. When Emma boldly proclaimed that "whether love lasts but one brief span of time or for eternity, it is the only creative, inspiring, elevating basis for a new world," none of her enraptured listeners knew that she not only felt degraded in her own love life but ashamed of her hypocrisy. "If ever our correspondence should be published," she wrote, "the world would stand aghast that I, Emma Goldman, the strong revolutionist, the daredevil, the one who has defied laws and conventions, should have been as helpless as a shipwrecked crew on a foaming ocean."

To the public, however—particularly to the guardians of morality—Emma was hardly helpless. When she lectured she seemed a threat to the very foundations of the republic. Where labor unrest led to massive strikes and police violence—Paterson, Ludlow, Lawrence—she spoke out on behalf of the workers and tirelessly raised money to support their cause. And *Mother Earth*—less sophisticated and exuberant than *The Masses*, more polemical and exhortatory—grew in circulation and influence.

Ben shared in the drudgery of revolution, as did Hippolyte and Sasha—who, after his release from prison, became Emma's closest confidant—and Emma's ecstatic sense of mission sustained them in lives otherwise drab, dismal, and impoverished. Almost constantly on the road, they arrived late at night in deserted cities, slept in cheap hotels or crowded apartments, exhausted themselves in lectures, meetings, and demonstrations, all the while facing the threat of beatings or prison. Their only indulgence was their ideals, their only comfort their prophecies.

One radical cause of the era received Emma's less than wholehearted support—the suffragist movement. Narrowing women's demands to the single issue of the vote, she argued, deluded women into thinking that power resided in the ballot, focused too much attention on middle-class concerns, showed indifference to the labor movement, ignored the need for radical structural changes in the economy and government, and, most important, completely misjudged the sources of women's oppression.

"Her development, her freedom, her independence," Emma wrote, "must come from and through herself. First by asserting herself as a personality, and not as a sex commodity. Second by refusing the right to anyone over her body; by refusing to bear children unless she wants them. . . . That is, by trying to learn the meaning and substance of life in all its complexities, by freeing herself from the fear of public opinion and public condemnation. Only that, and not the ballot, will set women free, will make her a force hitherto unknown in the world, a force for real love, for peace, harmony; a force of divine fire, of life-giving; a creator of free men and women."

Emma took a subjective, psychological approach to women's issues. She railed against the repressiveness of marriage—"an economic arrangement, an insurance pact, a safety valve against the pernicious sex-awakening of woman"—and asked why "the healthy, grown woman, full of life and passion, must deny nature's demand, must subdue her most intense craving, undermine her health and break her spirit, abstain from the depth and glory of sex experience until a 'good' man comes along to take her unto himself as a wife." She criticized feminists for emphasizing "external tyrannies" such as the denial of the vote while "internal tyrants were left to take care of themselves." She argued that "the revolutionary process of changing her external conditions is comparatively easy; what is difficult and necessary is the inner change of thought and desire."

To some of her fellow radicals Emma seemed to place too much of the burden of liberation on the assertion of will. But it was her genius to expand the realm of the political to include the merely "personal." Women's liberation? The move from the nineteenth-century values of self-sacrifice and submission to the twentieth-century values of self-expression and assertion? Decades ahead of her time, Emma insisted that "she must be an individual . . . before she can do anything for anybody else."

In the early and mid-teens, the women's issue to which Emma devoted more and more of her time and energy was the one that met with the most virulent resistance—birth control. Emma argued that women's right to control their own bodies couldn't be separated from their right to control their own destinies. "If everyone followed the injunction of the Bible and Teddy Roosevelt to be fruitful and multiply," she said, "every tenement house would be turned into a lunatic asylum by the excessive number of children." "I may be arrested, I may be tried and thrown into jail," she wrote in *Mother Earth*, "but I never will be silent, I never will acquiesce or submit to authority, nor will I make peace with a system and shall not rest until the path has been cleared for a free motherhood."

Though influenced by Margaret Sanger's pioneering work, Emma sharply disagreed with what she regarded as her pragmatic approach—limiting the birth control cause to the spread of contraceptive information and attempting to win the wider, more respectable constituency of middle-class women.

Emma helped distribute Margaret's pamphlets, but their personal relationship remained prickly. As she wrote a friend, she had "started out on birth control agitation long before the Sangers thought of it." "It is tragic but yet true," she told another friend, that Margaret "is not big enough to give credit to those who have paved the way for her. Then, too, she is evidently trying to interest people of means, so of course it will not do to mention the name of Emma Goldman. It is pitiful to be so small"—indeed it is, Emma's friends must have thought, as they witnessed her diminishing herself so pitifully.

The police certainly gave Emma credit, arresting her several times for violation of laws banning the spread of birth control information. On one occasion, she was given the choice between a forty-five-day sentence and a $100 fine, and unhesitatingly chose prison. "Women," she said — always eager to dramatize her defiance — "need not always keep their mouths shut and their wombs open. . . . If that is a crime, your Honor, I am glad and proud to be a criminal."

Her courage was frequently tested. On a trip to San Diego in 1912, Emma was greeted by a crowd screaming "we want the anarchist murderess," and while she met with the mayor and chief of police, who offered "protection" on the condition that she leave town immediately, a group of less official dignitaries kidnapped Ben, drove him to a secluded spot, and attempted to persuade him of the error of his ways. "These Christian gentlemen," said Ben, "subjected me to every cruel, diabolical, malicious torture that a God-fearing respectable business man is capable of conceiving. I was knocked down and compelled to kiss the flag. . . . With a lighted cigar they burned I.W.W. on my buttocks; then they poured a can of tar over my head and body. . . . One very gentle business man who is active in church work deliberately attempted to push my cane into my rectum. One unassuming banker twisted my testicles. . . ."

Such incidents intensified Emma and Ben's commitment to the cause and, for a time, to each other. Their affair continued to alternate between moments of erotic ecstasy and long periods of emotional turbulence. "Why," she herself asked, "did I ever make myself depend on you? A thousand things you have done should have killed my love, long ago. Instead [it] . . . has become light and air and food to me."

Like many people who fall into frequent fits of self-laceration, she had little self-understanding. Every cause she undertook confirmed for Emma the belief that no ideal could be achieved without unceasing struggle, so why shouldn't the ultimate ideal of uniting political revolution and personal fulfillment require the greatest struggle of all? And wasn't it also in some dark way desirable? Is it possible that Emma needed to have the necessity for struggle validated? Is it possible that, having set her goals so high, she regarded unattainability as the surest sign of authenticity? Anarchism and love — they couldn't be worth fighting for if they weren't almost impossibly difficult to achieve. Having been scorned by her parents for being a mere female, having been derided all her adult life as a frumpy harridan, she found that for a man to regard her as sexually desirable was worth any amount of pain.

But the almost sadomasochistic compulsiveness of Emma's behavior suggests deeper psychic sources. Unloved as a child, she seems to have felt unworthy of love. Lacking a strong sense of self, she had to invent one. Just as in her politics she mythologized herself as a martyr, in her love affairs she dramatized herself as a victim, elevating discontent into tragedy. Emma frequently signed her letters to Ben "Mommy"—and this intimation of maternal feeling must have involved both the sexual stimulation of breaking a taboo and the emotional gratification of infinite forgiveness.

For all her compassion, even her admirers conceded that Emma was often domineering and manipulative. Nearly every letter of love to Ben is also filled with hostility, nearly every proclamation of devotion accompanied by accusations and recriminations. "I will have your love if I have to drink it through your blood," she wrote him, "If I have to suck it out of W___, if I have to tear it out of you! It's mine! It's mine!"

But whatever the source of Emma's fixation, she chose as her lover a person who had to be continually confronted, and mixed with her revulsion at Ben's behavior was a compulsion to resign herself to the misery it caused her. "I will always want more than you will be able to give," she wrote Ben, "therefore I shall always be bitterly disappointed, it is inevitable and I must bow to the Inevitable." "Life is a hideous nightmare," she went on, "yet we drag it on and on and find a thousand excuses for it. I am mad, sick, worn, I must be strong, I must go away." And yet she stayed.

Compulsion requires even more energy than commitment, and in the early teens Emma's inner conflicts exhausted her to the point where she no longer had the strength to resist her reason. Furthermore, Ben's sexuality flagged after his beating in San Diego—"Your tender life-giving treasure box demands more than worn out Willie can give," he wrote—and he withdrew to his real mother for emotional support. A year earlier Emma might have been dismayed but she now found her sexual appeal confirmed from an unsuspected direction—another woman.

Almeda Sperry, a Pennsylvania prostitute, began to correspond with Emma after hearing her lecture on "White Slave Traffic." She came to New York to visit her mentor and after returning home wrote her about an encounter with Ben. "He asked Hutch Hapgood to suck on one of my breasts while he sucked the other. . . . He also asked me how many men there are in this town that I had not fucked yet."

But Almeda's letters also expressed her lesbian longings for Emma—"lovely bruised purple grape," she called her—and on a subsequent meeting the two women seem to have consummated their relationship. "Dearest," she wrote Emma. "If I had only had courage enough to kill myself when you reached the climax then — then I would have known happiness, for then at that moment I had complete possession of you."

Emma's brief affair with Almeda — assuming that Almeda's account was more than a fantasy — not only revealed her freedom from conventional constraints but also released her from her obsession with Ben, and for the first time since they'd met she began to feel attracted to other men. Ben felt his "Willie shrinking" at the very thought of Emma's relationship with Almeda and hoped that she hadn't taught her any "new techniques" that would supersede his — he was even more threatened by the possibility that she'd begin to emulate his own behavior. He had offhandedly suggested that she "go to it!" with other men, but now she actually might take his advice, a disturbing notion.

Their relationship dwindling, Ben set out on an affair with a tall blond woman who'd stopped by the *Mother Earth* office, while Emma set about revising her lecture on free love.

In "Misconceptions of Free Love," she discerned a difference between open and hidden sexual relations outside of monogamy and distinguished between spiritual and sexual union in nonmonogamous relationships. But in defining "good" and "bad" forms of free love, Emma wasn't merely rationalizing her troublesome response to Ben's promiscuity, she was determined to find some basis for free love that would honor the need for emotional stability. She wanted to place it outside the bounds of social convention yet within the bounds of personal morality — a distinction Ben wouldn't have understood, much less heeded.

Looking back on their relationship, Ben confided to Hutch, "When I came to 210 and was permitted to associate with the anarchists and the genuine intellectuals, . . . I knew nothing about literature or culture or movements. The only way that I could attract attention was to talk about sex and be vulgar, or shocking." Overshadowed by Emma, he retaliated with macho posturing, an aspect of the male psyche not covered by her anarchist theories.

But Ben could also have pointed out that for all Emma's talk about not being possessive, she often acted as if she wanted him completely at her command, and that for all her words of worship she was frequently delighted to make him guilty. He may have given her intolerable provocations, but part of her enjoyed playing the manipulative martyr, berating him while protesting her undying love, exploiting his lack of self-confidence even as she proclaimed his sexual prowess. Despite—or because of—his invaluable assistance to Emma for nearly a decade, acting as a kind of office boy of anarchism, she often humiliated him.

Emma's point of view, bowdlerized in her autobiography, was somewhat more exalted. There's nothing about her love affair with martyrdom. Nothing about her swings between sexuality and anger, between her assertion of self and her doubt of her worth, between her need for affection and her attraction to persecution. "Erotically Ben and I were of the same earth," she wrote, "but in a cultural sense we were separated by centuries of time. . . . The eternal struggle of man was rooted within me. That made the abyss between us." If Emma's view of herself was always so lofty, many a better man than Ben would have failed to bridge that abyss.

With the increasing possibility of American participation in World War I, Emma began to devote less energy to feminist issues and more to fighting conscription and the "blood and iron materialism" that was contaminating the country. By 1917—a year "excruciating even now to write about," she said over a decade later—as free speech and free assembly were routinely and violently suppressed, the U.S. government became a greater threat to the Constitution than the anarchists. Post office officials were on the verge of banning *Mother Earth*, government agents frequently outnumbered radicals at Emma's speeches, and on June 15, a U.S. marshal burst through the door at 210 East 13th Street and arrested Emma and Sasha for conspiring against the draft. Emma quickly packed a toilet case and a copy of James Joyce's *Portrait of the Artist As a Young Man*, and once more headed off to jail.

Emma and Sasha considered refusing to testify at their trial as a protest against the violation of their rights, but on the advice of friends—including Max and Jack, who called the proceedings the beginning of "the blackest month for free men our generation has known"—concluded that they'd serve their cause better by speaking out against the war effort. With unruffled dignity, Emma gave her occupation as a social student who diagnosed social wrongs and read from the Declaration of Independence—though, unlike Max at *his* trial, she remained seated during "The Star-Spangled Banner"—and lucidly disproved the government's charges.

The prosecutor had no recourse but rhetorical flourish and neglected to mention in his description of Emma's assaults on the rule of law that his own agents were confiscating manuscripts and mailing lists and financial documents from the *Mother Earth* office.

The jury reached a guilty verdict after only thirty-nine minutes, and the judge, though declaring Emma perhaps "the greatest woman of her time," imposed the maximum sentence—two years in jail. But after two weeks, Emma and Sasha were freed by Justice Louis Brandeis pending their appeal, and Emma immediately resumed committing the crime for which she'd been convicted.

From the day of her release, Emma and her comrades remained under surveillance, and within months, *Mother Earth* fell victim to the Espionage Act, which had doomed *The Masses*. It briefly resurfaced as a multigraphed newsletter called *Instead of a Magazine*. Still defiant, Emma undertook a speaking tour on behalf of the Bolshevik revolution. She held a huge New Year's Eve party, the invitation soberly recalling the "excruciating" events of 1917: "Wishes for any personal joy in the world's madness seem so commonplace that I can't gather up the courage to wish such things for the New Year, except that the world may come to its senses. I know that will bring us all joy."

Early in 1918, however, the Supreme Court rejected Emma and Sasha's appeal. What better place to celebrate her fiftieth birthday, she proudly reflected, than in prison?

By the time of Emma's release in late 1919, after serving twenty months of her sentence, the infamous Palmer raids had shut down most of the organizations involved in anti-war and radical activities, and Attorney General Palmer had signed a warrant for Emma's rearrest under the law authorizing the deportation of alien anarchists. From her new base on Grove Street, Emma used her few weeks of freedom to lash out, this time against prison conditions, the suppression of free speech, and the deportation proceedings themselves, the results of which were preordained. One guest proclaimed that "with prohibition coming in and Emma Goldman going out, 'twill be a dull country."

In Chicago, Ben was speaking at another banquet: "Emma came into my life years ago and seduced me from the old world. I dropped my old ideas. I dropped Jesus Christ. But today I'm thanking God I've learned the right road—and I learned it when I came to Jesus." He'd learned so much that he'd married that tall blond woman and fathered a son he named Brutus.

Emma remained committed to her cause. "One does not live in a country 34 years, live as I have lived, and find it easy to go. I found my spiritual birth here. All my dreams, hopes, aspirations, all the woe and pain, all the joy and ecstasy. . . . But I am proud. . . . The mad rush in getting us out of the country is the greatest proof to me that I have served the cause of humanity."

Exiled from the United States, Emma continued to serve the cause of humanity for another twenty years, especially in her prophetic assessment of the Soviet Union. She had written and spoken of the Bolsheviks as the forerunners of the liberation of mankind, but after a few months in Petrograd she had seen enough to say, "To remain silent now is impossible, even criminal. Recent events impel us Anarchists to speak out and to declare our attitude on the present situation. . . . Comrades Bolsheviki, bethink yourselves before it is too late." "I wish I had a tongue of fire," she told a New York reporter. "I would burn it into the hearts of the American people what a crime is being committed against [Russia]." "The only difference between Russia and other countries," she wrote a friend, "is that in Russia the very elements who have helped unfurl the revolution have also helped to carry the revolution to her grave."

Emma carried the anarchist message from country to country and was still at work in Canada in her early seventies when, in a rare moment of relaxation, she looked up at her partner in a card game, exclaimed, "God damn it, why did you lead that?," and collapsed from a stroke. Placed on a stretcher, the great exponent of revolution reached down in an instinctive gesture of modesty and covered her knees with the hem of her skirt.

Emma lived for three more months, but the great orator could only communicate with grunts and eye movements; she died on May 14, 1940.

Has anyone ever so fervently transformed personal memories into messianic politics, so ruthlessly universalized her life? Emma rarely considered such observations, but seemed to believe her dedication sprang full-blown from her observation of the world's injustices.

It wouldn't matter much except that Emma's lack of self-awareness resulted in a political and personal paradox. Her anarchism so strenuously stressed the institutional causes of social injustice and personal unhappiness, and so vigorously asserted that they could only be overcome by the structural transformation of society, that she paid too little attention to the motivating power of the human heart—the very power to which she so eloquently appealed.

As a result, Emma flipped back and forth between sacrificing her personal desires in the name of political activism and blaming herself for failing to dedicate herself unselfishly to the cause, unable to accept the fact that conflicting, unresolved feelings might be the price she had to pay for being so far ahead of her time. And in a final irony, what brought her shame seems as admirable as what brought her pride.

It wasn't ironic, however, that this champion of total freedom so often saw herself as driven and doomed, for it was her sense of psychological bondage that motivated her lifelong battle against all jailers of the spirit. And if it's true that Emma's attribution of injustice to institutions rather than to human nature was motivated in part by fear of her own frailties, that her commitment was energized by her unconscious desire to escape both her painful past and her dark obsessions, it's also true that if she'd been a happier person, she'd have been a less visionary leader.

When Emma said, "No life is worth anything which does not contain a great ideal," she spoke for the radicals and bohemians of the Village, and, in particular, to the New Women, many of whom, like Mabel and Louise, regarded her as a role model. Emma's greatest gift to feminism was to sense the connection between the transformative power of private life and the politicization of love.

As Emma prepared to leave the United States forever, one young member of the Justice Department, the twenty-five-year-old J. Edgar Hoover, wrote in a memo to his superiors, "Emma Goldman and Alexander Berkman are, beyond doubt, two of the most dangerous anarchists in this country, and if permitted to return to the community will result in undue harm."

And when Emma, Sasha, and 245 other victims of the "deportation delirium" boarded the *Buford* in New York harbor on the very cold morning of December 21, 1919, guarded by 250 armed soldiers, Hoover was among those seeing off "the Red Ark." Did the government treat her fairly? he asked Emma. Emma thought for a moment before replying, "We shouldn't expect from a person something beyond his capacity." Then she thumbed her nose.

Margaret Sanger

On the morning of February 9, 1913, Villagers reading the women's page of *The Call* found the left column completely blank except for the words, in large black type,

> What Every Girl Should Know. NOTHING! By Order of the Post Office Department.

A few months earlier, the popular socialist daily had commissioned a young nurse named Margaret Sanger to write a series of articles on sex for adolescents. She dealt with such subjects as masturbation, menstruation, defloration, and pregnancy with Victorian decorum, but when she turned to venereal disease—she actually used the words "syphilis" and "gonorrhea."

To Anthony Comstock, the bull-necked guardian of the nation's morals who served as semiofficial consultant to the postmaster general, the proper education for girls in such matters was ignorance, and Margaret's incendiary language was promptly censored. *The Call* challenged the decision, the ban was rescinded, the offending column ran a few weeks later, and the predicted plague never materialized.

But the pattern that would haunt Margaret for the next three decades was established. Seeking to protect the young, she was accused of defiling their purity. Hoping to help women, she was called the archenemy of the family. And committed to the spread of knowledge, she was vilified as a crusader for vice. As a writer in the *New York Times* put it, "the terrible Margaret Sanger whom thousands of the pious have been taught to regard as the female Anarchist . . . is engaged in no more iniquitous enterprise than the effort to help people be happy."

Margaret's "iniquitous enterprise" was inspired in part by the socialist ideas and feminist ideals she encountered soon after her arrival in New York in 1910—and in particular Mabel's Evenings, which were both intellectually intoxicating and emotionally alluring to the young nurse. In her "Every Girl" series, she tentatively suggested that the economic structure of capitalism enslaved women by forcing them to depend on men for support, and she argued that women should fight for greater freedom in choosing a husband and in deciding when to bear children. Though she was more a decorous observer than a participant in the discussions, Margaret found the unconventional, uninhibited lifestyle of the Village an exhilarating relief from the sterile, middle-class values she felt were stifling her emerging sense of self.

Several of the organizing meetings for Mabel and Jack's Paterson Pageant in Madison Square Garden were held at Margaret's apartment— Margaret herself spoke to the workers on the picket lines—but her husband, Bill, though an architect with artistic aspirations and socialist politics, felt considerably less enamored of the Village spirit than his wife. "Madame Pompadeau Dodge's salon—Oh! Gosh! How nauseating!" he wrote Margaret. "The I.W.W. in the parlor! . . . Parlor discussions, Parlor Artists, Parlor Socialists, Parlor Revolutionaries, Parlor Anarchists . . ." The Village was "a hellhole of free love, promiscuity, and prostitution masquerading under the mantle of revolution. A saturnalia of sexualism, deceit, fraud, and Jesuitism let loose. . . . If Revolution means promiscuity, they can call me a conservative and make the most of it."

Bill's view of bohemian radicalism as a mask for sexual license indicated that feminism was not threatening to unenlightened men alone. What did women want? The same freedoms men took for granted? Such licentiousness was intolerable! But Margaret, though increasingly dissatisfied with her marriage—and about to embark on the first of her extramarital affairs—attempted to reassure Bill that the success of their relationship depended on her self-expression, and she stubbornly pursued the Village vision of uniting individual liberation and social reform.

"In those years before the war," Margaret later recalled, "a new religion was spreading over the country. . . . This new faith was made up of the revolutionaries, anarchists, socialists of all shades, from the 'pink tea' intellectual to the dark purple lawbreaker. The term 'radical' was used to cover them all. But while all were freethinkers, agnostics, or atheists, they were as fanatical in their faith of the coming revolution as any primitive Christian was for the immediate establishment of the Kingdom of God. . . . There were martyrs aplenty—men and women who had served in prison for their beliefs and were honored accordingly. One had hardly any social standing at all in radical circles unless one had 'worked for wages,' or brushed up against the police, or had served at least a few days in jail. As in the early Church, most of the members of this order were of the working classes, though there were eccentric millionaires, editors, lawyers, and rich women who had experienced 'conversions' and were active in the 'movement.' "

Margaret's "awakening," as she called it, occurred in a shabby, dimly lit, and overcrowded tenement on Hester Street on the Lower East Side.

As Margaret told the story—and she repeated and refined it so often during the next fifty years that even its horror became idealized—she nursed a young Jewish immigrant woman named Sadie Sachs through the painful complications of self-induced abortion, and listened in dismay as Sadie said her doctor had dismissed her desperate pleas for birth control information by suggesting that her husband "sleep on the roof." Margaret suggested condoms or coitus interruptus (the other methods available at the turn of the century were vaginal sponges, rubber devices known as pessaries, the rhythm method, and postcoital douching, most commonly with either carbolic acid or the kitchen cleaning product Lysol), but when she returned to Hester Street three months later, she found Sadie dying of septicemia.

Sadie's tragic fate didn't so much traumatize Margaret as focus her energy and give direction and purpose to her still uncertain commitments. She vowed that from that day forward she would renounce "the palliative career of nursing in pursuit of fundamental social change."

"After I left [Sadie's] desolate house," Margaret recalled years later, "I walked and walked and walked . . . thinking, regretting, dreading to stop: fearful of my conscience, dreading to face my own accusing soul. . . . The miseries and problems of that sleeping city arose before me in a clear vision like a panorama: crowded homes, too many children; babies dying in infancy; mothers overworked . . . half sick most of their lives . . . made into drudges. . . . I knew a new day had come for me and a new world as well. . . . There was only one thing to be done: call out, start the alarm, set the heather on fire! Awaken the womanhood of America to free the motherhood of the world! I was now finished with superficial cures, with doctors and nurses and social workers who were brought face to face with this overwhelming truth of women's needs and yet turned to pass on the other side. . . . I resolved that women should have knowledge of contraception. They have every right to know about their own bodies. . . . I would scream from the housetops. I would tell the world what was going on in the lives of these poor women. I *would* be heard. No matter what it should cost, *I would be heard.*"

Enraged at the devastation of women's lives by economic exploitation, unwanted pregnancies, and $5 abortion mills, Margaret became a full-time nurse and sexual counselor and began her series of columns in *The Call*, the first systematic effort in this country to link the causes of sexual liberation and birth control. Indignant at the lack of support she found among her socialist colleagues, she spoke out forcefully at meetings of socialist Local No. 5, the Village chapter. "Poverty and large families go hand and hand." If workers "were fighting for better wages and shorter hours, they should equally be concerned with the size of the workingman's family." Yes, she would be heard!

In her early thirties, Margaret could have pointed to far earlier influences than the Village spirit of rebellion and the medical establishment's callous indifference to women. She was born in Corning, New York, in 1879, four years before Max Eastman and only fifty miles from his birthplace. Her father, an Irish stonecutter, was a supporter of Eugene Debs and a vocal unionist devoted to the liberating powers of alcohol. Her mother, an incurious Catholic, endured eighteen pregnancies, bore eleven living children, and uncomplainingly suffered from chronic tuberculosis. Despite all this, deep feelings of affectionate sensuality drew her parents together.

With a socially conscious father and a permanently ill mother, whose life surely revealed childbirth as a relentless burden—and with so few avenues open to young women in the late nineteenth century—Margaret almost inevitably decided to become a nurse. During her training, she met a glamorous Jewish architect named Bill Sanger, who, captivated by her mercurial high spirits, auburn hair, green eyes, and lithe figure, insisted that she become his wife after only a few months of assiduous courtship. Though Margaret had muddled misgivings, having briefly undertaken what she called "a trial marriage" with another suitor several months earlier, she reluctantly assented, and after their marriage in August 1902, the bride spent her wedding night working the night shift at the hospital.

Bill may have had artistic aspirations and socialist politics, but he had a middle-class view of marriage, and Margaret cut short her nursing career to bear three children within the next eight years. She soon found her own marriage repeating the same pattern as that of her parents. Bill proved incapable of providing economic security, and Margaret was suffering from a lingering case of tuberculosis that had been diagnosed during her nursing training. An improvident father, an ill mother, three young children, a sexually charged marriage but no reliable method of birth control (particularly necessary since her deliveries had been difficult and her illness made further pregnancies dangerous)—she was stunned to discover that she'd become almost exactly what she'd vowed to escape.

So it was in a mood of confusion, unarticulated dissatisfaction, and even guilt that she first became acquainted with the Village when she and Bill moved to New York in 1910. Bill's prestige as an architect (he helped design Penn Station), his interest in art, and, even more important, his involvement in socialist politics (he ran for alderman on the party ticket in 1911, garnering 352 votes), soon made them one of the Village's most prominent couples. Jack Reed visited their home, as did Big Bill Haywood, Walter Lippmann, Alexander Berkman, and Emma Goldman, but Margaret couldn't help noticing that they came to talk to Bill, while she played the silent, deferential hostess. Defiant talk and conventional behavior— she felt as if she were back in Corning.

Yet the talk of feminism, no matter how perfunctory, validated her vague unease, ameliorated her guilt over her shortcomings as a wife and mother, and suggested an outlet for her thwarted energies. As Bill devoted more and more time to painting, Margaret helped her fellow women—especially the poor of the Lower East Side, in whom she saw not the romance of immigration so celebrated by Jack and Hutch, but the misery of her mother.

Imagine Mabel's surprise when this demure, married lady with three children suddenly began to talk about her vision of liberated sexuality. Margaret, wrote Mabel, "told us all about the possibilities in the body of 'sex expression'; and as she sat there, serene and quiet, and unfolded the mysteries and mightiness of physical love, it seemed to us we had never known it before as a sacred and at the same time a scientific reality."

It was, wrote Mabel, as if Margaret "had been more or less arbitrarily chosen by the powers that be to voice a new gospel of . . . sex-knowledge about copulation and its intrinsic importance"; she was "the first person that I, personally, ever knew, who set out to rehabilitate sex," to make it "a scientific, wholly dignified, and prophylactic part of right living." Moreover, she was "the first person I ever knew who was openly an ardent propagandist for the joys of the flesh," Mabel concluded, characteristically transforming discreet conversation into passionate proselytizing.

Margaret had discovered sex early and experienced it voraciously. Sexual intercourse, she believed, brought her more deeply in touch with her yearnings and with her anxieties, and furthermore, she wasn't ashamed to confess, it helped her sleep. She wrote in her journal in 1914, "Emotion is that which urges from within, without consciousness of fear or of consequences." "The most far-reaching social development of modern times is the revolt of women against sex servitude," she wrote years later in an even more evangelical tone. "When women have raised the standard of sex ideals and purged the human mind of its unclean conception of sex, the fountain of the race will have been cleaned."

But Margaret was so discreet and so prescient in understanding that she couldn't allow her sexual behavior to compromise her birth control work that not even the omniscient Mabel knew that she had embarked on an affair with an editor she'd met while vacationing with her husband and children in Provincetown.

Margaret's "awakening" in Sadie Sachs's tenement apartment coincided with her awakening to the dissatisfactions of her own marriage. By now, Bill had given up architecture for painting and had transformed himself into something of a socialist bohemian, but like many he viewed women's issues as secondary in principle and nonexistent in practice. Self-fulfillment was the noblest of ideals—wasn't that what he sought for himself? But did self-fulfillment mean that women could abandon their responsibilities as mothers? Did the feminism he rhetorically supported mean women could forgo their loyalty as wives? Was this where fighting for the vote for women led?

No, Margaret answered, feminism meant struggling for women's autonomy over their own bodies and from suffocating marriages. Bill felt that the only way to save their marriage was to leave the licentious environment of the Village with its home-wrecking feminists, and he persuaded Margaret to accompany him to Europe. But Margaret had her own agenda. Big Bill Haywood had urged her, "If you want to know about contraception, go to Paris. The French have known things for years that we don't."

There, Margaret spent several months in "inactive incoherent brooding," and by the end of a year, "I had practically reached the exploding point. I could not contain my ideas, I wanted to get on with what I had to do in the world." She left Bill behind and on the boat back to New York reflected with increasing agitation on Sadie Sachs, the censorship of *The Call*, the sleazy abortionists, her mother's unfulfilled life, her own unfulfilled marriage. By the time she arrived home she had decided to start a magazine called *The Woman Rebel*, uniting her social commitment and personal rebellion in a coherent, determined, and courageous vision.

A young male colleague came up with the term "birth control" to describe Margaret's mission—"family limitation" and "voluntary motherhood" having been rejected as lacking in public appeal. And though the women of the Heterodoxy Club refused to support the project, ads in radical magazines elicited enough subscriptions to begin publication of the magazine in March 1915. In her inaugural manifesto, Margaret argued that such a magazine was necessary "because I believe that women are enslaved by the world machine, by sex conventions, by motherhood and its present necessary childrearing, by wage-slavery, by middle-class morality, by customs, laws, and superstitions." She called on women to fight for political liberation from patriarchal oppression, economic liberation from capitalist exploitation, and cultural liberation from male attitudes. Specifically, she attacked statutes criminalizing contraception and abortion, and promised that she would violate the law by providing practical birth control information in future issues.

Supportive letters poured in—most of them asking for more information about contraception—and articles about this brazen young woman and her outspoken publication appeared in newspapers across the country. Margaret expected to be attacked for her "extremist" approach, but to her surprise she found herself denounced from the left as well as the right. Many of the Village radicals who helped finance the magazine—including Mabel—withdrew their support, and many of the middle-class feminists felt she'd gone too far. In *The Masses*, Max reproved Margaret for "that most unfeminine of errors—the tendency to cry out when a quiet and contained utterance is indispensable." On the other hand, Emma wrote Margaret from Chicago that even though IWW women were "up in arms" over her audacity, *The Woman Rebel* was "the best seller we've got."

The postal authorities, in their fear that contraception would destroy the republic, didn't wait for Margaret's promise to violate the law. They confiscated the first issue and indicted its editor for sending "indecent" materials through the mails. She avoided the central post office by placing copies of the magazine in streetcorner mailboxes throughout New York, a tactic that resulted in criminal indictment—four counts carrying a possible sentence of forty-five years.

Margaret's father recommended "a rest cure," her lawyer advised plea bargaining, and a free speech advocate suggested psychoanalysis. But Margaret insisted that "birth control must not be set back by the false cry of obscenity. There must be no sentimentality in this important phase of sexual hygiene. Women must learn to know their own bodies." Rejecting the advice of her friends, she wrote a pamphlet entitled "Family Limitation" explaining withdrawal, condoms, douches, suppositories, sponges, and pessaries in layman's language and with accompanying diagrams. But when she took the manuscript to a printer well known in Village circles for his courage and radicalism, he turned white. "This can never be printed," he said. "It's a Sing Sing job." So Margaret saw twenty printers until she found someone willing. After preparing 100,000 copies for distribution, hiding them in a dozen cities, and sending telegrams to colleagues with a prearranged code signaling their release, Margaret sailed for Europe under the alias Bertha Watson, leaving her children with friends and leaving Bill forever.

In England, where she intended to stay until the hysteria abated, Margaret worked as a waitress in a tearoom and sought out birth control activists to learn the most up-to-date methods of contraception and the most effective tactics of agitation. Engrossed by one of Nietzsche's more poetic texts, she met a middle-aged, married Spanish radical-in-exile, with whom she promptly began a Nietzschean affair.

But the man she most longed to meet was Havelock Ellis, the famous English sexologist. In December 1914, having secured an invitation to tea through mutual friends, Margaret showed up at the great man's door and discovered "a tall, lovely, simple man with the most wonderful head and face and smile." To Havelock, Margaret seemed "quicker, more daring and impulsive" than the English feminists he knew, and he, too, was instantly charmed. Several scholarly discussions ensued over the next few weeks, but since neither the mentor nor his student was inclined to stay in the realm of abstraction, their conversations grew warmer, more suggestive, until the two finally became lovers.

Havelock, who accurately described himself as "a reserved, slow, undemonstrative person," was twenty years Margaret's senior, expressed shock at her radical politics, and furthermore—and of somewhat more immediate concern—frequently suffered from an inability to sustain an erection. In point of fact, he was currently married to a lesbian, to whom this affliction was rather a blessing than a curse. But Margaret's awestruck devotion, eroticism, and perhaps, most of all, willingness to keep their affair casual since she was still sleeping with her Spanish lover, overcame every obstacle. Throughout the spring and summer of 1915 the foursome continued their liberated arrangement—oddly enough, only Havelock's wife felt threatened—and in the fall, having reached a more sophisticated understanding of the birth control cause, Margaret decided to return to New York to stand trial on the obscenity charges.

During Margaret's ten-month absence, Anthony Comstock had died, birth control had received some degree of legitimacy in the national press, and she had become a celebrity. Shortly before her scheduled trial, she posed, at Jack Reed's suggestion, for widely published pictures wearing a lace-collared dress and embracing her two young sons (her daughter had died in 1915). And the night before the trial over two hundred guests crowded into the Brevoort Hotel for a testimonial dinner. Jack was there, and Walter Lippmann, and Herbert Croly of The New Republic, and several society women, including Mrs. Willard Straight, Mrs. Ogden Reid, and Mrs. Thomas Hepburn, whose daughter Katharine would become a model of the forthright, independent woman two decades later. When Margaret concluded her brief remarks, even those who condemned her tactics leapt to their feet in applause.

The prosecutor must have wondered how he could possibly win a conviction against this image of motherly respectability, this new icon of high society, and twice postponed the obscenity trial. In early 1916, the charges were dropped.

Ironically, the only person imprisoned in the case was Bill, who found himself hauled before a New York judge for his part in the birth control conspiracy. "Too many persons have the idea that it is wrong to have children," orated the enraged magistrate. "If some persons would go around and urge Christian women to bear children instead of wasting their time on woman suffrage, this city and society would be better off." He handed down a thirty-day sentence to the dismayed defendant, who must have reflected, as he was led off in handcuffs, that those sentiments weren't that far from his own.

But Bill's judge, in moving birth control from the realm of obscenity to the realm of women's place in society, inadvertently served the cause he meant to castigate. Increasingly regarded less as a family-hating radical than as a women's rights reformer, Margaret, after celebrating her own victory in a rousing rally, immediately took off on a cross-country speaking tour. Her basic speech—which she delivered over a hundred times in 1916 alone, and which benefited from her experience as an actress in high school—combined a socialist assault on the class system, a free speech condemnation of the government's efforts to suppress her movement, a scientific appeal for more information on contraception, and a feminist demand for women's control over their own lives.

Laborers and professors, social workers and bankers, IWW organizers and church leaders, poor mothers and society matrons—all heeded the part of her message that most reflected their own lives, but all heard her call for more rational family planning. So skillfully did she modulate her speech to fit her audience that she elicited enthusiastic support from both militant radicals and the respectable middle class, and left in her wake dozens of birth control organizations. "The impression she made on us," wrote a Boston Brahmin, "was one of a gentle, beautiful woman of unusual force of character. She appeared frail at first, but then her spirit and eloquence seemed to increase her stature as she molded us into an integrated group."

Birth control clinics were next. Margaret opened her first in October 1916, in a tenement storefront on Amboy Street in the Brownsville section of Brooklyn, then an Italian and Jewish working-class ghetto. Multilingual handbills distributed in the neighborhood read, "MOTHERS! Can you afford to have a larger family? Do you want any more children? If not, why do you have them? DO NOT KILL, DO NOT TAKE LIFE, BUT PREVENT."

Among the first visitors, however, was a "Mrs. Whitehurst," who purchased a sex education pamphlet, then returned the next day accompanied by three plainsclothesmen from the vice squad. Informed that she was under arrest, and that the clinic's furnishings and records were impounded, Margaret shrieked at "Mrs. Whitehurst," "You are not a woman, you are a dog!" "Tell that to the judge," replied the undercover agent, and Margaret, in the words of the *Brooklyn Daily Eagle*, was "half-dragged, half-carried" to a waiting patrol wagon. Upon being convicted in early 1917, and given the choice between a fine and thirty days in the workhouse, she unhesitatingly chose jail, and she was cheered on by a large crowd singing the "Marseillaise."

Margaret was now a national celebrity. She opened a two-room office on lower Fifth Avenue to which thousands of women flocked, and the Brownsville case resulted in a legal victory when the Court of Appeals, though upholding her conviction, ruled that her clinics did not violate the law if operated by medical professionals. Her cause had caught fire.

Margaret had an intuitive genius for finding the most effective balance between radical vision and pragmatic politics, advocating just enough civil disobedience to keep her cause in the public eye and indulging in just enough compromise to enlist an ever broader base of support. She remained a socialist throughout her life and was capable of the most sophisticated analysis of the link between capitalist exploitation and women's oppression. But for fear of alienating potential followers, she muted her socialism and her pacifism during the war, and focused exclusively on the single issue of birth control. She came to see her constituency as based on gender rather than on class, and though she privately disdained the socially elite "pink tea ladies" who provided much of her financial support, and was uncomfortable with the middle-class women who provided most of her troops, she came to see feminist solidarity as the crucial component of her cause. "We are interested in the freedom of women, not in the power of the state," she wrote. "Without that freedom for women—not only economic, but personal freedom as well—the right kind of state cannot exist and will not exist."

Margaret came to embody the Village vision by moderating her radicalism. To win the allegiance of reformers, without whose support her cause was doomed, she stressed such issues as infant mortality, birth defects, and child labor. Weren't they reason enough to champion freer access to contraception?

Relentlessly pursuing her unique brand of radical pragmatism, Margaret may have begun to win praise from both the left and the right, but both sides continued to denounce her as well. Authorities in several cities attempted to deny her the right to speak, and the FBI placed her under surveillance. And many prominent socialists attacked her for betraying the cause; even Emma—though her displeasure was aroused as much by jealousy and by an apparent affair between Margaret and Sasha than by any ideological dispute—complained that birth control was becoming "*too* respectable for decent folk" like bohemians and intellectuals.

The psychic source of most opposition to birth control was fear of female sexuality. Centuries of patriarchal prohibitions took on new and even more twisted forms in the nineteenth century with the emergence of secular capitalism. Since competitive individualism characterized the new ethos, new mechanisms of control were needed to replace religion and family. The myth of female sexual passivity, superficially the obverse of yet actually a disguise for the myth of female sexual insatiability, became the most repressive of these mechanisms, so that for a woman to even dare to raise sexual issues was seen as a sign of personal immorality and social chaos. No wonder, then, that when Margaret insisted on a woman's "absolute right to dispose of herself [or] to withhold herself" she was regarded as advocating licentiousness and debauchery.

Margaret was confronted with two insidious but powerful modes of repression—sexual control as an effective means of establishing broader forms of social control, and questioning of character as one of the most effective means of resisting attempts to empower women. "Pretty nearly everything and everyone has been against her," wrote an editorialist in the *New York Tribune*, "pulpits and legislatures and newspapers, public men and private citizens, and whole regiments of the prejudices, fears, bogeys, and dragons that still infest the mind of civilized man."

Even in the mid-twenties, many people continued to regard birth control as a bohemian cause. In 1924, the *New York Daily News* referred to Margaret as "a member of the advanced school of Greenwich Village philosophers." But as Margaret's support across the country increased, her stature in the Village diminished: she became too effective to continue as a focus of rebellion.

Margaret fell victim to fits of despondency and what her doctors called "nervous fatigue." Havelock continued to write longingly from London, and in early 1920, partly to renew their relationship, partly to recuperate from another attack of tuberculosis, Margaret sailed for England. Despite the tone of his letters, Havelock was deeply involved with another woman—somewhat to Margaret's relief, as it turned out, for she soon realized that their erotic communion, if not their intellectual compatibility, had dimmed.

Even while "resting," Margaret found time to engage in a series of bristling encounters with one of the leading English exponents of birth control, Marie Stopes, who had written a best-seller called *Married Love* (sex manuals being forced to adopt this kind of semi-sacramental tone even as late as the fifties). Marie declared that sexual intercourse energized both partners by a mutual exchange of "substances materially presented as chemical and ultrachemical molecules," and described orgasm in phrases even Margaret found a bit florid. "The half swooning sense of flux which overtakes the spirit in that eternal moment at the apex of rapture, sweeps into its flaming tides the whole essence of the man and woman."

When Havelock introduced Margaret to a debonair, upper-class aesthete and novelist named Hugh de Selincourt, she was soon enjoying "the apex of rapture" herself. Hugh and his wife had established a kind of sexual commune on a country estate, and though Havelock enviously argued that Hugh's erotic proficiency was merely a mask for his intellectual inadequacies, and that men like him were nothing but "sexual athletes," to Margaret "sexual athlete" was just the ticket. While Margaret was being denounced from virtually every other quarter as a harlot or a home-wrecker, what bliss to hear herself described as a "delicious blend of the great queen and a little girl."

While not necessarily going so far as to argue, as Hugh did, that those who loved the same person should also love each other, or that such liberated sexual revels were a revolutionary political act, Margaret enthusiastically took part whenever anyone suggested a ménage à trois or ménage à quatre. After their brief but joyous affair in 1920, whenever she visited England, she found time to relax in an environment that would always "radiate beauty, stimulate mental and spiritual growth . . . and entirely do away with the pettiness of jealousy, which so often occurs in regular marriage"—to say nothing, as she wrote Hugh privately, of "the joys and delights a certain English old thing has given me."

In her own writing on sex, Margaret compared the ordinary man's technique (Bill's?) to that of an orangutan attempting to play the violin, whereas an adept lover's (Hugh's) was like that of a symphony conductor, his baton (as it were) making sure that each passage flowed spontaneously into the next, leading to a melodic, harmonic, and rhythmic consummation. The woman's role was to attune herself to her conductor's movements, resulting in "a dance in which two humans are no longer separate and distinct persons, but in which their beings are commingled in a new and higher unity, a mutual rhythm and ecstasy."

In the summer of 1920 she had an exhilarating affair with H. G. Wells, at the time one of the most well-known writers in the world. There was "no aloofness or coldness in approaching him," Margaret wrote in her autobiography, "no barriers to break down as with most Englishmen; his twinkling eyes were like those of a mischievous boy."

Wells even based a novel on their affair, *The Secret Places of the Heart*, in which Sir Richmond Hardy seduced a Miss Grammont, intelligent, erotically liberated, in search of noncommitment. "He found that she was very much better read than he was in the recent literature of socialism, and that she had what he considered to be a most [unfeminine] grasp of economic ideas. He thought her attitude toward socialism a very sane one because it was also his own," he wryly wrote. He described her as a woman with "a scientific quality of mind," and it was this kind of intellectual respect that assured the occasional renewal of their affair and their enduring friendship.

Sexually refreshed and ideologically subdued, Margaret returned to the Village in the fall of 1920 for the publication of her first book, *Woman and the New Race*, which appeared the same year women finally won the vote. Havelock wrote an introduction for the book, which received generally favorable reviews. "She proclaims aloud what women have been taught they must smother to whispers," wrote a critic in *The New Republic*. The book quickly ran through its first printing, sold over a half-million copies in the next few years, and at last brought birth control into the mainstream of public discourse.

"Yesterday's criminal," said one of Margaret's colleagues, had been transformed into "today's heroine." But the campaign against birth control continued as fanatically as ever. In 1921, police invaded a conference at New York's Town Hall and dragged Margaret to a nearby station house, where she was booked for disorderly conduct. In the mid-twenties her speaking engagements in upstate New York were routinely barred or disrupted. In 1929, after another undercover policewoman had infiltrated Margaret's Brownsville clinic and been fitted with a diaphragm, eight policemen burst in and arrested the staff. That same year, Boston authorities refused to allow her to speak, but Margaret, by now skilled at co-opting acts of suppression, posed for a widely distributed photo with a band of tape covering her mouth. By now she had achieved worldwide fame: in India she even convinced Gandhi to encourage birth control for the populace.

Noah Slee was nothing if not respectable. A pious Episcopalian, a harrumphing Republican, a staid member of the Union League, he had become a multimillionaire by inventing and marketing 3-in-One Oil, and had been married for more than thirty years when he met Margaret at a dinner party in 1921. Within a few months, Noah had abandoned his wife, his business, and a good deal of his respectability in pursuit of this enchanting woman.

For her part, Margaret had always been candid on the subject of remarrying: in obeisance to her feminist principles she admitted that it would only be for money, and from the day she met him she rarely referred to Noah as anything but "the millionaire." They were improbably, but practically, married in the fall of 1922.

She returned to the Village, but this time to a five-story town house office on West 16th Street and a luxurious apartment at 39 Fifth Avenue.

Not only did Margaret accurately describe herself as "no fit person for love or home or children or friends or anything which needs attention or consideration," she insisted that she and Noah maintain separate suites and he was required to make a telephone call or write a note before he could enter her domain. Furthermore, she made him sign an agreement allowing her to keep her name professionally and to retain the freedoms she'd enjoyed as a single woman.

In his eyes, it was a fair exchange. After all, hadn't she been the means of his escape from a stultifying marriage? Hadn't she made him the gift of youth? If, in some respects, Noah was unable to take full advantage of this gift—in one poignant letter, he explained that he loved her "beyond life itself," then reminded her not to forget his enema tube—Margaret was unable to appreciate the constant tenderness he showered upon her. Both her activities and her inclinations kept her away from home much of the year, and in one of her letters, she wrote, "Dearest Noah—Darling—It is really always lovely to be away from you even one day," fortunately catching herself before sealing the envelope and carefully changing the "v" in "lovely" to an "n."

Still, if marriages can be called successful when both partners get what they want, Noah and Margaret's turned out better than most. From her point of view, the match completed her transition from disreputable rebel to respectable reformer. The woman who'd been jailed in New York on obscenity charges was now a registered Republican. For the remainder of his life Noah generously supported her movement, and though she suffered periodic fits of depression and enjoyed periodic affairs of passion, Margaret was increasingly regarded as a staid savior of the family.

In her autobiography, this ruthless forthright woman distorted her past, her passions, her personality to serve her mission. The psychic costs may have been incalculable, but the social consequences were monumental. As H. G. Wells put it, "The movement she started will grow to be, a hundred years from now, the most influential of all time in controlling man's destiny on earth."

Such remarks are usually meant as eulogies rather than as prophecies, but the reason this one seems so exaggerated is simple: the movement Margaret pioneered is now taken for granted as one of the conditions of everyday life. Some feminists complained that in focusing on a single issue, and in abandoning her initial beliefs in that cause's potential for a radical reconstruction of society, Margaret undermined, or at least delayed, the achievement of female autonomy in other aspects of life. Furthermore, they argued, even in terms of that single issue she too strongly stressed the virtues of motherhood and too narrowly defined the parameters of sexuality, merely assuring that women could enjoy intercourse without fear of pregnancy. Yet such arguments pay too much attention to her tactical politics and too little to her visionary principles. It's difficult to imagine a cause encompassing such a broad range of social, cultural, scientific, moral, and sexual concerns or one more significant in freeing women's energies to pursue autonomy in every other avenue of life.

Her social commitment moved beyond ideology and achieved what the radical ideologues only prophesied. Her yearning for erotic liberation remained concealed, and yet she freed herself from the moral conventions so many bohemians merely railed against—and in consequence lost both her marriage and her children to her cause.

Margaret's image fell short of the radical-bohemian ideal, but her work fulfilled its goals. Despite the conviction of the radical bohemians that revolution was imminent, the fusion of social change and personal liberation they advocated too often took place not in the lives of contemporary men and women but in some vague "socialist world order" in the distant future. Seldom has a political or cultural movement had such faith in persuasion and such ignorance of power. Margaret in contrast skillfully moved from salon rhetoric to social effectiveness. One of the most visionary of the Villagers, she was at the same time the most pragmatic.

Mabel Dodge, who gathered together the likes of Max Eastman, Walter Lippmann, and Alfred Stieglitz in her legendary salon at 23 Fifth Avenue

Max Eastman, editor of
The Masses

Max Eastman and his wife, Ida Rauh

Robert Minor's cartoon
from the back cover of
The Masses, July 1916

Army Medical Examiner: "At last a perfect soldier!"

New York Call, 22 November 1917

Outside the courthouse during the first *Masses* trial in November 1917, from left, Crystal Eastman, Art Young, Max Eastman, Morris Hillquit, Merrill Rogers, and Floyd Dell

Museum of the City of New York

Polly's Restaurant

Eugene O'Neill, right, and Charles Demuth in
Provincetown, July 1916

Preparing the set for the play *Bound East for Cardiff* by Eugene O'Neill
(top of ladder), produced by the Provincetown Playhouse, 1916

The Provincetown Playhouse at 133 Macdougal Street

George Cram (Jig) Cook,
the guiding force of the
Provincetown Players

Norma Millay and Harrison Dowd in rehearsal for Edna St. Vincent Millay's play *Aria da Capo* at the Provincetown Playhouse, 1919

The Hotel Brevoort, on the corner of Fifth Avenue and 8th Street

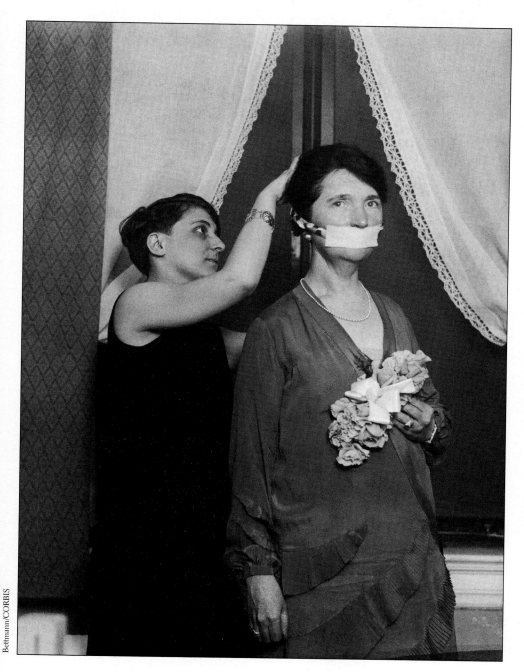

Margaret Sanger, April 17, 1929

Emma Goldman speaking about birth control at a Union
Square rally, May 21, 1916

Margaret Sanger with sons Stuart and Grant,
1916

Big Bill Haywood

Emma Goldman and Alexander Berkman, 1918

Elizabeth Gurley Flynn at the silk
workers' strike, February 1913

Brown Brothers

John Reed

John Reed and Louise
Bryant at Croton

Courtesy Houghton Library, Harvard University

Edna St. Vincent Millay

Front row, left to right: Susan Glaspell, Beatrix Hapgood, Mary Heaton Vorse, Hippolyte Havel; back row: Harry Weinberger, Neith Boyce (face hidden), Hutchins Hapgood, Miriam Hapgood (standing)

Culver Pictures

Hutchins Hapgood

Henrietta Rodman

Willa Cather on the cover of *Time* magazine, August 3, 1931

Hart Crane

Theodore Dreiser, ca. 1912

In Provincetown, Massachusetts, ca. 1916, from left to right: Kenneth Russell Chamberlain, Maurice Becker, and Harry Kemp

Harry Kemp, the Poet of the Dunes, at the door of his dune shack

Margaret always insisted, as she put it in the mid-fifties, "It was my duty to place motherhood on a higher level than enslavement and accident. For these beliefs I was denounced and arrested. Because I saw these as truths, I stubbornly stuck to my convictions." Only days before her death, the Supreme Court permitted the use of contraceptives on grounds of the right to privacy. "I am so happy in a cause," Margaret wrote. "All the world of human beings is a passing show. They come and go"—the denunciations and arrests, the trials, the rallies and demonstrations, fund-raising, organizing, lecturing and writing, even the time she was kicked in the teeth by a zealous guard—"but the idea of human freedom grows ever closer around one's heart and comforts and consoles and delights."

One of the most vilified women of the century, by the time of her death in 1966 at the age of eighty-seven, Margaret Sanger had become one of the most admired.

The Dormancy of Feminism

The feminist movement, envisioned by the remarkable Village women, virtually disappeared after World War I and lay dormant for many decades.

In the twenties, the flapper replaced the New Woman in the iconography not just of the Village, but of the entire nation. Superficially emancipated, the flapper needed no ideology. She was sexually uninhibited and erotically fulfilled—and still dependent on men. She went to dances instead of picket lines and dedicated herself to fashions instead of causes. She was free to take a glamorous job, free to have premarital sex, free to smoke and drink and wear lipstick—free to be frivolous? Stressing personal liberation and sexual experimentation: hadn't those been the preeminent goals of the Village women of the teens?

Of course, the feminists had sought a society where women could be gay, erotically fulfilled, free from the constraints of convention, but to the flapper it was an expression of bourgeois indifference. On a transatlantic voyage in the twenties, Mary Heaton Vorse scorned the shallow liberation of the young women aboard, their "willed freedom." "Well, here it is," she wrote in dismay of the emancipation she and her fellow feminists had fought for—"Look at them."

The leading feminists—what did the twenties usher in for them? Emma Goldman was in exile, Crystal Eastman jobless, Neith Boyce in a marriage like a truce, Heterodoxy abandoned. Louise Bryant and Susan Glaspell, women with independent, rewarding careers, remained linked in the public imagination with the high-profile men in their lives. The gap between ideology and reality swallowed up many of the feminist men in the Village as well, Floyd Dell forsaking bohemian radicalism for middle-class convention, Max Eastman confusing free love with philandering, Hutch Hapgood turning faithful only out of weariness.

Why did a movement with such passion, such energy, such ideological rigor disappear so quickly?

First, as has happened to so many American movements, much of the fervor of feminism was dissipated by its piecemeal successes. Women had won the vote, birth control was increasingly available (especially to middle-class women, a constituency crucial to a cause stressing cultural as well as economic oppression), repressive sexual codes were relaxed, and women were more welcome in the workplace during a period of rapid economic growth.

Second, the resurgence of patriotism meant the end of idealism. Americans often confuse the two, which are in fact usually in opposition — and the utopian thinking of the early teens instantly gave way to the jingoism of the war. Feminism required vision, and the vision of the twenties was the American Century. Peacetime and the economic boom quieted all reservations about the viability of the American system. Injustice, oppression, and exploitation, most Americans felt, had been swept away by the rise of prosperity.

Third, the link between radicalism and bohemianism, so characteristic of the teens, came apart in the twenties. Radicalism became moribund, partly because of government harassment, partly because of war-induced wealth, and bohemianism became meretricious because of self-conscious mimicry and commercial exploitation. The feminist movement had never been comfortable with either radicalism or bohemianism, but its emphasis on the politics of personal life had been nourished by the constant interplay between radical ideology and bohemian lifestyle. Personal life, in the twenties, had no politics, only prosperity.

Fourth, the increasing interest of the social sciences in the relationships of everyday life — sexual ones in particular — meant the "expert" replaced the advocate, amelioration took the place of vision. A utopian stance seemed naive to the mechanics of social change, leaving feminism deprived of its crucial moral energy, psychological insights, and cultural analyses. It could even be argued that feminism's emphasis on sexual liberation undermined its demand for a transformation of sexual relationships, for men proved all too ready to exploit women's sexual freedom while remaining unwilling to relinquish their sexual power. In any event, a more sophisticated understanding of the dynamics of interpersonal relationships and social change was not accompanied by a visionary attitude toward human potential; the feminist movement's commitment to possibility was undercut by the social sciences' commitment to engineering.

Measuring the impact of any movement is always problematic. The feminists, no matter what specific causes they advocated, sought to alter sexual attitudes and transform the social atmosphere, so their influence can't be judged solely, or even largely, in terms of political reform, economic advancement, or institutional structure. They may not have won many victories, but they changed the way daily life is apprehended.

The gap between the overthrow of the old order and the establishment of a new order, it has been said, is the definition of liberalism—and that could just as easily be said of feminism. The women's movement virtually disappeared for five decades before bursting forth irrevocably in the late sixties, the groundwork laid by the remarkable women of the Village in the teens—the Golden Age of Feminism.

V

Edna St. Vincent Millav

"A Lovely Light"

Running in the rain, her long hair streaming in the breeze, her bare feet skipping over puddles, a laughing young lover reaching out to embrace her as she dashes around the corner—Edna St. Vincent Millay!

A circle of friends reading one another their poems by the flickering flames of the fireplace. Young lovers riding back and forth on the Staten Island ferry until dawn. Speakeasy laughter, garret parties, midnight picnics in Washington Square Park.

> *My candle burns at both ends;*
> *It will not last the night;*
> *But, ah, my foes, and oh, my friends—*
> *It gives a lovely light!*

Though her carefree image masked an often troubled soul, for a few years her "lovely light" cast its glow over an entire generation. If Jack Reed was the Golden Boy of Greenwich Village, its Golden Girl was Edna St. Vincent Millay.

240

When Ferdinand Earle invited submissions for an anthology of the best in contemporary poetry, he had no idea how many would-be Miltons he'd unmute. Manuscripts poured in by the thousands, banal ballads, insipid odes, junk. In despair, Earle asked a professor friend to help him tackle the endless stacks of envelopes. After several hours of glancing at the first few lines, and discarding them, the professor reached back into the wastebasket.

"Renaissance," he read from the manuscript,

> All I could see from where I stood
> Was three long mountains and a wood;
> I turned and looked another way,
> And saw three islands in a bay . . .

The pages hit the wastebasket again. "Hey! That sounds good," Earle protested—well, maybe not good, but better than anything else he'd been reading.

They read through the entire poem, then read it again. "We both agreed," concluded Earle, "that it was tops." He promptly wrote a letter to the poet announcing that his submission—for surely such a fine poem could only be the work of a man—would receive the first prize of $500, and addressed the envelope to E. St. Vincent Millay, Esq., Camden, Maine.

Unfortunately, Earle neglected to consult the other two judges before writing Mr. Millay, and when they met to vote on the finalists a few weeks later, "Renascence"—the spelling of the title anglicized at Earle's suggestion—placed fourth, behind three poems of social protest. Upon receiving the published volume, the first-prize winner, Orrick Johns, "realized that the outstanding poem in that book was 'Renascence' by Edna St. Vincent Millay, immediately acknowledged by authoritative critics as such. The award was as much an embarrassment to me as a triumph." In protest—"I did not want to be the center of a literary dog-fight"—Johns declined to attend the award ceremony.

Earle's anthology was entitled *The Lyric Year*—1912 again—the year Edna St. Vincent Millay turned twenty.

Vincent—as nearly everyone called her—had sent her submission to *The Lyric Year* at the urging of her mother, Cora. Bright, brisk, even a bit raffish, Cora Millay had hoped to become a writer or a musician, but after her divorce in 1900 from Henry Millay—a charming but unreliable man who worked as a school principal but whose true vocations seemed to have been poker and alcohol—she uncomplainingly gave up her artistic ambitions to support their three young daughters.

Vincent, Norma, and Kathleen—three lively girls known to one another as Sefe, Hunk, and Wump—were eight, six, and four when their parents separated. "I remember," Vincent wrote years later, "a swamp of [cranberries]. . . . It was down across that swamp that my father went, when my mother told him to go & not come back. (Or maybe she said he might come back if he would do better—but who ever does better?)" Cheerfully idealistic, independent-minded, devoted to the arts, committed to liberal causes, Cora managed to raise her children in an atmosphere of urban sophistication and familial gaiety even in the dour gentility of small-town Maine. Few families were as impoverished as the Millays, few as merry. Vincent wrote—in a phrase she said perfectly characterized her childhood—"Meseems it never rained in those days."

Resourceful and high-spirited, Cora inspired her daughters to develop self-reliance and to cherish their close-knit family. She encouraged them to find wonder in the world of nature and delight in the life of the imagination. She was also wise enough to stimulate their individuality rather than impose her own aspirations. Fuel may have been scarce, food may have been inadequate, but books were abundant in the Millay household, as were music scores, painting sets, and improvised theatricals, and when the girls went to bed, Cora—who somehow found time to write poems and short stories for several New England newspapers and to help with the local orchestra—sang them to sleep with songs she'd composed herself.

Cora didn't protect her girls in a cocoon of fantasy. By forthrightly confronting the harshness of their life, she taught them to find joy in their deprivation. One winter, when the pipes burst, the kitchen floor flooded with several inches of water, then froze, and the girls skated on the indoor rink. They had "few of the necessities" of life, Vincent recalled of her fairy-tale childhood, but many of its luxuries.

Vincent's first love was music. At thirteen, she composed an opera based on "Little Boy Blue," and until sixteen, when she was forced to acknowledge that her hands were too small, she had hopes of becoming a concert pianist. Her literary gift was already apparent, however. Before she was ten she'd read "almost every word of Shakespeare," most of Milton, Pope, and Tennyson, and even dipped into Latin poetry. At fourteen she published her first poem, called "Forest Trees"—"And through it all ye stand, and still will stand / Till ages yet to come have owned your reign . . ."

The development of Vincent's sensibility proceeded in an unbroken line. No matter where she traveled, she never felt far from the rocky coast of Maine, and the richness of literature, with its classical forms and themes and allusions, formed as sensuous a part of her mental landscape as the ripeness of nature. Vincent's harmonious blending of familial interdependence and intellectual independence, of simple joys and sophisticated tastes, of lyric surrender and detached observation, was the gift of her childhood, which suffused her poetry. The only shadow that darkened her early years—the absence of her father—she attempted to transform into a gay acceptance of the impermanence of love.

Even an incident of near-tragedy in her childhood Vincent transformed into a celebration of rebirth. The award-winning "Renascence" was conceived when Vincent was ten, after she nearly drowned while swimming. Written when she was eighteen, the poem depicts the struggle between the allure of death and the embrace of life, the union of the yearning spirit and the beauties of nature, and the oneness of the soul with the divine—themes that would dominate her work.

Written in iambic tetrameter couplets, a technically risky form the teenage poet handled with astonishing finesse, the 214-line poem contains four sections. In the first, a sense of boundaries becomes increasingly confining, and the freedom-seeking spirit tries to reach out.

> The sky, I thought, is not so grand;
> I 'most could touch it with my hand!
> And reaching up my hand to try,
> I screamed, to feel it touch the sky.
>
> I screamed, and—lo!—Infinity
> Came down and settled over me . . .

In the second part, nearly crushed by the weight of Infinity, and hearing "The ticking of Eternity," the poet feels herself overwhelmed by omniscience—

> I saw and heard, and knew at last
> The How and Why of all things, past,
> And present, and forevermore . . .

—and succumbs to the craving for death.

But this capitulation soon ceases. In the third section, "The pitying rain" begins to fall on her grave.

> *I would I were alive again*
> *To kiss the fingers of the rain,*
> *To drink into my eyes the shine*
> *Of every slanting silver line,*
> *To catch the freshened, fragrant breeze*
> *From drenched and dripping apple-trees . . .*
>
> *O God, I cried, give me new birth,*
> *And put me back upon the earth!*

In the fourth and final section, the poet exults in her rediscovery of nature's beauties and in her reaffirmation of God's love.

The final stanza, so typical of Vincent's poetry, seeks a sense of restful repose, of almost ironic, cautionary detachment.

Though Vincent sometimes lapsed into strained metaphors and trite insights, and though she occasionally babbled on about "my tortured soul," too often resorted to archaic diction ("I would fain pluck thence"), and loaded the thing with solipsistic infinities of adolescence—faults for which a later generation of critics would dismiss her work as sentimental—her technique showed uncanny sophistication, her imagery contained precision and lyricism, and her transcendentalist vision skillfully modulated from deceptive girlishness to ecstatic wisdom.

The poem was a remarkable achievement for "Miss Twenty Years," as Earle addressed Vincent. Louis Untermeyer described it as "possibly the most astonishing performance of this generation." Floyd Dell rhapsodized: "Never has the simple beauty of earth been more poignantly captured in words than in this girl's poem: never, I think, in all poetry."

For months, praise poured in accompanied by astonishment that such an original, fresh, and accomplished poem had failed to win first prize. As one critic put it, "The young girl from Camden, Maine, became famous through *not* receiving the prize," and another called the judges' decision "poetry's scandal of the century."

One of the first letters Vincent received was from Arthur Ficke and Witter Bynner, both contributors to *The Lyric Year.* Witter was visiting Arthur, in Davenport, Iowa, and had casually leafed through a copy of the anthology. After reading the poem aloud, they immediately wrote the author, "This is Thanksgiving Day and we thank you . . ."

Convinced that the poet's name must be a pseudonym, Arthur also wrote Earle, "Witter Bynner, who is visiting me, and I read through most of the book. We grew somewhat downhearted over most of the poems . . . including our own. And suddenly we stumbled on this one, which really lights up the whole book. It seems to both of us a real vision, such as Coleridge might have seen. Are you at liberty to name the author? The little item about her in the back of the book is a marvel of humor. No sweet young thing of twenty ever ended a poem precisely where this one ends; it takes a brawny male of forty-five to do that."

"Mr. Earle has acquainted me with your wild surmises," Vincent replied. "Gentlemen, I must convince you of your error: my reputation is at stake. I simply will not be a 'brawny male.' Not that I have an aversion to brawny males; *au contraire, au contraire.* But I cling to my femininity! Is it that you consider brain and brawn so inseparable? — I have thought otherwise. Still, that is all a matter of personal opinion. But gentlemen: when a woman insists that she is twenty, you must not, must not call her forty-five. That is more than wicked: it is indiscreet. . . . When I was a little girl, this is what I thought and wrote:

> *Let me not shout into the world's great ear*
> *Ere I have something for the world to hear.*
> *Then let my message like an arrow dart*
> *And pierce a way into the world's great heart.*

"You cannot know how much I appreciate what you have said about my 'Renascence' . . .

"P.S. The brawny male sends his picture. I *have* to laugh."

The time had clearly come for Vincent to leave home, but Henry was no more able to pay for a college education than Cora. Fortunately, among the readers of "Renascence" was Caroline Dow, head of the National Training School of the YWCA in New York City, who had already been charmed by Vincent during a summer vacation in Maine. Dow urged Vincent to apply for a scholarship to Vassar, offered to solicit friends for financial help, and arranged for her to take preliminary courses at Barnard College.

New York! Skyscrapers, hurtling traffic, the noisy, filthy, rude crush — what an awesome sight it must have seemed to the girl who, even if she had felt the weight of infinity, had rarely ventured beyond the pastures of Camden. Vincent arrived on February 5, 1913, and the next day wrote her mother and sisters, "From my window [on the eighth floor of the YWCA on East 52nd Street] in the daytime I can see *everything*, —just buildings, tho, it is buildings everywhere, seven & eight stories to million and billion stories, washing drying on the roofs and on lines strung between the houses, way up in the air; —they flap and *flap!* In New York you can *see* the noise. . . ." And after a few weeks, "I feel that I am exceeding the speed-limit," she wrote home. "But I seldom skid, and when I do there is very lit-tle splash. Please give me some good advice in your next letter. I promise not to follow it."

In early March, she visited the Armory Show and reported to her family, "Saturday—Went to International Art Exhibition. Impressionistic school, you know, and perfectly unintelligible things done by people they call the 'Cubists' because they work in cube-shaped effects. Everything they do looks like piles of shingles. I'll get some postals of the pictures, I think—especially the one called 'Nude descending the stairs,' and if you can find the figure, outline it in ink and send it back to me." A few weeks later, she saw Sarah Bernhardt in *Camille*. "Just came back, and I'm all gone to pieces, but, oh, my soul."

To her astonishment, Vincent discovered she had become some-thing of a celebrity. Sara Teasdale, a minor poet but a major literary lion, in-vited her to tea, and Jessie Rittenhouse, socially prominent secretary of the Poetry Society of America, gave a dinner in her honor. Though too shy to read "Renascence" to the assembled guests—Witter Bynner read it in her place—Vincent was no more overwhelmed with wonder at her fame than she was intimidated by the metropolis, and her letters to Arthur Ficke ex-pressed girlish savoir faire. "I have been here since Wednesday and I am be-come a hardened citizen of a heartless metropolis." And in early March: "I wish very much that you were here in New York and that some of the peo-ple who are here were out in Iowa. I am not being a Bohemian. I am not so Bohemian by half as I was when I came. You see, here one has to be one thing or the other, whereas at home one could be a little of both."

Vincent soon sold two poems to the *Forum* for $25, the first pay-ment she received for her work. After keeping the check for several days, as if unconvinced it was real, she sent it off to her mother, "Promise me, please, that with some of this you'll do something to make something easier for yourself. Shoes, dear, —or have your glasses fixed if they're not just right. . . . And [she added to her sisters] I'd like it so much if each one of you would get some little tiny silly thing that she could always keep."

Of course, young men soon appeared on the scene, enchanted by her animated intellect and lively beauty. A young Nicaraguan poet named

Salomón de la Selva, a teacher of contemporary poetry at Columbia, became her frequent companion. Vincent and Salomón spent many a chaste but intimate hour taking in the five-cent view of the Manhattan skyline from the Staten Island ferry and passionately reciting poetry. "We were very tired, we were very merry— / We had gone back and forth all night on the ferry," Vincent later wrote in one of her most well-known poems, "Recuerdo" ("Remembrance"), perhaps named in honor of her Latin admirer.

Vincent entered Vassar in September 1913, and though many of her classmates held her in awe—not only was she a published poet, but she was a twenty-one-year-old freshman—she felt uneasy amidst the upper-class gentility. "I hate this pink-and-gray college," she wrote Arthur. "If there had been a college in *Alice in Wonderland* it would be this college. It *isn't* on the Hudson. They lied to me. It isn't anywhere near the Hudson. . . . They treat us like an orphan asylum. They impose on us in a hundred ways and then bring on ice-cream. I am thinking seriously of going to the University of Moscow, and taking a course in Polite Anarchy & Murder as a Fine Art."

Brought up in a home where the rules focused on kindness and lessons rather than clothing and curfews, Vincent resisted the regimentation governing the behavior of putatively Victorian maidens. When Vassar's president, Dr. Henry Noble MacCracken, called Vincent into his office for violating some trivial regulation, he acknowledged that he wouldn't expel her under any circumstances. "I know all about poets at college," he concluded slyly, "and I don't want a banished Shelley on my doorstep!" Vincent grudgingly responded, "On those terms, I think I can continue to live in this hell hole."

Despite being a mere "girls' school," Vassar had a stimulating faculty, and Vincent was soon engrossed in her courses. And despite the lingering restraints of puritanism, Vassar was committed to the emancipation of women—MacCracken had been enlightened when he heard the Pankhurst sisters face down a rancorous mob in Hyde Park—and Vincent joined the cheers when Inez Milholland spoke at the college's fiftieth-anniversary celebration in 1916.

According to MacCracken, "she was by fits an extraordinarily good student, then extraordinarily bad," but she took part in extracurricular activities with enthusiasm. She soon became one of the college's leading actresses, appearing in plays by Rostand, Synge, Lagerlöf, and Shaw (the poet

Marchbanks in *Candida*), and in her senior year she took the lead in her own drama, *The Princess Marries the Page*. But her greatest triumph came as the medieval French poet Marie de France, her hair adorned with pearls, in Hazel MacKaye's *Pageant of Athena*, "a cooperative story of women's intellectual advancement" presented as the centerpiece of that fiftieth-anniversary celebration.

Vincent's Vassar poetry ranged from a ditty she left for the maid,

> *Won't you come in bye and bye*
> *And sweep the cobwebs from my sky?*

to the baccalaureate hymn for her class, which began, somewhat to the astonishment of the assembled students, faculty, and parents,

> *Thou great offended God of love and kindness,*
> *We have denied, we have forgotten Thee!*
> *With deafer sense endow, enlighten us with blindness*
> *Who, having ears and eyes, nor hear nor see.*

How much more astonished they would have been if they'd known that Vincent had engaged in a number of lesbian affairs. Young men kept calling—de la Selva now taught at nearby Williams—but to a daring young feminist poet, brought up in a fatherless household and educated in a male-free enclave, lesbianism must have provided both the sensual gratifications she craved and the violations of convention to which she was always tempted.

Vassar averted its attention from behavior that challenged its unenforceable moral authority to focus on violations of its petty but enforceable codes. During spring vacation in 1917, Vincent saw Caruso in *Aida* at the Metropolitan Opera, but since the performance took place two days after she was due back on campus, she was forbidden to leave the school overnight for the rest of the term. But one lovely weekend in May, Vincent slept over with some friends at a nearby inn and an officious bureaucrat spotted her signature in the guest book. In view of such a clear-cut violation, the faculty exercised its usually thwarted power and suspended her indefinitely. Since Vincent was due to graduate in a few weeks, the suspension would bar one of Vassar's most famous students from her commencement exercise. MacCracken had a campus uproar.

Vincent reacted with outrage and tears, but soon informed her mother of the situation with bemused exasperation. "I can't stay here at all for Commencement: I can't graduate with the class,—my diploma will be shipped to me . . . & it all seems pretty shabby, of course, after all that I have done for the college, that it should turn me out at the end with scarcely enough time to pack and, as you might say, sort of 'without a character.'—The class is exceedingly indignant, bless 'em, & is busy sending in petitions signed by scores of names, & letters from representative people, & all that. It will do no good. But it is a splendid row. I don't pretend that I don't feel badly. I do—I have wept gallons, all over everybody. . . . But I never knew before that I had so many friends."

The administration finally relented—concern for its reputation winning out over reverence for its rules—and a few weeks later Vincent wrote Norma, "Tell Mother the class made such a fuss that they let me come back, & I graduated in my cap & gown along with the rest. . . . I went off in a cloud of glory"—and proudly signed herself, "Edna St. Vincent Millay B.A.!"

Vincent's early sonnets, and the love affairs they celebrated, made her famous, but the glow of her presence made her a myth. "Untamable as an egret, trailing long plumes through the upper air," in the words of Harriet Monroe, the founder and editor of *Poetry* magazine, Vincent could be animated, serene, carefree, austere—but she always conveyed an inaccessible independence, a delight in the separateness of a woman's soul. To the Villagers immediately following the war, she became the symbol of the liberated spirit, a lovely melody lingering on the breeze.

Like all representative figures, Vincent not only won the admiration of her generation but also bore the weight of its aspirations. That she bore them so lightly was part of her legend. She was quoted more than any poet since Shakespeare, courted more than any woman of her time, yet she understood herself less than almost anyone of her generation. Those who knew her best—especially her lovers—could never capture her in words, because what captivated them was her evanescence. From the first moment Vincent entered the Village, she was doomed to myth.

After graduating in June, Vincent hoped to find work as an actress, but an interview with the Washington Square Players had come to nothing and a tentative offer from a troupe in Milwaukee fell through, so she went to New York to look for a job. Finding nothing, Vincent spent most of the summer of 1917 back in Maine and finished her first book, *Renascence and*

Other Poems. In mid-September, she returned to New York and managed to eke out a meager income by giving occasional readings. In December, her book came out, bound in black with gold letters, its royalties totaling zero but its reception solidifying her reputation—though as she wrote a friend from Vassar, when she saw phrases like "one of the best known younger American poets," her reaction was, "I didn't know anybody had even heard of me." And in January 1918—though she'd briefly lived with friends on West 4th Street the previous June—Vincent finally moved to the Village, first to a temporary room on West 9th Street and shortly after to 139 Waverly Place, just down the street from the house in which Edgar Allan Poe had lived in the 1840s and written "Ligeia."

By January 1918, the Village could no longer take its joyous revolution of consciousness for granted, but was forced to define its role and articulate its identity. Its values denounced from without and exploited from within, its enclave invaded by thrill-seeking tourists and pseudo-bohemians, its coffeehouses and tearooms turning into avant-commerce, the Village was nearing the end of its age of innocence. But apartments remained cheap—rooms with fireplace for $15 or less a month—and nearly every block had its homey restaurants and cheerful bars. And it still retained its communal camaraderie in the midst of urban anonymity, its celebration of unconventionality, its unique blending of sophistication of thought and simplicity of lifestyle.

Vincent soon met dozens of Villagers—Theodore Dreiser, Malcolm Cowley, Hart Crane, E. E. Cummings, Alfred Kreymborg, Kenneth Burke, John Sloan, Eugene O'Neill, Susan Glaspell, Dorothy Day, Paul Robeson, Wallace Stevens, Djuna Barnes, Edmund Wilson, John Peale Bishop. Her mind reeled as she listened to her new friends talk of poetry, of course, but also all the isms, and especially feminism. Women could smoke in public, dress casually, spend evenings out unescorted—behavior still taboo in conventional society—and though Vincent took her independence for granted, she became an ardent advocate of women's rights, especially in matters of love.

Vincent sent her sister Norma $25 to come to New York, and in early 1918, she joined Vincent at her tiny apartment, "hardly large enough for a bed and a typewriter and some cups and saucers," a friend recalled, but with that quintessential bohemian luxury, a fireplace.

Soon after the first frigid winter, Kathleen Millay joined Vincent and Norma. "It was," said Malcolm Cowley, "one of the great Village events."

The three sisters moved into the top-floor apartment at 25 Charlton

Street. One of the favorite pastimes of the young men of the time was choosing the most charming of the sisters. As a putative poet put it, "One was beautiful, one was wise, and one was *mine*." The red-haired Vincent, tiny and delicate, the irregular features of her face ordinary in repose, but radiant when animated? The blond Norma, also an actress, somewhat taller and considerably "prettier" than Vincent though slightly resembling her? The brunette Kathleen, a recent Vassar graduate, writing a novel, taller still, the dark beauty of the family, not resembling her sisters at all? As Alexander Woollcott said, upon seeing Botticelli's *Primavera*, it should have been titled "The Multiplication of the Millay Family." A practical advantage of this admiration was that the sisters had to budget only a small portion of their meager funds for food. "Anyone who had not taken one of the Millay girls out to dine," said a Villager, "simply did not rate."

Vincent remained too committed to her poetry to seek a job, and having no money—so long as it was a matter of choice—was part of the romance of bohemia. "Would you mind paying me *now* instead of on publication for those so stunning verses of mine which you have," she wrote Harriet Monroe at *Poetry* in March. "I am become very, very thin, and have taken to smoking Virginian tobacco. P.S. I am *awfully* broke. Would you mind paying me a lot?" But Norma found work in a loft—"making airplanes," Vincent wrote their mother, adding, "she doesn't make quite all of them, just the screws, I guess, on maturer thought."

Unlike most newcomers, Vincent didn't have to make the giddy transition from small-town constraints to big-city independence, so no trace of adolescent rebelliousness or posturing eccentricity tainted her behavior. In some ways she was more sophisticated than her companions (lesbian affairs at Vassar hadn't been accompanied by so much *conversation*), in some ways more naive (in her mid-twenties, she had never been to bed with a man). A large part of her charm and artistic reputation, in fact, derived from how naturally she carried herself, for what so many of her friends had learned from Nietzsche or Marx or Freud, Vincent had learned from Cora. Still, Vincent needed the Village's paradoxical quality of simultaneous encouragement of individuality and sense of community in order to flourish as a person and as a poet. "Seems as if *somewhere* there ought to be something for me, doesn't it?" she wrote her mother with a kind of plaintive anticipation a few weeks before moving to the Village—and in the Village she found it. "There is a beautiful anonymity about life in New York," she wrote home, an anonymity without which she would not have become so famous.

With her dramatic instincts and the kind of beauty that was attractive in repose but mesmerizing when animated—the quality most mentioned by everyone who knew her—Vincent was naturally drawn to the Provincetown Players. On a blustery day in December 1917, she showed up to audition for the ingenue role in a drama called *The Angel Intrudes* by Floyd Dell. Vincent knew that the Provincetowners didn't pay their performers, but she hoped that an uptown scout might offer her a role on Broadway.

Floyd handled the auditions himself. "A sort of Celtic magic seemed to emanate from her like a perfume," he later wrote. "I thought of the Snow Princess whose kiss left splinters of ice in the hearts of the mortal men who loved her." During rehearsals, he remained distant, formal, but what better sign was there that he was falling in love?

The Angel Intrudes was "a forgettable one-act comedy" in Malcolm Cowley's undisputed estimation, but when it opened on December 28, it became one of the Players' most popular productions and Vincent one of their most promising performers. The company instantly voted her a full member on the basis of one "delicious performance."

During rehearsals, Norma stopped by the theater every night to pick up Vincent, and the two sisters soon found themselves accompanied by a young man named Charles Ellis, a painter who'd volunteered his services to the Players as a designer but who ended up as an actor and director as well. Norma was widely regarded as the prettiest of the Millay sisters. Cowley and Kenneth Burke fell in love with her and she and Charles eventually married; both appeared in the original cast of Eugene O'Neill's *Desire Under the Elms*.

Cora joined her daughters on Charlton Street for several months in 1919, less to chaperone them than to taste the Village herself. She bobbed her hair and delighted in being able to smoke in public without clucking disapproval. She made herself useful by sewing costumes for the Provincetown Players, and even joined her daughters in the ranks of their actresses. On one memorable evening Vincent, Norma, and Cora each performed in a different one-act play.

Floyd had written a one-act comedy, scheduled for the Players in late January, called *Sweet-and-Twenty*, and still thinking of himself as a playwright rather than as a suitor, he asked Vincent to dinner, read the play to her, and offered her the lead.

Eagerly open to moonstruck romance, the play's characters, Helen and George, simultaneously arrive to look at a house each wants to buy, and before even knowing each other's name, they decide it is love at first sight. On second sight, however, they reluctantly conclude that the only thing they agree on is their love for each other. A character called the Agent assures the couple that marriage is "an iniquitous arrangement devised by the Devil himself for driving all the love out of the hearts of lovers," and professes a typically Village solution. "If you are wise, you will build yourselves a little nest secretly in the woods, away from civilization. . . . And then you will come back refreshed to civilization . . . and . . . forget each other, and do your own work in peace."

Sweet-and-Twenty delighted the Players' subscribers as "a satire on marriage" and the playwright and his leading lady soon found themselves enacting its scenario. In her mid-twenties, Vincent was ready for her first sexual experience with a man—in his early thirties, Floyd was *always* ready for a sexual experience with a woman.

For all her flirtatious bravado, Vincent proved a timid beginner, and for all his sophistication, Floyd proved an awkward seducer. During their first night in bed together, Vincent refused to have intercourse. Undaunted, Floyd undertook an educational program, the goal of which was to convince Vincent of the superiority of Freud to Plato. After long discussions, Floyd tried to break through Vincent's reservations, this time with a less didactic approach. "I know your secret. You pretend that you have had many sexual love affairs—but [in] truth . . . you are still a virgin. You have merely had homosexual affairs with girls at college." Astonished at his "deductive powers," Vincent confessed, "No man has ever found me out before." Another lengthy discussion ensued, and they finally made love.

She called the experience "wonderful," and didn't need to be persuaded to repeat it. Within days the entire Village knew that the lovely young poet and the dashing young bohemian had become lovers.

When she and Floyd began their affair in January 1918, Floyd was considered the quintessential Villager. Managing editor of *The Masses*, under indictment by the federal government for anti-war activities, an active socialist and feminist, one of the first Americans to undergo psychoanalysis, and considered by many the finest literary critic in America, he was a leading spokesman for radical values and bohemian behavior. Others may have been more flamboyant, more idiosyncratic, but Floyd owed his reputation to the sober and efficient way he accomplished what they only aspired to. He talked with such common sense about joy, spontaneity, passion, beauty, love, and revolution that he seemed actually to embody them. A sensitive man, Floyd nevertheless seemed the kind of person who, in the dark night of the soul, would calmly set out to find a sensible solution—and succeed. A reasonable radical and cerebral bohemian, he was cheerfully, charmlessly *sane*.

Floyd also had a widespread reputation as one of the Village's great lovers. Like many men of otherwise deliberative character, Floyd could fall in love at a glance—a glimpse of stocking, a beguiling profile, and he felt he'd found his lifelong mate. But shortly after arriving in Chicago in 1909, he married Margery Currey, another émigré from Davenport, ten years older, not because he had fallen in love but because he hadn't. Free love seemed so much easier when love wasn't involved. A "liberated" woman, Margery provided a haven of intellectual companionship from which he would venture forth in search of romantic entanglements. As a token of their sophistication, Floyd and Margery hung a nude drawing of themselves on the wall of their apartment and hosted soirees where a frequent topic of conversation was not sex itself but the necessity for more candid conversation about sex.

Hardly settled into marriage, Floyd made love to a number of women, gratified that he was tearing down "the walls of custom and habit."

Enchanted by the "multitudinous" opportunities in their bohemian circle, Floyd could become enamored three times in a matter of months. Apparently he was able to enjoy sex only if he could convince himself that he was in love and violating taboos. When Margery inevitably discovered his infidelities and asked for a divorce—Floyd's view of their "arrangement" was another liberated "misunderstanding"—he promised to remain faithful, but succumbed after several weeks and congratulated himself when Margery agreed to end the marriage "without reproaches or recriminations."

"As for the love-affairs," Floyd wrote in his autobiography, ". . . which would not fit into the realities of my life as a married man, they were at least beautiful dreams. I don't think any of us quite knew what we believed about love and 'freedom.' We were in love with life, and willing to believe almost any modern theory which gave us a chance to live our lives more fully."

Still feeling that "intimacies were beautiful, good in themselves," Floyd fell in love again, this time with a beautiful twenty-year-old actress named Elaine Hyman, who took the stage name Kirah Markham. Floyd wrote Arthur Ficke that they were getting married, only to write again four days later that Kirah had fallen under the spell of Theodore Dreiser.

In the fall of 1913 Floyd left Chicago in search of yet more "liberated" environments. Sitting in the club car of the *Empire State Express*, Floyd wrote a thoughtful letter to the Chicago rabbi who'd officiated at his marriage to Margery—neither he nor Margery was Jewish, but they wanted their union to get off to an unconventional start—informing him that though he'd been "bruised" he was "ready to expose [himself] again to the dangers and pain of love." His problem, he told the no doubt astonished rabbi, had been an overreliance on "ideas," which had made him "hypocritical with women," "unsatisfactory as a lover," and "intolerable as a husband." Henceforth, he would discard his "superstitious reverence" for "reason and logic." As self-analysis, this seems a bit like an alcoholic blaming his addiction on his ability to speak the same language as the bartender, but as preparation for *Love in Greenwich Village*, as he titled one of his books, it perfectly captured the conflict between instinct and ideology that confused so many of the rebels against repression.

Floyd's psychic regime worked for a while. Immediately after arriving in the Village, he exposed himself once more "to the dangers and pain of love," first with a woman who kept an alligator in her bathtub, then with a photographer he'd known in Chicago named Marjorie Jones. Sharing an apartment, Floyd and Marjorie avoided the "misunderstanding" in his marriage to Margery by explicitly vowing to be completely open about their "inevitable faithlessness to each other." Floyd and Marjorie's "illicit domesticity," he later argued, had actually been intended "to keep [me] from becoming involved in other love affairs," as if he could only have a successful relationship by violating the premises on which it had been established.

But in spite of himself, Floyd carried out his vow of infidelity to Marjorie. The radicals and bohemians of the Village even regarded his behavior as proof of his feminism. But Floyd knew he was "a fickle and inconstant lover." He and Marjorie finally separated in 1916, a year before he met Vincent—they had become "too good friends," he wrote Arthur, "to be lovers any more."

As an editor and writer at *The Masses*, Floyd made perfunctory obeisance to feminism as an economic and class issue, but only sexual emancipation and nonmarital relationships aroused his enthusiasm. According to his argument, traditional domestic roles, marriage in particular, denied women the excitement of romance.

Furthermore, if women became free to venture into the world, men could initiate them into the formerly masculine "mysteries" of drinking and smoking, and even give "lessons in socialism, poetry, and poker, all with infinite tact and patience." Instead of traditional relationships, with men in the position of "sultans in little monogamous harems," men and women would become equal companions "in the adventure of life." "The Woman's Movement," Floyd wrote in an unconscious revelation of his actual agenda, was an expression "of that readiness of women to adapt themselves to a masculine demand," for since men were "tired of subservient women," a new woman would emerge, "the self-sufficient, able, broadly imaginative." The goal of women's liberation, in short, was to allow men to get laid.

To reconcile the conflict between the taboos of society and the imperatives of the flesh, he created both a concept of free love that rationalized impulse and a version of feminism that liberated women to serve male needs. Of course such a resolution of his conflicts proved as psychologically unsuccessful as it was ideologically suspect, and to his credit Floyd emerged from his lengthy psychoanalysis having resolved the discrepancy between his character and his instincts. What he really wanted was to settle down with a wife and children, and he promptly did just that.

Whether Floyd's arguments in *The Masses* ultimately aided the cause of women's liberation or momentarily diverted it from its more pertinent goals remains open to debate. But as Vincent's first male sexual partner, he involved her in an experience that certainly tinted her own legendary attitudes toward free love and feminism.

For several weeks Floyd and Vincent remained too engrossed in their explorations of sex—and the stir their affair had caused—to think about their suitability for each other. Floyd was convinced he'd found true love. Though at moments he saw Vincent as "a scared little girl from Maine," more often he felt that "one loved her hopelessly, as a goddess must be loved." "Melisande!" he began to call her.

Vincent remained too suffused with, if not exactly erotic delirium, at least the haze of awakened heterosexuality, to pay much attention to the personal qualities of her lover. Sex with a man! She gave herself up to the new sensation, then withdrew to ponder her experience, leaving Floyd feeling that she'd merged her soul with his, then suddenly disappeared beyond his reach. Bliss and agony for Floyd, a "wonderful" time for Vincent. As was to happen so often in Vincent's sexual adventures, gender roles were neatly reversed.

Still, Floyd's feminism obligated him to introduce his mistress to his larger world. He took her to the Liberal Club and made sure she met Jack Reed and Max Eastman, and got her a good seat at the conspiracy trial of *The Masses'* editors, where during the jury's deliberations she recited her latest poems to the defendants. He "earnestly discoursed upon Pacifism, Revolution, Soviet Russia, and Psychoanalysis," in the hope that if she shared his politics she'd be more eager to share her soul.

Unaware that he was trying to liberate her by making her more like

him, Floyd added socialism, atheism, and aesthetics to the curriculum—
but she resisted his socialism, rejected his atheism, and took only what she
wanted from his aesthetics. Nevertheless, their long conversations awakened Vincent to the intellectual ferment of the Village, a world she would
soon be speaking for.

One of the prominent themes of Vincent's poetry was an almost
joyous acceptance of the impermanence of love. Her feeling that sexual relationships were inevitably transient was no doubt due in part to her parents' broken marriage, but this simplistic explanation, favored by her
Freud-obsessed friends, fails to account for the gaiety with which she
greeted fleeting passion. Despite the absence of a father, she had had an
impossibly happy childhood—did she come to feel that though men
couldn't be relied on, feminine companionship was all she needed? More
likely, she retreated to some isolated part of her spirit where she could remain untouched by the yearning for love and the pain of its evanescence.
Her behavior toward Floyd—particularly the way she pulled further away
the further she drew him in—even suggests that her belief in the impermanence of love might have been an unconscious expression of resentment
for her father's betrayal, a way of abandoning men before they abandoned
her. In this light, many of her love poems might be read not only as a celebration of independence, as they were read by her admirers, but as denials
of need, protections against pain, forms of revenge.

Certainly Floyd came to their relationship with unresolved and
self-destructive drives of his own—part of what attracted them to each other
seems to have been the interlocking of their unfulfilled needs, an obsessive
dance of mutual neuroses. No doubt Floyd, eager to see himself as flamboyant, was enthralled by Vincent's blithe vivacity, and sensing her own
need for stability, she felt comfortable with Floyd's prosaic temperament.
But though both of them seemed artless, the unconscious can be calculating, and Floyd was to some extent drawn to the hopelessness of her inaccessibility, while she was drawn to the dependency she could wound.

If in public they seemed destined from the first, in private their enchantment soon began to dissipate. She grew resentful of Floyd's overbearing presence. When he persisted in asking her to become his wife—even
though they both considered marriage a relic of the past—she began to feel
suffocated and became restless and irritable. As Floyd's uncertainty increased, so did his protestations of love, yet the more he protested the more
she withdrew—a self-perpetuating cycle not unfamiliar to less liberated
couples. She responded to his wit and intellectual agility, but something
unreachable in her personality continued to disturb him. She'd try to make

him jealous—at a picnic with Salomón de la Selva, he recalled, she enjoyed "every moment of the encounter of her new beau with her old beau"—but she clearly didn't hope his jealousy would make him more ardent. "Vixen," he'd call her, half playfully; the name gave her pleasure. Inevitably, Vincent began seeing other men, not so much out of attraction as out of a desire to torment him with her independence. Yet her very effort to drive him away inflamed his desire; what could he do in his spasms of agony but insist that they get married at once?

In the early, erotic days of their affair, whenever Floyd broached the subject of marriage, they discussed it with the kind of dispassionate playfulness in which couples often engage when neither wants to admit they're threatened. "I'm not the right girl to cook your meals and wash and iron your shirts, as a good wife should," she would respond half teasingly. "You want to be loved," he would reply in the same teasing tone, "but you're afraid of being in love." Then the conversation would turn serious. Vincent didn't want to "belong" to anyone, and Floyd would argue that he wanted an equal partner. But love doesn't last, she'd go on, and he'd uneasily insist that the bond between a man and a woman was the highest purpose of life.

Vincent would shift the subject to her dedication to poetry. Didn't he see that marriage would tie her down, distract her from her work? But a loving husband would *free* her to work, he would protest, would *protect* her from distraction. They both thought Floyd wanted to settle down at precisely the moment Vincent wanted to explore her freedom—a mere case of bad timing—and so neither could see that their dispute wasn't between marriage and career but between his obsessions and her fears.

Floyd finally lost any chance when he began to psychoanalyze her. Too sophisticated to express disapproval of lesbianism, he disguised his alarm at her "sapphic tendencies" as curiosity about their sources. Are you still living "in the enchanted garden of childhood" where you knew no men? Why are you "terrified at the bogeys which haunt the realm of grown up man-and-woman love"? He pointed out how often she gave "dignity and sweetness to those passionate friendships between girls in adolescence"—in *The Lamp and the Bell,* for instance, or in her "Memorial to D.C.," about the death of one of her friends from Vassar. Was it possible that at the age of twenty-five she remained emotionally arrested in her teens? He wanted to know why she was so elusive.

"Floyd," Vincent would irritably interrupt, "you ask too many questions. There are doors in my mind you mustn't try to open." And as for Freud, Vincent considered his theories "a Teutonic attempt to lock women up in the home and restrict them to cooking and baby-tending." Floyd naturally took this resistance as the surest sign that she should undertake psychoanalysis and the sooner the better. The pressure would have been annoying in any case, but some dim sense that he was right, that he'd approached the inviolate sanctuary of her deepest emotions, must have been infuriating. It was too much—she told him their affair was over.

Except it wasn't. Vincent was dismayed by the possibility that she was pregnant. Floyd, who must have been secretly pleased, eagerly renewed his offer of marriage, she reluctantly accepted, and, as a sign of the reversal of roles she expected, she gave him an engagement ring. But when she learned she wasn't pregnant after all she broke off their relationship and sent Floyd back to his psychoanalyst.

For all their difficulties, Floyd remembered Vincent with adoration as well as exasperation. "One does not see 'Shelley plain' without some hurt," he recalled. "To know a great poet is a precious but painful privilege."

Vincent soon forgot Floyd in a haze of affairs, some of which she had begun while they were together. He had introduced her to the people and ideas of the Village, awakened her sexual interest in men, and precipitated the ambivalence about erotic love that was to become one of the major themes of the sonnets that made her famous. But rarely would she ever let someone come so close for so long.

In one of her best-known sonnets, entitled "Bluebeard," she wrote:

> This door you might not open, and you did;
> So enter now, and see for what slight thing
> You are betrayed . . . Here is no treasure hid. . . .
> Yet this alone out of my life I kept
> Unto myself, lest any know me quite;
> And you did so profane me when you crept
> Unto the threshold of this room tonight
> That I must never more behold your face.
> This now is yours. I seek another place.

This caustic condemnation of the invasion of her innermost being was thought by some Villagers to refer to her "secret" lesbianism and was regarded by most as a reaction to her affair with Floyd, though it was published a year before they met—a warning he failed to heed.

"Don't you think," Vincent once asked Floyd, "that our virtues as poets or artists may spring partly from the faults of our nature?" Lovely and liberated she may have been, but some part of her seems to have withdrawn to a remote chamber in her heart, to an inviolate solitude she could call "independence" and "art." Rarely have poems been so bold yet so distanced, so vulnerable yet so protected. Her popularity may have resulted less from her audacious candor than from her seductive evasions.

In February 1918, a tall, slim U.S. army major arrived in New York bearing important dispatches from the War Department for General Pershing in France. Major Arthur Ficke's ship wasn't sailing for three days, so he looked up his old Davenport friend Floyd Dell. The son of a wealthy, imperious lawyer, Arthur was sent to Harvard, then the University of Iowa Law School, and then into the family practice, rebelling only to the extent of collecting Japanese prints and publishing poetry in the academic/romantic mode. Bored by Davenport, by his work, by his marriage, Arthur welcomed the chance to escape into the army, though "probably there is no one alive who is less of a real soldier than I am."

The Masses' managing editor informed Pershing's courier with a sly smile that he was about to go on trial for conspiring against the war effort, and Arthur told Floyd he was eager to meet Edna St. Vincent Millay. Floyd did not mention that he'd begun an affair with her only a few weeks earlier, so the two men strolled over to her apartment at 139 Waverly Place. Arthur had continued writing to Vincent after their initial exchange of letters about "Renascence" and he was enchanted by her saucy charm. After six years of intimate correspondence, they were about to meet at last.

She wrote to him in December 1912: "All of my poems are very real to me, and take a great deal out of me. I am possessed of a masterful and often cruel imagination. All this is just the wee-est bit confidential, you know, and just because you asked me to be honest." When she concluded, referring to a collection of his work he'd sent her, "I was interested in your book's dedication, 'Cambridge days and *nights!*'"—establishing the tone of coy flirtatiousness that was to characterize her letters for the next six years—Arthur's heart must have somersaulted. Days and *nights!* Those suggestive italics! To have such virginal charm and at the same time to be so gaily "forward"—what man wouldn't be half in love?

A few weeks after: "I do not go to school, old man," she teased the man only nine years her senior. "I was honorably graduated from the Camden High School nearly four years ago. It is only because you are so very old that I seem to you a child, old man."

Spring 1913: "It isn't eccentric never to tell a poet which of his poems you like best, it's just plain lazy. I beg your pardon if I've said anything rude and hope I have. . . . Fancy, if you can, the horrible picture of you I am carrying in my mind at the moment."

Summer 1913: "If you hadn't written to me for as long as I haven't written to you I should be feeling bad just about now, thinking I had lost a friend. . . . Read me in the July *Forum* and see if you don't like me a little."

No teenage Circe, she said more than she meant and implied more than she realized. With a fellow poet, with a Spiritual Advisor, she yearned to be so close that, as she later wrote, "we sit in each other's souls." But if as a poet she wanted intense intimacy, as a woman she wanted cautious distance. "Think of this," she once wrote, "you may have told me a hundred things that you fancy still secreted in your esoteric heart!—Doesn't that make you awfully nervous?" She was writing equally intimate letters to other men at the same time, Witter Bynner, Louis Untermeyer, and John Masefield among them. Her candor and coquetry and flirtatiousness with Arthur, in short—much like her behavior with Floyd—allowed her to captivate men without giving herself.

In October 1915: "Do you recall writing to me last April, saying that you were coming to New York, & inviting me to an ice-cream soda?—I can't for the life of me think why I didn't answer that letter. It couldn't have been because I loathe ice-cream sodas,—for I must have realized, even as long ago as April, that you would make it something else, if requested,—a whiskey & soda, for instance. . . . Anyway, I am become superstitious about you. I think it is fated that we shall never meet.—And possibly that is just as well;—I might be terribly disappointed in you.—(You see I feel perfectly sure that you would like me.) . . . Sometime when you are in New York you might run up to see me.—Mightn't you?—Or mightn't you?—I suppose you mightn't.—But then, again, you might . . ."

What man could resist such invitations?

Vincent was home, but so were Norma and her boyfriend Charles. Vincent found herself captivated by Arthur's elegant self-confidence, courtly manner, and urbane wit, in contrast to the casual bohemians surrounding her. As they all laughed about the foibles of the Village and talked soberly about the horrors of the war, the others couldn't help noticing that the two poets seemed increasingly oblivious to everything but each other.

When Norma noticed a huge pickle in the midst of their feast, she held it aloft and declaimed in delight, "This pickle is a little loving cup!" Arthur exclaimed that Norma had provided a lovely line, and in only a few minutes improvised a poem on the cover of a pastry box, which he then read aloud:

> *This pickle is a little loving cup.*
> *I raised it to my lips, and where you kissed*
> *There lurks a certain sting that I have missed*
> *In nectars more laboriously put up.*

Their fate now sealed, Vincent and Arthur soon disappeared from the party, from the world itself, and only emerged from their rapturous lovemaking three days later, just in time for Arthur to catch his boat, leaving Vincent ecstatic, bereft—and dimly aware that she was still in the midst of her affair with Floyd.

Arthur's first letters avowed his undying love, but his ardor soon waned. Shortly after his arrival in Paris, he became involved with a pretty young painter named Gladys Brown, who was serving as an ambulance driver in a group sponsored by the Women's Suffrage Party, and when he finally divorced his wife it was Gladys he married.

Intensely affected by their affair and shaken by Vincent's even greater intensity, he, like so many of her lovers, was moved to transform his experience into poetry. Over the next several years, he composed nearly twenty sonnets, the unfashionable form he and Vincent were almost alone among contemporary poets in using, in which he expressed his response to the woman he now called his Spiritual Advisor.

Vincent wrote several sonnets expressing her exaltation and her agony, but more significantly, her sense that their love remained at once eternal and doomed.

> *There is no shelter in you anywhere:*
> *Rhythmic, intolerable, your burning rays*
> *Trample upon me, withering my breath:*
> *I will be gone, and rid of you. I swear:*
> *To stand upon the peaks of Love always*
> *Proves but that part of Love whose name is Death.*

This poem of agony and flight—with its veiled reference to the violence of sexual intercourse and its hint of anger at her father—reflects the shattering impact of Vincent's ecstatic and frightening affair with Arthur. Six years of physical distance and emotional intimacy, three days of erotic consummation, then a sudden rupture—what could be more threatening to her freedom, to her independence. What shelter did she seek that she could not find in Arthur? In one of her most famous sonnets—"written to you," she told him—she gives her answer.

> *The common soul, unguarded, and grown strong.*
> *Longing alone is singer to the lute;*
> *Let still on nettles in the open sigh*
> *The minstrel, that in slumber is as mute*
> *As any man, and love be far and high;*
> *That else forsakes the topmost branch, a fruit*
> *Found on the ground by every passer-by.*

In a third sonnet written to Arthur published with the other two in the spring of 1920, and read at his funeral two decades later, the death in love becomes literal.

> *And you as well must die, beloved dust,*
> *And all your beauty stand you in no stead;*
> *This flawless, vital hand, this perfect head,*
> *This body of flame and steel, before the gust*
> *Of Death, or under his autumnal frost,*
> *Shall be as any leaf that fell—this wonder fled. . . .*

While Arthur's love lingered in his memory largely as an occasion for poems of maudlin mysticism, their affair lodged in Vincent's memory as an ache around which accreted nearly all her sexual yearnings and terrors. In her first sonnet she fled from the tempests of eroticism, in the second she sublimated her voluptuous longings into the articulations of poetry, in the third she confronted, though with revealing equanimity, the conflict between love and death. But if, in all three, she avoided commitment to a sensual relationship, she remained faithful to a spiritual idea. Wonder may have fled, but Arthur remained beloved.

There's no reason to doubt the authenticity of Vincent's feelings, but to conclude, as did many admirers of her work, that her poems expressed her fierce independence, her tranquil acceptance of the passing of passion, her higher commitment to spiritual love, her belief in the primacy of art, her struggle with death—all the themes that characterize her poetry—is to ignore the spiritual turmoil that lay beneath their gay or melancholy or meditative surface and that she was never able to resolve.

Vincent's three days of "unleashed desire" with Arthur was the most intense and the shortest love affair of her life. Why did she so easily acquiesce to the feeling that their love was futile? Why didn't she make a greater effort to resume their affair after the war? Why did she so serenely transform their erotic connection into spiritual communion? Like celibates who cling to the memory of a tragic love as an excuse for avoiding sexual relationships, Vincent cherished the futility of her love for Arthur as an opportunity to escape into the lute-song of poetry. "It doesn't matter at all that we never see each other"? — on the contrary, it mattered above all else.

For much of 1919 Vincent devoted herself to a one-act poetic drama for the Provincetown Players called *Aria da Capo*. "You know the one," she wrote her mother, "Pierrot & Columbine & the shepherds & the spirit of Tragedy." Despite her flippant description and quaint material, this morality play, which she'd conceived at Vassar, expressed the bitter disillusionment that sometimes lurked beneath her lyric gaiety. Fusing contemporary farce and pastoral tragedy, creating two widely distinct sets of characters and two disparate tones, and employing a complex dramatic structure — three parts, as in the musical term from which the title was taken — *Aria da Capo* was one of the many pacifist parables inspired by World War I and one of the few to convey the tragic laughter that Santayana felt was the only appropriate response to the horrors of the new century.

In its counterpoint between brittle harlequinade and embittered pastoral disenchantment, *Aria da Capo* depicts mankind's inexorable evolution from Arcadian tranquillity to contemporary warfare. The barbarities of capitalism and nationalism, it suggests, are the result of well-intentioned but artless shepherds playing out their parts, while the silly and bored onlookers avert their eyes and allow the cycle to begin all over again.

The satire is occasionally deft, but more often it's ponderous — a socialist declaims, in an adolescent aperçu, "I love / Humanity; but I hate people." The thesis, if dramatically effective, remains philosophically murky. Are envy, mistrust, greed, and violence innate characteristics of human nature or merely the historical result of unjust social institutions? And the disillusioned tone, while capturing the mood of the moment, seems more ideologically imposed than felt.

When *Aria da Capo* opened on December 5, 1919 — under Vincent's direction, with Norma in the role of Columbine, and Charles, who also designed the sets and costumes, as one of the shepherds — Villagers wildly cheered at the final curtain. Alexander Woollcott of the *Times* called it "the most beautiful and most interesting play in the English language now to be seen in New York." Jig Cook called the play "a devastating indictment of man's folly, his greed, his quarrels, his war-like games." And Edmund Wilson, "thrilled and troubled" by Vincent's "bitter treatment of war," was impressed by her "less common sense of the incongruity and cruelty of life, of the precariousness of love perched on a table above the corpses." *Aria da Capo* was immediately mounted by scores of dramatic troupes and even became a triumph in Paris. "I find myself suddenly famous," wrote Vincent in amazed delight.

Besides *Aria da Capo*, the Provincetown Players' 1918–1919 season had opened with a production of her Vassar fairy tale, *The Princess Marries the Page*. In addition to Floyd's two plays, she performed in Rita Wellman's *The String of the Samisen*, Alfred Kreymborg's *Manikin and Minikin*, Wallace Stevens's *Three Travelers Watch a Sunrise*, and Eugene O'Neill's *The Moon of the Caribbees*, in which the three Millay sisters sang the offstage chorus.

Hoping for some income to supplement the glory, Vincent also tried out for the Theater Guild, the new troupe that emerged as a successor to the Washington Square Players, and appeared, ironically, as Columbine in their first bill in the spring of 1919. Floyd recalled that "when she did not get a hoped-for part in the next play, she cried like a heartbroken child," the only time, he said, he ever saw her cry. Paid very little for her poems, nothing at all for her acting, and shuddering, like any true Villager, at the mere idea of a job, Vincent decided to try writing short stories for mass circulation magazines, and in January 1919 raised the idea with W. Adolphe Roberts, the editor of *Ainslee's*. The preceding September, Vincent's old flame Salomón de la Selva had told Adolphe that Stephen Vincent Benét and Edna St. Vincent Millay were the most promising young poets in America. Adolphe had written Vincent asking her to stop by his office, then promptly fell in love with her.

A former war correspondent, a cheerful and forthright man who freely acknowledged that *Ainslee's*, as Edmund Wilson put it, was a "trashy" magazine, Adolphe took Vincent to places few of her other suitors could afford—Mouqin's on Sixth Avenue, the Lafayette on University Place, and fine French restaurants where he seduced her with soulful conversations about poetry and love.

Adolphe was in love, but Vincent was merely charmed. Just as he began to respond to her intimations that he was the only man in the world who truly understood her soul, she'd ruefully announce that she was unable to commit herself because the only man she'd ever loved was already married (a reference to Arthur more convenient than true), or dampen his ardor by blithely informing him when they parted that she was going off to see another lover (a revelation less candid than taunting). Whether this behavior was intended to safeguard her independence or to make men feel insecure—or perhaps her motives were inextricably connected—Adolphe kept his composure. "I took her temperament exactly as I found it and preached no sermons."

Adolphe continued to publish Vincent's work in *Ainslee's*, and beginning in 1918, her byline appeared in nineteen consecutive issues. He could pay only 50 cents a line for poetry even to the writer he considered "the greatest woman poet since Sappho," but when Vincent came up with the idea of a series of humorous stories and sketches her money worries seemed over. Choosing the pseudonym Nancy Boyd—not so much to hide her identity as to distinguish her prose from her poetry—Vincent published seven pieces in *Ainslee's* in 1919 and 1920, some of them written with the help of Cora and Norma, whose tart epigrams she gratefully borrowed. Gay, witty, and satirical Nancy Boyd proved so popular that *Vanity Fair*, a far more prestigious magazine, with far better rates, wooed her away. Adolphe said with amiable resignation, "*Vanity Fair* had the privilege of launching her as a success with a public that counted."

As usual, Vincent remained the most perceptive critic of her own work. "Some of my stories are good, some are bad," she wrote Arthur, but "almost invariably they are beautifully written, after a flippant fashion." The Nancy Boyd stories nearly all revolve around the conflict between love and independence and often involve the disparity between conventional values and Village sophistication—even in her commercial work, Vincent addressed the issues she struggled with in her life.

The artist heroine of "Young Love," her first story in *Ainslee's*, is relieved when a young man with whom she has been falling in love leaves her, allowing her to continue her musical career. The "improper" heroine of "Mr. Dalton Larabee, Sinner," her last, finally accepts a marriage proposal when her suitor, sensing her initial reluctance, declares that "the healing dispensation of divorce" is "an institution no less divine than that of matrimony itself." In a provocative parable called "The White Peacock," the heroine, after a night of rapturous lovemaking, abruptly orders her lover to leave. "Last night—pouf! What was it? A man and woman in each other's arms! Sweet, yes, perhaps you call it ecstasy, but, la! Not rare! As for me—ah, I slept after a little, and dreamed, and it was not of thee." What did she dream of? The white peacock, a symbol of art. The liberated young woman seeks both the love of men and revenge against their inevitable betrayal, a revenge disguised as a higher calling.

Vincent's friends frequently found what they considered lesbian themes in some of her poems. In 1918, Vincent wrote "Memorial to D.C.," an elegy for Dorothy Coleman, an intimate friend from Vassar who had just died. In 1921, for the fiftieth anniversary of the Vassar College Alumnae Association, Vincent wrote *The Lamp and the Bell*, a five-act verse drama set in the Middle Ages celebrating the almost erotic devotion between Bianca and Beatrice. "You are a burning lamp to me," declares Bianca, "a flame / The wind cannot blow out," to which Beatrice replies, "You are to me a silver bell in tower, / And when it rings I know I am near home." Bianca—who had sent her husband away on their wedding night in order to be with Beatrice—dies with Beatrice in her arms. At the end of the play, there is only Beatrice and her ecstatic memories of female friendship.

Vincent's Vassar friends could hardly have failed to sense the subtext, even if they missed the Freudian imagery, but apparently uneasy about the reaction in the Village—and disguising her unease as concern about the quality of the writing—she cautioned Norma not to let any of the Provincetown Players read the script. "They would hate it, & make fun of it, & old Djuna Barnes would rag you about it, hoping it would get to me"—Djuna Barnes, of course, being one of the Village's most prominent lesbians.

After a brief stay at 449 West 19th Street in the spring of 1920, and a trip to the artist colony at Woodstock that summer, Vincent moved into an apartment of her own at 77 West 12th Street in September. Her most prized possession was an old Victrola, and she set about to work to the "noble, mighty" harmonies of Beethoven's Fifth Symphony, soon finding that she could whistle the entire work. "It answers all my questions," she wrote a friend.

In June 1918 Vincent published five light verses in *Poetry* magazine (including her near-mythic candle quatrain), in April and May 1920 twenty sonnets appeared in *Reedy's Mirror* (including her three sonnets to Arthur), and in November 1920, the Village chapbook *Salvo*, in its first and only issue, carried many of these and several new poems in a collection called *A Few Figs from Thistles*, also brought out as a book a few months later by the prominent Village publisher Frank Shay.

If Vincent's earlier work had brought her fame, *Figs* made her a legend. The first edition of one thousand copies sold out in only a few weeks, and five more editions appeared during the next two years. Vincent became the most widely quoted poet in America. Floyd reported, during a leisurely cross-country trip to California, that wherever he stopped people were talking about her scandalous verses.

Many of her poems of this period dealt with themes other than love—rapturous invocations of the wonders of nature, hymns to the ineffable joys of poetry and music—but it was her love poems that entranced her readers. In her saucy dismissal of the conventions of Victorian love, in her celebration of the fleeting passions of lovemaking, in her demonstration of the emancipation of the female spirit, she embodied the vision of the Village.

Soon Villagers were delightedly quoting their favorite passages.

> And if I loved you Wednesday,
>   Well, what is that to you?
> I do not love you Thursday—
>   So much is true.
> And why you come complaining
>   Is more than I can see.
> I loved you Wednesday,—yes—but what
>   Is that to me?

She frankly depicted women's erotic desire, in imagery at once bold and ambiguous.

> Now will the god, for blasphemy so brave,
> Punish me, surely, with the shaft I crave!

Nothing quite like this voice had ever been heard before, and innocent as the poems now sound, to readers of the twenties they resonated with a carefree defiance that made Vincent "the lyric voice of the newly liberated, uninhibited young." What made Vincent's poetry seem all the more daring was that she didn't fiercely insist on women's sexual freedom but took it for granted. In Harriet Monroe's view, her work included "the most feminine sonnets ever written to prove the essential separateness of a woman's soul." "What sets Miss Millay's poems apart from all those written in English by women," said another critic, "is the full pulse which beats through them. . . . Rarely since Sappho has a woman written as outspokenly as this." Malcolm Cowley praised her for revolting against "the conventions that kept women from living honestly or recklessly." *Time* magazine wrote later that to most young people of the decade, "poetry meant simply Edna St. Vincent Millay."

Vincent's popularity was further enhanced by her enchanting readings on the lecture circuit and, later, on the radio. Her voice often dropped nearly an octave to grave intonations that were dramatically effective. Said Floyd, "Her reciting voice had a loveliness that was sometimes heartbreakingly poignant even in her lighthearted poems. I fell in love with her voice at once." Recalled Edmund Wilson, "Her authority was always complete; but her voice, though dramatic, was lonely."

Her influence could be seen in the sudden appearance of hundreds of light verse imitators in the popular press, and even such respected poets as Maxwell Bodenheim, Edith Sitwell, Max Eastman, and Louise Bogan modeled poems on her rhythms and tones.

She became so famous that her name began appearing in gossip columns, and she soon received the homage of parody. Samuel Hoffenstein, that master of light verse, wrote a quatrain that was almost as widely quoted as Vincent's:

> *I burned my candle at both ends,*
> *And now have neither foes nor friends;*
> *For all the lovely light begotten,*
> *I'm paying now in feeling rotten.*

Though regarded as the poet of sexual freedom, she actually celebrated spiritual independence—which meant not only the freedom to love but the freedom to forsake love for a higher calling. She should be, she audaciously declared, not a harlot *or* a nun, but a harlot *and* a nun, and as her lovers knew all too well, her aloofness was not sexual but emotional. She would never be possessed—she would always remain "stern in my soul's chastity"—for sexual rapture, even ecstatic love, was a diversion from the deeper dedication of her life, the pursuit of poetry.

In order to make Vincent a brazen symbol of sexual freedom, readers had to ignore her somber undertone of sexual unease. She eagerly succumbed to the fever and frenzy, then dismissed it as unworthy, and for all her surface merriment and romantic yearning, she treated her lovers as partners in animality and dispatched them with postcoital hostility.

For all her popularity, the critics reacted with a disdain that continues to this day. For one thing, Vincent had committed the sin of accessibility; for another, she had frivolously demeaned her gift. Wrote Louis Untermeyer, "In many of these self-conscious flippancies, Miss Millay has exchanged her poetic birthright for a mess of cleverness. Although there are a few poems which are worthy of her, the greater part of this volume smirks with a facile sophistication, a series of partly cynical pirouettes." But, more pertinently, nothing could have gone more against the grain of the modernism exemplified by T. S. Eliot, with its arid asceticism, weary disillusionment, and frayed nerve endings. Yet even those critics who disparaged her work admired her freshness and spontaneity, and acknowledged that whatever the aesthetic merit of her poetry, it reflected the ethos of the era.

With one volume, the girl from Camden, Maine, only three years out of Vassar, became the poet of the historical moment. Edna St. Vincent Millay—Poet Laureate of the Twenties!

In 1917, a young army corporal serving with a military hospital unit in France received a book of poems from his cousin entitled *Renascence*. In the few interludes between tending the bleeding and dying soldiers, an experience that irrevocably dislodged his cultivated complacency, he found a small measure of hope in what he called Vincent's courageous struggle "to embrace the world with love."

Edmund Wilson had read Vincent's poetry before. Only a year earlier, as a $15-a-week reporter on the *New York Evening Sun*, he had reviewed *A Book of Vassar Verse* containing some of her undergraduate work. He wrote, with starchy enthusiasm, "the contemporary verse [including, in particular, one of Vincent's poems] sounds a new note of frankness, intensity, and dramatic feeling . . . not unworthy of the American generation which has produced Miss Reese and Miss Teasdale."

Discharged in July 1919, Wilson returned to the Village, where he had lived briefly before the war, and moved into a room at 114 West 16th Street, only a few blocks from Vincent's apartment. He almost immediately found a job at *Vanity Fair*, where he soon became acquainted with the Nancy Boyd stories. He also saw *Aria da Capo*, "the first time I had felt Edna's peculiar power."

Another work of Vincent's moved him even more deeply, a sonnet called "To Love Impuissant" which appeared in the March 1920 issue of *The Dial* and which he promptly memorized and declaimed every morning as he showered.

> I, that have bared me to your quiver's fire,
> Lifted my face into its puny rain,
> Do wreathe you Impotent to Evoke Desire
> As you are Powerless to Elicit Pain!
> (Now will the god, for blasphemy so brave,
> Punish me, surely, with the shaft I crave!)

"The fascination that this poem had for me was due partly to its ringing defiance—at the time we were all defiant—but partly also to my liking to think that one who appreciated the poet as splendidly as I felt I did might be worthy to deal her the longed-for dart."

Edmund Wilson—Bunny to his friends, derived from "plum bun," his mother's nickname for him—came from an aristocratic family in Red Bank, New Jersey, where he was born in 1895. His father, who served as state attorney general and who was promised an appointment to the Supreme Court by Woodrow Wilson, was a brilliant but bleak presence, inspiring love but unable to express it, who succumbed to hypochondria, melancholia, and a series of "neurotic eclipses" that forced the family to place him in an institution. Bunny's mother, an indirect descendant of Cotton Mather, hardly alleviated this oppressive environment. Brusque and stern, she was also deaf—her son once said that even if she could hear they wouldn't have had anything to say to one another—and devoid of affection.

In this Calvinist and emotionally arid atmosphere, young Bunny found comfort in magic and puppetry and especially reading, as if he had to construct, in his imagination, his only means of communicating with the world. While he remained personally aloof, even afflicted with fear of inheriting his father's madness, in the realm of the imagined he discovered wonder and drama and the rich joys of human interaction and probed the psyches of the world's great writers with a lucidity, a *sanity* that eventually made him the stern but dispassionate chief justice of American letters.

At Princeton from 1912 to 1916, Bunny met his lifelong friends Scott Fitzgerald and John Peale Bishop, but he was regarded by most of his classmates as "a well-dressed . . . grind, a smug, conceited little fellow" unable "to engage with life, to experience it at first hand." He was voted the member of his class most likely to remain a bachelor.

The inevitable crisis came when Bunny volunteered for the American Expeditionary Force—already a curmudgeon in his early twenties, he refused to be drafted—and overnight he was plunged from the serenity of scholarship into the chaos of war. He could no longer bear "the falseness and dullness of my prewar life again. . . . My experience of the army had had on me a liberating effect."

But his wartime experiences didn't transform Bunny utterly. Though more confident when he returned to the Village, Bunny was a rather stiff bohemian. When he sauntered out for an evening his tie and socks matched; his defiance of convention extended little further than the Eighteenth Amendment. Despite his intellectual sophistication, he remained as he had been at Princeton, "too shy with proper young girls who were only just learning to be improper."

"I decided that I had now been innocent long enough," Bunny wrote in his typical tone of detached curiosity, "and decided to buy a condom. . . . The clerk . . . produced a condom of rubber, blowing it up like a balloon in order to show me how reliable it was. But . . . , thus distended, [it] burst, and this turned out to be something of an omen. . . . I was a victim of many of the hazards of sex—from which I might have been saved by previous experience: abortions, gonorrhea, entanglements, a broken heart."

Like most men of his generation, Bunny thought of women as divided into two types, either sexual partners to be utilized or romantic visions to be idealized, and his early sexual encounters were with shopgirls, waitresses, and prostitutes. His inability to get along with "ordinary" people meant, of course, that he sought out "ordinary" women, with whom he didn't have to "get along" once he'd satisfied his lust. A woman he might love, a woman he might marry? His sexual unease meant that she remained inaccessible.

Enamored of a sensibility, erotically bewildered, how could poor Bunny know that he was about to become involved with a woman who could give him only the illusion that he could unite romantic ideal and erotic adventure in a mature relationship—a woman who embodied the split between sexual availability and romantic inaccessibility?

Arriving late and exhausted at a party in the spring of 1920 after one of her performances at the Provincetown Playhouse, Vincent was persuaded to recite several of her poems. Bunny recalled, "She was one of those women whose features are not perfect and who in their moments of dimness may not seem even pretty, but who, excited by the blood or the spirit, becomes almost supernaturally beautiful."

Her verse appeared in the July 1920 issue of *Vanity Fair*, and by then her new editor was ready to admit that he "had fallen irretrievably in love with her." This mournfully accepting tone was to toll throughout their affair as if he realized it was doomed from the first—and as if he knew he would keep his balance even if his heart stumbled.

Falling in love with Vincent, as he admitted, was a rather common occurrence, an "almost inevitable . . . consequence of knowing her." He soon became one of her many lovers, but he had a quality she responded to more readily than she responded to adoration—a detached appreciation of her poetry that, from her point of view, gave their affair an intimacy far more satisfying than mere eroticism. "My most exalted feeling for her did not, I think, ever prevent me from recognizing or criticizing what was weak or second-rate in her work," he later recalled, though he never quite understood that this detachment turned him into what she wanted more than a lover—her friend.

When Bunny took Edna to parties, or when they attended concerts, operas, ballets, and plays, afterward, instead of joining their Village friends for an evening of bootleg booze, they'd return to his or her apartment, where they'd have ecstatic midnight discussions about what they'd seen or read, or, most often, about their love of poetry, the subject that brought them closest.

Rarely happier than when stimulating a woman's creative imagination, Bunny would wrap Vincent's legs in a blanket, pour her a peach brandy, and listen enraptured as she read her latest poems aloud. He'd praise her rhymes and rhythms, point out her weakest images and transitions—tranquil erotic foreplay for him, emotional intimacy to her.

On other occasions, Bunny would sit at his typewriter, a glass of bathtub gin at his side, and take down a Nancy Boyd sketch Vincent dictated to him, making suggestions for improvements and restraining her when "she insisted on putting in as comic lines remarks I had just made in earnest." His supportive tone, admiring but not uncritical, differed from Floyd's didacticism and Arthur's effusiveness, and she responded with her own sense of artistic rigor. It was this tough intellectual side combined with her feminine attraction that persuaded so many men they had found their ideal mate.

Vincent's aura of inaccessibility enchanted Bunny. But their affair never overcame a certain constraint. "There was something of awful drama about everything one did with Edna," he recalled years later, and while the drama exhilarated him, the word "awful" was not carelessly chosen, not by Edmund Wilson.

More psychologically acute than Floyd or Arthur, Bunny could even admit that "she was sometimes rather a strain, because nothing could be casual for her." Vincent's health, in fact, was poor during much of the first year Bunny knew her. In the spring of 1920, and again in the early winter of 1921, she suffered what she called "small nervous breakdowns," and though he never wavered in his support, he was the first to see signs of incipient neuroses in what her other friends and lovers called her independent spirit.

As for his rivals, Bunny knew that his colleague at *Vanity Fair*, John Peale Bishop, was also involved with Vincent. Frank Crowninshield even made a point of complaining that it was annoying to have both his top editors in love with one of his most important writers.

On another occasion, riding on a Fifth Avenue bus, Vincent recited a sonnet she had just composed entitled "Here is a wound that never will heal, I know." Bunny said it "plucked the strings of chagrin, for not only did it refer to some other man [Arthur, no doubt], . . . but it suggested that Edna could not be consoled, that such grief was in the nature of things." Even more to his chagrin, Vincent would sometimes announce, after an evening out, that she wanted to go home alone—not coyly, not to inflame his jealousy, and probably not as a way of asserting her independence, but most likely because she had a sudden attack of anxiety that she could only comfort in solitude. During a performance of Shaw's *Heartbreak House*, he noticed that she became "very tense" during the scene in which Ariadne complains, "I got my whole life messed up with people falling in love with me." Vincent was addicted to making men fall in love with her, and, like most addicts, she was frequently overcome with remorse.

Bunny accepted this behavior with the same equanimity that characterized his passion. Those who fell in love with Vincent, he recalled, "did not, I think, seriously quarrel with her or find themselves at one another's throats and they were not, except in very small ways, demoralized or led to commit excesses, because the other thing was always there, and her genius, for those who could value it, was not something that one could be jealous of." He soon realized—and it increased his admiration more than it frustrated his desire—that his real rival was her work, and recognized that the best he could hope for was a kind of ménage à trois with Vincent and her muse.

In the summer of 1920, Bunny traveled up to Truro, on Cape Cod, where Vincent was vacationing, to ask her to become his wife. His friends didn't think it wise—"Modern Sappho," one wrote in his diary, "18 love affairs and now Bunny is thinking of marrying her." Bunny himself didn't think it wise—but his head felt under an obligation to his heart. Knowing that John had also been invited to spend a weekend in Truro hardly encouraged his hopes, nor did the presence of Cora and Norma and Kathleen in the tiny house Jig Cook had lent the Millays for the summer.

Finally, Bunny and Vincent found themselves alone and he managed to propose—rather "formally," as he admitted. She said she would think about it. Bunny recalled, "It was plain to me that proposals of marriage were not a source of great excitement" to Vincent—nor to him either, he neglected to add.

Even Bunny seemed to realize that when his unromantic suggestion met with an equally unromantic response, he could hardly pretend he was heartbroken. Bunny returned to the Village almost relieved that Vincent had rejected him, for, of course, saying that she'd think about it was a kind way of saying no.

The person who wants less from a relationship than the other always gets what she wants. Yet when Vincent wrote to Bunny a few days after his visit, she seemed to fear that in rejecting his love she'd lost his friendship as well. "I don't know what to write you, either,—what you would like me to write, or what you would hate me for writing.—I feel that you rather hate me, as it is.—Which is false of you, Bunny. . . . I have thought of you often, Bunny, & wondered if you think of me with bitterness."

Vincent's plaintive "don't hate me" tone wasn't very far from the coy "please love me" tone she used in her letters to Arthur—a flirtatious manipulation in the guise of openhearted candor. Vincent yearned for a love she felt compelled to reject, a pattern that momentarily eased her anxiety and permanently frustrated her lovers. The repeated "you must hate me a little, don't you?" pleas in her letters became a perverse form of seduction, a way of making him give himself to her while she gave nothing in return.

What could poor Bunny do but what so many of Vincent's lovers had done? He would try to capture that unattainability in words. A born critic, he was compelled to understand her, not control her. He portrayed her in a play, in short stories and a novel, his efforts to capture her elusive spirit a sure sign, as he himself realized, that he remained dissatisfied.

The combination of encyclopedic erudition and lucid intelligence that served Bunny so well as a critic served him less well as an artist. For while he entered literature imaginatively, he responded to life intellectually. Even he admitted that his fiction suffered from the grid of schemes and constructs that kept his characters from taking on a life of their own.

In his play *This Room and This Gin and These Sandwiches,* a sensible, reserved architect named Arthur Fiske (!) repeatedly proposes marriage to an attractive, mildly neurotic actress. "I'm fond of you, you know that," she declares, "but you don't own me!" And later, "You flatter my defects," the Vincent character says. "Sometimes I love you very much." "Sometimes" seems enough for the put-upon Bunny character, for he responds, "You've given me a kind of repose."

It's hard to decide which is easier to accept—that the eminent writer had such a tin ear for dialogue, or that he and Vincent actually talked like that.

In "Ellen Terhune," one of the stories in his succès de scandale,

Memoirs of Hecate County, Bunny uses numerous details from Vincent's life to flesh out another maddening heroine. An allegory of the lure of beauty and its price in pain—an attempt to embody in fiction the themes of his classic *The Wound and the Bow*—it contrasts creativity and love, an all too frequent conflict in the lives of women artists in stories written by men. Unable to surrender to the narrator's love, Ellen/Vincent plunges more deeply into her art, until her tortured voice is "freed to a life of its own"—in death. Bunny seems to have intended the story as a kind of atonement for his failure to save Vincent from the loneliness of her devotion to poetry, but since he constructed a plot in which the price of Ellen's refusal of the narrator's love is "the peace of the grave," his atonement bears a striking resemblance to revenge.

I Thought of Daisy, Bunny's novel published in 1929, was his most sustained effort to explain his fascination with Vincent—and, in a sense, to understand why he remained so enamored of a woman whom he could never possess.

Much too subtle a man to divide women into madonnas and whores, he divided them into idealized intellectuals and earthy sensualists instead. The narrator of the novel sees in "the romantic poet" Rita Cavanagh not merely "the princess and the rake of the Village," but a somber, troubled, and elusive creative spirit with whom every man is in love. But he's also drawn to the vivacious showgirl Daisy and a symbolic rendering of what he called "the American reality," vital, vulgar, unreflective, resilient, spontaneous, and self-creating—her name certainly intended to evoke Henry James's Daisy Miller.

After first meeting Rita/Vincent at a party, the narrator/Bunny "should have asked nothing better of life than . . . to have passed my days alone with Rita in those high quiet rooms, hidden away among those crooked streets, with poetry and love!" But he soon comes to see in her an inexpressible but obsessive yearning for a beyond that no man can satisfy.

The narrator/Bunny can't quite comprehend why wonder should flee so fast. At first he tries to accept the simplest solution—Rita/Vincent is struggling with her identity as a woman and as a poet. The narrator briefly tries to meet Rita on her own terms. "If I could only keep up my spirit—if I could only play the game according to the sportsman's code which Rita had been trying to teach me, then in the long run, all might be right between us. If I could only remember that the days were not bricks to be laid row on row, to be built into a solid house, but only food for the fires of the heart, the fires which keep the poet alive as the citizen never lives, but which burn all the roofs of security!"

But what could have been more alien to Bunny's nature than "burning all the roofs of security"? Vincent's self "could not mate with others, because it held already, in one body, a union of female with male." Or perhaps it was "that dreadful isolation of the artist."

In her attempt to transform experience into art, he wrote of Rita, she seemed less interested in understanding others than in exploring herself. "She had the faculty of endowing her admirers with qualities which they themselves may hardly have hoped to possess," he wrote, so that they "seemed to have caught from Rita's own imagination some disturbing conception of themselves which they were straining to realize. It was as if, in their contacts with Rita, they had become somehow facets of herself."

Compare this description of Rita with Bunny's description of Vincent in an essay published after her death. "But her relations with us and with her other admirers had . . . a disarming impartiality. . . . What interests her is seldom the people themselves, but her own emotions about them; and the sonnets . . . dealt with a miscellany of men without—since they are all about *her*—the readers' feeling the slightest discontinuity. In all this, she was not egotistic in any boring or ridiculous or oppressive way, because it was not the personal, but the impersonal Edna Millay—that is, the poet—that preoccupied her so incessantly."

Acute as this passage is, what Bunny seems never to have understood is that this characteristic of Vincent's work paralleled the major flaw in his own fiction, and more important, this characteristic of her personality was the long-sought explanation for the failure of their affair.

If Vincent was offended by this portrait she didn't tell Bunny, but she did write him, rather tactfully, that she felt the manuscript was "uneven" and "not ready to be published," and elaborate notes clarifying her objections were discovered in her papers after her death.

No Floyd, Bunny would never wallow in insecurity. No Arthur, he'd never abandon himself to passion. Composed even as a lover, he became, almost to his relief, and certainly to hers, "dear Bunny," the deepest intimacy reserved for ex-lovers who have become lifelong friends. Even before their affair ended, Bunny remarked to Vincent in wry resignation that her ex-admirers ought to organize an alumni association—to which Vincent replied, "On en parle toujours, mais on ne le fait jamais" ("One always speaks of it, but one never does it").

Many rivals claimed Vincent's attention for brief periods—though after trying two "Greenwich Village ménages," as Bunny called them, she drew the line at married men. Her suitors ranged from Pieter Miejer, a Dutch artist from the East Indies who introduced batik to America, to Scudder Middleton, a soulfully good-looking and unmemorable poet, to an Italian baritone at the Metropolitan Opera ("a handsome and perfidious Don Giovanni," she said).

John Peale Bishop, Bunny's friend at Princeton and colleague at *Vanity Fair,* was an elegant Southerner who wrote loftily sensuous, fastidiously romantic poems to Vincent. A rather aloof dandy, he was Bunny's chief rival for several weeks in 1920, causing a strain in their friendship. On one melancholy evening the two men simultaneously hugged Vincent as she recited her latest poem — Bunny taking the top half, John the bottom.

Frank Crowninshield was a bit in love with Vincent himself — but adopted a pose of fatherly affection when it became apparent that she responded with little more than tender gratitude to her fond "Crownie."

Gene O'Neill and Max Eastman were ineligible for Bunny's alumni association — Gene because the last quality that would have attracted him in a woman was her troubled self-absorption, Max because, though he felt he *ought* to be in love with Vincent, and *attempted* to fall in love with her, and fantasized what a sensation it would cause if he *were,* he liked his women more robust. " I shall have to confess that I tried to fall in love with Edna Millay," Max wrote, "believing it for a time to be my romantic destiny, but regretfully failed."

Jack Reed, on the other hand, could at least be called an honorary member. In the fall of 1918, during the false armistice, Jack, Vincent, and Floyd celebrated by riding back and forth on the Staten Island ferry. And when Jack started to talk of his adventures in Mexico, Europe, and Russia, Vincent gazed at the Golden Boy of the Village and exclaimed, as Floyd no doubt wondered why he'd ever introduced them — "I love you for the dangers you have passed!" After Jack's death in 1920, she wrote "Lord Archer, Death" in his memory:

> *For know, this was no mortal youth, to be*
> *Of you confounded, but a heavenly quest,*
> *Assuming earthly garb for love of me,*
> *And hell's demure attire for love of jest:*
> *Bringing me asphodel and a dark feather*
> *He will return, and we shall laugh together!*

Perhaps Vincent's oddest romance was with Arthur's friend Witter Bynner. Witter showed the kind of ardent but not uncritical appreciation of her work that she most respected—while calling her a greater poet than T. S. Eliot, he found some of her verses "rather callow." She regarded him as a wise and humorous friend but hadn't showed the slightest spark of erotic interest—or seen any in him.

Then suddenly, in 1921, in a bizarre sequence of events even by Village standards, the two friends decided to get married. Witter, who was traveling with Arthur, sent Vincent a letter asking her to become his wife, but it got lost in the mail and she only learned of his proposal in a passing reference in a letter from Arthur. The idea rather pleased her, but that seemed the extent of it. She wrote Witter, "Do you really want me to marry you?—Because if you really want me to, I will." A few weeks later she wrote again, more cautiously. Wasn't "earthly marriage"—presumably in contrast to her celestial marriage to Arthur, which of course Witter knew all about—the most mixed of blessings, with its "series of disagreements, misunderstandings, adjustments, ill-adjustments, and readjustments"? Witter began to have second thoughts himself, and his correspondence took on a teasing tone implying that either one of them could gracefully back out. Arthur soon sent identical letters to Vincent and Witter expressing not second thoughts but downright disapproval—not because he was still in love with Vincent himself but because, though he didn't put it in so many words, he knew, and knew that Vincent knew, that Witter was a homosexual.

Vincent, for a moment at least, seems to have regarded this less as a drawback than as a virtue in a prospective husband. Given her exasperation at everyone falling in love with her, her distaste for "the adjustments and ill-adjustments" of conventional marriage, and her conviction that she remained mated to Arthur—marrying a gay man might be, as she responded to Bunny's proposal, "the solution." That such a union would enable her to remain emotionally chaste and give her the freedom to have affairs would have suited her belief that she shouldn't be asked to remain faithful to a single lover.

"Well, there's no denying that I love you, my dear," she wrote Arthur. But that wasn't any reason not to marry Witter, "and be happy with him. I love him, too. In a different way." The "different way" soon seemed an insurmountable barrier. As Arthur's wife remarked, Witter loved Vincent mildly but loved a man named Robert Hunt dearly—and the entire incident faded from memory.

Several months after the truncated marriage plans Vincent wrote Arthur, "There's not the slightest danger that I shall marry [Witter]: he has jilted me!" Even this obvious jest is revealing. Something in Vincent didn't merely believe that love was impermanent, she had to prove it—and something in Vincent remained convinced that men inevitably betrayed women, so even a man's homosexuality was a form of rejection.

But of all the members of Vincent's alumni association, Bunny remained the most active, and could always be counted on for emotional support and artistic advice. And despite her protestations that she never wanted a man to take care of her, Vincent grew increasingly dependent on his help. For one thing, she was all too aware of her fading youth. "I'll be thirty in a minute!" she wailed to Bunny, who had been thirty since the day he was born. For another, her health began to fail; burning one's candle at both ends worked better as a romantic credo than as a daily regimen. She felt ill with disturbing regularity, and her health was further compromised by the psychic tension that had always been part of her temperament. "Withdrawal is her natural condition," said Bunny. The legendary Villager was terrified of traffic and could hardly cross a street alone.

The swings between the poles in Vincent's personality grew more pronounced, more disquieting. Her effervescence would take on a hint of hysteria, her aloofness a tone of despondence. The woman whose company everyone had once sought was all too deeply disturbed. Besieged by suitors, harassed by fame, driven by perfectionism, she suffered what she plaintively called "a sort of nervous breakdown" in late 1920.

"The reason why I have not written you for so long," Vincent wrote her mother from her West 12th Street apartment in December, "is because I have been sick. I am all right again now, but I have been quite sick, almost ever since I moved in here—bronchitis for a while, & another small nervous breakdown after that. I didn't want you to know, for fear you would worry.—But now that I am all right again I have decided that the thing for me to do is to have a change,—change of everything,—so I am going to travel." Bunny persuaded Crownie to finance a year-long trip to Europe in exchange for two articles a month, one under her own name, one under the name Nancy Boyd.

The embodiment of the spirit of the Village in the twenties, she had lived there for only thirty-six months, and she left at the very beginning of the decade. On January 23, 1921—only a few weeks before Jig Cook and Susan Glaspell departed for Greece on *Themistocles*—Vincent boarded the *Rochambeau*, spending most of her savings on a stateroom with a bath, and set sail for Europe.

. . .

Vincent kept on the move—Paris, Rome, Vienna, Budapest, London—as if no matter where she fled, she sensed another nervous breakdown wasn't far behind. She met Scott and Zelda Fitzgerald in Paris, tentatively participated in the café bohemianism of half a dozen cities, and had several reckless affairs—one with a French violinist, which resulted in an abortion.

She was frequently ill, wretchedly lonely, and always short of money. When she did receive $500 advance money for a novel called *Hardigut*, she found it nearly impossible to write, and returned to the Village in February 1923 in worse shape than when she'd left.

Vincent's reputation continued to soar, however. Shortly after her return, she won the Pulitzer Prize for poetry on the basis of *A Few Figs from Thistles*, a second collection called *Second April*, and several poems collected in a third volume called *The Harp-Weaver*. Like most writers, she pretended to be more pleased by the cash accompanying the award than by the award itself. "My thousand bucks," she said, "which I ain't going to bust for god or hero—going to start a bank account with it."

Second April included several poems recalling ecstatic surrender to forbidden bliss, but a sense of loss, even despondency lay like a shadow behind her heart.

> *Life in itself*
> *Is nothing.*
> *An empty cup, a flight of uncarpeted stairs.*
> *It is not enough that yearly, down this hill,*
> *April*
> *Comes like an idiot, babbling and strewing flowers.*

Still suffering from the aftereffects of her abortion, Vincent took an apartment on Waverly Place and vowed to lead a more reclusive life until she recovered. But after turning down several invitations from a friend to spend the weekend in Croton-on-Hudson when spring arrived, she reluctantly agreed to visit the country for a few days. On the first evening, Floyd and his new wife dropped by, Arthur and *his* new wife showed up, and from across the road where they were sharing a weekend cottage came Max and his old friend Eugen Boissevain.

Vincent had met Eugen nearly six years earlier at a party at Max's apartment—but she had been in one of her aloof moods and Eugen, normally ebullient, was mourning the recent death of his wife, Vincent's feminist idol, Inez Millholland.

But in Croton, Eugen was his old jovial self. When the partygoers decided to enact "a delicious farcical invention, at once Rabelaisan and romantic"—Floyd's description—and when Vincent and Eugen found themselves paired off as the two lovers, the charade took on a life of its own. Recalled Floyd—who for the third time was having the unsettling experience of watching the love of his life becoming enamored of a man to whom he'd just introduced her—"We were having the unusual privilege of seeing a man and a girl fall in love . . . violently and in public, and . . . doing it very beautifully."

The next day, when Vincent awoke feeling more exhausted than ever, Eugen promptly moved her to his house, called a doctor, and nursed her around the clock. And only a few weeks later, Vincent wrote her mother, "I love him very much, I am going to marry him. There!!!"

Vincent's condition was worse than she suspected. Eugen insisted that she consult several doctors, forbade her to work more than an hour a day, and refused to let her see anyone except family and intimate friends, a regimen to which Vincent gratefully submitted. An intestinal operation was scheduled for July 18, 1923, and that morning Eugen announced that he wouldn't allow her to enter the hospital except as his wife. He hastily arranged for a justice of the peace, called Norma and Charles, Arthur and his wife, and several other friends, and gathered the wedding party on the lawn in front of his Croton cottage.

Despite her expressed contempt for marriage, Vincent decided she didn't look like a bride, so Norma improvised a veil out of some mosquito netting and picked some white roses for a bridal bouquet. Eugen didn't have time to buy a ring so he borrowed one from his maid. And under a canopy of trees, Edna St. Vincent Millay and Eugen Boissevain became man and wife—and immediately drove to the hospital in New York. "If I die now," Vincent wryly remarked to Arthur as she lay in bed, "I shall be immortal."

A hearty Dutch-born businessman who'd made a fortune as an importer of coffee and sugar from Java, an avid sportsman who'd rowed in the Henley regatta, and a philanthropist who'd helped raise money to send Jack to Russia for *The Masses*, Eugen seemed a most unlikely match for Vincent. Yet given her increasing physical frailty and emotional instability, her choice was predictable: the voice of defiant youth, the symbol of the liberated woman, the exemplar of the solitary artist, Vincent yearned for the kind of cocoon she'd known in childhood. At forty-three, twelve years older than his "Aidna," Eugen became a paternal presence in her life. He had an unusual capacity to take charge while remaining self-effacing. He was protective in precisely the way the independent Vincent needed—allowing her to draw upon both his dynamic energy and his burgher stability.

Eugen hadn't the slightest inclination to pry into the creative process, but he was a sophisticated connoisseur of poetry and appreciated her work to the point of idolatry.

Of course the intrigued response to Vincent's marriage—in the Village and across the country—failed to capture any of these undertones. "Has Happiness Come to Repay / Fair Edna St. Vincent Millay?" read a headline in the *Chicago Times*, with the subhead, "She Married as She Lived—On a Moment's Impulse." "She, to whom freedom is a religion, submitted to the matrimonial yoke," the story read, going on to call her "a feminist Percy Bysshe Shelley," "a gay free spirit of romance and joy." "Greenwich Village had predicted that she would never marry, that she was too fond of her freedom . . . that Edna would choose single blessedness in preference to the slavery of marriage." As for the widespread belief that Vincent had married a wealthy man, Eugen had lost most of his fortune during World War I, and she paid off all her own debts and those of her mother as well. "Everybody thinks it is my rich husband who has done it," she reported to Cora, "when in fact it is really I myself, every cent of it, with money that I made by writing."

After the operation, Vincent recuperated in Croton and in January 1924 settled into a house at 75½ Bedford Street, near the Cherry Lane Theater and Chumley's renowned restaurant. A three-story brick building, thirty feet deep and only nine and a half feet wide—the narrowest house in New York—with a fireplace in every room and a courtyard in back, it became "the Millay house," though Vincent lived there for only a few months. She almost immediately departed on a two-month reading tour, and when she returned, embarked on a six-month round-the-world trip with Eugen—pooling her receipts with the residue of his fortune. Shortly after their return in the summer of 1925, they sold the Bedford Street house—later to be occupied by John Barrymore—purchased a sylvan, seven-hundred-acre, run-down estate called Steepletop near Austerlitz in upstate New York, and left the Village forever, less than seven years after Vincent's arrival as "Edna St. Vincent Millay, B.A.!"

The return to country living wiped out whatever lingering attraction the city had held for Vincent. But her feelings for Arthur and Bunny, though she rarely saw them, remained strong for the rest of her life.

In 1922, after meeting Arthur and his new love, Gladys Brown, in Paris, she wrote him, "Isn't it funny about you and Gladys?—My god—it's marvelous. . . . And you didn't think we'd like each other!—men don't know very much. . . . I shall love you till the day I die." As late as 1937, she wrote Arthur how "terribly . . . sickeningly" she had loved him, and for the rest of her life wore "the red heart crumpled in the side."

Arthur and Gladys were married at Vincent's Bedford Street house in 1924, and in 1926, while living in New Mexico, the Fickes sent Vincent and Eugen money for a trip west, during which Vincent uncharacteristically asked for Arthur's help on an opera libretto and during which the two couples amused themselves by photographing one another in the nude.

When Bunny had traveled to Europe during Vincent's trip abroad, she'd intimated she might be willing temporarily to resume their affair. "She was tired of breaking hearts and spreading havoc, and wanted to start a new life," Bunny recalled her saying. "She was very broke . . . and she asked me to take her to the South of France; but I knew that she was not to be relied on." So though he'd made the trip largely to see her, he declined her invitation.

"She can no longer intoxicate me with her beauty," Bunny wrote, "or throw bombs into my soul; when I looked at her, it was like staring into the crater of an extinct volcano."

And after Vincent's marriage to Eugen, and after Bunny's marriage to Mary Blair—who'd caused such a scandal by kissing Paul Robeson's hand in the production of *Emperor Jones*—she wrote him playfully, "Am I a swine?—Oh, but such a little one!—Such an elegant and distinguished one!—So pink & white!—A truffle-sniffer, not a trough-wallower! I love you just as ever. I would go driving with you in Central Park in an open Victoria in a howling blizzard in a muslin frock. Do come, Bunny. . . . Let not the light tone of this communication put you off. I do want to see you."

So even after Vincent settled down with Eugen, Arthur and Bunny found themselves caught in her familiar, unsettling pattern. Only Eugen, with his fatherly stability, was a man with whom she could live. At Steepletop, named for the pinkish white steeplebush flowers that blanketed the meadows, Vincent could concentrate on her poetry while Eugen did the cooking and cleaning in addition to managing the farm and handling most of her correspondence. In the evening, he ran her bath and rubbed her neck.

Despite her continued ill health, Vincent undertook exhausting reading tours even when sales of her books proved insufficient to support them. Still the actress, she drew her audiences into the orbit of her intense theatricality. Seated on a thronelike chair, dressed in a flowing green gown and high-heeled slippers, she would remain silent for nearly a minute, focusing the audience's attention to a point of almost unbearable expectation, then with an abrupt toss of her head and in her deeply resonant voice, she'd begin to recite.

Vincent took a greater interest in politics than she had in the Village. Enraged at the Sacco and Vanzetti death sentence, she wrote her widely reprinted poem "Justice Denied in Massachusetts," and traveled to Boston on the eve of the execution to plead with the governor and to join the protesters outside the prison. Arrested with several leading literary figures, including John Dos Passos, she was bailed out by Eugen for $25.

She traveled to Washington to attend a ceremony honoring the early suffragists and read her poem "The Pioneer," dedicated to Inez Millholland. Her concluding line, "Take up the song; forget the epitaph," so stirred the assembled throng that she was asked to recite the poem a second time.

When Elinor Wylie was refused membership in the League of American Penwomen—presumably because she was a lesbian—Vincent sent off a letter protesting the "recent gross and shocking insolence to one of the most distinguished writers of our time." "It is not in the power of an organization which has insulted Elinor Wylie, to honour me . . . and indeed I should find it unbecoming on my part, to sit as Guest of Honour in a gathering of writers, where honour is tendered not so much for the excellence of one's literary accomplishment as for the circumspection of one's personal life. . . . I too am eligible for your disesteem. Strike me too from your lists."

Her feminism flared up a few years later when she was awarded an honorary degree by New York University but was not invited to a dinner honoring the male recipients. "On an occasion, then, on which I shall be present solely for reasons of scholarship," she protested, "I am, solely for reasons of sex, to be excluded from the company and the conversation of my fellow-doctors. . . . I register this objection not for myself personally, but for all women. . . . I beg of you, and of the eminent Council whose representative you are, that I may be the last woman so honoured, to be required to swallow from the very cup of this honour, the gall of this humiliation."

Vincent's feminist principles also played a part in her free love compact with Eugen. Word got back to the Village about a mysterious Russian; about last-minute telegrams to Eugen saying she'd be "delayed" a day or two returning from one of her reading tours; about unorthodox sleeping arrangements at Steepletop. But news of a long liaison with a handsome and sensitive young poet named George Dillon was based on evidence not innuendo.

Vincent was thirty-six, George twenty-two when she initiated their affair after a reading in Chicago—"I wish I did not feel like your mother," she once complained. Though he sometimes felt he was "being devoured," their relationship continued off and on well into the thirties, including an interlude of several months when they lived together in Paris while working on their joint translation of Baudelaire, and even a brief ménage à trois with the not wholly enthusiastic Eugen. For the most part, however, Eugen lived by the theory that "Unless you are a fool and so conceited as to think you are the greatest, the most wonderful man in the world, how can you expect a woman to love only you!"

People this open-minded about granting favors are often firm about expecting the favor to be returned, and Eugen would regale Vincent with tales of his erotic adventures with farmers' daughters and servant girls. By this time in Vincent's life, however, marriage *was* "the solution," and in the haven of marriage at Steepletop, she had at last found security.

But as her dependence on Eugen deepened, she was not so much shielded as virtually imprisoned. For a long time they refused to install a telephone, and when they finally did, they'd leave it off the hook for days at a time. They posted a sign reading "Visitors received only by appointment." Over the years, Eugen's subordination to Vincent even became a form of control, the way some people dominate their mates by encouraging a deeper and deeper dependence on their generosity. Vincent once pleaded with the organizer of an event, "I can't sit with strangers only. Please, I must have Eugen sitting beside me. . . . I don't know what will happen if he isn't here. Please, please—otherwise, I'll have to go home!"

And, of course, Vincent's psychic state affected her poetry as well. Lacking the tension that would have made her dig into her unconscious, her writing, at its best when defying and contrary, now had little to push against, and occasionally became soft and flabby.

"Eugen and I live like two bachelors," Vincent told friends. Increasingly withdrawn from the world, they clung to social ritual in social isolation. They'd dress for dinner even when they had no guests, share a bottle of wine, then a second, then a third, and the next day the routine would begin all over again, Vincent writing in her cloistered room, Eugen making sure nothing disturbed her work. After a series of minor quarrels, Eugen even refused to allow Norma to visit her sister.

Eugen's nursing didn't restore Vincent's health, but confirmed her identity as an invalid. She suffered constant anxiety headaches and minor ailments, her drug use exacerbating a situation it was intended to alleviate: "I am at present under the influence of hashish, gin, bad poetry, love, morphine, and hunger," she wrote a friend, "otherwise could not be writing you even this."

Friends who came to Steepletop expecting to find a sanctuary found something closer to a sanatorium. Max said that Eugen watched protectively over his "frail treasure like a dedicated dragon. . . . One felt on entering Steepletop that some very fragile piece of china, inestimable in value, was in an unstable equilibrium upstairs. . . . She cultivated for all that it was worth the privilege of being sick."

After a visit, Bunny surmised that "vigorously creative periods" continued to occur, but he also had the impression they alternated with "dreadful lapses into depression and helplessness that sometimes lasted for months."

One of the most widely read and acclaimed poets of her generation found her reputation reach its peak in her formative years, decline in the thirties and forties, and plummet in the fifties and sixties, to become virtually nonexistent. Well-known critics once praised the now unread poet's work—a phenomenon that rarely occurs. Allen Tate called Vincent's poetry on a par with that of Byron and Tennyson. Edmund Wilson wrote, "Edna Millay seems to me one of the only poets writing in English in our time who have attained to anything like the stature of great literary figures in an age in which prose has predominated," adding that she had the same talent for "giving supreme expression to profoundly felt personal experience" as Eliot, Auden, and Yeats.

But the praise gradually gave way to denunciation, often on the theory, so common among academics, that judicious criticism should concern itself primarily with moderating emotional reaction of any kind—except condescension and contempt. Vincent's wit came to be called merely clever, her technical adroitness facile, her irony cute. Her universal themes were regarded as clichés, her impudent attitudes flippant, her simplicity sentimental, her traditional forms hackneyed. She began to be viewed as a poet of a single subject, love, and a single mood, bittersweet—in short, the poet of adolescent girls. As Malcolm Cowley once remarked, the most striking quality of Vincent's poetry was the bad criticism it provoked.

Part of the problem remained that of all popular poets—much of the criticism had little to do with the quality of the work itself but with the enthusiasm for it. As a symbolic figure, Vincent was excessively praised for the attitudes she represented, and excessively denounced when those attitudes turned into conventions. And to the degree that her work advocated

social change—in particular sexual candor and female independence—
her very success soon made her seem outdated. Another part of the problem was the evolving nature of her poetry. As she turned from youthful
lyricism to mature meditation, as she focused less on love and more on nature, beauty, and death, her popularity waned with those who wanted to
continue to read about the vicissitudes of passion, and her stature diminished with those who found her losing her vibrant voice—the very readers
who had once charged her with sounding a single note.

But by far the largest part of the problem was the dramatic shift in
aesthetic fashion led by T. S. Eliot and resulting in the decades-long hegemony of the New Criticism. The year Vincent won her first Pulitzer Prize
saw the American publication of Eliot's *The Waste Land*, and no two poets
could have been more unalike. Though Vincent joined Eliot in revolting
against the Genteel Tradition, the qualities most characteristic of her
work—emotion and personality—were the ones his acolytes were most determined to expunge. "The death-bringer," Vincent called Eliot—and his
influence certainly brought death to her reputation.

But Vincent is neither a neglected master nor an overpraised mediocrity, and she deserves to be included in the pantheon—in an anteroom,
perhaps, reserved for those on the fringes of genius, the gifted minor poets,
the poets condemned for their popularity. One of the ways her reputation
might be revived would be to correct a misunderstanding upon which her
original reputation was based. Certainly Vincent's love poetry replaced the
languors and melancholy of traditional "women's poetry" with an audacious celebration of female sexuality and an impudent rejection of female
fidelity—an assault on respectability that seemed all the more shocking
for being so charming. But in truth, at the heart of her poetry, she emphasized the psychological more than the erotic—specifically, the constant
conflict between physical union and psychic distance and the belief that
yielding to impulse is at once emancipation of the body and betrayal of
the soul.

> *What lips my lips have kissed, and where, and why,*
> *I have forgotten, and what arms have lain*
> *Under my head til morning; but the rain*
> *Is full of ghosts tonight, that tap and sigh*
> *Upon the glass and listen for reply,*
> *And in my heart there stirs a quiet pain*
> *For unremembered lads that not again*
> *Will turn to me at midnight with a cry.*

When writing about nature and beauty Vincent often stressed the tension between ecstatic epiphany and inescapable impermanence. Nearly everything she wrote dealt with the transience of bliss and the disappearance of rapture.

Gaily defiant, and rarely tempted to "dicker with dying," Vincent never succumbed to the sentimentality of "tragic acceptance."

> *Down, down, down, into the darkness of the grave*
> *Gently they go, the beautiful, the tender, the kind;*
> *Quietly they go, the intelligent, the witty, the brave.*
> *I know. But I do not approve. And I am not resigned.*

But for Vincent, like many who adopt this attitude, her carefree defiance and her erotic abandon were ultimately prescriptions not for rapture but for something close to despair.

While revolting against conventional morality and overflowing with spontaneous passion, Vincent used traditional forms and displayed a masterly, controlled technique. She absorbed the lyric, the sonnet, the ballad so deeply into her consciousness that her expression always felt fresh. Her exact metaphors illuminated even the most commonplace ideas and she was a master of alliteration, assonance, subtle variations in rhyme and rhythm.

One of Vincent's signatures was her wit, most notably revealed in sudden reflections and in final lines that cast an arc of irony back over the poem that did not contract her meaning, as irony so often does, but expanded it with startling insights. The concluding couplet, which traditionally expressed an idea in Vincent's hands, opened into the mystery.

> . . . *"One thing there's no getting by—*
> *I've been a wicked girl," said I;*
> *"But if I can't be sorry, why,*
> *   I might as well be glad!"*

Or:

> *Till all the world, and I, and surely you,*
> *Will know I love you, whether or not I do.*

Despite changes in aesthetic standards, Vincent shares much of the responsibility for her declining reputation. Her emotionalism may have become unfashionable, but far worse were her occasional prosaic pronouncements, as if clichés could be redeemed by being made "poetic."

Fall follows summer, death devours life, art survives time—and trivial truths will always be with us. Limp generalizations ("The anguish of the world is on my tongue"), cleverness in the guise of insight, verbal pirouettes attempting to do the work of sustained thought, forceful assertion when quiet persuasion fails—of these she was too often guilty. Vincent saw many of her flaws as clearly as any of her critics, and more viciously than most. "Acres of ostentatious and pedantic drivel," she wrote her publisher of one of her works.

Yet the characteristic that keeps Vincent from joining the ranks of the enduring poets is the one that made her such a popular poet—the frequent superficiality of her treatment of love. For all her apparent boldness, she seldom faced her confusion, or grappled with her distress. What better prescription for popularity than candor without confrontation, audacity without challenge, confession without revelation? For though Vincent was seemingly the most confessional of poets, in some ways she was the most concealed. There was a deviousness in her directness, impressing her readers with her honesty so she wouldn't have to confront herself with the truth. Like those who confess a small sin in order to conceal a larger one—how can someone so frank about her failings be suspected of deceit?—she won a reputation for candor through the very process of remaining hidden.

The disparity between Vincent's surface revelations and her unconscious conflicts affected her lovers and her readers in much the same way. Her flirtatiousness captured their attention. Her frankness drew them into her orbit. Her intimations of intimacy promised sexual surrender to her lovers, poetic revelation to her readers. And then, just when she'd made them fall in love with her, she refused to yield to the very emotions she'd elicited, leaving her lovers frustrated at her inaccessibility, her more discerning readers dissatisfied with a certain falseness of tone. Whatever exasperation she may have caused her lovers remained of concern only to them—but what poetry she might have written if she'd been willing to penetrate her feelings and express their tangled complexity.

I don't know where you are," Vincent wrote Bunny from Steepletop in August 1946. "But I think, and I think it often, 'wherever he is, there he still is, and perhaps someday I shall see him again, and we shall talk about poetry, as we used to do.' " She recalled, with an almost painful nostalgia, those lovely, luminous moonlit nights back in the Village—bending under "the terrible weight of the perfect word," reading aloud "immortal page after page conceived in a mortal mind." She was only now beginning to recover from "a very handsome—and, as I was afterwards told, an all but life-size—nervous breakdown" she'd suffered two years earlier.

Vincent was also suffering the continuing decline of her lyric gift. During World War II her poetry even degenerated into jingoistic versifying. As she wrote Bunny of her "Pious Prostitution of Poetry to Propaganda," "I can tell you from my own experience, that there is nothing on this earth which can so much get on the nerves of a good poet, as the writing of bad poetry."

> *Make Bright the arrows,*
> *O peaceful and wise!*
> *Gather the shields*
> *Against surprise.*

Her reputation was as devastated as her health; neither would recover.

Bunny hadn't seen Vincent since 1929, but two years after her letter, in August 1948, while attending the Berkshire Music Festival, he drove over to Steepletop to spend an afternoon. "I'll go and get my child," Eugen said upon his arrival, and when Vincent appeared "It was a moment before I recognized her," Bunny recalled. Her hands shook, he noticed, and her eyes looked frightened, but even more disturbing was the way she submitted to Eugen's solicitude. "At moments he would baby her in a way that I had not seen him use before but that had evidently become habitual."

In his account of the visit in his journals, Bunny seemed almost cruelly detached. But in the memorial essay he published after Vincent's death he expressed a distressed compassion for the woman he'd once loved. Her recent poetry's "unrelieved blackness," the "terrible eclipse of [her] spirit"—"the changes in her were like the old images of dreams that come to us exaggerated, distorted, swollen with longing or horror. So she was still, although now in a different way, almost as disturbing to me as she had ever been in the twenties, to which she had so completely belonged—for she could not be a part of my present."

Bunny couldn't comfort Vincent—nor, by this point, could Eugen. The love she'd first felt for him had soon faded into the rituals of domesticity, then degenerated into abject dependency. For brief interludes her spirit would revive, particularly when she could find the strength to reenter the realm of poetry. She memorized her masters, from Catullus to Keats, with prodigious energy, and though she could no longer write, she could protect her past.

In a letter to her publisher in May 1943, responding to the proposal that she introduce a collection of her poems with gossip about her love affairs — more discreetly worded, of course, though that's what was wanted — Vincent gave a spirited reply, "Your proposition, that Harper's bring out a volume of 'The Love Poems of Edna St. Vincent Millay,' containing a 'mellow *Foreword in retrospect*' written by their author, in which foreword she confides to the public '*when, where, and under what impulsion*' (the italics are mine) those poems were written, leaves me strangely cold. You might . . . have come across the knowledge that I am the only poet in America (at least, I believe this to be true) who consistently and in all circumstances refuses to make in print any statement whatever regarding any poem whatever that she has published.

"You state that, in your opinion, such a book as you describe would 'make new readers' for me," Vincent continued. "I do not doubt it. People who never in all their lives, except when in school and under compulsion, have held a book of poems in their hands, might well be attracted by the erotic autobiography of a fairly conspicuous woman, even though she did write poetry. The indubitable fact that, even as I was winning my new readers, I should be losing entirely the good esteem of the more sensitive and by me the most valued, of the readers I already have, does not seem to have occurred to you."

Beguiling even in her indignation, Vincent wrote in a covering letter, "It is a fact, that you harass me so, you run me so ragged, with your one proposition after another, propositions which, more often than not, I feel unhappily obliged to turn down, that you destroy all my serenity of mind. If you really want a book from me, why not stop worrying me for a while, and give me a chance to write it? On which genial and diplomatic note, I close. Trusting, however, in closing, that for one year more it may be said of me by Harper & Brothers, that although I reject their proposals I welcome their advances."

The immortality of art proved a pale consolation when, after a short illness, Eugen died in August 1949. Vincent was utterly bereft. Her friends tried to persuade her to leave Steepletop, or at least have someone come live with her. But she stubbornly stayed on alone and survived the winter in a haze of alcohol. She managed to dull the agony of summer by sporadically resuming her writing. As another winter of unbearable loneliness approached, her dread grew.

On the night of October 18–19, 1950, Vincent stayed up for hours, drinking Alsatian wine and reading the galleys of a new translation of *The Aeneid*. At first flush of dawn, she finally started upstairs to her bedroom. She was found dead at the bottom of the stairs the next day.

VI

Eminent Villagers

Willa Cather

As an enclave of outsiders, the Village served two apparently contradictory functions—it provided both a sense of public unity and a sense of personal privacy. Those who felt odd or unconventional could express themselves publicly without head-shaking disapproval, and privately without prying curiosity. One could hide out in the Village as easily as one could put oneself on display—for it was a community in the service of individuality.

Willa Cather lived in the Village far longer than Mabel Dodge, Jack Reed, Jig Cook, and Vincent Millay—in fact, she wrote many of her frontier novels on Bank Street. Yet no one was less likely to show up at Mabel's salon, or *Masses* editorial meetings, or Provincetown Players opening night parties. Willa made the Village her home for the most creative years of her life, partly because she found its small-town domesticity and European bohemianism appealing, but mostly because she was attracted to its laissez-faire attitude toward unconventional sexuality—she didn't so much express her lesbian instincts as maintain the fierce sense of privacy they engendered.

Virtually from birth, Willa was called Willie. In one of her most autobiographical stories, her heroine changed her name from Theodosia to

Tommy, and was torn between her fondness for a young man and her obsession with a young woman. By her teens Willa had cropped her hair, was wearing boys' clothes, and took to calling herself William, and in college she often cross-dressed and frequently had crushes on other women. She began her career as a journalist, and in her mid-twenties at last escaped "Siberia"—as she datelined her letters from Red Cloud, Nebraska—by accepting a position as editor of a women's magazine published in Pittsburgh. In 1899, she met Isabelle McClung, the beautiful, cultivated, high-spirited daughter of a prominent judge, and soon afterward moved in with the McClungs—"chez the goddess," as she candidly put it. Willa and Isabelle were probably not lovers, but Willa was deeply infatuated.

In 1906 Willa received a job offer from Sam McClure, editor of the famous muckraking magazine that bore his name, and moved to the Village. Her first residence was a studio apartment at 60 Washington Square South, next door to the "House of Genius" where Stephen Crane, O. Henry, and Theodore Dreiser had once lived, and where Jack Reed would soon settle after graduating from Harvard.

Working for Sam McClure, said one of his employees, was like "working in a high wind, sometimes of cyclonic magnitude." Indeed, Willa had gotten her job when his two most famous contributors, Lincoln Steffens and Ida Tarbell, had resigned to form a rival publication. But the mercurial editor and the placid, efficient writer immediately hit it off, and after only two years, Willa was named managing editor, responsible for the daily operations of a magazine with nearly a million subscribers. In 1911, determined to devote herself full-time to her own writing, she left *McClure's*—but only after agreeing to ghost-write Sam's autobiography, a task that allowed her to develop her skill at speaking in a male voice.

While at *McClure's*, Willa made frequent trips to Pittsburgh to visit Isabelle, and traveled with her to Europe in 1908, but she also kept company with Edith Lewis—the daughter of a Lincoln, Nebraska, banker whom she'd met in 1903 and brought to *McClure's* as a copy editor shortly after her own appointment. Upon her return from her European vacation with Isabelle, she and Edith took an apartment together at 82 Washington Place, just off the Square. While Isabelle remained for Willa the luminous emblem of ineffable, unattainable erotic fulfillment, Edith became her quotidian companion, supportive, devoted to the point of servitude.

Willa continued to spend time with both women until Isabelle's sudden marriage in 1916, a devastating blow to Willa, and though it seems likely that her relationship with Edith was as chaste as her relationship with Isabelle—"Everything the world was entitled to know was in her books,"

Edith bluntly wrote after Willa's death—it certainly embodied lesbian longings. Both relationships expressed the duality of Willa's character and career—yearning and stability, obsession and renunciation, possessiveness and detachment, unconventionality and conservatism—the divided self so characteristic of so many major American writers and that, in Willa's case, was less a sign of suppressed sexuality than a challenge to contain and transcend ambiguity. Her novels, read for decades as simple tales of the frontier, are, in fact, complex tales of the frontiers of spirit.

Willa and Edith's years at Washington Place were comfortable, domestic—just what Willa needed as she embarked on her career as a writer. Early in 1913, they found a much larger apartment at 5 Bank Street—$42 a month for seven rooms—and discovered that they could even afford a cook and housekeeper, a French woman named Josephine Bourda, who was to remain with them throughout their stay in the Village.

Willa and Edith knew several openly lesbian couples, but Willa never lost her Midwestern sense of propriety. She remained reluctant to expose her most intimate feelings even to her most intimate friends, and insisted that she and Edith live in separate rooms. "My apartment," Willa even called 5 Bank Street in her letters to friends. Their fellow Villagers may have gossiped, but they also let it be known that they had a shrugging attitude bordering on indifference, which was precisely what Willa sought.

Willa's Bank Street years were uneventful. While other Villagers were advocating a socialist revolution and transforming the American theater, she sat at her spartan desk, and with sunlight pouring through the windows wrote O, Pioneers!, My Antonia, The Professor's House, and Death Comes for the Archbishop, the novels that by the mid-twenties would make her world-famous.

Willa traveled widely, often without Edith. She met Mabel Dodge when she stayed with her and Tony Luhan in Taos for two weeks in 1925 (Tony, it has been suggested, served as a model for the archbishop's Indian friend, Eusabio). But back at Bank Street, aside from her Friday afternoon "at homes," she remained reclusive. An occasional celebrity like D. H. Lawrence might be granted an hour or two, a select circle of friends including her publishers, Blanche and Alfred Knopf, might be invited for a quiet evening, but everyone else almost instantly felt how annoyed she could become at intrusions on her privacy. Villagers who encountered Willa on the street found it difficult to believe that this plain, stocky, almost dowdy woman in her apple-green coat and matching porkpie felt hat could be a renowned writer—until they saw the formidable fire in her eyes.

Willa's attitude toward the Village found expression in the short story "Coming, Aphrodite!," published in H. L. Mencken and George Jean Nathan's *Smart Set* in 1920. Don Hedger, a dedicated, hardworking, and unknown young painter, is alarmed to discover that a lovely young singer named Eden Bower—aha, the alert reader notices, Hedger and Bower— has moved into the adjacent apartment, but he soon realizes that he can spy on his new neighbor through a knothole—one lucky night, he watches as she languidly undresses. "The immortal conception!" Don thinks—after all, he's a painter. But he must get to know her better, he decides—after all, he's also a man.

Eden's impulses are more forthright—she's come to the Village for "the taste of freedom"—and the inevitable seduction proves a feeble test of Don's powers of persuasion. Their brief affair comes to an end when they quarrel about what Eden sees as Don's lack of worldly ambition and Don sees as Eden's lack of aesthetic appreciation—but not before he tells her a long and brutal Mexican folktale about a chaste princess and a tribal chief involving rape, castration, slavery, and burning at the stake. Years later, Eden returns to the Village, now an international star of superficial, crowd-pleasing gifts, and inquires after Don. To her surprise, he is also a "success," though only to a small coterie of painters to whom "he is one of the first men among the moderns."

"Coming, Aphrodite!" reflects Willa's nostalgia for the old Village—pigeons resting on the Garibaldi statue in Washington Square, solemn artists developing their craft in lonely studios—in vivid contrast in her imagination with the traffic, bustling hangouts, and faux artists of the Village of the teens. Her views of the "New Woman" may be glimpsed in her portrait of the frivolous Eden. And her opinion of heterosexual passion—for this story is one of the few works of fiction in which Willa dealt with an erotic connection between a man and a woman (so explicitly that several sentences were expurgated by the *Smart Set* editors)—is evident in her depiction of male voyeurism and primitive barbarity, and in the androgynous tone of the authorial voice.

The theme of the story seems to be the moral contrast between two different types of artistic ambition—Eden sees success as public adulation, Don sees it as aesthetic achievement. But an interlocking theme emerges, equally expressive of Willa's character and vision: the moral contrast between the destructiveness of desire and the chaste devotion to art. Don, by remaining in isolation, escapes the twin temptations of glamorous acclaim and erotic passion.

The quaint charms of the Village, as Willa wrote in "Coming, Aphrodite!," had "long since passed away," and in 1927, when "progress" meant that the building at 5 Bank Street would be torn down for the Seventh Avenue Subway, she and Edith moved to the Grosvenor Hotel at 35 Fifth Avenue, a "temporary" residence that lasted for five years, until they moved uptown to an apartment on Park Avenue and 62nd Street.

The connection between Willa's fiction and her sexuality was not a simple matter of sublimation or "encoding," as some critics have suggested, but a complex interaction involving, in a phrase she was fond of using, "the thing unsaid." Her fiction may be read as a "muscular" appropriation of a masculine tradition, as a woman's sensibility transcending the conventions of gender—few critics now label her a provincial or regional writer, a category in which she was condescendingly confined for decades—but her merit should be measured by her gifts of indirection and suggestion, through which she subtly conveyed the struggle to create an autonomous self. "She takes such pains to conceal her sophistication that it is easy to miss her quality," said Wallace Stevens. The key to understanding the relationship between her writing and her sexuality can be found in aligning Stevens's remark with a line of Swinburne's that Willa underlined in her copy of his poetry while still in college—"To love aloud is often to love amiss."

Willa never identified herself as a lesbian—or as a feminist, for that matter—and in one of her few comments on the subject of homosexuality fiercely disapproved of Oscar Wilde's "infamy." She never denied her lesbian impulses, but the crucial point was that she refused to define herself as a lesbian, or in any other way. The self was always in the process of silently emerging.

So the Village gave Willa order, comfort, security, and especially privacy—the very things most young people came to the Village to escape. As she wrote, "The business of an artist's life is not Bohemianism, for or against, but ceaseless and unremitting labor."

Theodore Dreiser

Three of the greatest American novels were written in Greenwich Village—*Huckleberry Finn, O Pioneers!,* and *An American Tragedy.* The irony is that all three, and the novelists themselves, are as far as possible from the Village ethos. Mark Twain lived there for nearly three decades because a perverse strain in his character desired respectability—in this case, association with the gentility of the rich families, including that of his compatriot Henry James, who lived on the north side of Washington Square. Willa

Cather sought the isolation that only a tolerant community could provide. And Theodore Dreiser, an avid reader of Balzac, wanted to enact the story of the ambitious young man from the provinces who seized literary glory in the great city—and where else in that great city could a boorish and graceless man, who also happened to be a writer, feel comfortable? A contempt for respectability, a sense of communal spirit, an air of sophistication—the enduring paradox of the Village, one of the reasons it was a source of so much creativity, is that its sensibility was both narrowly defined and all-embracing.

Theodore first came to the Village in 1894, taking a room in a dingy Bleecker Street hotel. As a successful journalist and struggling novelist, he traveled widely for the next twenty years, often living in cheap lodging houses in the Village or flophouses in the nearby Bowery whenever his work brought him back to New York. By 1912, he was something of a legend to the literary radicals of the Chicago Renaissance for his convention-shattering *Sister Carrie*. Floyd Dell, Arthur Davison Ficke, Sherwood Anderson, and Margaret Anderson were among his circle, but he took particular interest in an attractive and intellectual twenty-year-old woman named Kirah Markham. The daughter of a wealthy Jewish father and gentile mother, Kirah was not only half Theodore's age, but she was involved with Floyd. But since Floyd was rarely "currently involved" with only one woman, he had little cause for complaint when she and Theodore departed for New York with suspicious simultaneity in 1913. An ardent defender of Theodore's novels, Floyd was considerably less taken with his charms. "Dreiser," he recalled, "was hardly the young man's notion of a knight-errant—somewhat pudgy, no great talker."

In the summer of 1914, Theodore took a two-room apartment in a redbrick row house at 165 West 10th Street and for the first time in his adult life settled down for more than a few months. Bookshelves covered most of two walls and he hung two large and, in the judgment of some of his friends, lurid paintings—an abstraction consisting mostly of triangles and a portrait of a voluptuous reclining nude being served a tray of fruit by a black maid. He had little furniture—a daybed, a lectern, and a rocking chair, in which he sat for hours, folding a large white handkerchief into a tiny square again and again and again as he talked with visitors, a neurotic compulsion not even the Village Freudians could comprehend. But the centerpiece of his apartment was a square rosewood piano that had once belonged to his composer brother, Paul, and that Theodore had transformed into a desk. He continued his frequent travels, but for the rest of the teens he always returned to the rumpled comfort of his bachelor quarters—though he was a bachelor with a harem and a bohemian only in his scorn for bourgeois convention.

When writing his fiction, Theodore would work every day from nine to four, then walk in Washington Square Park to soothe his nerves, browse in the 8th Street Book Shop, and spend the evening with Floyd Dell, Max Eastman, Sinclair Lewis, Margaret Sanger, Hutch Hapgood, or Emma Goldman. Mabel's salon held no interest for him—he may have sympathized with her rejection of middle-class propriety, but he rejected even more fiercely the upper-class ambience within which she expressed it.

"The red-ink boys" of *The Masses* were more Theodore's style, but he seldom attended their beer-and-cheese editorial meetings over on Greenwich Avenue, and when he did, recalled Louis Untermeyer, he seemed "unhappy, uncomfortable, and yet pontifical." He frequently attended the productions of the Provincetown Players—where Kirah, no longer his lover, often performed. One of his own plays, *The Girl in the Coffin*, was produced by the Washington Square Players in 1917, and another, *The Hand of the Potter*, by Jig's group in 1921. A "conspicuously offensive" evening, said the critic for the *New York World* of the latter effort. "A repulsive play," added the New York *Herald*. "Give thanks, oh brother," a friend wrote Theodore, "that you were three thousand miles away." (Theodore blamed both Jig's poor production and the puritanical critics for the flop—annoying Jig, who lost $1,500 on the venture.)

Though not a man for congenial table-hopping, Theodore could occasionally be found at Romany Marie's in the Brevoort Hotel, and the Purple Cat on Washington Square—"the usual atmosphere of college boys trying to be devilish and finding it difficult," he noted sourly in his diary. But his favorite hangouts were Luchow's, the German restaurant on 14th Street, and Polly's restaurant on Macdougal Street, where he would play a popular game called Up Jenkins with half a dozen friends so late into the night that Polly would plead with them to go home. He grew particularly fond of Polly's paramour. "Hippolyte Havel is one of those men who ought to be supported by the community," he told Hutch. "If I ever have any money, I'll certainly settle some of it on Hippolyte." It wasn't only women who came to learn that Theodore's promises were at once heartfelt and meaningless, for when he *did* have money, Hippolyte certainly never saw a dime.

Theodore visited the Armory Show in 1913, joined the Liberal Club with Floyd as his sponsor, and attended *The Masses'* rollicking balls at Webster Hall—on one occasion, solemnly arguing anarchism with Emma

Goldman while simultaneously, as Sinclair Lewis noted, lubriciously eyeing a somewhat younger and thinner woman. Now and then he would even host a sitting-on-the-floor, candlelit party at his own apartment, but by and large he had less interest in Village gatherings than in Village obsessions.

Theodore's radical politics were intuitive, based more on class grievance than class analysis, and when Floyd tried to interest him in Freudianism, he proved "perfectly incapable of taking in these ideas." He did consult A. A. Brill while researching the psychological aspects of murder for An American Tragedy, and even proposed a jointly authored book. Brill, who couldn't help but notice the handkerchief ritual during their many talks, thought it must involve "sexual symbolism" of some sort, but, in those days, what didn't?

In one of his few stories about the Village, Theodore described it from the point of view of an outsider, but with a relish that must have come, at least in part, from his own feelings. "She was, or had been," reads a typical passage, "in the company of this, that, and the other individual . . . Greenwich Village ne'er-do-wells, pseudo and disgraced artists and poets, loafers, I.W.W. social wreckers—and the like—an unholy and disgraceful crew."

Theodore's closest friend wasn't a Villager at all—H. L. Mencken shared Theodore's vigorous contempt for middle-class values, a high esteem for Theodore's novels, and, it must be said, an anti-Semitism all the more despicable because they both insisted they had many Jewish friends. "N.Y. to me is a scream," Theodore wrote Mencken, "a Kyke's dream of a Ghetto. The lost tribe has taken the island." An inveterate practical joker, Mencken would journey down to West 10th Street to deposit various items in Theodore's mailbox—pamphlets on sex hygiene, say, or frankfurters tied with ribbons, or letters purporting to come from President Wilson inviting him to the White House—but Theodore could only make the most heavy-handed rejoinders. As Margaret Anderson once said, "Dreiser had no more wit than a cow."

Sour and humorless, he was hardly a likable man. Not to put too fine a point on it, he was in many ways a monster. He could be cruel, deceitful, gross, cold, and ungrateful—sometimes it seemed that the best thing that could be said about him was that at least he wasn't craven. He got into countless imbroglios with his publishers, whom he accused of cheating him. He was abusive to critics and landladies, tradesmen and secretaries, all of whom failed to meet his exacting standards—in other words, who failed to satisfy his whims. The waiters at the Brevoort were terrified lest they seat him at the wrong table, the clerks at the Jefferson Market trembled lest they fail to serve him promptly. Imperiousness without style — an unhappy combination.

Even Theodore's friends were frequently the recipients of his exasperation, sometimes his wrath. When a minister once piously said something about "loving one's enemies," he replied, "That's the easiest thing in the world, it's getting along with one's friends that's difficult." And according to Helen Dreiser, his wife for many long, miserable years, "Human emotions washed against him like waves against a stony shore."

Yet Theodore could be thoughtful, considerate, even charming, and dozens, *hundreds* of women momentarily adored him. He wasn't an ideologue of free love; he simply tried to bed every woman who caught his fancy. No hypocrite, he made it clear to whatever woman he happened to be involved with that he'd sleep with whatever woman he wanted, and made it equally clear that she'd better not even think of availing herself of the same freedom or he was through with her on the spot. On one occasion, he brought home a woman he'd met at a party and told the woman he was living with to sleep in the other room while he and his pickup had sex in the bedroom. Hundreds of affairs, thousands of lies — clandestine phone calls, secret liaisons, even false addresses. "A forest of intrigue," Mencken said. For months at a time, "he devotes himself largely to the stud." The ladies' man as brute.

And yet that charm — he could make a woman feel she was the center of his universe. "I wonder if ever there was a man," recalled Helen, "who so evoked the desire to confide one's joys, sorrows, and secrets." And Kirah, years after they'd parted, still spoke fondly of his "animal magnetism" and "utter sense of loneliness" (a pair of traits that lured countless Village women into his bed).

"Dreiser was never any good [at conversation] until some exchange of sex magnetism put him at ease," said Margaret Anderson. "But even when I listened to Dreiser in conversation with women with whom he could establish a quick sex sympathy, his talk had no flavor for me. Sex display puts you at your best if you're a tempered human being."

Part of Theodore's charm was merely a seduction ritual, but part reflected a genuine interest in hearing other people's experiences. Even that trait was tainted by egotism, however, for he candidly acknowledged that he used his affairs as research for his novels, and that he believed the conflicts of sexuality enhanced his creativity — a belief he had numerous opportunities to test, and a belief that angered his friend John Sloan, who condemned his "carelessness about women whose hearts were wrecked by an 'artist's desire for experience.' " And Theodore didn't merely use women sexually, he put his lovers to work for him as clerks, typists, even as editors responsible for getting his mammoth manuscripts into publishable form.

So potent was Theodore's "chemical attraction," as he himself called it, that few of the women he ruthlessly betrayed and abandoned expressed regrets—a situation that might have changed had they had a chance to read his diaries. Dozens of entries depicted his simultaneous obsession with sex and callousness toward women. "We lie on bed awhile, and she weeps still more, and finally we fall to screwing," reads a typical entry. Or: "Am horribly bored by her today. Nevertheless we screw." Well, at least he was honest on paper.

Duplicitous as a man, Theodore was forthright as a writer. The chief value of his novels remains the honesty, integrity, and plodding determination with which he wrenched American fiction from the realm of moral uplift to the realm of social truth. His battles with censorship were even more courageous than those of Max Eastman and the staff of *The Masses*. But as a stylist he was so graceless that it was a commonplace even at the height of his fame to call him the world's worst great writer. A Robert Benchley parody: "Up East Division Street, on a hot day in late July, walked two men, one five feet four, the other, the taller of the two, five feet six, the first being two inches shorter than his more elongated companion, and consequently giving the appearance to passers-by on East Division Street, or, whenever the two reached a cross street, to the passers-by on the cross street, of being at least a good two inches shorter than the taller of the little group." If the trouble with the graceless-great-writer formulation is that it assumes his greatness, he was one of those writers whose achievements must be measured by context rather than by content. Though little read these days, and less admired, he deserves homage for contributing to the liberation of American fiction from its Victorian optimism and puritanical hypocrisy.

During the long years of work on *An American Tragedy*, Theodore moved from 165 West 10th Street to 16 St. Luke's Place, an isolated byway in the far West Village. "In the corner was a washstand with the intimacies of toilet frankly displayed," wrote an interviewer from the *New York Times*. "There was a huge lump of coal in the grate. On the mantelpiece above it sat a fat Buddha."

Unlike most Villagers, Theodore was no host, no joiner, no mixer. In a community where everyone knew everyone else with an easygoing intimacy, he had few close friends. He referred dismissively to "the same old Village crowd," and was annoyed when Mencken said that one of his novels "suggests the advanced thinking of Greenwich Village"; he hankered after a materialistic success that was anathema to most of his neighbors. Still, it remained his favorite neighborhood, the one place in his entire life he felt most comfortable.

The young man from the provinces who seizes literary glory in the great city was a story thousands of Villagers were trying to emulate, but it was a nineteenth-century story. New York was only beginning to emerge as the cultural capital of America, and Greenwich Village was still an enclave of rebels and rejects. The difference between New York and the capitals of Europe, as one historian has pointed out, was that in New York one didn't so much make one's way as *find* one's way. So while the Village didn't shape Theodore's ideology or mold his sensibility, it allowed him the freedom to discover them for himself.

In the mid-twenties, Theodore's wife, Helen, and his publisher finally convinced him that his financial status allowed him more luxurious quarters and that his literary status demanded a more respectable address. Reluctantly he moved to a large duplex on West 57th Street. It wasn't as casual as the Village apartments of his younger years—but then Theodore had never really been young.

Guido Bruno

During the mid-teens, hundreds, *thousands* of uptowners and out-of-towners rode the Fifth Avenue double-decker bus downtown to the Washington Square terminal. Across the street at 58 Washington Square South, they climbed the stairs to the top floor, where two signs on the door announced, "Bruno's Garret," "First Aid for Struggling Artists." After paying 10 or 25 cents, depending on how business had been going, the sightseers entered a cluttered suite of rooms and beheld a dozen or more "struggling artists": bearded young men contemplating their half-finished paintings and bobbed-haired young women in smocks and sandals declaiming their imagist poetry. Posters and manifestos and sketches lined the walls, jugs of wine sat on the windowsills, dirty dishes littered counters, mattresses were strewn on the floor—the middle-class image of the artists' gay and irresponsible life! "To get it written, to get it spoken," read another sign, "to get it down at any cost, at any hazard, it is for this only that we are here"—this and the admission fee, for Guido Bruno had gathered together these "struggling artists," who, in return for an occasional meal and the use of the mattresses, carefully staged their bohemian behavior for the delectation of the thrill-seekers. "They came to me from England and Germany, from Bohemia and Italy, from France and Germany," bellowed Bruno with characteristic inaccuracy, "—even Japan and India send their visitors. Truly cosmopolitan days!" Guido Bruno—the Barnum of Bohemia.

From the moment the Village realized it was "the Village," capitalists emerged to exploit its image. In middle-class culture, style leads inevitably to fashion, self-consciousness to imitation, rebellion to commercialization—especially when a trend or a cause is regarded by the middle class as at once outrageous and innocuous. As early as the mid-teens, real estate operators began to publicize the low rents of the Village—a campaign aimed, of course, at raising them. Dozens of jewelry and clothing and knickknack stores opened on the main thoroughfares and every block seemed to have its cozy teashop where day-trippers could ogle one another under the mistaken impression that everyone else was an authentic Villager. No one was more eager to witness the bizarre behavior of bohemia, or to purchase its quaint artifacts, than those whom bohemia scandalized. And, of course, the bohemians were scandalized in turn, for no one likes to "amuse" those for whom one has contempt. Disdain for a commercial culture was being turned into a marketing strategy, the American cult of boosterism was exploiting a community that condemned consumerism, entrepreneurs were profiteering on those who'd turned their backs on mercenary values. While most Villagers were appalled by these ironies, a few were delighted by the opportunity they provided, and none more than Guido Bruno.

One has to be a bit of a bohemian in order to fake it successfully, and if Guido was a sham, a charlatan, a fraud, he was also a genuine eccentric. The only honest thing Guido ever did was remain true to his pose.

Guido arrived in the Village in 1906 at the age of twenty-two, took a menial job in the morgue, and subsisted largely on leftover pastries provided by a kindly French baker on West 4th Street. One of those people who prefer to leave false impressions rather than straightforwardly lie— vague intimations are so much more romantic—Guido let some of his friends believe he was Italian, others Serbian, still others an exiled officer of the Imperial Hapsburg Army, and when directly asked, would reply, "I, Bruno, have given birth to myself!" In point of fact, he was the son of a rabbi from a village north of Prague, and so, by happy coincidence, an authentic Bohemian. He spoke English with a German accent and conversed fluently, and floridly, in seven languages. He commuted daily from his home in Yonkers—yes, this quintessential "Villager" lived in the suburbs, and was even suspected, correctly as it turned out, of having a wife and daughter, to whom he returned most evenings.

At six foot three and weighing over two hundred pounds, Guido was swarthy and Teutonic, though the intimidating effect was diminished by a certain greasiness in his long hair, the way he slouched forward as he talked and averted his eyes from the person to whom he was speaking. He appeared at all hours in a checked suit, spats, and a brown derby or green felt hat, as if to say he didn't care if it was noon or midnight. His appearance was ostentatious, his manner obsequious—what better combination for a low-life con man?

The Garret wasn't Guido's first scam. A few years earlier, he had attempted to sell several fake Aubrey Beardsley drawings to a New York art dealer, claiming he'd purchased them in Paris. On another occasion he nearly bought a printing firm as the "agent" for eight millionaire backers, all of whom, it turned out, were in prison.

But Guido found his calling in 1914 when he noticed the thriving tourist trade at the ice cream parlor on the ground floor of the dingy building at the southeast corner of Thompson Street and Washington Square, the residence of New York's official gravedigger. Instantly realizing that the tourists hadn't come all this way for refreshments, he rounded up his "struggling artists" from among the gainfully unemployed youth and began to act as a kind of maître d' of bohemia. Bruno's Garret served as a combination art gallery, poetry center, lecture hall, and tourist orientation office—"All this on a strictly no-commercial basis," he boasted, implying, inaccurately, that the admission fee was distributed among the "struggling artists"—a kind of foreshadowing of the rent-a-beatnik-for-your-party fad of the early sixties.

Soon the Garret functioned as a publishing house as well, for twenty-five to fifty people a day paying 10 or 25 cents each could hardly support the lifestyle to which Guido aspired. *Bruno's Weekly, Bruno's Monthly, Bruno's Bohemia, Bruno's Review, Bruno's Scrapbook, Greenwich Village Edited by Guido Bruno in His Garret on Washington Square*—these were some of the small-format magazines and booklets and pamphlets and gazettes that issued prolifically from Bruno's Garret. But his best-known series, which appeared with astonishing regularity considering his lackadaisical work habits, was called *Bruno's Chapbooks*, the name appropriated from the London fin-de-siècle periodical. Using a dilapidated press donated by his Italian landlord, editing copy at cafés while drinking a concoction of Vichy water and milk, and hawking his handiwork on street corners—for he was already so renowned as a swindler that no store would carry his publications—Guido claimed a circulation of 32,000, though that figure was considerably closer to copies printed than to those sold.

The most prominent feature of every publication was an advertisement for Bruno's Garret, and, in a nicely circular touch, the most prominent feature in the Garret was a display of posters and flyers advertising the publications. He published his stories and poems, often under pseudonyms such as Mildred Meaker and Maude Martin, and his own bombastic and cryptic essays. But surprisingly—and probably accidentally—he occasionally lapsed into good taste. He introduced the work of the real Aubrey Beardsley to America, published Oscar Wilde, John Addington Symonds, Djuna Barnes, and Alfred Kreymborg, and was the first editor to accept a poem by an unknown young writer named Hart Crane.

Kreymborg, in particular, was indebted to Guido, who invited the poet to read at his Garret (uncharacteristically giving him the evening's entire proceeds, a grand total of $2.50), published his short story about a prostitute, and vigorously defended the story in court when the authorities brought charges of obscenity—even eliciting a letter of support from George Bernard Shaw, which he flourished before the astonished judge. Guido found a way for Alfred to repay him, however. When the charges were dismissed, he promptly published a second edition of the offending story at triple the price—and kept *those* proceeds for himself.

Guido was so obviously a charlatan that his efforts to find a benefactor were almost always fruitless, but a few people were so awed by his audacity that they gave him money just to see what he'd do with it. Guido's main source of financial support was Charles Edison, who'd inherited a fortune from his father, Thomas Alva Edison, and who wanted to try his hand at bohemianism. Charles bankrolled many of Guido's periodicals—one of which published a poem by one Charles Edison—and, since Charles's main interest was avant-garde drama, the two men established the 110-seat Thimble Theater at 10 Fifth Avenue on the corner of 8th Street, opposite the Brevoort Hotel.

Charles produced plays by Chekhov, Strindberg, Gogol, and Shaw, while Guido founded the Bruno Players (which put on the first pro–birth control play), sponsored concerts (though many in the audience were dismayed to discover that the sole instrument was a phonograph), and hawked his publications in the lobby before and after every show. Feeling that Guido wasn't pulling his weight, Charles took over sole management of the theater for a few years before turning it over to Harry Kemp, and decades later was forgiven his youthful indiscretions by the voters of New Jersey, who elected him governor.

Guido, despite his boastful claims to the contrary, had incessant difficulties with women. When word got around that he'd publish poetry for a fee, dozens of women showed up at his Garret with their verses and their money, then waited in vain to see their work in print. Finally realizing they'd been taken, several hired lawyers to inquire of Guido when they could expect publication—or reimbursement of their fee. Guido would protest his innocence, and then casually inform the lawyers that, of course, the women had offered him not only their verses but their bodies—"I, Bruno, sleep with all girls." If the matter ever came to trial, he intimated, he would be under solemn oath to tell the whole truth, and nothing but the truth, whereupon the thwarted lawyers would inform their clients that it was advisable, all things considered, to write off the publication fee as a bad debt.

One woman was persistent. Shortly after making $20,000 in a real estate deal, a middle-aged widow from New Brunswick, New Jersey, received a letter from Guido praising the poems he'd read in a New York newspaper and suggesting they meet to discuss a collection of her work. After giving Guido $1,500 to defray unspecified expenses, she slept with him in his Garret. Faced with the usual rigmarole with her lawyer she wrote a stinging letter to a local journalist. "I have met all sorts of men, in many walks of life," she fumed, "but never one so low and depraved as this wretch. He's not really human, he's a sinister shape of hell, without shame or pity or feeling for anything except money. I noticed a queer thing about his eyes, but did not note its significance until too late to be of use. A yellow light came into them when money was the subject of conversation—a queer wildfire sort of light." An interesting insight, but hardly worth $1,500.

The artist Clara Tice was one of the few women who had reason to feel grateful to Guido. She had an exhibition of caricatures of village denizens at his Garret, and painted a series of female nudes that the Society for the Suppression of Vice felt merited prosecution. But Guido soon turned against Clara and held a mock trial at one of his Monday night Bruno Cabarets, during which he accused her of "murdering art," and summed up his indictment in verse: "Clara Tice, you rhyme with mice."

Djuna Barnes, too, had reason to feel grateful to Guido. In 1915 he published her first book, *The Book of Repulsive Women*, and she later modeled the character of Felix Volkbein in *Nightwood* in part after him. "One day Guido Bruno was among us," Djuna wrote in 1919. "He did not nudge his way in, he did not rise in our midst, rather, one should say, he fell."

Djuna introduced Guido to Frank Harris when the notorious English editor and man of letters came to New York to rescue *Pearson's Maga-*

zine. Frank was a far more successful charlatan and self-promoter and womanizer, and he had the charm, wit, and talent Guido so sorely lacked. Naturally Guido became a dedicated disciple, and Frank, who had a fondness for people who worshipped him and whom he, in return, could abuse with impunity, made him a kind of literary secretary. Guido's duties remained imprecise. On occasion, he'd put together "literary evenings" at the Garret at which Frank would hold forth and on other occasions he'd propose schemes for conning money out of potential patrons of the arts, which Frank would reject as vulgar or embellish with more skillful touches. But mostly Guido served Frank as a drinking partner. After a few years Frank returned to England—but not before making sure that Guido published several of his pieces, and that he was paid for them.

Most Villagers loathed Guido for his character, which mocked their most cherished values, and for his enterprises, which attempted to turn their beloved community into a tourist trap. *The Quill*, not a magazine noted for its acerbity, repeatedly berated Guido for attracting "Thrillage Hounds to Greenwich Thrillage." The Village couldn't remain an enclave for bohemians and radicals forever, but Guido did his worst to make the Village a sideshow, a den of freaks. As Floyd Dell put it, he decided it was all over when a tourist came up to him at a local restaurant and asked if he were "a merry Villager."

On the heels of Frank's departure, a fire in the Garret, the expensive lawsuit over Alfred Kreymborg's short story—plus the intuition that many of his scams were about to catch up with him—Guido decided it was time to get out of the bohemia business, and in 1917 he disappeared as suddenly as he'd surfaced. Grace Godwin turned the Garret into a coffee shop and spaghetti joint called Grace's Garret. The rumor went around that he had decamped to Buffalo and was operating a secondhand bookstore, but after a few months as a rare book dealer on 14th Street—and rare indeed his books must have been—he moved to Wisconsin and worked sporadically and ineffectually for Senator Robert La Follette's Progressive party. Only years later did the Villagers learn Guido Bruno's real name—Curt Kisch.

Margaret Anderson

"I have never been able to accept the two great laws of humanity," wrote Margaret Anderson, "that you're always being suppressed if you're inspired and always being pushed into a corner if you're exceptional. I won't be cornered and I won't stay suppressed." It takes a person with a certain sense of privilege to call these "the two great laws of humanity," a person with an unusual form of rebelliousness, and Margaret was both privileged and rebellious. Raised in an oppressively respectable family in a small town in Indiana at the turn of the century—they moved into a new house every year, she claimed, so her mother would have an opportunity to redecorate—she was expected to confine herself to "the higher joys of country club and bridge." But by the time she reached her teens, "I already knew that the great thing about life"—in addition to a predilection for aphorism—"is not to do what you don't want to do."

One of the things Margaret didn't want to do was accept the "mediocrity" and "vapidities" of upper-middle-class life, so she typed up a series of twenty-page letters to her father "exposing the criminality of our family life and offering a program upon which he could act in every domestic crisis." Her father declined to follow her program, so she wrote to a *Good Housekeeping* advice columnist asking "how a perfectly nice but revolting girl could leave home." When the columnist asked her to come to Chicago to talk, she confronted her family once more. But she had everything she wanted, they said. "Yes, materially," she answered. Then what else did she want? "Self expression." And what was that? "Being able to think, say, and do what you believe in." "It seems to me," replied her father wearily, "that you do nothing else."

And so, in 1908, Margaret went off to Chicago—a city in the midst of a literary renaissance and soon to become a way station to the Village. She rented a small apartment overlooking Lake Michigan, and when her mother took away all her furniture in a vain effort to force her to return home, she simply went on living in the empty rooms, reveling in her freedom from housework. Virtually penniless, she sold two silk negligees and her calfskin-bound copy of Ibsen, and even when too poor to buy heating fuel, she insisted on buying a fresh yellow rose every day. Eventually she found work as a book reviewer, and, as Floyd Dell said, she wrote "more enthusiastically than anybody had ever written in the whole history of book reviewing." But Margaret had larger ambitions. "I will become something beautiful," she said. "I swear it!"

Margaret *was* beautiful—a regal five foot ten, with red-gold hair and blue eyes. As she put it, she was "extravagantly pretty in those days—extravagantly and disgustingly pretty. I looked like a composite of all the most offensive magazine covers."

One night, shortly after her twenty-first birthday, Margaret awoke before dawn. She'd been depressed, and she suddenly realized why. "Nothing inspired is going on," she thought, and "I demand that life be inspired every moment." What would be the best way to assure that? Inspired conversation. But most people don't have the time or the talent for that. She concluded, "If I had a magazine I could spend my time filling it up with the best conversation the world has to offer." "I had only to decide something and it would happen," she later wrote, and having decided, she promptly fell back to sleep.

Since Margaret's irrepressible personality—and, it must be said, her luminous beauty—had won her dozens of friends in the literary community, when she announced, virtually the next day, that she was "about to publish the most interesting magazine that had ever been launched," they were, she recalled, "unconcerned about the necessary money and optimistic about manuscripts." Her blithe assumption that money could be easily obtained—a residue of "the criminality" of her wealthy upbringing—charmed skeptical backers. And her insatiable and impeccable taste guaranteed that she'd publish the best of contemporary writers.

Finding a name for the new magazine proved the most difficult challenge. Many were solicited for suggestions, Floyd Dell and Edna St. Vincent Millay's friend Arthur Davidson Ficke among them. In desperation, Margaret decided to call it *Seagull*—"soaring and all that kind of thing." And then suddenly she thought of "the little theater" movement in Chicago and called together the city's leading literary lights—Dell, Ficke, Sherwood Anderson, Theodore Dreiser—to make the announcement. *The Little Review*—that's it—that's perfect!

Margaret was soon publishing one of the most audacious, influential literary magazines in the nation's history from her tiny office in Chicago's Fine Arts Building. From its first issue in March 1914—sixty-four pages with a plain brown cover—*The Little Review* was a kind of salon in print, its emphasis shifting from issue to issue with Margaret's enthusiasms. Free love, futurism, birth control, Nietzsche, the new paganism—she covered them all. Vachel Lindsay, Carl Sandburg, Amy Lowell, Wallace Stevens, William Carlos Williams, Marianne Moore, and Djuna Barnes were among her earliest contributors—and soon, from abroad, Ezra Pound, T. S. Eliot, William Butler Yeats, and James Joyce.

"Contributors" was the precise word, for authors were paid nothing for their pieces. When Gertrude Stein complained, Margaret responded, "Well, neither do I consider it a good principle for the artist to remain unpaid—it's a little better than for him to remain unprinted, that's all." Benefactors were found to pay the magazine's bills—Frank Lloyd Wright sent along a check for $100, one poet even pawned his wedding ring and sent

Margaret the money, and Amy Lowell offered financial support if Margaret would let her edit the poetry section, an offer Margaret politely declined. But the phone company wasn't interested in philanthropy and threatened to cut off service, and the printers were only appeased when Margaret went to fewer pages and cheaper stock. "We may have to come out on tissue paper pretty soon," she said, "*but we shall keep on coming out.*" Guests at one of her frequent dinner parties found that the menu consisted of frankfurters and pickles.

At Ezra Pound's suggestion, Margaret subtitled the magazine "Making No Compromise with Public Taste"—virtually the same motto proclaimed by *The Masses* and the Provincetown Players. How often bohemian and radical enterprises of the teens guaranteed quality by rejecting convention and exulting in their exclusivity. But Margaret, Max, and Jig adopted this elitism in the name of democracy, for such mottoes seemed to them, not assertions of privileged superiority, but prophecies of universal liberation. They didn't advocate an aristocratic enclave, they simply assumed that political justice and aesthetic quality would soon triumph and expand to include everyone.

"If you've ever read poetry with a feeling that it was your religion," Margaret breathlessly wrote in her first editorial, "if you've ever come suddenly upon the whiteness of a Venus in a dim, deep room, if, in the early morning, you've watched a bird with great white wings fly straight up into the rose-colored sun . . . if these things have happened to you and continue to happen until you're left quite speechless with the wonder of it all, then you will understand our hope to bring them nearer to the common experience of the people who read us."

The early reaction to *The Little Review*, in fact, was decidedly mixed. "Making No Compromise with Public Taste"—and, one reader responded, "having none of our own." Amy Lowell called the magazine "amateurish and effervescent," Pound described it as "scrappy and unselective," "a jolly place for people who aren't quite up to our level." But Margaret remained undaunted, and when more and more readers wrote in with phrases like "What an insouciant little pagan paper," she knew she had an audience.

Landlords and suppliers, alas, had rarely "come suddenly upon the whiteness of Venus in a dim, deep room." One had turned a different kind of white after opening an envelope from Margaret and discovering that in payment of his bill it contained all the money she had—5 cents. But Margaret jubilantly turned adversity into advantage. She had a fascination with poverty based in large part on the fact that she only had to endure it as long as she chose, and a conviction, even when down to her last 5 cents, that "life is beneficent if you insist upon its being so."

And Margaret was nothing if not insistent. *The Little Review* was finally evicted? She'd publish from a tent. Five tents, actually, on the shore of Lake Michigan, with wood floors, cots, deck chairs, and—for there was no reason penury couldn't be elegant—oriental rugs. There Margaret and her assistants would swim in the morning, work on the magazine in the afternoon, roast corn and bake potatoes over campfires, and sleep under the stars. This Gypsy life lasted from May to November 1915, and would have made Margaret a legend in bohemian circles even if two of her most frequent contributors, and two of her best publicists, Ben Hecht and Maxwell Bodenheim, hadn't walked out to her camp from Chicago one afternoon, found her away, and pinned their latest poems to the flap of her tent—a story they never tired of telling.

Margaret's politics were based less on social analysis than on romantic yearnings. "You want free people just as you want the Venus that was modeled by the sea"—that was more or less her credo. "When *will* people stop using that silly superfluous phrase 'free love'? We don't talk about 'cold ice' or black coal'!" "I like monarchies, tyrants, prima donnas, the insane." How could such a woman resist Emma Goldman? Margaret heard Emma lecture just as the third issue of *The Little Review* was about to go to press, and, turning anarchistic on the spot, wrote a stirring article questioning why anyone would want to own property and why people couldn't live as brothers. "Anarchism was the ideal expression for my ideas of freedom and justice," she exulted. And if "art and anarchism are in the world for exactly the same kind of reason," it naturally followed that "I began to find people in my own class vicious, people in clean collars uninteresting. I even accepted smells, personal as well as official."

One smell Margaret couldn't accept was the governor of Utah's refusal to pardon Joe Hill, who had been sentenced to death. When she wrote an editorial concluding, "Why doesn't someone shoot the governor of Utah?" detectives were dissuaded from arresting her only when a friend convinced them she was just a flighty society girl. Subscriptions flooded in, but advertisers didn't particularly like being associated with a magazine that expressed such sentiments, and soon *The Little Review* wasn't just poor, it was broke.

Margaret was less dismayed by the lack of money than by the lack of manuscripts. "I loathe compromising," she wrote in the August 1916 issue. "If there is only one really beautiful thing for the September issue, it shall go in and the other pages left blank." "*The Little Review* hopes to become a Magazine of Art," she explained. "The September issue is offered as a Want Ad."

Perhaps the Chicago Renaissance had run its course.

A year earlier, Margaret had met the wise, tart-tongued Jane Heap, and they soon began an affair that was to last for several years. Prior to Jane, recalled Margaret, "I was a very unrelaxed person . . . and all my sex manifestations were expended to ideas." But one of those "ideas" was adamantly held. "I am no man's wife," Margaret vehemently declared, "no man's delightful mistress, and I will never, never, never be a mother"—a "sex manifestation" that if "unrelaxed" could hardly have been more clear.

"Margaret could never think, never distinguish one thing from another," said a friend. "She could only feel in a glorious haze." Margaret was entranced by Jane's articulate flow of words, paragraph after polished paragraph. "There is no one in the modern world whose conversation I haven't sampled, I believe," said Margaret, "except Picasso's. So I can't say it isn't better than Jane Heap's. But I doubt it in spite of his reputation. . . . Jane Heap is the world's best talker."

But Jane balanced Margaret in other ways as well. Earth to Margaret's fire, and, it must be said, depressive to her hysteric, Jane anchored Margaret's disorganization and dilettantism with a focused and formidable intelligence. Having grown up in mental institutions where her father worked, Jane knew how to deal with writers—she was a writer herself, signing her monthly column "jh"—and as Margaret's assistant, in her dark men's suits and brusque manner, she intimidated anyone who missed a deadline or objected to editorial "suggestions." Even Emma Goldman recoiled at Jane's assertiveness—"I felt," she said, "as if she were pushing me against a wall." Djuna Barnes detected what she called "a deep personal madness" in Jane, to which Margaret briskly replied, "she has a supreme sanity." As for *The Little Review*, "it was all expressed in the formula Jane found," said Margaret, "to express the emotions of life is to live. To express the life of emotions is to make art."

Early in 1917, Margaret and Jane moved to the Village. Margaret had found another angel—Lawrence Langner of the Theater Guild, who gave her the $75 he'd received from *Vanity Fair* for one of his plays, allowing her to say with glee that an uptown magazine had paid her way to the downtown mecca. Margaret and Jane rented a studio apartment at 31 West 14th Street and resumed publication of *The Little Review*, hiring as its printer a Mr. Popovitch, who was not only the cheapest printer in the city but whose mother, or so he claimed, had been the poet laureate of Serbia. Raising money remained a persistent problem—but, as always, "We survived only because I *looked* as if we had money." Still, the magazine continued to grow "more articulate, more interesting," and she regarded the years in the Village as *The Little Review*'s best period.

As for the Village itself, Margaret was frankly disappointed. Mabel Dodge would soon depart for New Mexico, and though Max Eastman was editing *The Liberator* with his sister, Crystal, "He seemed to me," said Margaret, "to lack the fire I wanted to associate with him and his ideas. This was partly due to the fact that he was a socialist. I could never listen to socialists. Anarchism, like all great things, is an announcement. Your 'magnetic center' can do what it likes with that. Socialism is an explanation and falls, consequently, into the realm of secondary things." Margaret shouldn't have been surprised—both she and Max looked at the world with delight, both had the gift of gusto, but Margaret was an incipient mystic while Max was an unrepentant rationalist.

If Margaret couldn't find inspiration in the Village, she'd create her own. She and Jane next moved into a floor-through at 24 West 16th Street, a house in which William Cullen Bryant had once lived, and turned their apartment into a lush garden of exotic decor. They set aside one room "where all *Little Review* conversation would take place," painted the floor dark plum and the woodwork cream, and covered the walls with delicate gold Chinese paper. A large divan, hung from the ceiling by black chains, was covered with four silk cushions, emerald green, magenta, royal purple, and a color few but Margaret knew existed, tilleul.

Alfred Kreymborg came to the gold room with his poems, Maxwell Bodenheim, William Carlos Williams, and the young Hart Crane, whom they not only published, but put to work as an ad salesman. At first, Margaret recalled, the poets, writers, and artists regarded her with distrust—she was "heartless, flippant, ruthless, devastating." They soon realized, however, that these very qualities were partly responsible for her gift as an editor, and within weeks the room was brimming with conversation, "with the feeling that poetry was your religion." Not that Margaret was always so ecumenical. When an earnest young Village woman brought the magazine several stories about the miseries of miners—"and other tragedies of mankind in which she had never participated"—Margaret disabused her of the notion that genius was the capacity for hard work, then suggested that perhaps a little lip rouge would help, on the theory that "beauty may bring you experiences to write about."

The subscription list of *The Little Review* continued to grow, but among its readers were the U.S. postal authorities. In the same month that *The Masses*' mailing privileges were revoked, four thousand copies of Margaret's magazine were seized and burned in an attempt to eradicate from human consciousness a story by Wyndham Lewis called "Cantleman's Spring Mate," in which it was subtly suggested that a young man and a young woman might possibly have had, or were about to have, or were *thinking* about having sexual intercourse. But *The Little Review*'s greatest cause célèbre was James Joyce's *Ulysses*. It sometimes seems that *Field & Stream* is the only magazine never to have claimed it first published Joyce in this country, but the honor belonged to Margaret. "This is the most beautiful thing we'll ever have," she exulted after reading *Ulysses*. We'll print it if it's the last effort of our lives!" And "it almost was," one of her admirers said.

Ulysses came to Margaret from Ezra Pound, whom she'd named European editor—since he was bombarding her with vituperative letters, she might as well put him to work. Pound demanded "ABSOLOOTLY NO INTERFURRENCE," and added that "God willing, I shall make the L.R. a thorn in the face of the older generation, who have labored all their lives to prevent American literature." One older-generation reader complained that "An Ezraized *Little Review* is gargolytic, monstrously so," but this was exactly the response Margaret hoped for. As Jane put it, "We have let Ezra Pound be our foreign editor. . . . We have let him be as foreign as his likes: foreign to taste, foreign to country, foreign to our standards of Art."

Using "tears, prayers, hysterics, or rages" to raise extra money, Margaret began serialization of *Ulysses* in early 1918, and over the course of twenty-three issues ran nearly half the novel. The older generation was heard from once more—"I think this is the most damnable slush and filth that ever polluted paper," ran one letter Margaret was delighted to publish. And the *New York Times*, she recalled with a mixture of rage and gratification, took particular pleasure "in insulting us roundly as purveyors of lascivious literature." But the post office used a much simpler form of literary criticism, confiscating four issues and burning them for alleged obscenity.

In the fall of 1920, the Society for the Suppression of Vice, unsatisfied with the mere destruction of the offending material, brought suit against the Washington Square Book Shop for carrying the issue of *The Little Review* in which the Gertie MacDowell episode in *Ulysses* appeared.

A few days before the trial, Margaret ran into John Sumner, the head of the Society, on 8th Street, apparently in search of smut, and began to berate him for his deplorable lack of taste. To her surprise, she found him charming, even willing to concede a point now and then. Margaret concluded triumphantly, "He was the perfect enemy—I won every point and he seemed to like it!"

Margaret's attorney was John Quinn, who defended many radical causes; he was also a patron of the arts and had given *The Little Review* $750 a year to pay for Ezra Pound's services. "I am not in the defy business but in the law business," Quinn informed Margaret and Jane, pledging them to silence during the trial.

When the prosecuting attorney declared that he was about to have several of the allegedly obscene passages read aloud, one of the three judges awoke from his daily nap to protest that such language should not be uttered in the presence of a lady like Margaret. Perhaps we can assume she is familiar with the offending words, Quinn responded with a sly smile— after all, she is on trial for publishing them. At this point, the presiding judge gave it as his solemn opinion that while Margaret may have published such language, she surely hadn't understood it. When one of the defense witnesses remarked that the novel was in no way capable of corrupting the mind of a young girl, Jane responded—in a remark soon repeated throughout the Village—that if there was anything in the world she feared, it was the mind of a young girl.

In such a courtroom, the verdict was inevitable—guilty, with a fine of $100. As Margaret was led off to be fingerprinted, she demanded soap, eau de cologne, and a towel before she would "submit to such an obscenely repulsive performance."

And in such a country, even the valiant Margaret lost faith. She decided to cease publication of *The Little Review*; the magazine should come to an end with Ulysses, "the epoch's supreme articulation." "Ten years of one's life is enough to devote to one idea," she explained, "unless one has no other ideas." "It might be five years before I would become an interesting person, that is, one who had emerged from her adolescent admirations. Those years I [mean] to spend in my congenital lyricism." But Jane wanted to keep *The Little Review* alive. So Margaret simply gave her the magazine, and from its new offices in Paris, Jane continued producing it first as a quarterly, then as an annual.

Margaret and Jane's personal relationship ended as well. Margaret grew bored with Jane's grumpy depressions, and at a Washington Square salon she met a French singer-pianist name Georgette LeBlanc—who had once been Maurice Maeterlinck's companion—and promptly fell in love. In 1923, the two women joined the exodus from the Village and set sail for France as well. Margaret and Georgette soon became prominent figures in the city's fashionable lesbian set. Then, tiring of Paris, they moved into a country lighthouse overlooking the Seine. "I always thought of myself as the happiest person in the world," Margaret exclaimed—but her happiness was oblivious. Even as the Nazis were preparing to engulf Europe and without a trace of irony, she declaimed, "In the world outside us, the era of personal exaltation had waned."

She had found a satisfying expression for her "congenital lyricism" in the cosmological teachings of Gurdjieff. Her jaunty aestheticism, her delicate outrageousness, her voracious search for ecstasy—they weren't diminished by the end of *The Little Review*, by age, or even by the horrors of the thirties and forties, but expanded to include the universe. "My earthly story with a heavenly meaning," she wrote on the last page of her autobiography, "will go on for me forever."

When Jane folded *The Little Review* in 1929 she wrote in her final editorial, "Self-expression is not enough; experiment is not enough; the recording of special moments or cases is not enough. All the arts have broken faith or lost connection with their origin and function. They have ceased to be concerned with the legitimate and permanent material of art."

The Baroness

Quietly editing manuscripts one day, Margaret Anderson and Jane Heap looked up and saw an apparition. "She wore a red Scotch Plaid suit with a kilt hanging just below the knees," Margaret recalled, "bolero jacket with sleeves to the elbows, and arms covered with a quantity of ten-cent store bracelets—silver, gilt, bronze, green, and yellow." Even more striking were her enormous earrings of tarnished silver and the high white spats with a band of decorative furniture braid around the tops. But most remarkable were the long ice cream soda spoons dangling from the black velvet tam o'shanter on her head, and the two tea balls hanging from her bust.

After a long silence, the apparition finally spoke. "I have sent you a poem," she said in a thick German accent. "Yes," replied Jane, sorting through a stack of manuscripts and pulling out one signed "Tara Osrik." "How you know I wrote that poem?" the woman asked. "I," said Jane, with something close to haughtiness, "am not entirely without imagination."

So began the long association between *The Little Review* and the Baroness Elsa von Freytag-Loringhoven, whom everyone simply called the Baroness. Margaret and Jane told her the poem was beautiful, that they'd be using it in the magazine, that they wanted to see more of her work. After the Baroness had left, they discovered that she'd pilfered $5 worth of 2-cent stamps that had been lying on a table. "Knowing her as we did later," recalled Margaret, "it is safe to assume that she used them not for postal but for decorative purposes."

The assumption was correct, for on several occasions pedestrians were astonished to see a woman striding past them with pink 2-cent stamps pasted on her cheeks. The Baroness may have been an exquisite poet—one of the most gifted of the American Dadaists—but it was her flamboyant costumes that made her a Village legend. Only a few years after Henrietta Rodman had caused a scandal by appearing in public in bobbed hair, loose gowns, and sandals, the Baroness made such "dress reform" seem almost . . . Midwestern.

Sometimes, in a casual mood, the Baroness would stroll the streets in nothing but a Mexican blanket, sometimes she'd simply add a peacock fan (or Kewpie dolls or stuffed birds or cigarette premiums), but far more often she felt like dressing up. Standing in front of her mirror, admiring her black lipstick and bright yellow face powder, or the way she'd made up one half of her face in blue, the other half in red, she'd find something new to wear—the black dress made from crepe from a funeral parlor, with a wooden bird cage around her neck, a live canary chirping inside, or perhaps a bustle nicely accessorized by a battery-operated taillight. "Cars and bicycles have tail lights," the Baroness rationalized with strident gaiety, "why not I? Also, people won't bump into me in the dark." Now for the hat: the inverted coal scuttle? the chocolate cake complete with lit candles? the kitchen colander trimmed with carrots, beets, perhaps a couple of peppers?

But none of these outlandish costumes could compete with the Baroness's signature gesture—an event noted by nearly every memoirist of the period. She shellacked her skull and painted it purple. "Shaving one's head is like having a new love experience," she explained to Margaret. "It's better when I'm nude," and she promptly demonstrated.

Her colorful costumes were intended as a form of art, and her tall, lanky body was a canvas upon which she arrayed all kinds of bizarre materials. She created sculpture out of detritus as well—tinfoil, ironware, automobile tires, ash cans, bits of garbage, "horrors which to her highly sensitized perception," said an admirer, "became objects of formal beauty." With this juxtaposition of dissimilar forms, the elevation of the ordinary into the realm of art, the Baroness was one of the first artists to utilize "found objects," though "found" might be expanded to include "stolen." On more than one occasion visitors to her apartment were surprised to see, hanging on her sculptures, pieces of jewelry or other valuables that'd been unaccountably missing since the Baroness had visited *them*.

The Baroness actually was a baroness. She was the widow of a titled German businessman who'd come to New York in the early years of the century, lived in a suite at the Ritz Hotel, returned to Germany during the war, and soon after committed suicide in protest against his homeland's barbarism. Some said the Baroness was Danish, some Bulgarian, some Estonian. She encouraged the mystery, of course, but, in fact, she was born Elsa Ploetz, in 1874, in Germany, to a German father and a Polish mother. In her teens, she fled to Berlin to escape "the bourgeois harness of respectability," and became a prominent figure in artistic and literary circles while supporting herself by stripping in high-toned variety shows.

The experience proved valuable when the Baroness found herself alone and destitute in New York. Forced to move from the Ritz to a series of shabby, unheated apartments in the Village, she worked as a nude model for Robert Henri, George Bellows, and George Biddle. According to Biddle, she had "the body of a Greek ephebe, with small firm breasts, narrow hips, and long smooth shanks." Even in the nude the Baroness had a decorative imagination. Biddle recounted the day she undressed for him and revealed two tomato cans over her nipples and between them a small bird cage with "a crestfallen canary."

Every day between five and six, the Baroness walked her dogs in Washington Square Park. On several occasions, the police arrested her for . . . well, the charge was unclear, but the concept of "indecent exposure" was stretched to include her costumes. Angered at such restraint, Margaret recalled, "she leaped from patrol wagons with such agility that the policemen let her go in admiration." Tired of her tiny apartment, she asked a friend for a room in her much larger flat, then berated her friend for not moving out and leaving the place to her. Tired of not eating, the Baroness found work in a cigarette factory, "where she provoked such wrath" — Margaret again — "that one of her co-workers in a rage reminiscent of Bizet knocked out two of her side teeth. Oddly enough," Margaret added, "this did not detract from her distinction."

Not all the Baroness's anecdotes ended in contretemps, however. In one favorite story, a painter brought her a newspaper clipping of Marcel Duchamp's notorious *Nude Descending a Staircase*. He recalled that she "took the clipping. And gave herself a rubdown with it, missing no part of her anatomy" — allowing one Village wit to remark that "this must have been the one time Duchamp's 'Staircase' descended a nude."

But if most Villagers regarded the Baroness as nothing more than an aristocratic eccentric, a few considered her an accomplished poet. According to Margaret, she was "the only figure of our generation who deserved the epithet extraordinary." The Baroness was certainly a *prolific* poet, but the following excerpt from a poem entitled "Mineself—Minesoul—and—Mine—Cast—Iron Lover," published in *The Little Review* in 1919, can be called representative:

> *His hair is molten gold and a red pelt—*
> *His hair is glorious!*
> *Yea—mine soul—and he brushed it and combeth it—he maketh it* shining and glistening around his head—and he is vain about it—but alas—mine soul—his hair is without sense—the hair does not live—it is no revelation, no symbol! HE is not gold—not animal—not GOLDEN animal—he is GILDED animal only—mine soul! His vanity is without sense—it is the vanity of one who has little and who weareth a treasure meaningless! O—mine soul!—THAT soulless beauty maketh me sad! . . . we will play again that old WONDERFUL play of the "TWOTOGETHER"!—mine soul—if thus it will be willst thou flare around him—about him—over him—hide him with shining curtain—his that song of savage joy—starry eyes— —willst thou heat—melt—make quiver—break down— dissolve—build up— —SHAKE HIM—SHAKE HIM—O mine starry-eyed soul?
> *Heia! Ja-hoho! hisses mine starry-eyed soul in her own language.*
> *I see mine soul—we still understand each other!* I LOVE THEE *thou very great darling! we must wait and smile— —*PERHAPS SARDONICALLY— — —*mine very great soul— — —because we now are artists— — —and:* NOTHING MATTERS!!!

Despite the Baroness's best efforts, Man Ray wrote Tristan Tzara in 1921 that "Dada cannot live in New York," and enclosed a nude photograph of the Baroness to illustrate his point. Her legs formed the letter A in the word "l'amerique," and the picture was topped by several repetitions of the word "merdelamerde" in case Tzara should miss the point. The photograph was a still from a movie Ray had made for Marcel Duchamp in which Ray portrayed a barber shaving off the Baroness's pubic hair—a symbol of the death of Dada ("the mother of American Dada" losing the hair over her womb) that was rendered even more symbolic by the loss of the movie in the developing process.

Dada may have been dead in New York, but the Baroness, according to one observer, continued to act as if her "whole life was Dada." She once showed Biddle one of her "color poems," a portrait of Marcel Duchamp painted on a piece of celluloid, his face indicated by an electric light bulb from which hung icicles, and including "large pendulous ears and other symbols." "You see," she haughtily explained, "he is so tremendously in love with me." "And the ears?" Biddle asked. "Genitals," the Baroness replied, "the emblem of his frightful and creative potency." "And the incandescent electric bulb?" The Baroness, recalled Biddle, curled her lip in scorn. "Because he is so frightfully cold. You see, all his heat flows into his art."

Duchamp, in fact, did *not* love the Baroness—as any Village Freudian could have guessed, it was the other way around. She confirmed this herself when she recited one of her latest poems at a gathering of New York Dadaists. "Marcel, Marcel. I love you like Hell, Marcel." Indeed, the Baroness confessed that from her teens she had been "mansick up to my eartips—no, over the top of my head, permeating my brain, stabbing out my eyeballs."

The Baroness in love was a frightening phenomenon. So frightening that one Villager called her a "nymphomaniac"—a label they applied to women who not only advocated free love, but went so far as to enjoy it. William Zorach, one of the designers for the Provincetown Players, was undressing in his apartment one evening when she suddenly scrambled out from beneath his bed, stark naked. Zorach fled into the night. Wallace Stevens, after one meeting with the Baroness, said he never ventured south of 14th Street for years for fear of meeting her again. One afternoon Hart Crane was on his way to her apartment to get the typewriter she'd borrowed, when, on second thought, he decided to buy a new one instead.

George Biddle, one man who did succumb, escaped to tell the tale. "She looked at me through her blue-white crazy eyes," he recalled. "She said, 'Are you afraid to let me kiss you?' I knew she was suffering agony. I shrugged my shoulders and said, 'Why not, Elsa?' She smiled faintly, emerging from her nightmare. Enveloping me slowly, as a snake would its prey, she glued her wet lips on mine. I was shaking all over when I left the dark stairway and came out on 14th Street."

But the man who most permeated the Baroness's brain was William Carlos Williams. One day, visiting Margaret and Jane, Bill noticed, under a glass bell, "a piece of sculpture that appeared to be chicken guts, possibly imitated in wax." Told that the sculptor was an ardent admirer of his poetry, Bill made the fatal mistake of sending her a complimentary letter and asking to meet her. Learning that she was in the Women's House of Detention on Sixth Avenue for stealing an umbrella, he gallantly paid her bail and took her to breakfast at a nearby café.

He was so strongly impressed that he visited her at her 14th Street apartment, where two of her dogs were copulating on her bed, and where he compounded his error by telling her he had fallen in love with her. The Baroness confessed she had fallen in love with him as well, and suggested that to liberate his poetic imagination all he needed to do was contract syphilis from her. Perhaps he wasn't in love with her after all. On further reflection, he remembered that he was married. He politely excused himself and, like Zorach, fled into the night.

But the Baroness was not to be deterred, and deluged Bill with calls and letters, in one of which she enclosed a nude photograph of herself taken by Marcel Duchamp. "He might have stopped it," said Margaret, "by treating her like a human being (as Duchamp did) and convincing her that it was no use. But instead he acted like a small boy and wrote her insulting letters in which his panic was all too visible." The Baroness complained to Margaret that "he brought me peaches and now he won't look at me. Not just peaches—they were ripe peaches. Are American men really so naive as that?"

By now, Bill was so terrified that he planned to flee to Europe, but the Baroness traveled to his home in New Jersey, sat in his car, and arranged to have him called away to treat a sick baby—Williams being a doctor as well as a poet. Bill threatened to call the police—whereupon, according to one version of the story, she threw open her coat, disclosed that she was naked, and moaned, "Villiam Carlos Villiams, I vant you." All accounts agree that when Bill demurred, the Baroness smashed him on the neck and departed in a rage. He was a coward, she told Margaret. He was ignoble. He didn't understand what a great poet she might have made of him. And in a review of one of his collections in *The Little Review*, she accused him of bourgeois sentimentality and sexual timidity, and asserted that he lacked skill at juggling.

Nevertheless, the Baroness decided to give Bill a second chance. This time he was prepared—he had purchased a punching bag and had been working out regularly—and when she began to hit him, he "flattened her with a stiff punch to the mouth," and followed through on his threat to call the police. "What are you in this town, Napoleon?" she screeched, but her mood soon changed. She'd never do it again, she promised from prison, and Bill, in order to make her keep her promise, gave her $200 to leave the country—and another $200 a few weeks later when she informed him the first had been "stolen." The Baroness, of course, failed to keep her promise, but Bill—though confessing that he was still infatuated—kept his and never saw her again.

Another writer drawn into the Baroness's sticky web was Djuna

Barnes, but the two women managed to get beyond their first awkward encounter. On being introduced to Djuna at the offices of *The Little Review*, the Baroness exclaimed, "I cannot read your stories, Djuna Barnes. I don't know where your characters come from. You make them fly on magic carpets. What is worse, you try to make pigs fly." Though the Baroness never recanted her opinion, Djuna eventually became one of the most ardent champions of her poetry, and served as her major source of support during the final years of her life.

Village tolerance allowed countless eccentrics to express their individuality, but in a few cases, such as the Baroness's, tolerance turned into celebration that locked idiosyncratic personalities into the roles of "characters" and thwarted their creativity. The poor Baroness never had a chance in America, for everything she did was instantly transformed into anecdote.

In 1923—"her spirit withering in the sordid materialism of New York," recalled Biddle, and feeling that she had not long to live— the Baroness returned to Germany with the help of a small fund raised by friends. Ironically, when she arrived in the flourishing Dada scene of Europe, few thought of her as anything but a dotty old lady. She was institutionalized twice, forced to sell newspapers on street corners to make enough to eat, and in 1926, virtually friendless and penniless, moved to Paris when Djuna sold her own annotated manuscript of *Ulysses*, given to her by Joyce himself, to provide her with a small pension.

Her heart had become "an abode of terror and a snake—" the Baroness wrote Djuna from Germany. "I need, for a few quiet hours— human sympathy—talk—love—in my terrible plight. . . . —I am badgered about as if I had been a culprit. . . . I will probably yes, yes, yes, probably have to die. All persons who are ruthlessly lonely—must be mad. I have always been thus."

For years Djuna kept a portrait of the Baroness on her mantel, and the Baroness's words, she said, lingered in her memory long after everyone else's had disappeared. Indeed, she used excerpts from her letters as an obituary in the February 1928 issue of *Transition*.

"On the fourteenth of December, she wrote, "sometime in the night, Elsa von Freytag-Loringhoven came to her death by gas. . . . She was, as a woman, amply appreciated by those who had loved her in youth, mentally she was never appropriately appreciated. A few of her verses saw print, many did not. I now give parts, as they make a monument to this her inappropriate end, in the only fitting language which could reveal it, her own."

Some of the Baroness's friends suspected suicide, a few even suspected murder, but most felt like Djuna that it was a bizarre accident—"a stupid joke that had not even the decency of maliciousness."

Robert Clairmont

Robert Clairmont—as a Villager once said, and as he himself was fond of repeating—burned his money at both ends. If the Village of the teens had been an enclave where young men and women could find a life free from middle-class striving and materialistic values, where they could dedicate themselves to art, to anarchism, to feminism, to any movement that promised the total transformation of American society, in the twenties it was a district of frivolity and self-indulgence. If the quintessential Villager of the teens was an impoverished rebel, in the twenties it was a millionaire playboy—a role Robert Clairmont played with gusto and panache.

The Village had become the center of the city's bootlegging. The poetess was replaced by the prostitute. The gaiety had a shrill edge, a kind of enforced spontaneity. The speakeasies and parties and nightclubs were patronized primarily by well-to-do businessmen and adventurous uptown couples on a night out. In popular iconography, the Village was no longer a place one lived, but a place one went.

Villagers might have become decadent, but it was an innocent decadence—they hadn't lapsed into cynicism. They no longer believed in causes or movements, but continued to believe in irresponsibility and good times. In short, they were now as American as anyone else, and Robert Clairmont became their exemplary figure. "Come on," was Bob's motto, "we've got to try everything before they nail me in the eternity box."

Bob had made his fortune, everyone in the Village believed, when as a handsome teenage lifeguard at the Pittsburgh Athletic Club he saved a steel magnate named Sellers McKees Chandler from drowning, and, a few years later, an orphan working his way through college as a soda jerk, received a letter notifying him that Chandler had died and left him all his money. There was a grain of truth in the story—if teaching a man how to swim could be said to save him from drowning, and if $500,000 could be called "all the money" of one of the richest men in America. Bob thought of himself as a poet, but with half a million dollars he saw no reason why he couldn't be a stock market investor as well, and when he arrived in the Village in 1926, he was an unknown poet but a millionaire many times over.

Bob paid perfunctory attention to his stock market holdings. "It's a good thing I kept on sleeping through the clock again this morning," he once mentioned to a friend. "I was going to sell. Instead, I've got a few thousand extra bucks." No matter how much he spent today, he always seemed to have more tomorrow, and he was not a man who kept careful track of his spending. He became so rich that he could afford to adopt the unmercenary attitude that "If he woke in the morning, it was wealth enough."

But Bob's nonchalance was deeper than his wallet. He had a streak of true bohemianism, regarding his wealth as an opportunity to indulge his whims. Within a few weeks, the entire Village knew about the rich poet in the luxurious apartment at West 4th Street who, said a friend, "was like a sieve through which Wall Street poured money." A downtown Gatsby, Bob bought suits by the dozen and when his bed linen ran out, he'd take it to the local laundry and buy a new set while awaiting its return. He chartered taxis by the day, purchased tickets for plays and concerts in blocks, and sent telegrams announcing, "Will arrive in half an hour."

But what impressed Villagers even more than Bob's free spending on himself was his open wallet with others. Writers or painters low on cash had only to show up at his restaurant table for a free meal. Fellow poets unable to meet their rent found it paid three months in advance. Anyone eager for an evening on Broadway or the Harlem clubs had only to join his entourage, and discovered that he tipped the orchestra leader the equivalent of a month's rent to play his favorite songs. And any Village woman "in trouble" had only to let Bob know and he discreetly paid her "hospital" bill. So generous was Bob that he became a kind of weird hybrid of St. Francis and the Pied Piper.

Max Bodenheim was first in line but, as one of Bob's friends said, the moment he stepped out of his apartment, "artists popped from manholes, tumbled down doorways, and flowed from waterspouts." Potential editors of potential magazines appeared on his doorstep—everything was in place but potential cash. Playwrights needed only a small production to become the next O'Neill, women needed only a polite introduction to become the first Mrs. Clairmont; all but the latter succeeded in their appeal. Bob was greeted everywhere with outbursts of hyperbolic affection he always saw through but never resented. He didn't even begrudge those who, unwilling to humiliate themselves by begging, forged his name on their checks.

The few Freudians remaining in the Village speculated that Bob's generosity was motivated by guilt over his ill-gotten gains, but as far as Bob was concerned, they could hardly be ill-gotten, having simply fallen into his lap, and he seemed too sunny to have any dark corners in his psyche.

Even the largesse he empathetically lavished upon impoverished poets and hungry painters couldn't be given such a grand label as "motivation." He didn't behave as a one-man foundation or as a haughty patron promoting an aesthetic agenda, or as a moralizing welfare worker. Bob merely took pleasure in giving money to anyone who needed it.

As he once explained his philosophy of philanthropy, "It is a battle. . . . You listen. . . . The cause seems good. . . . Yes, it sounded good. Yes, it's probably true. . . . You can't get away, you can't run. . . . YES: NO. YES: NO. Your hand goes into your pocket."

What particularly appealed to him about the bohemians of the Village, recalled a friend, was "the very candor of their self-interest." He might graciously give half a grand to an actor or a composer or a novelist with a cock-and-bull story he saw through after half a sentence—"It'll make no difference in a billion years," he'd say with a shrug—but most Villagers understood that they'd be just as successful with a straightforward story. He mused, "It's mostly some slight sum—five or ten dollars—a real crisis runs about a hundred. I think I'd like a person who asked for a Steinway Grand or a trip to Asia." Once, when Bob entered a Village restaurant, a willowy woman asked him, before he could even sit down, "Are you alone?" Replied Bob with a wry smile, "never for long."

Bob soon became even more renowned for his Village parties—nonstop affairs lasting two, even four days, open to anyone who showed up at his unlocked apartment, and often continuing long after the host himself had left on a business trip or for a weekend in the country. "The lost tribes of the American Montparnasse passed through his rooms," recalled one of his friends. He'd simply tell a few friends he was in the mood for another shindig, word would get around that everyone was welcome—everyone but "rich dullards," that is—and the saturnalia began.

A young nightclub dancer would stand in front of a crowded couch carrying a lapful of glasses in her skirt. The poet Eli Siegel would entertain the guests with a shrieking rendition of Vachel Lindsay's "Congo." In one corner, a group would gather around Bob's phone, shouting to friends in Europe or California over the hubbub, while in another, a tall, almost catatonic young man in full Indian war regalia would stand impassively for hours. In the bedrooms, recalled one partygoer, couples would lie on the pile of coats "theorizing about or practicing love."

One inevitable feature was a 3:00 or 4:00 A.M. phone call from the local precinct ("What unearthly racket?") or an appearance by a couple of policemen on the beat. "Cops!" someone would call out, and Bob would gently explain that his friends would soon be leaving, that he was genuinely sorry he'd troubled his neighbors, and that here, perhaps a hundred dollars would make up for any inconvenience he might have caused the officers.

On one memorable night, according to the breezy memoir by Tom Boggs, Bob's idolatrous friend and unreliable Boswell, "Three young men were loudly discussing the subtleties of James Joyce, two girls had to cup their hands to their ears to catch the unrepeatable things Adolf Dehn was telling them, and a serious-faced gentleman was prowling around on all fours with an occasional plaintive 'Yark?' There was a cacophony of dishes in the kitchen, there were splashes of laughter from the 'opium bunks' and from pairings-off in the other rooms. Suddenly an attractive young woman in a short skirt and tight sweater loudly announced, 'Somebody's stolen my garters.' Bottles, books, cups, and glasses were set down and everyone joined in merry search. Finally, the garters were discovered in the bathroom, pinkly smiling from a large mirror to which they had been securely nailed." By dawn, several partygoers had dozed off or fallen into a drunken stupor on the bathroom floor. Then everyone would revive, open another case of liquor, and the whirl would resume. "Still the Caliph of Washington Square, Bob could see no way to abdicate."

The genial host would often leave in the middle of the festivities to drop in on another party, return a couple of hours later, make sure that the liquor hadn't run out, then leave again to take in a movie at the 8th Street Cinema. On one occasion, Bob bumped into an attractive young woman who was just leaving. "I've swiped two quarts of Scotch," she said, not recognizing her host. "There's plenty more—get yourself some, big boy, and meet me outside." So Bob hid two more quarts of his own Scotch in his fur coat and rejoined her. When Bob would return after two or three hours to find his apartment packed with revelers, he'd walk over to the Brevoort and take a room for the night. The Villagers began to say that if the lights were on at Bob's, he must be out.

Bob was obviously popular with the bootleggers. His greatest contribution to bohemia, wrote one chronicler of the period, was introducing fine vintage to the Village. There were always five-gallon jugs of cheap wine at every party—just in case the good stuff ran out—but every couple of hours he'd dial the local speakeasy for another case of fine wine or Imperial Scotch, his credit being even better than his cash.

Since Bob's presence wasn't necessary at Bob's parties, when he went out of town, Villagers would congregate at his well-stocked apartment and phone out for extra supplies in his name. Nothing could abuse his hospitality—not the three-figure long-distance phone calls, the telegrams charged to his account, not the broken crockery and appliances or the cigarette burns in his carpets, the missing shirts and ties, the purloined jewelry, not the antique chairs burned for firewood, not even the rare books that he would find in a Fourth Avenue shop, his signature on the flyleaf.

Only once did one of Bob's parties leave a sobering aftertaste. Among Bob's multitude of friends was the artist Hans Stengel, who had served in the German army during World War I and who, in Bunny Wilson's words, "cultivated . . . something of the imperious manner . . . of the traditional Prussian officer." Hans had a gift for mordant caricature that might have made him a widely recognized artist in another country at another time, but in America in the twenties he was reduced to hackwork to support himself—for a time he was the principal cartoonist for the Sunday *Herald Tribune*. According to Bunny: "He astounded even the inhabitants of Greenwich Village—by no means free, despite their reputation, from the pervasive indifference and tepidity of contemporary American life—by the violence of his despairs and exhilarations."

Despair had the upper hand on the night of January 26, 1928, when Hans hosted a party at Bob's apartment. Bob was in the country and knew nothing about the party, and when he returned home, he found his apartment in an even greater shambles than usual. Bookcases had been tipped over, his closets had been emptied. Must have been quite a blowout, he thought idly, until he learned what had happened.

Hans's guests arrived to find the apartment filled with tall black candles. Shortly after midnight, one of his friends knocked on the bathroom door, and opened it to discover Hans hanging from the door frame by a belt. To memorialize his suicide, Hans had drawn a caricature of himself hanging, with his tongue lolling out. The tragedy left the entire Village in shock for weeks, and even Bob—carefree, imperturbable Bob—decided it was time to move.

Bob moved to several apartments simultaneously—one at 61 Perry Street in the Village, another on West 72nd Street, another near Columbia University, and yet another on Edgecombe Avenue in Harlem. Each had a fully stocked wardrobe and kitchen and liquor cabinets. All he really needed, he explained, was a place for a change of shirts between Wall Street and Harlem. But he added, "no matter what part of town I'm in, I like to be near home." As he explained to his friend Duke Ellington, "I simply have to go places, and get so tired there'll be no place I want to go."

For a brief moment, he soured on the Village, uncharacteristically complaining about the hangers-on and leeches. "There is no rest for the rich—and weary," he said. "I really should wear some sort of disguise. They all dive at me like a fresh corpse in the jungle." He even went so far as to put a lock on the door of the Perry Street apartment.

One night, Bob was enjoying a rare quiet evening at home, when the theater producer John Rose Gildea burst in from the kitchen and exclaimed, "Clear out the place, boys! . . . Tonight . . . the future of the American stage will look, not to Broadway, but to Perry Street. For your instruction, . . . I have arranged an all-night vaudeville I guarantee to—"

"Hold it a minute," Bob interrupted. "How did you get in here? The door is locked!" "Well, if you must know," answered John, rather pleased with himself, "through the coal chute." "And who is paying for this spectacle?" inquired Bob. John tossed bills and coins onto the dining room table. "I'll give you double what's there," countered Bob, "if you disappear right now." But John persisted, and the "all-night vaudeville" proceeded.

It soon dawned on Bob that the inebriated and increasingly uncoordinated performers thought they were auditioning for a nonexistent Broadway show he was backing. "Leave your name and address," John told each of the performers at the end of their act, "and I'll notify you of Mr. Clairmont's opinion in a few days." Mr. Clairmont's opinion was already perfectly clear to most of them, for they couldn't help but notice that he'd quietly disappeared during a dog act. At the end of the evening, when a friend knocked on the upstairs bedroom door and suggested, "Come down, Bob, they're all gone," a woman's voice came through the door—"He's asleep."

Bob decided to move "the perpetual party" to a twenty-four-hour-a-day greasy spoon cafeteria called Hubert's Sheridan Square. Garishly lit, featuring a dark brown sludge called "coffee" at 5 cents a cup, Hubert's was little more than a hangout for all-night cabbies and local drunks working off their hangovers, but within a few weeks it had become the most popular meeting place south of 14th Street.

Hubert, hard-nosed businessman, initially expressed displeasure at the invasion of those "crazy artists," who were more interested in cadging money from Bob than in spending it on food. But when limousines showed up bearing Bob's friends from uptown, and when Walter Winchell arrived to check out the scene at the Village's "Two Maggots," Hubert raised the price of a cup of coffee to 10 cents, asked Bob for tips on the market, and instructed his cashier to seat the most picturesque customers at the front window—including the "socialite" dressed in nothing but her fur coat and a negligee.

Though now a patron of the arts, Hubert still had his headaches. Some of the "characters" bothered his paying customers by trying to sell books they'd just purchased as rare editions, or by passing notes that read, "I am a Poet, and I owe Hubert twenty-five cents for my coffee and sandwich. He won't let me out of here unless the bill is paid. I will write you a sonnet if you will give me a quarter." As one Village wit put it, "It was remarkable that their fare never exceeded twenty-five cents: perhaps they were aware of the maximum worth of their sonnets." After one of the "crazy artists" hurled a brick through the plate glass window, Hubert had to hire a bouncer — surely the first bouncer ever employed by a cafeteria.

The dynamic of even the most egalitarian subculture invariably creates an inner circle, and Bob's back table at Hubert's was a kind of downtown Algonquin Circle called the Greta Garbo Social Club. The club had its marginal members — including a former lieutenant of the Northumberland Fusiliers, now an occasional theater critic, with the imposing nom de plume Baron Charles Amadee Grivat de Grandcourt, and its lone woman, the poet Mary Carolyn Davis, who'd once been a bronco buster in the gold-mining camps of the Northwest and who was now renowned for writing spontaneous couplets on the cuffs of her dancing partners — but its three permanent fixtures, in addition to Bob and Tom, were the poets Maxwell Bodenheim, Eli Siegel, and John Rose Gildea.

Maxwell Bodenheim became the archtypical poet-bum of the Village. Eli Siegel was one of those poets unfortunate enough to become so well known for a single poem — "Hot Afternoons Have Been in Montana" — that the rest of his considerable body of work remained unknown. Showing his dark good looks to best advantage by always dressing in white, he was a bookish bohemian, with a stentorian, almost biblical style. As a kind of guru in the fifties, he formed a Village cult called Aesthetic Realism, based on the premise that "all opposites are alike." And John Rose Gildea had studied for the priesthood but had found a more congenial calling working for a theater producer. Long-haired and wild-faced, he often wore a red leather outfit and black hat, sported a diamond nose ring, and hung a tire chain around his neck with a glass doorknob attached.

The avowed purpose of the Greta Garbo Social Club was to give the acclaimed actress a chance to meet its members, and in case such an opportunity failed to materialize, to accept whatever other attractive young women might be willing to serve as her substitute. Its more obvious purpose was to carouse and to boast of sexual conquests — usually in anticipation rather than in the aftermath. But its *real* purpose was to form an inner circle so that one could say one belonged to an inner circle.

Even Bob grew bored of so much revelry, so, in the early spring of 1927, he decided to publish a small-format magazine called *New Cow of*

Greenwich Village (A Monthly Periodical Sold on the Seven Arts as Such).
Though the project had a hint of merriment—volume 1, number 1 appeared on April Fool's Day—his lead editorial expressed sentiments about
Hubert's artistic clientele that must have astonished them. "This editor's
dislike of the poets panhandling in Hubert's restaurant is mainly because
the forms are all so hackneyed," wrote Bob—what some might call biting
the hands he fed. "There are so many poets every night in Hubert's one
does not believe there are that many. The millennium will arrive when the
uptown laundered go to the counter and order a soft boiled lyric or sonnet
with cold rimes. Then Art will not only meet but eat at Hubert's." *New Cow*
was fully expected to operate in the red, but such was Bob's uncanny good
luck that even this short-lived venture turned a profit.

Bob's seriousness about poetry was revealed when he allowed
nearly everyone into his circle—the most blatant hypocrites, the most egre-
gious freeloaders—except his rich peers and pretentious poets. When it
came to his own poetry, he had to hide his wealth because no one would
have believed he got it published on merit alone. He was, in fact, a passable
poet, and in 1928, the Dial Press bought out a collection called *Quintillions*—his pleasure that the publishers didn't know he could have financed
the book with his pocket change was matched only by their chagrin when
they learned the truth.

"Sadness Couplet," the first poem in the book, showed an unsuspected side of Bob's feelings.

> *They tell who walk in love and all alone*
> *A mechanical piano has a sadness all its own.*

And those who joined in his crowded entourage must have been a bit bewildered to read:

> *There are much too many people:*
> *And, then again, not enough . . .*

Melancholy lines from a man renowned for his merriment. For
there remained one aspect of Bob's life not even his closest friends could
comprehend—his curious reluctance to get involved with a woman. Oh,
there were hundreds of women, but never *a* woman. When flattered by his
friends about his "successes," Bob moved from back-slapping camaraderie
to blasé savoir faire to indifference to something close to ruefulness. He was
simply looking for the perfect girl, he'd say. And who could blame him?

Soon, the suspicion grew that he was difficult to please. "I don't want to be tied down to even a Romanoff princess so early in the game." Overtly envious, his friends became covertly exasperated. Maybe Bob was growing disillusioned, maybe Bob was sated, or maybe Bob was homosexual.

Bob's uncharacteristic secretiveness, his eventual outbursts of exasperation when questioned too closely—none of it confirmed that he was a member of what the Villagers called "the nether sex," but it was consistent with the behavior of the "confirmed bachelors." Of course it's questionable to assert, as so many Village Freudians did then and do now, that one's deepest impulses are the opposite of one's most visible behavior—for if Bob's "wenching" can be interpreted as an obvious sign of his secret homosexuality, can Henry James's chaste deportment be interpreted as an obvious sign of his secret "wenching"? Nevertheless, Bob's protestations did have the peculiar elusiveness of a man pretending to partially conceal one part of his life so he can wholly conceal another. And those dozens of abortions he paid for? Why did none of the women claim he was responsible for their pregnancies? Remember, too, the millionaire's bequest of $500,000 to the handsome young lifeguard . . .

Partying, drinking, "wenching"—like the twenties, Bob seemed embarked on an endless bender. Even after years of spending his money as fast as he could, he was wealthier than when he'd arrived. Yet in the midst of the revelry, he had a foreboding of what was to come. "If my money ever goes . . ." he once told Tom, "I suppose I can make a living by selling postcards to my visitors." At times that prospect almost appealed to him. "You know," he told a friend wistfully, "this life of pleasure is *hard*."

Bob awoke in the late afternoon of Monday, October 29, 1929, casually called his broker, and with a nonchalant shrug realized the spree was over. He'd lost a good deal of his fortune and by the end of the day he'd lost it all. "It was Red Monday, Tuesday, Wednesday, Thursday, Friday, Saturday, and Sunday, too," he told a reporter from the *New York Telegram*. "Wall Street was flooded in red ink, and I happened not to have my water wings along."

"Poet Rhymes Himself Out of Million," "Spent $10,000 on Party Once—Now Broke," "Art Patron Loses Millions," read the headlines from Dallas to San Francisco. Bob received hundreds of consoling letters, even checks from the hundreds of people he'd helped. A Rhode Island woman sent him a basket of candies and cigarettes, which he shared with the members of the Greta Garbo Social Club. A woman in Pennsylvania sent him a money order, a woman in Oklahoma sent him another; he turned them over to a welfare shelter. A wealthy widow from Australia sent him passionate poems, and he even received an all-expenses-paid invitation from a love cult in Palo Alto, California.

But Bob and his cronies had one last spree. On New Year's Eve, 1929, when he was down to his last $1,000, the members of the Greta Garbo Social Club trooped into a tavern on Broadway and West 41st Street decked in fake ermine robes and gold cardboard crowns. After draining two black bottles of Irish whiskey, they piled into a taxi, shouting "Webster Hall!"— the site of *The Masses'* balls, of the Village's annual Pagan Routs: that was their destination.

"To the blare of trumpets and the thud of kingly drums, we were led to the center of the floor. Blue, green, white, and red curtains of light played over us. Then, as the orchestra broke into Ellington's 'East St. Louis Toodle-oo,' we were whirled away into the dance."

The rumor soon spread through the Village that Bob had been seen on a breadline. He *was* on a breadline, but as a temporary city employee passing out food vouchers to the destitute. "It could be plenty worse," he said. "I might have had to try selling apples at a medical convention. After all, there is a certain philosophical satisfaction in counting loaves of bread. Suppose there was [none] to count?"

"The perpetual party" abruptly came to an end, and Bob never looked back. Well, once. Recalling his Village days in a mood somewhere between resignation and resentment, he complained, "It cost me $800,000 to learn that the only art which mattered vitally to those apostles of aesthetics was the art of getting dollars for nothing. Education is rather expensive, isn't it?" But Bob accepted his fate philosophically, edited a poetry magazine called *Pegasus* for a couple of years, and lived quietly on the Upper West Side for decades.

Harry Kemp

The unkempt Harry Kemp now thumps our door:
He who has girdled all the world and more.
Free as a bird, no trammels him can bind.
He rides a boxcar as a hawk in the wind:
A rough, thin face, a rugged flow of words.—
A Man, who with ideal himself begirds . . .
Here's to you, HARRY, in whatever spot!
True poet, whether writing it or not.

—JACK REED, from "The Day in Bohemia"

Tall, broad-shouldered, and robust, Harry Kemp strode through the streets of the Village, filling his lungs with the intoxicating air of Bohemia. Harry had a gift—not so much for poetry as for the poet's life—not so much for self-expression as for self-dramatization. So deeply did he believe that he was "the greatest poet since John Keats" that the Villagers came to believe it, too. The King of Bohemia, he was called, the Byron of the Village!

Harry collected appellations the way poets of later generations collected grants. Unkempt Harry Kemp—that's the one no one could avoid. The Don Juan of the Village—that's the one he tried his hardest to earn. But the ones that describe him best and pleased him most evoke an era as forgotten as his verses: the Vagabond Poet, the Tramp Poet, the Hobo Poet. No wonder the Villagers of the teens and twenties, so contemptuous of the conventional, were as enamored of Harry's poetry as he was himself.

Born in Youngstown, Ohio, in 1883, he was the only child of a mother who soon died of consumption and a father who left him with his grandmother, an impoverished, nearly illiterate, but generous soul of whom he remembered little but her kindness to peddlers and tramps. Abandoned to his imagination, Harry was a bookish boy, reading Darwin, Shelley, Whitman, and especially Byron. Oh, what a god stared out at him from the frontispiece! Curly hair, shirt open halfway down his chest, an expression at once swaggering with worldliness and yearning for the ineffable. From the first, Harry was infatuated with the idea, the image, the posture of the poet, and at the age of seventeen he decided to wander the world, a pack on his back, a song in his heart.

Signing on as a cabin boy on a German cargo ship sailing out of New York, he traveled to the Far East, and when he returned to the States a year later he hit the road as a "blanket-stiff"—so called for the rolled blankets hobos carried. Hopping freight trains with a volume of Byron in his belt, Harry dreamed of transforming his picaresque travels into transcendent poetry.

> *Accept, and the world moves with you.*
> *Revolt, and you walk alone.*

But Harry was astute enough to realize that even self-created heroes need more than a boxcar education, and he was voracious enough to seek out spiritual vagabonds who might help him on his quest. In 1904, he spent several months at the Roycroft community in East Aurora, New York, a semi-utopian society led by Elbert Hubbard, who'd adopted the name Fra

Elbertus, and who disillusioned Harry by printing in one of his popular periodicals what would have been Harry's first published poem—had he not
omitted Harry's name, implying that he himself was the author.

A year later, Harry visited another semi-visionary, Bernarr Macfadden, whose Physical Culture City in the New Jersey pines attracted
hundreds of adherents with its emphasis on physical fitness, and flocks of
sightseers and reporters with its emphasis on nudity. Harry wore clothes as
seldom as possible for the rest of his life, but he learned another lesson just
as long-lasting. He saw that Macfadden (who later founded a publishing
empire that included *True Romances, True Detective,* and *Photoplay*),
though a sincere cultist, was also a skillful showman, a forerunner of the
genre of "advertisements for myself."

Harry had the instincts of a self-promoter but now he turned them
into a principle. One of the most important parts of poetry, he suddenly realized, was publicity. His own role was clear—an outcast genius misunderstood but forcing the world to accept him, no, to applaud him, by the sheer
bravado of his adventures, by the ineffable loveliness of his songs, and he
immediately set forth for . . . Lawrence, Kansas.

Harry had once studied a German textbook written by Professor W.
H. Carruth of the University of Kansas and decided that Carruth was to become his patron. Harry knocked on Carruth's door, announced that his
destiny was to become a great poet, and asked for the professor's help in getting a college education. Carruth was so taken with Harry's charming audacity that he financed his first semester's tuition.

Playing the outcast genius to the hilt—and skillfully exploiting the
irony that the role was one of the surest ways to social acceptance—Harry
set up an interview with a reporter from the *Kansas City Star,* which appeared under the headline "Tramp Poet Arrives; Kansas Enrolls Box-Car
Student," and which was widely reprinted. Harry was developing a technique he called "the Big Bass Drum," later amended to "the Art of Spec-
tactularism"—based on the theory that part of a great poet's task was to call
attention to his work by calling attention to his personality—and soon published an article of his own, headlined "Harry H. Kemp, the Studious
Hobo: He Reads Homer and Is Contented: Arrived by Freight: Ten Cents
in Pocket on Arrival." The myth was well under way—though Harry had
yet to publish a single poem under his own name.

Harry spent six years in Lawrence and worked summers with
threshing crews, on cattle trains, and on boats on nearly every river in the
Midwest. Occasionally, a small check for one of his poems would arrive in
the mail, for his widespread fame as a poet convinced the editors of local

newspapers and magazines that the least they could do was actually publish him. Understanding that a poet could never have too many patrons, Harry decided to call upon the most well-known person in Kansas—William Allen White, editor and publisher of the renowned *Emporia Gazette*. Making sure that the local journalists knew of his "pilgrimage," he walked the nearly one hundred miles from Lawrence to Emporia and spent the first nights of his journey in outhouses, reading a volume of Keats by candlelight.

Harry knew, of course, that White would be expecting him—but what he couldn't have known was that White's other house guest was the famous reformer journalist Ida Tarbell, and that they were in the midst of planning a new national magazine to be called *The American*. They were seeking a poet, they told Harry over dinner, who could "sing for them the life of present-day America, the dignity of labor, the worth of the daily, obscure endeavor of the world." Harry assured them they'd found their man. As charmed as Carruth, White and Tarbell told Harry he'd become their "official poet"—in fact they published more than two dozen of his poems in the next three years—and White added that he would write letters of recommendation to the editors of several national publications. This outcast business, Harry must have gleefully reflected, is certainly booming!

Harry found yet another well-connected patron in Upton Sinclair, author of the muckraking novel *The Jungle* and a frequent fellow contributor to *The American*. Harry, wrote Upton, was "the greatest promise for American poetry in my time," and since this was precisely Harry's own opinion, the two men began a long and mutually flattering correspondence. In July 1911, realizing that the young Byron wouldn't have spent the rest of his life in a small university town in the Midlands, Harry hopped a train east to achieve his "long-deferred fame." Upton suggested that they meet at a radical community in Arden, Delaware, and offered to pay all his expenses.

Upton believed that the emancipation of labor and of women were "the two great causes in which the progress of humanity was bound up." He was currently at work on a book demonstrating "the new attitude toward love and marriage, in which the equal rights of both parties to experiment and self-discovery are recognized"—"experiment" being a fancy word for fooling around. But Upton's notions of love fell considerably short of his practice. His wife, Meta, somewhat understated the case when she wrote that "his love advances had always failed to convince [her] of their reality," and in accordance with her husband's paeans to "experiment and self-discovery" had experimented and discovered herself with a number of other men—an ardent discipleship Upton failed to appreciate.

Harry arrived at Arden—"a rather raw and somewhat bashful boy," recalled Meta. Harry wholeheartedly endorsed Upton's theories, but was even more attracted to Upton's declaration that he would provide him with a "love program for a poet"—for at the age of twenty-seven, despite his reputation as a man with lust for "experience," he was still a virgin. Upton urged Harry to sleep with various and willing women, but Meta had a love program of her own.

Newspapers across the country gleefully reported the scandal. "Upton Sinclair Says Wife Has Left Him: Says He'll Seek Divorce: Blames Harry Kemp, a Kansas Poet, with Influencing Her" read one headline. Meta's characterization of her husband as "an essential monogamist without having any of the qualities that an essential monogamist ought to possess" delighted the press, but Harry came in for his share of the ridicule as well. He was called "the hairy scrivener," and one forgotten versifier wrote,

> *I am the hobo poet,*
> *I lead a merry life!*
> *One day I woo the Muse, the next*
> *Another fellow's wife.*

In order to win a divorce, Upton had to prove adultery. Among those who testified on his behalf was a landlady in Long Branch, New Jersey, who asserted that Harry and Meta had signed the register as a married couple, but who added that they seemed "too loving to be a man and wife." After the divorce Upton sailed to Holland, Meta soon found a new lover, and Harry was left alone, but at least he was no longer a virgin.

Harry was perhaps the country's best-known bohemian, but he had yet to set foot in the country's best-known bohemia. In 1912—that magical year again—he finally arrived in the Village. Having been liberated by Meta, he confessed he was now as "driven about by the oestrus of sex" as by the pursuit of poetic immortality—and, like hundreds of thousands of men and women over the decades, he saw the Village as synonymous with sexual license.

Harry, Henrietta Rodman warned her women friends, was "not the kind that carries a wedding ring about in his vest pocket," but they soon became fast friends and before long he was a regular at her famous spaghetti dinners. Harry regaled Henrietta's guests with tales of his travels and boasts of his sexual prowess, and—when not quietly taking one of them aside to ask if he might borrow a dollar or two—pontificated on various topics, the loudness of his opinions surpassed only by the gaps in his knowledge.

Harry had at last found a home uninhibited enough to gratify his gargantuan appetites. He visited the Armory Show, stood before a painting of a nude, and proudly proclaimed with gusto that he recognized the model from a recent night in her bed—only to realize, so the story went, that the man standing nearby was the painter himself, who was married to the model. At his room at 10 Vaness Place, he'd engage in all-night poem-reciting contests with Sinclair ("Red") Lewis, his fellow lodger, taking turns declaiming famous verses until the other finally came up blank.

Like many of his fellow Villagers, Harry made a fetish out of poverty—what could be more anomalous than a bohemian with a job? None of his friends begrudged the King of Bohemia an occasional hand-out, and Luke O'Connor at the Working Girls' Home on Sixth Avenue and 8th Street or Daddy Gallup at Gallup's restaurant on the corner of Greenwich Avenue and 11th Street let him charge his meals, "charge" being a code word for "free."

Harry momentarily considered making a living as a boxer. He installed a punching bag in his apartment, offered to trade lessons in writing poetry for lessons in boxing, and as "Battling Kid Kemp" even got into the ring for a not entirely encouraging round with legendary Harry Greb.

Harry continued to sell his poems, but magazines paid by the line, and Harry, in contrast to his conversation, wrote short. On one visit to the offices of publisher Frank Munsey, he confided that he was broke but that he had a poem in his head he'd write out on the spot. Munsey agreed, Harry wrote out two couplets, and Munsey mentioned that he paid 25 cents a line—whereupon Harry changed the couplets into quatrains, and doubled his fee.

Harry's first book of poetry, published by Mitchell Kennerley in 1914, was called *The Cry of Youth*, a collection reflecting his experiences as a hobo, sailor, and hired hand. "It has never been done before—since Villon's time at least," he wrote of his poems, "to have an outcast transcribe into definite literary language of verse his genuine vagabond moods—without dilettantism!" But despite his best efforts to link his poetry and his persona, he had to admit that people were considerably more interested in the latter. When Harry requested a royalty statement, Kennerley braced him for the bad news by saying, "At present more people are writing poetry than reading it," then informed him that his account came to $16.93.

Fortunately, H. L. Mencken and George Jean Nathan, the editors of *The Smart Set*, though neither radical nor bohemian, published several of his poems, sketches, and satiric aphorisms. Mencken defended the magazine against Theodore Dreiser's charge that it was filled with "prestige and badinage" and that Harry's work, in particular, was "not worth space": "Harry Kemp is the only tabble doty genius who has given us anything fit to print."

Max Eastman also admired Harry's work—like Mencken, he was engaged in a rearguard campaign against modernism—and in one of his rare miscalculations, offered him a part-time position as an editor. "Harry raised the banner of neo-classicism and bore it up, lonely and neglected," he recalled, "a voice crying in the wilderness, while T. S. Eliot and his confreres were still in short pants. And he anticipated Ernest Hemingway in his cult of red-blooded he-male bellicosity and death-in-the-afternoonism by about two decades. Harry used to come around to *The Masses* office . . . offering to take on John Masefield and Jack Johnson, Rudyard Kipling and Jess Willard, with his typewriter in hock and one hand behind his back. Underneath this mighty swagger he had good taste and a very honest mind."

After only a year Harry was growing restless. In the fall of 1913, he boarded the English liner *Oceania* and promptly went to the first-class deck, prepared for a luxurious crossing to Southampton. Except that he didn't have a ticket. He'd informed journalists on both sides of the Atlantic of his plan to stow away on first class, arranged to have it publicized when the ship reached mid-ocean, and even wrote a letter to the captain confessing his crime. Give me "the benefit of the imaginative break," he pleaded, but the captain was not a lover of poetry and put him to work washing dishes. When the ship docked, Harry was sentenced to three weeks at hard labor in solitary confinement—and upon completion of the sentence he was to be deported to the United States at his own expense. With the help of, among many others, the Labour party, George Bernard Shaw, Ford Madox Ford, and Ezra Pound (who privately called Harry "that ass"), the deportation order was overturned.

Harry was lionized in London as he had been in the Village. He was even credited with coining "sex for sex's sake." "The Villon of the Village," as he was now called, returned to America in the summer of 1914, this time with a first-class ticket paid for by the legendary litterateur Frank Harris.

How good it was to be home! "The Social Revolution . . . was still young," he wrote. "It had not yet got caught in the stale mud of economic and materialistic pessimism. . . ."

But Social Revolutions come and go, and Harry's longing for poetic glory and the quest for the perfect woman took precedence. One day, he found her.

The moment Harry saw Mary Pyne at a party in the fall of 1914 he knew he'd found his dream. After talking with her for a few minutes he rushed to his apartment, scribbled a poem in her honor, and ran back and presented it to her. In February 1915, only a few months after she'd turned twenty-one, they were married.

Everyone who knew Mary agreed she was the perfect woman. Red-haired, unearthly thin, with gray-blue eyes and a pale complexion, she was said to have stepped out of a page of Robert Burns, a painting by Titian. Theodore Dreiser compared her to a fragile flower, and Harry always thought of her as medieval Madonna. Mary's inner loveliness was even more striking. She was praised for her kindness and generosity, and her lack of vanity. Everyone agreed she had an intuitive appreciation of the arts, an almost mystical mind. Now she was Harry's "true and ultimate mate."

When she met Harry, Mary was living with her often unemployed father, working as a waitress or clerk or dance hall instructor. She wanted to become an actress, and with her dreamy beauty and artistic sensitivity seemed destined to become a star. In fact, as we have seen, she and Harry appeared in several of the early Provincetown Players productions. During a particularly impoverished period in her marriage, Mary approached the legendary Broadway impresario David Belasco for a job, but when Belasco's enthusiastic assurance that he'd make her a leading lady was accompanied by the veiled suggestion that they might explore a more personal relationship, she politely declined his offer.

In 1917, poorer than ever, Harry and Mary moved into a single room on West 10th Street. Theodore Dreiser was obsessed with Mary, and bewildered that she would prefer Harry to him.

As for Harry himself, Dreiser wrote, "To me he was a somewhat disorderly blend of the charlatan, the poseur, the congenital eccentric, and the genius, or honest, sincere, seeking thinker, the charlatan and the genius sectors being at times not too clearly discernible. . . . As I saw it, he was suffering from a rabid form of ego-mania."

But Dreiser was honest enough to set down Mary's account of *her* feelings about Harry. "I know that some people think that he is a little crazy. And he is a terrible egotist. . . . But there is something else there, a love of beauty, and what's more, he is not as strong as he pretends to be."

To the bafflement of their friends, Harry had several affairs during their marriage. "Few poets are monogamically inclined," he proclaimed.

"Their imaginations will not let them. Every woman is a new country for them." Men who are *not* poets, Harry neglected to add, often show the same tendency.

Some Villagers even suspected that Mary had a brief affair with Djuna Barnes, and Dreiser, who may well have made a clumsy pass or two at Mary, believed that she and Hutch Hapgood were romantically involved. Hutch denied it, claiming that their long daily meetings were confined to conversation, and given the mystical strain in both their temperaments, and Hutch's eagerness for "soul exchange," he was probably telling the truth. In any case, Harry more than once threatened to beat him up—a sexist reaction, considering his own behavior, but a natural one, considering how many Village husbands had threatened to beat *him* up.

But love, as Harry often wistfully said, was only "a brief immortality." From the first, Mary was chronically ill. Dreiser was particularly hard on Harry for hanging out in cafés and theaters while Mary was left in bed lacking "suitable heat and food, pleasant surroundings, satisfactory clothing, competent medical service." More likely, Harry was acting out of despair, or at least desperately trying to sell his poetry to pay for Mary's doctors.

One day Lawrence Langner, founder of the Theater Guild, learned that Mary had collapsed with a hemorrhage. "Harry was in a pitiable state, and at a loss to know what to do. I passed him on Sixth Avenue one day carrying some small parcels. 'I just sold a poem,' he said, 'and I've bought Mary some caviar, pâté de fois gras, pickles, and some other things she likes from the delicatessen.' "

Finally, Mary's condition was correctly diagnosed as tuberculosis, and she was sent to a Saranac Lake sanatorium. Hutch and Djuna visited her and Harry interrupted his bedside vigil only to go to New York to sell his poems and buy gifts for her. One day, in November 1919, Mary seemed "curiously, ecstatic, happy, and radiant"—an ominous sign in a TB patient—and the next day she wrote Harry's name again and again on a scrap of paper and feverishly drew several sketches of his head. That evening, Harry was visiting Langner in his Village apartment when the phone rang. It was for Harry. He listened for a moment, hung up, and burst into tears. "My little Mary," he sobbed, "my little Mary is dead."

Devastated as Harry was, he had a native gusto and a congenital self-absorption that sustained him, and soon he resumed work in the theater. Harry had met Jig Cook in the spring of 1916 at Renganeschi's restaurant on West 10th Street, and discovered that they shared a passionate distaste for what Harry called "the trinity of Sure-fire, Hokum, and Happy

Endings" of the Broadway stage, and a determination to create a theater in which playwrights, again in Harry's words, "wrote honestly of life as they saw it." Hearing about the group of amateur playwrights and actors in Provincetown, he decided to join them for the summer. "Poems to Swap for House: Kemp Would Gladly Exchange Some Jingles for a Cottage," read a headline in the May 10, 1916, edition of the *New York Times*, after Harry had placed an ad offering to exchange the manuscripts of several of a "well-known" poet's unpublished verses—and any royalties that might ensue—for a summer cottage on the Cape. Receiving no reply, he wangled a room from the grocer John Francis, Gene's benefactor, and joined the Provincetown Players for a glorious summer season.

In the fall, Harry rejoined Jig and his company in the Village, performing in three of the first season's plays. But though he could quote hundreds of his own poems from memory, he had trouble remembering even the few lines of Gene's dialogue.

As a playwright, Harry was only marginally more successful. Jig wasn't impressed by *Prodigal Son*, but lacking anything better, he produced it during the 1916–1917 season. Harry, sensing Jig's reluctance, and confessing that years of incessant poverty had filled him with "unreasonable belligerence" that he took out on his "well-meaning, bewildered associates," decided to try his hand at his own theater.

In his "miraculous naivete," Harry took over the Thimble Theater from Guido Bruno and Charles Edison. Subscriptions were 75 cents per performance, which also entitled patrons to become members of his amorphous League for the Defense of Bohemian Life. The proceeds were divided equally among the actors, most of whom, in accordance with Harry's emphasis on amateur spontaneity, were hired for their *lack* of experience.

"I have plays dealing with every century of recorded time," read one of Harry's flyers, "and with every kind of person from the caveman to the modern, civilized warlord. Some of my plays will be severe and classical, others comic even to the loud laying on of burlesque slapstick. Every play will be written, produced, and sometimes participated in by me. Come and traverse the ages with my imagination as your Mercury." One of his plays, he promised, would try to have a live crocodile on stage, a production, he didn't add, underwritten by Crocodile cigarettes.

In the late teens, real estate operators had become a prominent part of Village life, and in 1919 the tiny Thimble Theater was torn down to make way for a large apartment building. Who should come to Harry's rescue, however, but Vincent Pepe, the Village's leading real estate operator.

Pepe owned property in the Minettas, a tiny district centered around Minetta Lane and Minetta Street, and hoped to turn the area from a hangout for hoodlums and dope fiends into a kind of American Latin Quarter. Not realizing that he was about to become one of the earliest forerunners of gentrification, Harry gratefully accepted Pepe's offer to transform the building at 8 Minetta Street into a theater, and in 1920 he opened Harry Kemp's Playhouse featuring Harry Kemp's Players.

Pepe's plan wasn't immediately successful—one night, theatergoers had to step over a dead horse to enter the theater—but once inside they were greeted by an often arcane but amusing introductory talk from Harry, a brief biography of Boccaccio, or a little lecture on the history of kissing.

The Quill reported that Harry's little speeches were "worth the price of admission"; alas, the same could seldom be said for the plays. His poetic dramas, he boasted, aspired to "attain a sort of exalted, universal language that does not pass away." But disdaining the American vernacular he knew so well, writing in blank or rhymed verse, he attained instead an archaic, stilted, frequently florid poesy.

If Harry's first move foreshadowed the gentrification of the Village, his second foreshadowed the birth of the East Village. "Poet Quits Village to Start New Bohemia on East Side," read a headline in the *New York Evening Mail* in 1924, when Harry moved to East 11th Street. A year later he settled at 288 East 10th Street, where his Poet's Theater occupied the basement. This theatrical venture proved even shorter than the other two—notable only for Bobby Edwards's claim in *The Quill* that he left the theater in confusion, thinking that a play of Harry's called *The Rabbit's Foot* was actually *The Rabbi's Foot*, and for the debut of a nineteen-year-old apprentice actor named Clifford Odets.

When Harry moved to the Lower East Side, he took a new wife with him, another lovely, red-haired woman in her early twenties, a Barnard graduate who had wandered into the Village one day in 1922. Seeing a sign at 150 West 4th Street reading "Down the Rabbit Hole," she descended the steps into the Mad Hatter. Noticing her pronounced resemblance to Mary Pyne, Harry learned that her name was Frances McClernan, and exclaimed, "I'm going to marry you." A year later he did.

Soon after the ceremonies, Frances realized that though Harry was a nationally famous poet, "I had a husband to support." She took a part-time job managing the Mad Hatter three nights a week, modeled for the B. Altman & Co. catalogue, and served as the poster girl for Camay soap. One advantage of marriage to Harry was unanticipated. He had befriended the neighborhood gangsters, several of whom escorted her home when she had to work late, and one of whom, as a Christmas present, offered to bump off anyone she wanted.

There must have been times when Frances was tempted to point to Harry himself, but she resigned herself to his bizarre behavior and roguish swaggering. Even after she left him in 1926, she admitted, "You never knew quite what was going to happen next. . . . I had a wonderful time with him—no complaints. . . . And I got what I wanted. It couldn't have gone on. It was too fantastic."

Let others complain that their beloved Village community had degenerated into a night spot for tourists and thrill-seekers; to Harry it remained a magic kingdom. He could still be seen at Romany Marie's, back at the Poet's Table, fulminating and reciting his latest poems to whoever happened to be present—other poets, or Edgard Varèse, or Marsden Hartley, or Paul Robeson.

Still living from hand to mouth—"and sometimes," he said, "it was a long way from the hand to the mouth"—he would think nothing of squandering his last two dollars on a sumptuous meal at the Brevoort, then holing up in a small room for three months with a budget of only fifteen dollars for coffee, bread, and cheese.

Then the old wanderlust would reappear, and Harry would head out, no longer hopping freight trains but sponsored by rich patrons—the most prominent of whom was Joseph Fels, the Philadelphia soap manufacturer, who also aided Theodore Dreiser. In Paris, in 1923, Harry led a contingent of two hundred bohemians from seven countries on a march from the Dôme café to Montmartre to express their opposition to Prohibition. Drinking champagne in front of Sacré-Coeur, he announced that he was planning a League of Bohemian Republics to include every bohemian community from Paris to San Francisco. "When the earth is salted with bohemianism and the army of bohemians is so strong that the world will recognize its power will come the real revolution which will overturn bolshevism and capitalism and shock the people into thinking and understanding." Returning to Paris in 1925, he discovered his revolutionary league had dwindled to a single member.

But Provincetown was Harry's favorite retreat, and nearly every summer after 1916 he managed to live there on virtually nothing. Edmund Wilson, E. E. Cummings, and John Dos Passos would hike out to visit him in his shack in the dunes, and for a couple of seasons he ran yet another theater. But mostly he wrote his poems or read the classics by the light of a kerosene lamp. Or sometimes, reported a New York newspaperman, he'd stand on the highest dune and shout poetry at the sky.

Why did Harry continue to captivate the Villagers? As Mencken observed, "He swam into public notice at a time when the literature of the land was suffering from a bad case of respectability. The reigning novelists were beginning to take on the sober dignity of headwaiters or Episcopal rectors; . . . . He demanded, not the chautauqua salute, but a handout."

By the mid-twenties, like the Village itself, Harry's energy was increasingly expended in maintaining his myth. The uptown columnists turned him into one of the most frequently quoted figures of the decade. He published a best-selling autobiography, his verses frequently appeared in *The Saturday Evening Post*, and in 1926 *The Ladies' Home Journal* ran his picture in a feature on the best-known poets of the day. But as in the case of so many other American literary personalities, Harry's fame was not "long deferred," but arrived at almost precisely the moment he least deserved it.

Harry tried harder than any of the Villagers to fulfill the bohemian commandment to make living into an art, to invent oneself every day, but when he undertook his autobiography at the age of thirty-six, he seemed to make living a pose. One Villager suggested that he title his memoir "My Favorite Subject," and even Harry laughed. Still, *Tramping on Life* was in many ways his best book, for when narcissism threatened to spill over into vainglory on every page, he was able to mock his pretensions without surrendering them.

Not only did it become a best-seller, but it was widely acclaimed as one of "the great biographies of the earth," and marked a significant advance in the assault on what Max Eastman called the "blight on American expression," the conviction that the public and the private were separate spheres. But when Harry wrote a sequel a few years later the publisher sold fewer than four thousand copies, not so much a sign that his creative energies were flagging as that his bohemian image was outmoded. By 1919–1920, Sherwood Anderson's *Winesburg, Ohio* and Sinclair Lewis's *Main Street* had signaled a new revolt against traditional American materialism. F. Scott Fitzgerald and Ernest Hemingway expressed a new doctrine of disillusionment with American values while Harry was still celebrating his intoxication with bohemian life.

Like Max Eastman and Floyd Dell, Harry disdained modernism in poetry—"the crossword school" he called it—and continued to write verses blending swooning romanticism and the stilted formulas of neoclassicism long after both schools had been buried in anthologies. Louis Untermeyer wrote that his work was "full of every kind of poetry except the kind one might imagine Kemp would write. Instead of crude and boisterous verse, here is a precise and almost overpolished poetry." To Witter Bynner, Harry's verses were like "seven-league boots on a linnet."

During the Depression, Harry made headlines—"Poet Gets Job!"—by joining the Federal Writers Project, easily meeting the requirement that applicants be destitute. From the early thirties to the mid-forties, his poetry frequently appeared in the *New York Times*—the paper of record certifying his status only a decade or two too late. And in 1941, feeling that he had recaptured "the old sparkle and verve," he completed a third volume in his autobiography—only to have it rejected by Maxwell Perkins ("most of the figures who appear in it have somewhat faded out of interest") and dismissed by his old admirer H. L. Mencken ("your book is too windy and in large part rather too archaic in mood").

Harry may have been an anachronism for the last half of his long life, but that was only because he stayed true to the first half. His ideals—visionary self-expression, perpetual youth, impoverished genius, defiance of "the damnable conventions" of "false society"—may have passed into the realm of naive nostalgia, but almost alone among the prominent Villagers of the teens, he remained an authentic bohemian to the end. "He who has once learned the art of being young," he said, "can never grow old."

In his dotage, Harry took to parading around Provincetown in a wintergreen wreath and a black cape. In 1946, at the age of sixty-three, he even embarked on a "one-against-the-atom-bomb" campaign, walking all the way to Washington, selling poems along the way. But back on the Cape he drank more and more heavily, once getting so soused he accidentally downed an entire bottle of ink. He kept a pot of stew going for months, only to discover a missing glove at the bottom. And once he emptied a bottle of home-brewed wine and found a decomposed mouse in the dregs.

As Harry reached his seventy-sixth birthday, his friends insisted that he move into a cottage they constructed for him, and though he was grateful, when a friend asked if he wanted to revisit the dunes, he broke into sobs.

"I want to be burned up and not stink in the grave," Harry dictated into a tape recorder a little over a year later. "I want half my ashes to be scattered over the dunes in Provincetown, and the other half over Greenwich Village." When he died of a cerebral hemorrhage in August 1960—"the spirit that exalts the word" ceasing at last—his friends completed his long pilgrimage in front of the Provincetown Playhouse.

VII

William Carlos Williams, the Little Magazines, and the Poetry Wars

Exhausted after a full day of treating patients, William Carlos Williams angrily answered the phone. "Doctor," said a woman's voice, "my child has swallowed a mouse." "Then get him to swallow a cat," he replied, and slammed down the receiver.

That evening, he drove his Ford flivver from his home in Rutherford, New Jersey, into the Village to attend a party thrown by the poet Mina Loy. Off in a corner, a French girl in her teens reclined on a divan, attended by several young men, each of whom, Bill recalled in his autobiography, had "a portion of her body in his possession which he caressed attentively, apparently unconscious of any rival. Two or three addressed themselves to her shoulders on either side. Her feet were being kissed, her shins, her knees, and even above the knees, though as far as I could tell there was a gentleman's agreement that she was not to be undressed there."

It was a scene that intrigued Bill for years, and where else could it have happened but in the Village?

347

. . .

After the teens, hundreds of thousands of men and women in the metropolitan area remembered their nights in the Village as the nights of their youth, though they never slept there once, but Bill was the first and most prominent of the regular visitors.

After getting his medical degree, Bill "instinctively avoided a New York City practice," but after deciding his true passion was poetry, he spent as much of his free time there as possible. The new was what he was seeking in poetry—new forms, new rhythms, new subject matter, even a new vocabulary, "the better to ensnare the intangible," as he wrote his friend Marianne Moore in 1916.

Bill's head, recalled a friend, "was a dice-box rattling with ideas." As a young man he made his decision. "Words it would be and their intervals: Bam! Bam!" Poetry, direct and simple, dealing with the uniqueness of the commonplace, aiming at the exact transcription of reality. "No ideas but in things."

His wife, Flossie, did not accompany him to New York, which was fortunate, for one of the attractions that drew Bill to the Village was its sense of erotic energy. Modern marriages could best work, he felt—a modification of the code of free love to which only he subscribed—with a certain amount of emotional violence, but whether or not such emotional violence was necessary in a successful affair he never revealed.

Bill's Village friends were mostly poets and painters. As he explained years later, he cherished "the opportunity to know the important men of his epoch—as the men of past ages, living in city groups such as Florence, Paris, London once lived." But the socially conscious, literary-political rebels Walter Lippmann and Emma Goldman, with their conviction that literature should serve social goals, and Max Eastman and Floyd Dell, with their hostility to modernism in poetry, had no interest for him.

Bill held Jack Reed, in particular, in something close to disdain. When he first met Jack at a party, he knew him mainly as the author of a few conventional and undistinguished poems. And as for Louise Bryant, Bill showed no more instinct for feminism than for activism. Louise, he recalled, "had on a heavy, very heavy, white silk skirt so woven that it hung over the curve of her buttocks like the strands of a glistening waterfall."

As an intellectual who lived near Paterson, Bill might have been expected to take an interest in the textile workers' strike in 1913, but in a short story called "Life Along the Passaic River," published two decades later, he, like the New Jersey police, characterized Jack as an outside agitator. "That bright boy from Boston came down and went shooting off his mouth around in the streets here telling us what to do"—a complaint that would have had more moral force if Bill himself had done anything to help the strikers.

No, for Bill the poet's purpose had nothing in common with what he scornfully thought of as mere journalism, and his dedication shouldn't be compromised by what he regarded as do-good activism. On evenings when Big Bill Haywood was talking about the IWW at Mabel's salon, Bill could be found discussing the abandonment of capital letters or the "over-all musical design" of a poem with Kay Boyle or Louise Bogan at the 14th Street salon of Lola Ridge, "that Vestal of the Arts."

Bill was drawn to the modernist painters of the Village, for their aesthetic revolution seemed to him far more significant than the political revolution advocated by the anarchists, socialists, and IWW. "There was at that time a great surge of interest in the arts generally before the First World War," he recalled. "New York was seething with it. Painting took the lead." He frequently visited the Metropolitan Museum of Art and the galleries of the Village—when he saw a painting he liked, he said, it gave him an erection. When he saw Duchamp's notorious *Nude Descending a Staircase* at the Armory Show in 1913, he "laughed out loud," not in scorn but "happily, with relief." The exhibition represented in painting what he was hoping to achieve in poetry—not merely the dynamiting of stale traditions but an explosion of free, fresh, and vigorous sensibilities. Poets have much to learn from the modernists, he wrote Harriet Monroe soon after the show, and in 1917 he read his futurist poem, "Overture to a Dance of Locomotives," at the exhibition of the Society of American Artists.

Bill included Village painters among his closest friends. He was especially close to Charles Demuth, who had a studio on Washington Square South. During one of their long walks they decided to experiment by treating a common subject, selecting a fire truck that roared by with a large 5 painted on its side. Bill's Imagist poem "The Great Figure," though one of his best known, is one of his least successful, but Charles's painting *The Figure 5 in Gold*—a huge 5 in the center, with patterns surrounding it and the words "Bill" and "Carlos" clearly discernible—remains one of the masterworks of the American modernist movement.

Bill also enjoyed Marsden Hartley's companionship. He considered Hartley a seminal influence and a close friend, though he didn't much like his paintings, and found him distressingly unpredictable. But they were joined in their contempt for the artiness of the crowds at Village parties. "Yup," said Marsden, "they give me the gut ache, too, the arty art worshippers. . . . There ought to be laws against talking about poetry, art, or the social revolution"—the last of which, at least, Bill agreed with.

Marsden's "small Dresden china blue eyes under savage brows made him look as if he were about to eat you," Bill recalled. "None of us took him seriously—except in his work. He was too kind. He told me how once he had made rather direct love to Djuna Barnes—offering his excellent physical equipment for her favors. . . . I can see Marsden now, with his practical approach, explaining to Djuna what he could offer her."

Marsden's blunt seduction was either a fabrication or a failure—not only wasn't Djuna interested, neither was Marsden. Bill once referred to him as "a kind of grandpapa to us all, male and female alike," but on other occasions he was more direct, calling him a "tortured homosexual." That Marsden regarded life as "essentially comic" doesn't contradict this view, of course, for comedy is often the last resort of the tortured. In any event, Marsden made several futile passes at Bill, and once wistfully told him that he "would have made one of the most charming whores of the city." "He was one of the most frustrated men I knew," Bill wrote. "A tragic figure. I really loved the man, but we didn't always get along together, except at a distance."

Bill enthusiastically participated in the revolution of the theater both as an actor and as a playwright. In 1916, his friend the poet Alfred Kreymborg wrote his notorious one-act drama *Lima Beans* for Jig Cook's group—would Bill be interested in playing one of the three roles?

Kreymborg was no O'Neill, and in *Lima Beans* tackled the subject of a husband who liked lima beans and a street vendor who disrupted the man's marriage by trying to sell his wife anything *but* lima beans. No doubt Alfred had larger metaphorical resonances in mind, but when Bill called it "a fragile bit" he was being generous. In any case, Bill played the husband, Mina Loy was cast as the wife, and the artist William Zorach, who also designed the cubist set, portrayed the vendor. The better to satirize middle-class manners, Alfred instructed his actors to move and speak like mannequins—all jerky gestures and wooden line readings—a dramaturgical decision that, as it happened, allowed for the best possible expression of Bill's acting talents.

Bill's editorial collaboration with Alfred Kreymborg on *Others*, one of the first of the "little magazines," published from 1913 to 1919, became their most significant contribution to Village life. Alfred, though only modestly talented as a playwright and a poet, was not without experience with little magazines. From September 1913 to November 1914, with the help of Charles and Albert Boni of the Washington Square Book Shop, he'd brought out ten issues of a publication called *Glebe*, subtitled "Songs, Sighs, and Curses," each featuring the work of a single writer. Though *Glebe*'s circulation never rose above three hundred—approximately the number of Alfred's Village friends—he rationalized its failure as the fate of uncompromising genius in a hostile environment. But Alfred regarded even the Armory Show as a commercial exploitation of avant-garde experimentation—it was, he said, "a business coup d'etat"—and felt sure his time would come. A little magazine as a kind of Salon des Refusés, that was his idea. Alfred was no cynic, but hadn't the French painters become famous precisely because they'd been rejected? Properly promoted, couldn't the refusal of traditional outlets be turned into widespread acceptance?

(Another little magazine had also come and gone in New Jersey—this one lasting a single issue. In March 1915, Man Ray—born Emanuel Rabinovitch, also known as Rudnitsky—a painter, photographer, filmmaker, and writer who'd helped Alfred with *Glebe*, brought out *The Ridgefield Gazook*, a four-page magazine featuring his drawings of bugs copulating, plus a series of puns on his own name and those of Pablo Picasso and Hippolyte Havel. Man Ray soon moved to a tiny room on West 8th Street and became America's leading exponent of Dada. After the war he sailed to France, never to return.)

In the early teens Alfred got married, and founded a small artists' colony in a cluster of shacks in Grantwood, New Jersey, on the slopes of the Palisades. In the summer of 1915 he began planning a new magazine to be called *Others*, believing that what America needed was a poetry magazine devoted to experiment, one more radical than Harriet Monroe's *Poetry*, which would print the poems Harriet rejected. Dozens of Village poets, artists, and intellectuals took part in the effort, traveling across the river on Sundays for a brief "business meeting," then picnicking and talking of poetry, cubism, the coming war, Ty Cobb, free love. On one memorable afternoon Man Ray and Marcel Duchamp played an impromptu game of tennis without a net—the first Dada sports event. Later, Alfred suggested that they recite their latest poems. Most of the poets, though fiercely committed to dynamiting tradition, proved too shy to read their work in public, but Bill overcame his self-consciousness with sheer volume. At sunset everyone headed back to the Village, feeling, as Alfred put it, "joyous bewilderment in the discovery that other men and women were working in a field they themselves felt they had chosen in solitude."

Bill was "hugely excited" by the communal atmosphere—at Grantwood he first met Duchamp, Man Ray, Mina Loy, Malcolm Cowley, Maxwell Bodenheim, and Orrick Johns, who had beaten out Edna St. Vincent Millay for the Lyric Year prize but was equally famous for his wooden leg, "sometimes lost or stolen," Bill said, "after a drunken spree." He was invigorated by the opportunity to talk poetry with his fellow revolutionaries. "We'd have arguments over cubism which would fill an afternoon. There was a comparable whipping up of interest in the structure of the poem. It seemed daring to omit capitals at the head of each poetic line. Rhyme went by the board. We were, in short 'rebels.' " And *Others* was to be their banner.

So every Sunday, Bill would drive from his home in Rutherford, less than ten miles away, "to help with the magazine which . . . saved my life as a writer. Twenty-five dollars a month kept it going, and the scripts began to come in. Kreymborg got the money somehow" — in the beginning, from the art collector and Duchamp patron Walter Arensberg.

In the winter of 1915, *Others* was well on its way. Usually sixteen pages, with a goldenrod cover, and costing 15 cents a copy, the magazine consisted almost entirely of poetry, with a few short plays and hardly any criticism. The initial three issues were prepared at Grantwood — the first featured Alfred, Ezra Pound, Mina Loy, and Orrick Johns; the second, Bill and Wallace Stevens; the third, Maxwell Bodenheim and a recent Harvard graduate recommended to Alfred by Ezra Pound: T. S. Eliot. Needless to say, none of the poets were paid, though the printer, a Bronx anarchist who called himself "Mr. Liberty," charged only $25 for the five-hundred-copy press run as his contribution to the revolution.

But disturbing criticisms were leveled by some who might have been expected to be friends of the magazine. Mina Loy's "Love Poems" in the very first issue — especially "Pig Cupid," with its erotic imagery of pigs rooting through garbage — outraged not only the traditionalists but many of the modernists as well. Epithets from the mainstream press — "swill poetry," "hoggerel" — delighted the *Others* staff, but when Harriet Monroe called Mina "one of the long-to-be-hidden moderns," and Amy Lowell vowed never to submit any of her poems to a magazine that would publish such scandalous material, "the gang" realized that they had entered "the poetry wars" with a detonation.

Mina's scandalous poetry, lovely looks, and cosmopolitan personality made her one of the most talked-about women in the Village. "Looking for love with all its catastrophes," she once said, "is a less risky experience than finding it." She'd spent several years as one of Mabel Dodge's favorite guests at the Villa Curonia, and several months as the mistress of the Italian futurist leader Filippo Marinetti. A reporter for the *New York Sun* called her the symbol of the New Woman. "This woman is half-way through the door into Tomorrow," rhapsodized the writer, and quoted Mina as saying, "The antique way to live and express life was to . . . say it according to the rules. The modern flings herself at life and lets herself feel what she does feel, then upon the very tick of the second, she snatches the images of life that fly through the brain." Furthermore, "no one who has not lived in New York has lived in the Modern World."

Though Mina bore the brunt of the initial assault, the entire *Others* enterprise was soon under attack. Max Eastman, a radical in nearly everything but poetry, scorned what he called "lazy verse," and Louis Untermeyer, who, like Oscar Williams, turned to anthologizing as the only way to keep his mediocre verses in print, referred to the *Others* poets as "crank insurgents." Ezra Pound, congenitally hostile to artists, nevertheless began to bombard Alfred with pugnacious advice and splendid manuscripts. "While I concede this to be the liveliest sheet that has ever come out of the States," he wrote from London, "quite a few exhibits are frankly impossible." Soon afterward Alfred opened a large packet from him including several poems, Eliot's "Portrait of a Lady" among them, accompanied by a typically bilious letter—"Unless you're another American ass, you'll set this up just as it stands."

Alfred remained unperturbed. But since he was increasingly involved in his theatrical projects, and was more gifted at promoting than editing, *Others* was soon published by a series of revolving editors—the same kind of participatory democracy practiced by *The Masses* and the Provincetown Players, but without Max's genial efficiency or Jig's demented exuberance to hold the conflicting contributors together—and appeared with astonishing regularity, monthly for the first fourteen issues. It lived up to its motto, "The old expressions are with us and there are always others," and for a few years became the locus of the American poetry renaissance of the teens.

Bill, who'd been recommended to Alfred by his former University of Pennsylvania classmate Ezra Pound as his "one remaining pal in America," was not only enthusiastic about *Others*, he took over a "competitive" issue with twenty-two poets that came out in July 1916.

"Kreymborg is trying the experiment—God bless him—of letting a few of us who are near at hand take an issue and see what we can do with it," Bill wrote Marianne Moore. "My idea is this: to put into the thing what I think is the best work. I am not philanthropic. One piece by each person — some one thing that he or she is willing to stand to. Jam these various units together and forget the 'ensemble' — that will take care of itself." Then Bill returned Wallace Stevens's submission with a few suggested alterations. Ezra Pound wouldn't write without payment, but he sent the work of a protégé, with the comment that *Others* seemed to him to be doing rather well "for a dung continent that keeps Wilson as president."

A few months later a special *Others* booklet of Bill's poems appeared, featuring him and Alfred. They dealt with such quotidian subjects as his pregnant cat, a young housewife in a negligee, and water splashing in his kitchen sink, and demonstrated his poetic agenda at length. He explained years later, "No one knew [what our aims should be] consistently enough to formulate a 'movement.' We were restless and constrained, closely allied with the painters. . . . The thing that gave us most a semblance of a cause was not imagism, as some thought, but the line: the poetic line and our hopes for its recovery from stodginess." Bill was as much a revolutionary as any of the Villagers. If capitalism was a lie, if middle-class culture was a lie, if social conventions were lies, so, asserted Bill and his colleagues, was the very language of genteel poetry.

Like the other rebels, the new poets hoped to gain sustenance, energy, and support from the community — in this case, a community defined by sensibility, not geography. But jealousies, rivalries, and personality conflicts were inevitable even in a community of like-minded souls. As George Russell defined a literary movement: "Five or six men who live in the same town and hate each other."

Beyond the sensibilities of the Village, Bill's relationship with Amy Lowell was both opportunistic and brutally frank. He wooed her bank account, but that didn't stop him from abusing her character, her judgment, her poetry. Writing to tell her how much he'd liked one of her poems, he added, "much as I dislike you," and then went on to ask her to send along a small amount of her large fortune to help support *Others*; at least she couldn't accuse him of hypocrisy. Amy thanked him for his "love letter," reiterated her opinion that the poetry in *Others* was beneath her notice, and told him not to hold his breath until her check arrived. On another occasion he wrote that she had a "lamentable stinginess of spirit," and as for her imagist movement, "aside from what you stole from Pound your venture is worthless." One of her recent poems was "that piece of yours which I quite sincerely believe to be twaddle and which I have never yet heard anyone admire."

But privately Bill agreed with Amy and other critics that *Others* printed a lot of mediocre stuff, and that if money was always in short supply, so were aesthetic standards. Indeed, the attributes that had made the magazine a success—its democratic editing process, its willingness to publish unrecognized poets, its acceptance of new styles—also led to its failure. Its refusal to apply doctrinaire standards became a refusal to apply any standards at all. Harriet Monroe at *Poetry* magazine was often an overly strict editor, Margaret Anderson at *The Little Review* often exasperatingly mercurial, but Harriet had intellectual focus, Margaret firm enthusiasms. Alfred lacked the charisma to lead a group and the talent to articulate his vision. His main quality was egoless flexibility, which was enough to attract hundreds of poets, but not enough to make them cohere into a movement.

When the magazine folded in 1919, Bill was largely responsible. He agreed to edit the July and August issues, but wrote a savage attack on the magazine in July and canceled the August issue. In a blast called "Belly Music," he wrote, "I am in the field against the stupidity of the critics writing in this country today"—singling out Amy Lowell for "ginger pop criticism," and H. L. Mencken for "the braying of a superficial jackass."

Bill was just as fed up with the *Others* gang. Years later, he wrote that the magazine "had really no critical standards and offered only the scantiest rallying point for a new movement. . . . It helped break the ice for further experimentation with the line, but that was all."

Bill and the Village poets continued to look for a publication that would promote a common cause. Harriet's *Poetry* magazine wasn't the answer, at least not for Bill. He'd been feuding with Harriet for years, especially over her "vicious" changes to his poems. But he was also dismayed by the magazine's "epicurean" tone and intellectual inertness, its philistine insistence on paying its contributors, and finally, its hostility to greatness. *Seven Arts*, under the editorship of James Oppenheim and through the intellectual guidance of his associate Waldo Frank, was the first little magazine to argue that if America was a middle-class industrial nation, that was not a sign of sterility and oppression, but of vitality and progress. "In all such epochs, the arts cease to be private matters; they become not only the expressions of the national life, but a means to its enhancement. Our arts show signs of this change. It is the aim of *Seven Arts* to become a channel for the flow of these new tendencies: an expression of our American arts which shall be fundamentally an expression of our American life." Such cultural nationalism seemed a bit too celebratory to most Villagers. After all, "expressions of the national life" was pretty much what they had come to the Village to escape.

But the idea of a literary community, and an explicitly stated renascence, revealed a paradox; many writers, artists, and intellectuals regarded the Village as an enclave where they could escape the oppressions of capitalism and convention, while much of their work implied the radical transformation of that society. To what extent were they content with an alternative community as an end in itself, and to what extent were they committed to economic, social, and cultural revolution?

The debate over the role of arts in a capitalist democracy had scarcely begun before it was overwhelmed by war. The financial backer of *Seven Arts*, a food industry heiress, threatened to withdraw her support when it published anti-war essays by Jack Reed and Randolph Bourne. Then the staff split in half—between the pacifists and those who enlisted. After only twelve issues—in which it published Robert Frost, Eugene O'Neill, Carl Sandburg, Amy Lowell, Alfred Kreymborg, Sherwood Anderson, Theodore Dreiser, John Dos Passos, John Dewey, H. L. Mencken, and Van Wyck Brooks—the magazine folded.

Few of the little magazines survived the war. *Others* lingered for a few issues past the Armistice before Bill put it out of its misery, and even the solid old *Dial*, after nearly four decades in Boston, where it had been founded by Margaret Fuller with Emerson's encouragement, and nearly four decades in Chicago, seemed moribund by 1918 when it moved to new offices at 152 East 13th Street.

Fortunately for its survival, if not for the revolution, *The Dial* found a new formula—minimizing politics and stressing the arts with an international scope that more closely suited the temper of postwar America and the increasingly cosmopolitan outlook of American writers. Its editor and co-owner, Scofield Thayer, was a wealthy dandy who lived on the east side of Washington Square and collected Aubrey Beardsley drawings, and who, during his brief marriage, encouraged sexual experimentation less out of a commitment to free love than as a concession to his own uncertain sexuality.

Scofield bought enough stock in *The Dial* to become an unofficial contributing editor, and in late 1919, in partnership with other investors, took over the magazine entirely. Though Scofield had originally been drawn to *The Dial* by its anti-war stance, he sensed the country's flight from politics and early in 1920 an entirely new *Dial* appeared that reflected Scofield's conviction that "the world will never understand our spirit except in terms of art." Some of his friends regarded him as an overrefined aesthete, but everyone agreed he was an exquisitely refined editor, and he brought to the magazine not only most major American writers but also T. S. Eliot *(The Waste Land)*, Ezra Pound, William Butler Yeats, Ford Madox Ford, Marcel Proust, Oswald Spengler, and Thomas Mann.

At first circulation slipped from ten thousand to six thousand, leaving the magazine with a deficit of $100,000 at the end of Scofield's first year—enough to publish all the rest of the little magazines combined—but by the end of 1922 circulation had risen to fourteen thousand. *"The Dial* made a noise in the world," recalled its associate editor, Gilbert Seldes. "It directly affected the artistic life of a generation, and indirectly the life of our whole time."

When Scofield left the magazine in 1925, he was replaced by an editor who skillfully guided it through the rest of the decade—Bill's old friend Marianne Moore. Bill described her as "like a rafter holding up the superstructure of our uncompleted building, a caryatid . . . surely one of the main supports of the new order."

Born in a St. Louis suburb in 1887, she was raised in the home of her grandfather, a Presbyterian pastor, and educated at Bryn Mawr, where one of her classmates was the poet H. D. — Hilda Doolittle—and where she majored in biology, learning the fine art of dissection. After graduation, she taught at the Indian School in Carlisle, Pennsylvania, for three and a half years—the legendary Jim Thorpe was one of her students—then in the mid-teens moved with her mother and brother to Chatham, New Jersey, only twenty miles from Alfred Kreymborg's compound, when her brother took a position as a pastor. Finally, in 1918, she and her mother settled in a basement apartment on St. Luke's Place so they could be near her brother, by then a navy chaplain stationed in the city.

Marianne's life remained governed by the very propriety against which most of her neighbors were rebelling. Like a small-town spinster, she supported her mother by working as a tutor, secretary, and librarian. But behind her facade of propriety, she had a silver wit. Her conversation, said Alfred, was "a mellifluous flow of polysyllables which held every man in awe."

The Dial's policy—in the unfortunate, self-congratulatory Village tradition of basing self-definition on what one is not—was to print "works of merit not welcomed by commercial magazines," and Marianne, with her Village contacts and her fastidious tastes, proved a more than capable heir to Scofield. Once asked what made the magazine so extraordinary, "Lack of fear, for one thing," she replied. What was her editorial policy? "We . . . didn't have a policy, except I remember hearing the word 'intensity' very often. . . . That seemed to be the criterion. And we didn't care how unhomogenous they might seem. And didn't Aristotle say that it is the mark of a poet to see resemblances between apparently incongruous things!"

The Dial had found a way to survive World War I, but it couldn't find a way to survive the Crash. Its once wealthy owners decided that a magazine devoted to the arts was not the highest of their priorities, and, along with much else in America in 1929, *The Dial* suddenly ceased to exist. Not everyone mourned. Many writers agreed with Bill that by the end of the twenties, *The Dial* had served its purpose, that its internationalist, aesthetic eclecticism was outmoded; it had become "half-hearted," he said, characterized by "worthlessness"; it had been "found Freudian."

Bill exempted Marianne from his criticism; indeed, she was virtually the only poet of the teens and twenties to remain aloof from the "poetry wars"—partly because of her eclectic tastes as an editor, but mostly because of her saintly character and her unique poetry. She neither joined causes nor formed any causes for others to follow. If ever a poet was sui generis, it was Marianne Moore.

One of the signatures of Marianne's poetry was its idiosyncratic rhythms—as she put it, "a kind of pleasing jerky progress." Another was the precision of her language. Yet another was what she called her "conscientious inconsistency," especially in tone—often mingling the conversational and the taciturn, the whimsical and the devotional without the slightest loss of coherence—"Reticent candor," as one critic has described this aspect of her work. But most important was her refusal to separate the secular and the sacred. In examining the particularities of objects, she was interested not only in accuracy of depiction, but in an exploration of values. Unlike Bill, she expanded the subject of a poem until it revealed its moral. Or as Bill himself put it, "In looking at some apparently small object one feels the twirl of great events." This dutiful granddaughter and sister of pastors celebrated the most conventional values—decency, courage, endurance. Convinced that only masters like Chaucer, Dante, and Shakespeare deserved the name of poet, Marianne called her work "observations" (the title of one of her books), experiments in rhythm, exercises in composition.

In 1929, Marianne and her mother moved to Brooklyn, where she remained for the rest of her life, her famous black cloak and tricorn hat her only concessions to iconic flamboyance. She thrived, she said, on "tame excitement," and, nearing eighty, she was still insisting that "We need rigor—better governance of the emotions." But on the wall of her apartment hung a four-foot-square picture of a porcupine.

In the early twenties, most of Bill's closest friends went to Europe. But *everyone* went to Europe then. Puritanism had been intolerable, but Prohibition was worse. And what did America have to offer its artists and writers that could compare with the sophistication and permissiveness of the Left Bank?

Alfred had joined the exodus, and established a little magazine called *Broom* in Rome, which he co-edited with Harold Lobe (the model for Robert Cohn in *The Sun Also Rises*). It moved to Berlin, where it was co-edited by Lobe and Matthew Josephson, then, in a return to its ideological roots, to the Village, co-edited by Josephson and Malcolm Cowley. Fifteen issues were published in Europe and five in the Village before *Broom* fell victim to both its own internal squabbles and obscenity charges by the postal authorities.

But long after Alfred left the Village, Bill remembered their years of comradeship—and their years of alienation—and dedicated a book to him called *Sour Grapes*. Bill made new friends—Josephson, Cowley, Kenneth Burke, Louis Zukofsky, and Blaise Cendrars. New periodicals appeared, among them a magazine put out by the painter Stuart Davis, neatly encapsulating in its title its editorial attitude toward the America of the twenties—*Shit*. Bill noted disapprovingly that sooner or later "the intellectuals began to intrude on the terrain opened by the lunatic fringe."

The biggest blow to Bill's hope for poetry was the sudden prominence of T. S. Eliot's *The Waste Land*. Bill wrote: "Eliot's genius [gave] the poem back to the academics. . . . It wiped out our world as if an atom bomb had been dropped upon it and our brave sallies into the unknown were turned to dust."

Bill returned to the Village periodically for the rest of his life—get-togethers at Mattie Josephson's house, meetings with Allen Ginsberg and other beatnik poets to whom he had become an icon. In January 1959, when he was in his late seventies, Judith Malina and Julian Beck at the Living Theater mounted *Many Loves*, his verse play, which ran for 216 performances. But the Village hadn't changed as much as many people thought. Several weeks after the opening, Bill had to write Beck an irritated letter reminding him that he hadn't yet been paid.

VIII

Hart Crane

The Roaring Boy of the Village

Hart Crane was Harold Crane until his late teens, when his mother—whose maiden name was Hart—wrote him that she was proud of his "Harold Crane" poems in Village publications but plaintively added, "Do you intend to ignore your mother's side of the house entirely?. . . How would 'Hart Crane' be? No particularity there. You see I am always jealous, which is a sure sign I believe in your success." Years later, Hart insisted he'd changed his name because the memory of his mother's shrill "Haaaa-roooold" still grated on his nerves, but whether dutifully or defiantly, he now signed his name "Hart Crane."

Praising his work yet subtly demanding devotion, Mrs. Crane had needs of her own that were entangled in his psyche. His father was just as proud, and saw no reason Hart couldn't continue to write poetry while working in the family business. C. C. Crane was a candy manufacturer, and in the twenties, while his son was writing *The Bridge*, he expressed his creativity by inventing "the candies with the hole," Life Savers. The combination of parental pressure and filial piety largely determined Hart's sense of identity. If these emotional battles weren't disabling enough, the conflict *between* his parents was the central psychic event of Hart's life. As he wrote his mother shortly after turning twenty, "I think it's time you realized that for the last eight years my youth has been a rather bloody battleground for yours and father's sex life and troubles"—and a bloody battleground it would remain.

Yet another conflict left a scar across Hart's reputation. Hart Crane entered American iconography as the poet who exemplified the tortured genius destroyed by a materialistic culture. The transformation of Hart Crane's life into Hart Crane's legend is the story of the transformation of personal torment into public purpose and of the ways iconography both distills and distorts.

And yet another story runs parallel: the decline of the Village as a haven where artists could escape convention and find a supportive community of outcasts. Hart came to the Village to take part in what was still called "the literary life," but fled it in order to fulfill his creative destiny.

Born in Garrettsville, Ohio, in 1899, Hart was the child of one of those upper-middle-class marriages not uncommon in the Midwest at the turn of the century, uniting commerce and culture—a combination that encouraged artistic sensibility and discouraged its expression. Hart's parents enacted another common pattern—his father regarded his mother as sexually cold and his mother saw his father as sexually savage, but they both attempted, despite their frequent quarrels, to "keep up appearances." Of course the children of such marriages see through these "appearances," but unable to understand the hostility beneath them, they struggle both to keep up appearances themselves and to unconsciously choose between their parents.

At first, Hart saw his father through his mother's eyes—as a monster of greed and lust. And then he suddenly switched perspectives and saw his mother as a monster of selfishness and aloofness. For even as he hated first his father, then his mother, he craved the love of both; but they alternated between outpourings of affection and sudden spells of disapproval. In *The Bridge*, he wrote that he was forever "shouldering the curse of sundered parentage." Bearing both their names, always hating one of them, Hart, too, was sundered, always hating half of himself. And since he unsuccessfully sought the love of both, he felt he was always failing both—making him guilty even about his misery.

Hart saw only one recourse—to flee. At fifteen, he tried to commit suicide—first by slashing his wrists, then by swallowing sleeping powder. At seventeen, he moved to the Village—but this flight was no more successful, and he shuttled back and forth between New York and his parents' home in Cleveland for several years.

During that time, Hart felt guilty for rejecting both his father's repeated offers to take part in the family business and his mother's repeated attempts to reconcile. His father's offers were straightforward, but his mother was a master of manipulation. Possessive and capricious—always a psychologically destructive combination—she swung between smothering adoration and bitter complaints of his neglect.

"Nothing but illness and mental disorder in my family," he wrote a friend from the Village, "and I am expected by all the middle-class ethics and dogmas to rush myself to Cleveland and devote myself interminably to nursing, sympathizing with woes which I have no sympathy for because they are all unnecessary, and bolstering up the faith in others toward concepts which I long ago discarded as crass and cheap."

His very identity threatened by his parents' miserable marriage, Hart began to write in his early teens. If writing couldn't heal the fracture in his psyche, at least it could give words to his anguish. For Hart, poetry wasn't a means of escape, it was a means of discovery, a way to give solidity to his sense of self.

Hart first moved to the Village in 1916. He rarely lived in one place for more than a few months at a time, and often stayed in friends' homes, as if in search of a surrogate family. His mother even joined her "orphan," as she called him after her divorce, for a few miserable months.

While living in Cleveland, Hart had come across *Bruno's Weekly* in a local bookstore, and like thousands of sensitive, displaced young people, he became enthralled by the Village insurrection. In fact, his first published poem, written in Cleveland in 1916, was printed in *Bruno's Weekly* shortly after he arrived in the Village—a thirteen-line lyric in praise of Oscar Wilde, another artist, he must have felt, who found the inspiration to sing even while imprisoned. Called "O33" after Wilde's cell number in Reading Gaol, the poem surely appealed to the charlatan Guido Bruno less for its artistic merit—which he was unable to discern—than for its homage to his patron saint. Indeed, a series of articles on Wilde in *Bruno's Weekly* earlier in the year must have strengthened Hart's emerging conviction of the connection between poetry and pain.

While in Cleveland, Hart also came across another Village publication, *The Pagan*, and wrote its editor, Joseph Kling, "I am interested in your magazine as a new and distinctive chord in the present American Renaissance of literature and art. Let me praise your September cover; it has some suggestion of the exoticism and richness of Wilde's poems."

Hart looked up both editors as soon as he arrived in the Village. He sized up Guido Bruno as a bohemian hack within a few minutes, but he was impressed by Kling. Hart was such a frequent visitor to the offices of *The Pagan* that Kling decided to name the teenager an associate editor. In later years Hart called *The Pagan* "a fetid corpse," but during his apprenticeship it was his outlet for several essays and nearly a dozen poems. Kling felt Hart was "the equal of any American lyricist of the day"—praise to which Hart responded with astonishing maturity. "I don't trust Kling's criticism very far," he wrote, "judging by the 'tone' generally prevalent in the magazine. But I *am* improving and would just as soon be deceived a little as not."

Kling wasn't able to pay Hart, but did get him free tickets to Village theaters and published his review of three playwrights. Eugene O'Neill's *Ile*, Hart wrote, was a splendid "picture of the silence, solitude, and desolation of northern waters." "Although slightly reminiscent of Anatole France," he concluded of Edna St. Vincent Millay's *Two Slatterns and a King*, "its medieval satire was gratifying." But the works he liked best— though most Villagers found them silly—were Alfred Kreymborg's *Manikin and Minikin* and *Jack's House*, which he praised for their "lyric-dramatic dialogue."

The young Ohio poet exulted at finding himself at the center of Village literary life. He wrote a friend in Cleveland, "Illusions are falling away from everything I look at lately. . . . Still there is something of a satisfaction in the development of one's consciousness even though it is painful. There is a certain freedom gained—a lot of things pass out of one's concern that before mattered a great deal. . . . To one in my situation N.Y. is a series of exposures intense and rather savage. . . . New York handles one roughly but presents almost more remedial recess."

Among the "exposures" Hart found most rewarding was his friendship with Mary and Padraic Colum, who invited him to stop by their apartment two or three times a week to talk poetry. The Colums described him as "gangling, semi-literate," but listened to his work with increasing admiration, not only giving him encouragement and a kind of informal education, but becoming the first of dozens of surrogate families.

Growing disenchanted with *The Pagan*, Hart sought out other outlets for his poetry. Alfred Kreymborg's magazine represented the "newness" he was striving for in his own work. It published poets he admired, such as William Carlos Williams, and had accepted one of his poems—or so he thought for several months. "Damn good stuff," Williams wrote him of his submissions, but warned him that, at the moment, *Others* was short of the money to publish them. In his next letter, Williams was wise enough to suggest that Hart consider other magazines if he wanted to see his work published in the near future. "The literary life" may have seemed glamorous glimpsed from Cleveland, but it was becoming as disheartening and unstable as the life Hart had fled.

In his dejection, Hart found an unlikely ally—Maxwell Bodenheim—who promised him to get his poems into *Others*, where he was one of the rotating editors, and to help him place his work in *Seven Arts*. To Hart, Bodenheim was a poet who, "through the adverse channels of flattery, friendships, and 'pull,' " had finally succeeded "after four years of absolute obscurity." But Bodenheim had apparently used up his store of "flattery, friendships, and 'pull' " on his own behalf, and if Hart—or anyone else—had depended on him for support he would have remained in "absolute obscurity" for far more than four years. Hart had called Bodenheim "a first-class critic," but now decided his aesthetic credo was "inordinately precious." Hart may have been too proud, and too perceptive a judge of poetry, to let himself get dragged into the gamesmanship of the literary life, but at least he was learning the rules.

Even at his most dejected, Hart never believed that the poet's rejection by his culture was inevitable, so when he heard that *The Little Review* had recently moved to the Village, he was one of the first writers to knock on Margaret Anderson and Jane Heap's door.

Hart became a regular at Margaret and Jane's literary evenings, enthralled by their provocative conversation about poetry, but annoyed by their lack of enthusiasm for the examples he showed them. Hart would "sometimes leave us in a fury," recalled Margaret. But he always came back. When at last she accepted one of his poems, he exulted to a friend that he was going to be published in the same issue with Yeats and Pound! But Margaret had neglected to consult Jane, who strenuously objected to a line referring to the immaculate white ice of Norway. ("Immaculate is a dirty word to use," said Jane. "That ice is so white it looks black.") Hart was livid—was this going to be the same kind of runaround he'd experienced at *Others?*—but within weeks Margaret wrote, "Dear Hart Crane, poet! I'm using 'Shadow' in the December issue, now going to press. It's the best you've sent yet: I'll tell you details of just why when you come. It's quite lovely. Hurrah for you!!"

Margaret may have thought "Shadow" was Hart's "best yet," but according to Ezra Pound, the magazine's European editor, "beauty is a good enough egg, but so far as I can see, you haven't the ghost of a setting hen or an incubator." "Too good a douche to waste on one novice," Hart calmly responded. He might not have reached his twentieth birthday, but unlike Keats, he wasn't about to be killed by a review.

Hart had found a literary home in *The Little Review*, but ironically—given the magazine's precarious finances and his later reputation as a poet destroyed by a commercial culture—his closest association with Margaret and Jane was as their ambitious advertising manager. Hart had hoped to support himself by writing movie scripts—the first in a long line of Village poets with the same preposterous fantasy—but when his scenarios were repeatedly rejected, he took up Margaret and Jane's offer to solicit ads for their magazine.

"There is no reason why *The Little Review* could not be developed into as paying a periodical as *The New Republic*, *The Nation*, or *The Dial*," Hart wrote his mother, as eager as any Alger hero. But despite his hopes of making as much as $4,000 a year on commissions by mounting an assault on "all the great establishments on Fifth Ave.," advertisers proved unaccountably reluctant to peddle their products in an avant-garde magazine, and in his first couple of months Hart sold only one ad. Eventually he did persuade one "great establishment" to buy space, and for several issues *The Little Review* carried ads for Mary Garden candy—manufactured by Hart's father.

Heeding his mother's pleas, Hart briefly returned to Ohio in 1918, working in a munitions plant and as a cub reporter for the *Plain Dealer* of Cleveland, and late in 1919—having had his fill of the literary life—he went home for what he thought was forever. Now a local celebrity of sorts, he gave a newspaper interview and let it be known that as vulgar as he found life in Ohio, at least it was honest, and preferable to life in the "deplorable" Village. "It is utterly self-conscious, because it has been so much in the limelight. With so many uptown visitors coming in to observe from mere curiosity, and with so many 'artists' who are not artists at all living there, the Greenwich Village of a few years ago is gone."

Hart decided to go to work in his father's company after all, but he soon learned that with every step up the work grew more tedious. Stock boy, warehouse keeper, handyman, clerk, even branch manager—he tried his best, but what could be further from the empyrean realm of poetry than the daily burden of business? "The most revolting sensation I experienced," he wrote a friend in the Village, "is the feeling of having placed myself in a

position of quiescence or momentary surrender to the contact and possession of the insensitive fingers of my neighbors here. I am learning, just beginning to learn,—the technique of escape."

Hart was referring to escape into the world of the imagination, but
he was also learning to escape behind a facade of acquiescence, and, more
practically, by going to the office only when his father was in town. Selling
was the worst and he dreaded "this tramping around" to corporate execu-
tives, who, sensing his self-disgust, gave him the reaction he felt he deserved.

Hart's father's patience was not limitless, and in April 1921 they had
their inevitable confrontation. The scene ended when Hart cursed his father and bolted out. At first distraught, he soon turned the quarrel into a
noble act of rebellion. "Whatever comes now is much better than the past,"
he wrote a Village friend. "I shall learn to be somewhere near free again,—
at least free from the hatred that has corroded me into illness."

But Hart remained in Cleveland for nearly two more years, living
with his mother, and, far from fleeing the business world, he took a position
at an advertising agency. "I grew more pleased with my work and treatment
there every day," he said. "In short, I rather begin to feel sort of human
again." "Never guessed a commercial institution could be organized on
such a decent basis," he added. "And they actually will come of their own
accord and tell you that they are pleased with the work you are doing for
them!!!!!!!!!!"

Hart wrote poetry in his free time, and his gift matured rapidly, as
did his reputation. But he still wanted to prove to his father that he could
succeed in the business world; he might have rejected his father, but not
his father's values. He was beginning to believe that his role wasn't to express bohemian alienation but to explore American ideas. Working in advertising didn't strike him as a debasement of his talents, but as an
opportunity to participate in the emerging "American century."

When Hart left the advertising agency in early 1923, it wasn't out of
disillusionment; his employers didn't have enough business to keep him
on. With their assistance, he concocted a plan that would keep his father
from calling him a failure. They'd send him to New York "on business,"
he'd find a job, and then he'd "resign." So when he arrived back in the Village in March 1923, he was no sensitive young poet fleeing the provinces,
he was a job seeker on Madison Avenue. He landed a position with J. Walter Thompson, one of the premier advertising agencies in the country.
"They employ a lot of real writers as copy writers at Thompson's," he wrote
his mother, "and have an entirely different feeling about art and business

than you encounter any place west of N.Y. In fact it's a feather in your cap
if you know a little more than you're 'supposed to' here."

Though Hart fervently hoped his father would be impressed, and
wrote his mother of his happiness, he was living under considerable emotional strain, not just from his high-pressure job (his first account was the
Gutta Percha Paint Company), but from the intense demands of his writings. He'd begun work on what he hoped would be his masterpiece, *The
Bridge*, whose complex vision taxed his creative energies.

The one release Hart could always count on was alcohol. The first
drink took the edge off his nerves, the second calmed him, the third brought
a kind of euphoria; but unfortunately, he didn't stop there. The fourth made
him edgy, the fifth stirred up his anxieties, and the sixth brought a form of
psychosis in which he accused his friends of betraying him and occasionally
threw objects out of windows until he was physically restrained.

One particularly screeching hangover brought his career at J. Walter Thompson to an end after six months. Assigned to a cosmetics account,
he had arranged several vials of perfume on his desk. He arrived at work
one morning suffering from a bad headache, grew nauseated from the
odors, and in a sudden rage hurled all the bottles into the street. The legend
was born — the tortured, self-destructive, alcoholic poet displaying his contempt for commercial culture in an act of heroic defiance. But though his
nerves *were* frazzled by his job, he had no quarrel with his employer's values. His frustration was largely over his writing, and far from being proud of
his outburst, he was ashamed of it. The Villagers made a myth out of a man
whose deepest contempt was for them.

Hart still lived in the Village — it was one of the few places in the city
where he could afford the rent. And most of his friends were still Villagers. Allen Tate, Waldo Frank, Matthew Josephson, Kenneth Burke,
E. E. Cummings, and Gorham Munson hardly adopted the adversarial
attitude toward American culture of his former allies at *The Pagan* and *The
Little Review*. Instead they formed a kind of literary community seeking out
the aspects of American culture that they hoped to reinvigorate.

The change in Village literary life between the teens and the twenties — a change in which Hart was a leading figure — was at once seismic
and subtle. Most of the poetry published in *The Masses*, to give one instance, had been conventional in form and revolutionary in sentiment.
The writers for *The Masses* had sought the overthrow of the American po-

litical system on the basis of European theories, but had disdained developments in European poetry. In contrast, many in the new group of poets explored revolutionary forms in order to express traditional American values—the nineteenth-century ideals that had been lost in the postwar era. They sought a revitalization of American politics while being influenced artistically by the Europeans. The paradox can be overstated, of course, but the leading poets of the twenties shared little of the radical/bohemian spirit of the Village of the teens.

Allen Tate later summed up the attitude not only of his generation but of every generation of Villagers: "I think we were drawn together by three things. We were young, we were poor, and we were ambitious. That is, we thought that the older generation was pretty bad, and we were later going to replace them."

Among Hart's friends was Eugene O'Neill, whom he considered the model artist, not only a writer who made a decent living without compromising his work, but one who, as far as young Hart could see, led a relatively middle-class life complete with wife and dog.

He formed an even more influential friendship with the legendary photographer and patron saint of the arts, Alfred Stieglitz. Their meeting, Hart wrote Stieglitz, "was a tremendous one in my life because I was able to share all the truth toward which I am working in my own medium, poetry, with another man who had manifestly taken many steps in that same direction in *his* work. . . . We are accomplices in many ways that we don't yet fully understand." Hart *did* understand that he and Stieglitz shared the belief that the artist must deal with the raw turmoil of contemporary American life, with the thrust and rhythm of the city in particular. Their friendship soon faded, but Stieglitz's ideas remained crucial to Hart as he worked out the complex themes of *The Bridge*.

And one glorious night in 1923, Hart formed a brief but intense friendship with the artist he admired more than any other. In 1921, he had published "Chaplinesque," "a sympathetic attempt to put [in] words some of the Chaplin pantomime, so beautiful and so full of eloquence, and so modern."

He sent a copy of the poem to Chaplin, and received a brief note from his artistic hero, which he showed to all his friends in a daze of delight. Then, one evening a year later, while reading in his apartment in his pajamas, he heard a knock at the door. There stood Charlie Chaplin himself!

Fancying himself an intellectual—though he was the most intuitive of artists and described his work solely in terms of craft—Chaplin spent much of his free time in the Village whenever he came to New York, and on this occasion he looked up Waldo Frank, mentioned Hart's poem, and asked for an introduction. The two men strolled over to Hart's apartment and, to his astonishment, Hart found himself face-to-face with the "most pleasant-looking, twinkling little man in a black derby." " 'Let me introduce you to Mr. Charles Chaplin'—said Waldo," Hart wrote his mother the next morning, "and I was smiling into one of the most beautiful faces I ever expect to see. Well!—I was quickly urged out of my night clothes and the three of us walked arm in arm over to where Waldo is staying at 77 Irving Place (near Gramercy). All the way we were trailed by enthusiastic youngsters. People seem to spot Charlie in the darkness. He is so gracious that he never discourages anything but rude advances."

Chaplin was "so radiant and healthy, wistful, gay, and *young*," Hart went on. And best of all, "he remembered my poem very well and is very interested in my work. I am very happy in the intense clarity of spirit that a man like Chaplin gives one if he is honest enough to receive it. I have that spiritual honesty. . . . We (just Charlie and I) are to have dinner together some night next week. . . . Stories (marvelous ones he knows!) told with such subtle mimicry that you rolled on the floor. Such graceful wit, too—O that man has a mind."

Months later, in a letter to his father justifying his decision to pursue a poet's life, Hart mentioned his evening with Chaplin. He was beginning to gain a reputation, he wrote, and proved his point by listing "the many distinguished people" who admired his work, O'Neill, Stieglitz, Frank, and Chaplin prominent among them. Maybe his father couldn't understand his poetry, but certainly he'd be impressed by his famous colleagues. "I wish you could meet some of my friends," he continued, "who are not the kind of 'Greenwich Villagers' that you may have been thinking they were. If I am able to keep on in my present development, strenuous as it is, you may live to see the name 'Crane' stand for something where literature is talked about, not only in New York but in London and abroad."

After his evening with Chaplin, Hart decided that the time had come to devote all his energies to his work. He couldn't let himself be distracted by the partygoing and gossip and backbiting of the literary world, or get trapped in the deadly spiral of taking jobs to support his writing and ending up too drained to write. Nothing Chaplin said in particular influenced Hart—but "the intense clarity of spirit that a man like Chaplin gives one," and Chaplin's treatment of him as a fellow artist, were decisive. He had grown disgusted with the world of the Village once before and returned to Ohio. Now he fled for good, and for the rest of his life only returned for brief visits.

"Most of my friends are worn out with the struggle here in New York," he wrote in partial justification of his decision. "If you make enough to live decently on, you have no time left for your real work—and otherwise you are constantly liable to starve. New York offers nothing to anyone but a circle of friendly and understanding brothers,—beyond that it is one of the most stupid places in the world to live in. Of course, one's friends are worth it, but sometimes, when you see them so upset by the fever and crowded conditions, the expenses and worries—you wonder whether or not there is much use in the whole business."

For two months in the winter of 1923–1924, Hart lived with friends in a farmhouse in Woodstock, the emerging artists' colony two hours north of the city, where he replenished his creative energies for the long months of work on *The Bridge* that lay ahead. Early in 1924 he moved to a room at 110 Columbia Heights in Brooklyn overlooking the Brooklyn Bridge— "the finest view in all America," he exulted. By one of those resonant coincidences, it was the very room—though Hart didn't know it at the time—in which John Augustus Roebling, the architect of the bridge, had lived years earlier.

While the Village no longer entered Hart's consciousness except as a place to avoid, he remained in close touch with most of his Village friends, and formed new relationships with several others from his "exile" in Brooklyn Heights—Marsden Hartley for one, Marianne Moore for another. He didn't much like Moore's poetry—"too much of a precieuse for my adulation"—and he didn't much care for her editorship of *The Dial*, though he became edgily and reluctantly involved in a professional relationship. Back in 1919, *The Dial* had been the first publication to pay for his work—the grand sum of $10. In 1925—boom times in America!— Moore paid him $20 for "The Wine Menagerie." Moore cut the poem severely, rearranged several lines, and even changed its title, leading Hart's friend Kenneth Burke to assert that she'd taken all the wine out of the menagerie. "I never would have consented to such an outrageous joke," complained Hart, "if I had not so desperately needed the twenty dollars." As for Moore, "Hart complains of me?" she remarked years later. "Well, I complain of *him*. . . . His gratitude was ardent and later his repudiation of it commensurate. . . . He was so *anxious* to have us take that thing. . . . 'Well, if you would modify it a little,' I said, 'we would like it better.' "

Unfortunately for Hart, when he sought to publish a section of *The*

Bridge called "The Dance" two years later, *The Dial* was one of the few outlets left. "I've had to submit it to Marianne Moore recently," Hart wrote
Allen Tate, "as my only present hope of a little cash. But she probably will
object to the word 'breasts,' or some other such detail. It's really ghastly. I
wonder how much longer our market will be in the grip of two such hysterical virgins as *The Dial* and *Poetry!*"

Otto Kahn, the banker/patron, supported Hart during much of the
time he was writing *The Bridge*, but in 1928, the pressure to have a weekly
paycheck created a scene that helped cement the legend of the dissipated
genius. Working for a Wall Street brokerage house, where he frequently
didn't arrive until after noon, and often still drunk—he finally reached the
breaking point. "There's Scott's Emulsion," he roared, smashing his fist
down onto a stack of stocks and bonds. "There's Scott's Emulsion," he repeated even louder. "I never took a drop of that and I never will as long as I
live!" He shouted, "Never!" and bolted out of the building.

Hart's heavy drinking, which began in the early twenties, soon
turned him into an out-and-out alcoholic. Following the scent of "the wine
menagerie," he embarked on extended binges that became part of Village
lore. According to Malcolm Cowley, everyone in the Village came to recognize three distinct phases of Hart's drinking: warm affection, brilliant
monologue, and broken furniture. The trick was to give him one or two
drinks to bring out his mellow fellowship and loosen his articulate
tongue—then hide the bottle.

Hart drank to soothe his torment over his parents; he also had a romantic notion that alcohol gave him access to his muse. But there was another purpose—to give him courage to embark on his often dangerous,
long-after-midnight sexual adventures. He wasn't drowning his shame, as
some of his friends suspected; he was readying himself for ecstasy.

Hart's homosexuality was an open secret in the Village. He was compulsively confessional, and would regale his friends with hilarious accounts of his liaisons down on the docks or in sailors' bars—for he favored
"the nautical variety"—or, when the fleet was at sea, in the seedy saloons.
These encounters occasionally ended in threats of blackmail, but more
often in savage beatings. Policemen would find him in alleyways hung over
and badly bruised and robbed of his last dollar, and would drag him off to
the local precinct house. But such lurid evenings would enter his repertoire as well-polished, self-mocking anecdotes for the delectation of his
friends.

A spiritualized obsession and its droll aftermath—the *two* phases of his eroticism. "How I am stalked by lust these dog days!" he would write a friend in the first phase. "And how many 'shadowy' temptations beset me at every turn! Were I free from my family responsibilities I would give myself to passion to the final cinder. After all—that and poetry are the only things life holds for me." And in another letter the next morning, in the second phase, he would recount his escapades in a tipsy-ribald vein to another friend—"the passionate pulchritude of the usual recent maritime houreths"—concluding, "But here I am—full of Renault Wine tonics—after an evening with the Danish millionaire on Riverside—and better, thank God, a night with a bluejacket from the Arkansas."

Hart's sexual initiation had taken place in his early teens, when he was seduced by one of his father's employees. His first love affair was at the age of twenty while he was working at his father's candy outlet in Akron. "This 'affair' that I have been having has been the most intense and satisfactory one of my whole life," he wrote Gorham Munson back in the Village, "and I am all broken up at the thought of leaving him. Yes, the last word will jolt you. I have never had devotion returned before like this, nor ever found a soul, mind, and body so worthy of devotion. Probably I never shall again."

"Garden Abstract," one of his best early poems, seems a direct response to this affair, though despite its explicitly phallic imagery, it purports to express a female perspective. But a poem he wrote four years later, "Possessions," is a more direct depiction of his attitude toward sexuality. Overwhelmed by desire, erotically "possessed," the poet, driven by "the fixed stone of lust," wanders down Bleecker Street, finds a momentary partner, then returns to the solitude of the self. Having experienced the turbulence of sexuality, he has spiritualized his passion. Even when Hart ventured into waterfront dives or cruised the streets of the Village, he always hoped to transform his lust into love—and even if he failed, he felt his failure was redeemed by his quest.

> *I turning, turning on smoked forking spires,*
> *The city's stubborn lives, desires.*

In 1923, Hart met the man who would be the companion, soulmate, and love he thought he'd found in Akron. At the Provincetown Players he met the artist Ivan Opffer, and later his brother Emil, a sailor in the merchant marine, with whom he fell desperately in love.

"For many days now," Hart wrote Waldo Frank shortly after meeting Emil, "I have gone about quite dumb with something for which 'happiness' must be too mild a term. . . . I have seen the Word made Flesh. I mean nothing less, and I know now that there is such a thing as indestructibility. . . . And I have been able to give freedom and life which was acknowledged in the ecstasy of walking hand in hand across the most beautiful bridge of the world."

In Emil's long absences at sea, Hart fell prey to fits of jealousy, but he believed that happiness was spiritually transcendent only when it included moments of suffering. Partly to sustain him while Emil was away, Hart undertook a series of six poems, called "Voyages," about the sea that was Emil's home, and about the understanding and devotion they found in each other's arms.

Hart continued to see Emil for the rest of his life, although during the second half of the twenties their relationship dwindled from passionate love to casual friendship. In the spring of 1927, he met another urbane and literate sailor, whom he called "Phoebus Apollo." He was deliriously happy for a few weeks, until his new lover sailed off forever. But mostly he recanted his vow and returned to the "beckonings" of "the City's complicated devastations."

Hart's friends never considered his sexuality "perverted," in part because he refused to regard it that way himself, and they showed him the generosity of not trying to "explain" his homosexuality as the result of his parents' sexual hostility—though Allen Tate recalled Hart once saying "something to the effect that the constant quarreling of his mother and father, and the violent sexual reconciliations . . . had given him a horror of the normal sexual relation." Nor did anyone interpret his brief, passionate affair with Peggy Cowley, Malcolm's estranged wife, in Mexico in the last months of his life as "rescuing" him from "deviance." One of the reasons for everyone's tolerance was a subtler intolerance. Like Hart, they despised the effeminacy of the "usual" Village homosexuals, and while Hart had homosexual impulses, he was relieved beyond measure to realize he did not have what were called homosexual "mannerisms."

While Hart had no qualms about telling his friends he was a homosexual, telling his mother was an entirely different matter. He wrote her effusive letters about Emil—"He is so much more to me than anyone I have ever met that I miss him terribly during these eight-week trips he takes for bread and butter"—but this, he surely intended her to think, and she surely believed, was nothing but an intense friendship. However, when Hart and his mother visited Los Angeles in 1928, and she insistently asked to be introduced to the actor "friends" he was spending so much time with, he decided to tell her everything. He started with a long disquisition on the nature of homosexuality, its invariable appearance in all cultures, and the bigotry homosexual people had to contend with, even recommending several books. Yes, he finally confided, he was a homosexual, and seeing her shocked expression recalled experiences in his adolescence that had "conditioned" him toward his preference, and went so far as to intimate that he'd tried to "cure" himself by trying "normal" relationships.

Hart didn't regret confiding in his mother until he realized she now had a weapon she might use to hurt him, or worse, to turn his father against him should they ever seem about to reconcile. And, in fact, when he did reach a rapport with his father in the last years of his life, her threats to tell him of his son's homosexuality shadowed Hart's peace.

Hart was intimately familiar with two groups of people who led double lives—middle-class families and homosexuals—and while he resisted his parents' efforts "to keep up appearances" and refused to hide his homosexuality, in nearly every other way he remained a divided self. The Villagers of the teens had insisted that the integration of personal impulse and social behavior was the basis of cultural health—the gap between them was responsible for both the prevalence of oppression and the repression of creativity—but Hart's life was a rejection of this radical-bohemian ethos. Always in search of a surrogate family, he was both greedy for reassurance and wary of rejection, making him the most affectionate of friends and the most exasperating. As Waldo Frank put it, "he lived exacerbated in a constant swing between ecstasy and exhaustion."

His second self was the disciplined, patient, objective, dedicated poet, exemplifying intellectual equilibrium and ruthless self-examination. He once said, "I admit that the freedom of my imagination is the most precious thing that life holds for me,—and the only reason I can see for living."

Indeed, the means he used to free his imagination for his writing were often the very means that resulted in his erratic behavior. Unlike many of his Eliot-influenced friends, such as Allen Tate and Yvor Winters, who distrusted impulse and submitted themselves to the discipline of theory, Hart cherished spontaneity and felt that theory too often calcified into dogma. This attitude might make him seem "aimless and irresponsible," he admitted, but he believed that to be a poet meant to be open, trusting, unguarded. "You seem to think that experience is some commodity—that can be sought!" he wrote Winters. "One can respond only to certain circumstances, just what the barriers are and where the boundaries cross can never be completely known. And the surest way to frustrate the possibility of any free realization is, it seems to me, to willfully direct it. . . . One should be somewhat satisfied if one's work comes to approximate a true record of such moments of 'illumination' as are occasionally possible."

Like most poets of the twenties, Hart felt compelled to define himself in relationship to T. S. Eliot. *The Waste Land*, while seminal, was "so damned dead," he said, and again and again he asserted his "cry for a positive attitude" in opposition to Eliot's pessimism. "I take Eliot as a point of departure toward an almost complete reverse of direction. His pessimism is amply justified in his own case. But I would apply as much of his erudition and technique as I can absorb and assemble toward a more positive, or (if [I] must put it so in a skeptical age) ecstatic goal. I should not think of this if a kind of rhythm and ecstasy were not (at odd moments, and rare!) a very real thing to me." If Hart's credo could be summed up in a phrase, it would surely be, as he wrote Allen Tate in 1922, "Launch into praise!"

Also like most poets of the twenties, Hart defined himself in relationship to the decade's exuberant conviction of reawakened national greatness. An uneasy skepticism might moderate the optimism of many intellectuals, a despairing cynicism might dominate the exiles in Paris, but in *The Bridge* Hart dedicated himself to "a mystical synthesis of America" that would elevate the American consciousness. "Time and space is the myth of the modern world," he wrote of Lindbergh's flight, "and it is interesting to see how any victory in the field is heralded by the mass of humanity. In a way my Bridge is a manifestation of the same general subject. Maybe I'm just a little jealous of Lindy!"

Poetry, Hart felt, should be "an instrument of consciousness that could envision some absolute and timeless concept of the imagination with astounding clarity and conviction," that could create "a single, new *word*, never before spoken and impossible to actually enunciate but self-evident as an active principle of the reader's consciousness henceforward." "One must be drenched in words, literally soaked with them to have the right ones form themselves into the proper pattern at the right moment." At the same time, he sought intense compression rather than the slack free verse or imagistic mood-conjuring favored by so many Village poets of the teens. What poetry needs, he said, is "an extraordinary capacity for surrender"—not just to personal sensations but "to the sensation of urban life." He couldn't write, he said, without the "whispering approach of what I might call 'temperature'—the condition for organic fusion of experience, logical or no." "Alert blindness"—that was his aspiration.

Hart's masterpiece, *The Bridge*, linked him with the celebratory, prophetic strain of American poetry and in particular with the mystic nationalism of Walt Whitman—whose picture he carried in his wallet. Furthermore, "this epic of modern consciousness," as he also characterized his work, linked him to Van Wyck Brooks, Waldo Frank, Charles Beard, Sherwood Anderson, John Dos Passos, and many other writers who were also reexamining the American past in an effort to illuminate contemporary culture. Expanding a tradition that reached from Emerson's "wise passivity" to William Carlos Williams's "mirror on modernity," Hart's thematic concerns were a form of metaphysical patriotism.

The Bridge covers wide expanses of time and space, as if in a dream, juxtaposing legends of American history—Columbus, Cortés, Pocahontas, Rip Van Winkle, the Gold Rush—with realities of contemporary America—subways, skyscrapers, movie houses, and burlesque shows—and juxtaposing allusions to Plato, Marlowe, Shakespeare, and Blake with more recent writers like Whitman, Melville, and Poe. At the center of the poem, an exploration of America's consciousness and that of the poet parallels the discovery of "the new world" with that of a new self. The Brooklyn Bridge symbolizes "a mystic consummation," the union of myth and reality, the redemptive restoration of wholeness to history and to self.

In view of the poem's audacious ambitions, it's hardly surprising that many critics consider *The Bridge* a magnificent failure, and that Hart himself came to feel that it didn't fulfill his conception. *The Bridge* contains sections that belong in the canon of American poetry, but his success in building them into a coherent and revelatory design is more problematic. Nevertheless, his achievement remains as monumental as the edifice on which it was based.

So rapid was Hart's emotional and creative deterioration after he finished *The Bridge*, it seemed in retrospect that only the intensity of his dedication kept his psyche from splintering. The alcoholic binges became more frequent, the saloon brawls more violent. Poetry was initiated in ecstasy, abandoned in despair. He reconciled with his father, but his relationship with his mother remained as volatile as ever. His encounters with his friends began to develop signs of paranoia.

In 1931, Hart traveled to Mexico on a Guggenheim fellowship, and though he found momentary happiness with Peggy Cowley—"Boys, I did it!" he gaily announced to a barful of friends the day after first making love to her—and experienced a resurgence of poetic inspiration with "The

Broken Tower," his life disintegrated into chaos and anguish. In a particularly unpleasant scene, he was ejected from the American embassy and deposited in front of his friend Katherine Anne Porter's house, whereupon he cursed her, she recalled, "with words so foul there is no question of repeating them," and after which he profusely apologized. He even swallowed a large quantity of iodine in a halfhearted effort to end his life.

Virtually forced to leave Mexico, Hart and Peggy set sail for New York. A few minutes before noon on April 27, 1932—after three days at sea, a night of heavy drinking, and a sexual encounter in the sailors' quarters that left him severely beaten—he appeared dressed in his pajamas and an overcoat, strode to the railing of the afterdeck, neatly folded his coat, and leapt into the sea.

"Someone told me," wrote Hart's friend John Dos Passos, "that . . . the last his friends on deck saw of him was a cheerful wave of the hand before he sank and drowned." But the horrified passengers couldn't agree if the hand was waving goodbye or reaching for a life preserver. According to Peggy, Hart's last words were "I'm not going to make it, dear." He was thirty-two years old.

Many reasons were suggested for Hart's suicide. Some of his friends attributed it to a combination of financial insecurity, drinking, sexual anxiety, shame at his increasingly debauched and abusive behavior, and distress over his relationship with his parents (his father had died less than a year earlier). Some critics, reading backward, have argued that the central theme of his poetry was self-destruction—which makes about as much sense as the argument of one critic that in his suicide Hart sought transcendental unity with his favorite symbol, the sea. Allen Tate—almost obscenely gnawing at the bone of ideology even in the face of a friend's death—asserted that it was the "logical conclusion" of Hart's refusal to embrace an intellectual tradition, that it was "morally appropriate," and that it exemplified one of Eliot's fundamental tenets, the breakdown of "the integrity of the individual consciousness."

But inevitable as his suicide seemed, Hart had never been even half in love with easeful death. "I shall [never relax]," he wrote a friend, "into the easy acceptance (in the name of elegance, nostalgia, with splenetic splendor!) of death which I see most of my friends doing."

It's just as certain that his suicide was ultimately inexplicable, but those who stressed the creative stasis of the last several years of his life at least acknowledged that whatever else he was—a son, an alcoholic, a homosexual, the wild child of the avant-garde—in his very essence, he was a poet. And in the last five years of his short life, Hart lost his almost audacious confidence in his poetic gift. He began to have his doubts in the middle of writing *The Bridge*—"most of my energy is wasted in a kind of inward combustion," he complained—and after its completion he suffered from what can only be called imaginative exhaustion.

But perhaps the problem lay less in Hart's assessment of his talent than in his conception of his role as a poet. Valuing poetry more than life itself, he never accepted his inability to achieve his vision of an absolute poetry. As William Carlos Williams put it, "He continually reached 'up,' out of what he *knew*, to that which he didn't know."

The creative imagination, the poetic act—Hart staked everything on this ideal and remained willing to sacrifice everything for its attainment. Idealism as prophecy—what could be more American? And when he gradually came to realize that such a goal was unattainable, he had nothing left to live for. "In a profound sense," said R. P. Blackmur, "to those who use it, poetry is the only means of putting a tolerable order upon the emotions." So it seems most likely Hart decided to end his life when he understood that he'd reached a terrifying impasse—that he could never write the poetry he could imagine.

In any case—since no society is quite as obsessed with self-destruction as one that stresses cheerful individualism—Hart's suicide entered American iconography as the emblematic gesture of the anguished artist in a materialistic culture. The litany of the ills of America in the twenties—commercialism, corruption, cynicism, mendacious optimism, and meretricious idealism—was invoked to make his death a potent symbol of the poet's fate. The visionary had no role in America, the artist had no function—the only escape was death. "The ordeal of the artist" has become such a persistent theme in American mythology that it sometimes seems as much officially sanctioned as it was originally adversarial. Hart's life has been used to exemplify "the ordeal of the artist" by poets who themselves have been transformed from adversarial artists into icons. Robert Lowell, in his elegy "Words for Hart Crane," portrayed him as twice alienated—as an artist and as a homosexual—and called him "the Shelley of [his] age." And Allen Ginsberg, in "Death to Van Gogh's Ear!" linked him with other artists martyred by a dehumanizing society.

This transformation of Hart into an iconic figure had little to do with the facts of his life—and in some ways contradicted his convictions about American culture and his sense of his own identity. He contributed to the defining conviction of the twenties, that America was emerging into greatness. "The ordeal of the artist" argument makes Hart a victim of the very society he celebrated, it displaces attention from his poetry to his biography, and worst of all, when it does consider his poetry, it diminishes his achievements.

The twenties in the Village, Malcolm Cowley recalled, were years of "youth and poverty and good humor." For thousands of young writers, the pilgrimage to the Village was the fulfillment of a dream, but Hart's dream was at once less rebellious and more exalted, and when he left—almost at the same time as Edna St. Vincent Millay—he had become both disillusioned with bohemia and enraptured with his muse. The essential fact about Hart was stated by one of his oldest friends shortly after his death: "No one who has known Hart Crane very long or very well has failed to feel the silent, terrible sincerity of his purpose."

IX

Maxwell Bodenheim

"Poems Twenty-Five Cents Each"

P oems twenty-five cents each. Poems twenty-five cents each. Autographed copies fifty cents." Bearded, rheumy-eyed, toothless, his floppy pants held up by suspenders fashioned out of scraps of twine, his swollen ankles encased in laceless shoes, the old man shuffled from table to table at the San Remo, the Minetta Tavern, the Village Vanguard.

Oblivious to patrons who edged away from his rank smell, he coaxed them out of their quarters with a complicitous cackle. "What about you, sir, a poem for the lady? Yes?" With trembling hands, he withdrew a sheaf of wrinkled papers from his sweat-stained briefcase, pretended to look for a poem suitable for such a discerning patron of the arts — "Ah, here's the one I want you to have" and made the exchange with an almost dapper dignity. After a courtly bow, he shuffled to the bar, slid the coin discreetly across the counter, then emptied the shot of cheap whiskey with a single gulp.

One might depict a poetess:

She recites dripping verse with plenty
Of remarks on her spasmodic charms.

While some customers contended that the verses were fairly priced at 25 cents each, most were less interested in the poems than in the signature at the bottom, for they saw not a besotted bum, but a defiant spirit, debonair even in his degradation, the poet praised by Pound, the novelist pursued by smut-hounds, the notorious roué of a thousand amours, iconoclast, renegade, scourge of the philistines, "unwashed archpriest of Bohemia," Poet Laureate of Greenwich Village—Maxwell Bodenheim.

In 1915, at the age of twenty-two, Maxwell Bodenheim stood jauntily at the door of poet Alfred Kreymborg's Bank Street apartment, one arm in a sling, his bulging briefcase under the other. Despite his disheveled clothing and a slightly cynical smile, his pallid, ascetic face and golden hair gave him the appearance, as his friend Ben Hecht said, "of a pensive Christ." Kreymborg had already published several of the young man's poems in *Others*—but before the afternoon was over he found his guest to be "the queerest of the queer."

Kreymborg was spared Bodenheim's malodorous four-foot-long white Polynesian pipe, which he'd acquired in exchange for a sonnet, but not the items in Bodenheim's briefcase: poems, rejection slips, a change of socks and shorts, and a bottle of Tabasco sauce, which he poured over the meal to which Kreymborg invited him, having already doused his meat with a full bottle of his host's Worcestershire sauce and the contents of the salt and pepper shakers. But Bodenheim's enthralling conversation—anecdotes, baroque invective, woeful catalogues of his ailments, and dazzling denunciations of his enemies—diverted attention from his eating habits, and Kreymborg and his wife, Christine, immediately installed him in the room directly over their apartment. For several months they acted as surrogate parents, Christine making sure Bodenheim ate and dressed at least passably, Alfred introducing him to a wide circle of poets, novelists, and painters. At one "party of welcome," Kreymborg recalled, "there was no greater pleasure than listening to Bogie [as everyone called him] and Marianne Moore spinning long, subtle thoughts in colloquy." He intrigued Marcel Duchamp, William Carlos Williams, Conrad Aiken, and Malcolm Cowley with his peculiar mixture of ebullient vituperation, grungy manners, and poetic sensibility. He was soon acting as an associate editor of *Others*, moderating all-night poetry readings at Sam Schwartz's basement bar with an iron hammer as a gavel, and hanging out with Eugene O'Neill and Dorothy Day at the Hell Hole, where they composed a long poem together.

The legend that was already beginning to grow up around Bodenheim depended on his being a poet, a very good one. In this regard, the bohemians who were amused by his outrageous behavior weren't essentially
different from the philistines who were scandalized by it, for both focused
on the man and ignored his work. Still, in the years before 1920, critics
considered him a poet of extraordinary promise, worthy of mention in the
same sentence with Ezra Pound and Carl Sandburg. Margaret Anderson of
The Little Review remembered for decades a line from the first poem of his
she ever read ("moon paint on a colorless house"). William Carlos
Williams wrote Amy Lowell that *Others* was a valuable publication if only
because it "held the future of such a man as Bodenheim in its palms," and
Hart Crane wrote his mother in 1919 that "Bodenheim is at the top of
American poetry today" (although a few years later he referred to "an atro-
cious piece of dull nonsense by Bodenheim").

Bodenheim "sunned himself in this admiration," Kreymborg
noted, but he also noticed that the poet often "spoke with the weariness of
an aged man" and that he "more than once betrayed the impression that he
was about as happy as he would allow himself to be without neglecting to
keep an eye on the disillusionment soon to follow."

Bodenheim had left a trail of outrageous behavior in Chicago, and news
of the episodes preceded him to the Village. In one, he had told a rich
radical couple that he was being pursued by the police for refusing to register for military service, and so impressed them with this courageous resistance that they hid him in a luxurious apartment for several weeks, where
he was supplied with food and wine and even the occasional trollop. This
sumptuous life lasted until the couple discovered he'd been dishonorably
discharged several years earlier.

Villagers who hastened to befriend an amusing "character" soon
discovered that such characters are amusing in inverse proportion to their
proximity. Bodenheim's true genius was for alienation. It was as if he had
adopted his prickly pose to express his anti-authoritarianism only to find
that it expressed his self-destructiveness and confirmed his sense of self-
loathing by driving away even his friends.

Even people who were inclined to tolerate Bodenheim's idiosyncrasies for the sake of his art were stunned when, feeling he was not sufficiently the center of attention, he would bite off chunks of his wineglass
before reciting his latest poems, oblivious to the blood dripping from his
lips. His personality became so abrasive that when he visited London, Con-

rad Aiken said, in only three months he set back the cause of American poetry twenty years. And his personal habits were so filthy that at the Mac-
Dowell writers' colony Elinor Wylie refused to sleep in the same bed
Bodenheim had occupied. When he was invited to Amy Lowell's home,
her dogs, apparently under the impression that he was a beggar, attacked
him and shredded his already tattered clothes—and when he found a
check for $10 under his dinner plate, more than enough to replace his suit,
he demanded $90 more to soothe his nerves.

To the impoverished bohemian, money was something to be taken
from the rich and given to the poet. "Bodenheim was always asking for
money and from everyone," recalled a Village acquaintance. "He had mul-
tiple excuses: his health, his teeth (or lack of them), a fictional friend who
was on the point of committing suicide. . . . If you did not comply with his
request, you were attacked for your meanness. If you did comply, you were
insulted because of your affluence." He saved his deepest scorn for those
from whom he mooched, proud of nothing so much as his ability "to destroy people on my guillotine of phrases."

For several months in 1921, Bodenheim participated in an ingenious share-the-wealth scheme concocted by a Village character named
John Coffee. At a lavish banquet at the Brevoort Hotel, Coffee grandly announced he had stolen $2,000 worth of furs and intended to sell them and
distribute the proceeds to the needy. The neediest turned out to be Bodenheim, the poet Louis Grudin, and Coffee himself, who established a summer colony in Massachusetts, a kind of "Brook Farm in reverse"—an
expensive apartment with the fur thief paying all the bills. Coffee suddenly
vanished—later to resurface at Matawan State Hospital for the Criminally
Insane—but Bodenheim continued a truncated ménage for two years by
showing up at the advertising agency where Grudin had found employment and soliciting his "half-share" of his "partner's" paycheck.

If one ironic aspect of the bohemian's code in the twenties was their
obsessive, shabby, and often illicit scheming for money while expressing
contempt for the self-centered and acquisitive values of capitalist society,
another was the almost holy incompetence with which they handled the
money they'd so meanly acquired. Even when Bodenheim managed to eke
out a modest income from his scandalous novels, he remained indigent.
He once left the Liveright office on Fourth Avenue with $1,000 in royalties
and immediately squandered it in a fixed poker game. The man who would
show up at William Carlos Williams's doorstep and demand $200 simply
because he was thinking of getting married would give away even larger
sums to Village vagrants, drunks, and prostitutes.

"Nobody seems to like me," he once complained to Hecht, who sometimes gave the impression he'd invented Bodenheim—and who wrote a Broadway play about him after his death. "Do you think it is because I am too aware of people's tiny hearts and massive stupidities?" "They are too aware of your big mouth," Hecht replied, to which Bodenheim crowed with malicious delight, "I was born without your talent for bootlicking."

When Bodenheim finally received national attention for his work it was only as a succès de scandale. In 1925, his best-selling novel *Replenishing Jessica* attracted the scrutiny of the smut-hound John Sumner, self-appointed successor to Anthony Comstock, who brought obscenity charges against Bodenheim and his publisher, citing passages like "his fingers enveloped the fullness of her breasts quite as a boy grasps soap-bubbles and marvels at their intact resistance." At the trial, the defense strategy consisted almost solely of reading the book to the jurors, who, the newspapers reported, slept through the recitation. It was *Replenishing Jessica*, incidentally, which prompted New York mayor Jimmy Walker's famous remark that "no girl was ever seduced by a book," an aphorism resplendently characteristic of the twenties—if the spirit of an age can be captured in the sentiments it both advocates and disproves.

Easy as it is to mock the sexual etiquette of earlier eras, it's hard to read *Replenishing Jessica* as anything but unintended satire. The eponymous heiress goes to bed with over a dozen men from two continents in an attempt to awaken her erotic nature. Bodenheim's prose wanders haphazardly from true romance ("That was the kind of love she had never felt and was always searching for") to attempts at insouciant worldliness ("Jessica fled to Europe, where she drifted from one capital to another") to Victorian verbiage (love letters are called "missives").

Alas, she turns out to be a prude. "When he had striven to possess her again, she had allowed him to kiss her but had rejected his more amorous onslaughts and informed him that they would never reiterate the previous night." The jaded heroine decides that what she really wants is a man who's "not merely desirous of her physical favors."

Replenishing Jessica is typical of the twenties in that its raciness is so stilted, typical of bohemia in that its polarization of art and money, to say nothing of sex and love, is so socially and psychologically ungrounded, and typical of Bodenheim in that its view of male sexuality—in perhaps the only unconscious cynicism of his entire life—stressed deceitful, manipulative catering to a woman's whims for the sole purpose of enveloping her soap-bubble breasts.

Bodenheim, in fact, was a lecher. The most persistent rumor was that at dances he cut in on his friends and, with a cackling leer, suggested to their wives or girlfriends that he was prepared to demonstrate how much more satisfying sex could be with a poet. Bodenheim was among those, along with millionaire Robert Clairmont, Eli Siegel, and John Rose Gildea, who founded the Greta Garbo Social Club, whose sole agenda was to deflower all the virgins "who bobbed like so many ripe apples in the liberated Village barrel." But since, like Groucho Marx, Bodenheim usually chose to make his coarse invitations to the most improbable matrons, and since "he had already lost most of his front teeth . . . [and] was never," in Dorothy Day's saintly understatement, "a very prepossessing person," he was met with the disgusted rejections he seems unconsciously to have sought.

Almost all Bodenheim's books of poetry in the twenties were dedicated "to Fedya"—Fedya Ramsey, an actress and dancer who'd assumed the role of motherly muse during his years in Chicago. In 1916, as he boarded a train to join her in California, he happened to see a newspaper story of her death after a fall from a horse, blacked out, and regained consciousness several days later in a ditch. Even Bodenheim's first wife, Minna Schein, a writers' secretary and later IWW functionary, acted less as a sexual companion than as a maternal conscience, allowing him to fool around and then exercise his considerable talent for extravagant remorse. Alternatively dependent on and repelled by Minna's stability—just as he was attracted to and disgusted by the dance-hall girls and poet-chasers with whom he constantly betrayed her—he would abandon his casual partners and seek out confirmation of his sexuality with the harried woman to whom he refused to be faithful.

Nevertheless, with every failed affair, and with his added notoriety as the persecuted author of a "pornographic" best-seller, Bodenheim's legend as a libertine increased. Finally, a series of amorous episodes in the summer of 1928—Sixty Days That Shook the World, said the Villagers—brought Bodenheim and the Village tabloid fame. One of the many girls in search of the flaming lover and weaver of words was a raven-haired 18-year-old named Gladys Loeb, whose father was a physician on the Grand Concourse in the Bronx. After a disillusioning dalliance, Bodenheim told her the adoring poems she had written about him were revolting rubbish.

Gladys turned on her gas oven and stuck her head inside, only to be saved in the nick of time by her landlady, who found the nearly dead girl, a picture of the poet pressed tightly against her bosom.

A few weeks later, a twenty-two-year-old poetry lover named Virginia Drew rapturously wrote Bodenheim that she wanted to meet him to discuss her work. He invited her to his Macdougal Street apartment, where he informed her that her writing was insipid slush. Virginia "placated herself with a constant, conscious advertisement" of her availability until Bodenheim fled to a Times Square hotel. She soon discovered his whereabouts, and after he thought he had dissuaded her from killing herself, he bade her farewell. When she failed to come home for two days, her father tracked him down, but having been alerted by the hotel clerk, Bodenheim left for Harry Kemp's cottage in Provincetown. The police broke down his apartment door after Virginia's body was found in the Hudson River.

This time Bodenheim's love life was not confined to the tabloids—the *New York Times* put the story on page one under the headline, "Bodenheim Vanishes as Girl Takes Life," and reported that a nationwide search was under way for the Village seducer and murder suspect. "The poet by his absence has enmeshed himself in a case as bizarre as any of his own books."

Not even Bodenheim's books were as bizarre as the succeeding events. Gladys Loeb, apparently envious that another inamorata had succeeded where she had failed, showed up in Provincetown, but her father, two reporters, and a local constable had arrived only minutes earlier. Bodenheim, who knew nothing of Virginia's suicide, quickly placated the police and Gladys's father, who emerged from the cottage to say, "I think we've been doing Mr. Bodenheim a great injustice."

Gladys, her father, and Bodenheim shared a cab to Hyannis, but when a carful of reporters crashed into them, the fragile truce broke. The caravan continued to New York, where waiting police and press learned that Bodenheim had jumped a train in Stamford, Connecticut, and reappeared a few hours later in a Harlem ballroom flirting with a taxi dancer.

The press hooted with delight at the events they called "so typical of Greenwich Village," Bodenheim returned to MacDougal Street after turning down a $1,000 offer to tell his version of the story—some things were beneath even his dignity—and forlorn Virginia Drew was utterly forgotten.

The suicide of one's partner would seem an odd way to prove one's prowess as a lover, but the Village lecher became notorious throughout the world as a twentieth-century Casanova until two succeeding codas finally convinced the public that his erotic adventures were grotesque. Yet another teenage poetry lover wrote him yet another rhapsodic letter, and the correspondence lasted long enough for "Dorothy Dear" to have a purseful of the poet's love letters. She was killed in the worst subway accident in New York history, Bodenheim's throbbing "missives" found scattered over the blood-soaked tracks.

The fabled Aimee Cortez capped his erotic legend on a note of flamboyant pathos. Aimee would show up at parties, proudly announce that she had the most voluptuous body in the world, throw off her clothes, and dance with a stuffed gorilla, often climaxing her orgiastic gyrations by leading one of her entranced admirers to bed in an adjoining room, At the age of nineteen, she won the unofficial title Mayoress of Greenwich Village.

In his posthumous *My Life and Loves in Greenwich Village*, written by a charlatan named Sam Roth and based on the poet's alcoholic ramblings, Bodenheim is quoted as saying, "She never extended her favors to sterile, uncreative men, and the idea of sleeping with a banker or shopkeeper would have been as abhorrent to her as engaging in an affair with a daughter of Lesbos." But before the decade was out, Aimee, like Gladys Loeb, stuck her head inside her gas oven—but unlike Gladys she was found dead.

Almost overnight he was transformed from legendary lover into legendary bum. By the early thirties, Bodenheim was shambling through bars, selling his poems for a quarter each to buy booze. "They weren't really his own poems, not toward the end," says one old-timer. "I happen to know the guy who wrote them for him. He was a pest. If you saw him coming you crossed the street." When not panhandling, he managed to publish six novels during the decade, including the infamous *Naked on Roller Skates*, which had such an impact on the beatnik Villagers of the fifties. Though he flirted halfheartedly with radicalism and was later fired from the Federal Writers Project for alleged communist activities, the Communist party had denounced him as "a nuisance."

In 1934, to pursue the most irresistible temptation of the American Dream, Bodenheim went to Hollywood in the insane hope of selling one of his novels to the movies. But after waiting vainly for several weeks for the desired word from "Mr. Thalberg," he returned to the Village despondent and just as unemployable.

Bodenheim momentarily summoned up enough of his vituperative vigor to lead a ragtag battalion of writers in a march on City Hall to protest the inadequacy of the relief allowance—$14 a month for rent and $10 for food. According to the *New York Herald Tribune* of March 5, 1935, "Maxwell Bodenheim, poet, novelist, and some time night club entertainer—led a small delegation to the Home Relief Agency at 303 W. 17 St. at 1 p.m. yesterday and asked for funds to keep himself from starvation so that he would continue writing his novel on the class conflict in the US. . . . He was unshaven, very pale, and his hair was messed. He said that 5 or 6 weeks ago he had applied for relief, and that the agency had promised to send an investigator to his flat at 70 Seventh Avenue. 'I waited for a week,' he said, 'and was forced to leave then because I couldn't pay my rent. Since then I haven't had a roof over my head, and if it hadn't been for my friends I would have starved.' "

As a result of his protest, Bodenheim was given $20.10 ($15 for back rent and $5.10 for food), a victory which prompted another New York paper to anoint him "the mayor of New York." Bodenheim and his cohorts," the *Herald Tribune* concluded, "marched in formation to the Writers Union, 26 W. 88th St., to celebrate the government's recognition of letters."

Minna Schein finally divorced Bodenheim in 1938, having been separated from him for years. The fierce loner almost immediately remarried, as if he desperately needed stability he could resist. This marriage reversed the pattern. His wife, Grace Fawcett Finnan, soon developed cancer, and Bodenheim devotedly if haphazardly nursed her until her death a decade later. In a sense, Grace was now his only excuse for living. "A paradox of his life," a biographer has written, "was the tenacity with which he clung to existence while punishing himself to the point of destruction."

Ben Hecht recalled an alarming visit from the poet in the late forties. "He sits, unaware of me, like a man lost in some private Hell. . . . 'Honestly, Ben, I am sick of the whole thing. I know of no sensible reason why I should not commit suicide and put an end to this whole stupid nonsense. . . . I'd commit suicide tonight except that I am in love with my wife. . . . And she loves me. I can't imagine why—can you? A scarecrow body and a dead soul!' A smile touches his tear-wet mouth and he whispers, 'The falling snow is like a wreath of daisies in the night.' "

Hecht was deeply touched by this scene—so much so that for several hours he was unaware that when he left the room to call Grace, Bodenheim had stuffed his suitcase full of Hecht's clothes.

By the forties and early fifties, Bodenheim was a Village legend only to tourists who condescendingly purchased 25-cent poems from the toothless old poet. On occasion, he was capable of a memorable phrase — slumped on a barstool he muttered the famous remark, "Greenwich Village is the Coney Island of the soul" — but after Grace's death in 1950, he wandered the streets disconsolately, sometimes wearing an "I am blind" sign, in such a gin-soaked daze that he was sent to the alcoholic ward at Bellevue.

Only his rage remaining, Bodenheim would painfully shuffle over to "the waxworks," the Waldorf Cafeteria on Sixth Avenue near 8th Street — so named because its yellow-green lights cast a cadaverous glow over the drunks and prostitutes who lingered there — where, over his "supper," hot water laced with ketchup, a concoction called "bohemian tomato soup," he would engage in desultory arguments with cabbies or insomniac artists, arguments being, as Hecht often said, the only thing Bodenheim ever won. And in this dismal setting, Bodenheim began the last love affair of his life, a most improbable romance even by Village standards.

One rainy night in April 1951, after Bodenheim had vainly tried to peddle a sonnet in memory of Grace, a pretty, dark-haired young woman named Ruth Fagan said, "Here's my last quarter." Bodenheim gave her the poem, and shuffled off into the rain, but Ruth ran after him. Two days later at the waxworks — Bodenheim in a pressed shirt for the occasion — they announced that they were going to get married, and a week later they claimed to be man and wife (though there is no record of the marriage at City Hall).

When asked what an attractive woman of thirty-two could possibly see in a fifty-nine-year-old, decaying, and probably impotent derelict, Ruth was fond of explaining that "he had an umbrella and I did not." Villagers speculated that his helplessness aroused her maternal instincts, or that she was interested in his nonexistent royalties, or that she fantasized of attending to a declining genius. But since she was mentally unstable herself — at the age of fourteen she had set fire to her parents' home in Detroit, had suffered several nervous breakdowns, and had been confined for several weeks to a mental institution in Brooklyn — the umbrella explanation seems as rational as any.

Unlike her husband, Ruth sporadically held a job — doing needlework for a theatrical troupe, or working as a comparison shopper for Macy's — and they soon moved into a shabby apartment on Bleecker Street. But Bodenheim allocated virtually all of his wife's meager earnings for alcohol and they spent their few remaining years living in 75-cent-a-night flophouses, or in hallways and doorways when even that became too expensive.

Through it all, the wretched couple stayed together even when he'd blacken her eyes, even when she slept with other men. Ruth hopefully arranged a benefit performance at a Village restaurant for "one of those unfortunate men of genius for whom the economic struggle has been too much," and, in a final attempt to rehabilitate her husband, promoted a poetry reading at the Jabberwocky café on 4th Street. The event attracted a sizable crowd, but most of the audience came to see a Village curiosity, and after mumbling a few poems, Bodenheim stumbled off drunkenly.

In 1952, Bodenheim was invited to attend a reunion celebrating the Chicago Renaissance by Karl Shapiro and Ellen Borden Stevenson, Adlai Stevenson's ex-wife. In the words of one observer, he "looked as if he had been buried, or drowned for some weeks, a sort of living dead man, and he smelled that way too." He somehow managed to stay sober for a few days, but inevitably began drinking heavily, and scandalized the testimonial dinner by panhandling the guests. Ruth, by now as disheveled and rank as her husband, kept proudly informing everyone, "Anyway, I'm Mrs. Maxwell Bodenheim," but that didn't keep her from propositioning several guests or him from slapping her face.

Back in the Village, Bodenheim was taken by the anthologist Oscar Williams to meet Dylan Thomas at the Minetta Tavern. The two poets had barely heard of each other—though they'd won *Poetry* magazine's Oscar Blumenthal Award in consecutive years—but they listened to each other recite their latest compositions with a shared sense of defiant anguish. Bodenheim was unaware of the mucus dripping from his nose—until Thomas, to the astonishment of the onlookers, took a handkerchief from his pocket and gently wiped it away.

No one else was so solicitous of the grotesque old man except that sleazy Village operator Sam Roth, who had once owned a magazine that ran sections of James Joyce's *Ulysses* in the twenties without the author's permission, and who was now publishing erotic novels out of a fleabag office on Lafayette Street. He would soon serve five years for fraudulent use of the mails. Plying Bodenheim with alcohol, and dragging out his disordered memories, Roth compiled enough material to publish, after the poet's death, his so-called autobiography—a meretricious little volume that Roth wrote himself, including a chapter eulogizing Sam Roth.

. . .

While Sam Roth was exploiting Bodenheim's past, other men were exploiting his impotence. Though Ruth still loved her husband, she picked up men on the streets, but she'd never taken a regular lover until she met a scar-faced, itinerant twenty-five-year-old dishwasher named Harold Weinberg in the winter of 1953. As a child, he'd been placed in a Hebrew orphanage, then in a mental hospital at the age of ten, and had been discharged from the army as mentally unstable, a decision validated by his subsequent police record and frequent outbursts of violence.

The trio were soon sucked into a whirlpool of brutality. Bodenheim loathed both Weinberg and the arrangement, but by now he was emotionally as well as sexually incapacitated. He once screamed at Weinberg, "Leave her alone or I'll kill you." Another time, Weinberg slashed him with a knife.

On the night of February 6, 1954, wet and cold, Bodenheim and his wife accepted Weinberg's invitation to sleep in his dingy $5-a-week Third Avenue room, just off the Bowery. Apparently thinking he'd fallen into a drunken stupor, Ruth and Harold began to make love. Momentarily regaining consciousness, Bodenheim realized what was happening, and after a lifetime of humiliation, his rage flared up one final time. The two men scuffled, and Weinberg grabbed a .22-caliber rifle and pulled the trigger. The bullet burst Bodenheim's heart and lodged in his spine. As Ruth clawed at her lover, Weinberg plunged a hunting knife into her chest.

Attempting to leave the impression that the couple had been surprised by a burglar, Weinberg turned Bodenheim's pockets inside out, scattered the contents of Ruth's suitcase over the bed, padlocked the door, and fled. The next afternoon, when Weinberg's landlord knocked at the door to collect two weeks' overdue rent, he sawed off the lock and found the two bodies lying in a pool of cheap wine.

The police were unable to identify the victims until they discovered an envelope addressed to Ruth Fagan Bodenheim. Weinberg was apprehended on February 10. "I ought to get a medal," he ranted at his trial two months later. "I killed two Communists." Instead he was committed to Matawan State Hospital for the Criminally Insane. All his life, Bodenheim had assaulted respectability with what he considered inspired lunacy, only to die defending his honor against a madman.

Ben Hecht, who had always had more use for Bodenheim the legend than for Bodenheim the man, grandly announced that he would pay all the funeral expenses, then sent a check for only $50, leaving Minna Schein to bear most of the cost. Ruth Fagan's unclaimed body lay in the city morgue for three days before it was consigned to a Westchester crematorium, but Bodenheim's body was laid to whatever rest it could claim in a New Jersey cemetery on the day his murderer was apprehended.

"Who, possibly, could have wanted to kill poor, homeless Max," asked *Life* magazine in a full-page spread on his death—conceding that "once, practically anyone might have had the idea"—while as far away as Moscow, *The Literary Gazette* referred to the Village as "America's wilderness district" and declared him "a victim of the 'American way of life.' "

In his eulogy, Arthur Kreymborg called Bodenheim "a great lover and wit," and concluded, more charitably than prophetically, that "we need not worry about his future, he will be read."

Bodenheim is no longer read. The work of the writer considered by his contemporaries the exemplar of the bohemian spirit consists almost entirely of borrowed ideas, conventional novels, and pedantic poetry. Its only astonishing quality is its quantity. Despite his disordered life, he published twenty-one books in less than twenty years. Garrulous, unfocused, irrelevantly omniscient, Bodenheim's fiction rejects any and all forms of authority—familial, institutional, moral—and consistently ignores its economic, political, or psychological sources. In one of his novels, he asks his readers to pity "tragically valiant . . . Youth" because it has been forced to wear brassieres "to keep the breasts from bobbling a little with the walking of legs." As Marianne Moore noted as early as 1924, the novels are rooted in an "interest in retaliation," and they regard art as primarily an antisocial activity and sex as merely an act of rebellion.

The poems, while just as hackneyed in theme, are as rigorous and stylized as the novels are flaccid and shapeless. Louis Untermeyer, who contributed the respectful introduction to Bodenheim's first volume of poetry, pointed out even then that "Sometimes he gets drunk with his own distillation, and reels between precocity and incoherence." The avant-garde poet praised for his idiosyncratic "word tapestries" was very nearly as pedestrian, derivative, and timid as the valley dwellers he scorned.

This sarcastic, corrosive man exemplified a common Village type, compounded of anti-authoritarianism and self-destructiveness, the characteristic bohemian response to what the group perceived as the self-satisfied respectability of the American middle class. From the beginning, Bodenheim saw himself as a victim and did everything in his power to validate this perception.

Hecht, who was most responsible for romanticizing his character, shrewdly understood that he had "a mystic sense of himself as an unwanted one," and encouraged him to revel in it by applying to him such epithets as "the ideal lunatic."

At moments, especially in his poetry, Bodehheim could see through this pose. "We swept Main Street of shams and bric-a-brac / And slew vulgarities—tin sword crusades," he wrote late in life of his generation of poets.

But Bodenheim never understood the psychological deviousness of his oppositional stance—either the way it hoped simultaneously to berate his society's values and receive its plaudits, or the way it shocked his culture only to call forth its rejection, thus achieving aesthetic martyrdom. Bodenheim—and those bohemians who applauded what they considered his uncompromising nonconformism—verified his stature not by what he accomplished but by whom he alienated.

Two myths intersected in Bodenheim's life—the bourgeois myth of success and the bohemian myth of failure—illuminating their power over the American imagination and their price in human pain.

Bodenheim's story is usually told in terms of the decline of the Village from the gay days of the Jazz Age to the grim years of the Depression, but in fact it traces the decline only from the teens to the twenties. The bohemians of the twenties no longer believed that the values of the American middle class were to be confronted and altered, but rather that they were simply to be rejected and replaced—not by something more noble or idealistic, but by whatever the middle class happened most furiously to condemn.

It's not too much to say, in fact, that to many Villagers in the twenties—and this perversion of bohemian ideals continued for decades—disaffection from the middle class became an end in itself. When rejection by bourgeois society becomes a sign of merit, irresponsibility a sign of authenticity, incapacity a sign of sensitivity, and dismissal a sign of artistic temperament, it's not far to go until failure becomes the ultimate sign of integrity. Or until the bohemian manqué begins to ask, "Where else can a poet live in America but in the gutter?" Bodenheim and his ilk turned their outcast status into a racket. They became official renegades against the official culture, or even, in those rare cases where their work had lasting merit, Tragic Figures.

Two of the culture's dominant values—individualism and success—were coming into conflict, and the culture was entranced by images of splendid miseries and spectacular crack-ups. F. Scott Fitzgerald, for one, would hardly have remained a dashing, glamorous figure if he had lived, like Max Beerbohm's Lord Byron, to write long cranky letters to the *Times*.

But for Villagers to mythologize Bodenheim as the quintessential bohemian, as happened in the forties and fifties, was to legitimize the bourgeois view of the poet as a weird misfit—and further, to play into the middle-class facility both for dismissing bohemians as poseurs and for finding their misery quaint. Those who romanticized Bodenheim as a carefree spirit destroyed by a repressive society elevated individual psychosis to the stature of tragic destiny; they failed to understand that his success as a legend depended precisely on his failure as a human being. If it is true, as William Dean Howells suggested, that Americans want tragedies with happy endings, the Village bohemians too often wanted farces with tragic endings.

X

Thomas Wolfe and Aline Bernstein

"The Knife of Love"

Crumpled sheets of paper and discarded notebooks cluttered the floor, and ledgers filled with page after page of false starts. In one half of the huge room, flies hovered over plates of unfinished food. Dirty underwear was tossed into corners. The other half of the room was immaculate. A drafting table sat under a skylight—pens and ink, rulers, compasses, sketch pads neatly aligned on its surface. Drawings were pinned to the wall in precise rows; a smock was carefully draped over the back of a chair.

In 1926 and 1927, Thomas Wolfe and Aline Bernstein shared a room on the top floor of a dilapidated building at 13 East 8th Street. Plaster peeled from the walls, the floorboards sagged, the ceiling sloped at both ends so that Tom had to stoop. The heat was turned off at five, so on winter evenings he had to wrap himself in blankets, but in this cherished setting Tom began the novel he would eventually call *Look Homeward, Angel*—yet another novel of small-town America written in the Village—and Tom and Aline embarked on the most tender and most brutal of all the legendary Village love affairs.

. . .

A native of Asheville, North Carolina, he was a man of unquenchable appetites—and had the unappeasable narcissism of a boy who felt unloved by his parents and unappreciated by everyone else. At Harvard Graduate School, Tom rampaged through the stacks of Widener Library like a famished predator. And he was just as voracious in George Pierce Baker's playwriting workshop—the same class Eugene O'Neill had taken a few years before. He would pour his passion into plays, not yet realizing that his sensibility was more suited to the expansiveness of fiction than the tautness of drama.

Six feet five inches tall, heavyset, rawboned, Tom had a leonine presence, and the domed forehead, flowing hair, and far-off gaze of a nine-teenth-century poet. He seemed in permanent disarray. He had a sham-bling gait, and was often awkwardly shy, but nothing was tentative about his mercurial moods. He could be the most generous and trusting of men, and the most selfish and paranoid. He was, said John Dos Passos, "a gigantic baby," and Sinclair Lewis recalled, "You couldn't be a friend of Tom's any more than you could be a friend of a hurricane."

When in one of his "black moods," Tom would drink or sink into self-pity, and then lash out at his closest friends for "betraying" him. His most characteristic mood, however, was exuberance. He himself described a need for release, for "if energy of this kind . . . keeps boiling over and is given no way of getting out, then it will eventually destroy and smother the person who has it."

As for women, Tom was at once boyish and virile, a combination that meant he didn't have to try too hard. Having little trouble interesting women, he took little interest in them beyond sex, and at Village parties was known to disappear into a bedroom with a woman and an hour later not remember her name. As one of his conquests put it, "He was intolera-ble and wonderful and talked like an angel and was a real son-of-a-bitch"—something Aline would learn all too soon.

In 1924—the year Edna St. Vincent Millay left the Village and Jig Cook died in Delphi—Tom took a job as an English instructor at the Washing-ton Square campus of NYU. Drawn by the $1,800 salary for a small teach-ing load that would allow him time to write—as well as by its proximity to the Broadway theater he hoped to conquer—and seeking *la vie littéraire* where "all that was deathless and immortal" would flow from his pen, Tom was soon disappointed on all three counts. Despite his gregariousness, he made few friends among the writers and artists, finding them lacking in purpose and ambition—and "he dreamed a dream of glory," unconsciously regarding them as competition. His efforts to get his plays produced proved futile. And though he remained a conscientious teacher, he came to regard his classes as "an odious bondage," the three sections and over one hundred students frequently leaving him too exhausted to write.

Exhorting his students to appreciate the romance of language, Tom was dedicated, impassioned, eloquent—and miserable. It was drudgery. The faculty was too immersed in the rationalizations of Freud or Marx to comprehend the transcendence of literature. But worst of all were the girls, their "shamelessness" and "indecency" arousing an erotic frenzy he could scarcely contain.

"The girls, the proud and potent Jewesses with their amber flesh, schooled to a goal of marriage, skilled in all the teasings of erotic trickery, . . . pressed in around him in a drowning sensual tide." Girls, Jews, sex—they seemed inseparable—there was no escape.

Tom was drained but not defeated. "The world is mine," he wrote in a letter home, "and I, at present, own a very small but gratifying portion of it—Room 2220, at the hotel Albert." The venerable building on University Place between 11th and 12th Streets depended largely on a permanent clientele, and was home, at one time or another, to hundreds of Village writers, poets, painters, playwrights, and actors.

Tom roamed the streets of the Village, occasionally picking up a woman in a bar and bringing her back to his room for a night of sex as lonely as his days.

And then Tom met Aline.

In August 1925, Tom spent the summer in Europe and in August returned to America on the liner *Olympic*. On the last night of its voyage it lay in temporary quarantine outside New York harbor, and Tom, who had traveled over in third class, accepted the invitation of a shipboard acquaintance to join a gala in the second-class café. Aline and her traveling companion descended from their first-class cabin to take part in the festivities.

Tom's acquaintance and Aline's companion had previously met, so the four travelers shared a table. Tom's initial impression was of "a matronly figure of middle age, a creature with a warm and jolly little face, a shrewd, able, and immensely talented creature of action, able to hold her own in a man's world." As the evening wore on, he became enchanted. "A woman of incomparable loveliness," he decided. And in Aline's mind, as she later wrote in a fictionalized account of their meeting, "his size, his vitality, his insatiable hunger were magnificent."

In *his* fictionalized account of their meeting—for as throughout their relationship, Aline could hardly get a word in edgewise, even on paper—Tom transformed their instantaneous attraction into word-saturated revelation. "There was for him no beauty that she did not share, . . . no . . . hatred, sickness of the soul, or grief unutterable, that was not somehow consonant to her single image and her million forms—and no final freedom and release, . . . that would not bear upon its brow forever the deep scar . . . of love."

Tom and Aline talked and danced for hours, abandoning their companions to stand on the deck, gazing at the starlit sky, the waves, the lights of New York blazing in the distance. Impetuously, he kissed her. He had a bottle of brandy in his room, he said, and laughing, they made their way down to third class.

How could any two people be more unalike?—Tom a small-town Southerner and Aline an urban sophisticate, Tom Christian and Aline Jewish, Tom emotionally erratic and Aline self-possessed, Tom a self-enraptured visionary and Aline a cool-headed professional. And even more inauspicious, Aline was not only married and the mother of two teenage children, she was nearly twenty years older than Tom. They parted at dawn and didn't see each other as they disembarked. Nothing but a romantic last night at sea.

Tom went home to Asheville for a brief visit, but Aline entered his thoughts almost hourly. What a vivacious woman, with a kind of gentle exuberance, with such sensual abandon. But no, it was just a one-night fling. Yet when he returned to the Village, he was disappointed, almost angry, when he found no note from her.

Tom finally wrote Aline a letter that he carried in his pocket for several days—a ridiculous, pompous letter; he berated himself the minute he'd mailed it. "Whatever else the world may say of me, I have never truckled to the mob." He couldn't believe he'd written that!

So Tom felt relieved and delighted when Aline called the next morning and invited him to a play at the Neighborhood Playhouse. Both were a bit wary. After all, their initial encounter had been so erotically charged that disappointment seemed inevitable. They chatted amiably, visited backstage after the show, and parted by shaking hands. But they agreed to meet on the steps of the New York Public Library a few days later to celebrate Tom's twenty-fifth birthday. Over lunch he told her the story of his life—"every secret hope, every insatiate desire, every cherished and unspoken aspiration, every unuttered feeling, thought, or conviction"—a very long lunch indeed.

By the end of the tale, Tom was so sodden with alcohol that Aline had to put him in a taxi to take him home. When he realized she wasn't coming with him, he accused her of manipulating him, abandoning him, betraying him. When he called in remorse the next day, they knew they were in love—"the met halves," he said, "of a broken talisman."

"A very beautiful and wealthy lady who was extremely kind to me on the boat," Tom described Aline in a letter to his mother, who "has seen me daily and entertained me extensively." Discretion kept him from saying more—that her name was Aline Bernstein, for instance, or that she was forty-four years old, or that she was married to a prominent Wall Street stockbroker. The marriage was one of convenience since the birth of their two children, though she remained devoted to her family; she had an "arrangement" with her husband that allowed her to have occasional affairs.

The daughter of the famous Shakespearean actor Joseph Frankau, Aline had been raised in a theatrical boardinghouse on 44th Street, studied painting with Robert Henri, and shown a certain talent for writing fiction—a talent Tom would have cause to regret—and in the early twenties established herself as one of the first women set and costume designers on Broadway. Moving easily between Park Avenue and the Village, she was commonsensical and vibrant. In appearance she was alluring—petite, with liquid brown eyes, and a soft tilt to her head, the result of slight deafness in one ear, that made her seem to be listening with fond intimacy. Aline's conversation was unfailingly bright. Once, when paying a 10:00 A.M. visit to her Village theatrical wigmaker, and discovering that his establishment had been converted into a speakeasy, she said, "All right, then, give me an Old Fashioned instead." With her capacity for generosity and enjoyment, she fully deserved what she always regarded—even in the depths of despair—as the miracle of Tom's love.

Only a few months after they'd met, they wanted a place of their own and Aline found the loft space at 13 East 8th Street. The fourth floor had recently served as a sweatshop, but it could easily be cleaned up, and those skylights, they were ideal! And didn't she have a good excuse to give her husband? A studio near her work? So in January 1926 they moved in, Tom insisting on sharing the $35-a-month rent and, for the sake of propriety, keeping his room at the Albert.

For the first time since leaving Asheville, Tom had a home, and Aline brought emotional stability into his life. Her belief in his talent focused his writing. She knew he would never succeed as a dramatist, and gently persuaded him to devote his energies to fiction instead. Though he never became anything close to a disciplined writer, his imagination began to envision a form in which he could express his overflowing memories.

"My pet," Tom called Aline, "my lass," "my plum-skinned wench"—and, more and more often, "my Jew." The opposite side of his emerging anti-Semitism, of course, was the erotic allure of the other, of what he regarded as an alien race, sinister, sybaritic. Aline's age also excited him. She was old enough, he once suggested more meaningfully than he knew, to be his mother. She was the most maternal of women, allowing him to combine the fiery sex he craved with the tenderness he'd never known. But if much of Aline's attraction for him was based on displaced bigotry and neurotic need, what finally released him from the inhibitions that had always made sex so unsatisfactory was her erotic abandon. When he once asked her, "with proud crowing love," if she could feel him inside her, she moaned, "God, can I feel it! That pole, that tree!" So if sex remained something close to an act of masturbation practiced in the presence of a woman, at least he enjoyed it more than ever before, almost as much as he enjoyed writing.

Enflamed with ambition, he returned to his novel, writing in red, clothbound ledgers Aline had bought him—"one of the most important events in my life as a writer," he recalled years later. He was also engulfed by self-doubt, but Aline's faith was resolute. With her financial help, Tom managed to reduce his teaching schedule until two obsessions absorbed every minute of his life—his novel and Aline.

Tom loved with the love of a narcissist—he saw Aline as merely a part of the novel of his life—which meant that he at once thrived on her devotion and demanded his independence. He also loved with the love of a son—he both cherished her affection and became taunted by guilt. Aline was less self-absorbed than Tom, but her obsessive absorption in him proved just as destructive—her seductive need soon turning into repellent demand, her unconditional love driving away a man who had a thousand conditions. And her age soon became an obstacle, for every quarrel not only disturbed her equanimity, but threatened her perception of herself as a vivacious, youthful woman. How can he be so cruel to someone who loves him so much, she'd ask herself, and the answer would be all too clear—he can't love someone so old. And then she'd resent him for his youth as well as his cruelty.

Tom and Aline traveled to Europe in the summer of 1926, and she was able to introduce him to James Joyce—having worked on an American production of *Exiles*. When the time came for her to return to New York, leaving him feeling abandoned to several months of loneliness, he impetuously asked her to divorce her husband and marry him. The proposal was at once a desire and a challenge that he knew she wouldn't accept—he wanted proof that it was she who imposed conditions on their relationship, who wasn't willing to abandon everything for love. In some twisted way, he wouldn't take yes for an answer, he asked largely for the vindication of rejection—and from that moment on, the pattern of their relationship subtly but irrevocably altered.

Aline's letters to Tom in Europe poured out her love. She bled, she wrote, from where she'd been torn apart from him. She wished she could send him "elixir of Aline." Tom also declared his love, but his letters had the tone of formal proclamations, as if he were merely keeping his writing skills honed. He declared his lust as well, misguidedly mimicking Joyce. "I should like to be the Leusian Bull of Europa with my long Bull tongue . . . [my] raw gleaming Bullprick stretching and filling her throatwards."

Tom's attitude toward Aline was conflicted, for like so many men who become dependent on a woman, he resented her for depriving him of his freedom. He promised to remain celibate while they were apart, but he must have realized, if only half-consciously, that this promise, in addition to her lavish "loans" that made his trip possible, turned him into a kept person.

Tom's petulant jealousy had already led to quarrels. After they'd spent a day with theater people in England, he burst into angry sobs, declaring, "You love those people more than you love me." Being without her gave him the opportunity to mull over and sharpen his rage, and his jealousy turned vituperative, explicitly sexual. She was being driven by "the hungry flesh of forty" to lift "her skirts, behind the door, with sow grunts and belly burlesque."

Aline's rejection of Tom's proposal of marriage now began to serve its purpose—for it foretold a betrayal that he didn't so much discover as insist upon. While he was languishing in Europe, she was "giving 3,297.726 violent hours to . . . drawings, hammerings [in her stage work], beddings, fuckings, eatings, lyings," and only "2.374905 minutes" to "the high passionate and eternal things of life." He always apologized for what she called his "hellish dance on paper about my unfaithfulness," admitting that his "abominable ravings" revealed what a monster lay concealed in his character—but confession only liberated him from his guilt and allowed him to begin all over again.

In addition to his sexual jealousy, the ambiguities of his pet name "my Jew" began to surface. "My grey-haired Jew," he addressed her, "my dear Jew," or sometimes just "Jew." Aline deflected his hostility with fond teasing. "St. Rebecca," she would sign her letters, and wrote that she wished she could join a Jewish nunnery to convince him of her fidelity. And after a first-night party, she wrote with a pained effort at endearment, "You could have made a lovely pogrom, you could have cut all their throats and seen all the dollars trickle out." But while Aline pretended that Tom's attitude toward her Jewishness was affectionate, he was privately writing that she was "a titillative New York Jew with a constantly dilating and palpitative vagina."

On the boat back to America in midwinter, Tom made a foreboding entry in his notebook. "What rut of life with the Jew now? Is this a beginning or a final ending? Get the book done."

Tom and Aline resumed their relationship with Aline now paying all the rent, and though they had moments of joy, more often they were tense and quarrelsome. Tom had entered the all-engrossing stage of his novel, and all it took to trigger one of his tirades was a passing reference from Aline to the abominable world of the theater when he was struggling to achieve literary glory. Rage was followed by remorse, but as Aline tearfully tried to recapture their love, Tom withdrew. No, he wrote a friend, the rumor wasn't true that he was leading a dissipated bohemian life. He was "respectable, hard-working, poverty-stricken, dirty—and, I'm afraid, somewhat dull."

Tom discovered that he could write more fluently while fondling himself—his narcissism becoming explicitly masturbatory—and he frequently induced an onanistic giddiness that made long passages of his prose seem not lyrical but woozily adolescent. His hand, he wrote, explored "the male configuration—the long and dangling shaft," and with this "good male feeling," "he filled page after triumphant page."

Except on those days when the gap between his vision and his words seemed unbridgeable—then he vented his frustration on Aline. As Tom made it increasingly clear that her very presence was intrusive—for those desperately in love often conspire to destroy precisely what they most seek to save—she begged for reassurances. In the midst of an argument about the theater, which had escalated into his accusation that she "essentially" despised him, he "casually" asked if her daughter was a whore. "I said [it] because I wanted to hurt her," he later admitted.

Aline thought maybe she could allay his rages by letting him take a bigger part in her life beyond their room. He had escorted her to the New Year's Eve Fine Arts Ball in Webster Hall, just down the street, where they danced happily, but Aline made the mistake of taking Tom to meet her friends at the Neighborhood Playhouse. When a young man greeted her with a theatrical embrace, Tom turned truculent. "I'm sorry," he said, "but you must not put your hands on her." The young man protested. Tom pushed him onto a chair. Fisticuffs were averted when two men held Tom back. Walking home, Aline was adamant. "We must never go out among people again."

She soon recanted, and a few weeks later she invited him to go with her to a party and meet some of her actor, writer, and poet friends. Uneasy in his rented tuxedo, Tom was affable enough with Carl Van Vechten, but quickly assessed the rest of the guests as poseurs, hustlers, dilettantes. Elinor Wylie aroused his particular wrath—how condescendingly she'd asked him to sit on the floor while she recited several of her poems! When she finished, Tom made several sarcastic remarks directed at her and her husband, William Rose Benét. Tom may have felt proud but Aline was humiliated, and vowed never to take him to a Village event again.

"Get the book done." Entering the final, agonizing stages of his novel, he was on the verge of nervous collapse. The first thing he wanted was Aline, but their traumatic quarrels made his work even more difficult. And the woman whose succor was so crucial wasn't just spending all her time with the vile people of the theater—oh, he could understand it all now—she was a promiscuous whore flaunting her sluttish affair for all the world to see. And what was he doing with a middle-aged woman anyway, surrendering "the lonely wild integrity of youth which had been his" before they met?

Tom had no evidence Aline was unfaithful, for there was none, but two contradictory impulses drove his livid accusations. He needed to believe she was sleeping with other men to validate his turbulent emotions, and he needed to predict she *would* sleep with other men as a way of preventing her from doing so. In some perverse way it didn't matter, for he wanted to be, he said, "prepared for anything—either to be exalted by love, or to be sanctified by treachery." Such a chilling phrase—for a man who believes that treachery sanctifies will stop at nothing to be betrayed.

So Tom would work himself into a fury, berate Aline for her "bawdy missions," and even drunkenly call her home at two or three in the morning to see if she was actually there. And—for he needed her love as desperately as he needed to destroy it—the next day, the next hour, the next minute, he would sob with abject remorse. "I was obsessed by the work I was doing," he later told her, "driven on desperately to finish it. . . . The horrible pain lengthening out day by day, and no escape. . . . Love made me mad, and brought me down to the level of the beasts." And he tried to explain his behavior in a letter to a friend. "I wanted to own, possess, and devour her; . . . I began to get horribly sick inside . . . and my madness and jealousy ate at me like a poison."

By now, alas, Aline also had her suspicions about Tom. Walking along 8th Street one evening, she saw a woman's silhouette in the window of their room and charged up the stairs to confront him—only to discover that he was entertaining three colleagues from NYU. Chastened, she withdrew, leaving Tom to explain with a wink that the "violent middle-aged woman" was merely his jealous mistress who "had come up to catch him in the act." But if Aline was embarrassed on this occasion, from time to time Tom did, as she accused him, bring "silly cheap little tarts" up to their room.

It couldn't go on—it went on. The intensity of Tom's ambivalence was matched by the intensity of Aline's obsession, immobilizing them both. He couldn't write without the stability of her love—or the instability of their arguments. She wasn't just devoted to him, she was clinging to her youth—and the more she protested her love and mourned the loss of his, the further she drove him away.

One afternoon, Aline discovered two of her love letters unopened on the floor. She burst into sobs, and wrote him an anguished note. "I found upon the floor under rubbish two ardent letters of mine, to you. I tore them to pieces, it made me feel so sad, to think you could throw my loving letters to you around." But her emotions overcame her reason, and she added, almost as an afterthought, "Would you like to go to Europe with me? Vienna, Prague, Budapest?"

Tom accepted—he agreed with a friend that they'd become "emotional tinderboxes" who had to escape the pressure—and on their brief trip they quarreled only halfheartedly, both uneasily wondering if they'd exhausted their anger or if they were experiencing a momentary respite.

Upon their return, Aline looked for a larger space, and in October 1927 they moved into a spacious two-room apartment with kitchenette and bath on the second floor at 263 West 11th Street. Again they split the rent—$135 a month—and the space, Aline working in her usual orderliness in the front room, Tom working in his usual disorder in back, "a stinking lair," one of his NYU colleagues described it.

Though beginning to sense his "incestuous shame," and determined to sever the emotional shackles that chained him to Aline, Tom still couldn't end it and expressed his defiance by bringing women back to his room. Maybe he could force *her* to leave—at once freeing him from a torturing relationship and giving him the gratification of betrayal.

But while Aline grew despondent, her devotion—not only to Tom but to his genius—never wavered, and when he finished the first draft of his novel in March 1928, after twenty arduous months, she took it upon herself to find a publisher. Tom was deeply moved by Aline's faith, but remained troubled by her love, and when several publishers rejected his novel and his bitterness grew, he decided once more to make a final break. But immediately he equivocated—maybe they should just part for the summer.

Aline reluctantly agreed. "You are in terrible shape I know," she wrote him. "I do know how you are suffering. . . . With all of your imagination, you do not seem to know how it is to be constantly vilified and beaten by a loved being. You talk to me as though I were the lowest of the low, and I cannot stand it any longer." She added, "My presence seems to be so painful to you, that I will make no attempt to see you or speak to you again," but immediately offered, as if to acknowledge that the final break had come at last, "If you care to see me before I leave, will you let me know?"

So they both went off to Europe separately. Tom had been honest with her about the torment their affair was causing him, but not honest enough to tell her that he thought of his trip as "the Grand Tour of Renunciation." Like many men who want to break off a relationship, he'd given her hope only to make the separation easier on himself.

Yet as soon as Tom realized he was at last unchained, he realized how intensely he loved and needed her. It's never easy to tell the difference between love and need, but Tom's narcissism made it difficult for him to separate his lover from his fantasies. In any case, his letters in the summer of 1928 overflowed with pleas for forgiveness, even expressed a kind of melancholy tenderness he hadn't felt since their early days together.

Blaming the pressure of completing the novel and the anguish of its rejection, Tom wrote to Aline of his "unspeakable burden of pain and shame" over the way he'd behaved toward her. For the first time in months, his remorse wasn't merely an effort to alleviate his guilt, but a genuine effort to understand his cruelty and deceit, and in another letter he vowed to learn how to unroot "the snake-headed furies that drive us on to despair and madness."

Aline finally dared to ask if he would ever come back to her, and he wrote long, ardent paragraphs that never quite added up to an answer. Emboldened by his protestations of love, she responded tartly, "I will never be satisfied with this loving friendship you talk so much about. The phrase stings me to helpless anger. I am your true love."

When they were together Tom could think only of his desire to be free from an enslaving relationship, when they were apart he could think only of his desire to be enfolded in her arms—a paralyzing ambivalence based in part on his maleness, in part on his Oedipal guilt, but mostly on his vast and ruthless narcissism.

While in Europe, Tom heard that an editor at Scribners named Maxwell Perkins had expressed interest in his novel, but he'd had his spirits dashed too often to feel elated. He arrived home on New Year's Eve with only 27 cents in his pocket, and cautiously called Perkins on the morning after New Year's Day, 1929—a phone call that led, at last, to fulfilling his dreams of literary glory.

Laborious months of revision lay ahead, but Tom plunged into the work with manic enthusiasm. Gone were the uncertainty, the jealousy, the ambivalence. He and Aline found a new apartment, two rooms on the second floor of an old loft building at 27 West 15th Street. This time, however, they considered the place Tom's, with only a drafting table for Aline's occasional afternoon visits. They entered a period of wary calm. "Life is too short to be mixed up in nasty complications with other people," Tom told a friend, and he wrote another, "Because I was penniless and took one ship instead of another, I met the great and beautiful friend who had stood by me through all the torture, struggle, and madness of my nature for over three years." It was an elegy to a time he cherished but had no desire to recapture.

Tom tacked a motto from Horace on the wall of his apartment— "You can change your skies but not your soul"—and embarked on his revisions. He wrote on everything, even butcher paper, as the mammoth manuscript gradually filled several hat boxes. Coffee grounds collected in his huge pot until the sludge reached the top, and when he had to change his shirt, he'd sort through a pile of laundry until he found the one that was the least dirty—and on he worked, fourteen, sixteen, eighteen hours a day.

On October 18, 1929, *Look Homeward, Angel* was published by Scribners, dedicated "to A.B." He presented an author's copy to Aline, with the inscription, "To Aline Bernstein: On my twenty-ninth birthday, I present her with this, the first copy of my first book. This book was written because of her, and is dedicated to her. At a time when my life seemed desolate, and when I had little faith in myself, I met her. She brought me friendship, material and spiritual relief, and love such as I had never had before. I hope therefore that readers of my book will find at least a part of it worthy of such a woman. Thomas Wolfe. Oct. 3, 1929."

While Aline wasn't "entombed" in *Look Homeward, Angel*, she surely was in that inscription, for though heartfelt, it was unmistakably formal, and didn't so much celebrate as memorialize their friendship. That past tense—how it must have chilled her soul. Both of them knew that though they'd "reconciled," all that remained was what Tom called "the long and bitter war of separation." Unlike their previous tortured attempts to break apart, they behaved toward each other with ominous politeness. She hoped fame had liberated him from his insecurities, and he hoped it had liberated him from her. This man who had accused his mistress of duplicity almost daily now betrayed her regularly and with something close to glee. Enamored debutantes pursued him, he wrote a friend, begging "Fuck me, fuck me"; he made a long list of "Free Pieces of Cunt" in his diary, with the gratuitous explanation: "I fucked these women for nothing—the best price of all."

All too soon other entries began to appear—"a sobbing hell," "the old sensation of being caught, caught, caught." "I know you will say you still love me," Aline wrote him, "and want me to be your dear friend. Try to bear in mind that it is you who are turning from me and not I who go from you. . . . You have always said that I would leave you and stop caring for you first. Well, it's the other way, isn't it?"

But since Tom unconsciously understood that to take responsibility for breaking off their relationship would fill him with unendurable guilt, he desperately invented rationalizations that displaced responsibility onto others. He fantasized an encounter with Aline's husband. "What kind of man are you? Why don't you kill me? That's right, Goddamn it, kill me, . . . castrate me with a rabbi's circumcision knife, and feed my genitals to ladies' lapdogs." The hyperbole of the punishment at the hands of the betrayed husband momentarily eased his guilt, but not enough to confront Aline.

The Jews were to blame. "Intellectually," he noted, "they are sawdust and ashes," and sexually they were compulsively lascivious. After watching a Jewish woman at a restaurant, he wrote in his notebook, "Do you like to fuck Japs? Why not tell the truth? Jew women will fuck anything if it is in the mood."

He pretended to seek advice from friends of Aline's, describing the situation in such desperate terms that they could only tell him what he wanted to hear. He had no choice but to end the affair, they said—

one woman adding that since Aline was nearing fifty, "She's at the time of life when women get hysterical." Now he could tell her he'd sought advice from their friends, and since everyone thought they were bad for each other, maybe the time had come to separate. As he wrote Perkins, "I did not want to [leave her], but I yielded to what her friends wanted for her."

Aline only realized the seriousness of Tom's intentions when one day in the spring of 1930 he announced that he'd received a Guggenheim fellowship and was leaving for Europe alone. "Well, that's your way of informing me, is it?" Aline replied coldly. "If you go away and leave me this time, it will be for good. I know you'll never come back to me." He denied it, of course. In May, she saw him off on the SS *Volendam*, drinking champagne to ease the pain of separation and hanging around his neck a medallion Marsden Hartley had made for her, one of her most cherished possessions. In the agenda he'd made for himself a few days earlier, Tom had written, "I shall try to fuck beautiful women," and he proceeded to do so almost immediately after waving goodbye from the railing.

Somehow Aline managed to find out where Tom was and almost every day sent a letter, sometimes rueful, sometimes passionate, sometimes pleading.

"I love you with every fibre of my being, and I hate myself with the same intensity. I want to do away with so weak and miserable a soul . . . I love you." No reply. Another letter: "You would put upon my love the ugliness of your desertion and infidelity, but that does not change my undying fire." No reply.

She began to send desperate and despairing cables, saying she could not go on like this.

Tom was not tormented enough to answer, but he bought all the New York papers and anxiously scanned the obituaries. Instead of Aline's death notice, he found a review of Vicki Baum's *Grand Hotel* that praised Aline's set. Mutual friends said that she was "very radiant and happy." He even ran into her sister, who told him she "had never been happier or calmer or more joyful and successful than this fall." Then why, he asked, did she keep sending him these cables? Aline was an "emotional woman" who might "think she meant these things" for a few minutes, but he shouldn't take them "too seriously."

Nothing is quite as exasperating as having one's concern for a former lover turn out to be unnecessary—especially when that concern was only meant to alleviate one's own guilt—and Tom's exasperation, as always, turned malevolent. After talking to Aline's sister, he said with characteristic exaggeration, he vomited for two hours and wrote in his journal that the way she was behaving was "one of the vilest and basest things I have ever heard."

In relative tranquillity, Tom laid out his feelings in a long letter to Perkins. "No matter what breach of faith, truth, or honesty this woman may be guilty of, I want to come out of this thing with a feeling of love and belief in her."

Tom's tone was anguished and rueful, but in the privacy of his journal he reached new depths of venom. "I hope the whore dies immediately and horribly. I would rejoice at news of this vile woman's death."

Tom seethed in a cauldron of conflicting emotions, as permanently linked to Aline as to his mother. Guilty over violating this psychic taboo, ashamed of his cruelty, drowning in his need for her, suffocated by her need for him, he struggled to break free. Aline suffered from a single, simple emotion—anguish at his rejection. She saw her life slipping away and could no longer even cling to hope.

When Tom returned from abroad in March 1931, he moved to Brooklyn to escape his memories of their years in the Village—taking an apartment directly across the street from the building where Hart Crane had lived a few years earlier—but he didn't write her a word. When Aline read in the papers that Tom was back, she impulsively swallowed a handful of sleeping pills and for three days hovered between life and death.

Hearing of her suicide attempt, he was too distraught to visit her—distraught for himself. "Will help you all I can," he wrote in a telegram, but added, "You must help me. You must put hysteria and coercion aside: it does irreparable harm. . . . I send you my love which does not change."

Aline remained in the hospital for several weeks and developed a severe case of pleurisy and pneumonia. Tom wrote her of his eternal love. "Aline, I love you more dearly than anyone or anything in the world. I will love you all my life, and it will never change. . . . I want to tell you I would rather shed my own blood than cause you any pain. . . . I cannot tell you how I love you but I know that the thought and meaning of you is like a bullet through my brain"—an odd get-well sentiment to someone who's just tried to commit suicide.

Weakened by her illness, but cleansed by her attempt on her life,

Aline responded calmly. "What you want to say is that you no longer have sexual love for me. . . . Now let me tell you this, . . . my love for you is physical so long as I long to be near you, to share some of your life."

Tom gave in. When Aline recovered, she could visit him at his Brooklyn apartment on Thursday afternoons. But neither of them could keep their vows to be content with friendship. During the summer of 1931, he noted in his diary, they had sex only six times. And between her visits, Aline sent him piteous letters protesting her devotion. "Why I cling to you so, God only knows, but you are made of stuff so glorious, so terrible, and if I let you go, you will be lost." She signed herself "Scheherazade Bernstein."

Her love, he berated her, was merely glands, her need merely menopause. And in his diary, he hinted that his work on his next novel might be going better if she'd succeeded in killing herself.

Having failed in every attempt to break with Aline deviously, but without the courage to do it directly, Tom arranged a confrontation between her and his mother, who had been saying for years that "the Jew woman" should leave him alone. In January 1932, he asked Aline to lend him $500 and deliver it in person—the day after his mother arrived for a brief visit.

Tom began by precipitating a quarrel with Aline, and when she quietly responded, "You know how much I love you, Tom," his mother jumped in. "Well, it's all right if you love him as a friend, a dear friend—or do you love him as a mother?" "You don't understand," Aline started to explain, but Tom's mother interrupted her. "Well, I think I do understand. Any other kind of love I consider an illicit love. . . . you have grown-up children who are almost as old as Tom." Aline continued to protest that she didn't understand, but Tom jumped to his mother's defense. "My mother's not an ignoramus. She knows what she's talking about. Get away, let me alone," and he virtually threw Aline out of his apartment.

Aline sent him an embittered letter: "I had five one hundred dollar bills in my purse yesterday, which you asked me to bring you. . . . When I left you today, I took one out and threw it over the Brooklyn Bridge. I thought if they cannot understand how I love you, here is something to appease the gods your people worship. . . . The next four days I am going to throw a hundred dollar bill over the bridge into the river, just to show God I don't come from Asheville. . . . Tom dear, if only I could live backward from now on, to see where my fault with you has lain."

Tom and his mother had a good laugh. "I said [to Tom]," his mother recalled, "Call her up right now . . . [and] tell her that she's a Jew and I've never known one yet that if you drop a nickel but what they'd jump over and scramble for it. And tell her to leave the one hundred bill on the bridge."

Tom and Aline didn't see each other for two years after that confrontation, but Aline continued to write to Tom—once from a sanatorium—expressing her adoration and confirming her faith in his work. No matter how carefully they avoided seeing each other, they both knew they'd inevitably meet—but could they know it would be 3:00 A.M. in the men's room of the Plaza Hotel? Tom had passed out on the floor, and roused by an attendant, he sobbed that he wouldn't leave until "Mrs. Bernstein" came to take him home. The attendant managed to get a number out of him and called Aline. She came quickly, held him in her arms, and then deposited him, babbling, in a taxi to Brooklyn. So Tom still needed her! But the episode filled her with a mixture of pity and disgust that chilled any thoughts of reawakened love.

Nevertheless, she didn't have enough strength to resist seeing him again. A few months later, knowing that Tom and Maxwell Perkins stopped by the Chatham Bar nearly every evening, Aline sat at a corner table. Tom warmly greeted her, and understanding the delicacy of the situation, Max escorted them back to Scribner's offices. The two men left her alone for a few minutes, and when they returned she was holding a bottle of pills. Tom knocked it out of her hand. Aline fainted, and Perkins promptly called for a doctor. When she recovered, and the doctor assured them that none of the pills were missing, the scene ended in nothing but mutual embarrassment. She'd just felt faint, she explained, and was merely looking in her purse for a handkerchief.

Aline left, and Tom impulsively followed her. And as soon as she let him in, and he realized that there was little need for concern, he attacked her for being "a lecherous old woman." Remorse soon followed. He admitted that he couldn't get her out of his mind, even lying that since ending their relationship he'd been impotent. By dawn he'd projected his deceit onto her. She was, he concluded, "inwardly praying for nothing better than to be a leading character in a book of mine."

As it happened, she had been considering ways to prevent him from writing about her—but now, touched by his apparent devotion and flattered by his confession of impotence—she abandoned all her calculations.

Tom had always planned to write about Aline—to "entomb" her in his fiction—and several times over the years had asked her to write down her recollections of her childhood to help him in creating her character. The original manuscript of *Of Time and the River* had included a nearly thousand-page account of their affair, but Perkins—realizing that a two-thousand-page novel was commercially unfeasible, and fearing that Aline would sue for libel—persuaded Tom to save the Aline material for a later novel, a novel, he ardently hoped, and correctly foresaw, would never be completed.

The prospect of appearing as a character in one of Tom's novels had appealed to Aline when they were lovers, but after the painful scene with Tom and his mother, she made it known that she would not give her permission under any circumstances. Even this vow softened, and she wrote Tom that the only concession she wanted was "a personal and human agreement."

Tom interpreted this latest development to mean that she wanted to resume their affair, or, failing that, to be repaid all the money she'd given him over the years. Tom remained so suspicious of her motives that he determined to pay off all his "debts" to her to forestall her from bringing a lawsuit against him. When she refused to accept his offers of money, he demanded an acknowledgment that the ledgers in which he'd written *Look Homeward, Angel*—her gift to him in the first days of their affair, which he'd lovingly returned with the completed manuscript—canceled all his obligations. When Aline protested, he accused her of planning to rob him, but she sent him the written release he demanded.

Especially prolix about the unutterable, Tom had attributed muteness to Aline in *Of Time and the River*'s concluding passages. "Ah, strange and beautiful, the woman thought, how can I longer bear this joy intolerable, the music of this great song unpronounceable, the anguish of this glory unimaginable, which fills my life to bursting and which will not let me speak? It is too hard, too hard, and not to be endured, to feel the great vine welling in my heart, the wild, strange music swelling in my throat, the triumph of that final perfect song that aches forever there just at the gateway of my utterance and that has no tongue to speak!"

But Aline not only had a tongue to speak, she was brave enough to enter the morass Tom avoided. She might have threatened a lawsuit if he wrote about her, but she didn't hesitate to write about *him*. In 1933, she'd published *Three Blue Suits*, three short stories about men she'd known. Eugene—the very name Tom had chosen for himself in *Look Homeward,*

Angel—is a writer, his rich mistress brings a daily lunch in the studio they share, he reads her the same John Donne poem Tom used on the dedicatory page of *Angel*, and at the end he leaves her bereft by applying for a Guggenheim fellowship to go abroad.

Seeing how it felt to be turned into a fictional character, Tom was cool in a letter to Aline, questioning her portrait of him as an idle daydreamer and her omission of the difference in their ages, which might have explained his behavior. Privately, he bitterly complained about her "uncharitable and unjust" characterization, which he was convinced would "get pawed over and whispered about by wretched, verminous little people."

Encouraged by her psychotherapists, Aline began work on a novel in the mid-thirties, and in 1938 published *The Journey Down*, the story of two lovers. "She" is a stage designer, "he" is a writer, several years younger. They meet on a transatlantic crossing, begin an affair, share a Village studio, travel to Europe, begin to quarrel again, finally separate forever. At times the dialogue sounds virtually verbatim. "Where did you get your face," "he" berates her, "raised in that dung-heap the theater, among evil and rotten people, people bloated and foul and vile . . . strutting and showing their bodies; answer me, where did you get your eyes of love, your mouth of love, your flower face, did your mother cheat and lie with an angel? Answer me!" At times she even borrows Tom's vocabulary—"some day he would write into a magnificent book her beauty, her loveliness, their love, his passion and his tenderness, all would be entombed in his magic words."

Even in her anguish and bitterness, Aline remained incapable of revenge—*The Journey Down* is more a lament for lost love than an account of a woman's betrayal. Her portrait of Tom contains only a few harsh notes—"My Jewish blood," the narrator thinks, "he hates the Jews"—but even then, Aline was kind enough not to reveal the full virulence of Tom's anti-Semitism. But most amazing, Aline depicts Tom's ambivalence—which had tormented their relationship and nearly driven her to suicide—with a calm compassion. "You never knew, with him. He might be delighted, he might be furious, he might just retire into that vast interior region of his and give no sign of life, he might be like a graven image for hours on end. He was consistently uncertain."

Yes, despite everything, she still worshipped him. She took as her theme the interlocking of two souls destined to love and doomed to part. Aline went so far as to blame herself for their inability to sustain their love. And in a passage remarkable in its self-abasement, she described her *desire* to be devoured. "I should like to take the little vegetable knife [an echo of "the knife of love"?] . . . and cut a long, thin cut down one of his sides. Then I should like to make myself small and lay myself inside of him, take my needle and thread and sew up the seam neatly on the inside and so be at rest. Then, my darling, you would never have to look at me again."

. So ingrained was her masochism that her reawakened sense of self initially depended on her acceptance of her self's inadequacy. "I can stand pain," Aline wrote, "but my own ugliness and stupidity are what make me ill." She needed strength, "not against him, but against herself, she was afraid of her own weakness, she was afraid she would do all the horrible sordid things that women do, and that she longed to do." Such passages help explain why Aline continued in her relationship with Tom long after most women would have refused to tolerate any more of his incessant abuse. But this partial healing gave Aline the psychic energy to go further. By the end of the novel she was able to say, "Her life was her own, to do with as she wanted."

How did Tom react to this astonishing tale of transcendence? Even before it was published by Knopf, he angrily told his agent not to have any further dealings with the firm since it was obviously a Jewish house. He complained that Aline had egregiously portrayed herself as his victim, and the angrier he got, the more determined he became to banish her from his life forever. Finally, after a long evening of drinking, he stumbled to the Bernsteins' apartment. The Jews were the cause of all the world's problems, he bellowed, they should be wiped off the face of the earth—and he concluded by raising his arm and giving three cheers for Hitler.

Aline punched Tom in the face, and after a moment's dazed silence, called for the building's porter and ordered him ejected from her apartment.

Aline was at last free, Tom forever enslaved.

The bard of lyric exaltation whom William Faulkner once ranked as first among his peers—preposterous as it now seems, in the thirties Thomas Wolfe was widely regarded as *the* genius of American fiction—was, in later decades, read as the quintessential expression of adolescent emotions. Today he is hardly read at all. In the words of Harold Bloom, "There is no possibility for critical dispute about Wolfe's literary merits; he had none whatsoever. Open him at any page and that will suffice."

But not all Tom's contemporaries were stunned into unthinking admiration by his relentless prose. "He suddenly begins crying 'O this' and 'O that,' " wrote Frank Swinnerton, "as if he were parodying the Greek Anthology as a last resort." Robert Penn Warren declared that his novels were crammed with "chaos that steams and bubbles in rhetoric and apocalyptic apostrophe, sometimes grand and sometimes febrile and empty . . . the flotsam and jetsam and dead wood spewed up; iridescent or soggy as the case may be." Ernest Hemingway weighed in — "the over-bloated Lil Abner of literature" — and even Faulkner, despite his admiration, concluded that his novels were "like an elephant trying to do the hoochie-coochie."

These criticisms capture the glandular grandiosity of Tom's novels, but fail to acknowledge the pathos beneath the bombast. Tom was gifted with emotion, he was gifted with language, but he lacked the talent to link the two. His ranting efforts to bridge the gap not only account for the incoherence of his novels but explain the paradox of this most emotional of writers who so falsified feelings, of such an ambitious novelist with such a trite vision. As Bernard De Voto said of his work, genius is not enough.

Tom never lived in the Village again. The closest he came was in 1937, when he rented an eighth-floor corner suite at the legendary Chelsea Hotel on 23rd Street where artists and bohemians had lived since the time of O. Henry and Mark Twain.

And he never saw Aline again. After the shock of their final encounter had worn off, she was able to recall their years together without bitterness. Falling in love with him, she said, was like "a Japanese maiden's self-immolating leap into a volcano." She even became friends with Perkins — whom she'd once called her enemy — and wrote him years later when she was teaching at Vassar, "It gave me a pang when I saw my classes to think of what they all have in store for themselves, such wallops as they are going to have to take and nothing can save them."

Tom had always been haunted by premonitions of an early death — it seemed a necessary condition of genius — and in 1938, not yet forty years old, he developed tuberculosis of the brain and died in Johns Hopkins Hospital in Baltimore. Perkins persuaded Aline not to visit him — Tom's mother was at his bedside and no one wanted to risk the scene that would surely ensue if "the Jew woman" showed up — but before he drifted off into his final coma, he whispered, "Where's Aline? . . . I want Aline . . . I want my Jew."

The roots of Tom's psyche remained buried in Asheville, yet in one sense he was a quintessential Villager. The essence of the Village spirit was self-expression, and no one was more obsessed with self-expression than Tom.

But self-expression was an ideal all too easily debased. Its original goal had been the freedom of the individual from political, social, cultural, and moral constraints—which, the Villagers believed, would lead not to the chaos of unrestrained impulse but to justice, social harmony, cultural creativity, and moral honesty. But by the twenties, these noble and naive aspirations deteriorated into self-interest. Cynicism replaced idealism, self-consciousness replaced spontaneity, the Village ideal of self-expression was left without the higher purpose that had given it validity.

In Tom's case, self-expression degenerated into narcissism; his corruption of self went beyond even solipsism—the conviction of "genius." Bohemian communities, for all their apparent egalitarianism, too often regarded idiosyncrasy as a sign of superiority, and even encouraged the belief that "genius" wasn't just a higher level of creativity, but an order of being touched by the divine. Self-expression in such a culture became valueless if the self was anything less than transcendent. The concept of "genius," in short, was not only a burden on the artist but a debasement of art. Tom wasn't content with merely fulfilling his gifts, he was committed to expressing his "genius." And doomed to "genius," he failed even his talent.

The Village ideal of self-expression, unconstrained by Victorian repression and middle-class inhibitions, would liberate the self and harmonize the sexes. Of course free love failed from the first, falling victim not to social taboos but to the needs and neuroses of lovers, the Villagers' self-conscious adherence to theory even in the name of instinct, and mostly to male reluctance to surrender the prerogatives of patriarchy. The great love affairs of the Village—Mabel Dodge and Jack Reed, Louise Bryant and Jack Reed, Louise Bryant and Eugene O'Neill, Neith Boyce and Hutch Hapgood, Emma Goldman and Ben Reitman, Edna St. Vincent Millay and her man (or woman) of the moment—were affected by the Village only insofar as a liberated community gave them an unusual degree of freedom from custom and convention.

Custom and convention having further relaxed in the twenties, the only constraints on Aline and Tom's affair were self-imposed. The Village gave them the freedom to find their chains.

Unlike Aline, Tom never managed to overcome his sense of betrayal, his incestuous rage, but like her, he cherished his memories of their first years together. In the mid-thirties, when Perkins met him at the dock on his return from Europe, Tom exclaimed that he wanted to visit his favorite place in the city. The two men took a taxi to 13 East 8th Street, and when repeated knocking brought no response, they climbed a fire escape ladder to the top floor, broke in through a window, and wandered around the loft Tom and Aline had shared. Before leaving, Tom dug out a pencil stub and scrawled on the wall outside the door, "Thomas Wolfe lived here."

XI

Joe Gould

The Last of the Last Bohemians

Joe Gould always thought of himself as Joseph Ferdinand Gould, but to the bartenders and policemen of the Village, the poets and painters, the uptown visitors and out-of-town tourists, he was the Professor, or the Sea Gull, or Professor Sea Gull, or the Bellevue Boy, or sometimes—the only appellation that annoyed him—Little Joe Gould.

Joe Gould boasted of another name as well—the Last Bohemian. "The Village isn't what it used to be" was the nostalgic claim of those who left; "the Last Bohemian" was the defiant claim of those who stayed. And Joe Gould, youthful even in his decrepitude, dauntless even in his failures—a man who had no past or future because every day remained the same as the one before—deserves the title if only because the sole achievement of his pathetically heroic life was to stay.

Joe Gould never outgrew being Joe Gould. From his first appearance in the late teens to his death in the late fifties, he remained an unchanging fixture on the Village scene, mumbling to himself as he scratched his ribs and armpits and rummaged through garbage cans, leering at old friends or strangers as he asked for a handout. A man without a single gift except being Joe Gould, he fascinated Villagers with the purity of that achievement, his rejection of middle-class life, refusal to adjust or compromise or even "make a living." Joe Gould was widely acknowledged as the embodiment of Village values—an exemplary or a pitiful embodiment, as the case might be.

Sometimes, he said, he felt so low he had to reach up to touch bottom, but he remained adamant in his disdain for money and possessions. All Joe Gould ever wanted to own was, in fact, the Joe Gould Fund, which he maintained—with a balance that rarely reached beyond one figure—for four decades.

He transformed vagrancy into an ideal. But while he may have felt at home with the bums, in his heart of hearts he didn't consider himself *one* of them, for in the tattered cardboard portfolio that he carried was the manuscript of his masterpiece, *An Oral History of Our Time*, which he was convinced would make him the most renowned historian since Gibbon, and which, many Villagers believed, would record the true social history of the century. Constantly scribbling away, he estimated that by the early forties he'd written nine million words.

Joe Gould wasn't just a bum, he was a bum of a certain genius. He was the leading beneficiary of the Villagers' enduring fantasy of a link between the social misfit and the cultural rebel—after all, who better understood society's hypocrisies than society's outcasts? If Maxwell Bodenheim wrote poetry in the gutter, Joe Gould wrote history in the flophouse.

Joe Gould was born into one of the oldest and most respectable families in Massachusetts, and was raised among people who, at least in Little Joe's opinion, worshipped their names while ignoring their principles.

Joe Gould's father was an obstetrician and a member of the faculty of the Harvard Medical School. Joe showed little aptitude for medicine, or for anything else—he was, he said, ambisinistrous, or left-handed in both hands—and his mother despaired of his ever becoming a grown-up, a belief he did nothing to discourage. Still, he managed to graduate from Harvard. His classmates included a future president of the New York Stock Exchange, as well as T. S. Eliot and Walter Lippmann, none of whom showed any inclination to look him up in later years.

After some consideration, Joe Gould came up with a plan—he would dedicate the rest of his life to liberating the Albanians. For a few months in 1914, he collected money for the Friends of Albanian Independence, a society he founded and of which he was not the sole member, but one of the very, very few. It was the beginning of his lifelong panhandling, or, to look at it in a more positive light, his lifelong dedication to the under-dog, the leading example of which was Joe Gould himself.

Realizing that the Albanians remained indifferent to his efforts on their behalf, he moved on to the Chippewa of North Dakota, and spent the winter of 1915–1916 measuring the heads of fifteen hundred members of the tribe in a eugenics experiment.

Lacking any discernible talent, what could a young man do but go to the Village to write theater criticism and novels? In 1916, he got his first and last steady job, as an assistant police reporter for the *New York Evening Mail*. But a year later the idea of an oral history crossed his mind and his destiny was sealed.

Since the oral history would consume all his time and energy, Joe Gould renounced not only employment but even regular meals and a bed of his own. How he'd eat or where he'd sleep weren't his responsibility; it was society's task to support its geniuses—society, in this case, being strollers through the Village or patrons of its bars and restaurants whom he'd genially approach.

Soon Joe Gould became the Village's most recognizable character. Standing only five feet four inches and weighing only ninety to a hun-dred pounds, he had a dwarfish, emaciated look that was exaggerated by his clothes. Castoffs from friends, they were invariably several sizes too large, so that his overcoat nearly reached the ground and his shoes flapped like a tramp's. "Just look at me," he said. "The only thing that fits is this necktie."

In the winter, Joe Gould would stuff newspapers under his shirt to keep warm—"I'm snobbish," he'd say, "I only use the *Times*." He'd wear the same clothes until they became so ripped and filthy even *he* had to aban-don them. Still, he tried to counter his vagrant appearance by wearing berets and yachting caps, and using a long black cigarette holder—an ef-fect somewhat diminished by the fact that he only smoked butts he'd picked up off the sidewalk. He went weeks without bathing, so his presence could be detected by the odious combination of caked sweat and the fumi-gants used in flophouses. "People think I'm lousy because I'm always scratching myself," he complained.

Joe Gould had a frizzy beard, stained with coffee and littered with fragments of food. He was bald on top and the hair at the back of his head was long and scraggly—a fringed frieze, said a longtime Villager. He got a biennial haircut at one of the local barber colleges. His spectacles were lop-sided, and his eyes seemed constantly rheumy and bloodshot, not so much from drinking as from a persistent case of pinkeye. His toothless leer was positively alarming—even more so when his false teeth rattled in his mouth.

Anyone who ever watched Joe Gould eat would not be eager to repeat the experience. He'd gobble down huge mouthfuls of spaghetti or stew or his favored clams with his fork in one hand, his spoon in the other, pausing only to grab a piece of bread. He'd chomp his gums, run his dirty fingers inside his mouth, and belch as if exploding. Half his meal seemed to spill out of his mouth. He'd never have to worry where his next meal was coming from, a Villager once remarked, he could just pick it out of his beard.

Sumptuous repasts remained few and far between, however. (He said in the early forties that he hadn't eaten a square meal since June 1936, when he hitchhiked up to Cambridge to attend his Harvard class reunion.) Like Maxwell Bodenheim and other down-and-outers, Gould often had to make do with bohemian tomato soup. Every counterman in the Village knew the ritual. Gould would order a cup of tea, pay for it, ask for a second cup of hot water as if to make a second cup of tea with the same teabag, then, when the counterman looked the other way, add a liberal amount of ketchup to the hot water.

Year after year, Joe Gould dedicated himself to his twin projects— raising money for the Joe Gould Fund and using it to support himself while he wrote *An Oral History of Our Time.*

Joe Gould had two regular routes. First, he made the rounds of well-known Villagers—such soft touches as Malcolm Cowley, E. E. Cummings, Kenneth Fearing, Orrick Johns, the nightclub proprietor Barney Gallant—and, without deigning to mention money, would discreetly pocket whatever change they handed him. Villagers could be characterized, he said, as "the dime ones, the quarter ones, and the maybe tomorrow ones." Everyone understood that a dime would keep him away for a day, a quarter for a few days, and a dollar for a week. One writer, temporarily flush, once gave him $25, and, not pressing his luck, Joe Gould stayed away for six months.

On his second route, he made his way from Stewart's Cafeteria to Chumley's to the Athens to the Waldorf Cafeteria to the Jericho Tavern to the Samovar to Hubert's Cafeteria to the Village Square Bar & Grill to the Jefferson Diner to the Belmar to Goody's to the Rochambeau to the Minetta Tavern. Recognizing a Villager or spotting a thrill-seeking tourist, he'd introduce himself, describe his oral history project, and blithely ask for a contribution to the Joe Gould Fund. If a few coins were forthcoming he didn't act grateful, if he was turned down he didn't become resentful—after all, he never considered himself a beggar. On those rare occasions when someone rebuffed him by saying something like, "Get away from me, you old bum," he drew himself up to his full five foot four and showered him, almost literally, with expletive-filled invective. Otherwise he behaved with the courtesy and dignity befitting a scion of old Boston.

Once he had covered his two routes, he would hang out on street corners or at subway stops—Sheridan Square was his favorite location—and solicit contributions to the Joe Gould Fund. Even in downpours he could be seen trudging through the Village, a grin on his face, water running off his battered hat as if through a spout.

Joe Gould actually did inherit money after the death of his mother in 1939, and though the amount came to less than $1,000, even it seemed burdensome. To show his contempt for money and material possessions, the story goes that he spent the last of his mother's inheritance on a huge radio that he proceeded to smash to pieces in the middle of Sixth Avenue.

His life, Joe Gould often said, revolved around "the three H's"—hangovers, hunger, and homelessness—and after checking the Fund to see how much was left over from drinking and eating, he'd look for a place to spend the night. If he could afford it he'd take a room in a cheap hotel, but if not, he'd sleep in doorways, subway stations, on the floor in the offices of friends, sometimes even in one of the quarter-a-night flophouses, though they remained a last resort since his dignity was offended by the fact that the bums objected to his lice. Occasionally, when a new cop on the beat failed to recognize him, he was picked up for vagrancy and sent to Ward's or Rikers Island, and like Charlie Chaplin in *Modern Times*, he plotted to stay locked up as long as possible, since the city provided free cigarettes and three squares a day.

Joe Gould, it should go without saying, usually slept alone. Still, he didn't consider celibacy an ideal state, even for a historian, and though his most frequent erotic adventure was to visit Village galleries and leer at the nudes, he'd often come on to women at parties, at first kissing their hands with a courtly bow, then, emboldened by a few drinks, stealing a kiss with a gleeful cackle. These attempts at seduction were somewhat handicapped by his malodorous aura, and by his favorite pickup line, "You're the most beautiful woman I've ever seen," he'd gallantly proclaim, "with the exception of Eleanor Roosevelt." If he'd recently bathed and was in a mood more elfish than erotic, he'd manage to persuade the younger women to plant kisses on the top of his head, so that by the end of the evening his bald pate would be covered with lipstick.

He had more luck with down-and-outers like himself—at least with those who didn't threaten to call the police—women who'd come to the Village to write or to paint, but who'd gradually slipped from bohemianism to alcoholism, and, in some cases, from alcoholism to mental hospitals.

But always aiming higher—or perhaps just in search of free food and booze—the next night Joe Gould would be back at another high-toned party, wooing the most beautiful and unlikely women in the room.

To show that he wasn't disheartened by their inevitable rebuffs, Joe Gould was known to strip off his jacket and shirt and break into the Joseph Ferdinand Gould Stomp, which he claimed to have learned from the Chippewa—a flailing display of foot-stomping, hand-clapping, and chest-slapping, accompanied by a cackling rendition of the old Salvation Army song "There Are Flies on Me, There Are Flies on You, but There Are No Flies on Jesus."

If he felt his one-man floor show had been sufficiently appreciated—or even if not—Joe Gould would favor his audience with his most famous act: flapping his arms and bellowing, "Screeeech! Squawk! Screeeech!"—and, for the benefit of those few who might not recognize his impersonation, shouting, "I'm a sea gull!" This performance earned Joe Gould the nickname of Professor Sea Gull, and got him invited to many a Village party—and disinvited to many another.

But Gould had a special affinity with sea gulls, and boasted that he knew their secret language. "I can understand it better than I can speak it," he said, and had even translated several American poets into sea gull. Joe Gould thought a lot of poets sounded better in sea gull, and tried to use his translations to gain membership in the Raven Poetry Circle, the most prominent organization of poets in the Village in the thirties and forties. Allowed to attend a meeting at the insistence of Maxwell Bodenheim, Joe Gould took the opportunity to translate one of Bodenheim's poems into sea gull. "Screeeech! Squawk! Screeeech!" "Screeech! Squawk! Screeeech!" Bodenheim promptly withdrew his sponsorship.

Joe Gould persisted, however—for one thing, the Raven Poetry Circle served free appetizers and wine at its meetings—and he made himself such a nuisance that they gave him another chance to perform at their Religious Poetry Night. After listening to the members recite, he took the podium, announced that his poem was called "My Religion," and recited

In the winter I'm a Buddhist.
And in the summer, I'm a nudist.

Ejected once more and blackballed from future meetings, Joe Gould bad-mouthed the members of the Raven Poetry Circle at every opportunity. In the summer of 1942, he picketed their annual exhibition in Washington Square with a hand-scrawled placard: "Joseph Ferdinand Gould, hot-shot poet from poetville, a refugee from the Ravens. Poets of the world, ignite! You have nothing to lose but your brains!"

No wonder, then, Gould's reputation reached as far as Italy, where Ezra Pound referred to him as the "unreceived and uncomprehended native hickory," and even mentioned him in one of his cantos. He went on a cruise on J. P. Morgan's yacht, and took a three-week bird walk with an elderly countess, but though he considered himself something of a cosmopolitan, he had no desire to visit Europe. "Why should I go slumming? In the United States I meet a better type of European. And if I went abroad I would only meet second-rate Americans." In a section of his oral history entitled "Why I Am Unable to Adjust Myself to Civilization, Such as It Is, or Do, Don't, Do, Don't, a Hell of a Note," he characterized himself as an introvert and extrovert all rolled into one, a warring mixture of the recluse and the Sixth Avenue auctioneer.

Among those Villagers most fascinated by Joe Gould was E. E. Cummings. He not only felt a kinship with his Harvard contemporary, but he admired—envied, almost—Gould's uncompromising bohemianism. Cummings not only gave him much of his discarded clothing, but attempted, futilely, to help him get portions of his oral history published in *Esquire* and other periodicals. Joe Gould even made several appearances in Cummings's poetry, usually as a symbol of the virtue of the misfit.

> *a myth is as good as a smile but little joe gould's quote oral history unquote might (publishers note) be entitled a wraith's progress or mainly awash while chiefly submerges or an amoral morality sort-of-aliveing by innumerable kind-of-deaths*

Cummings also painted a portrait of Joe Gould, but the one that best captures his character was done by Alice Neel in 1933—an underground masterpiece that couldn't be shown in public for several years due to its putative obscenity. "It was one of the most shocking pictures I've ever seen," said one Villager.

A nearly life-size Joe Gould sits on a bench, so emaciated he seems nothing but bones, wearing a leering expression. That grotesque expression might have been enough to term the painting obscene, but Joe Gould posed stark-naked except for his spectacles, a nice Neel touch, and she gave him three sets of genitals, one set where one would expect to find them, a second set protruding from his navel, and a third set extruding from the bench.

One Villager felt neither admiration nor pity for Joe Gould. Maxwell Bodenheim was a lifelong competitor; the two men regarded each other with equal scorn. Bodenheim far outdistanced his rival in talent and alcoholism, but Gould got the upper hand in invective. Bodenheim described Gould "with his tonsured head, piebald ecclesiastical beard, and bent, shrunken frame . . . like a fugitive from a medieval monastery." Gould retaliated by focusing on Bodenheim's writing. "Max has written a whole shelf of books . . . that is, a whole shelf of no-good novels, a whole shelf of *long* no-good novels." And as for his poetry, he told Bodenheim to his face, "You're slipping. You were a better poet twenty-five years ago than you are now, and you weren't any good then. . . . You're only an artsy-craftsy poet. A niminy-piminy poet. An itsy-bitsy poet." This, from the author of "My Religion," Bodenheim chose to ignore.

Only one group, the communists of the thirties, looked on Joe Gould with open contempt—rather ironically, for while he certainly didn't qualify as a working man, he was one of the downtrodden of the earth they felt it was their mission to save. Joe Gould would have none of it. He mercilessly mocked the humorless self-importance of the radicals, their habit of saying "we," their Marxist jargon, their pompous proletarianism.

Finally, Joe Gould decided to write a poem expressing his disdain for the communists, which he called "The Barricades," and recited it wherever he could gather an audience.

> *These are the barricades,*
> *The barricades,*
> *The barricades.*
> *And behind these barricades,*
> *Behind these barricades,*
> *Behind these barricades,*
> *The Comrades die!*
> *The Comrades die!*
> *The Comrades die!*
> *And behind these barricades,*
> *The Comrades die!*
> *Of overeating.*

But Joe Gould's claim to fame wasn't his Joe Gould Fund or his Chippewa dance or his sea gull translations—and certainly not his poetry. No, he was famous in the Village—and would, he believed, become posthumously famous throughout the world, for *An Oral History of Our Time*. As he explained its premise, "What people say is history." His procedure was as artless as his project was grandiose. He'd just write down virtually everything he overheard, then append pithy commentary where he felt appropriate.

Villagers would see Joe Gould in bars and all-night diners, at Washington Square art exhibitions, at Union Square political rallies, at Salvation Army meetings, at soigné parties, among the bums on the Bowery. He'd move discreetly from group to group, writing down a verbatim account of what he overheard. Occasionally, he would abruptly ask impertinent questions, but mostly he'd eavesdrop anywhere, any time, compiling the word-for-word record, he claimed, of over twenty thousand conversations. His task, as he saw it, was to compile a complete chronicle of his era—a chronicle without coherence, discriminated by nothing but his legendary total recall.

And so Joe Gould could be seen scribbling away eight, ten, twelve hours a day at bus stops, in cafeterias, under the Sixth Avenue el, in flophouses, in the reading rooms of public libraries, writing with a pen he refilled almost daily at the post office on West 10th Street. He filled one composition book after another, never acknowledging that his dream of posthumous glory was seriously threatened by his nearly illegible scrawl.

When finished for the day, Joe Gould would place the composition book in a bulging, grease-stained cardboard portfolio secured by a rubber band, and also containing cigarette butts, bread crumbs, a paperback dictionary, ripped newspaper and magazine clippings, and a day's supply of sour balls. That portfolio was virtually his only possession. E. E. Cummings said he hardly recognized him the one time he showed up at his door without it.

Joe Gould wasn't nearly so protective of the composition books themselves, and he'd leave them with a flophouse attendant or a cafeteria counterman or in a painter's studio. He claimed that during World War II, they were hidden in a bale, wrapped in oilcloth, and stashed in the stone cellar of a chicken farm. Hundreds of Joe Gould's composition books gathered dust throughout the Village, on the top shelves of closets, under beds, in attics and basements. How could he possibly remember where they were, Villagers wondered. Had they forgotten that Joe Gould had total recall?

Eventually, he claimed, it would be the longest book ever published. In 1934, the *New York Tribune* reported that the oral history had reached 7,300,000 words, in 1937 the same paper reported that it had grown to 8,800,000 words, and by the early forties Joe Gould asserted that it was eleven million words long—a figure that, for some reason, remained stable for the rest of his life. Maybe at a certain point he decided that another million or two words, more or less, weren't worth mentioning. Maybe he simply liked the figure eleven million. Or maybe he felt that to claim to have written more than that would strain his credibility. In any case, he never ceased writing, he just stopped counting.

Those few Villagers who still regarded him as "just that nut Joe Gould" were taken aback to learn that he published several essays from his oral history in the prestigious little magazines of the twenties, including *The Dial*, the most prestigious of them all. In 1923, *Broom* published "Social Position"—originally titled "Chapter CCLXVIII." In 1929, Ezra Pound's *Exiles* took "Art." And in 1931, *Pagany* favored its readers with "Insanity" and "Freedom," two subjects that may have been more closely linked than their author or his editors knew. But his greatest triumph remained the April 1929 issue of *The Dial*, which included—alongside a poem by Hart Crane, a theater piece by Padraic Colum, and a book review by Bertrand Russell—his contributions on marriage, civilization, the auto (which he succinctly dismissed as "unnecessary"), skyscrapers ("bric-a-brac"), and the stock market ("a fuddy-duddy old maid's game"). As for the concept of progress, "If all the perverted ingenuity which was put into making buzz-wagons had only gone into improving the breed of horse, humanity would be better off."

He went so far as to claim credit for the demise of *The Dial* only three issues after he appeared in its pages. He even wrote one of his most famous poems to commemorate the occasion.

> *Who killed the Dial?*
> *Who killed the Dial?*
> *"I," said Joe Gould.*
> *"With my inimitable style,*
> *I killed the Dial."*

The Dial may have died, but Joe played a seminal role in the development of the "inimitable style" of another American writer, William Saroyan, who stumbled across that April 1929 issue in a secondhand bookstore in Fresno, California. Saroyan wrote years later that Gould remained "one of the few genuine and original American writers. . . . All other American writing was trying to get into one form or another, and no writer except Joe Gould seemed to have imagination enough to understand that if the worst came to the worst you didn't need to have any form at all."

Indeed, Joe Gould's *An Oral History of Our Time* didn't have "any form at all"—but that was precisely his plan. The rambling biographies of bums, the decline of Western Civilization, the graffiti in subway bathrooms, the nature and purpose of artistic expression, the flophouse flea, the jury system, the zipper, the treatment of the mentally ill—anything and everything found its place.

Joe Gould devoted special attention to the fads and foibles of the Villagers—their parties, their gossip, their drinking habits, their dress, their methods of birth control, and especially their cults, from free love to vegetarianism, from Freudianism to Swedenborgianism, from nudism to spiritualism. Naturally, the section on the Village was the longest, and, he thought, the most significant part of his oral history, consisting of seventy-five composition books, give or take a dozen here or there.

He had unshakable confidence in his gifts as a historian, but his ambition didn't extend so far as to hope his manuscript would actually be published. Well, at least not in his lifetime.

He decided that his oral history would be published only posthumously, and to facilitate this inevitability he carried in his breast pocket a wrinkled will in a sealed envelope bequeathing two thirds of the manuscript to Harvard and the other third to the Smithsonian, the division to be decided by weighing the composition books on a scale.

As the years passed, Joe Gould not only ceased seeking a publisher, he stopped pressing passages on friends and strangers. He could always be counted on to recite an excerpt, but these brief "lectures" always seemed to echo the portions he'd published back in the twenties. Yet oddly enough, as the years went by without completion of his project, Villagers who might have been expected to become more skeptical of the manuscript's existence found it more and more plausible. "I look upon Gould," said the poet and translator Horace Gregory, "as a sort of Samuel Pepys of the Bowery. If someone took the trouble to go through his manuscript and separate the good from the rubbish, as editors did with Thomas Wolfe's millions of words, it might be discovered that Gould actually has written a masterpiece." Even some of the radicals who scorned him saw a certain validity in his project. "The oral history," one admitted, "may very well turn out to be a sort of x-ray of the soul of the bourgeoisie."

Anti-Nazi demonstrators marching through the Washington Square Arch in the parade that drew 100,000 people to lower Manhattan on May 10, 1933

Edna St. Vincent Millay, with
Eugen Boissevain, left, and
Vincent Sheean

Floyd Dell

Thomas Wolfe and his mother in Asheville, North Carolina, 1937

Margaret Anderson, founder of *The Little Review*

Djuna Barnes, returning from
France, 1922

Dylan Thomas

Delmore Schwartz, ca. 1949

Maxwell Bodenheim
and Joe Gould, 1943

Joe Gould doing the Joseph Ferdinand Gould Stomp at his fifty-fourth
birthday party, ca. 1943

Peggy Guggenheim and Mina Loy in Paris in the 1930s

Willem de Kooning with his wife, Elaine, in his studio, 1950

Jackson Pollock and his wife,
Lee Krasner, in the Springs,
a community on eastern
Long Island, April 1949

The American Abstract Expressionists, "The Irascibles," who protested a show at
the Metropolitan Museum in 1950; front row, left to right: Theodoros Stamos,
Jimmy Ernst, Barnett Newman, James Brooks, Mark Rothko; middle row:
Richard Pousette-Dart, William Baziotes, Jackson Pollock, Clyfford Still,
Robert Motherwell, Bradley Walker Tomlin; back row: Willem de Kooning,
Adolf Gottlieb, Ad Reinhardt, Hedda Sterne

Hans Hofmann in his studio in 1950

Franz Kline at the Cedar Bar in Greenwich Village, 1957

No one knew Joe Gould better than Mitchell, who spent hundreds of hours with him over a period of nearly twenty years—and he, too, was a believer. In fact, Gould allowed Mitchell to read several chapters at a time when he'd become reluctant to show the manuscript to anyone else.

"Death of Dr. Clarke Storer Gould" was the title of the first excerpt Mitchell perused—an account of the death of Joe Gould's father. Mitchell then read "The Dread Tomato Habit," which included twenty-six pages of largely irrelevant statistics.

Mitchell was bewildered—these chapters didn't seem to bear any resemblance to the oral history as Gould described it. He managed to track down several more composition books Gould had stored with friends. "Death of Dr. Clarke Storer Gould," "The Dread Tomato Habit," "Drunk as a Skunk, Or How I Measured the Heads of Fifteen Hundred Indians in Zero Weather," "Death of My Mother."

More queries, and eventually Mitchell came across other chapters, but these brief, rambling essays didn't have anything to do with the project Joe Gould kept boasting about. Was the oral history a fantasy, a fraud?

Finally, Mitchell confronted Joe Gould. Gould mumbled something Mitchell couldn't quite hear, then turned his back and a few moments later disappeared.

Mitchell decided to keep Gould's secret as long as he was alive. And he didn't challenge him again. At first, Gould seemed wary when meeting Mitchell, but eventually he started referring to his oral history with the old confidence and zest. In some dim recess of his mind, he realized Mitchell knew the truth, but he could not acknowledge the truth to himself. He had to keep the dream alive—what else did he have?

Joe Gould may have been the most nonconformist of all the nonconformists in the Village, the most deadbeat of all its deadbeats, the craziest of all its crazies. He may even have had, as one Villager put it after his death, "the longest writer's block in the history of literature." But as he wrote in "Death of Dr. Clarke Storer Gould," "there are occasions when the facts do not tell the truth."

He would *cherish* the fact that he was a misfit, he would establish his idiosyncrasies and create a character for himself—"the greatest historian since Gibbon"—that he could perform with unquenchable conviction to the end. He belonged nowhere—not even in the Village, really—not unless he could make a career out of eccentricity itself.

As Joe Gould neared sixty—many Villagers asked, "Hasn't he been nearly sixty for decades?"—and his prodigious energy began to flag, a wealthy patron came to his rescue, allotting him $60 a month on two conditions, that he never be told her name, and that he use it for room and board at the Madison Gerard, a series of rooming houses on West 33rd Street. But after setting fire to his bed several times by dozing off while smoking, he was politely but firmly ejected. Soon he was once more soliciting contributions to the Joe Gould Fund and sleeping in a Bowery flophouse.

The Village had always found a way to exploit its legends, and in the late forties the proprietor of the Minetta Tavern "hired" Joe Gould as its resident bohemian. His job?—throughout the afternoon and early evening he was to sit by the window and scribble in his composition books to attract patrons in search of local color. His pay?—a free meal a day, so long as he stuck to low-priced items like spaghetti and meatballs.

In November 1952, Joe Gould collapsed on the street. Suffering from "confusion and disorientation," he was sent to Pilgrim State, an institution for the mentally ill on Long Island where, a few years later, he was joined by Maxwell Bodenheim's murderer. His doctors could do nothing for him as he sank deeper into listlessness. One of his symptoms particularly puzzled them. Every now and then, his apathy would lift and he would shamble through the wards flapping his arms, crying, "Screeeech! Screeeech! Squawk! Screeeech!"

Finally, on August 18, 1957, at the age of sixty-eight, Joe Gould died of arteriosclerotic senility. The Greenwich Village chamber of commerce paid for his funeral, at which he was virtually unrecognizable, the undertaker having shaved off his beard, and at which a Bowery friend read E. E. Cummings's "little Joe Gould." Several prominent Villagers formed a committee to search for the manuscript of *An Oral History of Our Time*, dozens of his friends and acquaintances conducted informal searches of their own—but all they could find was a single poem, a portion of an essay, and an unsent letter asking for a contribution to the Joe Gould Fund.

But no one needed to write Joe Gould's epitaph, for he'd written it himself—in his essay on "Insanity" published in *Pagany* a quarter of a century earlier. "I would judge the sanest man," he wrote, "to be him who firmly realizes the tragic isolation of humanity and pursues his essential purposes calmly, I suppose I feel about it in this way because I have a delusion of grandeur. I believe myself to be Joe Gould."

XII

Djuna Barnes

"One's Life Is Peculiarly One's Own When One Has Invented It"

The frail old woman shuffled through the gate into the courtyard of Patchin Place, when suddenly a huge male figure grabbed for her purse and groceries. She uttered a savage shriek and glared at her mugger. Startled, he bolted empty-handed.

All through the fifties, and into the early eighties, Villagers told stories about the august legend who lived in proud poverty and implacable isolation in her one-and-a-half-room apartment at 5 Patchin Place. On one of her few ventures out, the story went, she was asked by a department store clerk to show identification in order to pay by check. *"Identification?"* she responded haughtily. "I was a friend of T. S. Eliot and James Joyce!" "That's very nice, lady," replied the clerk, "but do you have a driver's license?" The old woman stiffened. "Do I look like the sort of person who would have a *driver's license?*" she said. On another occasion, a few weeks after she'd berated her publisher, James Laughlin of New Directions, and he'd restrained his own anger by telling her he'd learned at his mother's knees always to be respectful toward women, she waved her cane under his nose—"And how are your mother's knees, Mr. Laughlin?" E. E. Cummings, who also had an apartment on Patchin Place and frequently ran errands for his infirm friend, once bellowed across the courtyard, "*Are ya still alive, Djuna?*"

Djuna Barnes was still alive into her nineties, and over the forty-eight years she lived on Patchin Place, her legend grew—how she'd been a prominent journalist in the Golden Age of the Village, how she'd been the chic center of a circle of lesbian writers and artists in Paris in the twenties, how she'd been the only person to call James Joyce "Jim"; how her admirer Ernest Hemingway had given the hero of *The Sun Also Rises* her name, how T. S. Eliot had only two pictures hanging in his office at Faber and Faber, one of Groucho Marx, the other of Djuna Barnes. It was Eliot, in his introduction to her cult classic, *Nightwood*, who wrote, "What I would leave the reader prepared to find is the great achievement of a style, the beauty of phrasing, the brilliance of wit and characterization, and a quality of horror and doom very nearly related to that of Elizabethan tragedy."

Villagers would see Djuna in local markets, brandishing her cane at the clerks, or in libraries, where she read in an aura of severe silence, but they kept their distance, intimidated by her formidable reputation. But journalists and scholars rang her doorbell in vain. Readers of *Nightwood* came from across the country and sat on the sidewalk outside the gate of Patchin Place hoping to catch a glimpse of their idol. Carson McCullers, or so the story went, burst into tears as she rang the bell and called out to be let in, only to be answered by an imperious voice, "Whoever is ringing this bell, please go the hell away!"

Djuna lived out the last four decades of her life in a kind of defiant oblivion. Often going nearly a week without eating and as long as six months without talking, she would arise at 5:00 A.M., remain in her elegant nightgown, and spend the day typing out a line or two of poetry. She was nearly always ill or in pain—she suffered from arthritis, asthma, and emphysema, and nearly a quarter of a century before her death was diagnosed with cancer and told she only had six months to live—and had virtually no income other than a monthly stipend from Peggy Guggenheim. She was, she acidly remarked to one of the few visitors she admitted, "the most famous unknown writer in the world."

All the stories about all the great Village "characters" were a mixture of fact and fancy, and while the historical impulse is to separate the two, in the case of Djuna Barnes, her legend, compounded of scraps of biographical information, anecdotes, and numberless conjectures, came to have the heft of truth in the Village imagination. No matter how much exaggeration and distortion may have contributed to Djuna's image, stories told often are transmuted into iconography. Iconography expresses what people believe, and what people believe, whatever its basis in fact, becomes a crucial component of the texture of history.

The difficulty in sorting out fact and invention in Djuna's life is exacerbated by the peculiar nature of her art, for she systematically intertwined the two as if she could convince herself that by an act of imagination she had created a life not only emotionally more "truthful" but factually more "accurate" than her own. In a sense, her fiction was meant not so much to illuminate her life as to *replace* it, to distance her pain by transforming it into an aesthetic construction. Just as some people marry a person much like a despised parent in the hopes that this time it will come out right, Djuna wrote fiction about her family in hopes that this time she could *survive*. Her most ardent admirers admitted that her writing was often obscure, even impenetrable, and in an ironically revealing remark, Djuna expressed surprise that a critic had discerned autobiographical aspects she was sure she had concealed. As a writer and as a woman, she maintained her ruthless silence until the end.

Begin with her name—for even that's unclear. Djuna was apparently named Djalma, after a character in Eugene Sue's novel *The Wandering Jew*, and apparently became Djuna due to a brother's mispronunciation. Born in 1892 in Cornwall-on-Hudson, a bit of a bohemian enclave, Djuna was the only daughter among five children.

Wald Barnes, or so the story went, forced his children to eat small handfuls of pulverized gravel in the belief that, as with the poultry he haphazardly raised, it would clean out their digestive tracts. He seems to have carried his admiration of animals—or so Djuna hinted on many occasions—so far as to have frequent sexual intercourse with several of his prize specimens. Even more attracted to women, he used to carry a sponge on his saddle to wipe away the evidence of his erotic encounters in the neighborhood, though why he would want to keep them a secret remains unclear since he put up his many mistresses in his home—including an opera singer whose previous lover had been Oscar Hammerstein.

Elizabeth Barnes, an English émigré, tolerated these ménages, but took out her frustration on her children. She was, Djuna once remarked, "Mrs. King Lear," the world's strongest weak woman. Incest hovered in the air as well—Wald and his mother, Wald and his children, even Djuna's grandmother, who apparently seduced Djuna as a teenager.

These disturbing accounts, it should be pointed out, have been "authenticated" largely by casual comments Djuna made to her friends and by deductions readers have made from her fiction. In either case they are colored by her hatred for her father and her ambivalence toward her mother—perhaps the only two undeniable facts about her family. In any case, as Djuna once reported, her father told her it would take a lifetime to unravel her family background—and she still hadn't by the age of ninety.

As a child, Djuna never attended school, her father insisting, in the tradition of so many American eccentrics, that she could learn more at home, that he needed her services as a cook, seamstress, and farmhand. When Djuna was in her teens, the family moved to Long Island, driven out of Cornwall by poverty and the condemnation of the locals. Djuna already had every reason for bitterness toward her parents, but shortly after the move they were responsible for a trauma that alienated her permanently. According to some accounts, at the age of eighteen Djuna was "given" to the brother of one of her father's many mistresses, a man in his early fifties, and lived with him for a year in Connecticut in sexual servitude. But according to early drafts of a novel and a play that Djuna confessed were semi-autobiographical, her sexual initiation may have been even more brutal. In one case, her father raped her with her mother's passive assent, and in the other, her father attempted to rape her and, when she fought him off, strung her up from a rafter and traded her to a local farmhand for a goat. Whatever the facts of the matter, the young woman's psyche can hardly be faulted for failing to make nuanced distinctions, nor can the mature woman be blamed for seeking the "truth" in aesthetic reconstructions—or even for choosing not to "unravel" her past but to "ravel" it almost beyond recognition.

Djuna's weird, wretched life seemed more suited for the tabloids than for art, but by a characteristic act of self-definition she determined to write for the tabloids rather than serve as their subject—a decision that bizarrely foreshadowed her transformation of trauma into creativity. After living for a few months in Queens with her mother—who had finally found the sanity to separate from her lunatic husband—and after taking drawing lessons at Pratt Institute in Brooklyn, in the early teens Djuna moved to a tiny apartment in "The House of Genius" at 61 Washington Square South. She enrolled for classes at the Art Students League, started sending poems to magazines, and began to work as a freelance illustrator and feature writer for a number of New York newspapers.

Dozens of papers competed for the market, which meant that journalistic standards were virtually nonexistent. Ironically, this meant that there was space for stylish writers as well as for unscrupulous hacks—and even for a twenty-one-year-old woman in the male-dominated world. Paid $15 an article by the *Brooklyn Daily Eagle*, the *New York Tribune*, the *New York Press*, and the *Morning Telegraph*, at first Djuna covered the local beats—courthouses, old-age homes, orphanages, the occasional murder—but she quickly won a reputation for her offbeat features and idiosyncratic celebrity profiles.

It's unlikely that T. S. Eliot saw Djuna's account of a show-biz dentist who billed himself as "Twingeless Twitchell and his Tantalizing Tweezers," or her report on a visit to a firemen's training school during which she allowed herself to be rescued by three different procedures, or her mock interview with a baby gorilla named Dinah at the Bronx Zoo. And Carson McCullers probably never read Djuna's satirical story about a gathering of suffragette aviatrixes (she had little but scorn for the politics of feminism), or her gruesome piece about submitting herself to the kind of force-feeding then being practiced on arrested English feminists.

Among the celebrities Djuna interviewed—or rather, engaged in dialogue, for she preferred impressionistic portraits to conventional profiles—were Lillian Russell, Diamond Jim Brady, Flo Ziegfeld, Mother Jones, Billy Sunday, Alfred Stieglitz, David Belasco, and boxing champions Jack Dempsey and Jess Willard ("Now, on the level, Jess, aren't you plumb proud of this anatomy that goes with your name?"). Accompanied by her own Beardsleyesque illustrations and sassy headlines ("Nothing Ever Done Well That Wasn't Planned in Bed"), Djuna's articles seemed almost blithe in their surface innocence—the girl reporter having a lark—yet also revealed a tough self-confidence and absence of awe that must have baffled and impressed her swaggering male colleagues. And though her cheery faux-naïf approach was far away from the sophisticated, decadent facade of her fiction, it allowed her to sneak in tart insights, sarcasm, and nicking caricatures that prefigured her novels.

Among Djuna's sketches was her portrait of a character named Doris the Dope, a cocaine addict, part-time thief, and compulsive liar who led Villagers to believe she'd served in the Secret Service and had clandestinely borne a son to Oscar Wilde's paramour, Lord Alfred Douglas. A lesbian during the war and a heterosexual during peacetime—or at least that's what she told Djuna—she frequently greeted guests while lying naked on a mattress on the floor, an erotically inviting posture until her visitors discovered she was suffering from syphilis. After Doris the Dope cadged $15 from

Jack Reed by saying that she needed to bury her dead son, Jack surreptitiously followed her, heard her whistle, and saw the dead son emerge from behind a bush and stroll away with his now flush mother. She could piss like a man, she claimed, and when challenged she raised her skirt and promptly filled a bottle placed several feet away!

Now a figure of some notoriety, Djuna lived on Washington Square South, then on West 14th Street, and finally settled at 86 Greenwich Avenue, a seventeen-room apartment building called "the Clemenceau Cottage" for the French statesman who had once lived there in exile. But at one time or another it was the address of Djuna's friends Jack Reed, Floyd Dell, Ida Rauh, Gene O'Neill, Dorothy Day, Kenneth Burke, and Malcolm Cowley. One night, Djuna and Malcolm fell into a dispute regarding the advantages and disadvantages of male and female anatomy, and when Malcolm argued that men could urinate their initials in the snow, Djuna—perhaps remembering Doris the Dope—retorted, "Yes, but I can make a period."

Djuna had a regal presence—tall and slender, her angular features and pale complexion sometimes set off by blue, purple, or green makeup. Guido Bruno's description: "Red cheeks. Auburn hair. Gray eyes, ever sparkling with delight and mischief. Fantastic earrings in her ears, picturesquely dressed, ever ready to live and to be merry." She usually dressed completely in black, with a turban or tricorn hat and a cape, and pendent earrings that nearly reached her shoulders.

Contrary to her flamboyant appearance, Djuna's manner was aloof, expressed in her sardonic asides, abrupt, barking laugh, and intimidating silences. "I like my human experience served up with a little silence and restraint," she said. "Silence makes experience go further and, when it does die, gives it that dignity common to a thing one had touched and not ravished." Her friendships were usually based less on mutual intimacy than on shared disdain. For instance, Djuna and Edna St. Vincent Millay never got along, probably because they had too much in common, including reputations that made them rivals, and what the Villagers called "sapphic tendencies" that neither was ready to acknowledge.

Djuna and Margaret Anderson made no pretense of getting along—though Margaret published several of her early short stories in *The Little Review* when every other publication was sending them back, and though Djuna admitted that Margaret's support helped her move from journalism to fiction. "Djuna and *The Little Review* began a friendship which might have been great," Margaret wrote in her memoirs, "had it not been that Djuna always felt some fundamental distrust of our life, of our talk.

"To the more important luxuries of the soul she turned an unhearing ear. Djuna would never talk. She would never allow herself to be talked to. She said it was because she was reserved about herself. She wasn't, in fact, reserved—she was unenlightened. This led her into the construction of self-myths which she has never taken the pains to revise. It embarrassed her to approach impersonal talk about the personal element. It embarrassed us to attempt a relationship with anyone who was not on speaking terms with her own psyche. Her mind had no abstract facets. She is impatient of such facets."

Nothing was further from the truth—whatever else was in Djuna's mind, it surely contained "abstract facets." And as for "the personal element," she could have reminded Margaret of her furious embarrassment at a *Little Review* benefit held at Christine's restaurant. Sponsored by Souls in Revolt, an ad hoc group that proudly proclaimed themselves "an unorganized organization," the gathering featured a talk by the writer Sadakichi Hartmann. When the ubiquitous and impatient Hippolyte Havel had heard enough — "Sit down, Kichi!" he called out—the flustered Kichi toppled a plate of chicken à la king in Djuna's lap. A young man leaped to his feet to defend her from this outrage, fisticuffs were averted, and only Djuna, as fastidious in her way as Margaret and Jane were in theirs, remained unamused.

Djuna made the obligatory appearances at Polly's restaurant, at the Stieglitz gallery, and, of course, at Mabel's salon. "It was some time in the early fall, I think, of 1914," she wrote in 1917, "that I strayed into the house of Mabel Dodge toward evening, to show her my pictures. The nonchalant classes—the poet, the revolutionist, with their heads always on a sort of ball-bearing system, with bombs and other redeeming munitions of a future social order—were entirely new to me. This class struck me at first as entirely charming, not from the standpoint of wishing to cultivate their immediate acquaintance, but from a gratitude arising from the pleasure of being pointed out the way to the future with an index finger that had previously been dipped in gold ink.

"These were my grateful days," Djuna continues. "I was grateful to Mabel Dodge, who let me eat as many sandwiches as my suburban stomach could hold. I was grateful to Carl Van Vechten for having written the introductory card that had given access to so much. I remember how funny I looked in the midst of that artistic atmosphere. I remember that even at that time I asked myself the question, Why is it that all similarity of ideas and tastes has the same manner of dress, of speech and mode of living?

"I wonder a little, too, why old men have always had a peculiar liking for me where young men are entirely indifferent—and why at the same time for me there existed no man, young or old, who could draw the slightest, faintest word of interest from me apart from my drawing or some abstract thing connected with themselves. Perhaps it was because love had been discussed in my family circle, because all the old romances of man and maid had already been read to me. Perhaps it was because, and this surely was it, that art had been something that I felt and not saw, longed for and not possessed, to its outward fullness, hoped for and at last approached.

"And yet I was in awe of no one. I attempted not to show the arrogance of my upper lip that would persist in an attempt to curl, probably because I wanted to cry and wouldn't, and I felt cold because I wanted so dreadfully to feel warm and hopeful and one with them."

Djuna's closest connection to the Village was through the Provincetown Players, who staged three of her plays, and for whom she served as a part-time actress-usher and program-seller. Her drama, *Kurzy of the Sea*, appeared on a double bill with Eugene O'Neill's *Exorcism*. Gene was one of Djuna's earliest admirers, and suggested, perhaps disingenuously, that she was a better playwright than he was, and that they should collaborate on a play, a project both of them endorsed but never mentioned again.

Emboldened by Jig Cook's indiscriminate encouragement, Djuny—as the Provincetowners called her—decided to give her "abstract facets" full rein in a play called *Three from the Earth*. Stark and enigmatic, the story involves three young men who visit their father's former mistress after his mysterious suicide, in search of their long-lost love letters. The former mistress, it turns out, may or may not have been the mother of one of the sons. Jig selected the play for the opening bill of the 1919 winter season, in part because he hadn't the foggiest notion what it was about, an opinion shared by Alexander Woollcott of the *New York Times*, who concluded his review, "It is really interesting to see how absorbing and essentially dramatic a play can be without the audience ever knowing what, if anything, the author is driving at, and without, as we have coarsely endeavored to suggest, the author knowing either."

Guido Bruno put in his 15 cents' worth in a review entitled "Fleurs Du Mal à la Mode de New York," and in a first in the history of theater criticism, allowed the playwright to respond to his remarks. Djuna answered Guido's main objection to her script. "Morbid? You make me laugh. This life I write and draw and portray is life as it is, and therefore you call it morbid. Look at my life. Look at the life around me. Where is the beauty that I am supposed to miss? The nice episodes that others depict? Is not everything morbid? I mean the life of people stripped of their masks. Where are the relieving features?"

Djuna may or may not have known what she was driving at, but she knew what drew her to the Players. "So we talked, and so we went our separate ways home," she said, "there to write out of that confusion which is biography when it is wedded to fact. . . . Of such things were plays made. Eugene O'Neill wrote out of a dark suspicion that there was injustice in fatherly love. . . . I wrote out of a certitude that I was my father's daughter."

Years later, in an interview in the New York Times, Djuna expressed a mood of ambivalent nostalgia. "It was all so very, very desperate. Years ago I used to see people I had to, I was a newspaperman, among other things. And I used to be rather the life of the party. I was rather gay and silly and bright and all that sort of stuff and wasted a lot of time. I used to be invited by people who said, 'Get Djuna for dinner, she's amusing.' So I stopped it. Ghastly days—how I miss them."

Djuna wrote poetry as well as plays, and in 1915 she published a small volume of poems and drawings entitled A Book that contributed more to her reputation than to her income. That same year The Book of Repulsive Women, consisting of eight poems about female victims and five macabre drawings, was published as issue number 20 of Bruno's Chap Books, a series of 15-cent pamphlets put out by that Village charlatan Guido Bruno, who was later to serve as one of the models for the character Felix Volkbein in Nightwood. Realizing he had a hot number on his hands, he raised the price from 15 to 50 cents. If the censors couldn't comprehend what Djuna was saying, the Villagers certainly could, especially in the verses:

> Someday beneath some hard
> Capricious star—
> Spreading out its light a little
> Over far,
> We'll know you for the woman
> That you are.

.   .   .   .

See you sagging down with bulging
Hair to sip,
The dappled damp from some vague
Under lip,
Your soft saliva, loosed
With orgy, drip.

Djuna's quest for erotic fulfillment could be called frustrating, even futile, except that she harbored a certain sexual ambivalence herself—it was no coincidence that she got along so well with homosexual men. Her legendary remark that she spent an entire summer seeking an evening to go with her new nightgown reveals that for Djuna sex was sometimes as much a matter of style as of impulse.

Among her many lovers was a Harvard graduate named Putzi Hanfstaengl, who, two decades later, gained a certain renown as a court clown in the entourage of Adolf Hitler. Putzi's prowess was more reliable than his politics, for on one occasion, while dancing with Djuna, he allegedly became so excited a blood vessel burst in his penis. Other lovers included publisher Horace Liveright and Laurence Vail, who for a time inherited Jack Reed's reputation as the Golden Boy of the Village and who later married Peggy Guggenheim. Carl Van Vechten? Perhaps. Marsden Hartley? Almost certainly not. Like Carl, Marsden liked to call himself bisexual, a claim that entails at least an occasional effort. Djuna later said, of his imperious mannerisms, that Marsden was an eagle without a cliff.

Djuna's only relationship that lasted beyond a few weeks—for she was primarily attracted to abusive alcoholics, homosexuals, or heteosexuals whose common characteristic was indifference to her—was a common-law marriage to a man with the lovely name of Courtenay Lemon, with whom she and her pet parrot lived for two years in the late teens. A socialist, a libertine, an incipient alcoholic, and the descendant of an old American family—tautologies all—Courtenay held jobs on the copy desk at the *New York Times* and as a script reader for the Theater Guild while he wrote a multivolume history and philosophy of criticism, contributing to the glorious Village tradition of grandiose projects not a word of which has ever been published, in all probability because not a word was ever written. The relationship came to an abrupt end, either because Courtenay was unfaithful to Djuna, or because Djuna was unfaithful with the painter Maurice Sterne (who, a few months later, married Mabel Dodge)—or perhaps because, as Djuna later claimed, he disapproved of her earrings.

With neither a career nor a love to hold her to the Village, maybe it was time to move on. Although Djuna had found a following as a brash reporter and deft stylist—her employers paid her as much as $5,000 a year and she might even have become a Dorothy Parker figure a decade before *The New Yorker*—she had more audacious aspirations. In 1918, using an assignment for *McCall's* as an excuse, and armed with letters of introduction to Ezra Pound and James Joyce, she set sail for Europe.

Her journalistic eye and her savage wit liberated her from journalistic decorum soon after disembarking. "I came to Europe to get culture. Is this culture I'm getting? Then I might as well go back to Greenwich Village and rot there." But when she registered at the Hotel d'Angleterre in Paris, she spotted Alfred Kreymborg and a group of Village writers in the lobby—the expatriation had begun.

Ernest Hemingway and F. Scott Fitzgerald were in Paris, of course—and Gertrude Stein. But when Djuna met that grand lady, she reported, "D'you know what she said to me? Said I had beautiful legs! Now what does that have to do with anything?" Gertrude said it because, recognizing a kindred spirit, she felt compelled to cut her down to size. Edmund Wilson proved a less ambiguous admirer. He suggested over dinner with businesslike lasciviousness that they go to Italy and live together, a proposal she greeted with a shriveling burst of laughter.

Djuna's role in the expatriate community was already clear. As the man who later wrote *The Sun Also Rises* put it, she "dominated the intellectual night-life of Europe for a century." But she was often an unapproachable legend, drinking too much, smoking too much marijuana, unleashing her devastating repartee, but more often inflicting her even more devastating silences, all the while contemplating her great novel. "It's awfully hard to work in Paris," she said. "Everyone just sits around and says, 'Gosh, isn't it great to be here!' "

Realizing that the beasts roaming her psyche could be tamed only if she convinced herself that she'd imagined them, Djuna began work on a novel loosely based, like all her fiction, on her family. She found a regular income turning out articles, often under the pseudonym Lydia Steptoe, for *The Smart Set*, *Vogue*, and *Vanity Fair*. The latter she described as a magazine for people who want something French but who have never been to Paris.

Djuna's letter of introduction to Pound proved futile. He never liked her writing, and as he put it several years later, "There once wuzza lady named Djuna / Who wrote rather like a baboon." But she and Joyce soon became friends and mutual admirers. When she'd first read *Ulysses* in

The Little Review she raved, "I shall never write another line. Who has the nerve after this!" For his part, "Jim" was impressed enough by Djuna's abilities to present her with his annotated manuscript of the novel.

Djuna's awe at Joyce's talent didn't prevent her from writing about the man with an unwavering gaze. Her portrait of him for *Vanity Fair* was no less penetrating because it revealed so much about herself. "Because no voice can hold out over the brutalities of life without breaking," she wrote, "he turned [from singing] to quill and paper, for so he could arrange, in the necessary silence, the abundant inadequacies of life, as a laying-out of jewels—jewels with a will to decay. . . . If I were asked what seemed to be the most characteristic pose of James Joyce, I should say that of the head, turned farther away than disgust and not so far as death." Were her own work and "characteristic pose" ever so succintly described?

Then Djuna met Thelma.

"I'm not a lesbian," she said years later. "I just loved Thelma." Thelma Wood, a tomboyish sculptor from Missouri who claimed to have Indian blood—which no doubt contributed to Djuna's erotic enchantment—was tall like Djuna, wore black like Djuna, and drank heavily like Djuna. Thelma had always been a lesbian—she had a brief affair with Edna St. Vincent Millay in Paris in the early twenties—but Djuna seems to have had only two brief lesbian affairs before meeting Thelma.

In talking about her downtown days with the poet Mina Loy, Djuna disdainfully remarked that she'd tried nineteen male lovers before finally, in frustration, trying a female, most likely Mary Pyne, the ethereal poet and actress who had lived for years with Harry Kemp. After Mary's death, Djuna dedicated a series of sexually suggestive poems to her memory. As Maurice Sterne remarked in his memoirs, "When Mary Pyne died I found Djuna sobbing painfully, saying over and over that she would never get over the loss. These were the only times I had even a glimpse of the true intensity her controlled facade covered." "Your mouth and mine," Djuna wrote of Mary after her death, "and one sweet mouth unseen / We call our soul. Yet thick within our hair / The dusty ashes that our days prepare."

Maurice also speculated on Djuna's other affair. "One night at Polly's . . . [Djuna] took me over to a table where a mousy girl was dining. . . . Djuna began hissing, I hate you. I hate you. . . . They had an ominously quiet, violent fight before Djuna stalked out." The tan mouse?—Margaret Anderson. The quarrel?—over Margaret's lover Jane Heap. The antagonism between the two women was founded, at least in part, on sexual rivalry. Years later, Djuna confessed she'd had a crush on Jane back in the teens, and in a letter in the thirties she called Jane "a shit"—two remarks so contradictory they actually serve as evidence of an abortive affair.

As for Thelma, Djuna had fallen in love on the spot, and for a decade the two women lived together in an erotically charged, emotionally draining relationship—first in Paris on the Boulevard St. Germain, then at 45 Grove Street and on Washington Square South. Djuna was never a model of equanimity, but Thelma was the very portrait of volatility. She could be sparkling, tender, generous—then turn icy, grim, selfish. Many Americans in Paris agreed with Janet Flanner's description of Thelma as "the bitch of all time." But these qualities enthralled Djuna, especially the bizarre impulses that she could express only in sullen silences or Elizabethan prose.

Night after night Thelma wandered off through the arrondissements. Djuna would search for her companion, and at dawn they'd arrive home drunk and despairing. Thelma would threaten to leave, then Djuna would threaten to throw her out, and they'd sob in each other's arms, vowing lifelong love. Devoted, suspicious, enraged—for a decade they endured this tumultuous relationship until, in the early thirties, Djuna abruptly abandoned Thelma forever.

Despite this turmoil, Djuna published three books during her years with Thelma. A miscellany of twelve stories, eleven poems, three plays, and several drawings called A Book appeared in 1923. "In these stories of abnormality," wrote one critic, "Miss Barnes reveals an astuteness of manufacture and an intellectual tension verging at times on genius or insanity. Aside from the poetry, derivative in most cases, every piece in the book is almost too deeply disturbing."

And in 1929, a Dijon printer issued a private edition of Djuna's Ladies Almanack. Written under the pseudonym "A Lady of Fashion," it was structured as a bawdy "zodiac calendar" and sold by hawkers along the Seine. The book portrayed various types among Djuna's lesbian coterie—Daisy Downpour, Maisie Tuck-and-Frill, the Duchess Clitoressa, and so on. At once celebrating lesbian lust and satirizing Parisian promiscuity, Djuna detailed the days of the "Members of the Sect" and their "slips of the tongue" with a risqué bravado and an urbane wit. Less well disguised were Djuna's salacious allusions. Female anatomy, in particular, was described with pornographic gusto, including such phrases as "garden of Venus," "windy Space," and "cave's mouth," and in case any reader should miss the point, she slyly referred to "the consolation every Woman has at her fingertips." But since even her double entendres were expressed in a kind of arch Middle English, *Ladies Almanack,* like most of her books, was more talked about than read, and succeeded less as a succès de scandale than as a titillating curiosity.

Djuna's next book—on which her reputation was ultimately founded—came out of emotion recollected in anguish. The end of her affair with Thelma liberated her to write the novel that soothed her pain, brought her a measure of revenge, and inspired a cult renown that continues to this day. *Nightwood*—its title suggested by T. S. Eliot, who had no idea it echoed Thelma's surname—forsakes straightforward narrative and character development for oblique philosophical musing and evocative exploration of personality. Written in a style at once antiquarian, fevered, and convoluted, it presents an intimidating facade behind which lurks a grief-stricken heart.

Nora, reflective, nurturing, becomes enchanted by Robin, impulsive, insatiable, remote, their relationship as impossible as Djuna and Thelma's. In its contrapuntal structure, the novel contrasts the worlds of noon and midnight, of aristocratic tastes and bohemian sensations, the worlds of forbidden relationships and anguished solitude. Even more strikingly, it deals with the conflict between the human and the bestial. Robin—her very name signifying flight, fancy, freedom—desperately needs to be cherished, yet she cannot be confined by social commitment or moral responsibility. Having no center or self, no focus of will, she wanders from one relationship to another, leaving nothing but wreckage in her wake. Into this emotional maelstrom comes Jenny, petty, self-absorbed, blindly destructive—and Nora and Robin's affair, caught in a torrent of deceit and jealousy, crashes to an end. In the final scene, Robin hunts down Nora, and their wordless, almost liturgical meeting ends with an apparent act of sodomy between Robin and a dog on the floor of Nora's chapel.

Yet the Nora-Robin relationship is overshadowed by the austere grandiloquence of Dr. Matthew O'Connor, "an Irishman from the Barbary Coast . . . whose interest in gynecology had driven him half around the world," and whose virtuosity in matters epistemological, metaphysical, and theological drives him into a state somewhere between prophetic genius and prolix lunacy. Based on a legendary figure in the expatriate community named Dan Mahoney—who came from the Barbary Coast and, not incidentally, performed an abortion on Djuna—Dr. O'Connor serves as a kind of down-and-out transvestite Greek chorus, blathering about the depravity of innocence and the phosphorescence of decay, the imponderabilities of fate and the parameters of Time and Space. But the torrent of his talk does take on a kind of berserk majesty.

Understandably, only when T. S. Eliot agreed to contribute an introduction was *Nightwood* finally accepted in England in 1936. "Miss Barnes's prose is the only prose by a living writer which can be compared with that of Joyce," wrote Edwin Muir, "and in one point it is superior to his: in its richness in exact and vivid imagery entirely without that prettiness which so readily creeps into an Irish style." "One of the three great prose books ever written by a woman," added Dylan Thomas.

The American reviews, in 1937, were considerably less enthusiastic. The critic for the *New York Herald Tribune* wrote, "Call it poetry, call it caviar—it is the poetry of death; there is no life in those eggs. It is a book of Gothic horror, not of Elizabethan tragedy." *The Partisan Review*'s Philip Rahv—probably as annoyed by Eliot's introduction as by the novel, and perhaps detecting a slight whiff of anti-Semitism—concluded that the book displayed nothing but "those minute shudders of decadence developed in certain small ingrown cliques of intellectuals and their patrons, cliques in which the reciprocal workings of social decay and sexual perversion have destroyed all response to genuine value and actual things." The reading public seemed to share Rahv's view—a rare event, indeed—for Djuna's first royalty statements came to 43 pounds 8 pence from England and $350.23 from the United States.

This woman who would spend the last half of her life in a one-and-a-half-room apartment made numerous excursions to London, Vienna, and Berlin in particular, where she found Marsden Hartley and her old friend Charlie Chaplin, whom she'd met during the days of the Provincetown Players. She ventured as far as Tangiers, where she resumed a sporadic affair with the writer Charles Henri Ford and wrote her friend Mina Loy, "Never come to Tangiers!"

Back in Paris as the thirties came to an end—her obsessive wandering accompanied, as it so often is, by emotional immobility—Djuna lay in bed as the German army approached and said vacantly, "We'll be bombed in feathers."

Friends finally got her on a boat to New York, where she wandered from a dilapidated Midtown flat (she'd awaken to find mice in her bed), to two tiny rooms on East 54th Street she shared with her mother, to a larger apartment on Waverly Place she shared with her mother and one of her brothers. In September 1940, with the help of Helen Westley, Janet Flanner, and Eleanor "Fitzi" Fitzgerald, she moved to Patchin Place and began her "Trappist years," her years of legendary isolation.

Patchin Place, near the Women's House of Detention and the Jefferson Market, consisted of ten small brick houses surrounding a tiny courtyard full of towering ailanthus trees. Built in the nineteenth century, it was intended, like so many later fashionable Village locations, as housing for servants—in this case, the Basque waiters of the Brevoort Hotel. Laborers lived in many of the apartments as late as the teens, but they were gradually replaced by writers, artists, actors, and journalists—among them Jack Reed, Louise Bryant, Theodore Dreiser, Jane Bowles, E. E. Cummings, and for several years, an elderly woman known only as Dark Note, who sat all day in the courtyard dressed entirely in black and greeted everyone with savage, embittered invective.

Behind the chartreuse door of 5 Patchin Place, with its cardboard DO NOT DISTURB sign, Djuna had the walls painted robin's-egg blue and bought floor-to-ceiling bookcases to stand on either side of the fireplace. Cartons were jammed with documents and drafts; a doll broken in an argument with Thelma occupied a permanent place on the mantel. And beside her narrow bed stood a night table with a lazy Susan for her many medicines, including the opium suppositories on which she had become dependent.

Having settled at last, Djuna suddenly seemed old. She stopped drinking and smoking, but battled with asthma, arthritis, emphysema, cataracts, and heart trouble, and was so frail that she fell in traffic several times, once breaking an arm and fracturing her spine. She suffered what she called "my famous breakdowns" and was twice sent to a sanatorium. Djuna sometimes took as long as four hours to write a shopping list, though about all she ate was bread, tea, oatmeal, and Vegmato. Still, she continued to work—and would frequently arise at 5:00 A.M. and write in her Moroccan robe, her thinning white hair held in place by two combs. Her rent-controlled apartment cost only $49.50 a month and was maintained by the monthly stipend from Peggy Guggenheim, by an informal fund set up by the writer Glenway Wescott, and on one occasion by her old friend Samuel Beckett, who, on hearing of her destitution, promptly sent a check for several thousand dollars.

"See that you don't grow old," Djuna bitterly told one of the young, mostly gay Village men who ran errands for her. She added that he should make sure never to marry, never to allow himself to be operated on, never to find himself forbidden salt, sugar, tea, or sherry—and above all, never to be so foolish as to write a book. All she wanted, she said, was "to keep disorder at bay." "I *used* to be gorgeous," she insisted. "Don't think this is the real Djuna Barnes. The real Djuna Barnes is dead."

She wrote stories, poems, a series of cantos, but rarely published the results. She declined an offer from a film producer who wanted her to write a screenplay of *Nightwood* with Groucho Marx as Dr. O'Connor—either the most inspired or the most absurd casting suggestion in the history of cinema. But Djuna's major project throughout the late forties and early fifties was a play entitled *The Antiphon* that went through twenty-nine drafts, another apparent act of retribution against her father's sexual abuse, its style so oblique that all but a handful of poets found it impenetrable, and even they had to take refuge in words like "allusive" and "resonant" to express their bewildered admiration. No less a critic than T. S. Eliot had difficulty with the play's archaic dialogue, and offered one of the most ambiguous compliments in the history of criticism. "It might be said of Miss Barnes," he wrote, "who is incontestably one of the most original writers of our time, that never has so much genius been combined with so little talent."

Yet Djuna's reputation survived—indeed, the very obscurity of *The Antiphon* enhanced her legend, and tributes to her genius continued long after her muse fell mute. "One is glad to be living in the same epoch as Djuna Barnes," wrote Lawrence Durrell, and her friend Dag Hammarskjold translated *The Antiphon* into Swedish. Walter Winchell occasionally mentioned Djuna in his gossip column, alluding to her as "the femme writer." And the owners of one Village bookstore, responding to a sudden craze for Djuna capes and hats, asked for, but didn't receive, permission to call their establishment by her name.

Another tribute of sorts came from a woman in North Carolina who'd read *Nightwood*, felt she was destined to become Djuna's mate, and bombarded her with letters, declaring her eternal devotion, then protesting Djuna's rejection, and finally threatening to rape her if she didn't at least respond.

Both the tributes and the threats drove Djuna deeper into a kind of posthumous existence from which she only sporadically emerged. She would run into Marianne Moore on the street, and the two old friends would chat briefly. She would spend a rare evening in the theater, see Edmund Wilson in the audience, and join him for dinner. She occasionally stopped by the White Horse Tavern, and Marcel Duchamp once took her to a Village restaurant, where they spotted Salvador Dalí at a nearby table.

Such encounters marked the passage not of a year but of a decade. Only once did the legendary recluse emerge into the public eye. In 1963, a developer purchased Patchin Place for $630,000 and threatened to evict the tenants and erect a high-rise unless they agreed to a substantial rent increase. Djuna, who'd once vowed that the one thing she'd never become was a sweet old lady, spoke out at a protest meeting. She would die if she had to move, and added, to whooping cheers, that the character of the neighborhood had to be preserved so muggers would have a place to ply their profession.

The muggers, the letter writers, the admirers who camped on her stoop enraged Djuna; and Thelma, deceitful lovers, uncomprehending critics had all caused her pain; but it was surely her father and mother of whom she was thinking when she'd complained, in Dr. O'Connor's voice, of "the people in my life who have made my life miserable, coming to me to learn of degradation and the night." Dr. O'Connor also said, "In the acceptance of depravity the sense of the past is most fully captured," but Djuna so relentlessly distanced herself from the misery of the past, so ruthlessly transformed her biography into fiction, that she could regard her life itself as a creation of her imagination.

"Love is the first lie, wisdom is the last," she once wrote. She survived, she said, through "the lack of ability to hold memory too close." By now she was, as she once said, too old to take anything back and too cowardly to commit suicide. On June 18, 1982, a month after she'd been hospitalized with malnutrition, a few days after her ninetieth birthday, Djuna's spirit finally escaped. At her wish, her ashes were scattered in a grove of dogwood trees near her childhoood home in Cornwall-on-Hudson. "One's life is peculiarly one's own," said Dr. O'Connor—and one's death, as well, Djuna might have added—"when one has invented it."

XIII

E. E. Cummings and Dylan Thomas

The Village as Sanctuary, the Village as Stage

Hurrah!" was E. E. Cummings's first word. "Yesterday I noticed a lovely light blue [delphinium] who'd come to her beauty all alone!" were the last words he wrote in his journal. Celebration, beauty, singularity—from the beginning of his life to the end.

For nearly forty years E. E. Cummings lived on Patchin Place. Almost daily Villagers glimpsed the frail, stooped man chatting with his iceman, Dominic, or buying flowers from Psomas, or setting out for his late-morning stroll through Washington Square Park. He often dazzled his friends with his erudite, bawdy monologues, but he could be reclusive, irascible, brooding in impenetrable silence. Renowned for the spontaneity of his poetry, he was also a rigorous formalist. He was a rebel, an iconoclast, the embodiment of radical and bohemian aspirations, but many Villagers didn't know that he was as much a New England Yankee as Calvin Coolidge, a devout Republican, and a bit of an anti-Semite. In his later years, he was a fierce supporter of Senator McCarthy and a curmudgeon who felt that the beatniks were further desecrating an already despicable American culture with their sloppy writing and even sloppier appearance.

Cummings's first principle, he once said, was "Never take anyone's word for anything." And if many of his attitudes and values were antithetical to those of his neighbors, in his lifelong insistence on the freedom of thought and the integrity of self he was a quintessential Villager.

Estlin—as everyone called him—was born in 1894 in Cambridge, a child of genteel privilege. His father, who had been introduced to his future wife by William James, was a professor at Harvard and the minister of Boston's most prestigious Unitarian church. Tolerant, good-natured, and patricianly progressive in the manner of New England Unitarianism, Edward Cummings was the first man in Cambridge to install a telephone in his home—(his son, who had a phobia about noise, was one of the last Villagers to install one in *his*)—but more important, he taught Estlin that "gladness is next to godliness." But by his teens the incipient rebel began to resent the dominion of his father's gentlemanly tolerance, and improvised a tree house to which he frequently escaped.

Estlin went to Harvard as a matter of course, and what a roster of writers walked through Harvard Yard in the years before World War I— Conrad Aiken, Robert Benchley, Heywood Broun, Van Wyck Brooks, Witter Bynner, Malcolm Cowley, Bernard De Voto, T. S. Eliot, Arthur Davison Ficke, Walter Lippmann, John Dos Passos.

His promise as a poet already evident, Estlin was wooed by both *The Harvard Advocate* and *The Harvard Monthly*, and chose the latter, in part because it had been founded by George Santayana. He experimented with the radical changes in lineation and punctuation that would cause such consternation among traditionalists, and dealt with subjects his professors regarded as beneath the dignity of poetry. His description of a saloon brawl, for instance, led the legendary Professor LeBaron Briggs to write a gentle reprimand in the margin—"Please don't forget that a clean subject is never harmful." Briggs was more taken aback by two of Estlin's essays. The first, called "The New Art," praised Cézanne, Stravinsky, and the Duchamp of *Nude Descending a Staircase* and found links between modernist sensibilities in painting, music, dance, sculpture, and literature, and the second, "The Poetry of the New Era," extolled the revolt against convention of Mallarmé, Amy Lowell, and Ezra Pound.

Though Estlin's professors were discomfited by his idols, his classmates were enthralled by his spirit of rebellion and selected him to read a condensed version of his essays at graduation. His father forbade him to refer to Duchamp's *Nude* as a "a phallic fantasy," but even with this omission his address shocked his listeners, particularly President Lowell, who "turned to brick" when Estlin declaimed one of Lowell's sister Amy's racy lyrics.

Estlin's education, which was intended to turn him into a model citizen, instead turned him into a model iconoclast. Temperamentally unsuited to be a member of any group, he remained on the fringe of student escapades, but managed to take part in his share of alcoholic sprees and vomited as often into the Charles River as any undergraduate aspiring to Dionysian ecstasy. As for sex, he declared his determination to "get acquainted with the fair sex" before he graduated, a chivalrous attitude toward women that, alas, assured his acquaintances remained chaste. His most memorable moment came during a student production of a play called *The New Lady Bantock*, during which he kissed the leading lady with considerably more vigor than was called for in the script. The leading man, by the way, was played by "a cold and aloof" fellow student named T. S. Eliot, but Estlin outdid his rival on the night of the performance by presenting the actress who played Lady Bantock, not with a bouquet of roses, like the unimaginative Eliot, but with a poem he'd written especially for the occasion. As for prostitutes, like most undergraduates of the time he was more fascinated than experienced. One nervous night, while driving a friend to a Scollay Square liaison in the family car, he stopped to buy some fruit and returned to find the car had been towed away. He just barely avoided a juicy Boston scandal — Back Bay Minister's Automobile Found in Front of Brothel! — by slipping the court clerk a $5 bill.

But though far more innocent than he wanted to be, Estlin was rebelling against the father he'd once worshipped and the Harvard he'd briefly loved, even if his rebellion only took the form of attending church less often, cultivating an unshaven appearance, and responding to a moral code he found stifling. His professors confined themselves to weary shrugs at the ways of youth, but his father was reduced to tears. "I thought," he sobbed, "I'd given birth to a god!"

Estlin's rebellion against Cambridge values was matched by a rejection of traditional poetic modes. Seeking a distinctive style, he experimented with cubism, started to use verbs as nouns, and wrote parodies as a technique for both mastering and liberating himself from conventional forms. He began to use his then revolutionary violation of the rules of capitalization under the equal influence of the ancient Greek poets and the *Krazy*

Kat comic strip. Only in English, he asserted, is the word "I" capitalized. Shortly after his graduation Estlin's work appeared in a volume entitled *Eight Harvard Poets*, underwritten by Dos Passos's father.

Drawn to the allure of New York, but too dominated by his father to dare leave home without a job, Estlin halfheartedly tried to get a staff position on several magazines and on the *New York Post*, a strategy not measurably enhanced even by a letter of introduction from Amy Lowell. His real ambition was to take an apartment in the Village and devote himself to painting, and especially to writing. "I saw that to write *Hamlet* one must fathom life completely in his heart, & thus pitilessly spurn the world for months—a winter, say, in a N.Y. garret," he recalled with lighthearted facetiousness.

Finally, late in 1916, Estlin's opportunity arrived—a desk job at Collier's publishers, located on West 13th. When he and a Harvard friend rented a studio at 21 East 15th Street, an "enormous room," twenty by twenty with a ten-foot ceiling and a kitchenette, Estlin had his garret at last—though, a Harvard man in spite of himself, he had a garret with a piano.

Estlin devoted more time to his own work than to Collier's—one of his poems from this period was his famous homage to Buffalo Bill—and after only a few weeks, having convinced his father he was employable, he jauntily resigned, declaring, "My ability, if I have any, certainly does not lie in the direction indicated by a career in the publishing business." Intoxicated with the romance of the Village, and with the image of himself as a self-reliant young man liberated from convention, Estlin settled in to write and paint. He took time off to explore what he called "the stark irresistibly stupendous newness" of the city and to meet, as he wrote his mother, "several aggressively intellectual people of the literary world." He poured out poems, sang at his easel, and gave parties, where he pummeled his piano and spun monologues replete with recondite wordplay, burlesque slang, and his agile wit.

Independent at last! But after the United States declared war on Germany on April 6, 1917, Estlin's cherished freedom was threatened by something far more ominous than outmoded parental morals. Edward Cummings served as head of the World Peace Foundation, but his son's decision to volunteer for an ambulance unit serving the French army was motivated by a desire less to save the world for democracy than to save himself from the draft. Like many American writers who served in the ambulance corps, he realized that by ostensibly taking a "humanitarian" stand he could take part in a manly adventure while avoiding regimentation and minimizing danger. Starting in late April 1917 he spent five weeks strolling through Paris and was stationed in a series of French villages for several months. His only contribution to the war effort came when he more or less lost his virginity — an omission from his Harvard curriculum — with a Right Bank prostitute with whom, of course, he promptly fell in love.

Estlin's wartime vacation came to an abrupt end in September through a bizarre misunderstanding when the censors intercepted an allegedly suspicious letter from a Harvard friend who served in his ambulance unit. Estlin was questioned by a trio of French gendarmes, and blithely sailed through the interrogation until the last question, *"Est-ce-que vous detestes les boches?"* when he revealed a streak of stubbornness, especially when dealing with authority. "The question was purely perfunctory," he recalled in his thinly fictionalized version of the incident. "To walk out of the room a free man I had merely to say yes. . . . Deliberately I framed the answer: *'Non. J'aime beaucoup les français.'"* Although this reply was the extent of the evidence of his "spying," he was detained for a night that eventually stretched into three months. The internment center more closely resembled a hotel than a prison and Estlin couldn't help finding something amusing about his situation. But nothing dampens the comic spirit more than boredom, and when his father finally pulled the right strings to gain his release, he was happy to depend on parental patronage.

Only one thing remained before he returned to America. Technically still a virgin — fear of VD had kept him from consummating his affair with the Parisian prostitute — and remembering the kind of women he was likely to meet back home, on the night before sailing, he slept with a Parisian waitress and celebrated the occasion in verse.

> *how is that star*
> *called? She answers Berthe*
> *changing into a violet very stealthily*
> *O with whom I lay*
> *Whose flesh is stallions*
> *Then I knew my youth trampled with thy hooves of nakedness*

Back in the United States, Estlin immediately reasserted his independence from his father. In February 1918, he returned to the Village to share an apartment at 11 Christopher Street with the friend who'd written the intercepted letter. "The best studio in New York," he called it — three furnished rooms with tall windows for $30 a month. Since restaurant meals cost less than a dollar for two, they often ate out at Bartolotti's and the briefly fashionable Fortunio's and usually ended up either at McSorley's tavern on East 7th Street or at the burlesque show at Minsky's Winter Garden on Second Avenue and Houston Street or at one of the city's many vaudeville houses.

Estlin continued to write and paint, with the particular encouragement of two old Harvard friends, Sibley Watson and Scofield Thayer, who were about to purchase *The Dial* and move its offices from Chicago to New York. "Your sordid verses are now profaning the office-building gentility of the *The Dial*," Scofield wrote to him, adding that Merrill Rogers, the former business manager of *The Masses* now serving on *The Dial*'s board, found his submissions "pretty queer poetry." He was also hard at work on a novel that he called *The Enormous Room*, about his imprisonment in France. Depicting grim events and gross injustice in a lighthearted tone, anarchistic in its political perspective and narrative modes—cubistic set pieces, colloquial conversations, erudite allusions—with a gallery of grotesque characters and systematic parallels to *The Pilgrim's Progress*, the novel condemned authority and celebrated individualism in whatever form. Like his New England predecessor Thoreau, Estlin argued that in authoritarian times the free man had no choice but jail. His detention center, he wrote, was "the finest place on earth."

But the war intruded once again. Estlin was drafted in July and sent to Camp Devens in Massachusetts. Asked his occupation, he proclaimed, "Artist, and specialist in cubism," and, asked what duty he'd prefer, he responded, "Interpreter." But with its infallible instinct for putting the wrong man in precisely the wrong position, the army assigned him to the infantry, and then selected him for officer training, an offer he rejected with something close to horror. He spent much of his time reading *Ulysses*, and when he was discharged in January 1919, his proudest claim was that he'd never advanced beyond the rank of private, not an easy achievement.

Free again, Estlin rented a large studio apartment on the fourth floor at 9 West 14th Street. His new quarters had no heat and no water—he burned canned coal in a fireplace and lugged buckets of water up the seventy-four steps—but wasn't poverty, for those who could afford it, part of bohemia's charm? To support himself, he painted a sign for an Italian restaurant, executed a series of nudes for Scofield Thayer's apartment, and, best of all, sold several line drawings to *The Dial*, which also published several of his poems, including his paean to Buffalo Bill. He had at last reached the center of Village intellectual life. One evening, Villagers saw Estlin and a friend driving a garbage wagon through the streets as if it were a Roman chariot.

Always restless, Estlin spent much of the summer at Joy Farm, the Cummings family's New Hampshire retreat. In early 1921, with his Harvard friend John Dos Passos, who now lived at 3 Washington Square, he sailed for Europe on a Portuguese freighter, leaving behind his novel and a woman with whom he'd been in love since 1916.

Not only was Elaine Orr married, she was married to his most ardent champion, Scofield Thayer, and Estlin had first met her when she was Scofield's fiancée. To Dos Passos, the radiant, brown-haired young woman was "the Blessed Damozel, the fair, the lovable, the lily maid of Astolot. To romantic youth she seemed the poet's dream. Those of us who weren't in love with Cummings were in love with Elaine."

Estlin worshipped Elaine from the moment they met. Scofield asked his friend to write an epithalamium for their wedding, and his friend, thinking he was in love with both of them, cheerfully complied. Reciting the poem at his wedding lunch, Scofield came to the line, "Lover, lead forth thy love into that bed," paused with a sly smile, and exclaimed, "Ah, now we come to the interesting part"—a remark Estlin thought a bit in bad taste, probably because the same thought had occurred to him. The poem concluded with the line, "I beseech thee bliss / thy suppliant singer and his wandering word," and Scofield blissed the suppliant singer in a way Estlin hadn't intended by promptly writing out a check for $1,000.

Estlin let his feelings come closer to the surface in a sonnet he composed for the happy couple to read on their honeymoon.

> . . . the almost woman whose tresses are
> The stranger part of sunlight, in the far
> Nearness of whose frail eyes instantly stir
> Unchristian perfumes more remote than myrrh
> Whose smiling is the swiftly singular
> Adventure of one inadvertent star . . .

"The poem is really corking," Scofield wrote Estlin, so enamored of his bride he took pride in another man's adoration. Estlin agreed it was corking, but also felt it was un-Christian to adore another man's wife.

The Thayers remained away for over a year, but when they returned in the fall of 1917, their friends could see that the marriage was foundering. Elaine moved into the first floor at 3 Washington Square North, and Scofield returned to his room at the Benedict, the bachelors-only building at 80 Washington Square East, and began talking about free love, which in his case seemed less a desire to sleep with other women than to sleep with none.

When it came to sex, Estlin was not a man to seize the day. He dealt with his erotic energy within strict limits. He may have drawn dozens of sketches of copulating couples in the privacy of his studio, but he remained a model of decorum with the woman he loved.

Elaine was less restrained. She was unloved by her husband and falling in love with Estlin, who was too unsure of himself to sense her feelings. On one occasion, Elaine maneuvered him into her bedroom on some pretext, and gave him a longing look. "She couldn't mean me!" Estlin objected, "that I would Desire her—Because she is Another's and Belongs to Another Person." But loyalty to Scofield didn't drive him from her bedroom—fear sufficed, as did insecurity about his appearance: how unworthy he seemed next to the dashing Scofield. He sometimes affected a dapper little mustache in hopes of concealing his scrawniness, but there was nothing he could do about his diminutive stature.

For several weeks, Estlin brooded about his cowardice and forced himself to behave with increasing boldness—bringing Elaine flowers, taking her hand, even going so far as to stroke her cheek! Such advances may have seemed brazen to Estlin, but Elaine found them unnecessarily hesitant, and finally she took matters into her own hands, so to speak, and made her desires so unmistakably clear that even a Harvard man had to yield.

Elated at his luck, awed by Elaine, and guilty toward Scofield, Estlin dealt with his turbulent emotions through poems:

> i like my body when it is with your
> body. It is so quite new a thing . . .
> i like slowly, stroking the, shocking fuzz
> of your electric fur . . . i like the thrill
> of under me you so quite new
>
> . . . and the sly
> brutish paw-poems of him making love—
> shaped noises in the sharp jungles of my
> blood . . .

His Cambridge morals were nearly as demanding, and he vowed that he and Elaine must never descend to deceit—a pointless vow as far as Elaine and Scofield were concerned. The woman Estlin idealized had little of the vulnerability he attributed to her and none of the horror of adultery, and the friend he felt he'd betrayed actively encouraged the lovers; he sent Estlin a check to help him "entertain" Elaine.

A bit bewildered that his chivalry seemed so unnecessary, Estlin was just becoming accustomed to happiness when, only a few months after he and Elaine became lovers, she announced she was pregnant. Estlin and Scofield both counseled abortion, but she refused. Oddly enough, the pregnancy brought her and Scofield closer together, and by the time the baby girl was born in late 1919, the couple had resumed their relationship, and she and Estlin had become estranged.

Estlin departed for Europe with Dos Passos to flee the emotional and moral ambiguities of this bizarre triangle. He was still in love with Elaine, but he wasn't sure if he was ready for marriage, and he *knew* he wasn't ready for fatherhood; Elaine and Scofield's intention to raise his daughter as their own seemed at once a sensible decision and a heart-cracking defeat.

While traveling in Europe with Dos, as everyone called Dos Passos, Estlin ran into a number of friends—John Peale Bishop, Malcolm Cowley, Gilbert Seldes, Alfred Kreymborg. He tried his best to remain faithful to Elaine—who was presumably sleeping with another man—but this was one vow he wasn't unhappy to break, for like so many Americans who went abroad, and like so many Midwesterners and New Englanders who came to the Village, he felt that all he needed to overcome sexual inhibition was sexual opportunity.

Elaine and Scofield eventually realized their reconciliation was a sham and sailed off to Europe for a French divorce—and for a mutual reconciliation with Estlin, whom Elaine greeted with renewed devotion and whom Scofield wined and dined with cheerful relief. He introduced Cummings to Ezra Pound before leaving for Vienna to undertake psychoanalysis with none other than Freud himself. When her divorce came through, Elaine raised the issue of marriage. Did he want to give up his independence, even for a woman he loved? Did he want to be a father, even to his own daughter? And Elaine had lived in luxury—how could they reconcile the disparity in their incomes, especially since, as Dos said, "He thought a poet should be fed by ravens." But Elaine persisted, and when word came from Vienna that Freud thought Estlin and Elaine should get married, Estlin reluctantly relented. In March 1924 they became man and wife.

Returning to the Village, Elaine kept her apartment and Estlin took a studio at 50½ Barrow Street (Elaine may have detected a pattern, for Scofield had also kept his bachelor apartment after their marriage), but for a brief period her home once more became a social center, and Estlin, as

Dos recalled, became "the hub" of Village intellectual and social life. After sleeping until noon, he would write or paint or hang out at the *Dial* office on 13th Street. In the evening, Estlin and Elaine usually ate out, most often at a speakeasy called Marte's at 75 Washington Place—one of the reasons he'd returned from Europe was the blithe disregard for Prohibition in the Village—then moved on to raucous parties at friends' apartments or hers.

Dos recalled, "After a couple of brandies . . . Cummings would deliver himself of geysers of talk. I've never heard anything that remotely approached it. It was comical ironical learned brilliantly colored . . . and sometimes just naughty. . . . None of us wanted to waste time at the theater when there was a chance that Cummings might go off like a stack of Roman candles after dinner."

Estlin had never been happier. *The Enormous Room* had brought him wide recognition, his reputation as a poet was secure in little magazines like *The Dial* and *The Little Review*, his first collection of poems, *Tulips and Chimneys*, had been published, and against all odds, he'd married the woman he loved while maintaining the independence he cherished.

But all too soon, Estlin had more independence than he wanted, for Elaine went to Europe for the summer, fell in love with an Irish banker, and wrote Estlin that she wanted a divorce. Dazed, devastated—how many months had they been married? Three?—Estlin convinced himself that she'd succumbed to a momentary whim, but she was adamant. Had he been so self-involved he'd neglected her? Had his bohemian ways offended her—his sloppy dress, his refusal to take a job, his circle of friends? Was he sexually inadequate? Fresh from Freud's couch, Scofield took this last view when Estlin asked him to intercede. In retrospect, all these reasons seemed sufficient—but the most plausible explanation, ironically, was that despite his insistence on independence, he was an utterly impractical man married to a woman who wanted to be taken care of, a man too emotionally childish to assume the responsibilities of an adult.

Crushed, Estlin contemplated suicide, and even confronted her at her apartment and pointed a borrowed .38 at his head. Describing his "suicidal anguish" many years later, Estlin concluded "that all this was false & forced—that I was deliberately sucking the last semidrops of poison out of an otherwise empty experience; suffering as deeply as possible for fear that if I ever stopped suffering I'd be nobody—lose myself. Such was this period of self-inflicted pain."

In the end, he decided to respond like a gentleman, meeting Elaine's lover to discuss the situation and shaking hands as they parted. All the details of the divorce had to be worked out, especially regarding custody of their daughter, Nancy. She grew up thinking Scofield was her father, and only learned the truth decades later when the famous poet who had once been a close friend of her mother almost casually asked her, "Did anyone ever tell you I was your father?"

He never really recovered. Alone, shattered, Estlin was so incapable of taking care of himself he couldn't even find a place to live, until in 1924, Sibley Watson, a co-owner of *The Dial*—the man who'd lent him the pistol—located a room for him on the third floor of 4 Patchin Place. It had no facilities for cooking other than a wood and coal stove, but that was about the limit of his capacities in any case.

Having found all the comfort he required, Estlin resumed his daily routine—and gradually recovered at least some of his high spirits. He frequently exhibited in the Independent Show, an avant-garde showcase at which he once entered a doormat from his childhood home, but his reputation rested primarily on his writing. After publishing two more volumes of verse, he won the *Dial* award "for distinguished service to American letters" in 1925, which placed him in the company of T. S. Eliot, Sherwood Anderson, and Marianne Moore, who'd won the prize in the preceding three years, and William Carlos Williams and Ezra Pound, who won it in the following two. More important, the award carried a $2,000 check that allowed him to live for an entire year.

He wrote several humorous sketches for *Vanity Fair* under a series of "pseudonyms"—the most frequent being C. E. Niltse, an anagram no one had difficulty deciphering—parodies of theater reviews, mock interviews, spoofs of movies and poets including a devastating piece on Edna St. Vincent Millay, herself a *Vanity Fair* contributor, entitled "Helen Whiffletree, American Poetess," and signed P. E. Dunkels.

Most of Estlin's *Vanity Fair* pieces can't be called anything but trivial, but occasionally he expressed a heartfelt conviction. "From a thousand adjectives which fairly clamour of a chance to describe the Great American Mentality," he wrote, "there immediately stands forth one adjective in which our epoch finds its perfect portrait, in which our civilization sees itself miraculously mirrored, in which the U.S.A. shimmers in all the unmitigated splendour of its great-and-only-ness. This adjective is infantile."

"I can't get enough of you," *Vanity Fair* editor Frank Crowninshield told Estlin, "because you have exactly the touch we need." But Estlin resented the time taken from his poetry, privately regarded Crowninshield and his colleagues as "well-intentioned nit wit employers," and precipitated a falling-out in 1927.

Neither poetry nor painting brought in much money, of course, but Estlin lived with New England frugality. He hadn't forgotten Elaine—the pistol still rested beside his bed, and he even took boxing lessons to overcome his passivity—but at least he was getting up and around.

Making new friends, too, helped heal Estlin's loneliness. Allen Tate, poet and critic, became a member of his circle, prized for his learned and gentlemanly demeanor, as close to a Yankee as ever came from Kentucky. Hart Crane, too—Estlin admired his poetry, though "his mind was no bigger than a pin, which didn't make any difference (& may even have been an advantage)," and cherished his companionship, particularly at late-night parties. On one especially exuberant evening in the mid-twenties, Hart "won the cocktail contest," and verified his victory by insulting a policeman and spending the night in jail. "Beer with Cummings in the afternoon," Hart recalled, "which was almost better than the evening before, as C's hyperbole is even more amusing than one's conduct, especially when he undertakes a description of what you don't remember. Anyhow, I never had so much fun jounced into 24 hours before, and if I had my way would take both C'gs and Anne along with me to heaven when I go."

Anne? Anne Barton was her name, and she was heaven on *earth* to Estlin, a lovely, vivacious woman he'd met in mid-1925, and who pulled him out of despondency over Elaine. Anne lived at 55 Charles Street, worked as an artist's model, and was the embodiment of the Village flapper. At seventeen, she'd married Ralph Barton, a fashionable cartoonist who illustrated Anita Loos's *Gentlemen Prefer Blondes* (and who, after their divorce, took up with Carlotta Monterey, who would later marry Gene O'Neill). Now a divorcee in her mid-twenties, Anne quickly became a fixture on the Village party circuit—a heavy drinker and a dazzling conversationalist. The poet and the party girl soon became a favored couple of the literary set. If Hart Crane wanted them "along with me in heaven," Edmund Wilson included them on his guest list "for an ideal party." More important to Estlin, Anne was as adept in bed as he was inept, and provided him, as he later recalled, with his "first real introduction to sex."

But Anne provided the same service to other young men. Even in bohemian circles, a man who slept around was called a Don Juan, but a woman who availed herself of the same privilege was considered promiscuous, and Anne's "present capers," as Estlin called them, distressed him. Having been through two triangles with Elaine, he despaired at finding himself in an entire *series*. "She was a woman upon whom many men might go," he wrote in notes for a possible poem, "as if she were a ship. . . . And she was a woman into whom many men might go as many breaths inflate a balloon (which we admire for a moment) which is held for a moment & released: whereupon it jumps and exhausts itself, falling sillily, flops. And it must be reinflated."

And so they separated, reconciled, separated, reconciled. Had she had sex with other men, he asked when she returned from a brief trip abroad? Only once, she cheerfully replied, but he was "o-o-o-so handsome." During one of their separations, Estlin had a brief affair himself, with the socialite Emily Vanderbilt, who was also involved with F. Scott Fitzgerald and Thomas Wolfe, and who, Estlin confided to friends, had the loveliest breasts it had ever been his privilege to fondle.

But Anne remained the woman Estlin wanted, and as a last resort he suggested they both undergo psychoanalysis with Freud's translator, A. A. Brill. Familiar with Villagers since his sessions with Mabel Dodge back in the teens, Brill had apparently had enough of bohemian shenanigans. "For a large sum he could analyze her & *perhaps* remove her father complex"—Estlin's account of their negotiations—"but this would be useless unless she had money, so let her come back to him after she's married money!" Estlin managed to find a less mercenary analyst for himself, and after a series of sessions felt ready to attempt another marriage.

Estlin and Anne's wedding in 1929, with Dos as best man, was recorded in Walter Winchell's column—"e. e. cummings, the playwright (who spells it that way) is plotting to elope to Yurrup with Anne Barton, one of Ralph Barton's exes"—and in considerably more detail by Edmund Wilson. "They had been stewed for days—married in what they called 'The church of the Holy Zebra'—Dos had put them through it. . . . Anne went to sleep and slept for days and couldn't wake up—awful moment just before ceremony (Cummings' mother and sister were there) when, after everything had been most nonchalant and amiable, they all suddenly began snapping at one another."

After two days at the Brevoort Hotel, the newlyweds sailed for "Yurrup" where they spent much of the next three years, but marriage did nothing to alter Estlin's lack of steady income or Anne's sexual wanderings.

Back on Patchin Place, Anne continued to see other men, and when a friend asked Estlin why he didn't simply throw her out, he abjectly replied, "She has the keys." Anne called Estlin "my puny husband"—a fairy, a cocksucker. According to Malcolm Cowley, "She was at that time very entertaining, beautiful, a heavy drinker, and a perfect bitch," and, according to another friend of Estlin's, she "frequently made jokes about what she considered the inadequate proportions of his virile development."

Anne finally found adequate proportions in a New York doctor who made a house call. His fee, he said, was "one picture by E. E. Cummings or autographed copy of his next book," but he overcharged, taking E. E. Cummings's wife instead. In 1932, Anne went to Mexico for a divorce, and once more Estlin was left with nothing to sustain him but his independence.

During this troubled period, Estlin had undertaken one of his best-known and least successful projects. As with many intellectuals of the twenties, his enthusiasm for the theater was linked to his affinity for the popular arts, especially vaudeville, Tin Pan Alley, silent film comedies, and comic strips, which he felt captured the feverish energy of the decade far more effectively than the desiccated sobriety of high art. To treat Freudian theories in theatrical form — to deal with unconscious impulses through the modes of the vaudeville revue — Estlin dashed off a play called *him* in a few months in 1926.

"Him" — as Estlin called his "non-hero" — is writing a play in which elements of "the seven lively arts" take center stage and show the audience his innermost thoughts about the lyricism and pathos of contemporary life. "She" — or "me" as the female character is called — is a creature of pure feeling, unable to understand his creative struggles and concerned only with their relationship. In two parallel narratives, he writes his play and she goes through the nine months of pregnancy. Could the conflict between Estlin's commitment to poetry and his feelings about fatherhood have been far from his mind?

But to describe the play's plot is to distort its vision, for Estlin emphasized the serendipitous nature of life more than its linear development, the free-floating processes of the psyche more than the realistic depiction of character. As Him says of his own play, "It's about anything you like, about nothing and something and everything, about blood and thunder and love and death — in fact, about as much as you can stand."

The three Fates hover over much of the action, one section parodies Gene O'Neill, characters burst into irrelevant flights of fancy, entire scenes seem to have no point other than to display the author's verbal virtuosity, and when one of the characters is about to utter a colloquial word for penis a John Sumner figure rises in the audience to protest.

Estlin's aim may have been to demonstrate that our "digressions" are the truest portraits of the way our minds function, but his intellectual follies, while often inspired, had no more unity or resolution than the revue format upon which they were modeled. They are an excellent example of the kind of incoherence the avant-garde too often praises as "provocative" — its synonym for the one word it can never bring itself to utter, "incomprehensible."

Needless to say, producers didn't break down the doors of 4 Patchin Place to gain the performance rights and it was only after a section of the play was published in *The Dial* in 1927 that the Provincetown Players decided to take a chance. Eleanor "Fitzi" Fitzgerald — Gene O'Neill's friend, Hart Crane's benefactor — once more came to the rescue of a Village artist. "*Him* was only produced by the Provincetown Playhouse because Fitzi insisted it should be," Estlin said. Jimmy Light — though his approach remained considerably more self-effacing — once more proved himself an able successor to Jig Cook. "When actors wanted a reading of a line, they went to Cummings," he recalled. "They found out more from him than I could ever give them in directions." So *him*, its unusually large cast and high production costs severely straining the Players' budget, opened for just twenty-seven performances on April 18, 1928.

Estlin printed a "warning" in the program — something that would become standard stuff in avant-garde productions of the sixties. "Relax, and give this PLAY a chance to strut its stuff — relax, don't worry because it's not like something else — relax, stop wondering what it's all 'about' — like many strange and familiar things, Life included, this PLAY isn't 'about,' it simply is. Don't try to despise it, let it try to despise you. Don't try to enjoy it, let it try to enjoy you. DON'T TRY TO UNDERSTAND IT, LET IT TRY TO UNDERSTAND YOU."

In the event, many of the New York critics predictably resorted to jaunty dismissal, typified by Brooks Atkinson in the *New York Times*. "Resolving himself into an ectoplasm essence, the above-named playgoer accordingly drifted off into a state of Nirvana and projected himself across the footlights, hoping to be understood. It was no use."

The Villagers, as they do to this day, regarded the bad reviews from the daily press as the surest sign of artistic merit, but since even the producers realized that they weren't *always* the most reliable guide, they prepared a pamphlet of enthusiastic comments by Conrad Aiken, Waldo Frank, John Sloan, Edmund Wilson, and Stark Young, entitled "him AND the CRITICS," with an introduction by the editor of *Seven Lively Arts*, Gilbert Seldes.

Drawn by the controversy, audiences packed the two-hundred-seat theater every night of the run. "We went not once, but three times," wrote Jacques Barzun. "Now," wrote a columnist for the *New York Sun*, "if Mr. Cummings will only write a 'her.'"

In the midst of the *him* brouhaha, the *New York Daily News* Inquiring Photographer asked Estlin, "What do you consider has been the outstanding accomplishment in President Coolidge's administration?" "The most wonderful thing that President Coolidge did," he answered, "was to confuse the whole country about the true meaning of a simple English sentence. 'I do not choose to run' sounds simple, but nobody in the country except the President knows what it means." Estlin's reply may have seemed flippant, but he was expressing his disdain for the degradation of discourse in the political climate of the twenties. He'd been an offhand socialist in the teens, extolling the Russian revolution and praising Jack Reed—though he seemed more interested in annoying his father than in declaring a political vision—but, as was the case with most Villagers, his disillusionment after the war turned into aloof scorn for political activity of any kind.

In 1931, however, like many curious intellectuals, Estlin spent several weeks in Russia—an experience that led to a virulent contempt for leftist politics that remained his sole political conviction for the rest of his life. His travel diaries—published under the title *Eimi*, Greek for "I am"—portrayed life under the communist regime with unremitting hostility, not on the basis of any anti-Marxist analysis but in instinctive revulsion at regimentation. *Eimi*, in fact, was a kind of sequel to *The Enormous Room*, in which an entire country was regarded as a prison.

Estlin may have been a Yankee in temperament, but he remained a modernist in style, and he described his descent into the "unworld" of Soviet Russia in prose so dense, elliptical, and fragmented that *Eimi* became one of the most unread books in the history of publishing. About its only readers were its reviewers, and many of them confessed they either hadn't finished it or had waded through to the end only as a professional obligation. "A Super Atrocity in the Much Abused Name of the Novel," read a typical headline, the writer so baffled that he mistook a diary for a work of fiction, and George Jean Nathan honored it as "the Worst Book of the Month."

Gilbert Seldes and Marianne Moore came to his defense—but many others, including Malcolm Cowley and Edmund Wilson, couldn't disguise their disapproval of his anti-Soviet diatribes, and two other friends promptly crossed to the other side of the street when they saw Estlin walking toward them. Betrayal—what other word could be used for the anti-communist views of a Villager, a poet, the author of *The Enormous Room*?

Ironically, such was the fervor for Russia among intellectuals in the early thirties that Estlin's ardent defense of the individual isolated him within the very community dedicated to individualism.

No matter, Estlin had been transformed by his trip, and asserted his belief in the individual and his rage at authority with such dogmatic bitterness he could hardly talk about more innocuous political issues without flying into a reactionary tirade. Though he never read newspapers and wouldn't allow a radio in his home—and though his stance remained less a conviction than an attitude—he became a rabid Republican, felt Roosevelt might as well have been taking orders directly from Moscow, and called the United States "home of the slave." Sometimes his anti-communism had a hint of anti-Semitism. "Kikes," he often exclaimed, ran the country, and he showed appalling insensitivity to Hitler's treatment of the Jews. "Am I crazy?" he said in defense of his unpalatable opinions. "Sure. So were a few perfectly amazed individuals, standing bolt-upright in pitch-darkness among a lot of sheep." But while in private Estlin could be vicious, rabid, hysterical, in the popular imagination he remained the lovable iconoclast. Indeed, his philosophy seemed summarized in one of his most famous lines—"we're wonderful one times one."

Estlin had lost Anne, he'd alienated most of his friends. *The Dial* had ceased publication, the Provincetown Playhouse had closed its doors. As the country entered the Depression, the financial plight of the poet was hardly uppermost in anyone's mind. In the first half of 1934, Estlin's royalty statement came to a round zero. The first half of 1935 seemed a veritable boom, with fifteen copies of his poetry collections finding buyers. After fourteen firms turned down his new collection, what could he do but turn to his mother for $300 to underwrite its publication? *no thanks*, he entitled the book.

The Guggenheim Foundation came through with a grant, and on the opposite end of the spectrum, Hollywood beckoned. Like so many Village writers, Estlin was momentarily mesmerized by the prospect of writing for the movies—unaware that the studios were filling their lots with anyone who'd shown they could write a publishable sentence, paying them fabulous sums, then ignoring their work. In 1934, Estlin turned down an offer of $100 a week at Paramount, but the next year he decided to give it a go. He met Irving Thalberg, he auditioned for the Walt Disney organization—but nothing came of his trip. He was unemployable even at the golden teat of Hollywood.

Despite it all, the early thirties remained in his memory as one of the happiest periods of his life. "The curse wonderfully became a blessing," he recalled years later, "the disappearance an emergence, the agonizing departure an ecstatic arrival."

E stlin was referring to Anne—and to Marion. How did this timorous Harvard virgin, this inept seducer, this "puny husband" attract yet another lovely woman? Marion Morehouse, who was to become Estlin's third wife, was universally regarded as one of the most beautiful women in America. Marion wanted to become an actress, but when the only roles she could land were in shows like the *Ziegfeld Follies* she turned to fashion modeling. Marion was "the greatest fashion model I ever shot," said no less a photographer than Edward Steichen, and when she shared a room with the actress Aline MacMahon, Aline asked her to move because none of her suitors would look at her when Marion was present.

Estlin met her in 1932 through their mutual friend, Jimmy Light, the director of *him*, who took him backstage after a production in which she had a minor role. "This gal's too tall for me," Estlin initially thought, but by the end of the evening they were both captivated. "She's not my equal (can't follow me) mentally," he began to think after a few dates, but he soon realized her uncomplicated cheerfulness made her a far more congenial companion than the cosmopolitan and self-absorbed women he'd known. And what woman could resist a poet who wrote, "I'm tremendously glad of you," or who sent her a drawing of an elephant with the word "love" forming its penis, or who asked her to spend a weekend in the country by suggesting, "Let us move our minds out of smallness, out of ideas, out of cities; let us pack all our minds carefully (without breaking anything) and carry them carefully away and unfold them very carefully among the hills and rivers."

Estlin's timidity was irresistible, and he was so astonished at Marion's devotion that he returned it with an overflowing gratitude. For the remainder of Estlin's life, the couple's days were filled with mutual adoration.

After their marriage in 1934, they lived in separate apartments, Estlin in his fourteen-by-twenty studio on the third floor rear at 4 Patchin Place, Marion at 8 Patchin Place, until four tiny rooms on the ground floor at number 4 became available. Estlin painted during the day and wrote at night, and though they used Marion's apartment for meals and entertaining—Marion summoning him with an elephant bell—he'd always retire to his studio to sleep. In spite of his insistence on independence, Estlin remained utterly dependent on Marion the moment he left the realm of the imagination. And he was demanding. Lack of recognition, poverty, physical ailments—all made him increasingly irritable. He had a phobia about noise, developed the arrogant self-righteousness of the ill-informed, became more and more reclusive, unsociable. Marion shielded him from young admirers, protected him from importunate friends, and carried on graciously when, in the middle of entertaining guests, he'd suddenly rise without a word and retire to his studio. He couldn't make it through the day without her—he knew that better than anyone—but he exercised the tyranny of the helpless.

Poetic poverty may have been the Village style, but it's the style of the young. Even in middle age, Estlin depended on his mother for a monthly check. His collected poems were published in 1938—after legal vetting to be sure none of them were "obscene"—but though the volume was highly praised, his six-month royalty statements came to amounts like $14.94, $6.00, $9.75. Fortunately, Estlin's work was gaining a following among college students, and though they couldn't afford to buy his books they encouraged their teachers to invite him to readings. In the mid-thirties—at first abrasively, and always reluctantly—Estlin began to appear on campuses across the country, and readings soon became a kind of second career. His pay gradually rose from $25 to a high of $700, and hundreds of students would show up, chanting the Buffalo Bill poem even before its author took the stage.

An avid admirer of popular culture, Estlin knew how to play to his audience. They thought of him as a bohemian poet? He'd dress like one in a white turtleneck and scuffed sneakers. His platform style, on the other hand, mixed aristocratic indifference with actorly rapport. Audiences were entranced—they were in the presence of high culture and yet they were enjoying themselves! Estlin established firm rules for his appearances. "There will be no provision for autographing books," he wrote his hosts, or "attending dinners, receptions, and other social functions as part of the total reading engagement." The sponsor of one of his readings recalled that in person he was "charming, soft-spoken, and thoughtful," but little did his admirers know that "the bohemian poet" was a bit of a snob. "To me," he confided, "Hell holds few horrors worse than spending so much as a weekend in such a desolatingly mediocre hole as Indianapolis." He preferred readings at Southern, Catholic, and women's colleges because their students seemed better behaved.

Estlin's readings exhausted him and took away far too much time from his writing, but he needed the money, he basked in the adulation, and, best of all, he found a new and larger audience for his poetry. By the forties he'd become one of the best-known poets in America—and one of the most misunderstood. His charm was carefully crafted, in many ways misleading, ambiguous down to its commas, and his student fans were enamored of his verbal agility and ebullient idiosyncrasy and responded more to his persona than to his poetry.

> *I'd rather learn from one bird how to sing*
> *Than teach ten thousand stars how not to dance*

> *be of love (a little)*
> *More careful*
> *Than of everything*

> *—tomorrow is our permanent address*
> *and there they'll scarcely find us (if they do)*
> *we'll move away still further: into now*

For a poet who came to fame through his readings, he was always more moved, he said, by "the inaudible poem—the visual poem, the poem for not ears but eye." He would have agreed with Wallace Stevens, who said that "to a large extent, the problems of poets are the problems of painters, and poets must often turn to the literature of painting for a discussion of their own problems," for he considered himself "an author of pictures, a draughtsman of words."

As for his refusal to conform to "proper" punctuation and grammar, Estlin wanted to free his work from the constrictions of intellect and release the authenticity of emotion. Anti-authoritarian even toward language, he felt that the rules of syntax crippled inspiration, inhibited expression, distorted meaning. Capitalization assigned values he wished to violate. His arrangement of words on the page was far from random—he constructed elaborate charts of vowel sounds, made long lists of words, and sketched complex diagrams of themes before proceeding to write, but the goal of this preparation was to liberate intuitive responses. Anything dictated by tradition undermined the integrity of the individual.

" 'Art,' if it means anything," he once wrote, "means TO BE INTENSELY ALIVE." And to be alive means to be "original" and "naïve," not "second-hand" and self-conscious," to experience rather than to analyze, to feel rather than to think. A poem should be a verb, not a noun. And a poet should have "the child's vision" and "integrated simplicity," a commitment to "organic sensation." "The Symbol of All Art is the Prism. The goal is unrealism. The method is destructive. To break up the white light of objective realism into the secret glories which it contains." "Now, having paid tribute to so-called reality," he said at a lecture at the Museum of Modern Art, "we are free to enter Life."

In his response to a letter from a high school student, Estlin made one of his most explicit statements about the poetic process: "A lot of people think or believe or know they feel—but that's thinking or believing or knowing; not feeling. And poetry is feeling—not knowing or believing or thinking. Almost anybody can learn to think or believe or know, but not a single human being can be taught to feel. Why? Because whenever you think or you believe or you know, you're a lot of other people: but the moment you feel, you're nobody-but-yourself. To be nobody-but-yourself—in a world which is doing its best, night and day, to make you everybody else—means to fight the hardest battle which any human being can fight; and never stop fighting."

To feel rather than to think, to be "nobody-but-yourself"—the perfect prescription for a campus cult. Estlin addressed his readers in his preface to his *Collected Poems* as though he were speaking to each of them personally, assuring them of their unique perceptions and superior sensibilities. "The poems to come," he wrote, "are for you and for me and are not for most people—it's no use trying to pretend that most people and ourselves are alike. Most people have less in common with ourselves than the square root of minus one. You and I are human beings; most people are snobs. . . . You and I are not snobs." Rarely has snobbery been so nakedly expressed as in Estlin's explicit denial of it. So the lowercase "i" who captivated readers with his sensitivity and vulnerability was fully capable of disdain for other people. The sanctity of the private self had been a Village ideal—but it was an ideal that could easily turn into contempt for those outside the select circle.

During the thirties many Village intellectuals and political activists dismissed Estlin's poetry precisely for its celebration of the individual. The socialists of the teens had advocated a collectivist state as the best means of liberating the person, but by the thirties the Marxists talked only of liberation of "the people." Kenneth Burke, for instance, scorned Estlin's work for its lack of social consciousness. "For delights," he wrote, "there is sexual dalliance, into which the poet sometimes reads cosmic implications (though a communicative emphasis is lacking). For politics, an abrupt willingness to let the whole thing go smash. For character building, the rigors of the proud and lonely, eventually crystallizing in rapt adulation of the single star." *The Daily Worker* was more scornful. "Unlike Keats, who feared that his name might be writ in water, Mr. Cummings probably wants his epitaph to read: Here lies one whose name was writ in lower case." And imagine what Village communists would have thought if they'd seen the ad for Wanamaker's that appeared in 1939—"If you respond to Sibelius and e. e. cummings, this is your furniture." The avant-garde as a tool of capitalism!

If he remained skeptical about reaching a large audience—"am now confronted by the task of making my Voice Weedable for the Gwate Amewican Publick"—and was sensitive to the accusation that his work failed to show development, he had no reason to complain of most of his reviews. Marianne Moore wrote: "This writing is an apex of positiveness and of indivisible, undismemberable joy." Another critic noted that, in reading Estlin's poetry, "the imagination gets a little drunk." But whether praised or condemned, Estlin tried to remain serenely indifferent—or rather, his guise of indifference took the form, as it often does, of a secret desire for adoration. As he told an audience at a reading at Harvard, quoting Rainer Maria Rilke, "Works of art are of an infinite loneliness and with nothing to be so little reached as with criticism. Only love can grasp and hold and fairly judge them."

But long-deferred recognition didn't mellow Estlin. And the very contrariness that gave him so much of his subject matter, and that made him so popular with young readers, also alienated him from his culture and cost him many of his friends. Invited to the White House in 1962, he brusquely declined—he wanted no part, he said, of "the Kennedy-Kulchur (Mick-kike) tie-up." He never felt at ease anywhere but in his Patchin Place haven, and on Joy Farm, where he puttered around in overalls and still drove a 1929 Ford.

But, like his neighbor Djuna Barnes, he found his Patchin Place sanctuary under attack. A fourteen-story apartment building went up next door, and even worse, Robert Moses's "urban renewal program," as it was egregiously misnamed, had scheduled Patchin Place and the Jefferson Market for demolition. "A lively & indignant Jewish advertising writer & Marion leaped into action," he wrote, "a committee for defense was formed," and the project was defeated.

Like most poets, Estlin was possessed by many selves, many of them contradictory—timorous lover, helpless tyrant, uncompromising nonconformist, idealistic curmudgeon, anarchist Republican, reactionary icono-clast, and, most of all, crusty Yankee. He shared the Villagers' lifelong ro-mance with individualism, and no one was more eloquent in its defense, more self-righteous, more ardent.

He died in the fall of 1962 at Joy Farm at the age of sixty-eight, suc-cumbing to a brain hemorrhage a few minutes after sharpening his ax.

In 1950, Marion Cummings received a telephone call from the poet John Malcolm Brinnin from a basement bar on Christopher Street. Dylan Thomas was having a few late-afternoon drinks and had expressed a desire to meet Estlin. Why not come right over, Marion said. Estlin hated im-promptu visitors, she knew, but he'd attended one of Dylan's readings only a few days earlier and been so moved he'd wandered the streets for hours af-terward. Yes, come right over—we're only a few blocks away.

And so, at 4 Patchin Place, at mid-century, two of the most famous poets of their time met for a few quiet hours. "Once they had overcome a brief, exploratory, and mutual shyness," Brinnin recalled, "Dylan and Cummings seemed happily at ease and intimately sympathetic as they came upon ways to express the curiously double-edged iconoclasm that marks the work and character of each of them."

Long after Dylan's death three years later, Estlin would say that he reminded him of Hart Crane. Both poets could be the most "hearty" of men, he said, but also the most self-destructive. They were like lemmings: "Nobody could stop them—on they rushed—straight ahead—and plunged in." For his part, Dylan basked for days in the glow of a man "whose sim-plicity and easy humor had quite disarmed him."

What two poets could be more alike? Exuberant in their work, reaching larger audiences through their readings than their books, wor-shipped by the young. What two poets could be more unalike? The Yankee curmudgeon and the Welsh bad boy—the recluse and the gregarious wan-derer, the fastidious craftsman and the disruptive, flamboyant bard.

Estlin and Dylan represented rebellion against convention, but the iconography of rebellion took two diametrically opposed forms. Estlin saw the Village as a lifelong haven of privacy, and Dylan, for a brief, flaming moment, saw it as a platform for extravagant public display. The poet could withdraw and be mythologized for his inaccessibility, or be greeted at every gathering and mythologized for his theatricality.

Crowds would gather around Dylan's table whenever he stopped by the White Horse Tavern, and he'd stop by at all hours, for a midday beer, an early evening whiskey, a late evening double, then another to unwind before heading off to an after-midnight party somewhere, he scarcely knew where, he barely knew with whom. He'd then head off to bed somewhere, he scarcely knew where, he barely knew with whom. Then late the next morning he'd start the cycle all over again with a breakfast beer.

The crowd would listen, enraptured, as he lyrically described his native Wales, bawdily recalled the professors' wives he'd bedded, recited from his favorite poets, savagely satirized literary critics, burst into music hall ditties, called a fellow poet "a mock-barmy, smarmy, chance-his-army tick of a piddling crook who lives in his own armpit," and answered questions with self-deflating aphorisms, deadpan wit, and ebullient laughter. Dylan was the poet as performer, and the White Horse was his stage.

Established in the 1880s, the Horse became Dylan's favorite bar the moment he landed in New York for his first reading tour of America in 1950. Norman Mailer, Clement Greenberg, Michael Harrington, Gregory Corso, William Barrett, the Clancy brothers—all hung out there, "drinking in the front room if you wanted to get laid," recalled one regular, "drinking in the back room if you wanted to talk politics." When business was slow, the bartender would ring his cowbell an hour or two early and announce quietly but firmly, "Get out, boys and girls." But business was never slow if Dylan was drinking at his regular table at the window, and since he considered the Horse the nearest thing in New York to an English pub, and was reminded of his beloved Swansea by the seamen and stevedores who stopped by for a tankard, he rarely missed a night.

Everyone at the Horse had heard tales of Dylan's tours. From Miami to Vancouver, from Boston to Los Angeles, he maintained a hectic pace that often left him unsure exactly where he was—but never reluctant to perform, never unwilling to enact his role as the wandering bard, the outrageous genius. He needed the money, but more than anything, like Estlin before him, he needed the adulation.

Even as a boy back in Wales, Dylan had lusted after fame. He wanted to be known, he said, as "the Rimbaud of Cwmdonkin Drive." In an article he wrote while barely out of his teens, he expressed his aspirations more obliquely but just as unmistakably—and, alas, prophetically. "No one can deny that the most attractive figures in literature are always those around whom a world of lies and legends has been woven, those half mythical artists whose real characters became cloaked forever under a veil of the bizarre. They became known not as creatures of flesh and blood, living day by day as prosaically as the rest of us, but as men stepping on clouds, snaring a world of beauty from the trees and sky, half wild, half human. It is, on the whole, a popular and an entertaining fallacy." Of course it was a fantasy, but on his reading tours of America it seemed to be coming true.

No one could captivate an audience like Dylan Thomas. He'd approach the platform almost apologetically. He'd anxiously gaze at the rapt faces in the audience, blink, nervously fumble with his paper, wipe the sweat off his forehead. Dylan's audience wasn't surprised at his rumpled suit and tousled hair—this was a poet, after all—but they hadn't expected him to be so *short*. Yet when he gripped the rostrum and began to recite, he had an enormous presence. His sonorous voice, his emotional intensity, his exuberance filled even the largest auditorium. The audience listened spellbound, erupting in whoops and cheers after the last line of every poem. Dylan treated poetry as a *spoken* language, the voice rather than the page the source of enchantment.

But back at the Horse, Dylan was a legend for uninhibited, often outrageous behavior. He'd gulp down a handful of barbiturates for breakfast, followed by a couple of eggs in a tumbler of brandy. He'd break bottles if the bartender didn't serve him fast enough. He'd spew boozy invectives at pompous professors. He visited his idol Charlie Chaplin and pissed in a potted plant. He met many celebrities—Carl Sandburg, Thornton Wilder, W. H. Auden, Anita Loos, James Agee, Delmore Schwartz, Lionel and Diana Trilling, even President Eisenhower—but on more than one occasion his behavior was so rude he was sternly asked to leave.

Rude, too, were Dylan's responses to questions about his poetry. Though he'd sometimes reply self-effacingly, more often he'd mock his interrogators, or turn hostile. When someone at a staid academic gathering asked him to explain "Ballad of the Long-legged Bait," he replied, "It's a description of a gigantic fuck."

Dylan's rows with his wife were legendary, too. Much of the time Caitlin would resentfully disassociate herself from her husband by saying things like "I can't tell you how many times I've heard those poems; isn't there a bar?" In private, their quarrels often escalated into violence. "I can't remember where we were, or how it started," Caitlin recalled of one incident, "but we were in a hotel room, and I do remember the room when we left it; everywhere was covered in green toothpaste, the ceiling, the walls, everywhere." Rumor had it that when she'd had more than enough of his buffoonish behavior, she'd strike him with her fists, knock him down, and pound his head against the floor.

The habitués of the Horse also heard about Dylan's habit of stealing clothes. Hats, ties, pants, socks, would find their way from his hosts' closets into his suitcase. Again and again he'd come downstairs to dinner wearing a shirt uncannily resembling one in his host's dresser drawer. Caitlin took up the habit, too—how could she be less well dressed than her husband? Once, while staying with Ellen Borden Stevenson, Adlai Stevenson's wife, with whom Dylan was shamelessly flirting, she passed up a beautiful blue dress, considering it too audacious, and pilfered a humble gray flannel suit instead.

While no one complained of missing clothes—indeed, most of Dylan's victims were flattered that the famous poet admired their taste—money was a different matter. Dylan borrowed, cajoled, and wheedled whatever he could—money he promised to repay, but money they never saw again. After his first tour of America, he might have been relatively well off from his reading fees, recording royalties, and book sales, but like most congenital sponges, he fostered the myth that he remained deeply in debt—to deceive Caitlin, and to conceal his carelessness, for he'd spend hundreds of dollars a day and have no idea where the money had gone. "This round's on me," he'd announce to a crowd, which often included the very person from whom he'd "borrowed" the money he was now flaunting. He'd never pick up his change in restaurants or bars, often leaving a tip several times his bill. He'd give away money he'd just cadged to complete strangers and then plead poverty once more. The penniless poet was a myth he so carefully created that he came to believe it himself. Brinnin once secreted $800 in cash in a leather handbag he gave Caitlin as a going-away present so that when they unpacked back in Wales they'd have something to show for their trip.

Needless to say, nearly everyone in the Village regarded rudeness and thefts and lies as the forgivable flaws of genius. Academics might be appalled by his lack of decorum, but that was precisely why their students adored him. His admirers *wanted* him to be disreputable, for that was their image of the romantic poet and what entranced them. And sensing this need, Dylan did everything he could to satisfy it. Insecure in his person, he basked in his persona. Vulnerable in his life, he became vain of his legend. When a man whispered to him after a reading at Sarah Lawrence, "I'll tell you what, Dylan Thomas, if you hadn't written any poems, nobody would have heard of you," the inane remark bothered him for days. But he reveled in stories of his unruly behavior, for he seemed to think that without them, nobody would have *idolized* him.

· · ·

Of all the stories that made their way back to the Horse, the most enthralling were those about Dylan's drinking and womanizing.

Dylan often boasted that he was "the drunkenest man in the world." He'd be drunk by noon—so the stories went—then continue drinking throughout the day and night, never passing out, never sober long enough to have a hangover. Then the next day he'd go on a *real* bender. Then he'd pee on the carpet.

Dylan the actor had the gift of giving his audience exactly what it wanted—if they wanted him soused, he'd get soused—but alas, he became so enamored of applause that he lost the ability to distinguish between Dylan the actor and Dylan the man. Once, asked why he drank so much, he assumed the role of offhand wit, but speaking more truthfully than he knew, said, "Because they expect it of me."

They expected womanizing, too—ceaseless flirting and brazen come-ons. They expected Dylan to bed two, three, four women a night—for part of his legend was compulsive, uncontrollable satyriasis. Wasn't this the poet who, when asked why he had come to America, answered, "To continue my lifelong search for naked women in wet mackintoshes"? Weren't campuses across the country filled with girls who'd flung themselves at the famous poet? Hadn't he deflowered half the enrollment of Bryn Mawr and Bennington and Sarah Lawrence?

Dylan—so the story went—could no more say no to a woman than to a drink. He'd start with bawdy remarks—"Giraffes copulate at 80 miles an hour" was one of his favorite mood-setting lines. Then in precise detail he'd praise her anatomical attributes. Then, with an expression halfway between a swoon and a leer, he'd exclaim that he wanted to put his hands in a warm bosom. (At Harvard, he declaimed, "I would like to take you back with me to Wales, that I might suckle at your paps.") More than one Villager served as his procurer, sometimes even "loaning" his girlfriend for the night. If he'd become too drunk to articulate his desires, he'd kneel in front of the object of his lust and put his head under her skirt. Even if no woman were around, he'd make his lechery known. As cigars were being passed around at an all-male gathering, he suddenly boomed, "Gentlemen, I wish we were all hermaphrodites." "Why do you wish that, Mr. Thomas?" one of the gentlemen politely queried. "Because, gentlemen, then we could all fuck ourselves."

According to the legend, deans' wives were the most frequent objects of Dylan's randy attentions, but his two most notorious encounters were with a well-known writer and a Hollywood starlet.

Shortly after meeting Katherine Anne Porter at a New York party,

Dylan vaguely suggested what they might better occupy themselves with, and when she rebuffed him, he hoisted her up to the ceiling and spun her around the room—an awkward attempt at seduction that might have passed unnoticed if Porter hadn't been fifty-nine years old.

Shelley Winters, on the other hand, was a gorgeous young actress with a reputation for holding her own in salacious repartee. They had a conversation at a Hollywood dinner party, though accounts differ about the details. According to Brinnin—who served as Dylan's guide and whose book *Dylan Thomas in America* would do so much to enhance his legend—Winters "surprised him by remarks that showed she knew not only of him, but that she was acquainted with his work." According to Winters, however, when told that "he draws accurate and biting images of people and events," she concluded that he was a cartoonist. But the two accounts agree that Dylan came on to Winters. Brinnin, retelling what Dylan told him, reported that he was rebuffed, he said, in "language which was as direct as a stevedore's and notably more colorful." In Winters's version, when she asked him why he'd come to Hollywood, he answered that for one thing he hoped "to touch the titties of a beautiful blonde starlet." She could grant him his wish, she replied, and "When we had finished the dessert and brandy, I announced, 'You may touch each of my breasts with one finger.' . . . Then, with great ceremony, Mr. Thomas sterilized his index finger in the champagne and delicately brushed each breast . . . leaving a streak in my pancake body makeup. A look of supreme ecstasy came over this Welsh elf's face. 'Oh, God, Nirvana,' he uttered."

The Villagers believed every tale—*Dylan* believed every tale. Caught up in his role, eager to confirm his admirers' expectations, he no longer seemed to know which of his exploits actually happened, which were embellished, which were apocryphal. The more far-fetched the stories, the more believable they became—for when a man and his admirers conspire to make a myth, the parameters of truth become the dimensions of delusion.

Who would believe that on Dylan's nonstop, cross-country tours he frequently felt lonely, confused by attention, exhausted by the pace? A large part of him thrilled to the adulation, but another part—shy, insecure, provincial—remained disconcerted by the hoopla. He had the illusion that his shyness, insecurity, and provincialism could be overcome, but as thousands cheered his readings, as the parties merged into one continuous extravaganza, as every unconventional gesture was interpreted as a display of spontaneous outrageousness, they weren't so much overcome as overwhelmed. Back in Wales, Dylan could understand what had happened to him. When traveling abroad, he said, "one is given a foreign license to *be* a Welshman, and the odder one is the more typical is it thought to *be* of the character and behavior of those brutal and benighted songbirds who cluster together, hymning on hilltops, in the wooad and llanwigwams." And as Caitlin succinctly observed, "In America they make too much fuss of poets; in London they make too little."

As for the stories of prodigious drinking, before he came to America, he rarely drank at home, confining himself to beer, and turned to whiskey and bourbon only on his tours. Beer for the world's most famous imbiber? No, no, exclaimed his hosts, nothing but the best! Too eager to please, to maintain the myth, he never hesitated to do anything anyone asked of him, especially when away from his desk, when with strangers, when never given a moment alone. Monumental drunkenness followed — that part of the myth needed no embellishment. But he became soused after only a glass or two — *that* must never be known. And who suspected — other than Caitlin — that the raucous poet turned to drink not so much to heighten as to escape his sensations?

As for Dylan's supposedly insatiable sexual appetite, that, too, was the myth of excess. His poetry provided a fountain of erotic imagery, his conversation a geyser of lascivious abandon. But when it came to sex itself, Dylan was largely bluff and bravado — and even then only when drunk. Even Brinnin — who, if the truth be told, probably hoped to be propositioned himself — recognized that most of Dylan's propositions were performances. "Since his addresses to women were made publicly," he wrote, "they were almost always answered by public rebuff. . . . More than one of the women who had humored him through such episodes told me that there was nothing clearer than the fact that he did not really want them to respond."

Dylan did have several one-night stands and a few brief affairs — considering the multitudinous opportunities that came his way, and the sodden state he was usually in when they did, it would have been astonishing if he hadn't — but these, as a member of his circle explained, remained merely "a hiatus from his marriage." He cherished his freedom even more than he cherished women, and no woman should have expected even a minimal commitment from him when he was with her to flee his commitment to Caitlin. Who was he deceiving more, his wife or himself? As one of his biographers astutely noted, "He always wanted women to look after him when he was ill, or in trouble, but not to prevent him from making himself ill or getting into trouble." Still, nothing could convince the Villagers that Dylan wasn't in a state of perpetual rut. And as for those rumors of impotence that began to filter back to the Horse, weren't they simply signs of excess, of a man not so much lacking in libido as completely fucked out?

Back in Wales and while accompanying Dylan on his second tour, Caitlin became enraged by the stories of her husband's ceaseless philandering, and by the love letters she found in his pockets, often unopened. Her frequent answer when told that Dylan had been unfaithful was, "But who would ever go with a comical man like that? It's not possible. These rich women wouldn't want to bother with him, stinking of beer and sweat and stale cigarettes and God knows what." And she also knew what none of the mythmakers knew—that Dylan was helpless in bed—so inept that she never had an orgasm in all the years of their marriage. He had "an almost juvenile approach to sex," she recalled after his death; he had been "so lacking in sexual drive" that "It was like embracing a child rather than a man; he felt so young and tender, so soft and sweet. He wasn't aggressive in a masculine sense; he wasn't strong enough. He was able to make love; he functioned, but I can't remember much about it because it didn't make much impression on me; somehow, the actual fucking didn't touch me."

A friend back home in Wales remembered Dylan as a chameleon who could adapt to any company and play any role. "We would decide in the morning what role we were going to play when we went out for a drink. . . . The role of the drunken Welsh poet with 'fag in the corner of the mouth, and dirty raincoat, and polo sweater' sometimes lasted for a week or more, but no longer." When he came to America, he expanded the role and never ceased performing it. Once again, Caitlin knew another Dylan. "His home was to Dylan a private sanctum where for once he was not compelled, by himself admittedly, to put on an act, to be amusing, to perpetuate the myth of the infant terrible, one of the most damaging myths and a curse to grow out of."

Dylan suffered from another curse—his failure to distinguish between achievement and accolades. Not the first poet to fall under the spell of the spell he cast on his audience, he was the first to be confronted by mass media fame. His radio appearances, his recordings, his readings, the hundreds of articles about his outlandish antics—it's not too much to say that the whirlwind in which he found himself presaged the hysteria that greeted rock stars a decade later.

Crazes and cults had swept up poets before, but in the mass publicity of the postwar years, a poet could instantaneously be transformed from the idol of a select few — as Estlin had been — into the icon of an entire generation. Moreover, fame floated free of the poetry itself and almost overnight Dylan found himself a superstar. And he was completely unprepared for the outpouring of adulation, the expectations of his followers, and, worst of all, the isolation of celebrity. Even a poet who cultivated irony and detachment would have been overwhelmed.

The curse was transformed into something close to a tragedy — for Dylan had achieved his long-awaited breakthrough at precisely the moment he began to dread he could no longer write. Acclaimed at last! And the words that brought him acclaim no longer flowed from his pen! Once asked if he'd ever give up poetry for prose, he answered, "You don't give up poetry. It may give you up, but you don't abandon it." He even confessed that "My need — as I imagine it — to write may be all conceit. The bellows that fan the little flicker is nothing but wind after all." He'd always been, he said, "at the mercy of words" — but now they seemed to have given him up.

Was Dylan frozen by fame, debilitated by its distractions? — or was he so warmed by it that he forgot the struggle to achieve it? He'd yearned for recognition, but did its magnitude so terrify him that he could only handle it by exaggerating his persona? In any case, he feared that his talent was rapidly fading, and dealt with the anxiety in ways that further diminished his gifts. And in a final irony, the more he squandered his genius, the more famous he became.

The wine-soaked poet — rebelling against decorum, unconstrained by convention, lying, stealing, drinking, wenching, shocking academia, scandalizing the middle class — this was the role assigned to Dylan and he performed it to perfection. Unfortunately, no one seemed to notice that those who enacted it were destined for self-destruction.

The Horse is packed, awaiting Dylan's arrival, and when he comes in at last, Ernie, the proprietor, sends over a tankard of ale on the house. The crowd laughs uproariously at every lame joke, no one minds when he answers questions with brusque obscenities. He announces he's going to recite a poem:

> *There was a bloody sparrow*
> *Flew up a bloody spout*
> *Came a bloody thunderstorm*
> *And blew the bugger out.*

No, it's not one of Dylan's best performances, but the legend has so transcended the reality no one can tell the difference—certainly not Dylan himself.

It seemed he'd been a fixture forever. But he had arrived in America only a little over two years earlier. How had it all gone so wrong?

"My darling far-away love, my precious Caitlin, my wife dear," he wrote home shortly after his arrival in America, "I love you as I have never loved you, oh please remember me all day & every day as I remember you here in this terrible, beautiful, dream and nightmare city. . . . I am staying right in the middle of Manhattan, surrounded by skyscrapers infinitely taller and stranger than one has ever known from the pictures . . . and the noise all day & night: without some drug, I couldn't sleep at all. The hugest, heaviest lorries, police-cars, firebrigades, ambulances all with their banshee sirens wailing & screaming, seem never to stop. . . . And I have no idea what on earth I am doing here in the very loud, mad middle of the last mad Empire on earth."

Dylan was even insecure about his readings—"I felt a very lonely, foreign midget orating up there." "I've been to a few parties, met lots of American poets, writers, critics, hangers-on, some very pleasant, all furiously polite & hospitable. But apart from one occasion," he reassured Caitlin, "I've stuck nearly all the time to American beer."

Still, as for New York itself, "It's nightmare, night & day: there never was such a place; I would never get used to the speed, the noise, the utter indifference of the crowds, the frightening politeness of the intellectuals, and, most of all, these huge phallic towers, up & up, hundreds of floors, into the impossible sky. I feel so terrified of this place, I hardly dare to leave my hotel room—luxurious—until Brinnin or someone calls for me. . . . The rest of America may be all right, & perhaps I can understand it, but that is the last monument there is to the insane desire for power that shoots its buildings up to the stars & roars its engines louder & faster than they have ever been roared before."

But the rest of America seemed even more insane. Writing Caitlin a few weeks later from "my pilgrimage of the damned," Dylan described "this vast mad horror, that doesn't know its size, or its strength, or its weakness, or its barbaric speed, stupidity, din, self-righteousness, this cancerous Babylon."

So, ironically, on Dylan's first trip to America, the Village had seemed a quiet refuge. Coming back to the Village, Dylan told Brinnin, "was like coming home to the most wonderful place of all."

Before discovering the Horse, Dylan patronized Village restaurants and bars like the Grand Ticino, the Silver Rail, Goody's, and the Minetta Tavern, where he fell under the spell of Joe Gould and for once found himself out-cadged. For a brief period he frequented the San Remo on Bleecker Street—"the restlessly crowded hangout of the intellectual hipster," Brinnin described it, "and catch-all for whatever survived of dedicated Bohemianism in Greenwich Village." At first the regulars stared at him as a curiosity and occasionally came over to his table to buy him a drink, but the San Remo crowd was too self-consciously "sophisticated" to acknowledge any idols; soon Dylan found himself just another carousing celebrity, and he bar-hopped until he found his home at the Horse.

When he received a second invitation to America, Caitlin insisted on coming with him, and though he eagerly anticipated the attention, he downplayed the hoopla to Caitlin. "Darling darling dear my dear Caitlin," he had written her during his first trip from the Hotel Earle on Washington Square, "oh God how I love you, oh God how far away you are, I love you night, day, every second, every oceanic deep second of time, of life, of sense, of love, of any meaning at all, that is spent away from you and in which I only think of coming back, coming back, to you, my heart, my sacred sweetheart, Caitlin my dear one." But if part of him rejoiced that his "sacred sweetheart" was accompanying him, another part couldn't help fearing she'd cramp his style.

Unable to find free lodgings with friends—the Villagers may have idolized Dylan, but having him in their homes was another matter—the quarreling couple took a cheap apartment with kitchenette at the Chelsea Hotel, the already dilapidated artist and bohemian haven on West 23rd Street. With her no-nonsense attitude and the clear-eyed skepticism with which she recognized her own volatile temperament, Caitlin soon saw a side to the Village that Dylan never acknowledged. "A feebler Soho but with stronger drinks," her husband had told her, but after she'd witnessed the behavior of the bohemians for a few weeks she found them "cellophane-wrapped, chic, sleek, showroom models." "The bohemians of America are not, by a very long well-creased leg, the same as that original romantic Parisian article, starving in a garret, in an atmosphere reeking in equal proportions of beards, misunderstood genius, and plain filth." And as for her husband, he only loved America as a land of opportunity for "flattery, idleness, and infidelity"—an accusation he sheepishly defended himself against by amending it to "appreciation, dramatic work, and friends." To Caitlin, Dylan remained a wonderful poet but a miserable husband, a liar, a lout, even a bit of a buffoon. And worse. "Dylan," she said years after his death, "was a shit." Dylan came back to America two more times—but both times alone.

When Dylan arrived in New York for his fourth tour in the fall of 1953, he was fleeing marital and monetary crises and embarking on major new projects—his play *Under Milk Wood* and an opera libretto for Igor Stravinsky. But his abundant vitality had been replaced by an edgy listlessness. He complained of feeling unwell. And his gout made him feel, he said, "as if I were walking on my eyeballs." He seemed alternately lethargic and frenetic, went without food for days at a time, and drank more heavily than ever. But now his drinking didn't have the spirit of conviviality, but that odd combination of indifference and compulsion that signals the desire to reach oblivion.

The Villagers couldn't help noticing that Dylan seemed to have a steady girlfriend. A Bennington graduate in her thirties, a sometime painter and dancer, Liz Reitell served as Brinnin's assistant at the Poetry Center—her assignment during this period was to take charge of Dylan. Her destiny, for a few weeks, was to become Dylan's lover. Despondent over his bitter quarrels with Caitlin, who had made her objection to his trip unmistakably clear, and dejected over his ill health, Dylan expressed his feelings with an odd and uncharacteristic obliqueness—Caitlin, he told Liz, was his widow.

The story of the last three weeks of Dylan's life would be told over and over again in every bar in the Village.

Dylan arrived on October 19, 1953, and once more took up residence at the Chelsea Hotel—where, he said, "the cockroaches have teeth." A few days later, he took part in a staged reading of *Under Milk Wood* at the Poetry Center, and after the performance, suddenly became so nauseated he had to vomit. "I can't eat, I can't drink, I'm even too tired to sleep," he groaned. "I have seen the gates of hell tonight." At a cast party the next evening, he seemed to have recovered his high spirits, but everyone suspected something must be wrong—he politely turned down every offer of a drink. Asked why, he repeated his phrase from the previous day—"It's just that I've seen the gates of hell, that's all." "The words," Brinnin said, "had already become something to say at a party." A matinee of *Under Milk Wood* the next day "was by every report its greatest performance"—Brinnin again. "A thousand people were left hushed by his lyrical harmonies and its grandeur. . . . Dylan himself said he had at last heard the performance he wanted to hear."

In 1953, *Time* magazine had reported with its characteristic breezy cynicism, "When [Dylan] settles down to guzzle beer, which is most of the time, his incredible yarns tumble over each other in a wild Welsh dithyramb in which truth and fact become hopelessly smothered in boozy invention. He borrows with no thought of returning what is lent, seldom shows up on time, is a trial to his friends, and a worry to his family." Although Dylan would have been hard pressed to find a single untrue word in this account, he instructed his solicitor to sue for libel. To defend itself, the magazine hired a detective to trail Dylan and compile a dossier detailing the authenticity of its article.

The detective wouldn't have seen Dylan taking barbiturates for breakfast, or washing down sleeping pills with tumblers of Old Grand-dad, his favorite American brand. But he may have seen a corner table at the Algonquin Hotel when Dylan, Liz, and a Dutch businessman quietly talked about the war—until Dylan burst into such loud and obscene ravings that a waiter insisted that he lower his voice. Liz tried to soothe him, and he burst into tears. When Liz finally managed to get him to leave, Brinnin remembered, "Dylan continued in drunken behavior that seemed to be touched frighteningly with a streak of insanity. He made gargoyle faces at people passing by in the street, walked in a tottering and lunging parody of drunkenness, spoke four-letter words loudly with complete disregard for who might hear them. As they stopped for a traffic light, Dylan turned to her, 'You really hate me, don't you?' he said. 'No,' said Liz, 'but it's not for your lack of trying.' "

And the detective certainly followed Dylan down to the Horse and witnessed enough to fill pages—for Dylan not only got drunk nearly every night, he became contentious at the slightest provocation, ranted at imaginary enemies, and blustered incoherently. He would have become a figure of ridicule—if he hadn't been so pathetic.

At a get-together at a Sutton Place town house, after downing several Irish whiskies, Dylan joined his hostess, a refugee countess, in her bedroom for over an hour while the rest of the guests chatted uneasily with Liz. And on his thirty-ninth birthday, October 27, he had drinks at the Horse with Liz and Howard Moss, poetry editor of *The New Yorker*, left for a dinner party, but could hardly manage to say a word to the guests gathered in his honor. Just as a sumptuous feast was being served, he complained of feeling so ill he had to go back to his hotel. "What a filthy, undignified creature I am," he moaned as he dropped onto his bed and burst into sobs.

· · ·

Ten days after his arrival in New York, Dylan made his last public appearance, at a reading at CCNY—spent most of the afternoon drinking, participated with a semblance of coherence in an evening symposium at a film society called Cinema 16, and headed off to the Horse. By now Dylan rarely went an hour without a drink, his only food was raw eggs in a glass of beer, and he managed to stay on his feet only with the aid of Benzedrine. Attending a party on Central Park West, he chased a dancer around the room with such awkward abandon that she suffered a concussion.

During the last few days of October, he became even more erratic, one moment brawling with anyone he encountered, sobbing in maudlin remorse the next. He was so ceaselessly drunk he seemed to be only dimly conscious. Wretched, so wretched—that was all he could manage to say when asked how he felt. "He had all the devils," Liz later recalled of those terrible days, "and some of the angels, too"—but now only the devils remained.

On the night of November 3, Dylan broke down in Liz's arms and said he wanted to die, "to go to the garden of Eden." After a few hours of restless, groaning sleep, he got up at 2:00 A.M., announced he had to have a drink, and despite Liz's desperate protests, bolted out of the room. When he returned an hour and a half later, he proudly declaimed the words that soon became a part of Village lore—"I've had eighteen straight whiskies. I think that's the record." Collapsing into Liz's lap, he added "I love you, but I'm alone."

Dylan's remark about eighteen straight whiskies, though endlessly quoted, was never believed. No one even seemed to know where he'd gone, until, thirty years later, an artist came forth with an eyewitness account. He'd seen Dylan at the Horse that night. "His color was horrifying. The man seemed a monster puppet. His condition was clearly a source of amusement and contempt to his companions. The 'tart' [as he called the woman at Dylan's table] progressively dipped thin cigars in one of the eight highballs before him and slid them into his mouth. . . . I thought, now all that's needed is a red robe, a crown of thorns, and the final casting of dice."

The next morning, Dylan announced he was suffocating—he needed fresh air, he said, and more than that, he needed a drink. But two beers at the Horse were all he could manage before becoming so sick he had to return to the Chelsea, where Liz finally decided the time had come to call for medical help. Half an hour later, a doctor administered various medications that allowed Dylan to sleep for much of the afternoon, but he awoke with an attack of nausea and vomiting. Summoned once more, "the doctor with the winking needle," as Dylan now called him, gave him a cortisone shot. Dylan slept a few more hours, again awoke with an attack of nausea and vomiting. "The horrors," Dylan kept repeating, "the horrors"—and pleaded to be "put out."

After dozing for a few more hours, Dylan awoke and gripped Liz's hand. Suddenly his face began to turn blue. Liz called the doctor again, and Dylan was taken by ambulance to St. Vincent's Hospital on West 12th Street at 1:58 A.M. on November 5.

At first, the doctors suspected diabetic shock, but after several hours changed their diagnosis to "a severe insult to the brain" caused by alcohol poisoning and called in a brain specialist. Breathing spasmodically in an oxygen mask, Dylan remained in a coma for twenty-four hours, thirty-six, forty-eight. The doctors gave him blood transfusions. They performed a tracheotomy to ease his breathing. His temperature rose, fell, and rose again to 105.5.

Rumors spread—Dylan had fallen down a flight of stairs in a drunken stupor, he had been mugged outside the Horse, he had passed out from an overdose of drugs, he had suffered a cerebral hemorrhage—and the anxious vigil began within hours after he was admitted. Dozens of people congregated in the waiting room, in the hallways, and outside his room.

But who were all those appalling strangers? Who was that woman, for instance, who stood at the door of Dylan's room for half an hour, quietly gazing at his wracked body, then suddenly vanished? Who were the dozens like her who came and went without saying a word? Had they once asked him for an autograph after a reading? Had they once had a drink with him at the Horse? Had he spent a night in their bed? Everyone in the overflowing crowd seemed to feel they alone had been close to him, they alone deserved to be there at his vigil.

Factions developed, people eyed one another suspiciously, silent accusations filled the air. Dylan had a death wish, some whispered, his entire life a long and ceaseless suicide; others murmured he was a fallen angel destroyed by "friends" who made remarks like that.

Within a few days Dylan's table at the White Horse would be turned into a shrine. Within a few years the beatniks would worship him as one of their "holy fools," the country's most popular folk singer would take his name, and his face would appear among a row of icons on the cover of a Beatles album. But now, what might have been a vale of tears was being transformed into a bitter farce. Everyone at St. Vincent's blamed everyone else for slowly killing Dylan with their selfish disregard for his privacy, his health, his genius. They expressed contempt for the mob that was turning the vigil into a gathering of vultures. The dying man had become property, they said—scandalized by everyone's presence but their own.

And then Caitlin arrived from Wales, accompanied from the airport by a motorcycle escort—and word quickly spread that the first words she spoke upon entering the hospital were "Is the bloody man dead or alive?" Shocked at his condition, she hurled herself upon his body—leading to another rumor that she'd tried to rip away the oxygen mask. Everyone feared she'd run into Liz, about whom she knew nothing, but she'd become too hysterical to notice anything.

Never regaining consciousness, far away from the Wales he loved, Dylan did not go gently. In every hour that brought him closer to death, his body grew inert, his breathing nearly inaudible. Finally, at 12:40 on the afternoon of November 9, as a nurse was washing him, he gave a final gasp and stopped breathing. John Berryman, the only other person in the room, emerged a few minutes later—the nurses already dismantling the oxygen tent—and cried, "He's dead! He's dead!"

Dylan Thomas, someone said, died of being Dylan Thomas.

XIV

Delmore Schwartz

Alien in Residence

In the summer of 1935, when Delmore Schwartz was twenty-one years old, his mother's nagging drove him out of their Brooklyn apartment to a boardinghouse in the Village. Like so many young men and women before and after him, he was determined to become a writer. In a dingy room at 813 Greenwich Avenue, over a steamy July weekend, he wrote "In Dreams Begin Responsibilities." Ecstatic, he immediately showed the story to his friend William Barrett, who would later become the leading American authority on existentialism. "The friends of youth thrust manuscripts upon one often enough, God knows," Barrett recalled nearly fifty years later, "and here and there one would encouragingly find glimmerings of talent amid much stumbling and awkwardness. But here was something completely formed and wonderfully perfect."

The story stayed in Delmore's desk for two years, until the fall of 1937, when he submitted it to *Partisan Review*, which announced that it was resuming publication as a noncommunist literary magazine. The editor barely knew his name, but they made it the first piece in their premiere issue. A year later, when Delmore published his first book, a collection of stories and poems, he was immediately acclaimed the wunderkind of American letters.

November 11, 1953, Delmore Schwartz is now thirty-nine. "Five s.t.s. (second time in past two or three weeks), jarful of whiskey at 10, two glasses of Zinfandel. Yesterday unrest/dissatisfaction/resentment/anger, in several directions before sleep. . . . Looking at Faulkner's stories & Sound & Fury & As I Lay Dying—looking for story [it turned out to be "The Leg"] and the nostalgic paragraph which started me off eighteen years ago, that July afternoon in 1953 at 8 [13 Greenwich Avenue]—'IDBR.' At 6:15 began to drink." Despite intermittent periods during which his mind functioned with clarity and vigor, Delmore began to lose that struggle between his past and his promise from the moment he engaged it, and finally succumbed to a madness he always suspected was foredoomed.

As a poet, he not only inherited and extended the modernist aesthetic of Rilke, Yeats, Eliot, Pound, and Joyce, but, in his tormented life, he seemed to his contemporaries to embody the curse of genius. As an editor and essayist at *Partisan Review,* the most influential journal of his generation, he exemplified a post-Stalinist politics and a Europeanization of literature and defined the role of the intellectual in postwar American culture. In Greenwich Village bars and on Ivy League campuses, he became the archetype of the "alien in residence"—witty, quarrelsome, lyrical, despondent, extravagant in both his gifts and his flaws, the exemplar of an entirely new sensibility, the urban, ironic, cosmopolitan, mockingly self-analytical outsider, at home only in the realm of ideas. Delmore Schwartz, in short, was renowned as the quintessential "New York Jewish intellectual," whose legendary stature in American culture in the forties and fifties was based precisely on his alienation from American life. Wrote Saul Bellow in *Humboldt's Gift,* his novel based on Delmore's life, "Humboldt was just what everyone had been waiting for."

The emotional brutality of his childhood assured that "nothing good will come of it." Even his conception was an act of deceit, Delmore learned: his mother became pregnant against his father's wishes. Before he was three years old, his parents' marriage had reached such embittered contentiousness that they woke him one night and demanded that he choose between them, and shortly before they finally separated a few years later, his father offered to buy Delmore from his mother for $75,000. Besieged by his father's recriminations and his mother's self-righteous lamentations, the boy must have felt there was only one authentic emo-

tion—rage—and that it was the only response to the one primal instinct—
treachery.

Delmore couldn't resist, he could only flee, and he sought refuge
from his parents' emotional squalor in the serene, empyrean abstractions of
poetry and philosophy. Since to risk feeling was to invite betrayal, and since
he could secure approval only through the detached rigors of the intellect,
he announced, as a freshman at the University of Wisconsin—embracing
the pompous effusiveness of undergraduate mysticism as well—that "I
shall devote myself to vision alone."

But the taint of Delmore's wretched self-image could be only momentarily alleviated. "From the time I first met him," recalled William
Phillips, one of the editors of *Partisan Review*, "his psychic distortions were
full-grown. . . . He acted as though he hated his mother, refusing to see her
or even talk to her. . . . He admired, somewhat grudgingly, his father's success as a real-estate operator, though he talked about him as if he were a distant, mythical figure."

Barrett recalled that Delmore's mother "did everything she could
to prolong his narcissism, exaggerate his ego with praise, and yet in her
clever and poisonous way insinuate[d] in the child, then the boy, and then
the young man, that the love and trust of anybody was not to be believed."
Delmore could cry out, in his imagination, "Don't do it," but he could only
acknowledge, in his life, that "memory is all we get from existence"—as he
wrote plaintively to Gertrude Buckman shortly before she became his first
wife. In a gesture all too typical of his family's hysterical manipulations, his
mother's response to confrontations was to threaten to kill herself.

The young author of "In Dreams Begin Responsibilities," though enslaved to his memories, was not yet corrupted by egotism, and Delmore
burst on the literary scene in the late thirties like a bright nova in the firmament. He was praised by the poets and critics he had assiduously cultivated
(Wallace Stevens, R. P. Blackmur, John Crowe Ransom, Mark Van Doren)
and showered with honors he had eagerly sought (two Guggenheims, an editorial position at *Partisan Review*, a teaching post at Harvard). His first book
of poetry, said F. O. Matthiessen, received "more critical acclaim than has
come to any other American poet of his generation." Allen Tate wrote that
"Schwartz's poetic style is the only genuine innovation since Pound and
Eliot." There was even a letter from Eliot himself, which, Barrett recalled,
"he handled like a sacred relic, reading it to me, not letting me touch it, but
showing me the signature as if to guarantee its authenticity." A correspon-

dence with Pound culminated when the young poet discovered the master's anti-Semitism, and grandiosely announced in a letter, "I want to resign as one of your most studious and faithful admirers." Delmore had become, in Irving Howe's words, "the poet of the historical moment."

Overflowing with an almost intimidating eagerness, his conversation exuded an edgy, intellectual gaiety. Mary McCarthy was awed by his "monstrous" erudition and Dwight Macdonald felt that "his open, ardent manner, large, dreaming eyes, sensitive mouth, and proud good looks" gave him the appearance of "a newly fledged eaglet." Although he was the youngest member of the *Partisan Review* gang, he immediately became its magnetic center, the person who dominated every debate, who had read every book, who made the witticisms everyone quoted, and who took perhaps his greatest delight in knowing everybody's secrets. Standing in the middle of a dozen listeners, reeking of cigarettes and whiskey, hopping around as if he couldn't contain his energy, clutching his head in mock dismay, shuddering at the obtuseness of an antagonist's argument, Delmore enthralled his contemporaries not only as a kind of stand-up intellectual, but as the quintessential embodiment of the disheveled genius.

"The Mozart of conversation," Bellow called him, and he explicated poetry, debated politics, dissected personalities, teased his friends with affectionate anecdotes about their foibles, or denounced his enemies with savage tales of their stupidity, duplicity, and malicious motives. He was renowned for his lethal verbal caricatures. "When [Morton Dauwen] Zabel starts to write, he puts on a uniform." "Nothing that Auden likes so much as a good death." Hannah Arendt was "that Weimar Republic flapper!" He captured Arthur Mizener in the single perfect word, "courtier," and in a phrase with prophetic overtones for his own future, brilliantly characterized Robert Hutchins of the University of Chicago as "a boy-wonder emeritus." Bellow considered him "a wonderful talker, a hectic nonstop monologist and improvisator, a champion detractor. To be loused up by [Delmore] was really a kind of privilege. It was like being the subject of a two-nosed portrait by Picasso."

But there was another side to Delmore. If many people, like Dwight Macdonald, regarded him as "an intellectual equivalent of the Borscht Circuit tummeler, a stirrer-upper," others, like Philip Rahv, saw him as an embittered neurotic. "He had a great need for affection, both to give and receive," Barrett recalled, "except that . . . this deep-seated force, whatever it was . . . made him ultimately destructive and suspicious of affection." The man who one night would regale his audience with Chaplin impressions would the next night brood in the corner, immobilized by self-loathing. The same man who last week greeted a friend with a joyful bear hug, the next week would pass him on the street with only a glower. When his nervous and intellectual energy subsided, his mood would shade into gloomy, twitching self-consciousness, a sure sign that his energy was about to return, only this time in outbursts of vituperation or provocation. The ingratiatingly clumsy and exuberant charm was replaced by hostility and rage.

Delmore's obsession with intrigue would take a demonic turn. If, in his periods of affability, his hyperactive ego entangled his friends in elaborate fantasies, in his blacker moods—which came with increasing frequency in his mid- and late twenties, soon lasting for months at a time—he abused them for constructing webs of conspiracy. Colleagues were mocking him behind his back. Critics were secretly ridiculing his poetry. "Even paranoids," he said in his most famous aphorism—retaining enough irony to construct the phrase but not enough to forestall the thought—"even paranoids have enemies."

"He took an exceedingly comfortless view of the conduct of human beings, of whose motives he was chronically distrustful," Rahv recalled, "and his habit was to denounce endlessly what he saw as their moral lapses while taking care to exculpate himself." Although he began a journal in 1939 in an effort to reconcile, or at least comprehend, the polarities in his personality, he seemed doomed to intensify his psychic conflicts. "The self," he cried out in one of his stories, "the self is a wound."

Delmore was two distinct and extravagant personalities to his friends and colleagues in the Village and at the *Partisan Review*, but this duality enhanced his stature: they assumed he was a genius because he was so unpredictable. He would hold his hand perpendicular to his face from the scar down his nose to the cleft in his chin to show how different the two sides of his face were from each other—a difference that reflected his split personality.

Delmore, in fact, had no center to his personality through which his contradictions passed. It was as if his emotions existed not on the radii but on the circumference, as if he flipped from intimacy to hostility, from ecstasy to despair, from grandiose self-esteem to histrionic self-loathing without a moment's modulation. And since he was always seeking in vain for some way to reconcile his feelings, he became that most tragic of figures, a schizoid narcissus.

• • •

But how else could an American intellectual survive in the thirties and forties but by embracing his alienation? The split in Delmore's personality that was the source of both his poetic gift and his doomed life magnified the dualities of his era, and was one way his generation defined "genius." Delmore's tragedy, in short, was regarded not as singular but as exemplary.

But while Delmore was deeply committed to the exalted vocation of poetry, when it came to his career, he behaved like a shameless hustler. The ingenious plotting and scheming that later fed his paranoid fantasies at first went into promoting his work. He ingratiated himself with critics for whom he had little respect, insisting that "one had to know the right people." He solicited letters of praise from poets he disparaged. He arranged to meet Allen Tate in a bar on West 8th Street, and when Tate praised him as the best poet since Eliot, he announced to all his friends that Tate had simply shown up at his door. He bombarded James Laughlin, the publisher of his collection *In Dreams Begin Responsibilities*, with imperious directives—get quotes from I. A. Richards, Wallace Stevens, John Dos Passos. "It might help to get one from Hemingway," he advised, adding, in one of those sudden switches that revealed an ironic awareness of his deviousness, "if you can reach him before Franco arrives in Barcelona and cuts out his black heart." He urged him to send the book to W. H. Auden without its jacket, on which Delmore was labeled "the American Auden." "He won't be pleased," Delmore noted wryly, "to see that he is the English Schwartz."

Delmore took candid delight in such stage-managing of his career, but his manipulations only concealed his anxiety, and when it became apparent, to him as well as to Laughlin, that the many delays he imposed on the book's publication had mostly to do with a fear of failure, his anxieties turned to dread. "Fear of review," he wrote in his journal. "Laurels contesting my laurels." "Published and punished."

Delmore ruefully confessed his "fabulous dream." "I don't try to deceive myself that I would not like the fame, the success, and the money which I daydreamed about as an adolescent," he wrote in his journal. But when it came—the fame and the success, if not the money—it heightened rather than diminished his anxiety. "All these fine reviews and all the rest of the things that I've been getting during the last few months," he wrote Laughlin in 1940, "are accumulating to the point where I am going to be terrified. It can't last." The pressure of praise proved intolerable precisely because he needed it so much he was certain it wouldn't continue. Since approval now depended on his talent, what if that talent failed him? In a letter to Mark Van Doren, he described "that remorse which seems insepa-rable from publishing."

"I would soon accustom myself to the idea that I am not a really good poet," he wrote R. P. Blackmur. "What is hardly bearable is the end-less shift between the illusion that I am, and the disillusion and disappoint-ment when again and again the whole poem looks bland or foolish, until the illusion returns." In one of the most revelatory entries in his entire jour-nal, he wrote, "Give me poetry and strength of character, give me strength, goodness, and knowledge, give me humility and indifference (freedom from remorse) from my own sins"—but then he adds, without even the ironic beat of a comma, "and from all that is said against me."

What was said against him? Only marginal reservations, but Del-more magnified them into devastating critiques, and was even more wounded by slights he only imagined. The ingenuity that had embroidered elaborate anecdotes for the delight of his Village coterie now concocted convoluted scenarios of rejection. And when his second and third books—*Shenandoah*, a verse play, and *Genesis*, a poem with prose commentary—received less than ecstatic reviews, he denounced his critics and moaned inconsolably that he had squandered his talent.

Before Delmore was even thirty, the major theme of his poetry be-came the failure of hope. The leading characters in his short stories were writers whose dreams of glory had been shattered. And he was so convinced his friends would betray him that he made sure to alienate them before they had the chance; he was so certain his genius would desert him that he tried to come to terms with failure before it happened—not understanding, in either case, that in so obsessively preparing himself for the dreaded pos-sibility he insured its inevitability. But it's too easy to say that too much praise too soon is the enduring curse of too many American writers, for as destructive as acclaim was to Delmore's beleaguered psyche, indifference or disapproval would have been more devastating. His mind quickly turned everything—affection, hostility, acclaim, criticism—into an assault on his hopes, his needs, his very identity.

I pity the girl who marries you," his mother had once admonished him for failing to hang up his coat—but every woman with whom Delmore was involved had deeper cause for concern. If being called the greatest poet of his generation cast him into insecurity, how could he accept the love of a mere woman? But the man who imagined himself, in his most famous story, standing up in a darkened theater and crying out "Don't do it," badgered Gertrude Buckman into a hasty, ill-considered marriage. And the desperately needy man who understood that "the demon of an absolute has me in thrall" chose a woman who was emotionally undemonstrative and sexually unresponsive.

As the wedding date approached—June 14, 1938—Gertrude continued to confess her reluctance, Delmore's apprehension expressed itself in fits of nausea and vomiting, and his mother announced that she wished she were dead. At the ceremony, in a gesture that a Freudian devotee like Delmore was certain to understand, she suddenly lost the use of her legs and had to be carried up the stairs of the synagogue. Delmore, panicked at actually finding himself married, frantically telegrammed Barrett to join the couple on their honeymoon in Vermont.

Delmore's mother had lamented throughout his childhood that sexual intimacy could only lead to betrayal; so, while he celebrated love in his poetry, and yearned for it in his life, he undermined what he most cherished. After he and Gertrude separated in 1943, he courted the most unsuitable women, and when he did find a likely match, either she was in love with someone else or he immediately began seeing someone else as well. He even spied on his lovers, perhaps in hopes of discovering their infidelity and confirming his premonitions—for he found it easier to live with an excruciating revelation than with an intolerable uncertainty.

Delmore left the Village to teach at Harvard in 1940 and stayed until 1947 (with a year's sabbatical back in the Village in 1945)—another ideal shattered. Though weary of the quarrels and jealousies of the literary world, he at once realized that academia made the Village scene, even the *Partisan Review* crowd, seem as benign as a nunnery. Although he was justifiably proud of his appointment and hoped that at last he had found a community of intellectuals with whom he could feel at ease, he immediately felt humiliated and excluded. "I never thought about anti-Semitism," he told Harold Rosenberg, "because everyone was [already] against me as a poet." "Harvard," he noted in his journal, "home of the 'nervous breakdown.'"

His letters are filled with tales of animosities, pettiness, and pusillanimous feuds. To be sure, his paranoias came closer to the surface with every year. "How often snubbed in the Square," he wrote in his journal. He confided to his colleague John Berryman, "They're threatening to send an observer to one of my sections to judge my teaching," and complained that the "big guns" were conspiring against him, and "AT A TIME WHEN I CAN BARELY TALK." To be sure, he was hardly a model of the disinterested scholar, often responding to his colleagues with the envy and contempt that characterizes so many ambitious young academics, and adopting the pose of belligerent bohemian when confronted by academic propriety.

Still, Delmore knew enough about his own pathological obsessions to recognize them in others, and he perceived the pettiness, malice, and arrogance of his Harvard colleagues with uncanny lucidity. "I have never seen so many friends hate each other with such intensity," he wrote his publisher. "Harry Levin, speaking of [F. O.] Matthiessen," he wrote R. P. Blackmur, "seems to have fixed me with M., by repeating something I said to M., who then called me up to ask about it. This was in June and I made a special point of asking Harry not to repeat it. M. smiles sweetly when he sees me, but we have since not been asked to his house, not even to the Christmas punch when all are asked." Oh Groves of Academe! Of the same Harry Levin, he said, "though learned [he] identifies criticism with sneering." "They are on the right side," he described other members of the faculty to Allen Tate, "they mean well, they are nothing if not courteous, they always occupy the high places and are well paid, and it is just this 'type' that is incapable of serious and exact perception and judgment"—the kind of insight that, if bruited carelessly about Cambridge, could get a young instructor fired.

Whether in the Village or at Harvard, Delmore was always riding what he called his "manic-depressive roller-coaster." The manic side was best typified by his gossip about T. S. Eliot, the poet whom he most revered and whose career he most wished to emulate, but the man he was determined to demolish—for those very reasons. He began his well-rehearsed set piece with a few disparaging remarks about Eliot's work—"East Coker" became "East Coca-Cola"—slid into an outraged description of Eliot's shameless literary politicking, and built to a crescendo of hilariously salacious anecdotes about the sex life of Tom and Viv, "as if," Berryman remarked, "he had a pipeline to their bedroom." The depressive side expressed itself in his unrelenting insomnia. "History is a nightmare: during which I am trying to get a good night's sleep," he noted in his journal.

The plots grew more frequent, more insidious—the measures against them more desperate. Delmore was so hypersensitive to betrayal that even before *Genesis* appeared in 1943, he accused his publisher of trying to get out of his commitment and was convinced that a "cabal of enemies" was eagerly awaiting the opportunity to destroy his reputation. "When I get scared, I get devious," he confessed to Blackmur—and he countered their malicious campaign with a Machiavellian one of his own. Letters, phone calls, review copies "to the right people"—another torrent of shameless directives to his publisher. "I do not intend to forget," he told Laughlin, "that we are living in this world where dog eats dog and books of noble poetry. The main thing, obviously, is to be perfectly aware that one is not being noble: it is only when one begins to deceive oneself about the character of one's manoeuvres that one is really lost and damned forever." In the months after *Genesis* was published, to largely negative but hardly hostile reviews, he grandiosely claimed he was about to sign a deal with Hollywood and intimated that his publisher was stealing his profits.

Money was increasingly the focus of Delmore's complaints, for while he may have been the greatest poet since Eliot and Pound, he virtually had to beg to eke out a living on the grant and teaching circuit ("the game of poetical chairs," as it was called by Berryman's wife, Eileen Simpson). Here another of his conflicts came into play. He believed he could keep separate the realms of "books of noble poetry" and "this world where dog eats dog," but neither his character nor his culture would let him. Rather than modulating between dedication to his work and advancement of his career, he flipped wildly between naively noble devotion to his poetry and devious campaigning for his survival, throwing the two poles of his life into unremitting opposition.

But Delmore's early letters are filled with a dedication to disinterest. "So long as neither of us think we are of angelic intelligence, perfect at all times," he wrote a friend in 1937, "there's a good deal to be learned by these disputes. . . . It seems to me that without the assumption that any act or work might have been better or worse than it was, all judgment, literary and moral, becomes impossible." "I've heard nothing but surprising praise," he wrote Ransom about one of his essays, "and I can't think unanimity is ever accurate or just." And to Tate, "You are quite right in reproving me for making critical remarks in passing and without arguing the point. I hope that you will reprove me whenever you see fit and with brutal frankness."

He wasn't being disingenuous. The conviction that when it came to poetry, to ideas, the intellect should be utterly disinterested was at the center of his being. But how could such a man survive on a college campus? This attitude almost immediately got him into trouble. When he wrote Tate a long letter critiquing Tate's book *Reason in Madness*, and called many passages "shocking in their inaccuracy and misunderstanding," demonstrating the "incoherence and misrepresentation" of others, he was stunned by the anger in Tate's reply. "Now I don't know what to make of your present letter," Delmore wrote back, "personality, temperament, and repudiation of friendship have suddenly made an appearance, to my immense surprise." "I have not turned on Allen," he protested to Blackmur, "only on his last book." But the correspondence between these two old friends ceased for two years.

Delmore learned quickly. He modulated his idealism to the extent that he declared "one owes it to literature to be virtually Machiavellian for the sake of good writers." Regarding himself foremost among those good writers, he began to vacillate between his commitment to honesty and his instinct for scheming. Furthermore, since he had staked his precarious identity on his poetic reputation, and since the latter now rested on what he came to see as the annuities, jealousies, and stupidities of his critics, he was thrown back into his primal insecurities.

Delmore would write Berryman scorning Blackmur's "stupidity" in certain remarks in a review of one of his books, then three days later turn around and write Blackmur himself that he found the review "the only one which could be considered an act of genuine criticism" and ask that he be "charitable enough to help me" by clarifying those points for which he had called Blackmur stupid. Frankness was fine when it came to ideas—but flattery was better when it came to careers. "If I must choose between friendship and what I think (rightly or not), I choose friendship," he wrote Dwight Macdonald in 1943, referring to a previous letter that had wounded even the imperturbable Macdonald—but the disingenuousness of that "if" was revealed in a postscript when his "honesty" compelled him to add, "If I had wanted to hurt you, why did I withhold most of my [previous] letter?" If he hadn't wanted to hurt him, why point this out? And when his correspondence with Tate finally resumed, he swallowed his pride and asked a favor.

"The remark about the first symptom of dishonesty being a belief that everyone is dishonest," Delmore wrote Tate in a letter in 1938, "is the kind of observation that I write in the blank pages of my Nicomachean Ethics"—one of those remarkable insights he was able to formulate precisely because he was unable to perceive its application to himself. For if anyone ever believed "everyone was dishonest," it was Delmore. Where at first he was simultaneously blunt and polite with his friends or with poets and critics he admired, when it became a matter of gaining favors, the strain of the contradictions began to overwhelm him.

Look carefully at an apparently innocuous passage in a letter to Ransom. "There is one matter about which I am eager and that is the teaching job, the possibility of one, at Kenyon College. I was supposed, I think, to wait until the proper moment arrived and Allen Tate, who has in a very short time been kind to me in many ways, proposed my name to you. At any rate, although this may be premature, I would welcome an opportunity to teach very much, and I may have certain qualifications, academic ones, I mean, of which you do not know, and I would be grateful indeed if my name was kept in mind." The hesitations in the syntax, the truncated phrases, the apologetic qualifications all show him trapped in emotions he felt compelled to conceal. Beginning in the graceful rhythms of courtesy, he seems to grow embarrassed, even angry, at finding himself forced to adopt such an ingratiating tone, and gradually collapses into awkward cringing—"if my name was kept in mind" instead of the more natural "if you would keep my name in mind," because to say "you" again would be imposing too much, and rather than risk alienating a potential patron, he's even willing to grovel. It's not too much to say that passages like this— which appear with increasing frequency in his letters—reveal the emotional turmoil of a man so enraged and humiliated that he has to play this game that he finally loses control and falls into an obsequiousness that must have made his skin crawl. Machiavellianism was never supposed to descend to this!

All the while Delmore was behaving so duplicitously, he was writing poems of candor, irony, and exemplary dignity, lucid critical essays, and hundreds of letters filled with sparkling wit and devoted friendship. His lapses into hostility, manipulation, and self-abasement were not the deepest expressions of his spirit, but tragic signs of the pathology that was gradually destroying his psyche.

When Delmore returned from Harvard to the Village in 1945, he was still, at thirty-one, the boy wonder of American letters. One evening that fall, Delmore and Barrett dropped in on a crowded bar just off Washington Square. They sat down with a group of people and listened, engrossed, to David Diamond, a composer and old friend of Delmore's, describe the scene in Paris—how he had debated literature in Left Bank cafés, tracked down Joyce's home, and even followed the master on one of his daily walks. Paris! But to Delmore, the Village was humming with the same electric energy that burned in the City of Light when it was released from World War I and embarked on its fabled decade as the capital of art. "It's 1919!" Delmore shouted at Barrett, "1919! 1919! It's 1919 over again!"

Now, at the dawn of "the American century," it was the Village's turn to become the new capital of art. The intellectuals and bohemians of the Village may have been contemptuous of patriotism, but when it came to art, they were as jingoistic as any Republican. That was the grandiose dream that energized Delmore, rekindling his hopes of both poetic glory and intellectual community. "I was born," he exulted, "with a post-war soul!"

Although Delmore was convinced the exhilarating ambience of bohemia would prove more congenial than the suffocating atmosphere of academia, he soon fell into the familiar pattern of melancholy and restless despondency. When Barrett ran across him in Washington Square Park one day and attempted to soothe his anger, Delmore shouted at him, "We live in the world of Hitler and Stalin, and you want me to be gentle!" When an old friend saw him drinking alone in the Minetta Tavern and went over to praise his latest book, Delmore burst into uncontrollable sobs.

Delmore couldn't stay in one apartment for more than a few months at a time, but wherever he moved, he took his solitude with him. When Barrett tried to locate him, the switchboard operator at *Partisan Review* reported that Delmore had taken a cold-water flat on Bedford Street, without a telephone, and that whenever they wanted to contact him they sent someone over to leave a note in his mailbox.

And so his years in the Village passed—too troubled to write more than a few poems, a few essays, gloomy passages in his journals. He listened with only desultory attention at *Partisan Review* editorial meetings, wandered into Chumley's bar as soon as it opened, or into Stewart's cafeteria to loiter with friends like Saul Bellow and Isaac Rosenfeld, and even tutored an eccentric millionaire named Hy Sobiloff who harbored the eager but vain hope of becoming a poet just like Delmore.

And the paranoia. Out to dinner with John Berryman and Eileen Simpson, he suddenly seemed anxious, distracted, and finally he asked Simpson if she'd mind changing places with him, he had to have his back to the wall, he couldn't stand having anyone sitting behind him. "Do they whisper behind my back?" She found herself recalling the words of one of Delmore's poems—"Do they speak / Of my clumsiness? Do they laugh at me, / Mimicking my gestures, retailing my shame?"

Distressed as he was, Delmore was also falling in love—with a woman on the verge of marrying another man, and when he was virtually living with someone.

When asked how he and Elizabeth Pollet met, Delmore liked to say, "In the pages of Oscar Williams." She was a novelist and short story writer, and it seems likely that he was attracted to her idealization of him — and to her demurely glamorous appearance — more than to her talent. Pollet lived on Hudson Street, Delmore's other lover on Sullivan Street, and he continued to see both of them until the day, some six months later, they appeared simultaneously at his door at 91 Bedford Street and he fled in disarray to Barrett's apartment.

Thus the course of love: Delmore vacillated; Elizabeth announced her intention to marry his rival; Delmore showed up at her apartment in a wild-eyed rage; Elizabeth fled down the fire escape; Delmore returned to Boston in despair; Elizabeth got married, but soon the lovers reconciled in 1948; took their vows in 1949, and lived together in a climate of recrimination, suspicion, and emotional violence until their divorce in 1957. "I got married the second time," Delmore said, "in the way that when a murder is committed, crackpots turn up at the police station to confess the crime."

Disillusioned with academia and bohemia, disappointed in love, Delmore seemed to find a haven only in the free-floating world of radical intellectuals that he inhabited during the forties and fifties, mostly as an editor at *Partisan Review* from 1943 to 1955, later as an editor and critic at *The New Republic* and at *Perspectives USA*. Although he refused to accept the political ideology of *Partisan Review*, he was enthralled by its quarrelsome characters and argumentative atmosphere. "He thinks," Randall Jarrell said, referring to Delmore's "personally involved, New Yorkerish" obsessions, "that Schiller and St. Paul were just two *Partisan Review* editors."

Partisan Review began as a Village ménage à trois among Marxism, modernism, and bohemianism, with bohemianism soon feeling neglected and moving out, and Marxism and modernism continuing to cohabit, but finally going their separate ways. Delmore lived in the modernist wing, contributing his own poems, reviews of other poets, essays on masters such as Yeats, and magnificent short stories, and at first refused to become an editor because "I would get a Marxist label without being a Marxist." When he finally agreed, his motive was less the attractions of conversion than "the delights of conversation."

Just as Village artists and writers fantasized their preeminent role in "the American century," the *Partisan Review* radicals fervently fantasized themselves, after years of embattled neglect, at the forefront of a cosmopolitan and socialist postwar America. If their ideological commitment, though more sustained than that of the bohemians, was just as doomed, their rigorous, disputatious, ironic, intellectual style was far more seductive to Delmore — and indeed, ideology was almost beside the point. This polemical milieu allowed him to be an idealist about poetry, a skeptic about ideas, and a gossip about friends, until his idealism, his skepticism, his friendships were all consumed by paranoia.

"The PR boys" with whom Delmore had the most consuming relationships were Dwight Macdonald and Lionel Trilling, Macdonald because they shared polemical styles, Trilling because they did not.

Delmore's intimacy with Macdonald was based on an incessant exchange of insults. "And he could take it as well as dish it out," Macdonald recalled. "I can't remember him irritated by the most drastic counterattack: indeed he seemed to welcome direct onslaught on himself and his ideas like a skillful swordsman who knows he can deflect the thrust." A typical passage in one of Delmore's letters to Macdonald: "It occurred to me reading the last issue of P.R. that perhaps you were not a member of the advance guard, but rather an archaism, born too late: a great muck-raker, a greater [Lincoln] Steffens?" A typical passage in his journal: "I spoke with Dwight amiably: You must come over here so that I can throw you out [of] the house."

As for Trilling, at worst he possessed the magisterial intelligence Delmore scorned, at best the civilized humanism he envied and thus felt compelled to condemn. Trilling's intellectual composure seemed a personal affront to his own distorted life. In one of his most famous essays, "The Duchess's Red Shoes," he took his profound disagreement with Trilling's increasing conservatism and unresponsiveness to modernism as an opportunity to express his even deeper hostility to Trilling's "manners." "He entertained social views (and social misgivings), which would be intolerable if they were presented nakedly, as social criticism of a political program, instead of being united with literary considerations."

One of his most satirical stories, "New Year's Eve," about a *Partisan Review* party at the end of 1937, was published in the journal in 1945.

The guests in "New Year's Eve" are shown to be locked in "what was soon to be a post-Munich sensibility: complete hopelessness of perception and feeling." The literary critics F. W. Dupee and Lionel Abel appeared in quasi-fictional form, Dupee as a failed and cynical novelist, "an interesting and unfortunate human being," and Abel as an intensely disliked critic whose "chief activity was to explain to all authors that they were without talent"; Dwight Macdonald appeared as a frantic editor suffering from a "pathological excess of energy." Delmore's self-caricature was more kindly. He was the author of "a satirical dialogue between Freud and Marx," and "had for long cherished the belief that if he were an interesting and gifted author, everyone would like him and want to be with him and enjoy conversations with him." "The idiom which prevailed"—at the party, at the *Partisan Review* itself—"might perhaps be said to be that of unpleasant cleverness."

But unlike Mary McCarthy's novel *The Oasis*, which also skewered a number of *Partisan Review* types, including Rahv, a former lover, "New Year's Eve" didn't entirely burn bridges. Shenandoah, the Delmore character, is in despair "at his inability not to get into arguments with other human beings, especially those he liked." "He always tells other human beings what he regards as the bitter truth about each one of them and then he is astonished that they get angry." " 'Some other world,' he said to himself, 'some world of goodness, some other life, some life where the nobility we admire is lived; some life in which those who have dedicated their being to the examination of consciousness live by the laws they face at every turn.' " Delmore could still see his own faults as clearly as everyone else's.

Finally Delmore's mood became so dispirited, his work so perfunctory that even his old friend Barrett complained. He was doing Delmore's work as well as his own, wouldn't somebody talk to him? Rahv had given up, so William Phillips took on the task. Feeling sympathy for his condition, even feeling helpless "in dealing with what was obviously a psychic disorder," Phillips walked over to Delmore's apartment on Perry Street and confronted him. Snarling and screaming, Delmore bitterly accused him of going behind his back and lashed out with "vague threats and all kinds of ominous insinuations." Since he could hardly get in a word, Phillips left the issue unresolved. "I could make no headway with pathology."

Pathology. Even his closest friends started using the word. They began to recall signs—his sudden rages, his unappeasable self-doubt, his devious scheming—that indicated something more problematic than a paradoxical character. His mockery of his friends lost its affection and became ridicule. He was no longer avid for approval so much as suspicious of treachery. As Rahv noticed, he even began to ritualize his own unhappiness. As Bellow put it, "The pathologic element could be missed only by those who were laughing too hard to look." "Delmore Schwartz committed suicide piecemeal," Barrett recalled, "day by day."

Delmore saw it coming before anyone else, and fought it harder than anyone imagined. In his first entry in his journal, December 8, 1939, after referring to "time wasted," "work which is not good enough," "sickening excitement," and "the usual tendency to retaliation by means of the written word," he vowed to try to master or at least moderate what he already acknowledged were the excesses of his nature. "The long conversation of the soul with itself ought now, by the help of this exercise, to turn more frequently to objective observation."

At the age of eighteen he confessed in a letter, "I always cause those who are near me more suffering than pleasure." To Gertrude Buckman in 1943: "Perhaps an immense illusion—what a good boy, with all my short-comings, I was then, how full of the desire to be good, generous, because I have always wanted to be good and became evil because I expected too much of other human beings and tried to force them to behave as I thought they should."

In Delmore's poetry and short stories, the confessional acknowledgment of his destructive instincts, the remorseful vow to master them, became a persistent theme:

> *I am my father's father,*
> *You are your children's guilt.*
>
> *Well: The heart of man is known:*
> *It is a cactus bloom.*
>
> *So many surround you, ringing your fate,*
> *Caught in an anger exact as a machine!*

And from his fiction: "Mrs. Fish had concluded her story by saying that it was peculiar but an assured fact that some human beings seemed to be ruined by their best qualities. . . . He turned from the looking-glass and said to himself, thinking of his mother's representation of the Baumanns, 'No one truly exists in the real world because no one knows all that he is to other human beings, all that they say behind his back, and all the foolishness which the future will bring him.'"

Delmore was astute enough to seek professional counsel. It was a common witticism among his friends that Delmore was so immersed in psychoanalytic jargon that he paid his analyst to teach him his profession. He partially recognized the failure of his self-analysis—"the intellectual criticism of his own emotions," he wrote in one of his stories, "was as ever of no avail whatever."

Indeed, it was Delmore's ironic fate that his compulsive introspection hastened rather than forestalled his mental collapse. As he wrote of a character clearly modeled on himself in an unfinished story, "Wherever I go, he said to himself, I have an important thing to watch, to guard against, to deny. . . . I begin to watch myself. I think only of whether I am cutting a fine figure before [my friends]. Not to be laughed at, but to be respected, that would be one way of stating my motive. . . . I do not gaze upon the others except to see the effect of my actions upon them, or to suspect their glance, their look, their voice, of irony, contempt, or ignorance."

Such convoluted self-consciousness, combined with his deepening self-doubt, was paradoxically both a form of solipsism and a surrender of ego. The more self-absorbed Delmore became, the more he allowed others to establish his self-image—and the only way he could resolve this paradox was by uniting his low self-esteem and his dependence on the judgments of others into the coherence of paranoia. The syllogism in Delmore's psyche thus took on a doomed logic—I am worthless, yet I am nothing but what others think of me, therefore others are determined to destroy me.

"Soon he succeeded in putting everyone in the wrong," Delmore wrote in his journal—able to see what was happening, but unable to put it in the first person—"the one art learned from his mother."

Delmore left *Partisan Review* in 1955, and managed to land teaching positions at Kenyon, Princeton, and the University of Chicago, and writing jobs at *The New Republic* and *Perspectives USA*—where he was reduced to synopsizing other writers' articles. By the mid-fifties he was an alcoholic, and reliant on sleeping pills at night and amphetamines in the morning. "My narcissistic supplies," he called them. Friends who hadn't seen him for only a few years were shocked at the change in his appearance. His face was mottled and swollen, and he had a frantic, haunted look in his eyes that made him seem mad.

Even Delmore's sense of shame deserted him. As he desperately tried to hang on, his letters were characterized by disdainful begging for jobs and money—and no one feels more victimized than one so willing to grovel—and even by whoring of the work he once held sacred. Submitting a story to *Partisan Review*: "As you know, it is a question of money and nothing else right now. I hardly have to add that I'll make any changes of any kind to make the story usable." And eventually this—from the heir to Eliot and Pound: "Looking at copies of *The Dude* [a girlie magazine], it occurred to me that the present story might be too long for periodical publication: I'd be glad to make any cuts or changes which would help to make the story usable."

Delmore found no solace in his marriage. Envious of Elizabeth's success (one of her novels had become a best-seller), suspecting her of betrayal (he had to be restrained from striking her when she merely accepted a light from Ralph Ellison), he sank into domestic squalor and drunken rages. On the way home from a party, his driving was so erratic that Elizabeth insisted he let her drive. He refused; she got out; he crashed into a telephone pole and spent the night in jail, shouting at the police, "I'm guilty, guilty, punish me!"

The crisis in his marriage precipitated his descent into psychosis. Elizabeth left him for seven months in 1956. By the following summer, feeling she was "living on the side of a volcano," she decided to separate from him once more. With the collusion of their mutual psychiatrist, the day before they were scheduled to sail for Germany on a Fulbright, she left Delmore a note saying she refused to see him again unless he consented to be hospitalized, and, fearing violence, went into hiding.

Why would she do this to him? She must be deserting him for another man! Fixing on a passing reference to Hilton Kramer in her note — then the editor of *Arts* magazine, he had asked her to write some articles — he was convinced Kramer had betrayed him. All that summer, Delmore harassed him with threats of lawsuits, until over Labor Day weekend, he appeared at Kramer's room at the Chelsea Hotel, demanding to see Elizabeth, and screamed he'd break down the door if Kramer didn't let him in. Kramer convinced a desk clerk to intervene, fled to a friend's home in Hoboken, and obtained a restraining order. Apprehended by the police, Delmore was committed to Bellevue, where he had to be confined in a straitjacket.

Diagnosed as suffering from "acute brain syndrome" and "diffuse brain disease," Delmore was only released after a group of friends began an escrow account to be used for treatment at the Payne-Whitney clinic. He was so trapped in the web of paranoia, however, that anyone who showed any interest in his situation was suspected of complicity in his humiliation. The very people who'd contributed money to help him, he ranted when he vainly tried to collect funds for his living expenses, were now trying to steal from him! A series of bizarre lawsuits ensued. "The case of Delmore Schwartz," read one affidavit, "versus Hilton Kramer, Elizabeth Pollet, James Laughlin [his publisher], Marshall Best [an editor who had rejected a manuscript], Saul Bellow, The Living Theater, William Styron, Perry Miller [the Harvard scholar with whom his Cambridge girlfriend was in love], [and] Harry Levin," plus, Delmore added, "other names [that] will be added when an investigation has occurred, or perhaps sooner."

He also became convinced he had suffered a heart attack and had come "close to dying" while at Bellevue — but he gradually refocused his psychic energy on Kramer, demanding $150,000 for his "illicit relationship" with Elizabeth and for the "false arrest" leading to his incarceration. The lawsuit proceeded with Dickensian speed, and only several years later did Delmore finally penetrate to the core of the conspiracy. From his journals, July 22, 1964: "It is now seven years to the day since my wife, Elizabeth Pollet, left me suddenly. . . . The man for whom she left me—after many preparations over a period of two years designed to conceal the real motives of her actions—was NELSON ROCKEFELLER. His great wealth, his status as a married man, and his political ambitions were all very much involved in her effort to conceal the real reasons for her actions."

Alfred Kazin described a visit with Delmore in the late fifties. "He sat in his squalid little box of a room on Greenwich Avenue. . . . It was the kind of room that could have been chosen only by someone with an extraordinary knowledge of all the murderously bad rooms put aside and carefully preserved by the heartless state for poets to die in. . . . It needed remarkable self-knowledge, long practice in disaster, even to discover a room like that. And there he was, buried alive up to his fine eyes in 'betrayal,' . . . as he twisted and spat in the rage of his unhappiness."

Lists began showing up in his journals, long lists of the *nice* things people had said about him—" 'What a marvelous human being,' 'He told me how very talented you are,' 'Highly amusing,' 'Ransom thinks that you're wonderful,' 'Dr. G. thinks that you're a genius' "—as if they could provide him a kind of incantatory reassurance. The mirror image of his paranoia was a childishly naive trust that would momentarily cleanse his spirit of anxiety. "I don't know why," he wrote Dwight Macdonald during the same year he was suing half the Village for betraying him, "I always believe what people say."

While Delmore's insane ravings made him unwelcome in his old haunts, another side of his madness brought him a new circle of friends, acolytes, actually. In the bars of the Village—the White Horse Tavern on Hudson Street, in particular, where he took over the role of house poet from Dylan Thomas—among the lumpenbohemians, the failed poets, the dropout intellectuals, the callow college graduates, he found at last the milieu he had always craved, a band of adoring listeners.

Delmore played the famous poet, the powerful *Partisan Review* editor, the legendary raconteur with a raucous fervor. He would expound on Marx and movies, Freud and tabloids, Yeats and baseball, sarcastically recount his days at Harvard and *Partisan Review*, and read from his heavily annotated copy of *Finnegans Wake* for as long as eight hours at a stretch. He would parody Joyce Kilmer ("only man can make a Christmas tree"), or describe how Queen Elizabeth had visited the Far East to discover the secrets of fellatio and displayed her newfound prowess, when she returned to Buckingham Palace, on Danny Kaye. Gazing in an alcoholic haze at the crowd drinking in his every word, he was actually happy. It had all come true, all his dreams of genius, of glory, of approval!

Girls flocked to the White Horse to meet the glamorous writer they had idolized in college. Whispers of madness only added to the allure, and a series of mistresses, all in their teens or early twenties, provided him with the intellectual awe and sexual submission that was all he wanted and all they had to offer. But these episodes only added to the battalions of disenchanted Village women. When he announced one evening to a barful of cronies that he was going to get married—a marriage that everyone knew would never take place—he suddenly blurted out, "I don't know why I'm getting married, I can't fuck anymore."

Barrett's last encounter with him took place in the early sixties. Seeing Delmore with a young woman across the room, Barrett invited them to join him and his companion for an after-dinner brandy. For a minute or two Delmore was almost amiable, but then he exploded into incoherent bellowing. When the young woman finally persuaded him to leave, Barrett burst into tears. "There's nothing to be done," his companion consoled him, "he's beyond salvaging"—the man who had once been "the most magical human being I've known."

The few people who had the patience to try to help him could think of no other recourse than to send him to various hospitals. But he always escaped, rejecting psychiatric treatment as the culmination of the ever-widening conspiracy. In 1960, when he received his invitation to attend the Kennedy inauguration four months late—he was moving too frequently to be tracked down, even by the White House—he declaimed that the delay was part of the plot to destroy his reputation. In 1961, he was present at the party at which Norman Mailer stabbed his wife and was convinced that the entire episode "may have been—probably was—a setup" to humiliate *him*. He telephoned his psychiatrist's wife to tell her the FBI would be interested in her relationship with Bertolt Brecht. The Empire State Building was sending out rays to damage his brain. He smashed all the windows in his apartment on West 12th Street, was again taken to Bellevue, and wrote to Howard Moss, at *The New Yorker*, "If I sound a little hectic, I am: last week I was almost killed a second time, at Bellevue, just like four years ago. But it's impossible to exaggerate, so I will be silent." But how could he be silent when, while visiting Phillips, he kept pointing at the sky and screaming that "little children" were plotting to kill him?

For a few years in the early sixties, Delmore taught at Syracuse University, surviving only though his cunning and the faculty's compassion, but he left abruptly in January 1966 and moved into a shabby hotel near Times Square. He informed no one of his whereabouts. "You don't recognize me," he told Matthew Josephson outside the White Horse on one of his few forays downtown, "because the whole shape of my head has changed."

On the evening of July 10, 1966, Delmore left his room at the Hotel Columbia three or four times to wander listlessly through Times Square. At 3:00 A.M., a Mrs. Kruger in room 506 called the desk to complain that "Mr. Schwartz was dropping and throwing things again." After promising to quiet down, Delmore took out his garbage, but then got off the elevator on the fourth floor instead of the sixth. At 3:30 A.M. the desk received another call. A Mr. Klineman in 406 complained that a man was "making strange noises outside his door." When the police arrived at 4:15, they found Delmore unconscious, his lip bloodied from a fall, his shirt and pants ripped open in his frantic attempts to breathe. This was not a conspiracy, this was a heart attack, and a few minutes later Delmore Schwartz died in the streets of New York, in a shrieking ambulance.

His body lay unclaimed in the Bellevue morgue for three days; all the friends from whom he had cut himself off learned of his death by reading his obituary nearly thirty-one years to the day after he had written "In Dreams Begin Responsibilities." Among the newspapers, manuscripts, girlie magazines, and empty bottles in his lonely room lay a last notebook in which he had scrawled,

> *The poisonous world flows into my mouth*
> *Like water into a drowning man's.*

XV

Dawn Powell

The Village as an Idea of Itself

Dawn Powell, wrote Diana Trilling in 1942, "is our best answer to the familiar question, 'Who really says the funny things for which Dorothy Parker gets credit?' " For over four decades, Villagers were fond of quoting Dawn's witticisms, all the more scathing for being expressed offhandedly. "He seems to have let his toupee go to his head," she once said of a pompous acquaintance at a Village party. Characterizing one young woman-about-town, she wrote, "With her increasingly extravagant tastes she really could not afford to work." Another was "proud as punch" of her virginity, "you would have thought it was something that had been in the family for generations." And about going on the wagon—a temptation Dawn did her best to resist—"I like the way everything looks so crazy when you aren't drinking." Puckish, spontaneous, Dawn never had to rely on *l'esprit d'escalier*. My motto, she said, is *allez-oop!*

In her duplex apartment at 35 East 9th Street, just off University Place—where for many years she carried on a casual ménage à trois with her husband and her lover, and where she filled an aquarium with gin the afternoon before her famous parties—Dawn regularly hosted gatherings of her friends: Edmund Wilson, Djuna Barnes, Van Wyck Brooks, Malcolm

Cowley, John Dos Passos, Matthew Josephson, Gore Vidal, J. B. Priestley, and even, on occasion, Ernest Hemingway. Wilson's diaries of the period are littered with references to yet another "knock down and drag out party at Dawn's."

But far more frequently—nearly every night, in fact—Dawn presided over an informal salon at various hangouts, especially at the Lafayette Hotel café, directly across the street from her apartment. I can look down, she told Mattie Josephson, and see my checks bouncing. A three-story Federal building owned by a French family, the Lafayette—one of the more elegant of the Village meeting places until it was torn down in 1950 to make way for a high-rise apartment house—featured tall windows, mirrored walls, marble-topped tables, and magazine racks filled with French periodicals. But the two features Dawn most appreciated were the coffee cups in which the management discreetly served wine to regulars during Prohibition and a telephone girl who could always be counted on to call her away whenever the company proved dull. Dawn rarely had to avail herself of this latter service, however, for with the regulars at her corner table including John Cheever, A. J. Liebling, Joseph Mitchell, Stuart Davis, and Reginald Marsh, the conversation rarely foundered.

Dawn's novels were full of clever language—caustic characterizations, tart epigrams, sly asides—but her wit was always accompanied by artistry, her satire by compassion. Dawn made no secret of her loathing for Diana Trilling's much quoted remark about Dorothy Parker. For one thing, as her biographer Tim Page has pointed out, nowhere was it written that there could be only one witty woman in New York, but more important, too much stress on her wit reduced her carefully crafted comedies of manners to glib collections of one-liners. "True wit should break a wise man's heart," Dawn once wrote. "It should rest on a pillar of truth and not on a gelatine base, and the truth is not so shameful it cannot be recorded."

If this was Dawn's public credo as a novelist, in private she revealed the personal cost. "Wits are never happy people," she wrote in her diary in 1939. "Their anguish has scraped their nerves and left them raw to every flicker of life."

During World War II and the Eisenhower era, the American imagination turned increasingly toward a romanticized past, especially in the pacifying melodramas of popular fiction and the technocratic fantasies of film; it was only natural that a country with a weak sense of tradition should have a strong sense of nostalgia. And Villagers, too, romanticized their reminiscences. If the Villagers of the teens saw themselves as anticipating social and cultural and political transformation, those of the forties and fifties luxuriated in almost placid disaffection, the hope of transformation turned into a desire to be left alone.

Nostalgia can be insidious, particularly in a culture dominated by the media, for it's all too easy not merely to cherish the past but to imitate it. Too many Villagers, especially in the forties and fifties, reenacted Village rituals as if they were a substitute for faith. Village bars and cafés imitated the hangouts of lore. In their logos, in their tone, downtown publications exploited the suggestion of past glories. Real estate entrepreneurs capitalized on the quaint charms of the teens and twenties. And Villagers themselves lived out their gay adventures according to an idea of *la vie bohème* that hadn't existed for decades.

In this atmosphere of secondhand dreams, Dawn became "the bard of Greenwich Village," caricaturing a galaxy of Village "types" (the young man from the provinces, the dissipated painter, the neophyte actress, the artsy hanger-on with no talent except for flattery and jargon), memorializing the hangouts (the seedy bar, the salon-of-the-moment), and documenting the changes in Village customs and mores over the decades (its attitudes toward worldly success, artistic goals, and sexual behavior, in particular, with little concern for political commitments).

But most important, though rarely overtly, Dawn's Village novels dealt with the *idea* of the Village, with the ways in which its inhabitants imbued their community with a magic that in turn imbued *them* with a sense of uniqueness no less flattering because unearned. The aura of a mythic past hovers over her pages—a mythic past that has resulted in a self-conscious present—making her novels what one critic has called "a wicked ethnology." Only a writer who knew the Village intimately and yet regarded it with detachment could simultaneously celebrate and satirize its people and places and values —and only Dawn, who lived in the Village all her adult life yet observed it from the perspective of her Ohio childhood, so acutely possessed this double vision. She found herself at the center of its social life and felt herself a visiting alien—giving her novels both the detailed knowledge of the insider and the discernment of the outsider.

We were on a farm with a new stepmother who didn't know what to do with us," Dawn recalled of her childhood, "so she put us outdoors and locked all the doors." She'd been born in Mount Gilead, Ohio, in 1897. Her mother had died when she was six, and her father, a traveling salesman, had married a woman who couldn't cope with his three daughters while he was on the road. Dawn tolerated the locked doors, but when her stepmother burned all the stories she'd been writing—"a form of discipline that the ego could not endure," even at the age of twelve—she carefully counted out the thirty pennies she'd saved by berry-picking and ran away to her maternal aunt's in nearby Shelby. Her aunt lived directly across the street from the train station, and the mournful whistle of the departing trains entered her nightly dreams. Cleveland! If only she could go to Cleveland! And why not New York!

Dawn couldn't afford to go to college, so she wrote the president of Lake Erie College for Women lobbying for a scholarship. "I will do anything to work my way through," she said, assuring her success by adding, "anything from washing down the back stairs to understudying your job." At Lake Erie she worked in a print shop, put out an alternative newspaper called *The Sheet*, acted Puck in a production of A *Midsummer Night's Dream*, and wrote a paper for her ethics class entitled, "The Inhibiting Effects of the Family upon the Individual"—her destiny was clear. Dawn knew what most Villagers had dreamed of in adolescence, for it had been her dream, too. "Most of my childhood," she wrote years later, "was spent waiting for New York."

When Dawn arrived in New York in 1918, she immediately joined the U.S. Naval Reserve as a yeoman, but the war ended only ten days later so she moved to a cheap rooming house and began writing. A tiny, black-haired woman, with a round face and snub nose, she was far from a classic beauty, but her lively eyes and droll wit attracted a number of boyfriends. In 1920, Dawn met Joseph Gousha, an advertising executive in his early thirties. On one of their first dates, as she was playing ragtime on her roommate's piano, he noticed a copy of Schopenhauer's *Essay on Pessimism*. Dawn hastily denied the book was hers—as if in a scene from one of her novels, she was convinced not even a Village man would be interested in an intelligent woman—but Joseph found her name on the flyleaf, her lie was exposed, and he fell in love. Brought together by ragtime and Schopenhauer—a quintessential Village romance!—they were married a few months later.

In August 1921, she gave birth to Joseph Junior, but the baby suffered from a combination of cerebral palsy and schizophrenia, exacerbated by a difficult childbirth. Institutionalized most of his life, Joseph Junior was a financial burden and great emotional strain. Jojo, as Dawn called him, "is really very intelligent," she told Mattie Josephson, "and just *different* from other people." But the lifelong affliction of the person she most loved forever shadowed her joie de vivre.

Most of their friends agreed that Dawn and Joseph would have divorced but for the bond of Jojo. Dawn, in fact, began an affair in the early thirties with a dapper bachelor named Coburn Gilman, and found the perfect Village solution to her dilemma—a ménage à trois. Coby, as everyone called him, worked in the tweedy reaches of publishing, but lost his job during the Depression, and at the end of the decade moved into Dawn and Joseph's 9th Street duplex—Joseph using the upper floor, with its separate entrance.

Joseph and Coby frequently met, of course, but greeted each other with dignified formality, "just like two old clubmates," said one of Dawn's friends. Both men were heavy drinkers, but while Joseph sank into alcoholism, Coby carried himself with patrician elegance despite his seedy, secondhand clothes. As one of her characters said in an early novel, "A woman needed two lovers, one to comfort her for the torment the other caused her."

Dawn began her career by writing articles for several New York newspapers, and tried her hand at plays as well, one produced by the Group Theater in 1933 (a satire on business in which a salesman tries to clinch a deal by forcing his wife to respond to the advances of an out-of-town buyer), another by the Theater Guild in 1934 (a facile Broadway comedy starring Spring Byington and Ernest Truex in which a divorcee tries to seduce her daughter's fiancée).

But Dawn's metier was fiction, and over four decades she published fifteen novels, roughly divided into two categories—her Ohio novels, in which her characters dream of escaping to the big city, and her New York novels, in which her characters often recall their Midwestern backgrounds. Dawn's unstable childhood—frequently finding herself a newcomer in strange surroundings—meant that she constantly had to prove herself anew, and in order to survive she became preternaturally observant and articulate, detached and skeptical. The dialectic between these qualities informed her Ohio novels, for she depicted the pieties of small-town life with a precise realism and dissected its hypocrisies with sly irony.

One of the most common themes in Dawn's fiction—and one of the most common experiences of those who lived in the Village—was the desire of the sensitive, imaginative young man or woman to escape the stifling constrictions of small-town America, but this escape was often achieved not so much by moving as by writing about moving. Liberation from the past can sometimes come with a change of address, but exorcism of the past more often comes by transforming it into fiction.

Most revolt-against-the-small-town novels—so many of which were written in the Village in the twenties—end when the protagonist discovers a new and more creative life in the big city. But Dawn's Ohio novels frequently end with the protagonist on the *verge* of leaving the small town, but not making the move—as if some unarticulated ambiguity holds her back until she realizes she doesn't have to leave her cherished memories, that in escaping the taboo against being herself, she is at last free to write about her new life as well.

Her New York novels often begin with the main character arriving from Ohio—if not in their literal narrative, in their emotional resonance—and in making this leap she liberated her sensibility and her fiction flourished. Her novels for the next three decades frequently had the same pattern—a Candide figure from a small town, earnest and naive, arrives in the big city, where he (or sometimes she) is soon voluble with awe. Bookstores and theaters and concerts and galleries, sophisticated parties, fabulous people—it's even more than they imagined. "This—this was Life. This was Beauty." Their romantic daydreams have come true.

The ingenue's indiscriminate wonder and awe are soon put to the test, for the enchanted city turns out to be not so much the realm of glamour, nobility, and creativity as the realm of vanity, chicanery, and pretension. The disparity between the fantasy and the reality—which affects not just the ingenue but the "fabulous people," for they are often dupes of their own illusions—is the gap in which Dawn's satire operates, as charged as a flash of electricity between two poles. By the end of the novel, most of the characters suffer from a kind of moral hangover—but, enlightened by experience, the ingenue retains enough of the decency and optimism that are the residue of her Ohio background to give the novel an upbeat ending. However, the ingenue is invariably the least convincing character in the novel.

The *most* convincing character is the city itself, for Dawn reveals how its moods and its rhythms insidiously invade the psyche, color perception, motivate behavior. The Village—a kind of contemporary Vanity Fair—can be gay, openhearted, overflowing with opportunities, but it can also be dissipated, thoughtless, destructive of dreams.

Twisting streets and tree-shaded sidewalks; quaint old Federal houses and sterile high-rise apartment buildings; the Washington Square

Book Shop; the dozens of bistros and saloons where your reputation was only as big as your tab; New York University, the New School, the Little Red School House, Cooper Union; the spire of the Jefferson Market Courthouse; "Washington Square Arch at the foot of Fifth Avenue like a gate to freedom"—Dawn's novels remain the best record of the Village landscape of the thirties, forties, and fifties.

The New York novels require a subdivision, for they fall into two groups—uptown and downtown. *Turn, Magic Wheel* (1936), an example of the uptown group, reveals Dawn at her most psychologically probing—she herself called it "very likely my best, simplest, most original book." Dawn offers a particularly devastating parody of an Ernest Hemingway figure (he forgave her) and a ruthlessly serene dismissal of the Marxists (they didn't)—but her focus is on a writer named Dennis Orphen, a recurring character in her novels, loosely based on herself, his surname both recalling her family background and suggesting her view of the writer's role in society.

Dennis is involved in a romantic triangle—a situation Dawn almost compulsively brought from her life into her fiction—but he's even more tormented by the moral ambiguities of his calling. He's written a novel about one of the women with whom he's involved that's caused her pain, and he agonizes over the relationship between pure imagination and literal re-creation. Doesn't the woman he's "fictionalized" have "a frailty to be protected rather than shrewdly analyzed"? "How clever I was, how damnably clever, Dennis thought, furious with his own demon that now made him see so savagely into people's bones and guts that he could not give up his nice analysis even if it broke a heart, he could not see less or say less." *Turn, Magic Wheel* has intimations of Dawn's sardonic wit, especially her deadpan use of paradox—"having said so many nasty things about Dennis her heart was filling with love for him"—but it has an elegiac tone, a sense of despair, and a moral anguish that were rarely to reappear in her fiction.

Dawn may have purged herself of the temptation to write too intimately about her personal life, but public figures remained fair game. In *A Time to Be Born* (1942), her novel about high-stakes, low-ethics journalism, her unmistakable targets—though she futilely denied it—are Henry and Clare Boothe Luce. The media mogul has nothing in his mind but jingoistic platitudes and circulation figures, while his cat-eat-cat writer wife has nothing in hers whatsoever, for she signs her name to whatever her "assistants" have written. Dawn had finally found the voice that would characterize her fiction for the rest of her life—it was in a review of *A Time to Be Born* that Diana Trilling made her remark about Dawn and Dorothy Parker.

*T*he Wicked Pavilion and *The Golden Spur* can justly be called the most accurate, the most penetrating, the most outrageously comic of all the hundreds of novels written about the Village.

The terrain of *The Wicked Pavilion* (1954) is the art world of the early fifties, the social whirl at the Café Julien in particular, where painters, patrons, critics, and gallery owners begin or end affairs, complain about prices, or even discuss aesthetics—though that's the fastest way to empty the room. Tourists in search of "the real Village" gaze at them in awe, though the café is described in a guidebook as providing "a typically French evening in New York."

Among the characters whose lives intersect in this setting of musty elegance—which, it must be acknowledged, bears scant resemblance to the world of the abstract expressionists who were revolutionizing American art during this exact period—are the Dawn surrogate Dennis Orphen, a wealthy collector named Cynthia (a Peggy Guggenheim figure), and a snooping journalist ("Briggs had hoped for assignments in the field of sports but the editor felt that literary training and education were required for that, whereas art was a department where inexperience and ignorance would not be noticed"). But the narrative focuses on the *ingénu* Rick's efforts to win his girl and the careers of the painters Dalzell, Ben, and Marius.

The danger, adventure in the city turn out to be a young woman named Ellenora, for, like so many young men, Rick's urban planning is actually a guise for his erotic longing. Dawn, now in her fifties, and a woman in a long-standing ménage à trois, pokes the gentlest of fun at the way Rick and Ellenora "skipped gracefully around the edge of love." Like all young women of the time, Ellenora intended to stalwartly resist Rick's advances, "but she was desperately eager for the opportunity to show her strength."

When it comes to the other habitués of the Café Julien—the painters and the leeches who cluster around them—gentle fun gives way to lethal mockery. Marius has recently died, the prices for his paintings have skyrocketed, and Dalzell and Ben, his oldest friends, begin to turn out fake Mariuses instantly hailed as masterpieces. "The greatest favor Marius, the man, had ever done for Marius, the artist, was to die at exactly the right moment." Dalzell and Ben begin to suspect another kind of sham, however, and eventually track down Marius, who's only pretended to die in order to paint in peace and escape the creditors and sycophants, ex-wives, critics, and gallery owners who'd turned the city of *his* dreams into one of the circles of hell. And in a supremely satirical touch, Marius decides the best place he can hide from the Villagers—the one place no one will ever track him down—is Staten Island.

The Wicked Pavilion ends with a kind of rueful vaudeville. The Café Julien—like Dawn's beloved Lafayette Hotel, on which it's modeled—is to be torn down to make way for yet another towering defacement of the Village. As Dennis Orphen writes in the novel's final words, "The Café Julien was gone and a reign was over. Those who had been bound by it fell apart like straws when the baling cord is cut and remembered each other's name and face as part of a dream that would never come back."

In *The Golden Spur* (1962), Dawn once more describes the rapture of the first vision of the Village. Jonathan's mission isn't to discover "the city of his dreams," but to find his father, for he has learned his real father is a man with whom his mother had an otherwise inconsequential affair during her brief but carefree stay in the Village in the late twenties. Her diaries lovingly recall the charms of her Horatio Street apartment, of the Brevoort Hotel, of the Washington Square Book Shop, of Romany Marie's—but he can find none of them in the directory.

The focal point of *The Golden Spur* is its eponymous bar—a kind of cross between the Cedar Tavern and the San Remo—one of the few places remaining from the Golden Age of the Village, somewhat seedier than the Café Julien but just as central in the lives of its clientele. "The Golden Spur, they explained, was the cultural and social hub of New York City, which was bounded on the south by the San Remo, on the east by Vasyk's Avenue A bar, on the west by the White Horse, and on the north by Pete's Tavern." "Before you look for a job or a home or a girl," one of the regulars instructs the newcomer, "you must establish your bar base. . . . Look them all over carefully. . . . Compare their advantages and disadvantages. Is this a tourist trap, a 'Left Coast' hangout, or is it on the Bird Circuit, a meeting place for queers? Once you've made your choice, you conduct your social and business life there, since your home, mate, and job are bound to switch constantly."

Jonathan "thought wistfully of the pack of gallery-flies prowling through the night, battering on doors to be let in, brawling and bruising down to the The Golden Spur, and he thought those were real backers of art, those were the providers, the blood-donors, and [the] salon of critics, guides, and millionaires were the free-loaders, free-loading on other people's genius, other people's broken hearts, and, when it came to that, other people's money."

And what Villager could fail to recognize the summer bachelors hoping they'd at last meet one of those fabled nymphomaniacs or the adult education students dropping by for a pick-me-up after classes in Nietzsche and pasta, or the Jersey commuters who were "likely to shout 'Yippee!' when they went to a Village spot"? Jonathan encounters all these characters—plus, more crucially, a duo of painters' girlfriends who make him feel like a diaphragm tester, another young woman who's leading a double life as a dutiful suburban daughter / aspiring Village actress, and an irascible painter whose abundance of talent is matched only by his absence of charm.

But Jonathan remains obsessed with finding his father, and finally narrows his quest to three candidates—a tipsy professor, a stuffed-shirt lawyer, and a dismally depressed best-selling novelist, each of whom rather takes to the idea of finding a long-lost son who might redeem his disappointed life. On one level the novel is a parody of the "search for identity" theme so popular in the fifties, on another it's a depiction of the ways in which a rediscovered past at first vitalizes but ultimately disrupts the lives of middle-aging Villagers.

The mid-fifties Village of *The Golden Spur* is a place in decline, but if Dawn's previous novels treated the follies of the Villagers with a mixture of venom and compassion, her final novel has a tone of almost rueful amusement. Now in her sixties, she is in an elegiac mood. As one of the writers muses in a momentary spasm of joy, "All that he remembered as they passed the lane of lights on Fourteenth Street was the feeling of excitement, promise, and youth, a wonderful feeling that he had never expected to recapture"—but that feeling, like the Café Julien, also passes away.

In a world of destruction," Dawn wrote at the end of *The Locusts Have No King*, "one must hold fast to whatever fragments of love are left, for sometimes a mosaic can be more beautiful than an unbroken pattern." "My novels," she once said, "are based on the fantastic designs made by real human beings earnestly laboring to maladjust themselves to fate. . . . My characters are not slaves to an author's propaganda. I give them their heads. They furnish their own nooses." Her theme, wrote her friend Edmund Wilson, was "the provincial in New York who has . . . made himself a permanent place there, without ever, however, losing his fascinated sense of an alien and anarchic society."

"Hard iron." Dawn had that in her character, especially as a writer who had to support herself, her curious ménage, and her disabled son. This was the woman, after all, who wrote in *Turn, Magic Wheel*, "She had learned long ago that there was no one on earth who could afford to weep, no occasion worthy of it. . . ."

In an age when the word "feminism" had left the Village vocabulary, she also knew a bit about the difficulties faced by working women. As one of her female characters says, she often feels she has to make a choice between being "a woman and therefore less of an achieving individual or an achieving individual and therefore less of a woman."

Emotionally vulnerable, psychologically haunted, she was always clear-eyed, worldly-wise. Like Hart Crane, her Ohio contemporary—an otherwise bizarrely anomalous comparison—this complex woman had a kind of joyous fortitude. But while Hart came to loathe the Village, Dawn never lost her love, and in 1932, soon after Hart committed suicide, she wrote her cousin, "New York, it's the only place where people with nothing behind them but their wits can be and do everything."

In the last seven years of her life, after her eviction from 35 East 9th and the painful, lingering death of her husband, she had to move several times, finally settling at 95 Christopher Street. Outside her windows she could witness "the riveters and wreckers pulling down my beloved city around my ears." Still she kept her relentless cheer. "The fact that it is getting more and more bedlamish, dirtier, more dangerous, and more impossible," she wrote, "seems to heighten my foolish infatuation."

In 1965, as thousands of young men and women flooded into the Village, none of them knew of the elderly woman who lay dying of cancer in St. Luke's Hospital and who'd once been young like them and just as full of dreams.

XVI

Jackson Pollock and the Abstract Expressionists in the Village

Rearranging the Stars

The night after Jackson Pollock's death in August 1956, the Cedar Tavern was packed. Dozens of his fellow painters had gathered in their favorite watering hole, stunned and grief-stricken. Remember that night Bill de Kooning socked him in the jaw and Jackson just stood there for several seconds, wondering whether to sock him back, and finally turned away and said, "What? Me? Hit an artist?" Yeah, but Jackson hit plenty of them in his time—those fights he'd get into with Franz Kline, throwing him off the bar stool, the two of them wrestling on the floor? Or the time Jackson, drunk to his eyeballs, sat down in a booth beside a woman he'd never seen before and slurred, "Wanna fuck?" Or the time he stood outside after he'd been temporarily banned from the bar, peering through the window, silently begging to be let in. "The reason I miss him," said Franz Kline, tears running down his cheeks, "the reason I'll miss him is he'll never come through that door again."

The New York painters of the forties and fifties—Willem de Kooning, Franz Kline, Hans Hofmann, Arshile Gorky, Mark Rothko, Barnett Newman, a dozen others—were part of the most famous generation of artists in American history. They virtually reinvented painting and moved the center of the art world from Paris to New York. Whether they were called the 8th Street School, the 10th Street School, the Action painters, or the abstract expressionists, they created a new image of the painter in the American imagination: ruggedly handsome men in spattered blue jeans, back-slapping drinkers, crude womanizers, impetuous brawlers. They were driven by existential anxieties, tormented by psychic demons. Confronting the cataclysms of the Holocaust and nuclear Armageddon, they dedicated themselves to painting as an act of redemption, as a sacred calling.

This image of the New York painter as an unstable mixture of the romantic and the apocalyptic resulted from a combination of self-dramatization and media myth. The legend stressed their personalities more than their painting, but its hyperbole about their lives was innocuous compared to its simplification of their work. The popular image of a unified abstract expressionist movement distorted its historical role. For one thing, though the artists shared a few guiding principles—rejection of traditional "content," or emphasis on the flatness of the canvas, or reliance on unconscious impulses—they pursued them with such an idiosyncratic obsessiveness that each developed a signature style. And though as a group they were regarded as exponents of a uniquely American approach to painting who made a radical break from all the painters who'd preceded them, they had crucial links to the past and none of them was uninfluenced by the masters of European modernism. And finally, though all of the leading abstract expressionists eventually received critical acclaim and huge commercial success, the latter was unanimously disdained, and in many cases, destructive to their personalities, their lives, their painting itself.

Jackson Pollock was not necessarily the most representative of the abstract expressionists, but he was certainly the most mythic. Widely regarded as an inarticulate primitive, he became the icon of the abstract expressionist painter pouring his unconscious impulses onto his canvases. Acclaimed for his drip technique—and widely mocked for it, as "Jack the Dripper"—he became the most famous painter of his generation.

Born in 1912 on a sheep ranch in Cody, Wyoming, Jackson was named after nearby Jackson Hole, and though the family almost immediately moved to San Diego, he always relished his image as the "cowboy painter," striding up Fifth Avenue in his boots. A rebel in high school, Jackson briefly attended communist meetings, but was more deeply influenced by the teachings of Krishnamurti. Taken to several of the "new messiah's" rallies by his art teacher, Jackson absorbed the message that alienation from society was a virtue and the insistence that intuition take precedence over intellect. Anti-intellectual by temperament, Jackson may have been regarded as a noble savage from the Wild West—an image he encouraged—but even by his teens, he had developed a sophisticated understanding of Eastern mysticism.

In the fall of 1930, encouraged by two of his older brothers who were painters, Jackson moved to the Village. "If you want to be an artist," one of them told him, "there is only one place to be, and that's where it's all happening. That's New York." He took a room a few blocks from Union Square and enrolled in a free sculpture class at Greenwich House, a Village institution on Barrow Street that provided activities for young artists. But he was only marking time until the fall term of the Art Students League on West 57th Street, where he began several years of study with the well-known painter Thomas Hart Benton. Jackson's father had abandoned his family when Jackson was only nine, and Benton almost immediately became a father figure to his teenage student—even a kind of model for his aspirations, combining his father's virile swaggering and his mother's artistic sensibility. But if Benton was a man to emulate, he was a painter to resist, for after briefly experimenting with modernism he had turned to a muscular but sentimental regionalism—and as Jackson said years later, "My work with Benton was important as something against which to react very strongly."

Even as a teenager, recalled his classmate, *New Yorker* cartoonist Whitney Darrow Jr., Jackson painted "with frenzy, concentration, wild direct energy . . . never polished or graceful." Like Benton, he insisted on touching the life-study models to get the right feel of their bodies, a habit that kept many women from working in Benton's classes. Despite their artistic differences, Jackson remained Benton's favorite student and virtually became a member of his family on Hudson Street—rumors even circulated that he was sleeping with Benton's wife. Never one to discourage legends, particularly about his manhood, Jackson declared flatly, "I used to fuck her," but there had only been a few awkward advances, lightheartedly rebuffed.

Too unstable to live by himself, Jackson shared small, cheap, unheated apartments with one or the other of his brothers, first at 47 Horatio Street, then at 46 Carmine Street, and on the top floor of a five-story building at 76 West Houston Street, until, in 1935, he and his brother Charles moved into a large floor-through at 46 East 8th Street, almost directly across the street from the building in which Thomas Wolfe had written *Look Homeward, Angel* a few years earlier. He worked sporadically as a cafeteria busboy, as a janitor at Greenwich House and at the City and Country School on West 13th Street. He also found occasional work as a "stonecutter" through a federal relief program for artists, "stonecutter" serving as a euphemism for statue cleaner—first the statue of Peter Cooper on Cooper Square, then the equestrian monument of George Washington on Union Square. "A big crowd gathered around the statue," recalled a friend, "and there were Jackson [and his brother] hamming it up, scrubbing the horse, making a big point of scrubbing the rear end and the underparts. Everybody was howling."

When flat broke, he subsisted on 5-cent meals or day-old bread for a penny, or on the outer leaves of heads of lettuce that kindly clerks slipped him—even rolls and apples he'd steal off the grocery shelves.

In the two decades after the Armory Show in 1913, the American realist tradition of Thomas Eakins and George Bellows gave way to the influence of the Parisian modernists, the cubists in particular, until in the early thirties, in a kind of counterrevolution led by Benton, many American painters turned to regionalism and social realism. But Jackson wasn't interested in subjects outside himself. He experimented with many modes moving toward symbols, myths, archetypes. Many of the emerging American modernists who shared his resistance to realism faced a seemingly insoluble dilemma—their socially conscious political convictions clashed with their elitist painting styles, so that they thought like proletarians, but pursued their art like aristocrats. This paradox never disturbed Jackson, who had only the most hazy political ideas and whose artistic ideas were largely intuitive. No credo, no ideology motivated his work—from the beginning, he sought a style that would allow all his feelings to bypass his consciousness and appear spontaneously on the canvas.

Jackson first exhibited his work in public in April 1932 at the second annual Washington Square Outdoor Art Show on the sidewalk in Macdougal Alley. Then, as now, the show featured tourist kitsch—gaudy watercolors, adorable renderings of kittens, portraits of sad-eyed clowns, that kind of thing. Not surprisingly, Jackson's paintings, priced at $5 and $10, went unsold. His sales throughout the thirties, in fact, were almost nonexistent, though he did manage to trade a painting entitled *Cody, Wyoming* for a suit of clothes.

On August 1, 1935, came the announcement that the federal government had established an Art Project that would pay painters over $20 a week simply to paint! "People dashed through the streets of the Village," according to one account, "clutching paintings under their arms, spreading the news from door to door." Jackson signed up that very day, and the following week received his first check as a painter—$23.86. Mark Rothko worked for "the project," Adolf Gottlieb and Ad Reinhardt took part in its easel-painting program; Arshile Gorky and Philip Guston were put to work as muralists; Willem de Kooning quit his job designing window displays for shoe stores to join in—"I decided that if I worked at a job I was poor," he explained, "but if I painted, I just didn't have any money."

In a sense, "the project" gave birth to the artistic movement that a decade later would revolutionize Western painting. All across the Village, painters used their government stipends to transform abandoned lofts, installing wiring, plumbing, and heating to create spacious working studios. More important, they began to regard themselves as a community, the government's relief program drawing them together the way the Left Bank cafés drew together the painters of Paris. "A fraternity of painters," Jackson's brother Charles called gatherings at places like the Waldorf Cafeteria and Chumley's bar. As in many fraternities, this sudden sense of affiliation encouraged the macho swaggering, heavy drinking, and competitiveness that would damage so many of the Village's prominent painters. But it also gave them a sense of common purpose, of almost arrogant confidence that they were on to something new, subversive, revolutionary.

During the mid-thirties, these vanguard painters sarcastically labeled social realism and regionalism "paint proletarian" and "paint American." Rejecting both approaches, they formed no school of their own, but abstraction was increasingly in the air. As Adolph Gottlieb put it, with the audacity that characterized their attitude, "I was looking for subjective images stemming from the unconscious because the external world . . . had been totally explored in painting." Some of the painters who would soon lead the abstract expressionist movement were slow to adopt the new style. Barnett Newman painted figurative works in the thirties, all of which he destroyed. Philip Guston painted socially conscious murals, most of which left him dissatisfied. Franz Kline remained a figurative painter for years, as did Mark Rothko, though with hints of an evolving expressionism. Willem de Kooning alternated between classical figure studies and the "all-over" intensity of abstraction, flattening and fragmenting his figures. Clyfford Still, who began with landscapes of the American West, turned to a distorted, nonfigurative style. Hans Hofmann moved closer to abstraction with every year, and Arshile Gorky—accounting for his maître status with most of the avant-garde community—was a full-fledged abstractionist from the first, fusing cubism and surrealism.

Nonobjective art, open-formed and dynamic, became their credo. Some saw painting as a form of autobiography; others regarded their work as supra-personal. But all began to repudiate mere representation and what they regarded as the banality of propaganda and the sterility of formalism. Distrusting Marxism and Freudianism—ideologies fellow Villagers embraced—they sought a style that would express the personal, idiosyncratic experience of the individual. They found visual traditions and a new vocabulary in several significant shows at the recently opened Museum of Modern Art. By the beginning of the forties they weren't a band of untutored primitives, but the most knowledgeable group of painters in the world. As a leading critic wrote, "By 1940, 8th Street had caught up with Paris as Paris had not yet caught up with herself, and a group of relatively obscure American artists already possessed the fullest painting culture of their time."

The 1939 arrival of Picasso's *Guernica* at the Museum of Modern Art had an enormous impact on Jackson, but he was even more affected by the legendary Mexican painter David Alfaro Siqueiros, who arrived in New York in 1936 under the sponsorship of George Gershwin, and began a series of workshops. Siqueiros was a political rebel, "the naughty boy of Mexico art," but what fascinated Jackson was his aesthetic rebellion—his insistence on new materials (including industrial paint), on new methods (including pouring rivulets of paint directly onto the canvas), and on new attitudes toward art itself (especially working without reliance on preconceived plans or sketches). "As early as 1936," said one of Jackson's fellow students, "we had already announced the death of easel painting," and while Jackson remained indifferent to such large pronouncements, after his studies in Siqueiros's loft he increasingly relied on spontaneity, learned to value "accidents," and, as early as the mid-thirties, experimented with dripping paint onto a canvas laid on the floor.

But if Jackson became a kind of enfant terrible, it was less because of his audacious thinking about painting than because of his belligerent temperament, his frequent alcoholic binges in particular. Beer-soaked brawls had become a ritual in his crowd, but no one approached him in his consumption of booze—and no one was a meaner drunk. "Out of the mildest and most recessive person I knew," recalled a friend, "emerged a fire-breathing dragon." His fellow painters didn't exactly forgive his bellicose behavior—particularly when he tried to choke them or when he tore their paintings from the walls of their galleries—but they felt they understood its source, and on some level were in awe of its courageousness. After all, in this community, scandalous conduct, anguish, and despair were among the surest signs of genius.

On one occasion, Jackson destroyed one of his brother's paintings with an ax. On another, he challenged oncoming traffic to "run me down." He tore up a Village nightclub, assaulted a policeman, and spent the night in the Jefferson Market jail. He slammed his fist through plate glass windows, brutalized women at parties, then fell comatose into the gutter. Was it the frustration, the tension, the anxiety caused by his search for a radical new means of expression in his paintings—especially since he was so inarticulate in every other way? Was it insecurity, self-doubt, self-loathing? Was it tormented confusion over his sexual identity? Was it a longing for self-obliteration? Whatever the cause, in 1938 he went on a four-day bender, stumbling into every bar on the Bowery for a shot of rotgut, his clothes covered with vomit, his body covered with excrement. Finally he was picked up and sent to Bellevue, and, a few weeks later, committed to a mental hospital in White Plains.

Jackson dried out and underwent therapy, but two years later he went on still another monumental bender, this time shredding dozens of his paintings with a kitchen knife and tossing the remnants out the window onto 8th Street. More episodes followed—most directed at his rivals. He assaulted Arshile Gorky, raving that his paintings were "nothing but shit." He stood sodden and enraged outside a building at 25 Vandam Street that was managed by another rival and hurled stones until he'd shattered all the windows. Village bartenders had to break up his fistfights or ban him from their establishments altogether.

When conscription came in 1941, his psychiatrist wrote his draft board that he had "difficulties over adaptation to the social environment," and that "there is a certain schizoid disposition underlying the instability." The army had no choice but to classify him 4-F, unfit for service.

Jackson may have felt moments of shame, but he continued to pour his manliness onto his canvases. And into his abusive treatment of women. Though Jackson had a boyish charm when sober, when drunk he turned obscene. At parties and bars, he'd simply go up to a woman, grab her breasts, and kiss her, or if particularly plastered, thrust his hand into her crotch and mutter "Wanna fuck?" When this approach was inevitably rebuffed, he'd call the woman a bitch, a whore. His method of seduction was so unlikely to succeed that many of his friends became convinced that unconsciously he didn't want it to. But it was such an important part of his image of himself as a legendary cocksman that he insisted it often worked, and even claimed to have had several conquests that in fact existed only in his imagination.

At an Artists Union party in the winter of 1936, Jackson cut in on a dancing couple, moved his body against the woman's in a crude parody of sexual intercourse, and hoarsely whispered, "Do you like to fuck?" The woman stepped back and slapped his face. Stunned, Jackson not only apologized, but was immediately on his best behavior—so charming the woman that they ended the evening in his apartment. A one-night stand, instantly forgotten. It was Lee Krasner, but Jackson didn't remember her name when he met her again five years later.

Through poverty, alcoholism, and breakdown, Jackson continued to seek ways to capture his turbulent inner life on canvas. Moving closer to Siqueiros and Picasso every year, he grew steadily more subjective, more direct, more vehement.

In the winter of 1941, when an uptown gallery planned a show of French masters and their American followers, Jackson sensed a breakthrough, but didn't suspect that it would change his life as well. Included in the show was a young painter named Lee Krasner, who, upon learning the names of the other artists, asked her friends, "Who the hell is Jackson Pollock?" She discovered that he lived right around the corner from her place on 9th Street, and to her great surprise, when he answered the door she recognized the lanky, prematurely balding man with whom she'd spent a night five years earlier—though neither of them referred to it. Lee later claimed she fell in love with Jackson on the spot—and with his paintings—but, like nearly everyone else, she had an impulse to mythologize him, and she certainly mythologized their relationship. In fact, though Lee was sexually uninhibited—"She never went anywhere without a diaphragm," recalled a friend—and had seduced many a painter, apparently failing only with Bill de Kooning, months passed before she and Jackson became lovers.

The man from Wyoming and the woman from Brooklyn, the handsome, sexually confused man, the unattractive but voluptuous woman, the man of silence and the woman who, friends said, never stopped talking, the man who scorned careerism and the woman who, enemies said, treated nearly everyone in the art world in terms of their power—it was a match of interlocking incompatibilities. At night, Lee worked for tips at a restaurant and nightclub on 3rd Street called Sam Johnson's, part-owned by the poet Eli Siegel. Of course she had larger ambitions, but either sensing Jackson was far more talented, or realizing that the misogyny of the art world was unconquerable, she quickly shifted her ambitions from her career to his.

Taking charge of their relationship, promoting his paintings because he couldn't be bothered, Lee courted prominent critics and collectors, and introduced Jackson to several young painters, including de Kooning. But she thought her greatest coup would be to arrange a meeting between Jackson and the legendary Hans Hofmann, the eminent émigré painter whose classes she was attending.

Like Lee, most Village painters felt that Hans "really brought the word." Born in Bavaria in 1880, and having studied in Paris from 1904 to 1914, he knew Picasso, Braque, and Matisse personally, and had come to America in 1931. In 1933 he established his school in a single large room over the 8th Street Playhouse at 38 West 8th Street. His vibrant paintings — with their lyrical colors, tactile energy, and what Elaine de Kooning called "violent immediacy," especially after he turned completely to abstraction in the forties — were prized by his colleagues, though he had to support himself as a teacher until 1958. He resisted a signature style in order to allow himself the maximum spiritual freedom — "If I ever find a style, I'll stop painting," he insisted, for "unconditioned, unrestricted creativeness" was his goal. He even painted in the nude in order to feel uninhibited. As a critic wrote of his later work, "It is so full of joyful good spirits that one becomes convinced he never suffered a bad day in his life."

But Hans's greatest legend was as a teacher. Despite his sometimes impenetrable accent — his students imitated his favorite phrase, "Nicht wahr?" with affectionate laughter — he cast a spell over his classes with his emphasis on a kind of "loosened up cubism," demonstrations of modernist technique, lectures on metaphysical values, and, most of all, enthusiastic critiques of his students' work. He helped them develop their own styles rather than "paint Hofmanns." The word he brought from Europe was to escape "the tyranny of reality," to integrate the natural world with an individual temperament, and to treat the inherent qualities of the medium — the flatness of the canvas, the passivity of paint — not as limitations but as spurs to creativity. Hans saw art as a spiritual quest, and scornfully rejected psychological subtexts or ideological preconceptions — his gospel was the purity of painting.

Hans encapsulated his method in a phrase, "Push-pull." The canvas was an area of tension. "Put a spot on the surface and let the surface answer back!"; "Activate the surface!" Every stroke set off competing "push-pull" forces and counterforces. "To create the phenomenon of *push and pull* on a flat surface, one has to understand that by nature the picture plane reacts automatically in the opposite direction to the stimulus received. . . . *Push* answers with *pull* and *pull* with *push*."

"Combining equal parts of temperamental artist, supportive teacher, and irrepressible showman," in the words of one account of the period, Hans wielded influence that was deep and far-ranging. But when Lee insisted that Jackson meet him, she failed to grasp that Jackson was too competitive and self-confident to idolize anyone—and certainly would think concepts like push-pull were nothing but "a load of crap."

Prevailing on Hans to visit Jackson's studio—for Jackson was too proud to observe decorum and visit the elder, more established painter in *his* studio—Lee led him up the five flights of stairs, whereupon Hans was "absolutely aghast" at the "incredible mess," so unlike his own impeccable work space. Cigarette butts and Martinson coffee cans, many of them filled with dried paint, littered the floor; dozens of canvases leaned haphazardly against the walls. According to a story Lee told over and over, Hans picked up a brush that was lying on a palette, and the palette came with it. "With this you could kill a man," he said. "That's the point," said Jackson.

Hans then asked him about painting from nature; Jackson, edgy about being questioned, bluntly offered a phrase that entered Village lore, "I am nature."

Always the teacher and intellectual, Hans launched into a long aesthetic discourse, until Jackson, frustrated by what he took to be pedantry, bristled, "Your theories don't interest me. Put up or shut up! Let's see your work!"

Hans was appalled, Lee felt humiliated, but Jackson? Jackson thought it was all bullshit.

Jackson's own work during the early forties didn't evolve in an orderly progression, but leapt forward in exhilarating spurts between periods of frustrating stasis. "I am particularly impressed with their concept of the source of art being the unconscious," he said in 1944. "I want to express my feelings rather than illustrate them." His quest was to turn art into ritual, depicting not images, but creativity itself. He eliminated specific references, and refused to rely on a focal point. He depended on spontaneity, slashing paint onto the canvas in dense, turbulent strokes, as if his only subject was his own energy. He still hadn't solved the problem of how to "order" a painting without "content," but standing over his canvas, a cigarette dangling from his lips, he worked in a kind of feverish trance. He accepted "accidents"—even drips on the canvas. And he kept a painting "open" for days and weeks at a time—waiting for the moment when the canvas and the vision he'd been seeking suddenly coincided. His goal?— "memories arrested in space."

Jackson's fellow painters recognized his emerging genius, but they were alone—the market for his work was virtually nonexistent. But they were embarked on a crusade, not a career. Jackson supported himself as a part-time "squeegee man," silk-screening arty patterns onto ties and scarves, as a designer of department store window displays, as a vocational trainee in aviation sheet metal, and as a custodian at the Museum of Non-Objective Painting on East 54th Street—a job he secured with the help of the painter Robert De Niro Sr., the actor's father. When all else failed, he resorted to shoplifting.

Jackson may not have had any hopes of selling his paintings, but he *did* want to show them, and in the spring of 1943, the eccentric and legendary art patron Peggy Guggenheim asked him to participate in an exhibition at her Art of This Century gallery at 30 West 57th Street. A singularly unattractive woman, she tried to make up for her lack of natural grace with a unique style. She wore vermilion lipstick, lizard-green eye shadow beneath shaved eyebrows, and enormous unmatched earrings—at one art opening she wore one by Yves Tanguy and the other by Alexander Calder, in order, she said, "to show my impartiality between surrealist and abstract art"—and brandished a nearly two-foot-long cigarette holder which more often than not held no cigarette. She wore cheap, usually torn, but carefully disarrayed dresses, a costume whose primary function, her friends suspected, was to reveal her lack of underwear. Nearly every word she uttered seemed intended to scandalize, and she made no secret of her obsession with sex, earning a reputation for promiscuity even in one of the few segments of society that professed indifference to sexual decorum. Among her hundreds of lovers was Samuel Beckett, and among her several husbands was Laurence Vail, the so-called King of Bohemia who'd briefly been Djuna Barnes's lover. Everyone called her a nymphomaniac, the word reserved for women who liked sex as much as men, and it was generally believed that if a painter agreed to accept her patronage, he must also sleep with her.

Peggy had inherited a small fortune when her father went down on the *Titanic,* and formed a salon in Paris in the twenties, where she hosted Ernest Hemingway, Ezra Pound, Djuna Barnes, André Gide, and Jean Cocteau. When she returned to New York in 1941 with her husband, Max Ernst, she decided it was time to ensnare American avant-garde artists, and Jackson was one of the first she approached. Initially unsure about the quality of his work, she asked her friend Piet Mondrian. "This young man has serious problems," she said as the two of them stood before a canvas, "and painting is one of them." Mondrian simply stared at the picture for several minutes. He finally mused, "I'm trying to understand what's happening

here. I think this is the most interesting work I've seen so far in America."
"You can't be serious," said Peggy. "You can't compare this and the way you
paint." "The way I paint and the way I think," replied Mondrian, "are two
different things."

"Mondrian's nod," as it became known in Jackson's legend, was
enough to gain him inclusion in Peggy's next show. But when her advisors
suggested she give Jackson a one-man show, she asked Marcel Duchamp
for *his* opinion. She didn't know that Jackson had already met him at her
gallery, where he had ripped a copy of one of Duchamp's posters to shreds,
handed the pieces to the artist, and angrily muttered, "You know where this
goes." When Duchamp laconically declared Jackson's work "pas mal,"
Peggy needed no further encouragement. Jackson instantly became her
newest "find," with a monthly stipend, a promise of a one-man show—his
first—and, most important, a commission to paint a mural for the entrance
hall of her apartment on the Upper East Side.

Though Jackson was freed from financial worries for the first time
in his life, months passed before he touched the nearly ten-by-twenty-foot
canvas he'd purchased for Peggy's mural. He'd stare at it for hours, then get
roaring drunk. Finally, the evening before his deadline, he picked up a
brush and began to paint. "I had a vision," he later recalled. "It was a stampede." A literal stampede—mustangs, bulls, buffalos, antelopes, "every animal in the American West" hurtled across the canvas. But as he worked
into the night, a single fifteen-hour session, images of the animals began
to combine, to dissolve, covered over by swirling lines and spatters of paint,
disappearing under a combustion of calligraphy until all the figurative
elements with which he'd started were obliterated. "Nothing remained
of the original stampede," reported one account, "except furious energy,
panoramic chaos, and primal alarm."

Exhausted and exhilarated, Jackson impatiently waited for the
paint to dry, rolled the canvas, and raced to Peggy's apartment. But after re-
assembling the stretcher and canvas, he discovered that the mural was almost a foot too long. Peggy had taken the precaution of hiding all her
liquor, but it didn't take him long to find it. Drunk, hysterical, he called her
at her gallery. She dispatched Duchamp, who immediately solved the
problem—he lopped off eight inches from one end of the painting. Jackson
was too soused to complain. He stumbled into the living room, where
guests had already gathered to celebrate the installation, unzipped his fly,
and urinated in Peggy's marble fireplace.

•   •   •

Many critics greeted Jackson's shows at Peggy's gallery in the early and mid-forties with baffled disparagement—but several wrote with a keen appreciation of what he was attempting.

While the critic for the *New York Sun* said that Jackson's work resembled "a kaleidoscope that has been insufficiently shaken," and one observer recalled Stuart Davis's remark that abstraction was nothing more than "a belch from the unconscious," Manny Farber in *The New Republic* cited his "continuing effect of virile, hectic action . . . great sweeping continuous lines . . . emphatic contrasts . . . [demonstrating] that abstract art can be as voluptuous as Renaissance painting." But the most acute observation came from Robert Motherwell, the most intellectual and analytical of all the abstract expressionists, who wrote, "His principal problem is to discover what his true subject is. And since painting is thought's medium, the resolution must grow out of the process of his painting itself."

Jackson was merely annoyed at hostile criticism—even in the case of the critic who said his work had "an air of baked macaroni." But he became *enraged* when he read the laudatory introduction to the catalogue for one of his shows. "Pollock's talent is volcanic," wrote the prominent critic James Johnson Sweeney. "It has fire. It is unpredictable. It is undisciplined."

Undisciplined! Jackson expected the accusation from the uninformed—it would come, for the rest of his life—but in the catalogue for his own show! Despite his reliance on spontaneity, even chance, he knew he was among the *most* disciplined of artists, repainting every inch of his canvases until all his feelings, no matter how discordant or unresolved, were integrated into a unified, expressive whole. He reluctantly wrote a brief note to Sweeney, only because Lee persuaded him that a certain amount of politicking was necessary for his career. He expressed his pleasure with the catalogue and his belief that self-discipline would come with experience.

Still, the charge of lack of discipline rankled Jackson—probably because he clearly saw no paradox in the fact that his life was utterly lacking in discipline and that his life and his work were one. He had discovered that the only way not to succumb to his emotional turmoil, the only surcease from chaos, was to confront and capture that turmoil in his paintings. Virtually all the abstract expressionists saw art as salvation, but none more than Jackson.

But despite his inarticulateness and his disdain for theory, Jackson wasn't as unsophisticated and primitive as he so often behaved. As Willem de Kooning put it, "Pollock was suspicious of intellectual talk. He couldn't do it—at least not when he was sober. But he was smart enough—oh boy—

because when he was half-loaded . . . he was . . . very good, very provocative." But in one of the supreme ironies of his life, in the early forties his career became inextricably linked with that of a critic who espoused a
doctrinaire aesthetic theory and who aspired to become a reputation-
builder—and who had a temperament as arrogant and insecure as his.

When Clement Greenberg first saw Jackson's mural in Peggy's
apartment, he later recalled, "I took one look at it, and . . . I knew Jackson
was the greatest painter this country has produced." And he echoed this
opinion for the rest of the decade, to such an extent that Jackson's painting
and Clem's criticism almost seemed like a collaboration.

A young critic whose intellect hadn't caught up with his pomposity—he had picked up most of what he knew about contemporary painting
in the late thirties by attending several of Hans Hofmann's classes and
going to galleries with his close friend Lee Krasner—Clem began his career writing about art and literature for the *Partisan Review* and became the
art critic for *The Nation* in 1942.

In the later thirties and early forties, Clem formulated the doctrine
that systematically articulated the principles of the abstract expressionists so
clearly that he became known as "the pope of modernism." And as pope, he
had the power to defrock the painters of whom he disapproved and to
anoint the painters of whom he approved, Jackson foremost among them.
Clem argued—or rather proclaimed—that the painter shed all inessentials
in his quest for pure painting. "Let painting confine itself to the disposition
pure and simple of color and line, and not intrigue us by association with
things we can express more authentically elsewhere." The flatness of the
canvas must be honored, the intensity of the painting, its invention and
arrangement of surface, space, color, line. This also meant refusing to
allow elements of the other arts to encroach on the process, for "readable"
imagery of any kind corrupted the purity of painting. Clem scorned
iconography, verbal analogues, literary references, mythological allusions.
The painter should allow nothing extrapictorial into his work. How American—a program for purity, an elaborate intellectual system to reject ideas.
Rarely has a critic so articulately rationalized the absence of meaning.

Fortunately for Jackson's career—but disastrously for his life—
Clem's theories found their perfect embodiment in his paintings. From his
first review of Jackson's work, in *The Nation* in November 1943, to the end
of the decade, Clem championed the painter he began to see less as a pro-
genitor than as a protégé. "Being young and full of energy," that first review
read, "[Pollock] takes orders he can't fill. . . . [But these are] among the
strongest abstract paintings I have yet seen by an American. . . . Pollock has

gone through the influences of Miró, Picasso, Mexican painting . . . and has come out on the other side, . . . painting mostly with his own brush." Jackson's second one-man show, Clem wrote, "establishes him, in my opinion, as the strongest painter of his generation and perhaps the greatest one to appear since Miró. . . . He is not afraid to look ugly—all profoundly original art looks ugly at first." At last, Jackson must have felt—at last a critic who didn't talk about his lack of discipline!

The problem was that Clem wrote as if Jackson were a preeminent painter only because he exemplified Clem's theories. Here was a painter who could validate his doctrines—whatever it was *Jackson* was seeking in his paintings didn't concern Clem in the slightest. Squinting at a picture, his forehead furrowed, Clem seemed less interested in what he could learn from a painter than in what the painter had learned from *him*. Furthermore, Clem's aesthetic retained a certain Marxist cast of mind, a belief in historical inevitability in particular, so Jackson's work was, in his view, doubly detached from his own impulses—he was not only an intuitive agent of Clem's intellectual theories, he was an unconscious agent of historical necessity as well.

Jackson was awed by Clem's erudition and grateful for his praise—how could he dismiss as "bullshit" a critical theory that called him "the greatest painter this country has produced"?—but he also felt ill at ease under this kind of attention. And when Clem began to show up at Jackson's studio—partly at Lee's encouragement, partly to keep his acolyte in line—their relationship became an odd inversion of the usual interaction between critic and artist, the critic not so much evaluating the work as promulgating its premises. Aspiring to be the critic-as-artist, Clem influenced the way Jackson painted, then promoted the results.

In many ways, Clem and Jackson were alike—hesitant in conversation, earnest and ambitious in their work, temperamental provocateurs. But Clem was intellectual and Jackson intuitive; Clem was a rigorous formalist, while Jackson was ruthlessly committed to emotional expression. But recognizing that they needed each other, they became allies in the cause of abstract expressionism.

Many abstract expressionists resented Clem's role as intellectual bully, and privately scorned him as "a mediocrity with an education." Jackson was never as obedient as Clem wanted, but found himself mesmerized by his certitude, his sense of mission, his implication that they were fellow rebels. When Clem said, "To be attacked universally is a favorable sign, if you're not against most opinion something is off," Jackson recognized an impulse he had felt since he'd listened to Krishnamurti in his teens. He didn't completely comprehend Clem's theories—indeed, one of Clem's favorite phrases was "as stupid as a painter"—but he shared his conviction that together they would determine the future of painting.

Jackson had "arrived," but the most painful part of his journey lay ahead. "Probably the catalytic moment in his art, " wrote Robert Motherwell, "was the day he painted the mural [for Peggy Guggenheim]. . . . Dancing around the room, he finally found a way of painting that fitted him, and from then on, he developed that technique and that scale." Yet not all the abstract expressionists greeted his "success" as unambiguous— as one painter opined, "I guess you have to piss in the right fireplace."

After a decade and a half of struggle, torment, and exaltation, a way of painting, an increasing notoriety, an influential patron, acclaim from the most influential critic of the day. In the most encouraging sign of all, the Museum of Modern Art acquired his most groundbreaking painting to date, *The She-Wolf*.

Jackson's fellow painters understood the psychic costs of his struggle, but Lee had to *live* with it. She virtually stopped painting herself—such was the chauvinism of the art world that few of their friends took her work seriously, thinking of her only as "Jackson's girl"—and devoted her energy to keeping him sober and to promoting his career.

"Pollock was rather difficult," Peggy recalled in her autobiography. "But as Lee pointed out when I complained, 'He also has an angelic side,' and that was true. To me, he was like a trapped animal who never should have left the prairies of Wyoming." But when it came to being "difficult," Peggy was no prize herself. She chastised Lee for minor clerical errors; she invited Lee and Jackson to a party for fifty people, then made it known that she expected Lee to prepare the dinner. As far as Peggy was concerned, Lee was just a painter's girlfriend—in other words, another servant. And as accustomed as Lee had become to artists' eccentricities, even she was shocked when Peggy once ordered a taxi driver to pull over, got out, lifted up her dress, and peed into an open manhole.

Worst of all, Peggy tried to steal Lee's man. "He was grateful for the chance to do the mural," Lee recalled, ". . . but she wanted him in her bed every night to prove it." "Every night" was an exaggeration, Peggy's inclinations running to a *different* man every night—but finally, in early 1944, she intimated to the inebriated Jackson that he could show his gratitude for all she'd done for him by joining her in her bedroom. Peggy gave varying accounts of the "very unsuccessful" seduction: Jackson had fallen in a drunken stupor, or he'd vomited all over her sheets, or he'd defecated in the midst of their grappling, and/or "he threw his drawers out the window." No details were forthcoming from Jackson, whose only comment was, "To fuck Peggy you'd have to put a towel over your head first"—which, some of his friends wryly speculated, might well have been what actually happened.

Partially because of the anxiety his good fortune caused him, Jackson entered another self-destructive cycle. Nearly every bartender in the Village recognized him the moment he walked through the door, and many of them had had enough of his vituperative outbursts, and instantly ordered him to leave. Passing out in gutters in puddles of urine, disappearing for days at a time, Jackson seemed on the verge of a breakdown as serious as the one in 1938. One night a friend saw him peeing into a snowbank. As he weaved from side to side, he bellowed, in the kind of arrogance that only comes with despair, "I can piss on the whole world!"

Though frantic, Lee never thought of leaving Jackson. She had a more radical solution. They'd get married. They'd leave New York. In his rare moments of sobriety, Jackson scoffed at both ideas, but during the summer and fall of 1945, his resistance evaporated. In late October, Jackson and Lee were married, and in early November they moved to the Springs, a small community near Amagansett on the eastern tip of Long Island.

Jackson never explained why he left the Village, where he'd lived for a decade and a half, but his friends instantly understood. He wasn't moving to the country, said one, "he was moving *away* from something."

He had dozens of painter friends—but that meant he had rivals. He had a prestigious dealer—but that meant he had to start thinking of paintings as objects to sell. He had been acclaimed by important critics—but that meant he felt pressure to perform.

After years of worshipping at the shrine of the European masters, the American art world was discovering native artists—and, in the eyes of some critics, challenging the hegemony of Paris. The second half of the forties would be an era of artistic ferment, critical hubbub, media hoopla.

Jackson got out just in time.

Most of the painters in the loose-knit Village community never considered themselves part of anything as dramatic as a "movement." For one thing, though they turned away from representation, they all valued their idiosyncratic styles more than their shared commitment to abstraction. For another, one of the few convictions they held in common was that they would never be recognized by the middle class, or even by the art establishment, which they regarded as the guardian of its own tastes—and they saw no contradiction in the belief that they would both remain marginal and revolutionize American art. Another contradiction troubled them even less—the disparity between their dedication to their painting and the carelessness with which they led their lives, for what other response could a sensitive, intelligent person have to the existential anxieties of the modern world? Indeed, this combination of artistic seriousness and personal self-destructiveness led one critic to write, "Not since the Renaissance has there been a group of artists whose real lives have been so fascinating."

If the abstract expressionists had a mythic figure of their own, it was Arshile Gorky—"the Picasso of Washington Square." A generation older than most of the vanguard painters, he was a fully committed abstractionist when they were still struggling to find their styles. At six foot four he affected an Old World look, wearing a flowing black cloak, but behind the cosmopolitan veneer lurked an engaging peasant. He performed foot-stomping Armenian dances at parties—and he told self-dramatizing stories, especially how, on a sudden whim, he'd changed his name from Vosdanik Adoian in honor of the Russian novelist, and how his mother had died of starvation in his arms.

He was, said Willem de Kooning, "a Geiger-counter of art." He painted with blazing ferocity, expressing his psychic states on his canvases in semi-transparent cascades of color. Linking surrealism and abstraction, he nevertheless remained deeply respectful of tradition, and one of his many appellations was "the Ingres of the unconscious." Art historians often call Gorky a "transitional figure," which at once patronizes his achievement by placing him in a kind of limbo and diminishes his seminal influence on his contemporaries, who were mesmerized by his intense personality and encouraged by his fierce convictions. In 1946, a fire destroyed his studio and he developed colon cancer. Two years later, an auto accident left his painting arm paralyzed. A few weeks after that, knowing he'd never paint again and having been abandoned by his wife, Gorky left a simple note—"Goodbye my Loves"—and hanged himself.

Like Gorky, several of the leading abstract expressionists were immigrants and several others were the sons of immigrants—which helps explain not only their status as outsiders in America (doubly outsiders if they were Jewish) but their paradoxical commitment to both universality and Americanism.

Mark Rothko was born Marcus Rothkowitz in Russia in 1903 and emigrated with his family to Portland, Oregon, when he was ten. In one of his rare lighthearted moments, for few were so ruthlessly austere as he, he said he decided to become a painter when he wandered into an art class and saw a nude model. He came to New York in the twenties and supported his painting by taking jobs as a bookkeeper, a garment worker, and an actor—and in one of his rare lapses into self-mythologizing claimed that Clark Gable had once been his understudy. Conservative by nature, never at a loss for dignity, Rothko lived in the Village for only three years, on Jane Street and on the Bowery between Prince and Spring, and from the late thirties on he was a member of the small branch of uptown abstract expressionists who rarely visited the Village or hung out at the Cedar.

Beginning in a more or less representational mode, Rothko turned to nonrepresentational biomorphic forms in the forties, and from the fifties on painted almost exclusively in his signature style—horizontal rectangles of saturated color stacked on top of one another, a distillation that seemed renunciatory to some critics but a drama of spiritual freedom to others. "Portraits of states of the soul," he called these paintings—or occasionally "portraits of ideas"—for though he felt that his works were "skins that are shed and hung on a wall," this least autobiographical of artists sought transcendence over the physical world, identification with the cosmos.

Indeed, in his blend of Russian melancholy and Jewish mysticism, Rothko was "the rabbi of abstract expressionism." A bear of a man, his wire-rimmed glasses nearly always smudged, he could be urbane, reserved, combative, or morose—but at the core of his being was a messianic zeal to discover sublime, universal truths. Of all the abstract expressionists, he was the most dedicated to painting as a sacred act. He yielded to the seductions of worldly success, then felt contaminated when it arrived. Finding himself in the world of opinion, power, and commerce, his spiritual isolation deepened—at social gatherings, he would suddenly leave the room in the middle of a sentence—and as his first wife said, he had "a tremendous emotional capacity for despair." Late in life, his gloom engulfed him, his paintings were suffused with black, and at the age of seventy he, too, committed suicide.

Nearly all the leading abstract expressionists met tragic ends; in fact, many of them, if not actually suicides, certainly brought about their own deaths. It's not even too much to say that the Village romance of the outsider and contempt for success contributed to their self-destruction, for most of these artists insisted that marginality was a sign of authenticity. Rothko himself often said that rejection was one of the greatest spurs to creativity. "The unfriendliness of society to his activity is difficult for the artist to accept. Yet this very hostility can act as a lever for true liberation." And as for recognition, "As soon as the public has caught up with a painter," he once said, "it's time for him to take another direction."

In postwar America, however, the increasing sophistication of the middle class began to make this conviction, if not outmoded, as least more ambiguous. How do self-appointed outcasts respond when their work is recognized, even lionized by the very segments of society they scorn? In the fifties, with the sudden success of the abstract expressionists, the old answers of isolation and repudiation no longer seemed adequate.

Rothko had two encounters in Washington Square Park that traced the trajectory of his generation of painters. In the mid-thirties, he struck up a park bench conversation with a stranger. When they discovered they were both artists, Rothko and Willem de Kooning began a friendship based in large part on their feeling that they shared a lonely, dedicated passion. Three decades later, as the now famous Rothko strolled through the park, a mutual friend introduced him to another well-known painter—Andy Warhol. Rothko's revulsion at pop art, his disgust at the glibness with which a later generation had turned the artist from a lonely seeker after sublimity into a media-obsessed seeker after celebrity, so overcame him that he turned his back on Warhol and strode away without a word.

Like Rothko, Barnett Newman was an immigrant from Eastern Europe, had a strong streak of Jewish mysticism, and regarded art as a metaphysical endeavor. Rejecting the federal government's Art Project as a form of welfare, and twice failing the city's test for certification as an art teacher, he worked for most of the thirties as a permanent substitute instructor in the New York City school system. An ardent anarchist, he ignored the irony and ran for mayor in 1933 on a platform advocating free art and music schools, a free university, expansion of the public parks, and strict limits on automobile traffic.

Unlike most of the Village painters, who experimented with a wide variety of styles, even painting over their old works when they didn't have enough money to buy canvases, Newman went years at a time without painting at all, or he destroyed the few works he did produce, believing that "anonymity is the truest heroism" and patiently waiting to be struck by a vision that would embody his "transcendental self." "I am bored by the too easily inspired," he said in declining to attend the opening of a show by his friend Mark Rothko—who then declined to speak to him for years. Newman could articulate the principles of abstract expressionism with a rare clarity and erudition, and with a pontifical flair that flattered the painters' conviction that they were embarked on an exalted mission. But they were drawn to his affable disposition and genial eccentricities, his habit of wearing a monocle attached to a black ribbon, or his tailored tweeds made, he claimed, by the same man who'd outfitted Al Capone. But while they regarded Newman with affection, they had little respect for him as an artist—an amiable blowhard, they said, an opinion his first major show did nothing to dispel.

Rectangles of single colors interrupted by thin vertical bands of contrasting colors he called "zips"—and that's about all Newman's fellow abstract expressionists saw. What could be so lacking in voluptuousness, so unreliant on virtuosity? Barney's not a painter, they said, he's a kibitzer, a polemicist. After Willem de Kooning and Adolph Gottlieb saw his first show of zip paintings, they walked in silence for several blocks. "Well," said de Kooning at last, "now we don't have to think about *that* any more." About the only painter who didn't dismiss Newman's work was Franz Kline. When a friend described Newman's zip paintings, then disparaged them as simplistic, Kline responded, "It sounds complicated as hell to me."

To Newman, "complicated" wasn't the right word. "Iconic" was more appropriate, or "holistic," for he was attempting, he said, to paint "pure idea," to express "a metaphysical hum," to evoke the infinite. Of the centerpiece of the show, titled with redoubled immodesty *Vir Heroicus Sublimus,* he boldly announced, "It took a second, but that second took a lifetime." As a Villager slyly remarked, "If Jackson Pollock said 'I am nature,' Barnett Newman said 'I am art.' "

The abstract expressionists appropriated the most exalted vocabulary, aspiring to tragic profundities—and Newman was the worst offender. "We don't simply paint, we make cathedrals out of ourselves." "The present movement in America transcends nature," he wrote in 1945. "It is concerned with metaphysical implications, with the divine mysteries." The coolly ironic pop artists who followed reacted as much against what they regarded as metaphysical babble as to the exclusion of figuration. Still, it was Newman who made the famously wry remark, "Aesthetics is for the artist as ornithology is for the birds," and in an irony equaling anything that would emerge from pop art, the work of the painter who twice flunked the city's art test was soon hanging in the city's most prestigious museums.

Who could be more unlike in temperament and talent than Jackson Pollock and Barnett Newman? Yet each regarded himself as a revolutionary on the same barricades.

Clyfford Still was the most evangelical of the abstract expressionists—even de Kooning called him a fanatic. By the age of twenty-five, he had already vehemently rejected "the aesthetic puerility" of most American painting. From his monastic studio on Cooper Square came huge canvases covered with molten, ragged-edged shapes. At once messianic and ascetic, always a disturbing combination, Still exalted the isolated, tragic individual not only in his vehement paintings but in his vitriolic rhetoric. "When I expose a painting, I would have it say, 'Here am I, this is my presence, my feeling, myself. Here I stand implacable, proud, alive, naked, unafraid.' . . . I am simply asserting that the totality of my being can stand stripped of its cultural camouflage."

A recluse, Still proudly proclaimed his "Puritan reflexes"—which is another way of saying he could be the most uncivil of men. He berated his fellow painters, condemning the spiritual corruption of their aesthetic and moral standards. He shot off self-righteous letters to those he felt had degraded the artist's calling. This included critics, of course—"the butchers who make hamburger of us for the public gut"—and he once fired off a note to Harold Rosenberg calling him "a salon raconteur" and "intellectual lout." And though he'd been supportive of Jackson Pollock, when he wasn't invited to one of Jackson's shows in 1956, and knew that the artist was in emotional distress, Still didn't hesitate to write him to ask if he hadn't been invited because Jackson was ashamed of his work or because he was ashamed of the way people were using him. Like all people who appoint themselves a kind of freelance conscience, Still inflicted more pain than remorse, and it's tempting to speculate what moral degeneracy he sensed in himself that made him so eager to find it in others.

At times as ascetic as Still, Robert Motherwell also had a strong strain of sensuality—a combination that tinged many of his paintings with evocations of guilt. At times as polemical as Newman, he had more eloquence and erudition, making him one of the leading theoreticians of abstract expressionism. "Abstract art represents the particular acceptance and rejections of men living under the conditions of modern times," he wrote. "One's art is just one's effort to wed oneself to the universe. . . . For make no mistake, abstract art is a form of mysticism . . . [stemming from] a primary sense of a gulf, an abyss, a void between one's lonely self and the world. Abstract art is an effort to close the void that modern men feel."

Such melodramatic effusions seemed philosophic certainties to the Village intellectuals, and Motherwell provided them by the bushel. Indeed, he was speaking for most of the abstract expressionists when he said, "I allow no nostalgia, no sentimentalism, no propaganda, no selling out to the vulgar, no autobiography, no violation of the nature of the canvas as a flat surface, no clichés, no illusionism, no description, no seduction, no charm, no relaxation, no mere taste, no obviousness, no coldness." As for

Still's assertion that painters should refuse to be the pallbearers of tradition, "Every intelligent painter carries the whole culture of modern painting in his head," Motherwell wrote. "It is his real subject, of which everything he paints is both an homage and a critique, and everything he says a gloss." And as for the apparently contradictory claims of existentialism and formalism, Motherwell managed a reconciliation—"Painting," he said, "is . . . the mind realizing itself in color and space."

A banker's son and a former philosophy student, Motherwell moved with such cosmopolitan grace among the roughnecks of abstract expressionism that he had difficulty convincing them he wasn't merely a wealthy dilettante—"He *smells* rich," said de Kooning. He worked for several years in an Astor Place studio before moving to the Upper East Side like Rothko and Newman. Apollonian in temperament, he had a Dionysian side that emerged in his paintings—especially in his famous *Spanish Elegy* series, majestic, foreboding meditations on sex and death. Though Motherwell's admirers found in his work a striking blend of the soulfully sophisticated and the sensually primitive, to many of his fellow painters he seemed nothing but a man with cultivated manners, verbal ingenuity, and a bank account. "Even his elegies," said one, "look like they were painted to become expensive."

Nearly all the great American painters of the forties and fifties experimented with various styles before finally settling into abstract expressionism; Philip Guston was virtually alone in passing *through* abstract expressionism on the way to his mature style. The son of Russian-Jewish immigrants, he worked as a bit player in movies, as a factory hand, and a truck-driver, but he always regarded his old high school classmate Jackson Pollock as a kind of conscience for his artistic aspirations. Guston was high-strung and haunted—at the age of eleven, he'd discovered his father hanging from a beam. As a young man, he'd dropped his birth name Goldstein and never got over his guilt. But like many of the abstract expressionists, he rejected the Village craze for psychoanalysis—"I am afraid if my devils leave me," he said, quoting Rilke, "my angels will take flight as well." "Frustration is one of the great things in art," he said, "satisfaction is nothing. . . . My whole life is *based* on anxiety—where else does art come from, I ask you?"

Though highly praised for his socially conscious murals of the thirties, Guston increasingly found them shallow. He wanted something, he said, that would leave his blood on the canvas. So in the mid-forties he decided to turn to abstraction—a decision that left him virtually paralyzed for three years, chain-smoking Camels as he stared at a blank canvas. Finally, in the early fifties, in a West 10th Street building in which Winslow Homer had once lived, and later on University Place, he began to paint delicate, lyrical, abstract forms, influenced by Monet, that earned him the label "abstract impressionist." When his emotions became increasingly melancholy and despairing, and as his palette grew denser and darker, he decided to make another radical break, but the strain of beginning again proved nearly intolerable. As he explained, "It was two equally powerful impulses at loggerheads"—figuration and abstraction—and figuration finally won.

Jackson scorned the later work as "easel paintings," as "embroidery." Guston felt that he was rebelling against the depersonalization of abstraction, the absence of meaning—but the frequent appearance of flagellants in his final works reflected a far deeper sense of betrayal. Guston died of his self-destructive appetites, his friends said, and while the raw, blunt, cartoonlike paintings and drawings of his last years evoke guilt and fear, they also express a kind of nostalgia for a peace he'd never known.

David Smith, a sculptor who brilliantly blended the organic, was as much an abstract expressionist as any of the painters. He was a burly man, standing six feet four, a former steelworker who frequented longshoremen's bars as well as painters' hangouts. He could be as gentle as a St. Bernard, but could fly into violent rages, especially at women. As driven and as unhappy as Jackson Pollock, he met much the same end—in 1965 he was killed in a truck accident that was at least partly his own fault.

One can hardly deny the self-destructiveness that characterizes so many of the abstract expressionists. The ethos of the Village, especially in the forties and fifties, valorized the artist as an outsider. But the double strain of cultural isolation and painting in a radically new style caused many of them to find relief in alcohol. And more important, their conviction that to be authentic an artist must be in touch with his deepest feelings, his most forbidden fantasies, released feelings and fantasies that they could not always express in their work. The irony was that their quest for apocalyptic transcendence often blinded them to daily survival.

All the talk of apocalyptic transcendence also made them vulnerable to mockery. Ad Reinhardt was known to the public as a painter; he was known to the painters as a parodist. His fellow artists, he wrote, could be categorized as "the café-and-club primitive and neo-Zen-bohemian, the Vogue-magazine-cold-water-flat-fauve and Harpers-Bazaar-bum . . . the Modern-Museum-pauper and international-set-sufferer, the abstract-'Hesspressionist' and Kootzenjammer-Kid-Jungian, the Romantic-ham-'action'-actor." When he incautiously identified one of his subjects as Barnett Newman, the artist, amused until then, promptly sued.

Reinhardt's own paintings, especially his all-black works, were so cerebral, so homogenous, so devoid of painterliness, so ruthless in their exclusion of the artist's presence, that a witticism went around that Newman closed the door, Rothko pulled down the shades, and Reinhardt turned out the lights. Reinhardt *did* want to exclude emotion from his work—and where is it written, he asked, that an artist has to be anguished?—but he replaced feeling by attempting to create absolute, suprapersonal, timeless art. Unfortunately, Reinhardt never turned his provocateur's wit on himself.

Franz Kline, who didn't have a trace of pomposity in either his personality or his painting, was never a victim of Reinhardt's mockery. In fact, he was virtually the only warmhearted, easygoing man among the abstract expressionists, and the only one, said a friend, who "didn't in some way push his work at you." Everyone loved him, even the nonartist bohemians whom none of the other painters so much as acknowledged. He cherished the work of his fellow painters as much as his own—after seeing Motherwell's *Spanish Elegies*, he clasped the artist in a bear hug and exclaimed, "That's it!"

Standing only five foot three, Kline often had a doleful expression that belied his cheerful energy. His droll, earthy monologues were as inconclusive as they were unstoppable. His mind was so elliptical, his sentences so circuitous, that his stories seemed like jazz riffs. Fingering his thick mustache, finding a baseball metaphor for anything and everything, he'd talk about his bohemian days—a bohemian, he said, was someone who could live in places where an animal would die—the anecdotes so seamlessly linked that his listeners felt his life was a shaggy-dog story.

Actually, Kline's story was fairly straightforward—a lifelong commitment to art. He began as a cartoonist for his high school paper, then supported himself by making and repairing frames. He worked as a sidewalk caricaturist on Minetta Lane, hawked his paintings in Washington Square, and had a pencil portrait concession at the 1939 World's Fair. He also claimed he was on the state dole until 1953.

Kline came late to abstraction. In 1949, hoping to express more urgency in his work, he began to paint stark, startling canvases, largely in black and white—"a drunken Mondrian," a friend said. "Painting experiences," he called his work—paintings that seemed at once emotionally spontaneous and aesthetically controlled. Lionized by his colleagues, he remained virtually unknown to the public until near the end of his life. But his ambition was internal—"If you meant it enough when you did it," he said, "it will mean that much."

Kline, Pollock, and de Kooning formed a kind of best-buddies triumvirate upon which the other painters looked with admiration and envy.

Kline's courtliness and generosity, darkened by moments of eloquent mournfulness—"Truth," he once said, "is the nail of anguish"—were the perfect foil for de Kooning's anxieties and Pollock's anger. He'd often bait Pollock, claiming that whenever the two of them went on the town, he always seemed to end up getting punched in the face. But he was one of the few who recognized that much of Jackson's macho bravado was a form of baiting, that he wanted to be answered in kind. Their famous wrestling matches, in fact, were a form of bonding—on one occasion, as they lay entangled on the floor of the Cedar, Jackson was heard whispering, "Not so hard, Franz, not so hard."

Pollock and de Kooning were uneasy rivals from the first, deeply respecting each other's work but well aware that they represented opposite poles of the movement. "Jackson Pollock broke the ice," de Kooning graciously acknowledged. But if Pollock was an icon to the public, to the painters themselves, de Kooning was a cult. And as a critic put it, "Jackson may have been the genius, but the *painter* was Bill." The poet Robert Creeley wrote: "It used to be said of William Carlos Williams that the literal fact of his being there gave us one *clean* man we could utterly depend on, that nothing could buy his integrity. We had the same feeling and respect for de Kooning."

A native of the Netherlands, de Kooning entered the United States illegally in 1926, when he jumped ship in Hoboken. Even three decades later, hardly a day passed that he didn't worry he'd be deported. Almost alone among the abstract expressionists, he felt that painting wasn't so much a sacred calling as a job like any other—a low-paying job, as it turned out, and he was one of the first Villagers to discover that a bed folded into the wall would fool the building inspectors and that a rigged meter could provide free electricity. He was always ready to help younger painters, exuding the charisma of the unpretentious genius. He stirred his paint in Pyrex bowls, at times mixing in mayonnaise, and when he was too broke to afford oils, he used housepainter's enamel. Though short and stocky, he was blond, fair-skinned, the Adonis of the movement, who, said a friend, "took home a different tart every night."

Intelligent and articulate, de Kooning spoke with brusque exclamations and a thick Dutch accent. Hans Hofmann's theories, he said, were nothing but "bullsheet," he dismissed work he didn't like as "ridicklus," and he frequently expostulated, when asked why he'd become a painter, "Vat else is der?" He also displayed a wry wit—when asked by a jealous rival at a Village party, "Doesn't it bother you to be so overrated?" he promptly responded, "No, but it seems to bother *you*."

Traditionally trained, de Kooning both exemplified and subverted classic painting. Like Picasso, he ceaselessly shifted from one style to another—"I keep changing in order to stay the same," he once said. In the thirties he worked in both figurative and cubist modes, and in the forties he turned to abstraction—his work, in the words of one critic, fragmenting anatomy so fluently it became "the liquified residue of cubism." De Kooning never completely abandoned the human figure—"Flesh," he once said, "is the reason why painting was invented." His most famous works, his series of *Women* paintings done in the early fifties, were hysterical, mutilated figures, slashed onto his canvases as if in a frenzy of worship and loathing—monstrous goddesses.

The other painters admired de Kooning for his virtuosic draftsmanship, for his quicksilver touch, for his almost gaudy colors—"an elegant vulgarian," said one Villager—but they idolized him for the way the structure of his canvases seemed to emerge spontaneously as he painted, fluid, open-ended, and magisterially ambiguous. De Kooning was more laconic—"slipping glimpses," he called his canvases.

De Kooning once summed up his thinking quite simply. "Painting isn't just the visual thing that reaches your retina, it's what is behind it and in it. . . . Through your eyes it again becomes an emotion or an idea. It doesn't matter if it's different from mine as long as it comes from the painting which has its own integrity and intensity."

In the lush dynamism of his studio days, in the binges of his barroom nights, de Kooning was the quintessential abstract expressionist. When at the end of a boisterous party a woman asked him what his paintings meant, he thought for a moment, managed to mutter, "They mean . . . ," and before he could finish the sentence, passed out.

In the myth of abstract expressionism, the painters formed tight, self-protective bonds when unknown, then bitterly split with the arrival of fame. In fact, they gathered in a series of small, loose, and ever-changing clusters in the early years, coalesced into a volatile, faction-ridden community in the late forties and early fifties, then gradually went their separate ways.

In the thirties and early forties, small groups of painters spent their evenings at Romany Marie's, the San Remo, Hubert's, Sam Johnson's, the Albert Hotel bar, Rappaport's, Louis's, the Horn and Hardart automat, and several places that constituted "cafeteria culture," especially Bickford's,

Stewart's, and Riker's. They also congregated in two locations that couldn't have been more different: Peggy Guggenheim's soigné uptown town house and on the benches in the northwest corner of Washington Square Park. Over the years, so many of them met at the Waldorf Cafeteria at Sixth Avenue and 8th Street that by the late forties they were pushing three or four tables together and leaving latecomers to kibitz over their shoulders. They soon began to talk about starting an informal club.

Rothko, Motherwell, and Still had already formed the Subjects of the Artists School in a loft at 35 East 8th Street. The name, suggested by Newman, served as an implicit rebuke to Greenberg—we *do* have subjects, they insisted, even if the students were encouraged to find them within themselves—and as a subtler rebuke to Hofmann's school just down the block.

In the improvisatory spirit of their painting, from the fall of 1949 to the spring of 1950, casual classes were taught by whoever happened to be in the mood. On Friday evenings, the school sponsored lectures by such artists as Jean Arp, Willem de Kooning, and Ad Reinhardt, and on one memorable evening John Cage presented his "Lecture on Nothing." Lacking leadership or structure, the school soon disbanded so quietly that no one seemed to notice but the landlord.

Informal as the Subjects of the Artists School was, many of the painters wanted a place even less organized, a place where they could get together for a few beers and talk about anything and everything—except painting itself. Recalled de Kooning, "We didn't want to have anything to do with art. We just wanted to get a loft, instead of sitting in those goddamned cafeterias." And so, in the fall of 1949 they rented a fifth-floor loft at 39 East 8th Street, just two doors down from the school. Wanting to keep the group free of ideology—and happily exposing their inability to agree even on something so apparently simple as a name—they decided to call it simply "the Club."

Casual as it was, the formation of the Club was a pivotal moment in the movement. For the first time, though few of the painters realized its significance at the time, they acknowledged that they *were* a movement. Whether bohemian, radical, avant-garde, or some permutation of the three, many Village institutions followed the same pattern. A number of isolated individuals, gradually realizing they were working toward the same goals—even if those goals were self-expression, freedom from convention, and opposition to social hierarchies—would begin to gather in informal groups, then would form loose organizations to help advance their cause. Then, inevitably, they would discover that the moment they coalesced into an institution and formalized their principles they began to dissipate their energy and dilute their vision.

But the essence of the Village was to create a miniature society where personal idiosyncrasy could flourish through communal solidarity. Even Americans who have remained hostile to the Village have been fascinated by it because it has been a kind of laboratory in which a nation at once dedicated to militant individualism and to middle-class conformity could witness attempts to overcome that paradox.

The abstract expressionists never wrote a manifesto, and the manifestos written by their critical supporters were either disregarded or scorned. What they shared, instead, was an aesthetic climate consisting of a few open-ended principles, a virtually self-willed poverty, and the welcomed rejection of the cultural establishment—that the president of the United States himself, Harry Truman, dismissed their work as "scrambled eggs" seemed proof enough of their authenticity. Several of them warned of the dangers of even so simple a project as a social center. To give themselves any kind of structure was to acknowledge that they formed a movement, and doing so would inevitably diminish their individuality and confine their creativity. They were all aware of one another's work, they'd always managed to gather together in a spirit of freewheeling anarchism, so why formalize their relationships? Wasn't institutionalization the surest sign of waning vitality? Next thing you know we'll be coming up with a name to describe our painting. All this horseshit, several of the abstract expressionists asked, just because we want to start a club? And though this was hardly an argument, no argument was necessary. Once the initial twenty members rented the loft, the rest of the painters simply followed.

The Club began as a casual gathering place with no name on the door, no rules, and no agenda—and no paintings on the walls. A committee of ever-shifting volunteers was nominally in charge, though the sculptor Phillip Pavia found himself making most of the decisions. Collecting dues was his hardest job, of course, and cleaning up the loft after their get-togethers ran a close second; de Kooning, the former seaman, was one of the few members who stayed behind to sweep up and wash the dishes.

Intrepid loners the abstract expressionists may have been, but by the following summer, the Club had gained cachet and increased its membership from the initial twenty to sixty.

Institutions have a life of their own, independent of the unanimous feelings of their members, and invariably need to justify their existence. The members considered mounting exhibitions of their work—and actually managed to put one together at 60 East 9th Street in 1951—but soon decided that such projects were too formal and would inevitably favor some painters over others. Still, before anyone quite realized what was happening, the casual evenings were supplemented by an occasional guest speaker, even an occasional panel. Friday nights were formal affairs of as many as 150 people, with such speakers as William Barrett, Hannah Arendt, Edgard Varèse, Paul Goodman, John Cage, Joseph Campbell, and Dylan Thomas, followed by questions and discussion.

The Club was now a structured institution, but structure didn't bring decorum. The topic for the evening might be "the nature of the artist's moral commitment," or "the artist's existential role," or the need for community, or how to tell when a painting was finished, or the alternatives to mass culture, or how to deal with failure, but factions formed on every issue. The Friday discussions quickly degenerated into taunts, even fistfights. De Kooning fled one night, crying, "They're a bunch of baboons!"

And they didn't need Jackson's help. Uneasy in crowds, afraid he'd expose his inarticulateness, feeling that the other painters resented his celebrity, he attended few meetings. When he did, he either brooded at the back of the room or, if he'd had a few drinks, mocked the speakers with profane outbursts. This was the man, after all, who so disliked conversation about art that the night after Franz Kline appeared on a panel at the Museum of Modern Art he stood beneath his window and yelled up, "I heard you talked. You talked!" "Painters don't need clubs," he'd grumble, and they especially didn't need pedantic pronouncements about their work— "bullshit like that."

Despite the combative polemics, the Club served several purposes. The critic Thomas Hess cited its "semi-public auto-criticism"; another critic called it "an aesthetic version of group therapy." Most of the younger members felt that it was, as one put it, "like belonging to a church." It continued throughout the fifties, but as an ignored subculture rapidly became a cultural phenomenon, the scene fragmented and the informal hangout finally closed its doors in 1962. Abstract expressionism was no longer fashionable in the art world, but to the rest of the world it was legendary. The money—that was the key.

By the end of the decade the name of the movement was firmly established, and despite the virtually unanimous feeling that to name themselves was to write their own obituary, the subject refused to go away. As David Smith put it, "Names are usually given to groups by people who don't understand them or don't like them," and Bill de Kooning joined in—"It is disastrous to name ourselves." The most vehement was Mark Rothko. "To classify is to embalm," he fumed. "Real identity is incompatible with schools and categories except by mutilation."

"The New American Painting," the Museum of Modern Art called the movement, but even if that name was an admission of failure to come up with anything better, the painters weren't about to be labeled by a museum. "The New York School," Robert Motherwell suggested, but while the allusion to the School of Paris had a nice ring, few of the painters liked Motherwell. "Abstract-symbolist" was briefly floated, and "abstract-objectionist," and "subjectivist," and "intra-subjectivist." "Abstract expressionist"? The movement was revolutionary, but that phrase had actually been around since 1929, when MOMA's director, Alfred Barr, had used it to describe Kandinsky. It popped up again in 1944 in a book by the art dealer Sidney Janis, who wrote that current painting seemed "a merging of abstract and expressionist streams," and again in 1946 in a New Yorker column by Robert Coates, who referred to Hofmann as "certainly one of the most uncompromising representatives of what some people call the spatter-and-daub school of painting and I, more politely, have christened abstract expressionism."

"Abstract expressionism" caught on—if nothing else, the triumvirate of museums, media, and critics needed a label to make their task of embalming and mutilating easier—and the painters were stuck with what Pavia called "the unwanted title." With a name they lost their consciousness of being on the frontier and became famous—and with fame they lost their consciousness of being on their own and entered history.

They refused collective action—with one significant, well-publicized exception. On learning the names of the critics and curators who would form the jury at an upcoming show of contemporary painting at the Metropolitan Museum of Art, several painters were so outraged that they momentarily forgot their conviction that rejection by the art establishment validated an artist's originality, and decided to write a letter of protest. Gottlieb and Newman prepared a draft, and on May 22, 1950, an article appeared on the front page of the New York Times under the two-column headline "18 Painters Boycott Metropolitan: Charge 'Hostility' to Advanced Art." "Boycott" may have been the wrong word, since the artists had little chance of being invited, and "18" overlooked the five sculptors who'd also signed the letter, but at least their accusations came to public attention. The selection of the jurors, the letter stated, "does not warrant hope that a just proportion of advanced art will be included," and indeed showed "contempt for modern art," a conclusion seconded by a prominent critic who later wrote that the panel selected works that "might have been chosen by the Elkhart Bide-a-Wee."

The *New York Herald Tribune* published a supportive editorial entitled "The Irascible 18," and *Life* magazine, once more sensing a catchy headline and a subject for titillated coverage, asked the eighteen to pose for a group portrait. "The Irascibles" debated the propriety of appearing in a mass circulation magazine—could they flirt with middle-class acceptance without being seduced? Wasn't their stand against bourgeois taste compromised by appearing in the quintessentially bourgeois publication? But Jackson had become famous through *Life*, and they set aside their rivalries to join in protest, to find themselves united by something close to envy. So in November, fourteen of the eighteen gathered in a studio on West 44th Street—all conservatively dressed, at the insistence of Newman, who argued that their protest would have more impact if they looked like bankers—and on January 15, 1951, the full-page photo ran under the headline "Irascible Group of Advanced Artists Led Fight Against Show." The text took a swipe at the man the abstract expressionists had taken to calling "the *Life* painter" (after their 1947 piece on him), referring to "the drippings of Pollock." Even so, said one of the painters sullenly, *Life* saw its article as just "the next installment in the continuing saga of Jackson Pollock, the cowboy painter."

But enough of group action and respectability—it was time to take off their jackets and ties and head downtown to the Cedar.

The Cedar was the center, the scene. It was just what the painters wanted—a working-class, nondescript bar, a "no atmosphere" bar in de Kooning's phrase.

Located on University Place between 8th and 9th Streets, the Cedar Street Tavern was a long, narrow room, dim and smoke-filled, with leatherette booths, a few rickety wood tables; nothing on the dull green walls, no TV, no jukebox. Behind the bar stood the two regular bartenders, Sam and Johnny, ex-Marines keeping a stern eye on the patrons, who behaved very much like the laborers who had been the Cedar's regular customers only a couple of years earlier. Few women came in, a hand-lettered sign briefly appeared on the door reading "No Beatniks Allowed," and homosexuals were greeted with vicious taunts. "I'm ten inches long and all man," claimed a graffito in the men's room, under which someone wrote, "Great! How long's your dick?"

"The Cedar was like a secular church," said one painter, "like a flying circus," said another. It served a dual purpose—it was a place where artistic genius was appreciated, and it was a place where no one talked about art. John Cage might stop by for a drink to two, or the composer Morton Feldman, or Tennessee Williams, or Clement Greenberg and his girlfriend Helen Frankenthaler, or Harold Rosenberg, or Jack Kerouac, who made himself at home by pissing in a stand-up ashtray—but everyone acknowledged that the painters reigned. Especially Jackson.

And the king set the style. "The booze explosion," Elaine de Kooning, Bill's wife, called it. When they'd been poor, they'd nursed their beers and attended gallery openings as much for the free drinks as for the aesthetic shiver—but now that they were starting to sell their paintings, they turned to the hard stuff. "It is expected," said one painter, "because [as an artist] you're supposed to be tragic, lonely, passionate, dissipated, and doomed."

When Jackson entered the Cedar, de Kooning recalled, "He had that cowboy style. It's an American Quality with artists and writers. They feel they have to be very manly. . . . We'd run, fight, jump on each other. Such joy, such desperate joy."

According to one painter, "The Cedar was the cathedral of American culture in the fifties." But the critic Leslie Fiedler saw it differently. "In all that aggression and machismo, there was always a trace of hysterical desperation." Clem Greenberg was even more dismayed—the Cedar scene was "awful and sordid," it ate the painters alive, and after the first few years of back-slapping camaraderie, all he saw when he came through the door were "doomed artists," doomed partly as a pose, but one that all too soon became a destiny.

By the mid-fifties, after Jackson's death, the Cedar became a kind of intersection between the first and second generation of abstract expressionists, and a group of poets called "The New York School." If Jackson was the unofficial center of the scene in the first half of the decade, Larry Rivers and Frank O'Hara became its twin centers in the second half.

Yitzroch Loiza Grossberg, born in the Bronx in 1923, became Larry Rivers, some said, because it sounded black, or, others claimed, because he saw the name on the side of a truck, or more likely—accepting his own account, despite his congenital unreliability—because he was playing jazz in a group called the Mudcats. At the Cedar, Rivers was the court jester as king, and he was one of the first painters to turn the avant-garde into a career.

Rivers's early-fifties *Washington Crossing the Delaware*, with its mixture of traditional iconography and art history parody, anticipated pop art—but he gained greater fame by anticipating pop art's self-conscious transformation of the artist into a celebrity. His medium, in fact, wasn't so much paint as character. A proto-hipster, he drove a motorbike, would leave his apartment to buy a pack of cigarettes and return four days later, and so delighted in art world gossip that O'Hara called him "a demented telephone."

As a painter, Rivers had extraordinary facility, but also, alas, what a fellow Villager called "a genius for the vulgar." He himself proudly called it "natural bad taste," for he was among the first Villagers to realize that if mass culture could raid avant-garde art, why couldn't avant-garde art raid mass culture in return? Still, Rivers's genius, everyone at the Cedar understood, wasn't so much for being an artist as for being an art world climber. If painters wanted to become culture stars, he realized, they had to become showmen first—perhaps the last word on his career was from the Villager who called him "a grin without a cat."

The Cedar was suspicious of intellectuals, hostile to homosexuals—until Frank O'Hara arrived in the mid-fifties. With his hypergregarious personality—and with his lucid passion for vanguard painting—O'Hara quickly became a kind of mascot to the regulars at the Cedar and "the Boswell of abstract expressionism." Educated at Harvard with his improbable classmates Henry Kissinger and Daniel Ellsberg, he worked as a curator of contemporary painting at the Museum of Modern Art, but his true vocation was poetry and almost immediately he became the catalytic figure at the juncture of abstract expressionism and the New York School.

O'Hara had "a punk angel face"—John Ashbery's phrase—and a peripatetic personality. But perhaps his dominant traits were his flaming mind and his ceaseless search for enchantment—in poetry, in painting, in friendship, in sex, in alcohol and drugs. He had, said a friend, "a willingness to be happy." And everyone marveled at his bitchy wit—when Jack Kerouac confronted him, on a panel at the Club, with the accusation that he'd ruined American poetry, O'Hara promptly replied, "That's more than you ever did for it."

O'Hara wrote poetry the way he lived his life—on the fly. "You just go on your nerve," he said, and wrote in a kind of fusion of Walt Whitman and James Dean, highbrow culture and pop imagery, colloquial idiom and jazz improvisation—hot-rod poetry, said a fellow habitué of the Cedar. Though not anti-intellectual, he remained anti-metaphysical, and this approach to his art, combined with his insistence on being in the moment, allied him even to those abstract expressionists who constructed elaborate philosophical rationales for spontaneity. They went so far as to overlook his homosexuality—even Jackson, whom some suspected of homosexual impulses himself. O'Hara was killed when struck by a beach buggy on Fire Island in the summer of 1966, and was buried in the same Springs cemetery as Jackson Pollock. In his eulogy, Larry Rivers said that there were at least sixty people in New York who regarded him as their best friend.

After Pollock and Lee Krasner moved to eastern Long Island, Jackson traveled into the city once a week for a fifty-minute session with his uptown psychiatrist—and promptly headed downtown to the Cedar to undermine whatever he'd accomplished. He had spent several months in therapy with a Jungian analyst after his 1938 breakdown. Finding his patient "extremely unverbal," his doctor had asked him to bring in examples of his work, drawings he then analyzed for their "archetypal symbolism." Some, he'd concluded, revealed "violent agitation," others "paralysis or withdrawal of vital energy," and still others "a pathological form of introversion." "His own highly developed function of intuition needed no help from anyone," the doctor had said in summing up their sessions, "but [he] did need to be rescued from time to time from a crucifying sense of isolation."

Many of the painters resisted psychoanalysis as a threat to their creativity, but throughout the forties, Jackson tried other therapies—Freudian, Sullivanian, group, even hypnosis and homeopathy. He consulted a Park Avenue "organic healer" who claimed he could cure his alcoholism by a daily bath in a solution of rock salt and a daily drink concocted of guano and ground beets that would give him "a proper balance of gold and silver in his urine." Nothing seemed to work, however—nothing except those intermittent periods when he could express his unconscious in his paintings. But his alcoholic rampages recurred with a regularity that dismayed his friends and terrified Lee.

At a party at Jack the Oysterman's restaurant on 8th Street celebrating a show by Bill de Kooning, Jackson "came in like a cannon," an observer recalled. "He was insulting to his good friends in a way I'd never seen before. Everyone was white with fear. I mean there was the threat of physical violence." De Kooning, who liked to witness brawling even more than to participate, recalled another evening. "We were at Franz's place. . . . Pollock looked at this guy and said, 'You need a little more air' and he punched a window out with his fist. At the moment it was so delicious—so belligerent."

As his dealer Betty Parsons put it, "His whole rhythm was either sensitive or very wild. You never quite knew whether he was going to kiss your hand or throw something at you." At a dinner party at the home of a proper gallery owner in her fifties, Jackson was the soul of courtesy until she intimated that perhaps he'd had enough to drink, whereupon he started abusing her—"What does an old lady like you do for sex?" He smashed several of her precious antiques, then passed out as she called the police.

Jackson didn't drink as heavily in Springs—or when he did, he took out his fury in private—and though he remained destitute, claiming that he'd lived an entire year on the sale of one painting "and a few clams I dug out of the bay with my toes," he managed to work with a regularity he'd found impossible in the hurly-burly of the Village. And when he happened to meet an East Hampton doctor named Edwin Heller, he seemed at last to have found someone who could help him overcome his alcoholism. He wasn't addicted to alcohol, Heller told him, he was addicted to the release alcohol provided for his psychic demons. This was hardly a sophisticated diagnosis—many of Jackson's friends had been telling him more or less the same thing for years—but as is the case with so many addicts, the "cure" comes when the fragments of a chaotic personality suddenly coalesce around an incantatory "solution" and despair turns into faith. The tranquilizers Heller prescribed helped, but Jackson would have flushed them down the toilet if some corner of his psyche hadn't been ready to listen. Lee remained skeptical for months, many of his friends scoffed, but he stayed more or less sober for three entire years. There's no record of how or when he began the series of "drip" canvases, but from 1947 to 1949, he entered his most sustained period of creativity and he completed several of the masterpieces that have entered the pantheon of American art.

Day after day, Jackson followed the same routine. He'd sleep until late morning, sit silently over several cups of coffee for two hours, then work until nightfall in his barn studio. Then he'd sit on the stoop all evening, staring at the landscape, rarely saying a word to Lee, and never talking about art—he agreed with Matisse that "artists should have their tongues cut out."

Maybe the drip paintings began when he had to lay a canvas flat on the floor. Maybe he accidentally spilled paint or angrily hurled paint at a canvas that refused to conform to his vision. Or maybe the explanation was psychological—when he was leading a more or less stable life, his roiling emotions were at last given coherence by his innate genius.

The only certain truth about the genesis of Jackson's drip paintings is that the media myth is untrue—Jackson Pollock, the existential cowboy, defying convention, history itself, suddenly unleashed his defiant impulses.

For all his aversion to theory and inarticulateness about his work, Jackson had a sophisticated knowledge of art history. For all his reliance on unconscious feelings, he rigorously experimented with styles, methods, paints, and materials—rejecting the brush in order to gain more direct contact with the canvas, trying palette knives and basting syringes, squeezing paint directly from the tube, even incorporating sand, pebbles, broken glass, nails, buttons, and cigarette butts in his work. He and many other painters as far back as Siqueiros had included drips, accidental or not, in their completed paintings. Jackson's breakthrough lay in using the technique to cover the entire canvas.

The drip paintings liberated Jackson. He'd always wanted to express his unconscious feelings on his canvases. Now he'd eliminated the brush itself; now he could, as he said, "literally be *in* the painting." From 1947 to 1950, he refined the drip technique, learning how heavily to load his stick, how to thin his paint, how high above the canvas to hold his hand, when to stride around the painting with looping gestures, when to stand still and simply flick his wrist. He didn't want complete control over the canvas, or complete chance—he sought a revelatory balance between order and chaos, between discipline and spontaneity, a balance that itself required absolute *mastery*.

And in the process, Jackson didn't merely discover revelations, he *created* them. The white void of the canvas had been covered with a shimmering web of colors, the entire painting was a celebratory abstraction of creativity itself. Paint and spirit, as a Villager said, had become indistinguishable. His vision had at last been fulfilled—"energy made visible."

Significantly, during this period when Jackson did talk about his work, he avoided the overheated pronouncements of many of the other abstract expressionists. "I feel nearer, more a part of the painting," he said in describing his new procedure, "since this way I can walk around it, work from the four sides and literally be *in* the painting." In a radio interview: "The thing that interests me is that today painters do not have to go to a subject matter outside of themselves." And on another occasion: "When I am *in* my painting, I'm not aware of what I'm doing. It is only after a sort of 'get acquainted' period that I see what I have been about. I have no fears about making changes, destroying the image, etc., because the painting has a life of its own. I try to let it come through." Finally, when someone asked him how he knew when a painting was finished, he replied, "How do you know when you've finished making love?"

Nothing remotely like Jackson's drip paintings had ever been seen and many of Jackson's fellow painters greeted the works with extravagant praise. De Kooning said simply, "Jackson paints without a brush like a god."

Some critics mocked them, some rhapsodized, but all were stunned. The critic for the *New York Times* was appropriately restrained in his disapproval: "More than ever before . . . it seems to me that Pollock's work is well over toward automatic writing and that its content (not definite subject-matter but content) is almost negligible—that what one gets out of it one must first put there." As happens so often to artists who make radical departures, a contest of disparaging metaphors began: "Baked macaroni," "a mass of tangled hair," "a pleasant design for a necktie." Jackson reacted to such criticism with remarkable equanimity, but when a critic wrote that his work showed "chaos, absolute lack of harmony, complete lack of structural organization, total absence of technique, however rudimentary, once again chaos," he replied angrily, "no chaos, damn it!"

Time noted: "A Jackson Pollock painting is apt to resemble a child's contour map of the Battle of Gettysburg," but was compelled to add, "Nevertheless, he is the darling of a highbrow cult which considers him 'the most powerful painter in America.' " "Highbrow cult" could mean only Clement Greenberg, who escalated his admiration of Jackson's work with each exhibition. He wrote, "[His new show is] a newer and loftier triumph. We have at last produced the best painter of a whole generation." A few months later he extolled Jackson as a candidate to become "the greatest American painter of the 20th century."

Greenberg's claim piqued the interest of the editors of *Life* magazine, and on August 8, 1947, a two-page color spread appeared under the headline "Is He the Greatest Living Painter in the United States?" and changed Jackson's life.

"Recently a formidable high-brow New York critic hailed the brooding, puzzled-looking man shown above as a major artist of our time," the article began, "and a fine candidate to become 'the greatest American painter of the 20th century.' Others believe that Jackson Pollock produces nothing more than interesting, if inexplicable decoration. Still others condemn his pictures as degenerate and find them as unpalatable as yesterday's macaroni." But if the editors did quote from one of Jackson's favorite comments about his own work—"When I am *in* my painting, I'm not aware of what I'm doing"—the phrase was ripe for mockery, and the tone of the piece was slyly satirical in the manner of people who consider themselves sophisticated but who, when confronted by art they find baffling, conceal their unease not by straightforward condemnation but by facetious condescension.

Ironically, the supercilious text had far less impact than the headline and it was dramatically overshadowed by the huge photo of Jackson standing in front of one of his drip paintings. "Look at him standing there," remarked Bill de Kooning. "He looks like some guy who works at a service station pumping gas." De Kooning may have meant his comment sarcastically, but he got the point—the image overpowered the article. This wasn't some effete European, this was a he-man, a Hemingway hero, tough, taciturn, virile, this was a rugged *American*. Jackson had entered the realm of iconography.

Jackson's reaction to the *Life* spread was ambivalent. On the one hand, he felt vindicated, proud to the point of smugness—he was a star, let those sons-of-bitches at "21," where he'd once been turned back at the door, let them try to keep him out now! On the other hand, he felt self-conscious, disoriented, even a bit embarrassed—he'd been struggling to express his soul, only to end up in the pages of a glossy magazine. He remained the most ferociously competitive of all the abstract expressionists, but while he preened in the spotlight, he was among the most reclusive, the most dedicated to his work, the most suspicious of acclaim, and recognized not only that such attention was suspect, but also that it would inevitably be turned against him.

After all, one of the things Jackson had learned in the Village—it was in the very air he breathed on 8th Street—was that approval from the uptowners led to self-doubt about the value of one's work and suspicion from one's fellow artists. Hadn't he begun to hear the stories circulating at the Cedar that Lee's shrewd politicking accounted for most of his success? And he was astute enough to realize that in the postwar proliferation of the mass media, the very publications that heralded new cultural trends would be the first ones to deride them. Worst of all, since he felt such a profound connection between himself and his painting, assaults on his work, and even benign misunderstandings, amounted to personal attacks. All too soon, fame caused him little but torment. As he told Lee shortly after the *Life* article appeared, "I feel like a clam without a shell."

His reputation among his fellow painters began to suffer because they resented his celebrity. Some who had once admired his daring now referred to his "excesses." He'd stolen the drip technique from them, several claimed—including Hans Hofmann. Even Philip Guston, his old friend from high school, accused him of becoming a "non-artist," "our primitive break-through boy." "The myth of the great artist somehow diminished the rest of us," said yet another painter in summing up their rancor. "He is the sun and we are the black hole."

Still, Jackson managed to stay sober, and he completed one masterpiece after another—*Autumn Rhythm, Lavender Mist, Blue Poles*. Part of him reveled in the public perception of him as the manly cowboy painter; a deeper part knew he was a far more sensitive, complex artist than the readers of *Life* magazine would ever know. Much of himself remained unexpressed in his paintings, and he was competitive not only with his contemporaries but with art history itself. Swinging uncontrollably between extremes of self-confidence and self-doubt, he succumbed to the seductions of publicity he'd vowed to resist. He'd been acclaimed as the Great American Painter, but he became ensnared in the media hoopla. And magazine celebrity hadn't done anything more for his sales than had critics' praise. The worst thing about the distractions of fame was that they kept him from his work—but the best thing about the distractions of fame was that they kept him from his work.

In the summer of 1950, largely at the urging of Lee, Jackson agreed to a series of photo sessions in his Springs barn with a young photographer named Hans Namuth. Jackson had always refused to allow anyone to watch him work, but this would be different, this would be a way to turn the paraphernalia of celebrity into a document for the ages, this would be a portrait of genius in action. "It was great drama," wrote Hans of their sessions, "the flame of explosion when the paint hit the canvas; the dancelike movement; the eyes tormented before knowing where to strike next; the tension; then the explosion again."

Since Jackson's art was an art of ceaseless motion, wouldn't a film be even more dramatic? For weeks throughout the fall, the two men collaborated on a movie, improvising a trestle to hold a large sheet of glass upon which Jackson painted lines of kinetic energy while Hans filmed from underneath.

The movie was completed late in the afternoon on Thanksgiving weekend, and Jackson and Hans went back to the house to join a dinner party Lee had arranged. Jackson headed straight for the kitchen, poured himself a stiff drink, and downed it in ravenous gulps. Did he instinctively know that he had reached the end of his extraordinary burst of creativity? Did he fear that in agreeing to the photos and the film, despite all his misgivings about the allure of publicity, he had turned himself into a commodity?

Within minutes Jackson became roaring drunk for the first time in years, and took out his rage, his sense of betrayal, on Hans. Seated at the dinner table, he mumbled ominously, "You're a phony. I'm not a phony, you're a phony," then, suddenly, he grabbed the end of the table with both hands, and upended it, sending plates and silver, turkey and gravy and salad, crashing to the floor. Jackson stared at the wreckage, walked out of the room, and slammed the door behind him.

Tuesday night at the Cedar. Everyone's awaiting the arrival of the legendary painter. The door swings open and in walks Jackson Pollock— bloated, his once jutting jaw covered with a scrawny beard, his fierce eyes deadened. He listlessly greets a few friends, downs several beers, recognizes a woman at one of the tables and sits down beside her. After a few coarse, slurred remarks, her date mildly protests. Jackson just smiles and casually pushes everything on the table onto the floor, glancing defiantly at the woman's date—what are you going to do about it? A typical night at the Cedar.

"Painting is no problem," Jackson told Lee, "the problem is what to do when you're *not* painting." The blank canvas became less a challenge than a threat. "It's drawing, as so many of the great masters seem to tell us," Frank O'Hara wrote, "that holds back the abyss"—and increasingly frustrated by his inability to draw, Jackson turned inward. All the turbulence of his soul seemed to coalesce into one, overpowering emotion—self-loathing. He'd reached a creative cul-de-sac. He lacked concentration, he had no energy. All he had left was his genius.

He couldn't paint "Pollocks" anymore. The drip technique now immobilized him with self-consciousness, the very condition it was intended to overcome. He was too proud to allow himself to become a painter by rote, too dedicated to turn himself into a painter who merely gratified the expectations of others. Perhaps he remembered the conversation he'd had with Hans Hofmann back in the early forties—how he'd answered Hans's questions about working from nature by saying, "I am nature." Hans had thought for a moment and quietly replied, "Ah, but if you work from inside, you will repeat yourself."

So at the very height of his fame, Jackson renounced the very style that had brought it. No further radical changes appeared in his canvases— that period of his life was over—and he returned to styles he'd explored in the past, reintroducing figurative elements, biomorphic shapes, calligraphic passages, totemic images, still incorporating drips but emphasizing passages of brushwork. In 1951 and 1952, he painted almost exclusively in black and white.

Although the post-drip paintings momentarily eased Jackson's anguish, and a few have even entered the Pollock canon, the praise of some of the critics—as when the *New York Times* referred to "his happy advance over the impersonality of much of his early work"—angered more than encouraged him. Harold Rosenberg made his point plain—Jackson had "narrowed" his art with "stridency" and "paranoia." Even his most ardent champion, Clem Greenberg, deserted him. "Forced," "pumped up," "going downhill"—in his reviews, he argued that Jackson's work lacked the old energy and inspiration.

Worst of all, Jackson felt betrayed by his fellow abstract expressionists, who saw his new painting as retrogressive, desultory, crudely imitative, even of himself. And of them as well. After looking at one of Jackson's latest works, Barnett Newman remarked, "My blood is in that painting."

Jackson had hit rock bottom before, but this time he stayed there. He seemed permanently drunk. He hurled vicious taunts at the customers in Nedick's and Riker's cafeterias; he wandered through the Village cursing passersby and peeing in the street. He peed in potted plants at gallery openings—word began going around that if he could no longer paint, he could certainly pee. Once he staggered into the middle of oncoming traffic, braying at the cars hurtling past. He stumbled into a show by Philip Guston and tore several paintings from the walls—painters who were actually working were the objects of his deepest rage.

Lee desperately tried to keep Jackson away from the painters at the Cedar, who, she thought, both scorned his work and encouraged his drinking—but he was determined to confront them. At the Club—which he believed had turned into a shrine to Bill de Kooning—he'd curse the speakers and stomp out to the accompaniment of jeers. And at a talk by the critic Thomas Hess, who'd just published a book on the abstract expressionists in which he had defended Jackson against his detractors—Jackson slurred profanities and, in unendurable frustration, threw the book at de Kooning. "Why'd you do that?" the startled de Kooning asked. "It's a good book." "It's a rotten book," muttered Jackson. "He treats you better than me."

But the Cedar was the main stage of Jackson's disintegration. "If the audience wasn't big enough for his big dramatic entrance," Franz Kline recalled, "he would come back later, loaded slightly more."

Patrons who were waiting for another pathetic performance of self-destruction they could relate to their friends didn't have long to wait. Jackson would lift a drink: "Who's the greatest painter in the world?" "You are," everyone would answer. "It's me," he would reply, "they know it's me."

Throughout the evening he would approach patrons and challenge, "Who the fuck are you?" or "Ya call yourself a painter?"—and no matter what they answered, he would mutter contemptuously, "You're a phony," or "Fuck off." The more isolated he felt, the more compelled he felt to establish his preeminence.

The critics in the highbrow magazines were no more immune to competitiveness than the painters they wrote about. For a time, Jackson had clung to his reputation as a defense against the void, and now, when he was merely clinging to his image, another critic entered the fray who seemed at once to valorize and to tarnish that image.

Harold Rosenberg, a tall, urbanely intimidating man who'd moved from Marxism to existentialism in the postwar years, had long hoped to challenge the hegemony of Clement Greenberg as the leading spokesman for abstract expressionism—"a tipster on masterpieces," he called his rival, "a taste bureaucrat." In *Art News* in late 1952 he published a polemic entitled "The American Action Painters" that became the talk of the Village for months.

"At a certain moment," Rosenberg's article began, "the canvas began to appear . . . as an arena in which to act—rather than as a space in which to reproduce, re-design, analyze, or 'express' an object, actual or imagined. . . . On the one hand, [the gestures were] a desperate recognition of moral and intellectual exhaustion; on the other, the exhilaration of an adventure over depths in which [the artist] might find reflected the true image of his identity."

Rosenberg seemed to be freeing the painter from history altogether. "A painting that is an act is inseparable from the biography of the artist."

Rosenberg's article didn't name names, but most readers felt that Jackson was the central figure in his argument—even Jackson called it "Rosenberg's piece on me." Who else could he be talking about when he referred to "gestures of liberation," "a revolution against the given in the self and in the world," forming the self out of an event, "encountering" the canvas, "the outer spaces of consciousness," and especially—for everyone had heard of Jackson's encounter with Hofmann—paintings that don't reproduce nature but are themselves nature?

Rosenberg admired Jackson's process but dismissed his paintings— or so concluded many readers. He praised Jackson's "daily annihilation," but felt that the quality of his work had seriously declined. But most agreed that he was referring to Jackson when in his most memorable, most cutting phrase he labeled some of the canvases produced by the abstract expressionists "apocalyptic wallpaper."

"The modern painter," Rosenberg had written a few years earlier, "begins with nothingness. That is the only thing he copies. The rest he invents." "The man who started to remake himself," he now wrote, "had made himself into a commodity with a trademark." Rosenberg claimed he was merely describing an aesthetic climate, but didn't he intend those two passages to delineate the beginning and the end of Jackson's artistic biography?

As far as Lee and Jackson were concerned, Rosenberg was now the enemy. An enemy with a vendetta—for hadn't Jackson at a party at Rosenberg's house several months earlier muttered, "What a lot of shit" and "Horse piss" as their host pontificated about art? Why was he always put in the position of having to enact a role a critic assigned him, first as "pure painter," now as "existential hero"? Worst of all, he felt that Rosenberg's article didn't just ridicule his work, it was at the center of the cabal to overthrow his position as the preeminent painter of his generation and replace him with Bill de Kooning.

Jackson was so furious that he momentarily displaced his paranoia about his fellow painters onto the critics who underestimated them. As the two poles of abstract expressionism, Jackson and Bill de Kooning had always had a respectful rivalry—expressed, of course, in insults. Jackson called Bill's *Woman* series "that shit" and once told him, "You know more but I feel more." Bill believed "artists should have a brotherhood" but in the face of such taunts he gave as good as he got. When Jackson said he didn't like one of Bill's shows—"You painted it too fast"—Bill shot back, "Who the hell are you to speak? You paint like a chain smoker!"

Sharing a bottle of booze outside the Cedar one evening not long after Jackson had read Rosenberg's article and thrown Hess's book at Bill, the two painters commiserated about their lack of recognition. "Jackson, you're the greatest painter in America." "No, Bill, *you're* the greatest painter in America." "No, Jackson," said Bill, grabbing the bottle, "*you're* the greatest painter in America." Both knew the other didn't really believe what he was saying—but the scene was all the more poignant because both knew Jackson was no longer painting masterpieces, and never would again.

Inside the Cedar, another group was gathering—Village women, or "girls," long-haired, leotard-clad, artists and models and sculptors or just hangers-on in bohemia. In their macho camaraderie, the painters regarded them as "on the make," seeking a night of sex with fame, maybe even an affair that would bring them in touch with genius. One young painter who bore a passing resemblance to Franz Kline liked to regale his comrades with the story of the night he picked up a woman at the Cedar, took her home for a bout of torrid sex, and awoke the next morning to the words "How do you like your eggs, Franz?"

Jackson, of course, was the painter most of the "girls" wanted to meet—though his habit of slurring "You got great tits, wanna fuck?," then showing himself too polluted to do so, soon disabused them of the notion that he was the sexiest man in the Village. One night—or so the story went—Franz Kline became so annoyed with his bluster about his cocksmanship that he hired a prostitute to say, "Okay, let's go" when Jackson encountered her, whereupon the flustered Jackson instantly disappeared.

Jackson's marriage was a shambles. He felt smothered by Lee's self-sacrifice, he'd taken to calling her a "Jewish cunt," he'd even begun to strike her. Now he wasn't seeking sex so much as adulation. And when a twenty-five-year-old woman named Ruth Kligman showed up at the Cedar one night in February 1956 he found both.

A voluptuous and flirtatious artist's model from Newark who bore a slight resemblance to Elizabeth Taylor, Ruth was more systematic in her approach than most of the women who wanted to meet the legends. She asked a friend the names of the leading abstract expressionists. Pollock, de Kooning, and Kline, her friend replied. "Which one is the greatest?" When her friend said "Pollock," Ruth headed for the Cedar. She said she idolized Jackson "as other girls adored Brando or Elvis." And when they finally met, his legend and her fantasy surmounted his gross behavior, his bloated body, and his drunken impotence.

Legend and fantasy dominated Jackson's feelings as well. Far from concealing his relationship with Ruth, he made sure everyone at the Cedar knew about it. Now he had a "girl," a *gorgeous* girl; now let the other painters mock him. They even spent a night in his Springs barn while Lee slept in the house. Lee had long realized that Jackson was having an affair, but this was too much. "White with rage," she ordered Ruth off the property and soon after sailed for Europe to give herself and Jackson time and space to decide whether they could save their marriage.

Their marriage wasn't uppermost in Jackson's mind—in some dim recess of his consciousness he had to decide whether or not he could save his *life*. He felt he hadn't painted anything worthy of his talent for years, he was drinking as much as a case of beer a day, his relationship with Ruth had turned as abusive as his relationship with Lee. His only goal in life, his friends sensed, was self-obliteration.

"There's wildness in me, " Jackson said to a friend at the beach. "There's wildness in my hands." He picked up a handful of sand and let it fall through his fingers. "There *was*," he said softly. And now, awaiting Ruth's arrival for a weekend in Springs, he visited a friend on Friday night, and as he was about to leave, said softly, "Life is beautiful, the trees are beautiful, the sky is beautiful," then added, "but I only have the image of death."

Ruth arrived the next morning, accompanied by Edith Metzger, a twenty-five-year-old beautician from the Bronx—she wanted a friend with her in case Jackson was in one of his foul moods, as she instantly saw he was. Jackson spent most of the afternoon drinking gin; everything Ruth said seemed to make him angry. The women wanted to go to the beach—he refused. They wanted to go to a party in the evening—he sourly agreed, but changed his mind halfway there, then changed his mind again.

"He's drunk, let's go home," Edith whispered to Ruth on the way out, and when they stopped at a bar for a bite to eat, she refused to get back in the car; she would call a cab. Jackson passed out for a moment, awoke in a fury, and ordered the women to get in. Almost hysterical, Edith begged to be left behind, but finally, she gave in.

Jackson had gotten his green 1950 Oldsmobile V8 convertible in exchange for two paintings and his reckless driving was well known to the police. He pushed the accelerator to the floor. Within seconds Edith was shrieking, "Let me out!" but her screams only made him drive faster. "Please stop!" Ruth begged. "Don't do this!" But he careened through the night as if he could outrace his demons. The car came to a curve, and Jackson lost control. The car hit an embankment, surged through underbrush, turned end over end, and stopped. It was 10:15. They were only a few hundred yards from home. Ruth was thrown clear and suffered a fractured pelvis. Edith was killed instantly. Jackson was hurled from the car, flew fifty feet in less than a second, and slammed headfirst into a tree, at last finding the oblivion he'd sought for so long.

The son of a bitch," said Clement Greenberg when he heard of Jackson's death, "he did it." But after the shock and grief had worn off, after the eulogies and reminiscences, the words of another critic seemed grimly prophetic. "Death," said Herbert Read, "is the greatest thing that can happen to an artist." Read meant his words ironically, of course—death enhances an artist's reputation in a sudden rush of sympathy, and assuring that his output is finite, almost immediately inflates its value.

Only a few years after Jackson's fatal accident, paintings that once sold for a few thousand dollars, when they sold at all, were selling for three or four times that much. Eight thousand dollars was the highest price he'd ever received for a painting in his lifetime, but little over a decade later the same painting sold for $350,000, and if the owner had waited a few more years he could have made several million. And a leading museum, having refused to pay $10,000 for *Autumn Rhythm* in the last years of Jackson's life, purchased it for three times that amount a year later. Jackson's paintings were not only auctioned off as masterpieces, they became templates for fabrics, linoleum, even jigsaw puzzles. After all the years of tortured striving to transform self-destruction into self-expression, Jackson's life was turned into legend—and his legend into cash.

Death and success—since the flowering of Romanticism and the flourishing of bohemianism, the two have been linked in the popular image of the artist, as if to be an artist is to live in squalid neglect, die too soon, and achieve posthumous acclaim. "Success kills" was virtually a motto for the downtown artists, and "selling out" was the commonplace phrase of the day for painters who managed to make a living. "If anybody sold anything," said one painter, "the rumor went around that the quality of his work had gone down." "The minute success entered into the art world," said another, "everything changed. It was all ruined."

So the ambiguities of success led to the cult of failure. Indifference and isolation may have caused despair and dissipation, and even premature death, but only by passing through failure could the painters achieve the one kind of success they wanted. Despite their contempt for contemporary success, they never for a moment doubted historic achievement. They scorned the way their ideas were transformed into property, but if the myth of the artist's heroic failure was inevitably linked to the myth of his posthumous acclaim, they themselves were at least partially responsible.

When Robert Rauschenberg erased a Willem de Kooning drawing and exhibited the blank sheet of paper as a work of art, he was at once honoring a master, rejecting the concept of art as object, and confirming the death of abstract expressionism.

Pop art, the next chic school, emerged in the early sixties as an almost systematic repudiation of everything abstract expressionism stood for. The abstract expressionists had achieved fame and wealth in spite of their principles, while fame and wealth were among the first principles of the pop artists. Rejecting what they regarded as the emotionalism and elitism of their immediate predecessors—their evangelical ardor, their high-art condescension to mass culture—the pop artists were encouraged by a voracious art market that treated paintings as commodities that were either obsolescent or "hot," and by an insatiable media culture that was eager to renounce what it had so recently embraced. To demystify the pomposities of abstract expressionism, to replace the inner necessities of the individual with the fascinating facades of society, and, above all, to emphasize the irony between fine art masterpieces and mass media iconography—the backlash was so annihilating that when Sidney Janis, who had represented many of the leading abstract expressionists, mounted a pop art show in 1962, his old-line painters withdrew from his gallery in a gesture as futile as it was angry. Art, they felt, was no longer a quest for salvation, it was a dedication to entertainment.

Frank Stella spoke for most of the cool, irony-drenched younger artists who saw their predecessors as increasingly hollow and outmoded when he said he wanted to purge "the Romance of Abstract Expressionism." "I began to feel very strongly about finding a way that wasn't so wrapped up in the hullabaloo [of abstract expressionist rhetoric] . . . something that was stable in a sense, something that wasn't constantly a record of your sensitivity, a record of flux." And Roy Lichtenstein sarcastically announced that he was "anti- all those brilliant ideas of preceding movements which everyone understands so thoroughly." Meyer Schapiro had written of the abstract expressionists that, "The impulse becomes tangible. . . . We see, as it were, the track of emotion, its obstruction, persistence, or extinction." But what use was such an aesthetic to a movement that had no use for emotion?

As one prominent critic explained, "Andy Warhol said that he wanted to be a machine. What could be further from the emotional excesses of Pollock, the muscular dynamism of Kline, the transports of Rothko, the savage grandeur of Still and de Kooning, and the transcendentalism of Newman?"

Yet how brave the voyage into the unknown to reinvent painting itself. How compelling the hunger for transcendence. A French painter once remarked of the abstract expressionists, "They dive into the water before they know how to swim." But wasn't that the point? Wasn't the only failure a "failure of nerve"? Yet if the popular imagination had turned the abstract expressionists into icons largely because that was the safest way to deal with genius, in the art world the myth was moribund.

Nevertheless, the *work* of the abstract expressionists continued to influence painters until the end of the century. Yet in another sense, the movement didn't *lead* anywhere. Everything it stressed—stripping away convention, relying on performative energy, freeing the self not only from culture but from history itself—culminated in masterpieces, but also in a creative dead end. Freedom as disconnection from society, freedom as the absence of content or context—such a concept may have liberated the abstract expressionists to explore the outermost possibilities of painting, and it may have made them quintessential Americans, but it also left them adrift. To believe that the painter can achieve originality only by abandoning traditional form, space, content, and technique—to believe, moreover, that the individual can only make a self through liberation from limits—led to a thrilling sense of open-endedness, but also to an aesthetic that had no followers and, for the individual artists, to lives of loneliness and isolation.

The community of the abstract expressionists began to fragment soon after Jackson's death. They joined in contempt for the merchandisers of visions, of course, but the sudden prosperity that followed in their wake engendered rivalries over money far more bitter than any rivalries over aesthetics.

To the world, the abstract expressionists had never been Villagers—they were New York painters, American painters. Like the beats, who were seen in increasing numbers, but who also developed communities in San Francisco and on college campuses across the country, by the fifties they were part of the increasing popularity of bohemia across the nation, culminating in the counterculture of the sixties.

The abstract expressionists never really regarded themselves as Villagers, either. While nearly all of them shared several aspects of the Village ethos—sacrificing everything for art, disdaining the cultural establishment, regarding marginality as an impetus to creativity, romanticizing the renegade individual, and dedicating themselves to self-expression, their rebellion was confined to their personal and professional obsessions. With few exceptions they showed little interest in radical politics (or politics of any kind), their attitude toward sexual freedom was little more than macho chauvinism, and far from seeking a broad social and cultural revolution, they remained as insular as the middle class they despised. The only past that concerned them was art history. They had no sense of the heritage of insurgency that surrounded them—the very idea of a radical bohemia seemed irrelevant. They regarded their neighborhood primarily as a place of low rents, cheap bars, and willing women.

Clement Greenberg wrote frequently of the desocialization of the artistic community. The Village painters, he said, had an "intimate and habitual acquaintance with isolation . . . or rather the alienation that is its cause. . . . [It] is the condition under which the true reality of our age is experienced. And the experience of this true reality is indispensable to any ambitious art." "The fate of American art," he wrote on another occasion, "is being decided by young people, few of them over forty, who . . . have no reputations that extend beyond a small circle of fanatic, art-fixated misfits isolated . . . as if they were living in Paleolithic Europe."

Yet the media and the middle class voraciously assimilated rebellion and quickly transformed this isolation and hostility to mass culture into celebrations of Americanism—these men exemplified the pioneering spirit! And the Village was increasingly regarded as a charming community of American eccentrics, at once irrelevant and prophetic, as if everything it stood for could be both rejected and absorbed, as if all the Villagers' efforts to subvert American ideals could be made to confirm them.

The Cedar closed its doors in 1962—the same year the Club came to an end—and moved to a new location a few blocks north. By then few of the abstracts were left. As one Villager put it, "By the time most people heard of the painters at the Cedar, the painters were no longer going to the Cedar." The ten-year party was over.

In the new Cedar, a new generation of Villagers reminisced about the legendary artists. I heard one of the old-timers claim that he'd actually seen Jackson Pollock on a horse—you know, the cowboy image—and he said he'd never seen anyone more nervous in his life. Larry Rivers told me that Franz Kline was always at the Cedar when he got there and always there when he left. And did you hear the story about the painters gathering in the old Cedar the night after Pollock's death? Someone asked Franz Kline what he thought of Jackson's work. "Jackson's work? He painted the whole sky," he said softly. "He rearranged the stars."

Afterword

Rachel Wetzsteon

My father died on February 20, 1998, of complications from heart surgery. If he had lived longer, he'd have written a last chapter to this book in which he briskly outlined the history of the Village from the 1950s to the present, and also expounded on the nature and future of bohemianism. I was tempted to do something similar, or at least attempt to tie up the various loose ends of his epic narrative. But I can't help feeling that the book seems pretty complete as it stands. And besides, I'd rather consider what led him to the subject of the Village in the first place. Why would he want to spend ten years of his life passionately immersed in the intricate history of this particular square mile, in the love lives and creative careers of the rebels, outcasts, and visionaries who ended up there? And why did a native of Montana turn out to be the perfect person for the task?

He came to Greenwich Village in the early 1960s, after equally unpleasant stints in graduate school and the army, with dreams of becoming a writer. It was love at first sight: he adored the energy and electricity of the Village, and years later—the very antithesis of a jaded New Yorker—continued to insist that he couldn't live anywhere else. I love the way his enthusiasm pervades this book. As a non-native New Yorker, my father

571

could understand, on both an intellectual and an instinctual level, the rest-lessness that drove so many people here; he'd felt the same restlessness, and made the same journey, himself.

My father could also have passed as one of the gallery of eccentrics he so lovingly describes in these pages. In a poem I wrote for his memorial service, I coined a term that I hoped would demonstrate why: he was a "walking reader." Trotting from the *Village Voice* offices to his apartment on West Twelfth Street, sneaker-clad for greater speed, head bowed low in earnest perusal of *Daniel Deronda* or the latest issue of *American Theater*, he cut a bizarre figure, to be sure, but also one that wonderfully epitomized the manners and morals of Villagers past. His idea of hell, like that of many New York intellectuals, was being stalled on a street corner with nothing to read—or being so hopelessly conventional as to do only one thing at a time!

Treasured images don't vanish easily. Only weeks after my father died, I'd catch sight of a bustling, bearded man in the Village and imagine for a moment that it was him—only to realize, after a brutal reality check, that this couldn't be true. Even three years later I still think I see him, and many others have reported similar sightings. I'm almost tempted to believe that my father's last wish was to haunt the streets he so loved as a kind of wandering benevolent ghost, and that the wish was granted.

But is it true—as this book's opening line, after all, suggests—that the Village isn't what it used to be? Admittedly, it's hard to imagine Dawn Powell checking proofs of her new novel while sipping café latte on a plush couch at Starbucks, or Maxwell Bodenheim jotting down ideas for his lat-est mad poem on a napkin at super-slick Xando. The creative types, unable to afford the soaring rents, have mostly packed up and departed—for other boroughs, other cities, other crucibles of change.

Although it's easy to lament the death of the Village, perhaps we're missing the point when we do so. Even in its glory days (as this book demonstrates over and over) the Village was more a state of mind than a spot on a map, and therefore whether the center of this community is Perry Street or Paris or Williamsburg hardly matters; what's important is that the vitality, the fervor, the passion continue *somewhere*. As long as there are restless rebels and determined dreamers, there will be a Republic of Dreams. And so, as my father might put it in one of his characteristic para-doxes: the Village is dead; long live the Village.

Selected Bibliography

The creation of Republic of Dreams *was, to a great extent, an act of synthesis. While writing the book, the author consulted innumerable sources for information, stories, background, context, color, and inspiration. It was his intention to acknowledge his gratitude to these many sources. The following is a selected list of individuals, publications, and materials the author consulted while writing this book (along with a few pertinent additions to the scholarship on the subject published subsequent to the author's death).*

PREFACE AND INTRODUCTION

Abel, Lionel. *The Intellectual Follies: A Memoir of the Literary Venture in New York and Paris.* New York: Norton, 1984.

Abrahams, Edward. *The Lyrical Left and the Origins of Cultural Radicalism in America.* Charlottesville: University Press of Virginia, 1988.

Allen, Oliver E. *New York, New York: A History of the World's Most Exhilarating and Challenging City.* New York: Atheneum, 1990.

Amram, David. Personal interview, 27 May 1987.

Anderson, Sherwood. *The Portable Sherwood Anderson.* Rev. ed., Horace Gregory, ed. New York: Penguin, 1977.

———. *A Story Teller's Story: Memoirs of Youth and Middle Age.* 4th ed. New York: Penguin, 1989.

Aronowitz, Al. "Gate Keeper: Art D'Lugoff and the Future of Jazz." *Village Voice* 19 July 1994: 36.

Baldwin, James. *No Name in the Street.* New York: Dial, 1972.

Banes, Sally. *Village 1963: Avant-garde Performance and the Effervescent Body.* Durham: Duke University Press, 1993.

Bannon, Ann. Telephone interview by Martha Lagace, 23 January 1987.

Baraka, Amiri. *The Autobiography of LeRoi Jones.* New York: Freundlich, 1984.

Barrett, William. *The Truants: Adventures Among the Intellectuals.* Garden City: Anchor, 1982.

Beard, Rick, and Leslie Cohen Berlowitz, eds. *Greenwich Village: Culture and Counterculture*. New Brunswick: Rutgers University Press, 1993.

Berdan, Pamela, and Roberta Everett. Personal interview.

Beretta, Joanne. Personal interview.

Berman, Avis. *Revels on Eighth Street: Juliana Force and the Whitney Museum of American Art*. New York: Atheneum, 1990.

Berman, Paul. "Democracy and Homosexuality." *New Republic* 20 December 1993: 17–31.

Brightman, Carol. *Writing Dangerously: Mary McCarthy and Her World*. New York: Clarkson Potter, 1992.

Brooks, Van Wyck. *An Autobiography*. New York: Dutton, 1965.

———. *John Sloan: A Painter's Life*. New York: Dutton, 1955.

Brossard, Chandler. *As the Wolf Howls at My Door*. Elmwood Park, NJ: Dalkey Archive Press, 1992.

Broyard, Anatole. *Kafka Was the Rage: A Greenwich Village Memoir*. New York: Southern-Crown, 1993.

———. *Men, Women and Other Anticlimaxes*. New York: Methuen, 1977.

Burke, Carolyn. *Becoming Modern: The Life of Mina Loy*. New York: Farrar, Straus & Giroux, 1996.

Campbell, James. *Talking at the Gates: A Life of James Baldwin*. New York: Viking, 1991.

Cantwell, Mary. *Manhattan, When I Was Young*. Boston: Houghton Mifflin, 1995.

Carpenter, Humphrey. *W. H. Auden: A Biography*. New York: Houghton Mifflin, 1981.

Carr, Virginia Spencer. *Dos Passos: A Life*. New York: Doubleday, 1984.

Charters, Ann, ed. *The Portable Beat Reader*. New York: Viking, 1992.

Chauncey, George. *Gay New York: Gender, Urban Culture, and the Making of the Gay Male World, 1890–1940*. New York: Basic, 1994.

———. "The Way We Look." *Village Voice* 1 July 1988: 31.

———. "The Way We Were." *Village Voice* 1 July 1988: 29–30.

Cheever, John. *The Enormous Radio and Other Stories*. New York: Funk, 1953.

Churchill, Allen. *The Improper Bohemians: A Re-creation of Greenwich Village in Its Heyday*. New York: Dutton, 1959.

Clayton, Bruce. *Forgotten Prophet: The Life of Randolph Bourne*. Baton Rouge: Louisiana State University Press, 1984.

Clayton, Douglas. *Floyd Dell: The Life and Times of an American Rebel*. Chicago: Ivan R. Dee, 1994.

Coles, Robert. *Dorothy Day: A Radical Tradition*. Reading: Addison-Wesley, 1987.

Cowley, Malcolm. *Exile's Return: A Literary Odyssey of the 1920s*. New York: Compass-Viking, 1951 (originally published 1934).

———. *The Flower and the Leaf: A Contemporary Record of American Writing Since 1941*. Donald Faulkner, ed. New York: Viking, 1985.

Coxe, Louis. *Edwin Arlington Robinson: The Life of Poetry*. New York: Pegasus, 1969.

Cunningham, Sis, and Gordon Freisen. Personal interview.

Curtis, Thomas Quinn. Personal interview.

Day, Dorothy. *Loaves and Fishes*. San Francisco: Harper, 1981.

——. *The Long Loneliness: The Autobiography of Dorothy Day*. New York: Harper, 1952.

Dearborn, Mary. *Queen of Bohemia: The Life of Louise Bryant*. Boston: Houghton Mifflin, 1996.

Dell, Floyd. *Homecoming*. New York: Farrar, Straus & Giroux, 1933.

——. *Love in Greenwich Village*. N.p.: n.d.

Dennis, Patrick. *Auntie Mame*. New York: Vanguard, 1955.

Dickstein, Morris. *Gates of Eden: American Culture in the Sixties*. New York: Basic Books, 1977.

Diggins, John Patrick. *The Rise and Fall of the American Left*. 2nd ed. New York: Norton, 1992.

Di Prima, Diane. *Memoirs of a Beatnik*. 2nd ed. San Francisco: Last Gasp, 1988.

Dos Passos, John. *John Dos Passos: An Informal Memoir: The Best of Times*. New York: New American Library, 1966.

Douglas, Ann. Personal interview.

——. *Terrible Honesty: Mongrel Manhattan in the 1920s*. New York: Farrar, Straus & Giroux, 1995.

Duberman, Martin. *Stonewall*. New York: Plume, 1993.

Edmistan, Susan, and Linda C. Cirino. *Literary New York: A History and Guide*. 2nd ed. New York: Gibbs Smith-Peregrine Smith, 1991.

Elliot, Bruce. *Village*. New York: Avon, 1982.

Farnan, Dorothy J. *Auden in Love: The Intimate Story of a Lifelong Love Affair*. New York: Simon & Schuster, 1984.

Frank, Elizabeth. *Louise Bogan: A Portrait*. New York: Knopf, 1984.

Frank, Waldo. *Memoirs of Waldo Frank*. Alan Trachtenberg, ed. Amherst: University of Massachusetts Press, 1973.

Freeman, Joseph. *An American Testament*. London: Victor Gollancz, 1938.

Gallagher, Dorothy. *All the Right Enemies: The Life and Murder of Carlo Tresca*. New Brunswick: Rutgers University Press, 1988.

Gayle, Addison. *Richard Wright: Ordeal of a Native Son*. Rev. ed. New York: Doubleday, 1980.

Gaylord, Bruce R. *The Only Complete Guide to Greenwich Village*. 2nd ed. New York: Bruce Cranor Gaylord, 1984.

——. *The Picture Book of Greenwich Village*. 2nd ed. New York: Carol, 1991.

Gee, Helen. Personal interview, 29 March 1987.

Gilmer, Walker. *Horace Liveright: Publisher of the Twenties*. New York: David Lewis, 1970.

Gold, Herbert. *Bohemia: Where Art, Angst, Love and Strong Coffee Meet*. New York: Simon & Schuster, 1993.

Gordon, Lorraine. Personal interview.

Gordon, Max. *Live at the Village Vanguard*. New York: St. Martin's, 1980.

——. Personal interview.

Grazia, Edward de. *Girls Lean Back Everywhere: The Law of Obscenity and the Assault on Genius*. New York: Random House, 1992.

Green, Martin. *New York 1913: The Armory Show and the Paterson Strike Pageant*. New York: Scribner, 1988.

Gross, Steve, et al. *Old Greenwich Village: An Architectural Portrait*. New York: Wiley, 1995.

Gruen, John; Photography, Fred W. McDarrah. *The New Bohemia*. Chicago: Capella—Chicago Review Press, 1990.

Grumbach, Doris. *The Company She Kept*. New York: Coward, 1967.

Hahn, Emily. *Romantic Rebels: An Informal History of Bohemianism in America*. Boston: Houghton Mifflin, 1967.

Hale, Nathan G., Jr. *Freud and the Americans: The Beginnings of Psychoanalysis in the United States, 1876–1917*. New York: Oxford University Press, 1971.

Hamill, Pete. "Lion's Head Revisited." *Village Voice* 21 January 1984: 10.

Hapgood, Hutchins. *A Victorian in the Modern World*. New York: Harcourt, 1939.

Hayes, Elizabeth. Personal interview.

Hecht, Ben. *Letters from Bohemia*. London: Hammond, n.d.

Heide, Robert. Personal interview, 7 April 1987.

——, and John Gilman. *Greenwich Village: A Primo Guide to Shopping, Eating, and Making Merry in True Bohemia*. New York: Griffin, 1995.

Heller, Adele, and Lois Rudnick, eds. *The Cultural Moment: The New Politics, the New Woman, the New Psychology, the New Art, and the New Theater in America*. New Brunswick: Rutgers University Press, 1991.

Herrmann, Dorothy. *S. J. Perelman: A Life*. New York: Putnam, 1986.

Herschberger, Ruth. Personal interview by Martha Lagace, 16 January 1987.

Hoffman, Abbie. Personal interview.

Hoffman, Frederick. *Freudianism and the Literary Mind*. Baton Rouge: Louisiana State University Press, 1945.

——. *The Twenties*. 2nd ed. New York: Collier, 1962.

Holmes, Charles S. *The Clocks of Columbus: The Literary Career of James Thurber*. New York: Atheneum, 1972.

Hoopes, James. *Van Wyck Brooks: In Search of American Culture*. Amherst: University of Massachusetts Press, 1977.

Hornsby, George, and Veronica Hornsby. Personal interview.

Hoyt, Nancy. *Elinor Wylie: The Portrait of an Unknown Lady*. Indianapolis: Bobbs-Merrill, 1935.

Humphrey, Robert. *Children of Fantasy: The 1st Rebels of Greenwich Village*. New York: Wiley, 1978.

Jackson, Kenneth T., ed. *The Encyclopedia of New York City*. New York: Yale University Press, 1995.

Jacobs, Jane. *The Death and Life of Great American Cities*. New York: Vintage, 1961.

——. Personal interview, 8 April 1987.

Joans, Ted. Personal interview.

Johnson, Helene Mullins. Personal interview.

Johnston, Joyce. "Her Candle Burns at One End." Review of *In the City*, by Joan Silber. *New York Times Literary Supplement* 29 March 1987.

Jones, Hettie. *How I Became Hettie Jones*. New York: Dutton, 1990.

Josephson, Barney. Personal interview, 18 February 1987.

Josephson, Matthew. *Life Among the Surrealists*. New York: Holt, 1962.

Kaplan, Justin. *Lincoln Steffens: A Biography*. New York: Touchstone, 1974.

Kazin, Alfred. *A Walker in the City*. New York: Harcourt, 1951.

Kellner, Bruce. *Carl Van Vechten and the Irreverent Decades*. Oklahoma: University of Oklahoma Press, 1968.

Kisseloff, Jeff. *You Must Remember This: An Oral History of Manhattan from the 1890s to World War II.* San Diego: Harcourt, 1989.

Klein, Carole. *Alive.* New York: Harper, 1979.

Knopf Guides. *New York.* New York: Knopf, 1994.

Koch, Kenneth. Personal interview, 23 March 1987.

Kramer, Robert. Personal interview.

Kreymbourg, Alfred. *Troubadour: An Autobiography.* New York: Liveright, 1925.

Krim, Seymour. "Chandler, WWD, and, Inevitably, Hopefully Not Intrusively, Me." *The Review of Contemporary Fiction* Spring (1987): 87–90.

Kupferberg, Tuli. Personal interview.

Lanier, H. U. *Greenwich Village Today and Yesterday.* New York: Harper, 1949.

Lasch, Christopher. *The New Radicalism in America, 1889–1963: The Intellectual as a Social Type.* New York: Knopf, 1965.

Laucanno-Sawyer, Christopher. *An Invisible Spectator: A Biography of Paul Bowles.* New York: Weidenfeld & Nicolson, 1989.

Laughlin, James. Personal interview, 9 March 1987.

Leisner, Marcia. *Literary Neighborhoods of New York.* Washington: Starrhill Press, 1989.

Levine, Lawrence W. *Highbrow Lowbrow: The Emergence of Cultural Hierarchy in America.* Cambridge: Harvard University Press, 1988.

Lewis, Sinclair. "Hobohemia." *The Saturday Evening Post* 7 April 1917.

"The Lion Sleeps Tonight: The Brothers McCourt Sing a Legendary Pub's Lullaby." *New York Times,* 13 October 1996.

Lopate, Phillip. "Bohemia Died, but Life Went On." Review of *In the Night Café,* by Joyce Johnston. *New York Times Book Review* 30 April 1989: 11.

Loughery, John. *John Sloan: Painter and Rebel.* New York: Holt, 1995.

Luongo, Christopher. "Only the History Changes at Chumley's." *The Villager* 16 February 1989: 1.

Mabel Dodge: The Salon Years, 1912–1917. New York: Barbara Mathes Gallery, 1985.

Madden, David, ed. *Remembering James Agee.* Baton Rouge: Louisiana State University Press, 1979.

Madison, Charles. *Critics and Crusaders.* New York: Ungar, 1947.

Manso, Peter. *Mailer: His Life and Times.* New York: Penguin, 1985.

Marcus, Greil. *Lipstick Traces: A Secret History of the 20th Century.* Cambridge: Harvard University Press, 1989.

Markson, David. Letter to the author, 30 November 1988.

Marquis, Alice Goldfarb. *Alfred H. Barr, Jr.: Missionary for the Modern.* Chicago: Contemporary Books, 1989.

McAlmon, Robert, and Kay Boyle. *Being Geniuses Together: 1920–1930.* Rev. ed. San Francisco: North Point, 1984.

McCarthy, Mary. *A Charmed Life.* New York: Harcourt, 1955.

——. *Intellectual Memoirs: New York, 1936–1938.* New York: Harcourt, 1992.

——. Letter to the author, 1 December 1986.

McDarrah, Fred W., and Gloria S. McDarrah. *Beat Generation: Glory Days in Greenwich Village.* New York: Music Sales, 1996.

McDarrah, Fred W., and Patrick J. McDarrah. *The Greenwich Village Guide: Sixteen Walks.* Chicago: Capella-Chicago Review Press, 1992.

McKenney, Ruth. *My Sister Eileen*. New York: Harcourt, n.d.

Miles, Barry. *Ginsberg: A Biography*. New York: Simon & Schuster, 1989.

Miller, Charles. *Auden: An American Friendship*. New York: Scribner, 1983.

Miller, Terry. *Greenwich Village and How It Got That Way*. New York: Crown, 1990.

Mills, Hilary. *Mailer: A Biography*. New York: Empire, 1982.

Moody, Howard, Rev. Personal interview.

Morgan, Ted. *The Life and Times of William Burroughs*. New York: Holt, 1988.

Murger, Henry. *Scènes de la Vie de Bohème*. Paris: Gallimard, 1998.

Murnaghan, Brigid. Personal interview, 21 May 1987.

Muson, Gorham. *The Awakening Twenties: A Memoir History of a Literary Period*. Baton Rouge: Louisiana State University Press, 1985.

———. "Greenwich Village That Was: Seedbed of the Nineteen-Twenties." *The Literary Review*.

Nagrin, Lee. Personal interview.

Naumann, Francis M., with Beth Venn. *Making Mischief: Dada Invades New York*. New York: Harry Abrams, 1996.

Nelson, Raymond. *Van Wyck Brooks: A Writer's Life*. New York: Dutton, 1981.

Nichols, Cicely. Personal interview.

Nin, Anaïs. *Diary of Anaïs Nin, 1944–1947*. Vol. 4. Gunther Stulman, ed. New York: Harvest, 1971.

O'Brien, Geoffrey. *Dream Time*. London: Secker & Warburg, 1988.

O'Connell, Shaun. *Remarkable, Unspeakable New York: A Literary History*. Boston: Beacon, 1995.

O'Connor, Richard, and Dale L. Walker. *The Lost Revolutionary: A Biography of John Reed*. New York: Harcourt, 1967.

Olsen, Stanley. *Elinor Wylie: A Biography*. New York: Dial, 1979.

Osborne, Charles. *W. H. Auden: The Life of a Poet*. New York: Harcourt, 1979.

Ostrender, Gilbert. *American Civilization: The First Machine Age*. New York: Harper, 1970.

Parry, Albert. *Garrets and Pretenders: A History of Bohemianism in America*. New York: Covici, Friede, 1932.

Prager, Emily. Personal interview, 3 February 1987.

Prager, Peggy. Personal interview, 2 February 1988.

Raphael, Malcolm. Personal interview.

Rathbone, Belinda. *Walker Evans: A Biography*. Boston: Houghton Mifflin, 1995.

Reed, Susan. Personal interview.

Rogers, Gaby. Personal interview, 7 March 1987.

Rose, Mark. "Getting Out and About at Night in New Village." *Los Angeles Times* 15 June 1986, Part VII: 11–12.

Rosenstone, Robert. *Romantic Revolutionary: A Biography of John Reed*. New York: Knopf, 1975.

Rothchild, Charles. Personal interview.

Rubin, Joe. Personal interview.

Russ, Lavina. Personal interview.

Sante, Luc. *Low Life: Lures and Snares of Old New York*. New York: Farrar, Straus & Giroux, 1991.

Schorer, Mark. *Sinclair Lewis: An American Life*. New York: McGraw Hill, 1961.

Seigel, Jerrold. *Bohemian Paris: Culture, Politics, and the Boundaries of Bourgeois Life, 1830–1930*. New York: Sifton, 1986.

Seldes, George. *Witness to a Century: Encounters with the Noted, the Notorious, and the Three S.O.B.s*. New York: Ballantine, 1987.

Selzer, Jack. *Kenneth Burke in Greenwich Village: Conversing with the Moderns, 1915–1931*. Madison: University of Wisconsin Press, 1996.

Sennett, Richard. *Flesh and Stone: The Body and the City in Western Civilization*. New York: Norton, 1994.

Shattuck, Roger. *The Banquet Years: The Origins of the Avant-garde in France 1885 to World War I*. Rev. ed. New York: Vintage, 1968.

Shechner, Mark. "New York Intellectuals." Review of *The New York Intellectual: The Rise and Decline of the Stalinist Left from the 1930s to the 1980s*, by Alan Wald.

Shelton, Robert. *No Direction Home*. New York: Morrow, 1986.

Shi, David E. *Matthew Josephson: Bourgeois Bohemian*. New Haven: Yale University Press, 1981.

Silber, Joan. *In the City*. New York: Viking, 1987.

Simon, John. Personal interview.

Slater, Miriam. Personal interview.

Sloan, Helen, ed. *John Sloan: New York Etchings, 1905–1949*. New York: Dover, 1978.

Sloan, Mark. Personal interview, 10 March 1987.

Smith, Howard. Personal interview, 19 April 1987.

Solotaroff, Theodore. *The Red Hot Vacuum: And Other Pieces of the Sixties*. Boston: Nonpareil Books, 1970.

Spencer, Elizabeth. "Transformation." In *Boulevard*. Richard Burgin, ed. Philadelphia: Drexel University Press, 1995, pp. 140–49.

Spoto, Donald. *The Kindness of Strangers: The Life of Tennessee Williams*. Boston: Little, Brown, 1985.

Stallman, R. W. *Stephen Crane: A Biography*. New York: George Braziller, 1968.

Steckel, Anita. Personal interview.

Steffens, Lincoln. *The Autobiography of Lincoln Steffens*. New York: Harcourt, 1931.

St. John, Bruce, ed. *John Sloan's New York Scene: From the Diaries, Notes and Correspondence, 1906–1913*. New York: Harper, 1965.

Stokes, Geoffrey, ed. *The Village Voice Anthology, 1956–1980: Twenty-five Years of Writing from the Village Voice*. New York: Quill, 1982.

Stoler, Shirley. Personal interview.

Styron, William. *Sophie's Choice*. New York: Random House, 1976.

Sukenick, Ronald. *Down and In: Life in the Underground*. New York: Beech Tree, 1987.

——. "The N.E.A. and the Avant-Garde." *Nation* 11 October 1993: 400–401.

Thurber, James. *The Years with Ross*. Rev. ed. Boston: Atlantic Monthly Press, 1959.

Timms, Edward, and Peter Collier, eds. *Visions and Blueprints: Avant-garde Culture and Radical Politics in Early Twentieth-Century Europe*. Manchester: Manchester University Press, 1988.

Tomkins, Calvin. *Duchamp: A Biography*. New York: Holt, 1996.

Towne, Charles Garsen. *This New York of Mine*. New York: Cosmopolitan, 1931.

Trilling, Diana. *The Beginning of the Journey*. New York: Harcourt, 1993.

Trilling, Lionel. *A Gathering of Fugitives*. New York: Harcourt, 1956.

——. *The Liberal Imagination: Essays on Literature and Society*. 11th ed. New York: Anchor, 1950.

Tytell, John. *The Living Theater: Art, Exile and Outrage*. New York: Grove, 1995.

Van Doren, Mark. *Autobiography of Mark Van Doren*. New York: Harcourt, 1958.

Van Leer, David. *James Baldwin: A Biography*. New York: Knopf, 1995.

Van Ronk, Dave. Personal interview, 6 February 1988.

Wakefield, Dan. *New York in the Fifties*. Boston: Houghton Mifflin, 1992.

Wallman, Jan. Personal interview.

Wallowitch, John. Personal interview, 22 May 1987.

Ware, Caroline E. *Greenwich Village, 1920–30: A Comment on American Civilization in the Post-War Years*. 2nd ed. Berkeley: University of California Press, 1994.

Wertheim, Arthur Frank. *The New York Little Renaissance: Iconoclasm, Modernism, and Nationalism in American Culture, 1908–1917*. New York: New York University Press, 1976.

White, E. B. *Essays of E. B. White*. New York: Harper, 1977.

White, Robert L. *John Peale Bishop*. New York: Twayne, n.d.

Winter, Ella, and Granville Hicks, eds. *The Letters of Lincoln Steffens*. 2 vols. New York: Harcourt, 1938.

Wolfe, Gerard R. *New York: A Guide to the Metropolis*. 2nd ed. New York: McGraw Hill, 1994.

Woliver, Robbie. *Bringing It All Back Home: 25 Years of American Music at Folk City*. New York: Pantheon, 1986.

Wood, Sally, ed. *The Southern Mandarins: Letters of Caroline Gordon to Sally Wood, 1924–1937*. Baton Rouge: Louisiana State University Press, 1984.

Wouk, Herman. *Marjorie Morningstar*. New York: Doubleday, 1955.

Wreszin, Michael. *A Rebel in Defense of Tradition: The Life and Politics of Dwight Macdonald*. New York: Basic, 1968.

Wright, Dorothy. Personal interview.

Yates, Richard. *Young Hearts Crying*. New York: Delacorte, 1984.

Young, Izzy. Personal interview, 17 October 1987.

I: MABEL DODGE'S SALON

Aldington, Richard. *D. H. Lawrence: Portrait of a Genius But . . .* New York: Collier, 1950.

Brown, Patricia Leigh. "The Muse of Taos, Stirring Still." *New York Times* 16 January 1997.

Crunden, Robert M. *American Salons: Encounters with European Modernism, 1885–1917*. Oxford: Oxford University Press, 1993.

Eisler, Benita. "Georgia and Beck and Tony and Mabel." *Vanity Fair* April 1991: 117–24.

Everett, Patricia R., ed. *A History of Having a Great Many Times Not Continued to Be Friends: The Correspondence Between Mabel Dodge and Gertrude Stein, 1911–1934.* Albuquerque: University of New Mexico Press, 1996.

Foster, Joseph. *D. H. Lawrence in Taos.* Albuquerque: University of New Mexico Press, 1972.

Hahn, Emily. *Lorenzo: D. H. Lawrence and the Women Who Loved Him.* New York: Lippincott, 1975.

——. *Mabel: A Biography of Mabel Dodge Luhan.* Boston: Houghton Mifflin, 1977.

Hicks, Granville. *The Story of John Reed.* New York: Cooperative Press, 1935.

Lawrence, Frieda. *The Memoirs and Correspondence.* New York: Knopf, 1964.

Lee, Sue Davidson. *From Stieglitz: A Memoir/Biography.* New York: Farrar, Straus & Giroux, 1983.

Luhan, Mabel Dodge. *Intimate Memories,* vol. 3: *Movers and Shakers.* New York: Harcourt, 1936.

Mellow, James. *Charmed Circle: Gertrude Stein and Company.* New York: Praeger, 1974.

Merrild, Knud. *With D. H. Lawrence in New Mexico: A Memoir.* Rev. ed. London: Routledge & Kegan Paul, 1969.

Moore, Henry, and Warren Roberts. *D. H. Lawrence and His World.* New York: Viking, 1966.

Page, Jake. "Mabel Dodge: A Charged Particle Among the Force Fields of Her Times." *Smithsonian Magazine* June 1991: 122–26.

Rudnick, Lois Palken. *Mabel Dodge Luhan: New Woman, New Worlds.* Albuquerque: University of New Mexico Press, 1984.

Sagar, Keith. *The Life of D. H. Lawrence.* New York: Pantheon, 1980.

Spacks, Patricia. *The Female Imagination.* New York: Knopf, 1975.

Steel, Ronald. *Walter Lippmann and the American Century.* Boston: Little, Brown, 1980.

Stein, Gertrude. *The Autobiography of Alice B. Toklas.* New York: Vintage, 1933.

II: MAX EASTMAN AND *THE MASSES*

Aaron, Daniel. *Writers on the Left.* New York: Harcourt, 1961.

Conlin, Joseph R. *Big Bill Haywood and the Radical Union Movement.* Syracuse: Syracuse University Press, 1969.

Diggins, Jack. Letter to the author, 21 November 1988.

Eastman, Yvette. *Dearest Wilding: A Memoir with Love Letters from Theodore Dreiser.* Philadelphia: University of Pennsylvania Press, 1995.

Fishbein, Leslie. *Rebels in Bohemia: The Radicals of The Masses, 1911–1917.* Chapel Hill: University of North Carolina Press, 1982.

Haywood, Big Bill. *The Autobiography of Big Bill Haywood.* New York: International, 1929.

Lippmann, Walter. *Drift and Mastery: An Attempt to Diagnose the Current Unrest.* Madison: University of Wisconsin Press, 1985.

Untermeyer, Louis. *From Another World: The Autobiography of Louis Untermeyer.* N.p., 1939.

Wilson, Edmund. *Classic and Commercials: A Literary Chronicle of the Forties.* New York: Farrar, Straus & Giroux, 1950.

Zurier, Rebecca. *Art for The Masses: A Radical Magazine and Its Graphics, 1911–1917.* New Haven: Yale University Press, 1985.

——. Letter to the author, 14 November 1988.

III: JIG COOK, EUGENE O'NEILL, AND THE PROVINCETOWN PLAYERS

Boyce, Neith, and Hutchins Hapgood. *Intimate Warriors: Portraits of a Modern Marriage, 1899–1944.* Ellen K. Trimberger, ed. New York: Feminist Press at City University of New York, 1991.

Gelb, Arthur, and Barbara Gelb. *O'Neill.* 4th ed. New York: Harper, 1973.

——. *O'Neill: Life with Monte Cristo.* New York: Harper, 1979.

Glaspell, Susan. *The Road to the Temple.* New York: Frederick Stokes, 1927.

——. *Suppressed Desires: A Comedy in Two Episodes.* Rev. ed. Boston: Baker's Plays, 1951.

——. *Trifles: A Play in One Act.* Rev. ed. Boston: Baker's Plays, 1951.

O'Neill, Eugene Gladstone. *Eugene O'Neill: Complete Plays, 1913–1920.* Travis Bogard, ed. New York: Library of America, 1988.

——. *The Hairy Ape, Anna Christie,* and *The First Man.* 3rd ed. New York: Boni & Liveright, 1922.

Sarlos, Robert Karoly. *Jig Cook and the Provincetown Players: Theater in Ferment.* Boston: University of Massachusetts Press, 1980.

Waterman, Arthur E. *Susan Glaspell.* New Haven: Yale University Press, 1966.

Wetzsteon, Ross. "This Little Group of Friends: The Triumphs and Travails of Jig Cook and the Provincetown Players." *Village Voice* 11 August 1987: 87–88.

Williams, Gary Jay. Letter to the author, 14 December 1988.

IV: THE FEMINISTS OF THE VILLAGE

Adickes, Sandra L. *To Be Young Was Very Heaven: Women in New York Before the First World War.* New York: St. Martin's Press, 1997.

Alland, Alexander, Sr. *Jessie Tarbox Beals: First Woman News Photographer.* New York: Camera/Graphic, 1978.

Berman, Paul. "Emma Goldman Is Alive and Well and Making Trouble on the Lower East Side." *Voice Literary Supplement* October 1995: 13–21.

Cather, Willa. *My Antonia.* 7th ed. Boston: Houghton Mifflin, 1988.

——. *Willa Cather: Stories, Poems, and Other Writings.* New York: Library of America, 1992.

Chesler, Ellen. *Margaret Sanger and the Birth Control Movement in America.* New York: Simon & Schuster, 1992.

Cook, Blanche Wiesen, ed. *Crystal Eastman on Women and Revolution.* Oxford: Oxford University Press, 1978.

Douglas, Emily Taft. *Pioneer of the Future: Margaret Sanger.* New York: Holt, 1970.

Faderman, Lillian. *Odd Girls and Twilight Lovers: A History of Lesbian Life in Twentieth-Century America.* New York: Penguin, 1992.

Falk, Candice. *Love, Anarchy, and Emma Goldman.* New York: Holt, 1984.

Flynn, Elizabeth Gurley. *The Rebel Girl: An Autobiography: My First Life, 1906–1926.* Rev. ed. New York: International, 1973.

Garrison, Dee. *Mary Heaton Vorse: The Life of an American Insurgent.* Philadelphia: Temple University Press, 1989.

Gilligan, Carol. "Red Emma's Other Passion." Review of *Love, Anarchy, and Emma Goldman,* by Candice Falk, and *Emma Goldman: An Intimate Life,* by Alice Walker. *New York Times Book Review* 4 November 1984.

Goldman, Emma. *Living My Life.* New York: AMS Press, 1931.

Gray, Madeline. *Margaret Sanger: A Biography of the Champion of Birth Control.* New York: Putnam, 1979.

Makowsky, Veronica. *Susan Glaspell's Century of American Women: A Critical Interpretation of Her Work.* New York: Oxford University Press, 1993.

Reid, B. L. *The Man from New York: John Quinn and His Friends.* New York: Oxford University Press, 1968.

Schwarz, Judith. *Radical Feminists of Heterodoxy: Greenwich Village, 1912–1940.* Rev. ed. Norwich: New Victoria, 1986.

Sochen, June. *The New Woman: Feminism in Greenwich Village, 1910–1920.* New York: Quadrangle, 1972.

Trimberger, Ellen, ed. *Intimate Warriors: Portraits of Modern Marriage, 1899–1944.* New York: Feminist Press at City University of New York, 1991.

Vorse, Mary Heaton. *Time and the Town: A Provincetown Chronicle.* Adele Heller, ed. 2nd ed. New Brunswick: Rutgers University Press, 1991.

Wexler, Alice. *Emma Goldman in America.* Boston: Beacon, 1984.

V: EDNA ST. VINCENT MILLAY

Berman, Paul. "Edmund's Castle." Review of *From the Uncollected Edmund Wilson,* by Janet and David Castrono, eds., and *Edmund Wilson: A Biography. New Republic* 1 June 1996: 32–41.

Castronovo, David. *Edmund Wilson.* 2nd ed. New York: Ungar, 1987.

Cheney, Anne. *Millay in Greenwich Village.* University of Alabama Press, 1975.

Clampitt, Amy. "Two Cheers for Prettiness." Review of *Edna St. Vincent Millay, Selected Poems,* Colin Falck, ed. *New Republic* 6 and 12 January 1992.

Falck, Colin, ed. *Edna St. Vincent Millay: Selected Poems.* New York: Harper, 1992.

Gould, Jean. *The Poet and Her Book: A Biography of Edna St. Vincent Millay.* New York: Dodd, Mead, n.d.

Meyers, Jeffrey. *Edmund Wilson: A Biography.* Boston: Houghton Mifflin, 1995.

Millay, Edna St. Vincent. *A Few Figs from Thistles: Poems and Four Sonnets by Edna St. Vincent Millay.* New York: Salvo, 1921.

Russell, Isabel. *Katherine and E. B. White: An Affectionate Memoir.* New York: Norton, 1988.

Wilson, Edmund. *I Thought of Daisy.* New York: Farrar, Straus & Giroux, 1950.

——. *Letters on Literature and Politics, 1912–1972.* Elena Wilson, ed. 3rd ed. New York: Farrar, Straus & Giroux, 1977.

——. *The Stories of Light: A Literary Chronicle of the Twenties and Thirties.* New York: Farrar, Straus & Giroux, 1952.

——. *To the Finland Station: A Study in the Writing and Acting of History.* 2nd ed. Garden City: Doubleday, 1953.

——. *The Triple Thinkers: Twelve Essays on Literary Subjects.* 5th ed. New York: Farrar, Straus & Giroux, 1976.

——. *Upstate: Records and Recollections of Northern New York.* 4th ed. New York: Farrar, Straus & Giroux, 1974.

——. *The Wound and the Bow: Seven Studies in Literature.* 7th ed. New York: Oxford University Press, 1965.

VI: EMINENT VILLAGERS

Aaron, Daniel. *Writers on the Left: Episodes in American Literary Communism.* 2nd ed. New York: Columbia University Press, 1993.

Anderson, Margaret. *My Thirty Years' War.* New York: Covici, Friede, 1930.

Brevda, William. *Harry Kemp: The Last Bohemian.* London and Lewisburg, Ohio: Bucknell University Press, 1986.

Kisch, Arnold I. *The Romantic Ghost of Greenwich Village: Guido Bruno in His Garret.* New York: Peter Lang, 1976.

Lee, Hermione. *Willa Cather: Double Lives.* 2nd ed. New York: Vintage, 1991.

Swanberg, W. A. *Dreiser.* New York: Scribner, 1965.

Wetzsteon, Ross. "The Baroness of Greenwich Village: The Mother of American Dada Sparks a New Show at the Whitney." *Village Voice* 26 November 1996: 47–49.

VII: WILLIAM CARLOS WILLIAMS, THE LITTLE MAGAZINES, AND THE POETRY WARS

Anderson, Margaret, and Jane Heap, eds. *The Little Review: Quarterly Journal of Art and Letters.* XII:2 (1929).

Hoffman, Frederick J., Charles Allen, and Carolyn F. Ulrich. *The Little Magazine: A History and a Bibliography.* Rev. ed. New York: Kraus, 1967.

VIII: HART CRANE

Unterecker, John. *Voyager: A Life of Hart Crane.* New York: Liveright, 1987.

IX: MAXWELL BODENHEIM

Bodenheim, Maxwell. *Sixty Seconds.* New York: Liveright, 1929.

Williams, Ellen. *Harriet Monroe and the Poetry Renaissance: The First Ten Years of Poetry, 1912–22.* Urbana: University of Illinois Press, 1977.

Yagoda, Ben. "Maxwell Bodenheim: Catastrophe and Corrective." In *Boulevard*. Richard Burgin, ed. Philadelphia: Drexel University Press, 1995, pp. 199–209.

X: THOMAS WOLFE AND ALINE BERNSTEIN

Bernstein, Aline. *The Journey Down*. 2nd ed. New York: Knopf, 1938.

XI: JOE GOULD

Klonsky, Milton. "Squash and Stretch." *Esquire* December 1963: 162.
Mitchell, Joseph. *Joe Gould's Secret*. New York: Viking, 1965.

XII: DJUNA BARNES

Barnes, Djuna. *Greenwich Village As It Is*. University of Alabama Press, 1975.
———. *New York*. Alyce Barry, ed. Los Angeles: Sun & Moon Press, 1989.
———. *Nightwood*. New York: New Directions, 1937.
———. *Smoke and Other Early Stories*. Messerli, Douglas, ed. Los Angeles: Sun and Moon Press, 1993.
Barry, Alyce, ed. *Djuna Barnes Interviews*. Washington, DC: Sun & Moon Press, 1985.
Field, Andrew. *Djuna: The Formidable Miss Barnes*. Austin: University of Texas Press, 1985.
Ford, Charles Henri, and Parker Tyler. *The Young and Evil*. Watson, Steven, ed. Illustrated with Paintings by Pavel Tchelitchew. New York: Sea Horse Books-Gay, 1988.
Herring, Phillip. *Djuna: The Life and Work of Djuna Barnes*. New York: Viking, 1995.

XIII: E. E. CUMMINGS AND DYLAN THOMAS

Cummings, E. E. *1 x 1*. 2nd ed. New York: Harcourt, 1972.
Kennedy, Richard. *Dreams in the Mirror: A Biography of E. E. Cummings*. 2nd ed. New York: Liveright, 1994.

XIV: DELMORE SCHWARTZ

Dike, Donald, and David H. Zucker, eds. *Selected Essays of Delmore Schwartz*. Chicago: University of Chicago Press, 1970.
Phillips, Robert, ed. *Letters of Delmore Schwartz*. New York: Ontario Review Press, 1984.

Pollet, Elizabeth, ed. *Portrait of Delmore: Journals and Notes of Delmore Schwartz, 1939–1959*. New York: Farrar, Straus & Giroux, 1986.

Schwartz, Delmore. *The Ego Is Always at the Wheel: Bagatelles*. 4th ed. Robert Phillips, ed. New York: New Directions, 1986.

XV: DAWN POWELL

Powell, Dawn. *The Diaries of Dawn Powell, 1931–1965*. Tim Page, ed. South Royalton, VT: Steerforth Press, 1995.

———. *My Home Is Far Away*. 2nd ed. Tim Page, ed. South Royalton, VT: Steerforth Press, 1995.

XVI: JACKSON POLLOCK AND THE ABSTRACT EXPRESSIONISTS IN THE VILLAGE

Breslin, James E. B. *Mark Rothko: A Biography*. Chicago: University of Chicago Press, 1993.

Friedman, B. H. *Jackson Pollock: Energy Made Visible*. New York: McGraw Hill, 1972.

Gruen, John. *The Party's Over Now: Reminiscences of the Fifties—New York's Artists, Writers, Musicians, and Their Friends*. New York: Viking, 1972.

Kingsley, April. *The Turning Point: The Abstract Expressionists and the Transformation of American Art*. New York: Simon & Schuster, 1992.

Mayer, Musa. *Night Studio: A Memoir of Philip Guston*. New York: Penguin, 1988.

Naifeh, Steven, and Gregory White Smith. *Jackson Pollock: An American Saga*. New York: Potter, 1989.

Ratcliff, Carter. *The Fate of a Gesture: Jackson Pollock and Postwar American Art*. New York: Farrar, Straus & Giroux, 1996.

Sandler, Irving. *The Triumph of American Painting: A History of Abstract Expressionism*. New York: Icon, 1970.

Acknowledgments

The author and the estate are most grateful to the following individuals and organizations for their contributions to *Republic of Dreams* (and regret any inadvertent omissions): Rosemary Ahern, Wade Boggs, Fred Chase, Robert Christiansen, Robert Coe, Roger Copeland, Fred Courtwright, Ann Davidson, Loretta Denner, Karen Durbin, Margot Ebling, Jason Epstein, Beatrix Faust, Ruth Fecych, Jules Feiffer, Michael Feingold, Randy Gener, Richard Gilman, Lyman Gilmore, Vivian Gornick, Robert Heide, Nat Hentoff, Edward Hoagland, the Humanities Council of New York University, Tina Jacobson, Paul Johnston, Jonathan Kalb, Stanley Kauffmann, Kerri Kivlin, Seymour Krim, Martha Lagace, Robert Langs, Kay Larson, Deanna Leo, Michael MacDonald, David Markson, Kim Massie, Fred McDarrah, Charles McNulty, Taylor Mead, Terry Miller, Tim Page, Francine Prose, Anna Puga, Phyllis Raphael, Carolyn Reidy, Marc Robinson, Emily Remes, David Rosenthal, Francine Russo, David Savatteri, David Schneiderman, Harvey Shapiro, Raven Snook, Alisa Solomon, Lauren Stein, Daniel Stern, Gloria Stern, Laurie Stone, Ronald Sukenick, Zanthe Taylor, Theatre Communications Group, Alexandra Truitt, *The Village Voice*, Steve Watson, Scott Wetstone, Sandi Wisenberg, and Israel Young.

Index

abortion, 223–24, 227, 457
Absence of Mabel Dodge, The (Dasburg), 42, 97
abstract expressionism, 520–69
  Cedar Tavern as center for, 520, 538, 551–55, 560–64, 569
  decline of, 566–69
  European modernism and, 521, 524
  as movement, described, 520–21, 524, 536–37, 546–51
  name of, 521, 549–50
  origins of, 524–25
  public acceptance of, 538–39
  theory of, 533–35, 541–42, 562–63
  Village as home to, 568–69
  see also specific artists
A Club, 169
Addams, Jane, 199
Aeneid, The (Virgil), 292
Aesthetic Realism, 330
Ah, Wilderness! (O'Neill), 121
Aida (Verdi), 248
Aiken, Conrad, 95, 382–83

Ainslee's, 265–66
Albee, Edward, xiii
Albert Hotel, 397, 399
All God's Chillun Got Wings (O'Neill), 153
American, The (periodical), 336
"American Action Painters, The" (Rosenberg), 562–63
American Century, 238, 498–99
American Civil Liberties Union (ACLU), xi, 192, 200
American Communist party, 173, 175
American Tragedy, An (Dreiser), 297, 300
American Union Against Militarism, 198
anarchism, 17, 18, 19, 23, 36, 95, 203, 205–7, 221, 312, 314, 348
Anderson, Margaret, 308–17
  background of, 308–9
  Barnes's relationship with, 436–37, 442–43
  the Baroness as viewed by, 317–20, 322
  Dreiser as viewed by, 300, 301

589

Anderson, Margaret *(cont.)*
  Goldman's relationship with, 206,
    207–8, 312, 313
  Heap's relationship with, 313, 316–17
  as *Little Review* editor, 309–18, 355,
    364–65, 382, 436–37
  as Village resident, 313
Anderson, Sherwood, 345
Angel Intrudes, The (Dell), 136, 252
Anna Christie (O'Neill), 151, 152
Anthony, Katherine, 180
Anthony, Susan B., 173–74
Antiphon, The (Barnes), 447
anti-Semitism, 300, 400, 401–2, 407,
    410–11, 413, 414, 449, 465, 489–90,
    494
Arendt, Hannah, 490
Arensberg, Walter, 352
Aria da Capo (Millay), 147, 264–65, 270
Aristophanes, 101
Aristotle, 358
Ark, 44, 45
Armory Show (1913), 2, 20, 28–29, 67,
    246, 299, 338, 349, 351, 523
art:
  Ashcan School of, 60–61
  avant-garde, 67–68
  Dadaist, 320–21, 351
  modern, 349–50, 521, 524
  nonobjective, 524–25
  politics vs., 73–75
  proletarian, 20
  realist, 523, 528
  see also abstract expressionism
"Art" (Gould), 427
"art for art's sake," 73–75
Artists Union, 526–27
Art News, 562
Art of This Century Gallery, 530
Art Project, 523–24
Arts (periodical), 505
Arts and Politics Evening, 20
Art Students League, 169, 434, 522
Ashbery, John, 553
Ashcan School, 60–61
Associated Press (AP), 68–69
Atkinson, Brooks, 463
Atlantic Monthly, 70, 166, 169
Auden, W. H., 287, 490, 492
Austin, Mary, 163
Autumn Rhythm (Pollock), 559, 566

"Babs" (Villager), 18–19
Bacall, Lauren, xiv
Baker, George Pierce, 113, 119, 142, 396
Baker, Sara Josephine, 180
Baldwin, Roger, 95, 193–94, 200
Ball, Lucille, ix
Ballantine, Stella, 175
Balzac, Honoré de, 9, 298
Barnes, Albert C., 141
Barnes, Djuna, 313, 431–48
  Anderson's relationship with, 436–37,
    442–43
  background of, 433–34
  the Baroness and, 322–24
  death of, 448
  at Dodge's salon, 437–38
  Eliot's views on, 431, 435, 445, 447
  feminism as viewed by, 435
  finances of, 432, 445, 446, 448
  Joyce's relationship with, 323, 431,
    432, 441–42, 445
  legend of, 431–33, 446–48
  as lesbian, 267, 341, 350, 442–44
  marriage of, 440
  name of, 433
  as newspaper reporter, 435–36, 439,
    441
  in Paris, 441–45
  in Provincetown Players, 438, 439, 445
  pseudonym of, 441
  as Village resident, xv, 431–32, 441,
    446–48
  Wilson's friendship with, 441, 447–48
  writings of, 157, 306, 307, 438–40,
    443–45
Barnes, Elizabeth, 433–34
Barnes, Wald, 433–34
Baroness, the, *see* Freytag-Loringhoven,
    Baroness Elsa von
Barr, Alfred, 550
Barrett, William, 487, 490, 494, 498, 499,
    502, 507
"Barricades, The" (Gould), 425–26
Barrymore, John, xii, 142, 283
Barton, Anne, 460–62, 465–66
Barton, Ralph, 460, 461
Barzun, Jacques, 464
Baudelaire, Charles, 286
Baum, Vicki, 408
Beardsley, Aubrey, 305, 306, 356
beatniks, 449, 568

Beck, Julian, 359
Becker, Maurice, 69, 73
Beckett, Samuel, 446, 530
Bedford Street, xii, 283
Beerbohm, Max, 393
Beethoven, Ludwig van, 267
Before Breakfast (O'Neill), 128, 130
Belardi, Jenny, 125, 141
Belasco, David, 129, 154, 340
Bell, Josephine, 80
Bell Laboratories, xi–xii
Bellow, Saul, 488, 490, 499
Bellows, George, 76, 523
Bell Syndicate, 133
"Belly Music" (Williams), 355
Belmont, Mrs. O. H. P., 59–60
Beloved Vagabond, The (film), 64
Benchley, Robert, 126, 302
Benedict, Wallace, 195, 197
Benét, Stephen Vincent, 265
Benét, William Rose, 403
Benton, Thomas Hart, 522
Berkman, Alexander "Sasha," 18, 36, 77,
    203–4, 208, 213, 218–19, 221
Bernhardt, Sarah, 246
Bernstein, Aline, 395–417
Berryman, John, 486, 494–95, 497,
    499
Betts Academy, 110
Beyond the Horizon (O'Neill), 135, 142,
    147–48
Bible, 214
Biddle, George, 319, 321, 323
Biograph Films, xii
birth control, 221–37
    clinics for, 230–31, 234
    legalization of, 237, 238
    liberal support for, 65, 166, 179, 196,
        209, 213–14
    Sanger's crusade for, 19, 23, 36, 38, 67,
        83, 176–77, 197, 214, 221–37
    as term, 227
    see also abortion
Bishop, John Peale, 271, 273, 274, 278
Blackmur, R. P., 378, 493, 495, 497
Blair, Mary, 151, 152, 153, 284
Bloom, Harold, 414
"Bluebeard" (Millay), 259
Blue Poles (Pollock), 559
Bodenheim, Maxwell, 380–94
    autobiography of, 387, 390

bohemian lifestyle of, 325, 383–84,
        392–94
    eccentric behavior of, 382–84
    in England, 382–83
    first marriage of, 385, 388
    Gould and, 419, 421, 423, 425, 430
    in Hollywood, 387
    as legend, 382, 386–94
    love affairs of, 385–87
    murder of, 391–92
    poems sold by, 380–81
    press coverage of, 386, 388, 392
    reputation of, 364, 381–82, 392
    second marriage of, 388, 389
    third marriage of, 389–92
    Thomas's meeting with, 390
    as Village resident, 330, 380–84, 572
    Williams and, 382, 383
    writings of, 312, 380–82, 384–85, 387,
        392, 393
Bogan, Louise, 349
Boggs, Tom, 327
bohemianism:
    artists and, xii, 20, 297, 303–8
    disillusionment with, 369–70, 379
    as fashionable, 9–10, 55, 325
    feminism and, 162–66, 222–23, 435
    "genius" and, 416
    Greenwich Village as center of, ix, xi,
        xvi, 5–12, 87–89, 137
    middle class values vs., 7–12, 63,
        73–74
    origins of, 8–9
    as "perpetual revolution," 9–10
    philanthropy and, 324–33
    romanticism of, 392–94
    self-fulfillment in, 12–13, 22, 62, 66,
        74–75, 88, 91, 161, 164, 208, 308,
        416
"bohemian tomato soup," 389, 421
Boissevain, Eugen, 201, 281–87, 290292
Bolshevik revolution, 78, 80, 81, 83, 84,
        91, 92–93, 135, 145–46, 158–59,
        200, 220, 282
Bond, The (Boyce), 181, 186, 189
Boni, Albert and Charles, 81, 102, 351
Boni & Liveright, 81
Book, A (Barnes), 439, 443
Book of Repulsive Women, The (Barnes),
        307, 439–40
Book of Vassar Verse, A, 270

Booth, Edwin, 108
Booth, John Wilkes, xii
bootleggers, 324, 327
Borden, Lizzie, 150
Boston Globe, 122
Botticelli, Sandro, 251
Bound East for Cardiff (O'Neill), 113, 119, 126, 130, 171
Bourda, Josephine, 295
Bourne, Randolph, 356
Boyce, Neith, 181–92
  Dodge's correspondence with, 189–90
  as feminist, 181–82, 237
  marriage of, 171, 181–92, 238
  peyote tried by, 31–32
  in Provincetown Players, 104–5, 106, 128, 182, 190–91
  writings of, 181, 186, 189–91
Boyle, Kay, 349
Boy Scouts, 67
Brandeis, Louis, 219
Brecht, Bertolt, 507
Brevoort Hotel, 130, 138, 140, 230, 299, 300–301, 306, 327, 383, 446, 461
Bridge, The (Crane), 360, 367, 368, 370–71, 375–76, 378
Briggs, LeBaron, 450
Brill, A. A., 22, 35, 62, 63, 65, 88, 195, 300, 461
Brinnin, John Malcolm, 471, 474, 476, 477, 480, 482, 483
Brisbane, Arthur, 90
"Broken Tower, The" (Crane), 376–77
Brooklyn Daily Eagle, 231, 435
Broom (periodical), 359, 427
Broun, Heywood, 129, 150, 152
Brown, Gladys, 262, 283–84
Browne, Maurice, 101, 150
Bruno, Guido, 303–8, 342, 363, 436, 438–39
Bruno Cabarets, 307
Bruno Players, 306
Bruno's Chapbooks, 305–6, 439
Bruno's Garrett, 303–4, 305, 307, 308
Bruno's Weekly, 362
Bryan, William Jennings, 11, 96
Bryant, Louise, 93–98, 129–33
  Croton-on-Hudson house of, 130–31
  death of, 161
  as feminist, 93–94, 237, 348

first marriage of, 93–94
as *Masses* contributor, 98, 121
O'Neill's affair with, 118, 120–21, 124–25, 129–33, 135, 137, 138, 139, 142–43
O'Neill's correspondence with, 142–43
in Provincetown, 97–98, 118, 119, 120–21, 131–32
in Provincetown Players, 124, 126, 127, 131
Reed's correspondence with, 96–97, 98, 132–33
Reed's marriage to, 124–25, 127, 129–33, 142–43, 157, 159, 160, 237–38
Reed's relationship with, 93–98, 118, 120, 121
in Russia, 135, 139, 142, 158
third marriage of, 161
as Village resident, 94–95, 131
as war correspondent, 132–33
writings of, 98, 119, 120–21, 126, 127, 158
Bryant, William Cullen, 314
Buckman, Gertrude, 489, 493–94, 503
Bullitt, William, 161
Bunyan, John, 454
Burke, Kenneth, 252, 370, 469–70
Burt, Frederic, 119
Bynner, Witter, 244–45, 261, 278–80, 346
Byron, George Gordon, Lord, 287, 334, 393

Cage, John, 547, 552
Calder, Alexander, 530
Call, The (newspaper), 221–22, 224, 227
Cannell, Kathleen, 137
"Cantleman's Spring Mate" (Lewis), 315
Carlin, Terry, 116–17
  background of, 116–17
  bohemian lifestyle of, 32, 116–17
  death of, 158
  drugs used by, 32, 34, 140, 141
  O'Neill's friendship with, 98, 108, 116–18, 119, 141, 146, 157–58
  in Provincetown, 108, 118, 119, 134–35
Carruth, W. H., 335, 336
Caruso, Enrico, 248

Cather, Willa, 293–97
  background of, 293–94
  Dodge's meeting with, 295
  lesbian instincts attributed to, 293, 294–95, 297
  privacy maintained by, 293, 294–98
  as Village resident, xiii, 293, 295–98
  writings of, 294, 295–97
Cedar Tavern, 520, 538, 551–55, 560–64, 569
"Celebrated Jumping Frog of Calaveras County, The" (Twain), 6–7
Cézanne, Paul, 450
Chamberlain, Kenneth Russell, 57, 69
Chandler, Sellers McKees, 324
Change Your Style (Cook), 106
Chaplin, Charlie, 65, 368–70, 445, 473
"Chaplinesque" (Crane), 368, 369
Chaucer, Geoffrey, 358
Chelsea Hotel, 415, 481, 482, 505
Chicago Renaissance, 298, 390
Chicago Repertory, 151
Chicago Times, 283
Chippewa Indians, 420, 423, 426
Christianity, 13–14
Churchill, Allen, x
Claire-Marie Press, 30–31
Clairmont, Robert, 324–33
Clapp, Henry, 6–7
Clare, Ada, 7
class struggle, 17–18, 53, 75, 81, 82, 87, 173
Cleveland Plain Dealer, 365
Club, 547–49, 553, 561, 569
Coates, Robert, 550
Cocaine (play), 129
Cody, Wyoming (Pollock), 523
Coffee, John, 383
Cohan, George M., xi
Coleman, Dorothy, 266–67
Coleridge, Samuel Taylor, 245
Collected Poems (Cummings), 469
Collier, John, 189
Collier, Lucy, 189–90
Collier's, 49, 96
Colt, Samuel, xi
Colum, Mary, 363
Colum, Padraic, 363, 427
Columbia Gardens bar, 115, 146–47, 338
"Coming, Aphrodite!" (Cather), 295–297

communism, 84–85, 86, 146, 160, 173, 175, 200, 219, 387, 424–25, 449, 464–65
  see also Bolshevik revolution
Comstock, Anthony, 70, 222, 229, 384
Confessions of a Feminist Man (Dell), 162
"Congo" (Lindsay), 326
Constancy (Boyce), 104–5, 106, 190
Constitution, U.S., 69, 76, 77, 78, 80, 81, 202, 218, 271
consumer cooperatives, 49, 50
Contemporaries (Steele), 106
Cook, George Cram "Jig," 104–5, 123–29, 145–55
  as actor, 119
  ancient Greek drama as interest of, 101, 145, 154–55
  background of, 98–100
  death of, 155–56, 161, 396
  dome constructed by, 148–49, 150
  early marriages of, 99–100
  Glaspell's marriage to, 100, 101–2, 104, 123, 154–55, 171, 237–38
  in Greece, 152, 153–54, 280
  O'Neill's relationship with, 122–23, 139–40, 145–55
  personality of, 99–100
  in Provincetown, 98, 104, 134–35, 145, 171, 274
  Provincetown Players founded and managed by, 3, 98–99, 104–8, 123–26, 128–29, 133–37, 141–42, 145–55, 161, 299, 353, 438, 463
  theater as interest of, 101–4, 264, 341–42
  as Village resident, xvii, 100–101
  writings of, 100, 103–4, 105, 106, 150
Coolidge, Calvin, 449, 464
Cooper, Peter, 523
Cortez, Aimee, 387
Cosmopolitan, 197
Count of Monte Cristo, The (Dumas), 108–9, 112, 122
Cowley, Malcolm, 12, 250, 252, 267, 287, 359, 371, 379, 436, 461–62, 464
Cowley, Peggy, 373, 376–77
Crane, C. C., 360–61, 362, 365–66, 367

Crane, Hart, 360–79
  at advertising agency, 366–67
  background of, 360–62
  Brooklyn residence of, 370, 409
  correspondence of, 360–63, 365–66,
    372, 382
  drinking by, 367, 371, 377–78
  Eliot compared with, 374, 375, 377
  Guggenheim fellowship of, 376
  homosexuality of, 371–74, 377–78
  legend of, 367, 371, 377–79
  as *Little Review* advertising manager,
    314, 365
  in Mexico, 376–77
  name of, 360
  O'Neill's friendship with, 368, 369
  Powell compared with, 519
  reputation of, 366, 369, 460, 471
  suicide attempts of, 361, 377
  suicide of, 377–79, 519
  as Village resident, 321, 361–62,
    368–70
  Williams's views on, 363–64, 378
  writings of, 306, 360, 362–65, 367,
    368, 370–71, 375–76, 378, 427
Crane, Stephen, 6
Creeley, Robert, 545
Croly, Herbert, 230
Crowninshield, Frank, 273, 278, 459
Cry of Youth, The (Kemp), 338
Cummings, Edward, 450, 451, 452, 453
Cummings, E. E., 449–71
  in ambulance corps, 452–53
  anticommunism of, 449, 464–65
  anti-Semitism of, 449, 465
  background of, 450–51
  "Buffalo Bill" poem of, 452, 454, 467
  daughter of, 457, 459
  death of, 449, 471
  in Europe, 453–54, 455, 457
  financial situation of, 459–60, 461,
    465, 467–68
  first marriage of, 457–60
  Gould and, 424, 426, 430
  Guggenheim fellowship of, 465
  journals of, 449
  Joy Farm retreat of, 455, 470, 472
  Kemp and, 344
  love affairs of, 452, 455–57, 460–61
  noise phobia of, 450, 467
  paintings by, 452, 462

  pseudonyms of, 459
  readings given by, 467–68
  as Republican, 449, 465
  reputation of, 458, 463–65, 467–70,
    479
  Russia visited by, 464–65
  second marriage of, 461–62, 465–66
  third marriage of, 466–67
  Thomas's meeting with, 471
  as Village resident, 431–32, 449, 452,
    453–54, 457–58, 466, 470
  wartime internment of, 453, 454
  Wilson's friendship with, 460, 464
  writings of, 449, 450, 451–52, 453,
    454, 455, 458, 459–60, 462–64, 465,
    467–70
Currey, Margery, 254–55
Czolgosz, Leon, 202

Dadaism, 320–21, 351
Daily Worker, 470
Dalí, Salvador, 448
"Dance, The" (Hart), 370–71
Dangerous Characters Evening, 17–18,
    21, 206
Dante Alighieri, 358
"Dark Eyes" (Bryant), 120–21
"Dark Note," 446
Darrow, Whitney, Jr., 522
Dasburg, Andrew, 31–32, 33, 42–43, 44,
    97, 160
Davis, Bette, xiv
Davis, Mary Carolyn, 330
Davis, Stuart, 57, 69, 359, 532
Dawson, N. P., 129
Day, Dorothy, 137–38, 140–41, 381, 385
"Day in Bohemia, A" (Reed), 3, 37, 48,
    333
"Death of Dr. Clarke Storer Gould"
    (Gould), 429
"Death to Van Gogh's Ear!" (Ginsberg),
    378
Debs, Eugene, 18, 59, 82, 207, 225
Declaration of Independence, 218
Dehn, Adolf, 327
de Kooning, Elaine, 528, 552
de Kooning, Willem, 527, 537, 540, 542,
    548, 566
  as abstract expressionist, 520, 524, 539,
    544–46, 549–50, 561, 563, 564,
    567

Pollock as viewed by, 532–33, 552, 554, 556–57, 558
Pollock's friendship with, 520, 528, 544–45, 552, 563
Deland, Margaret, 166
de la Selva, Salomón, 246–47, 248, 258, 265
Dell, Floyd, 244, 255–56, 309
    Cook and, 100, 154, 156
    feminism as viewed by, 162, 255–56
    as intellectual, 238, 348
    love affairs of, 207, 238, 253–54, 298
    marriage of, 254–55
    as *Masses* managing editor, 3, 66, 71, 76, 253, 255–56, 260
    Millay's relationship with, 252–53, 256–60, 267, 268, 273, 277, 278
    in Provincetown Players, 126, 136, 154, 156
    trial of, 137, 260
    as Village resident, 4, 9, 168, 308
    writings of, 126, 136, 252–53, 255
de Mille, Agnes, 175
de Mille, Agnes George, 175
Demuth, Charles, 140–41, 349
De Niro, Robert, Sr., 530
de Selincourt, Hugh, 233
Deshon, Florence, 64–65, 201
Desire Under the Elms (O'Neill), 252
De Voto, Bernard, 415
Dewey, John, 53, 79, 86
Dial, 158, 186, 270, 356–58, 365, 370, 371, 427, 452, 458, 459, 463
Dial award, 459
Diamond, David, 498
Diff'rent (O'Neill), 151
Dillon, George, 285–86
Dodge, Edwin, 26, 46
Dodge, Mabel, 15–47
    advice column of, 35
    aristocratic background of, 16, 26–27
    Boyce's correspondence with, 189–90
    Cap Cod property of, 146, 158
    death of, 47
    domineering personality of, 3, 24–25, 26, 34–36, 44, 51, 88
    Evans's letters to, 30–31
    feminism and, 23, 24, 40, 163, 174, 228
    fictional portraits of, 25
    Fifth Avenue apartment of, 15, 16

Florentine villa of, 26–27, 39, 40, 43, 353
Hapgood's friendship with, 16, 19, 38, 42
love affairs of, 19, 27, 36–43, 96–97
in Paris, 39–40
peyote tried by, 31–34
physical appearance of, 35–36
press coverage of, 23–24, 42–43
psychoanalysis of, 22, 26, 34–35, 62, 461
as "Queen of Bohemia," 3, 25, 41, 46
Reed's affair with, 3, 37–43, 48, 85, 92, 95–96, 104–5, 120, 121, 130, 190
salon of, 3, 12, 15–26, 29–31, 33, 36–37, 47, 67, 68, 100, 112, 161, 168, 173, 176, 182, 206, 222–23, 226–27, 293, 295, 299, 314, 349, 437–38
second marriage of, 44–45
Steffens's friendship with, 16–17, 19, 21, 22–23, 25, 44
Stein's relationship with, 19, 20, 27–29, 35, 36, 42, 45
suicide attempts of, 41
in Taos, New Mexico, 45–47, 295
third marriage of, 46
Doolittle, Hilda (H.D.), 357
"Doris the Dope" (Villager), 435–36
Dos Passos, John, 172, 285, 344, 452, 455, 457–58
Douglas, Lord Alfred, 435
Dow, Caroline, 245
"Dread Tomato Habit, The" (Gould), 429
Dreiser, Helen, 301, 303
Dreiser, Paul, 298
Dreiser, Theodore, 297–303
    anti-Semitism of, 300
    difficult personality of, 300–302
    Dodge's salons avoided by, 20, 299
    financial situation of, 299, 303, 344
    Goldman's meeting with, 299–300
    handkerchief-folding ritual of, 298, 300
    love affairs of, 254, 298, 300, 301–2, 340

Dreiser, Theodore (*cont.*)
  Mencken's friendship with, 300, 301,
    302–3, 339
  as Village resident, xiii, 174, 297–99,
    302–3
  writings of, 297, 299, 302–3
Drew, Virginia, 386–87
Drick, Gertrude, 1–3
drug experimentation, 31–34, 140–41
Duchamp, Marcel, 1–3, 29, 319, 320–21,
    322, 349, 351, 352, 448, 450, 531
"Duchess's Red Shoes, The" (Schwartz),
    501
Dude, The (periodical), 504
Dumas, Alexandre, père, 108–9, 112, 122
Du Maurier, George, 9
Duncan, Isadora, 43–44, 45
Dunsany, Edward J.M.D. Plunkett,
    Lord, 102
Durrell, Lawrence, 447
Dylan Thomas in America (Brinnin), 476

Eakins, Thomas, 523
Earle, Ferdinand, 141, 244, 245
"East Coker" (Eliot), 495
Eastman, Annis, 193
Eastman, Crystal, 192–202
  background of, 192–94
  death of, 201
  education of, 193
  as feminist, 192–202, 237
  first marriage of, 195, 197
  Goldman compared with, 196
  influence of, 201–2
  as lawyer, 194–95
  as *Liberator* editor, 80, 199–200, 201,
    314
  Max Eastman's relationship with, 80,
    192, 193, 195
  nephritis of, 201
  as noninterventionist, 198–99
  personality of, 193–94
  physical appearance of, 194
  second marriage of, 197, 201
  sexual liberation supported by, 196–97
  as socialist, 198
  as Village resident, 13, 194, 195
  writings of, 197
Eastman, Max, 48–91
  anticommunism of, 84–85, 86
  autobiographies of, 65, 87–88

  background of, 50–51, 86–87,
    224–25
  on Columbia philosophy faculty, 50,
    79
  contradictory personality of, 50–51, 52,
    61–62, 84–89
  Crystal Eastman's relationship with,
    80, 192, 193, 195
  as Deweyite pragmatist, 53, 86
  Dodge as viewed by, 35–36
  Dodge compared with, 51, 88
  at Dodge's salon, 3, 12, 19, 21, 22, 31,
    33, 173
  editorials of, 54–55, 65–66, 68–69
  as feminist, 50, 51, 65, 167, 238
  as fundraiser, 59–60, 70
  Goldman's relationship with, 77, 206,
    207, 218
  indictments against, 68–69, 78–83,
    137
  as intellectual, 53, 79, 84–89, 90, 345,
    348, 353
  lectures by, 51, 60, 70, 78
  as *Liberator* editor, 80–84, 192, 200,
    201, 314
  love affairs of, 51–52, 61–65, 85,
    87–88, 278
  marriage of, 52–53, 61–62, 63, 95,
    195
  as *Masses* editor, 3, 50–91, 94, 100,
    161, 167, 171, 178, 228, 302, 339,
    353
  as noninterventionist, 75–83
  physical appearance of, 51
  press coverage of, 52–53, 69, 70
  psychoanalysis of, 62–63, 65
  Puritanism of, 51, 86–87
  reputation of, 51, 52–53, 65, 69, 79,
    84–85
  Russia visited by, 84
  salary of, 50, 53, 58
  as socialist, 53, 54–55, 76, 82, 84–89
  trial of, 78–83, 218, 256
  as Village resident, 51, 52–53, 60,
    88–89
  women's suffrage supported by, 50, 51,
    65
  writings of, 62, 65, 85
Edelson, Buddy, 114
Edison, Charles, xi, 308, 342
Edison, Thomas Alva, xi, 308

Edwards, Bobby, 91, 343
Eight, group of, 60–61
Eighteenth Amendment, 271
Eight Harvard Poets (anthology), 452
8th Street, xii, 525
8th Street Book Shop, 299
8th Street Playhouse, xi
Eimi (Cummings), 464
elections:
   of 1912, 18, 207
   of 1916, 97, 199
Eliot, T. S., 339, 352, 419, 451
   Barnes as viewed by, 431, 435, 445,
    447
   Crane compared with, 374, 375, 377
   influence of, 269–70, 288, 359, 374,
    375, 377
   Millay compared with, 279, 287, 288
   poetry of, 288, 353, 359, 375
   Schwartz compared with, 488, 489,
    492, 495, 496, 504
Ell, Christine, 115, 135, 137, 138–39,
   144
"Ellen Terhune" (Wilson), 275–76
Ellington, Duke, 328
Ellis, Charles, 2–3, 252, 261, 282
Ellis, Havelock, 229, 232–33, 234
Ellison, Ralph, 504–5
Elsa (Eastman's lover), 61
Emerson, Ralph Waldo, 7, 87, 356, 376
Emperor Jones, The (O'Neill), 148–50,
   151, 284
Employer Liability Commission, 194
Emporia Gazette, 336
Enemies (Hapgood and Boyce), 190–91
Engels, Friedrich, 53
Enjoyment of Living (Eastman), 65
Enlightenment, 87
Enormous Room, The (Cummings), 454,
   455, 458, 464
Equal Rights Amendment, 196, 200
Ernst, Max, 530
Espionage Act (1917), 76–83, 200, 219
Esquire, 424
Essay on Pessimism (Schopenhauer), 512
Evans, Donald, 30–31
Evening on Proletarian Art, 20
Everybody's Magazine, 62
Exiles (periodical), 427
Exiles (Joyce), 400–401
Exorcism (O'Neill), 438

Fagan, Ruth, 389–92
Family, The (Parsons), 179
Farber, Manny, 532
Faulkner, William, 414, 415, 488
Federal Bureau of Investigation (FBI),
   172, 221, 232, 507
Federal Writers Project, 346, 387
Fels, Joseph, 344
feminism, 162–66
   bohemianism and, 162–66, 222–23,
    435
   British, 194–95, 228–29
   dormancy of, 200, 237–39, 519
   male support for, 50, 51, 65, 133, 162,
    167, 177, 238, 255–56
   noninterventionism and, 198–99
   organizations for, 164, 168, 174–81,
    198, 227, 237
   sexual liberation and, 164–65, 196–97
   socialism and, 164, 166, 198
   social legislation and, 194–95
   of specific women, 166–237
Feminist Alliance, 164, 168
Few Figs from Thistles, A (Millay), 267,
   281
Ficke, Arthur, 244–45, 246, 254, 260–64,
   273, 277, 283–84
Ficke, Davison, 31
Fiedler, Leslie, 552
Fifth Symphony (Beethoven), 267
Figure 5 in Gold, The (Demuth), 349
Fine Arts Ball, 403
Finnan, Grace Fawcett, 388, 389
Finnegans Wake (Joyce), 506
First Amendment, 69, 76
First Feminist Congress (1919), 198
Fitzgerald, F. Scott, 271, 281, 345, 393,
   441, 461
Fitzgerald, Mary Eleanor "Fitzi," 142,
   144, 158, 211–12, 446, 463
Fitzgerald, Zelda, 281
Flanner, Janet, 161, 443, 446
Fleischmann's Model Viennese Bakery,
   xiii
"Fleurs Du Mal à la Mode de New York"
   (Barnes), 438–39
Flynn, Elizabeth Gurley, 39, 66, 173–74,
   180–81
Fog (O'Neill), 130
"Fog" (Reed), 127
Ford, Charles Henri, 445

Ford, Henry, 97
Forel, August, 70–71
"Forest Trees" (Millay), 242
Forrest, Edwin, xii
Forum (periodical), 246, 261
Four Lights (newsletter), 199
Fox, John, 60, 64
Francis, John, 120, 134–35, 342
Frank, Waldo, 355–56, 369, 372–73, 374
Frankau, Joseph, 399
Fredricks, H. C., 80
"Freedom" (Gould), 427
free-love doctrine, xi, 18–19, 36, 96, 177,
    179, 181–92, 204, 205, 209, 217–18,
    254, 301, 321, 348
Freud, Sigmund, 267, 332, 457, 458
    Brill as advocate for, 22, 35, 62, 63, 65,
        88, 195, 300, 461
    influence of, 22, 34–35, 62, 86, 87,
        103, 105, 128, 185, 188, 258–59,
        332, 462
    Marx compared with, 86, 87, 501, 525
Freytag-Loringhoven, Baroness Elsa von,
    317–24
Frick, Henry Clay, 18, 203–4, 208
Friday Literary Review, 100
Friends of Albanian Independence,
    419–20
Fuller, Margaret, 356
Fuller, Walter, 197, 201

Game, The (Bryant), 126, 127
Gandhi, Mohandas K., 235
"Garden Abstract" (Crane), 372
Genesis (Schwartz), 493, 495–96
Genteel Tradition, 20
Gentlemen Prefer Blondes (Loos), 460
Gershwin, George, xv, 525
Gershwin, Ira, xv
Gibran, Kahlil, xiii
Gildea, John Rose, 329, 330
Gilman, Charlotte Perkins, 175
Gilman, Coburn, 513
Gilpin, Charles S., 149–50
Ginsberg, Allen, 10, 359, 378
Girl in the Coffin, The (Dreiser), 299
Glaspell, Susan, 154–55, 237–38
    background of, 100
    Cook's marriage to, 100, 101–2, 104,
        123, 154–55, 171, 237–38
    in Greece, 154–55, 280

    in Heterodoxy Club, 179–80
    in Provincetown Players, 119, 122,
        123, 126, 134–35, 148, 156, 158
    as Village resident, 22, 101–2
Glebe (periodical), 351
Glintenkamp, Henry, 78
Glittering Gate, The (Dunsany), 102
Godwin, Grace, 308
Gogarty, Oliver, 27
Gold, Mike, 138
Golden Spur, The (Powell), 517–18
Goldman, Emma, 202–21
    as anarchist, 17, 18, 19, 95, 203,
        205–7, 221, 312, 348
    Anderson's relationship with, 206,
        207–8, 312, 313
    arrests and imprisonments of, 203–4,
        206, 208–9, 211, 214–15, 218–
        219
    autobiography of, 218
    background of, 203–4
    birth control supported by, 209,
        213–14
    childhood rape of, 203
    correspondence of, 210–11
    death of, 220
    deportation of, 160, 212, 219–20,
        221
    at Dodge's salon, 17, 206
    Dreiser's meeting with, 299–300
    East 13th Street residence of, 202, 206,
        218
    FBI surveillance of, 221
    as feminist, 196, 209, 213–15, 237
    free-love doctrine of, 204, 205, 209,
        217–18
    Frick assassination attempt and, 18,
        203–4, 208
    Havel's relationship with, 30, 204–5,
        213
    as idealist, 205, 212–13, 215, 220–
        221
    love affairs of, 30, 185, 203, 204–5,
        209–18
    Max Eastman's relationship with, 77,
        206, 207, 218
    as *Mother Earth* editor, 18, 89, 99, 202,
        206, 210, 213, 217, 218–19
    as noninterventionist, 77, 218–19
    notoriety of, 204, 206, 208–9, 212–13,
        221

occupations of, 203, 205–6
personality of, 207–8, 211, 215–16, 220–21
physical appearance of, 204, 209
press coverage of, 204, 206, 208
public lectures of, 206, 207, 208–9, 211, 212–13
Reed's relationship with, 160, 206, 218
in Russia, 160, 220
Sanger and, 214, 228
as suffragist, 196, 213
Good Housekeeping, 309
Gorky, Arshile, 520, 524, 526, 537
Gottlieb, Adolf, 524, 540, 550
Gottschalk, Louis, 7
Gould, Joe, 418–30
background of, 419–20
Bodenheim and, 419, 421, 423, 425, 430
bohemian lifestyle of, 418–24
Chippewa dance of, 423, 426
Cummings and, 424, 426, 430
death of, 430
Fund of, 419, 420–21, 430
as "Last Bohemian," 418
legend of, 418–19, 429–30
Neel's portrait of, 424–25
oral history of, 419, 420, 424, 426–29, 430
poetry of, 423–24, 425
Thomas's meeting with, 481
Gousha, Joseph, 512
Gousha, Joseph, Jr. "Jojo," 512–13
Grace's Garrett, 308
Grandcourt, Baron Charles Amadee Grivat de, 330
Grand Hotel (Baum), 408
Grant, Percy Stickney, 167
Grantwood colony, 351–52
"grapevine" metaphor, xiii
Great Depression, xiii, 346, 387–88, 393, 465, 523–24
"Great Figure, The" (Williams), 349
Great Garbo Social Club, 330, 332–33, 385
Greb, Harry, 338
Greeley, Horace, 7
Greenberg, Clement, 533–35, 547, 552, 561, 562, 565, 569
Greenwich House, 522

Greenwich Village:
as "American Ward," 5
artists in, xiv, 20; *see also* abstract expressionism
black population of, 5
bohemianism of, *see* bohemianism
commercialization of, 137, 304
cultural importance of, ix–xvii, 19–20
drug culture of, 31–34, 140–41
early history of, 4–7
East, 343–44
economic prosperity in, 11–12
in fifties, 517–19, 520, 538, 566–69
as film location, xii
"firsts" of, xi–xii
in forties, 509–17
gentrification of, 342–43
geographical boundaries of, 10–11
Golden Age of, 10–14
as "Green Village," 4
iconography of, x, xv–xvi
immigrant population of, 5
as "independent republic," 1–4
institutions and organizations founded in, xi–xii
intellectual milieu of, ix–x, xiv, 5–14, 21, 25–26, 206–7, 572
language of, xiii
as literary center, xiii–xiv
literature on, x
middle-class disapproval of, 7–12, 63, 73–74
mythology of, x, xv–xvii
name of, 4
novelists in, xiii
perceived decline of, ix, xvi, 4, 9–10, 80, 393, 572
performing artists in, xiv–xv
photographers in, xviv
playwrights in, xiii
poets in, xiii–xiv, 20
political activism in, 12–14, 17–18
population increases of, 4
post-war period of, 510–11
press coverage of, 7, 13, 23–24, 103
real estate values in, 5, 342–43, 511
religious movements in, 13–14
as "republic of dreams," xvi–xvii
"revolution of consciousness" in, xvi, 10–14, 185, 191–92

Greenwich Village (*cont.*)
  sexual emancipation in, xvi, 18–19, 36,
    61, 63, 164–65, 181–92, 196–97
  social movements started in, ix–x
  in teens, 10–14, 25, 182, 510–11
  as "The Village," xvi, 1–14, 171,
    572
  in thirties, xiii, 346, 387–88, 393,
    523–24
  tourism in, 137, 303–8, 344
  in twenties, 324–33, 393
*Greenwich Village and How It Got That
  Way* (Miller), x
"Greenwich Villageism," 89
Greenwich Village People's Institute,
  177
Gregory, Horace, 428
Group Theater, 513
Grudin, Louis, 383
Guernica (Picasso), 525
Guggenheim, Peggy, 432, 440, 446, 516,
  530–31, 532, 547
Guggenheim Foundation, 376, 408, 413,
  465
Guston, Philip, 524, 542–43, 558–59,
  561

Hairy Ape, The (O'Neill), 151–52
Hale, Ruth, 175
Hamlet (Shakespeare), 452
Hammarskjold, Dag, 447
Hammerstein, Oscar, 433
Hand, Augustus, 78–79, 80
Hand, Learned, 77
Hand of the Potter, The (Dreiser), 299
Hanfstaengl, Putzi, 440
Hapgood, Hutchins, 67, 117, 181–92
  Dodge's friendship with, 16, 19, 38,
    42
  feminism as viewed by, 162, 177
  Holladay's death and, 140–41
  love affairs of, 341
  marriage of, 171, 181–92, 238
  peyote tried by, 31–34
  in Provincetown Players, 123, 126,
    182, 190–91
  writings of, 181, 185, 186–91
Hardigut (Millay), 281
Harlem Socialist Club, 173
Harper's Bazaar, 58, 180
Harp-Weaver, The (Millay), 281

Harrington, Raymond, 31–32, 33
Harris, Frank, 307–8
Harry Kemp's Playhouse, 343
Hartley, Marsden, 42, 98, 349–50, 370,
  408, 440, 445
Hartmann, Sadakichi, 437
Harvard Advocate, 450
Harvard Monthly, 450
Harvard University, 450–51, 452, 475,
  494–95, 553
Havel, Hippolyte, 204–5, 351, 437
  at Dodge's salon, 15, 18, 19, 30
  Goldman's relationship with, 30,
    204–5, 213
  Holladay's relationship with, 19, 30,
    98, 299
  in Provincetown Players, 98, 123, 126
  as Village resident, 11, 30, 182
Haymarket Affair (1886), 203
Haywood, Big Bill, 17, 20, 23–24, 37, 39,
  171–72, 173, 207, 227, 349
Heap, Jane, 313, 316–17, 364, 442–43
Heartbreak House (Shaw), 274
Hecht, Ben, 312, 381, 384, 388, 391,
  392–93
Heller, Edwin, 555
Hell Hole bar, 32, 34, 115–16, 117, 125,
  137, 138–40, 146–47, 381
Hemingway, Ernest, 85, 172, 339, 345,
  359, 415, 432, 441, 492, 510, 515,
  558
Henri, Robert, 399
Henry, O., 6
Hepburn, Audrey, xii
Herland (Gilman), 175
heroin, 140–41
Hess, Thomas, 549, 561, 563
Heterodoxy Club, 174–81, 227, 237
Hill, Joe, 312
Hillquit, Morris, 80
him (Cummings), 462–64, 466
Hitler, Adolf, 414, 440, 465, 499
Hoffenstein, Samuel, 269
Hofmann, Hans, 520, 524, 528–29, 533,
  545, 547, 550, 558, 560, 562
Holladay, Louis, 114–15, 140–41
Holladay, Polly, 19, 30, 98, 114, 130, 140,
  174, 176, 299, 437
Hollywood, xii, 387, 465, 476
Homer, Winslow, 542–43
Home Relief Agency, 387–88

homosexuality, 42, 185, 350, 371–74, 377–78, 551, 553, 554
Hoover, J. Edgar, 221
Hope, Will, 75
Horace, 406
Horgan, Paul, 46
"Hot Afternoons Have Been in Montana" (Siegel), 330
"Hound of Heaven, The" (Thompson), 138
"House of Genius," 37, 294, 434
Howdy Doody, xii
Howe, Irving, 490
Howe, Marie Jenney, 176, 177–78, 180–81
Howells, William Dean, 7, 394
Hubbard, Elbert, 334–35
Hubert's Sheridan Square cafeteria, 329–31
Huckleberry Finn (Twain), 297
Hudson Dusters, 116, 147
Hughes, Charles Evans, 199
Humboldt's Gift (Bellow), 488
Hunecker, James, 18
Hunt, Robert, 279
Hurst, Fannie, 176
Hutchins, Robert, 490
Hyman, Elaine, 254

Iceman Cometh, The (O'Neill), 116, 121
Ile (O'Neill), 363
Imagism, 349, 354
Improper Bohemians, The (Churchill), x
Independent Show, 459
In Dreams Begin Responsibilities (Schwartz), 492
"In Dreams Begin Responsibilities" (Schwartz), 487, 489, 508
Industrial Revolution, 9
"Inhibiting Effects of Family upon the Individual, The" (Powell), 512
"Insanity" (Gould), 427, 430
Instead of a Magazine (newsletter), 219
Interior (Maeterlinck), 103
Internal Revenue Service (IRS), 147
International Workers of the World (IWW), 17, 23, 34, 38–39, 54, 64, 173, 207, 228, 349
In the Zone (O'Neill), 135–36
Irwin, Elizabeth, 175, 180
I Thought of Daisy (Wilson), 276

Jabberwocky café, 390
Jack's House (Kreymborg), 137, 363
James, Henry:
    as Village resident, 5, 6, 297, 332
    writings of, 276
James, William, 19, 450
Janis, Sidney, 550
Jarrell, Randall, 500
Jefferson Market, 301, 470
Jefferson Market Courthouse, xii, 173
Jefferson Market Jail, 526
Jelliffe, Smith Ely, 35, 62, 63, 65
Jesus Christ, 14, 69, 82, 219
Jimmy the Priest's, 112
Joe Gould Fund, 419, 420–21, 430
Johns, Orrick, 241, 352
Johnson, Grace Neil, 175
Jones, Ellis, 2
Jones, Marjorie, 255
Jones, Robert Edmond, 31–32, 102, 105, 153
Joseph Ferdinand Gould Stomp, 423, 426
Josephson, Matthew, 359, 508, 510, 512
Journey Down, The (Bernstein), 413–414
Joyce, James, 27, 327, 498
    Barnes's relationship with, 323, 431, 432, 441–42, 445
    writings of, 218, 315–16, 323, 390, 441–42, 454, 506
Jung, Carl Gustav, 22, 67
Jungle, The (Sinclair), 336
"Justice Denied in Massachusetts" (Millay), 285
Justice Department, U.S., 221
J. Walter Thompson, 366–67

Kahn, Otto, 135, 371
Kandinsky, Wassily, 550
Kansas City Star, 335
Kazin, Alfred, 506
Keats, John, 334, 365, 470
Kelly, Grace, xii
Kemp, Harry, 138, 208, 211, 333–46
    autobiography of, 345, 346
    "Big Bass Drum" technique of, 335
    death of, 346
    education of, 334–36
    in England, 339

Kemp, Harry (*cont.*)
  first marriage of, 190, 340–41, 343
  in France, 344
  as "King of Bohemia," 334, 337, 338
  love affairs of, 336–38, 340–41
  as *Masses* editorial assistant, 60
  Mencken's views on, 338–39, 345, 346
  in Provincetown, 341–42, 344–46, 386
  in Provincetown Players, 119, 340,
    341–42
  second marriage of, 343–44, 442
  self-promotion by, 333–36
  theater run by, 306, 341–43
  writings of, 335–36, 337, 338–39, 342,
    343, 345–46
Kempf, M. A., 75
Kempton, Murray, 170, 172
Kennedy, John F., 507
Kennerley, Mitchell, 338, 429
Kenton, Edna, 136, 155, 156
Kerouac, Jack, 553
Key, Francis Scott, 16
Kilmer, Joyce, 507
King Arthur's Socks (Dell), 126
Kligman, Ruth, 564–65
Kline, Franz, 520, 524, 540, 544–45, 549,
    554, 561, 564, 567, 569
Kling, Joseph, 362–63
Knopf, Alfred A., 295, 414
Knopf, Blanche, 295
"Knowledge and Revolution" (Eastman),
    54–55
Krafft-Ebing, Richard von, 205
Kramer, Hilton, 505–6
Krasner, Lee, 527–28, 529, 533
Kreymborg, Alfred, 314, 392, 441
  obscenity charge against, 306, 308
  as *Others* editor, 350–55, 356, 357,
    359, 363–64, 381
  in Provincetown Players, 128, 136–37,
    350, 363
Kreymborg, Christine, 381
Krishnamurti, 521–22, 534
Ku Klux Klan, 153
Kurzy of the Sea (Barnes), 438

labor movement, xi, 37–39, 54, 66–67,
    69, 101, 170, 171–73, 212–13, 222,
    348–49
Ladies Almanack (Barnes), 443–44
Ladies' Home Journal, 345

Lafayette Hotel, 510, 517
La Follette, Fola, 175, 178
La Follette, Robert, 69, 178, 308
Lake Erie College for Women, 512
Lamp and the Bell, The (Millay), 258,
    267
Lange, Jessica, xiv
Langner, Lawrence, 102–3, 313, 341
Laughlin, James, 492, 495–96
Lavender Mist (Pollock), 559
Lawrence, D. H., 46–47, 295
Lawrence, Frieda, 47
Lawrence, Mass. strike, 54, 170, 213
League of American Penwomen, 285
League of Nations, 83
LeBlanc, Georgette, 316–17
"Lecture on Nothing" (Cage), 547
Lemon, Courtenay, 440
Lenin, V. I., 81, 83, 84, 158
"Lenin's Testament," 84
lesbianism, 180, 216–17, 229, 248, 251,
    253, 258, 266–67, 285, 341, 350,
    442–44
Levin, Harold, 495
Lewis, Edith, 294–95
Lewis, Sinclair, 338, 345
Lewis, Wyndham, 315
Liberal Club, 101, 102, 103, 125,
    167–68, 256, 299
Liberator, 80–84, 192, 199–200, 201,
    314
Lichtenstein, Roy, 567
Life, 2, 392, 551, 557–58, 559
"Life Along the Passaic River"
    (Williams), 348–49
"Ligeia" (Poe), 250
Light, Jimmy, 145, 147, 152, 463, 466
Lima Beans (Kreymborg), 128, 136,
    350
Lincoln, Abraham, xii
Lindbergh, Charles, xii, 375
Lindsay, Vachel, 326
Lippmann, Walter, 11, 17, 22, 23–24, 44,
    229, 348, 419
Literary Gazette, 392
literature, avant-garde, 67–68, 73–75, 89,
    348, 353, 367–68
Little Africa, 5
Little Italy, xii
"little magazines," 350–59
Little Red School House, 175

Little Review, 309–18, 320, 322, 323, 355, 364–65, 367, 382, 436–37, 441–42, 458
Liveright, Horace, 383, 440
Lobe, Harold, 359
Locusts Have No King, The (Powell), 518–19
Loeb, Gladys, 385–86
Loew, Maurice, xii
London, Jack, 50, 146
Lonesome Pine, The (Fox), 64
Long Day's Journey into Night (O'Neill), 108, 112
Long Voyage Home, The (O'Neill), 135
Look Homeward, Angel (Wolfe), 395, 402, 404, 406–7, 412–13, 522
Loos, Anita, 460
Lorber, Harry, 33–34
"Lord Archer, Death" (Millay), 278
Los Angeles Times, 181
Love and Revolution (Eastman), 65
Love in Greenwich Village (Dell), 255
"Love Poems" (Loy), 352–53
Lowell, Abbott Lawrence, 450–51
Lowell, Amy, xiv, 20, 177, 311, 352, 354–55, 383, 450–51, 452
Lowell, Robert, xiv, 378
Loy, Mina, 347, 350, 352–53, 442, 445
Luce, Clare Boothe, 515–16
Luce, Henry, 515–16
Luchow's restaurant, 299
Lucy Stone League, 175
Luhan, Antonio, 45–46, 47, 295
"Lyrical Left," 25
Lyric Year, The (Earle, ed.), 241, 352
Lysistrata (Aristophanes), 101

McCall's, 441
McCarthy, Joseph, 449
McCarthy, Mary, 490, 502
McClernan, Frances, 343–44
McClung, Isabelle, 294
McClure, Sam, 294
McClure's, 294
MacCracken, Henry Noble, 247, 248
McCullers, Carson, 432, 435
Macdonald, Dwight, 84, 490, 497, 501, 506
McDowell writers' colony, 383
Macfadden, Bernarr, 335
Macgowan, Kenneth, 153

McKay, Claude, 194
MacKaye, Hazel, 248
McKinley, William, 202
MacMahon, Aline, 466
Macready, Charles, xii
Madison Square Garden, 37, 38–39, 114, 222
Maeterlinck, Maurice, 103
Mafia, xii
Mailer, Norman, xiii, 507
Main Street (Lewis), 345
Malina, Judith, 359
Manikin and Minikin (Kreymborg), 137, 363
Mann, Forrest, 2–3
Mantle, Burns, 136, 147
Many Loves (Williams), 359
Marie, Romany, 130, 140
Marinetti, Filippo, 353
Markham, Kirah, 298, 299, 301
Marquis, Don, 159
"Marriage Customs and Taboos Among the Early Heterodites" (Woolston), 174, 179–80
"Marriage Under Two Roofs" (Eastman), 197
Married Love (Stopes), 233
Marte's speakeasy, 458
Marx, Groucho, 432, 447
Marx, Karl, 53, 67, 86, 87, 159, 501, 525
Marxism, 53, 84, 86, 469–70, 500, 515, 525
Masefield, John, 115, 261
Masses, The, 48–91
    advertisements in, 67, 70–71
    avant-garde literature ignored by, 67–68, 73–75, 89, 348, 353, 367–368
    bohemian radicalism of, 55, 88–89, 91
    cartoons of, 14, 20, 54, 57, 59, 66, 67, 69, 72, 73, 75, 76, 77, 79–80
    circulation of, 68, 70, 84
    contributors to, 48, 58, 60–61, 67, 74, 75, 91, 95, 97, 98, 121, 131, 135, 169, 171, 182, 282
    cooperative ideology of, 49–50, 56
    covers of, 57
    criticism of, 58–59, 68–69
    Dell as managing editor of, 3, 66, 71, 76, 253, 255–56, 260

Masses, The (cont.)
　Eastman as editor of, 3, 50–91, 94,
　　100, 161, 167, 171, 178, 228, 302,
　　339, 353
　eclecticism of, 89–91
　editorial board of, 3, 49–50, 53–54, 56,
　　57, 71–73, 75–76, 80–81, 89, 128,
　　293, 299, 353
　final issue of, 91
　financial support for, 55–56, 59–60, 64
　founding of, 49–50, 112, 169
　influence of, 24, 68, 84, 89–91
　"insurrection" at, 71–73, 75–76, 89
　legacy of, 89–91
　legal proceedings against and
　　suppression of, 68–69, 76–83, 218,
　　256, 314
　Liberator compared with, 84
　mainstream publications compared
　　with, 49, 59, 67, 69, 311
　manifesto of, 48
　as noninterventionist, 71, 75–83
　organized religion attacked by, 14,
　　69–70
　political agenda of, 48–49
　Post Office interdiction of, 76–78,
　　314
　propaganda in, 73–75
　racial segregation as viewed by, 67
　realistic aesthetic of, 67–68, 73–75,
　　89
　revolution supported by, 54–55, 66, 78,
　　90
　as socialist publication, 14, 49–50, 53,
　　54, 55, 58, 59, 65–66, 72, 73–75
　staff of, 60–61, 137–38
　subscriptions to, 94
　tone of, 68, 69–70, 84, 213
　unorthodox content of, 49–50
　"Virgin Mary" ballad published by,
　　70
　working-class readership of, 74–75,
　　89–90
Masses balls, 63–64, 299–300
Masters, Edgar Lee, 136
Mather, Cotton, 271
Matisse, Henri, 555
Matthiessen, F. O., 489, 495
"Maurice" (Villager), xv
Mazeppa (play), 7
Melville, Herman, 6

Memoirs of Hecate County (Wilson),
　276–77
"Memorial to D.C." (Millay), 258,
　266–67
Mencken, H. L., 355
　Dreiser's friendship with, 300, 301,
　　302–3, 339
　Kemp as viewed by, 338–39, 345,
　　346
　as *Masses* reader, 84, 90
　as *Smart Set* editor, 296, 338–39
Menken, Adah Isaacs, 7
Men's League for Women's Suffrage, 50,
　51
Metropolitan Magazine, 20, 97, 131
Metropolitan Museum of Art, 349
Metropolitan Opera, 248
Metzger, Edith, 565
middle class, 7–12, 63, 73–74
Middleton, Scudder, 278
Midsummer's Night Dream, A
　(Shakespeare), 512
Miejer, Pieter, 278
Milholland, Inez, 51–52, 60, 199, 247,
　285
Millay, Cora, 241–42, 245, 246, 248–49,
　251, 252, 257, 266, 274, 278
Millay, Edna St. Vincent, 240–92
　as actress, 136, 247–48, 249, 284
　arrest of, 285
　background of, 241–43, 257
　at Barnard, 245–47
　at Cape Cod, 274–75
　correspondence of, 245, 246, 248–49,
　　275, 279–80, 283–84, 285, 290–91,
　　292
　critical disdain for, 244, 269–70,
　　287–90
　death of, 292
　Dell's relationship with, 252–53,
　　256–60, 267, 268, 273, 277, 278
　drug addiction of, 286–87
　early poetry of, 241, 242–45, 246, 249,
　　266–67, 352
　Eliot compared with, 279, 287, 288
　in Europe, 280–81
　as feminist, 247, 258–59, 285
　Ficke's relationship with, 260–64, 273,
　　277, 283–84
　financial situation of, 245, 265, 266,
　　281, 283

ill health of, 273, 281, 284, 286–87, 290–92
legend of, 240, 249, 267, 379
lesbian relationships of, 248, 251, 253, 258, 266–67, 442
love affairs of, 85, 246–47, 256–67, 272–80, 285–86, 292
marriage as viewed by, 257, 258, 274–75, 278–80
marriage of, 281–87, 290–92
music as interest of, 242, 248, 267
"Nancy Boyd" pseudonym of, 265–66, 270, 273
personality of, 240, 253, 256–60, 278
physical appearance of, 251–52
plays of, 147, 248, 264–65, 267, 363
press coverage of, 264–65, 283
in Provincetown Players, 136, 137, 147, 251–52, 264–65, 267, 272
public readings by, 268–69, 283, 284–85
Pulitzer Prize awarded to, 281, 288
reputation of, 240, 244–45, 250, 265, 266, 267–70, 280, 281, 287–90, 292, 436, 459
sonnets of, 249, 259, 262–63, 267–71, 274, 277
Steepletop estate of, 283, 284, 286–87, 290–92
at Vassar, 245, 247–49, 264, 266–67
as Village resident, xii, 249–52, 267, 280, 281, 396
Wilson's relationship with, 272–77, 280, 283, 284, 290–91
Wilson's views on, 264–65, 269, 270–71, 275–77, 287
Millay, Henry, 241–42, 245
Millay, Kathleen, 242, 250–51, 274
Millay, Norma, 136, 242, 249, 250–51, 252, 261, 264, 266, 267, 274, 282, 286
Miller, Terry, x
Minettas (neighborhood), 342–43
Minetta Tavern, 390, 430, 499
Minor, Robert, 57, 75, 172
Miró, Joan, 534
"Misconceptions of Free Love" (Goldman), 217
Mizener, Arthur, 490
Moise, Nina, 133–34, 137, 142
Mondrian, Piet, 530–31

Monet, Claude, 543
Monist Society, 100
Monitor, USS, xii
Monroe, Harriet, 100, 249, 251, 267, 349, 351, 352, 355
Moon for the Misbegotten, A (O'Neill), 115, 152
Moore, Clement, xii
Moore, Marianne, 348, 353–54, 357–58, 370, 371, 381, 392, 447–48, 464, 470
Morehouse, Marion, 466–67, 470, 471
Morgan, J. P., 424
Morse, Samuel F. B., xi
Moses, Robert, 470
Moss, Howard, 483, 507–8
Mother Earth, 18, 89, 99, 202, 206, 210, 213, 217, 218–19
Motherwell, Robert, 532, 535, 541–42, 547, 550
Mourning Becomes Electra (O'Neill), 151
"Mr. Dalton Larabee, Sinner" (Millay), 266
muckrakers, 294, 501
Muir, Edwin, 445
Munsey, Frank, 338
Munson, Gorham, 372
Murger, Henri, 8–9
Museum of Modern Art, 525, 535, 549, 550–51, 553
Museum of Non-Objective Painting, 530
My Life and Loves in Greenwich Village (Bodenheim), 387, 390
Mylius, E. F., 84

Naked on Roller Skates (Bodenheim), 387
Namuth, Hans, 559–60
Nathan, George Jean, 111, 151, 296, 338–39, 464
Nation, The, 145, 202, 365, 533–34
National League, xi
National Women's Party, 200
Neel, Alice, 424–25
Neighborhood Playhouse, 403
neurasthenia, 26
"New Art, The" (Cummings), 450
New Cow of Greenwich Village (periodical), 330–31
New Criticism, 288

New Freedom, 11
New Lady Bantock, The (play), 451
Newman, Barnett, 520, 524, 539–40, 542, 543, 544, 547, 550, 551, 561, 567
New Psychology Evenings, 22, 35
New Republic, 234, 365, 500, 504, 532
New Statesman, 59
New Woman, 162–66, 182, 221, 237, 296, 353
"New Year's Eve" (Schwartz), 501–2
New York City:
    grid system of, 4
    northward expansion of, 4–5
    see also Greenwich Village
New York City Board of Education, 167
New York Daily News, 232, 464
New Yorker, xiii, 441, 483
New York Evening Mail, 343, 420
New York Evening Post, 90, 103
New York Evening Sun, 126, 270
New York Globe, 16, 129
New York Herald, 129, 299
New York Herald Tribune, 328, 388, 445, 551
New York Mail, 136
New York Morning Telegraph, 24, 435
New York Post, 452
New York Press, 435
New York School, 552, 553
New York Society for the Suppression of Vice, 70–71, 153, 307, 315–16
New York Stage Society, 126
New York Sun, 464, 532
New York Telegram, 332
New York Times, xii, 7, 29, 30, 136, 161, 166, 186, 189, 206, 222, 302, 315, 342, 346, 386, 420, 438, 439, 440, 463, 550–51, 557, 561
New York Tribune, 129, 232, 427, 435
New York University, xi, 285, 396–97
New York World, 42–43, 52–53, 204, 299
Nietzsche, Friedrich, 87, 99, 110, 228–29
Nightwood (Barnes), 158, 307, 432, 439, 444–45, 447, 448
Nineteenth Amendment, 202
Norris, Frank, 6
no thanks (Cummings), 465
Nude Descending a Staircase (Duchamp), 2, 29, 319, 349, 450

"033" (Crane), 362
Oasis, The (McCarthy), 502
O'Brien, Joe, 104, 170
O'Connor, Luke, 115, 147, 338
Odets, Clifford, 343
Of Time and the River (Wolfe), 411–12
O'Hara, Frank, 552, 553–54, 560
Old Grapevine, xiii
O'Neill, Agnes Boulton, 138–40, 143–44, 146–47, 157
O'Neill, Carlotta Monterey, 108, 152, 157–58, 460
O'Neill, Ella, 109–10, 152
O'Neill, Eugene, 108–58
    background of, 108–13
    in Baker's playwriting class, 113, 119, 142, 396
    bohemian lifestyle of, 112–18, 120, 137
    Broadway productions of, 142, 146, 151
    Bryant's affair with, 118, 120–21, 124–25, 129–33, 135, 137, 138, 139, 142–43
    Bryant's correspondence with, 142–43
    Carlin's friendship with, 98, 108, 116–18, 119, 141, 146, 157–58
    Cook's relationship with, 122–23, 139–40, 145–55
    Crane's friendship with, 368, 369
    drinking by, 114–18, 125, 130, 137, 140, 141, 143–44, 146–47, 156, 381
    early plays of, 108, 113, 114, 119, 121–22, 126, 127, 128, 130, 134, 135–36, 363, 438, 439, 462
    education of, 110–11, 113, 119, 142, 396
    financial situation of, 111–12, 130, 150, 368
    first marriage of, 111, 156
    love affairs of, 111, 115, 120–21
    as newspaper reporter, 112–13
    Nobel Prize awarded to, 161
    as noninterventionist, 134, 135
    personality of, 109–14, 116–17, 122–23, 139, 143–44, 278
    as playwright, 3, 122, 135–36, 141, 144–45, 147–48, 150, 155–56
    press reviews of, 122, 136, 144–45, 150

in Provincetown, 98, 108, 118–23,
    125, 130, 131–32, 134–35, 139–40,
    141, 142–44
in Provincetown Players, 3, 108,
    119–23, 126, 127, 128, 130, 133,
    134, 135–36, 139–40, 141, 144–58,
    171, 252, 284, 342, 438
Pulitzer Prize awarded to, 142,
    147–48, 152
Reed's friendship with, 113–14, 120
religious sentiment of, 110, 138
reputation of, 122, 136, 142, 144–52,
    161
seafaring experience of, 111, 119
second marriage of, 143–44, 146–47,
    156, 157
suicide attempts of, 112
theatrical experience of, 111
third marriage of, 157–58
tuberculosis of, 113, 135
as Village resident, xiii, 32, 113–18,
    125, 137, 141, 157–58
O'Neill, James, 108–12, 122, 130, 146,
    147–48
O'Neill, Jamie, 109, 139, 152
O'Neill, Kathleen, 111
Onslow, Genevieve, 32, 33–34
Opffer, Emil, 372–73
Opffer, Ivan, 372
O Pioneers! (Cather), 297
Oppenheim, James, 14, 355–56
Oral History of Our Time, An (Gould),
    419, 420, 424, 426–29, 430
orgasm, cult of, 36
Orr, Elaine, 455–60
Oscar Blumenthal Award, 390
Other Players, 136–37
Others (periodical), 350–55, 356,
    363–64, 381, 382
"Overture to a Dance of Locomotives"
    (Williams), 349

Pagan (periodical), 362–63, 367
Pagany (periodical), 427, 430
Page, Tim, 510
Pageant of Athena (MacKaye), 248
Paine, Thomas, 4
Palmer raids, 160, 219
Paracelsus, 145
Parker, Dorothy, 441, 509, 510
Parsons, Betty, 554–55

Parsons, Elsie Clews, 179
Partisan Review, 487, 488, 489, 490, 491,
    494, 499, 500, 501–2, 504, 506, 533
Patchin Place, 431–32, 446–48, 449, 466,
    470
Paterson strike (1913), 37–39, 67, 101,
    173, 213, 222, 348–49
Pavia, Phillip, 548, 550
Peace That Passeth Understanding, The
    (Reed), 159
Peaked Hill house, 146
Pearson's Magazine, 307–8
Pegasus (periodical), 333
Pepe, Vincent, 342–43
Pepys, Samuel, 428
Perkins, Maxwell, 85–89, 346, 406, 409,
    411, 415, 416–17
Perspectives USA (periodical), 500, 504
peyote, 31–34
Pfaff, Charles, 6, 7, 8
Phillips, William, 489, 502, 508
Philpott, A. J., 122
Physical Culture City, 335
Picasso, Pablo, 313, 351, 490, 525, 527,
    546
"Pig Cupid" (Loy), 352
Pilgrim's Progress (Bunyan), 454
Pinchot, Amos, 60
"Pioneer, The" (Millay), 285
Poe, Edgar Allan, 6, 250
poetry:
    modernist, 287–90, 345–46, 348, 488,
        489–90, 496, 501, 504
    New York School of, 552, 553
    political, 348
Poetry, 100, 249, 251, 267, 351, 355, 371,
    390
Poetry Center, 482
"poetry wars," 350–59
Poets Evening, 20
Poet's Theater, 343
Pollett, Elizabeth, 499–500, 504–6
Pollock, Charles, 522, 523, 524, 526
Pollock, Jackson, 520–36
    as abstract expressionist, 520–21,
        529–36, 543, 544–45, 549, 558–59,
        561, 562–63, 564, 566, 567
    abusive behavior of, 554–55, 559–62,
        564–65
    anti-intellectualism of, 521–22,
        532–33, 555–56

Pollock, Jackson (*cont.*)
    artistic reputation of, 529–36, 540
    at Cedar Tavern, 552, 554–55, 560–64
    death of, 520, 552, 565–66, 568, 569
    de Kooning's friendship with, 520,
        528, 544–45, 552, 563
    de Kooning's views on, 532–33, 552,
        554, 556–57, 558
    drinking by, 520, 525–27, 531, 535–36,
        554–55, 559–65
    drip technique of, 521, 525, 551,
        555–60
    early career of, 522–27
    financial situation of, 522–24, 555
    Greenberg's relationship with, 533–35
    Guggenheim mural painted by, 531,
        533, 535
    Guggenheim's relationship with,
        530–31, 532, 535–36
    influences on, 522, 525, 527, 528–29,
        555–56
    Krasner's marriage to, 527–28, 529,
        532, 534, 535, 536, 554, 555, 558,
        563, 564
    Krishnamurti studied by, 521–22, 534
    legend of, 521, 531, 555–60, 565–66,
        569
    Life story on, 551, 557–58, 559
    Long Island home of, 536, 554
    Namuth's film on, 559–60
    one-man shows of, 531, 532, 533–34,
        541, 557
    post-drip paintings of, 560–61
    press coverage of, 532, 533–34, 551,
        557–58, 559, 561
    in psychotherapy, 554
    as Village resident, 522–27, 536,
        555
pop art, 539, 552–53, 566–67
Porter, Katherine Anne, 377, 475–76
"Portrait of a Lady" (Eliot), 353
"Portrait of Mabel Dodge at the Villa
    Curonia" (Stein), 27–29
Portrait of the Artist as a Young Man
    (Joyce), 218
"Possessions" (Crane), 372
Pound, Ezra, 339, 381, 424, 427, 441,
    457
    Crane and, 364–65
    as *Little Review* foreign editor, 311,
        315, 316

as *Others* correspondent, 352, 353, 354
    Schwartz and, 488, 489–90, 496, 504
Powell, Dawn, 509–19
    background of, 511–13
    death of, 519
    feminism as viewed by, 519
    gatherings hosted by, 509–10
    Greenwich Village as described by,
        511, 513–19
    marriage of, 512, 513, 519
    as Village resident, xiii, 509–13, 572
    Wilson's friendship with, 510, 518
    wit of, 509
    writings of, 510, 513–19
Pratt Institute, 434
Price, Mollie, 99–100
Primavera (Botticelli), 251
Princess Marries the Page, The (Millay),
    248, 265
Prodigal Son (Kemp), 342
Prohibition, 147, 271, 324, 327, 359,
    458, 510
Prophet, The (Gibran), xiii
prostitution, 18–19, 41, 115, 184, 196,
    306, 324, 451, 452, 564
Provincetown Players, 104–58
    amateurism of, 136–37, 141–42, 145
    Barnes in, 438, 439, 445
    Boyce in, 104–5, 106, 128, 182,
        190–91
    Bryant in, 124, 126, 127, 131
    Cook's management of, 3, 98–99,
        104–8, 123–26, 128–29, 133–37,
        141–42, 145–55, 161, 299, 353, 438,
        463
    Dell in, 126, 136, 154, 156
    dissident faction in, 136–37
    as experimental theater troupe, 3,
        141–42, 145–58, 293, 311, 353
    finances of, 105–6, 126–27, 135, 141,
        145, 147, 150, 151, 155
    first season of, 104–6
    founding of, 98–99, 104–8, 123–26,
        171, 182
    Glaspell in, 119, 122, 123, 126,
        134–35, 148, 156, 158
    Greenwich Village performances by,
        123–25, 133–37, 141–42, 144–58
    Greenwich Village theater of, 81, 124,
        125–27
    Hapgood in, 123, 126, 182, 190–91

Havel in, 98, 123, 126
Kemp in, 119, 340, 341–42
Kreymborg in, 128, 136–37, 350, 363
Millay in, 136, 137, 147, 251–52, 264–65, 267, 272
O'Neill in, 3, 108, 119–23, 126, 127, 128, 130, 133, 134, 135–36, 139–40, 141, 144–58, 171, 252, 284, 342, 438
organization of, 123–24
press reviews of, 122, 128–29, 136, 141, 144–45, 147, 150, 299, 438, 463–64
Provincetown performances by, 105–108
Reed in, 123, 124, 127, 131, 133, 159
rehearsals by, 133–34
Season of Youth in, 145
second season of, 107–8, 119–23
tax problems of, 147
ticket sales of, 126, 141, 147, 151, 463–64
Wharf Theater of, 105–6, 158
Williams in, 130, 350
psychoanalysis, 22, 34–35, 62–63
Puritanism, 51, 86–87
Purple Cat café, 299
"push-pull" technique, 528–29
Pyne, Mary, 138, 139, 190, 340–41, 343, 442

Quill, 308, 343
Quinn, John, 316
Quintillions (Clairmont), 331

Rabbit's Foot, The (Kemp), 343
Rahv, Philip, 445, 490, 502
Ramsey, Fedya, 385
Ransom, John Crowe, 496, 497–98
Rathburn, Stephen, 126–27
Rauh, Ida, 19, 31, 52–53, 61–62, 63, 69, 95, 102, 103, 147, 193, 195
Rauschenberg, Robert, 566
"Raven, The" (Poe), 6
Raven Poetry Circle, 423–24
Ray, Man, 320, 351
Read, Herbert, 565–66
Reader's Digest, xi
Rear Window, xii
Reason in Madness (Tate), 496–97
"Recuerdo" (Millay), 247

Red Scare, 85, 146, 160, 200, 219
Reed, John, 37–43, 78–98
Bolshevik revolution reported by, 78, 80, 81, 83, 91, 92–93, 135, 145–46, 158–59, 282
Bryant's correspondence with, 96–97, 98, 132–33
Bryant's marriage to, 124–25, 127, 129–33, 142–43, 157, 159, 160, 237–38
Bryant's relationship with, 93–98, 118, 120, 121
in China, 131
Croton-on-Hudson house of, 130–31
death of, 160–61, 278
Dodge's affair with, 3, 37–43, 48, 85, 92, 95–96, 104–5, 120, 121, 130, 190
as feminist, 133
Goldman's relationship with, 160, 206, 218
government prosecution of, 78, 80–82, 137, 145–46, 256
indictment against, 78, 80–81, 137
kidney ailment of, 97, 121, 124, 127
lectures by, 81
as Liberator contributor, 80–81, 83–84
love affairs of, 183, 278
as Masses contributor, 48, 67, 74, 75, 91, 95, 97, 131, 135, 282
in Mexico, 42, 43
as noninterventionist, 75, 76, 131, 135, 356
O'Neill's friendship with, 113–14, 120
Paterson Pageant organized by, 37–39, 101, 222, 348–49
personality of, 51, 81, 88, 94–95, 113–14, 240, 440, 463
in Provincetown, 97–98, 118, 119, 120, 145–46
in Provincetown Players, 123, 124, 127, 131, 133, 159
reputation of, 37–39, 81–82, 91, 145–46, 158–61, 240, 440, 463
in Russia (1919), 158–61
as socialist, 74, 75, 80–81, 83–84, 145–46
Steffens's friendship with, 37, 92
trial of, 81–82, 256
as Village resident, ix, 3, 37, 48, 93, 94–95, 146, 294, 333, 435–36

Reed, John (*cont.*)
  as war correspondent, 48, 71, 92, 131
  writings of, 3, 37, 97–98, 158–59, 333
Reedy's Mirror (periodical), 267
Reinhardt, Ad, 524, 543–44
Reitell, Liz, 482, 483, 484–85, 486
Reitman, Ben, 185, 209–18
"Renascence" (Millay), 241, 243–45, 246
Renascence and Other Poems (Millay),
  249–50, 270
Replenishing Jessica (Bodenheim),
  384–85
Rhapsody in Blue (Gershwin), xv
Richmond Hill estate, 4
Ridge, Lola, 349
Ridgefield Gazook (periodical), 351
Rilke, Rainer Maria, 470, 488, 542
Rittenhouse, Jessie, 246
Rivers, Larry, 552–53, 554, 569
Roberts, W. Adolphe, 265–66
Robeson, Paul, 150, 153, 284
Robinson, Boardman, 158–59
Robinson, Edward Arlington, 20
Rockefeller, John D., 90
Rockefeller, Nelson, 506
Rodman, Henrietta, 166–68, 318,
  337–38
Roebling, John Augustus, 370
Rogers, Lou, 180
Rogers, Merrill, 71, 78–79, 452
Rolland, Romain, 59
Romany Marie's café, 299, 344
Roosevelt, Eleanor, xii, 422
Roosevelt, Franklin D., xii, 465
Roosevelt, Theodore, 11, 97, 214
Rosenberg, Harold, 494, 541, 561,
  562–63
Rosenfeld, Isaac, 499
Roth, Sam, 387, 390, 391
Rothko, Mark, 520, 524, 537–39, 542,
  544, 547, 550, 567
Roycroft community, 334–35
Rubinstein, Artur, 27
Russell, Bertrand, 427
Russell, George, 354
Russia:
  Bolshevik revolution in, 78, 80, 81, 83,
    84, 91, 92–93, 135, 145–46, 158–59,
    200, 220, 282
  Bryant in, 135, 139, 142, 158
  Cummings in, 464–65

Eastman in, 84
Reed in, during 1919, 158–61
Reed's reports on Revolution, 78, 80,
  81, 83, 91, 92–93, 135, 145–46,
  158–59, 282

Sacco and Vanzetti case, 285
Sachs, Sadie, 223–24, 226–27
Salvo (periodical), 267
Sandburg, Carl, 57, 83
Sanger, Bill, 222–23, 225–26, 227, 228,
  230, 233
Sanger, Margaret, 221–37
  arrests of, 231
  autobiography of, 236
  background of, 224–26
  as birth control advocate, 19, 23, 36,
    38, 67, 83, 176–77, 197, 214,
    221–37
  clinics organized by, 230–31, 234
  death of, 237
  at Dodge's salon, 222–23, 226–27
  in England, 228–29, 232–33
  "Every Girl" series by, 221–22, 224,
    227
  FBI surveillance of, 232
  as feminist, 225–26, 235, 236
  first marriage of, 222, 225–26, 227,
    228, 230, 233
  Goldman and, 214, 228
  influence of, 227–32, 236–37
  love affairs of, 228–29, 232–34, 236
  as nurse, 223–24, 225
  obscenity trial of, 23, 228–30, 236
  press coverage of, 222, 231, 232
  public lectures of, 230, 234–35
  Sadie Sachs episode of, 223–24,
    226–27
  second marriage of, 235–36
  as socialist, 231–32
  tuberculosis of, 225, 232–33
  as Village resident, 222–23, 234
Sanger Defense Committee, 23
San Remo bar, 481
Santayana, George, 20, 59, 90, 450
Sapokanickan Indians, 4
Sappho, 266, 267
Saroyan, William, 427–28
Saturday Evening Post, 49, 345
Scènes de la Vie de Bohème (Murger),
  8–9

Schapiro, Meyer, 567

Schein, Minna, 385, 388, 391

Schopenhauer, Arthur, 512

Schwartz, Delmore, 487–508
  background of, 488–89
  death of, 508
  Eliot compared with, 488, 489, 492, 495, 496, 504
  financial situation of, 496, 504
  first marriage of, 489, 493–94
  as intellectual, 490–93, 496–97, 500–502
  Jewish ancestry of, 489–90, 494
  journals of, 488, 502–3, 506, 508
  mental illness of, 488, 489, 490–96, 499–508
  as modernist poet, 488, 489–90, 496, 501, 504
  as *Partisan Review* editor, 487, 488, 489, 490, 491, 494, 499, 500, 501–2, 504, 506
  Pound and, 488, 489–90, 496, 504
  reputation of, 487–90, 492–93, 496, 504
  second marriage of, 499–500, 504–6
  teaching positions of, 494–95, 497–98, 508
  as Village resident, 487, 491, 492, 494, 498–502
  at White Horse Tavern, 506–7, 508
  writings of, 487, 489–90, 492, 493, 495–96, 498, 499, 503

Schwartz, Sam, 381

Scofield, Nancy, 457, 459

Scribner's, 406, 411

Scudder, Janet, 20

Second April (Millay), 281

Secret Places of the Heart, The (Wells), 234

Sedition Act (1918), 200

segregation, racial, 67

Seldes, Gilbert, 357, 463, 464

Seven Arts (periodical), 135, 355–56, 364

Sex Antagonism Evening, 18–19, 21

Sex Question, The (Forel), 70–71

"Shadow" (Crane), 364–65

Shakespeare, William, xii, 242, 249, 358, 452, 512

Shapiro, Karl, 390

Shaw, George Bernard, 59, 103, 274, 308

Shay, Frank, 267

Shearer, Norma, xiv

Sheet, The (newspaper), 512

Shenandoah (Schwartz), 493

Shepard, Sam, xiii

She-Wolf, The (Pollock), 535

Shit (periodical), 359

"Should That Took Off Its Stockings and Threw Its Shoes Away, The" (Drick), 2

Siegel, Eli, 326, 330, 527

Simpson, Eileen, 496, 499

Sinclair, Meta, 336–37

Sinclair, Upton, 89, 158, 160, 336–37

Siqueiros, David Alfaro, 525, 527, 556

Sister Carrie (Dreiser), 298

Six Red Months in Russia (Bryant), 158

Sixty bar, 114–15

Slee, Noah, 235–36

Sloan, Dolly, 61

Sloan, John, 1–3
  Dreiser as viewed by, 301–2
  as *Masses* contributor, 58, 60–61, 67
  on *Masses* editorial board, 50, 56, 57, 72–73

Smart Set, 296, 338–39

Smith, Dave, 543, 549

Sniper, The (O'Neill), 134

Sobiloff, Hy, 499

socialism:
  anarchism and, 206–7, 314
  class struggle as doctrine of, 53, 75, 81, 82, 87, 173
  feminism and, 164, 166, 198
  Masses as forum for, 14, 49–50, 53, 54, 55, 58, 59, 65–66, 72, 73–75
  as "secular religion," 84–85

Socialist party, 18, 49, 207

"Socialization of Money, The" (Mylius), 84

"Social Position" (Gould), 427

Society for the Suppression of Vice, 70–71, 153, 307, 315–16

Society of American Artists, 349

Souls in Revolt, 437

Sour Grapes (Williams), 359

Spanish Elegy series (Motherwell), 542

"Spanish Willie," 147

Sperry, Almeda, 216–17

Spoon River Anthology (Masters), 136

Spring, The (Cook), 151

Stalin, Joseph, 84, 85, 499
"Star-Spangled Banner, The," 64, 78–79, 218
Static Dances (Cannell), 137
Steele, Wilbur Daniel, 104, 106, 119
Steffens, Lincoln:
    Dodge's friendship with, 16–17, 19, 21, 22–23, 25, 44
    Liberal Club founded by, 167
    as muckraker, 294, 501
    Reed's friendship with, 37, 92
Steichen, Edward, 466
Stein, Gertrude, 19, 20, 27–29, 35, 36, 42, 45, 67, 310, 441
Stella, Frank, 567
Stengel, Hans, 328
Sterne, Maurice, 44–45, 46, 440, 442
Stevens, Wallace, 147, 321, 354, 468
Stevenson, Ellen Borden, 390, 474
Stewart, Jimmy, xii
Stieglitz, Alfred, 368, 369, 437
Still, Clyfford, 524, 540–42, 547, 567
stock market crash (1929), 332, 358
Stopes, Marie, 233
Story of a Lover, The (Hapgood), 181, 185, 186–89
Stravinsky, Igor, 450, 482
Strunsky, Papa, xv, 175
Strunsky, Rose, 175
Subjects of the Artists School, 547
Sue, Eugene, 433
suffrage, women's, 50, 51, 65, 163–64, 166, 178, 180, 196, 199, 213, 238
Sullivan, John L., xi
Sumner, John, 70–71, 315, 384
Sun Also Rises, The (Hemingway), 359, 432, 441
Suppressed Desires (Cook), 103–4, 105, 106
Supreme Court, U.S., 200, 219, 237
Sweeney, James Johnson, 532
Sweet-and-Twenty (Dell), 252–53
Swinburne, Algernon Charles, 297
Swinnerton, Frank, 414–15
syphilis, 322, 435

Tammany Hall, xii, 16, 116, 147
Tanguy, Yves, 530
Taos, New Mexico, 45–47, 295
Tarbell, Ida, 294, 336

Tate, Allen, 287, 368, 371, 373, 374, 375, 377, 460, 489, 492, 496–97, 498
Teasdale, Sara, xiv, 246, 270
Ten Commandments, 14
Ten Days That Shook the World (Reed), 91, 145–46, 158–59
Tennyson, Alfred Lord, 287
Thalberg, Irving, 387, 465
Thaw, Harry, xii
Thayer, Scofield, 356–58, 452, 455–57, 458
theater clubs, 125–26
Theater Guild, 265, 440, 513
"Their Last Supper" (Becker), 69
Thimble Theater, 306, 342–43
Thirst (O'Neill), 122
This Room and This Gin and These Sandwiches (Wilson), 275
Thomas, Caitlin, 473, 474, 477–78, 480, 481–82, 486
Thomas, Dylan, 445, 471–86
    background of, 472–73
    Bodenheim's meeting with, 390
    Cummings's meeting with, 471
    death of, 484–86
    drinking by, 471–72, 479–80, 482–86
    financial situation of, 474, 482
    Gould's meeting with, 481
    legend of, 472–74, 476, 480, 484, 486
    love affairs of, 475–78, 482, 483, 484–85, 486
    marriage of, 473, 474, 477–78, 480, 481–82, 486
    reading tours of, 472, 473, 474, 476–78, 480, 481, 483
    reputation of, 471, 478–79
    self-destructive personality of, 471, 479, 482–86
    Time article on, 483
    at White Horse Tavern, 471–74, 479–81, 483, 484–86, 506–7
Thomas, Norman, 89, 200
Thompson, Francis, 138
Thoreau, Henry David, 454
Thorpe, Jim, 357
Three Blue Suits (Bernstein), 412–13
Three from the Earth (Barnes), 438
Three Steps Down café, 95
Tice, Clara, 307
Time, 483, 557
"Time of Her Time, The" (Mailer), xiii

Time to Be Born, A (Powell), 515–16
Toklas, Alice B., 28
"To Love Impuissant" (Millay), 270–71
Tolstoy, Leo, 99
Tramping on Life (Kemp), 345
Transition (periodical), 323
Tresca, Carlo, 173
triangle at Christopher Street and
   Seventh Avenue, xii
Triangle Shirtwaist Company fire (1911),
   170
Trilby (Du Maurier), 9
Trilling, Diane, 509, 510
Trilling, Lionel, ix, 501
Trimordeur Evening, 30
Trotsky, Leon, xv, 81, 83, 84
Trullinger, Paul, 93–94
Truman, Harry S., 548
Truth About Preparedness Campaign,
   198–99
tuberculosis, 113, 135, 225, 232–33, 341
Tulips and Chimneys (Cummings), 458
Turn, Magic Wheel (Powell), 515
Turner, Betty, 2–3
Twain, Mark, 6–7, 50, 87, 99, 170, 297
Two Slatterns and a King (Millay), 137,
   363
Two Sons, The (Boyce), 128
Tzara, Tristan, 320

Ulysses (Joyce), 315–16, 323, 390,
   441–42, 454
Under Milk Wood (Thomas), 482
Unemployment Evening, 23
Unitary Household, xi
United States:
   capitalist economy of, 198, 356, 383
   class conflict in, 17–18
   mass culture of, 553
   urbanization of, 9, 11–12
United States v. Eastman et al., 78–83
University of Wisconsin, 70, 489
Untermeyer, Louis, 50, 56, 244, 261,
   269, 299, 346, 353, 392
U.S.A. (Dos Passos), 172

Vail, Laurence, 440, 530
Vanderbilt, Emily, 461
Van Doren, Mark, 492–93
Vanity Fair, 266, 270, 272, 273, 313, 442,
   459

Van Vechten, Carl, 16, 21, 22, 25, 39, 42,
   403, 437, 440
Varèse, Edgar, 140
Vassar College, 193, 267, 270
Verdi, Giuseppe, 248
Versailles, Treaty of, 159
Viereck, George Sylvester, 20
Vietnam War, 172
Villa, Pancho, 42, 43
Villa Curonia, 26–27, 39, 40, 43, 353
Village Voice, xv, 572
Villon, François, 338, 339
Virgil, 292
Vir Heroicus Sublimus (Newman), 540
Vlag, Piet, 49–50, 54, 169
Vorse, Bert, 169, 170
Vorse, Heaton, 122
Vorse, Mary Heaton, 56–57, 97, 108, 115,
   168–73
"Voyages" (Crane), 373

Wait Until Dark, xii
Waldorf Cafeteria, 547
Walker, Jimmy, 384
Wallace, Tom, 115, 147
Walling, English, 17, 18
Wandering Jew, The (Sue), 433
"War Against War" exhibit, 199
Ward and Gow, 70
Warhol, Andy, 539, 567
"War in Paterson, The" (Reed), 38
Warren, Robert Penn, 415
Washington, George, 4, 523
Washington Crossing the Delaware
   (Rivers), 552–53
Washington Square Arch, xii, 1–4, 515
Washington Square Book Shop, 81, 102,
   315, 351
Washington Square Outdoor Art Show
   (1932), 523
Washington Square Park, 5, 299, 319,
   449, 539, 547
Washington Square Players, 102–4, 114,
   135–36, 249, 265, 299
Waste Land, The (Eliot), 288, 359, 375
Watson, Sibley, 454, 459
Webster, Daniel, 82
Webster Hall, 299, 403
Weeks, Rufus, 49
Weinberg, Harold, 391–92
Wells, H. G., 234, 236

Wescott, Glenway, 446
Westbeth housing complex, xi–xii
West 4th Street, 4
Westley, Helen, 103, 175, 446
Where the Cross Is Made (O'Neill), 144–45
White, Stanford, xii
White, William Allen, 336
White Horse Tavern, 471–74, 479–81, 483, 484–86, 506–7, 508
Whitman, Walt, 7, 87, 376, 553
Wicked Pavilion, The (Powell), 516–17
Wilde, Oscar, xi, 297, 306, 362, 363, 435
Willard, Jess, 435
William Morris agency, xi
Williams, Flossie, 348
Williams, Oscar, 353, 390, 499
Williams, Tennessee, xiii
Williams, William Carlos, 347–59
   art as interest of, 349–50
   autobiography of, 347
   the Baroness's infatuation with, 321–22
   Bodenheim and, 382, 383
   Crane as viewed by, 363–64, 378
   medical practice of, 347
   as *Others* contributor, 350–55, 363–64, 382
   in "poetry wars," 350–59
   in Provincetown Players, 130, 350
   Village visited by, 347–50, 359
   writings of, 347, 348–49, 354, 355, 359, 363, 376, 545
Wilson, Edmund, 151, 270–72, 328, 344
   background of, 270–72
   Barnes's friendship with, 441, 447–48
   Cummings's friendship with, 460, 464
   Eastman's influence on, 62, 85
   Millay as viewed by, 264–65, 269, 270–71, 275–77, 287
   Millay's relationship with, 272–77, 280, 283, 284, 290–91
   Powell's friendship with, 510, 518
   writings of, 275–77, 510
Wilson, Woodrow, 81, 83, 90, 111, 131, 159, 199, 271, 300, 354
Winchell, Walter, 329, 447, 461
"Wine Menagerie, The" (Crane), 370
Winesburg, Ohio (Anderson), 345
Winter, Charles, 53–54

Winters, Shelley, 476
Winters, Yvor, 374–75
Wobblies, 17, 23, 34, 38–39, 54, 64, 173, 207, 228, 349
Wolfe, Thomas, 395–417
   anti-Semitism of, 400, 401–2, 407, 410–11, 413, 414
   Bernstein's fictional portrayals of, 412–14
   Bernstein's relationship with, 395–417
   Brooklyn residence of, 409–10
   correspondence of, 398, 401, 404–5, 408, 409, 413
   death of, 415
   education of, 396
   European trips of, 397–98, 400–401, 404, 408–9, 413, 416
   Guggenheim fellowship of, 408, 413
   love affairs of, 461
   personality of, 400, 401, 403–4, 415–16
   plays written by, 396, 397, 400
   reputation of, 407, 414–15
   sexual jealousy of, 401, 402–4, 408–9
   in Taos, New Mexico, 46
   teaching position of, 396–97
   as Village resident, xiii, 395–96, 404–5, 415, 522
   writings of, 395, 402, 404, 406–7, 411–15, 428, 522
Wolheim, Louis, 151
Woman and the New Race (Sanger), 234
Woman of Genius, A (Austin), 163
Woman Rebel (magazine), 227–28
women:
   economic independence of, 166–67, 169
   emancipation of, 162–66, 185, 191–92, 255–56
   equality of, 164, 188, 196, 198, 200
   fashions of, 168
   "flapper" image of, 200
   male double standard for, 165, 171
   married, 167, 179, 213
   "protective" legislation for, 164, 194–95, 200
   sexual liberation of, 164–65, 178–79, 181–92, 196–97, 212, 213, 233–34, 238–39

suffrage for, 50, 51, 65, 163–64, 166, 178, 180, 196, 199, 213, 238
  see also feminism
Women series (de Kooning), 546, 563
Women's Peace Party, 192, 198, 199
Wood, Thelma, 442–43, 444, 446, 448
Woollcott, Alexander, 150, 152, 156, 251, 264, 438
Woolston, Florence Guy, 174, 179–80
"Words for Hart Crane" (Lowell), 378
working class, 74–75, 89–90
"Working Girls' Home," 115, 146–47, 338
World Peace Foundation, 452
World War I, 48, 92, 171, 178, 264, 283, 358
  noninterventionist sentiment in, 71, 75–83, 131, 134, 135, 137, 164, 179, 198–99, 218–19, 356
World War II, 172, 291

Wound and the Bow, The (Wilson), 276
Wright, Frank Lloyd, 310
Wylie, Eleanor, 285, 383, 403
Wylie, Ida, 180

Yeats, William Butler, 287, 364
yellow fever epidemic (1822), 4
Young, Art, 9, 49–50
  Ashcan School named by, 60–61
  as cartoonist, 57, 66, 69, 79–80
  indictments against, 68–69, 79–80
  on *Masses* editorial board, 49–50, 53, 72
"Young Love" (Millay), 266
YWCA, xi, 244–45

Zabel, Morton Dauwen, 490
Ziegfield Follies, 466
Zorach, William, 101, 321, 322, 350
Zukor, Adolph, xii

About the Author

Ross Wetzsteon was a journalist, critic, and editor in New York City for thirty-five years. From 1966 until his death in 1998, he worked at the *Village Voice* as a contributor and editor, and for several years served as its editor in chief. During his tenure at the *Voice*, he oversaw coverage of everything from politics to sports, but his abiding interest and the majority of his writing was on the theater. For twenty-eight years he was the chairman of the Village Voice Obie Committee, responsible for bestowing awards for excellence on Off- and Off-Off-Broadway artists and writers. His articles appeared in *New York Magazine, Men's Journal, Playboy, The New York Times, Inside Sports, Condé Nast Traveler, Mademoiselle,* and many other publications. He edited several anthologies, including *The Obie Winners in 1980* and *The Best of Off-Broadway* in 1984. He also contributed a preface to a collection of Sam Shepard's works, *Fool for Love and Other Plays,* and many essays to theater yearbooks and almanacs. He lived in Greenwich Village for thirty years.

Grateful acknowledgment is made to the following for permission to reprint previously published material:

Margaret Anderson, various quotations, reprinted with the permission of Professor Mathilda Hills, editor of Forbidden Fires (Naiad Press, 1996).

Djuna Barnes, various excerpts, reprinted with the permission of The Authors League Fund as literary executor of the Estate of Djuna Barnes. Excerpt from "From Fifth Avenue Up," in The Book of Repulsive Women (Los Angeles: Sun & Moon, 1994), copyright © 1915 Djuna Barnes; Sun & Moon edition, copyright © 1994 by Douglas Messerli; reprinted with the permission of the publishers.

Aline Bernstein, excerpts from My Other Loneliness: Letters of Thomas Wolfe and Aline Bernstein, edited by Suzanne Stutman, with a Foreword by Richard S. Kennedy, copyright © 1983 by Edla Cusick; copyright © 1983 by The University of North Carolina Press; reprinted with the permission of the publisher. Excerpts from The Journey Down, copyright © 1936, 1938 by Aline Bernstein; copyright renewed 1966 by Edla B. Cusick; reprinted with the permission of Alfred A. Knopf, a division of Random House, Inc. Letters of Aline Bernstein, copyright © The Estate of Aline Bernstein; reprinted by permission of The Estate of Aline Bernstein and Susan Schulman, A Literary Agency, New York.

George Cram ("Jig") Cook, quotations, reprinted with the permission of the Estate of G. C. Cook.

Hart Crane, excerpts from The Letters of Hart Crane, 1916–1932, edited by Brom Weber (Berkeley: University of California Press, 1965); reprinted with the permission of the Estate of Hart Crane.

E. E. Cummings, excerpt from "A Poet's Advice to Students," in A Miscellany Revised, edited by George J. Firmage, copyright © 1958, 1965 by George J. Firmage; copyright © 1958, 1965 by the Trustees for the E. E. Cummings Trust; reprinted with the permission of Liveright Publishing Corporation. Excerpts from the Introduction to New Poems, and excerpts from "The moon-lit snow is falling like strange candy into the big eyes of the," "S.T.," "I like my body when it is with your," "you shall above all things be glad and young," "be of love (a little)," "all ignorance toboggans into know," and "little joe gould has lost his teeth and doesn't know where," in Complete Poems 1904–1962. Copyright © 1923, 1925, 1926, 1931, 1935, 1938, 1939, 1940, 1944, 1945, 1946, 1947, 1948, 1949, 1950, 1951, 1952, 1953, 1954, 1955, 1956, 1957, 1958, 1959, 1960, 1961, 1962, 1963, 1966, 1967, 1968, 1972, 1973, 1975, 1976, 1977, 1978, 1979, 1980, 1981, 1982, 1983, 1984, 1985, 1986, 1987, 1988, 1989, 1990, 1991 by the Trustees for the E. E. Cummings Trust; copyright © 1973, 1976, 1978, 1979, 1981, 1983, 1985, 1991 by George James Firmage; reprinted with the permission of Liveright Publishing Corporation.

Mabel Dodge, various excerpts, reprinted with the permission of The Beinecke Rare Book and Manuscript Library, Yale University.

Crystal and Max Eastman, various excerpts, reprinted with the permission of Yvette Eastman.

Arthur Davison Ficke, poem; these lines were later revised to form the first four lines of "Fantasy for a Charming Friend" (with the word "pickle" changed to "goblet"), in Selected Poems (New York: George H. Doran Company, 1926); reprinted with the permission of the Estate of Arthur Davison Ficke.

Susan Glaspell, excerpts from The Road to the Temple (New York: Frederick A. Stokes, 1927); reprinted with the permission of the Estate of Susan Glaspell.

Hutchins Hapgood, excerpts from A Victorian in the Modern World: An Autobiography; reprinted with the permission of Harcourt, Inc.

Samuel Hoffenstein, "Songs of Fairly Utter Despair" (Part VIII), in A Treasury of Humorous Verse, copyright © 1928, 1930 by Samuel Hoffenstein; copyright © 1946 by Liveright Publishing Corporation; reprinted with the permission of Liveright Publishing Corporation.

Edna St. Vincent Millay: All quotations from Edna St. Vincent Millay's poetry, prose works, and letters appearing in this volume are protected under the copyright laws of the United States and are reprinted by permission of Elizabeth Barnett, Literary Executor.

Robert Motherwell, excerpts, copyright © Dedalus Foundation, Inc./Licensed by VAGA, New York, NY.

John Reed, various excerpts, reprinted with the permission of the Estate of John Reed.

Bill and Margaret Sanger, excerpts, reprinted with the permission of Sanger Resources and Management, Inc.